World Gazetteer
and
Geographical Dictionary

World Gazetteer
and
Geographical Dictionary

Volume – One

A - K

General Editor

J. Gunn, M.A., D.Sc., F.R.S.G.S.

LOGOS PRESS

New Delhi-110 002

ISBN -13 : 978-81-7268-167-8 (Set)
ISBN -10 : 81-7268-167-4 (Set)

ISBN-13: 978-81-7268-168-5 (Vol. I) ISBN-10: 81-7268-168-2 (Vol. I)
ISBN-13: 978-81-7268-169-2 (Vol. II) ISBN-10: 81-7268-169-0 (Vol. II)

Edition 2008

Printed and Published by

LOGOS PRESS

Building No. 4788-90, Street No. 23, Ansari Road, Darya Ganj,
New Delhi-110 002 (India)

Phone : 23272187

PREFACE

THERE is more need to-day than ever before for a handy, comprehensive, and reliable Gazetteer of the World. The extraordinary changes in the means of communication, not only by sea and land but also by air and ether, have so reduced the effect of distance that the whole world lies open to our view. Almost every day, therefore, the question arises in the home, the office, and the classrooms of our schools, "Where is that place?" The further questions are hardly less insistent, "What sort of a place is it?" and "How should its name be pronounced?"

The present volume has been compiled with the aim of providing answers to these and similar questions. The following are some of its chief features:

Comprehensiveness.—This Gazetteer and Geographical Dictionary contains over 10,000 entries. Its aim has been to include the name of every place in the world that is likely to be met with in the course of general reading or study, and about which any fact of geographical, historical, or other importance is known. In the interests of space, it is obvious that in the larger units only the most outstanding facts could be given. The work is intended as a book of reference for the general reader and for pupils in senior and advanced classes, and not for the specialist.

Reliability.—Care has been taken to base the facts and figures upon the latest available official or other authoritative sources of information. The populations given are those of the latest published Census figures—in the case of Great Britain, those of 1931.

Spelling of Names.—The published lists of the Royal Geographical Society have been taken as a guide in this matter, but in the main only so far as the sounds can be represented by the ordinary English alphabet. Special characters such as those adopted in certain countries of Central and Eastern Europe are of service to the specialist but not to the ordinary English reader.

Pronunciation.—In every case guidance to the pronunciation sufficient for the ordinary reader has been given. Where it has seemed necessary the name has been re-written, so that by reference to the " Key to Pronunciation," on page vii, at least an approximation to the sound is easily obtained.

Special English Forms.—Where custom has sanctioned a special English form or pronunciation for a foreign name, this is adhered to though differing from that used in the foreign country, as, for example, the spelling of Naples, Brussels, Florence, etc., and the pronunciation of Paris, Trafalgar, etc. The function of any such book is not to prescribe what the form or pronunciation ought to be, but to record what is commonly accepted among English-speaking people. In all cases where it has seemed desirable, however, the foreign as well as the accepted English usage is given.

The Geographical Dictionary.—The Dictionary of Geographical Terms gives in handy form an explanation of the terms most commonly used in Physical Geography, Meteorology, World Commerce, and other allied topics. This will be found of service not only in the school classroom but also by the general reader, and is a distinct novelty in works of this character.

The Publishers claim that no Gazetteer has ever before been produced which contains so much information in so compact and handy a form. Every care has been taken to ensure that the information is trustworthy and up-to-date, and it is hoped that the book will be found equally valuable in the School, the Office, and the Home.

The task of compiling and editing so comprehensive a work required the services of highly qualified experts, and the staff employed included Messrs. G. S. Dickson, M.A., B.Sc., J. Hamilton Birrell, M.A., Ph.D., F.R.S.G.S., A. P. Gray, M.A., W. Carnon, M.A., and others, together with the General Editor.

KEY TO PRONUNCIATION

ä as in mar (*mär*), psalm (*säm*), hurrah (*hurä'*).
a, *ă* ,, cat (*căt*), battle (*bătl*), abbot (*ăb'ot*).
ā ,, mate (*māt*), pain (*pān*), weight (*wāt*).
au, *aw* as in call (*cawl*), appal (*apawl'*), brought (*brawt*).
e as in sell (*sel*), ferry (*fer'i*).
ĕ ,, her (*hĕr*), fur (*fĕr*), gird (*gĕrd*).
ē ,, meet (*mēt*), leaf (*lēf*), mere (*mēr*).
i, *ĭ* ,, knit (*nit*), *silly* (*sil'i*), busy (*biz'i*).
ī, *ȳ* ,, white (*whīt*), arise (*arīz'*), might (*mīt*).
o ,, pot (*pot*), watch (*woch*), lorry (*lor'i*).
ō ,, grow (*grō*), know (*nō*), loaf (*lōf*).
ö ,, lord (*lörd*), resort (*rezört'*).
oo ,, room (*room*), glue (*gloo*), shoe (*shoo*).
u ,, full (*ful*), book (*buk*), could (*cud*).
ŭ ,, shun (*shŭn*), mud (*mŭd*), above (*abŭv'*).
ū ,, mute (*mūt*), few (*fū*), pure (*pūr*).
ou, *ow* as in doubt (*dout*), knout (*nowt*), aloud (*aloud'*).
oi as in coin (*koin*), buoy (*boi*), royal (*roi'al*).
ch ,, chime (*chīm*), catch (*kăch*).
ch ,, loch (*lo*ch), pibroch (*pē'bro*ch).
g ,, good (*gud*), linger (*ling'ger*).
j ,, jam (*jăm*), gem (*jem*), judge (*jŭj*).
n (nasal) as in entente (*äntänt'*), savant (*sävän*).
sh as in shove (*shŭv*), tension (*ten'shon*), action (*ăk'shon*).
zh ,, leisure (*lezh'ūr*), vision (*vizh'on*).
th ,, think (*think*), theme (*thēm*), health (*helth*).
th ,, thine (th*īn*), wreathe (*rē*th), though (thō).
wh ,, while (*whīl*), somewhere (*sŭm'whār*).

When the accent is placed immediately after a vowel, that vowel is long; when the accent is placed after a consonant, the vowel of that syllable is short, as

ca'ble	cab'in	o'ral	or'ange
se'cret	sec'ond	pu'ny	pun'ish
pi'lot	pil'lar	ty'rant	tyr'anny

ABBREVIATIONS

ac.	acres.
alt.	altitude.
anc.	ancient.
bor.	borough.
Brit.	British.
c.	about (*circiter*).
cap.	capital.
cent.	century.
co.	county.
comm.	commune.
dep.	department.
dist.	district.
div.	division.
E., E.	east, eastern.
eccles.	ecclesiastical.
episc.	episcopal.
est.	estimated.
exp.	exports.
Fr.	French.
ft.	feet.
govt.	government.
I., isl.	island.
I.F.S.	Irish Free State.
in.	inches.
L.	Lake.
l. bk.	left bank.
m.	miles.
mkt.	market.
Mt., mts.	mount, mountains.
munic.	municipal.
N., N.	north, northern.
par.	parish.
parl.	parliamentary.
pop.	population.
prod.	products.
prov.	province.
R., riv.	river.
r. bk.	right bank.
rep.	republic.
rly. (jn.)	railway (junction).
R.S.F.S.R.	Russian Socialist Federal Soviet Republic.
S., s.	south, southern.
sq. m.	square miles.
str.	strait.
terr.	territory.
tn.	town.
trib.	tributary.
U.K.	United Kingdom.
univ.	university.
urb. dist.	urban district.
U.S.A.	United States of America.
U.S.S.R.	Union of Socialist Soviet Republics.
vil.	village.
W., w.	west, western.
wat.-pl.	watering-place.
yds.	yards.

WORLD GAZETTEER

A

Aabenraa (*ōb'en-rō*), formerly APENRADE, port and wat.-pl., Sleswick, Denmark, 30 m. N. of Flensburg; trades in grain, fodder, and timber; fishing. Pop. 8,000.

Aachen (*ä'chen*), or AIX-LA-CHAPELLE, tn., Prussia, Germany, 44 m. W.S.W. of Cologne; Charlemagne's cap. and burial-place; coal and iron fields, hardware and textile manufactures; sulphur baths. Pop. 156,000.

Aalborg (*ōl'borg*), port, Liim Fjord, Denmark; shipbuilding yards. Exports: fish, grain. Pop. 43,000.

Aalesund (*ō'le-soond*), port, Norway, 160 m. N. of Bergen by sea; cod and herring fisheries; burned down (1904), but since rebuilt. Pop. 18,000.

Aalst. See ALOST.

Aar or **Aare** (*är*), largest Swiss riv.; flows through Bern and joins Rhine near Waldshut; 181 m. long; area of basin, 6,800 sq. m.

Aarau (*ä'rou*), cap. of Aargau, Switzerland. Products: silk, cotton, tiles, cement, scientific instruments. Pop. 12,000.

Aargau (*är'gou*), N. Swiss canton; agriculture, cattle, wine, fruit, salt mining. Cap. Aarau. Area, 548 sq. m.; pop. 247,000.

Aarhus (*ōr'hoos*), port, Denmark, on E. coast; good harbour; tobacco, silk, cotton, distilleries. Pop. 76,000.

Ab'aco, GREAT, one of Bahama Islands; E. of Great Bahama; lighthouse. Pop. 4,000.

Abadan', isl., delta of Shatt-al-Arab, Persia, 10 m. below Mohammerah; has large refinery of the Anglo-Persian Oil Co.; tn. (pop. 30,000) rapidly extending.

Ab'ana, or AMANAH (modern BARADA), riv. flowing from Anti-Lebanon Mts. through Damascus; loses itself in marshy lakes.

Abbazia (*ä-bat-sē'a*), tn., Italy, at head of Gulf of Fiume; popular health resort. Pop. 2,500.

Abbeville (*äb'vēl*), tn., on R. Somme, N. France; woollens, linens, hemp goods, sugar; has old churches; Brit. base in Great War. Pop. 20,000.

Abbeyfeale (*äb-be-fēl'*), mkt. tn., S.W. Limerick, I.F.S.; ruins of stronghold of Geraldines. Pop. 1,000.

Abbeyleix (*äb-e-lēs'*), mkt. tn., Leix, I.F.S.; famous Brigidine convent (1840); oat mills. Pop. 760.

Ab'bots Brom'ley, par. and mkt. tn., Staffs, England, 10 m. E. of Stafford; Norman church of St. Nicholas (restored 1855). Pop. 1,500.

Ab'botsford, on R. Tweed, Roxburghshire, Scotland, 3 m. W. of Melrose; home of Sir Walter Scott from 1812 to 1832.

Ab'bots Lang'ley, par. and vil., S.W. Herts, England; reputed birthplace of Pope Adrian IV. Pop. 4,200.

Abbottabad', hill station, N.W. Frontier Province, India, 100 m. W. of Srinagar; alt. 4,200 ft.; military cantonment; on one of main roads to Kashmir. Pop. 11,500.

Abeo'kuta, tn., s. Nigeria, W. Africa; palm oil, timber, yams, shea-butter. Pop. 38,000.

Aberav'on, now part of Port Talbot, Glamorganshire, Wales; tin works. Pop. 15,000.

Aberay'ron or **Aberae'on,** wat.-pl., Cardigan Bay, Cardiganshire, Wales; fishing, coasting trade, flour and saw mills. Pop. 1,200.

Ab'ercarn, urb. dist., Monmouthshire, England, 10 m. N.W. of Newport; coal, iron. Pop. 20,600.

Ab'ercorn, trading station, N. Rhodesia, 15 m. S. of L. Tanganyika; alt. 6,000 ft.

Abercynon (*ab-er-koo'non*), dist., Glamorganshire, Wales, in Mountain Ash urb. dist.; coal, iron.

Aberdare', tn., Glamorganshire, Wales, 4 m. S.W. of Merthyr Tydfil; exports coal; tin industries. Pop. 48,800.

Aberdar'on, par. and vil., Carnarvonshire, Wales, 28 m. S.W. of Carnarvon; Norman church and tumulus. Pop. (par.) 1,100.

Aberdeen'. (1) Port, royal burgh, and co. tn., Aberdeenshire, Scotland, on Rs. Dee and Don. Tn. built mainly of grey granite (the 'Granite City'); consists of Old and New Aberdeen. Great educational centre. Four bridges over Dee. Principal N. seaport of Scotland, chiefly coasting trade; deep-sea fisheries, centre of trawling. Industries include quarrying and polishing granite, textile, paper, comb, jute, jam manufactures; flax spinning, brewing, distilling. Pop. 167,300. (2) Tn., Cape Prov., S. Africa, 140 m. N.W. of Port Elizabeth; alt. 2,850 ft.; stock fairs monthly. Pop. (white) 2,600. (3) City, S. Dakota, U.S.A., 118 m. N.E. of Pierre; artesian wells; chemicals, foundry products. Pop. 15,000. (4) Port, Washington, U.S.A., at head of Gray's Harbour; lumber industry; salmon cannery. Pop. 22,000.

Aberdeenshire, maritime co., N.E. Scotland; has five dists.—Mar, Formartine, Buchan, Garioch, Strathbogie; among chief peaks of Grampians are Ben Macdhui, Cairntoul, Lochnagar; chief rivs., Dee and Don, noted for salmon; largest lake, Loch Muick; geological formation is mainly crystalline schists; climate mild; grouse, partridges, red deer abundant; has ash, fir, larch trees. Principal industry agriculture; many small holdings; oats, barley, turnips grown; shorthorn and polled Angus cattle bred. Very productive coast fisheries. Other industries: granite quarrying, brick making, brewing, distilling, paper and wool making. Chief tns., Aberdeen, Peterhead, Fraserburgh, Huntly. Area, 1,980 sq. m.; pop. 300,400.

Aberdour', seaside resort, Fife, Scotland, on Firth of Forth. Inchcolm is close by. Pop. 3,000.

Aberdov'ey, wat.-pl., Merionethshire, Wales, on estuary of R. Dovey.

Aberfel'dy, vil., Perthshire, Scotland, on R. Tay. Black Watch embodied here (1739). Pop. 1,500.

Aberfoyle', vil. and pass, Perthshire, Scotland, 34 m. N. of Glasgow. Associated with Scott's *Rob Roy.* Pop. of par. 1,200.

Abergavenny (*ab-ĕr-gav-en'i* or *ab-ĕr-gen'i*), tn., Monmouthshire, England, 20 m. N. of Newport. Ironworks. Pop. 8,600.

Abergele (*ab-ĕr-gĕ'li*), wat.-pl., Denbighshire, Wales. Pop. 2,700.

Aberlour', or CHARLESTOWN OF ABERLOUR, police burgh, Banffshire, Scotland, on R. Spey, 2¼ m. S.W. of Craigellachie; distilleries; orphanage. Pop. 1,200.

Aberneth'y. (1) Vil., Perthshire, Scotland, 8½ m. S.E. of Perth; anc. Pictish cap.; round tower. Pop. 600. (2) Par., Speyside, Inverness-shire, containing Nethybridge; favourite holiday resort.

Abersychan (*ab-ĕr-sooch'an*), tn., Monmouthshire, England, 2¼ m. N.N.W. of Pontypool; coal and iron dist.; manufactures sheet steel and tin plates. Pop. 25,600.

Abertillery (*ab-er-til-ā'ri*), tn., Monmouthshire, England, in S.W. coal dist. Pop. 31,800.

Aberystwith (*ab-ĕr-ist'with*), munic. bor., wat.-pl., and univ. tn., Cardiganshire, Wales, on Cardigan Bay; has National Library of Wales (1911). Pop. 9,500.

Abesh'r, cap. of Wadai dist., Chad Colony, Fr. Equatorial Africa; caravan centre. Pop. *c.* 25,000.

Ab'ingdon, munic. bor. and anc. tn., Berks, England, at junction of Rs. Thames and Ock. Agricultural trade; clothing and carpets. Pop. 7,200.

Abitib'i, lake, Canada; forms boundary between Ontario and Quebec; drained by R. Abitibi (200 m.), trib. of R. Moose. Gold found in dist.

Abkhas'ia, Soviet rep., Transcaucasia, U.S.S.R., on Black Sea; cattle, maize, fruit. Pop. 200,000.

Åbo (*ō'bō*). See TURKU.

Abo, tn., Nigeria, Africa, near mouth of R. Niger; exports palm oil.

Abomey (*ab-ō-mā'*), tn., Dahomey, Fr. W. Africa; formerly slave market. Pop. *c.* 20,000.

Abor Hills, dist., border of Assam, India; traversed by R. Brahmaputra; inhabited by wild Mongolian Abors.

Aboyne (*a-boin'*), or CHARLESTOWN OF ABOYNE, vil., Aberdeenshire, Scotland, on R. Dee, 10½ m. E. of Ballater; holiday resort. Pop. 900.

Abraham, PLAINS (or HEIGHTS) OF, S.W. of Quebec, Canada, above St. Lawrence R.; here Wolfe defeated Montcalm (1759).

A'bram, urb. dist., Lancs, England, 2 m. S.E. of Wigan; coal mining; engineering; cotton manufacture. Pop. 6,700.

Abran'tes, tn., Estremadura, Portugal, on R. Tagus; wine, fruit, grain, olive oil. Pop. 10,000.

Abruzzi and Molise (*ăbroot'sē; molē'sā*), territorial div., central Italy, embraces Aquila, Chieti, Teramo, and Campobasso provs.; cereals, wine. Pop. 1,480,700.

Abu', MOUNT, hill station (alt. 5,650 ft.), Aravalli range, Rajputana, India. Has Jain temples.

Abu Kle'a, WELLS OF, tn., Anglo-Egyptian Sudan, Africa, 90 m. N. of Khartoum; British defeated Arabs here (1885).

Abu Qir, formerly ABOU'KIR, small tn. and bay, Egypt; Nelson destroyed Fr. fleet in bay (1798).

Aburi (*ab-oo'ri*), tn., Gold Coast, W. Africa, 25 m. N. of Acora; govt. sanatorium; botanical station; alt. 1,540 ft.

Abu-Simbel, or IPSAMBUL, site of anc. temples, Egypt, on l. b. of R. Nile, *c.* 40 m. N.E. of Halfa; temples cut out of solid rock, with four colossal figures of Rameses, 65 ft. high.

Abyssin'ia, inland empire, N.E. Africa, surrounded by Brit., Fr., and Ital. terrs.; includes provs. of Tigré, Amhara, Gojam, Shoa, and Harar. It is a high plateau (average alt. 8,000 ft.) falling abruptly towards Red Sea, more gradually towards Nile. In N.W. the Simen Mts., of steep and bare rock, reach 15,000 ft. Chief rivers: Blue Nile, which flows through Lake Tana, and Atbara. Rivers have cut deep gorges in carrying fertilizing mud to Egypt. Lowlands up to 5,500 ft. (known as Kolla) have a tropical climate, but the Voina Dega, between 5,500 and *c.* 8,000 ft., with a subtropical climate and excellent pastures, is chief seat of pop. Above this region the Dega has horses and long-wooled sheep. Rainy season, June to Sept.

Abyssinia is rich in minerals, but only a little gold is exported to India. Other exports are hides and skins, ivory, coffee, civet, native butter, and wax; the chief imports are cottons (Amer., Brit., and Ind.), woollen fabrics, cutlery and hardware, Ital. and Swedish matches. There are practically no roads; goods carried mainly on pack animals. A railway runs from Jibuti to Addis Ababa.

The Abyssinians are deep brown in colour, well-formed and handsome, intelligent and fond of gaiety. They eat and drink heavily. Marriage is easily dissoluble and polygamy common. Abyssinian houses are rough circular stone huts, thatched with grass. Christianity was introduced in the 4th cent. by Frumentius, and the Abuna or head bishop is still appointed by the Coptic Patriarch of Alexandria, and in ritual, etc., Abyssinian Christianity resembles Coptic. Education of the people has only begun; there are two schools at Addis Ababa. Upon the old feudal government is now grafted some imitation of European civilization. Chief tns.: Addis Ababa (cap.), Diredawa, Harar. Area, 350,000 sq. m.; pop. *c.* 10,000,000.

Aca′dia (French *Acadie*), name first applied to all Fr. possessions s. of R. St. Lawrence; later to New Brunswick, Nova Scotia, and part of Maine. Cap. Port Royal (Annapolis).

Acajutla (*ak-a-hoot′la*), Pacific port, Salvador, Central America; exports coffee.

Acapul′co, Pacific port, Mexico; sheltered harbour. Pop. *c.* 6,000.

Acarna′nia, region, anc. Greece; now joined with Ætolia; chief tn., Missolonghi. Pop. 220,000.

Accra (*ak-rä′*), port and cap., Gold Coast, W. Africa. Exports cocoa, rubber, ivory; railway to interior. Pop. 38,000.

Ac′crington, tn., Lancs, England, 20 m. N. of Manchester; cotton and dye works; textile machinery. Pop. 43,000.

Achæa (*ak-ā′ya*), with Elis, prov., Greece; chief currant-producing dist. of Greece, the ports being Patras (cap.) and Ægion. Area, 2,000 sq. m.; pop. 321,000.

Achelo′us (modern *Aspropotamo*), famous riv. of anc. Greece, rising in Mt. Pindus; enters Ionian Sea. Its deposits have built up the Echinades Is. at its mouth.

Achensee (*äch-en-zā′*), or L. ACHEN, finest lake in N. Tyrol, Austria, source of Achen riv.; alt. 3,000 ft; area, 2½ sq. m. The Pertisau, a famous pleasure resort, is on the s.w. bank.

Achill (or EAGLE) **Island** (*äk′il*), isl., Mayo, w. coast of Ireland, three vils. on isl.; fishing. Pop. 5,300.

Achin′, or ATJEH, dist., N. Sumatra. Interior mountainous. Important trading centre from 17th cent.; exports pepper, copra, palm oil. Cap. Kota Raja. Area, 20,544 sq. m.; pop. 750,000.

Achin′sk. (1) Prov., Siberian Area, U.S.S.R.; forests; rye and wheat. Pop. 392,000. (2) Mkt. tn. in above, on Abakan R. and Trans-Siberian Rly.; gold found near. Pop. 7,000.

Achray′, LOCH, s.w. Perthshire, Scotland, at entrance to Trossachs; 1¼ m. by ¾ m.

Acireale (*ä-chē-rä-ä′lä*), tn., Catania, Sicily; thermal springs. Pop. 35,000.

Ack′worth, par. containing High and Low Ackworth, W. Riding of Yorks, England, 3 m. s. of Pontefract; quarrying. Pop. 4,800.

Aconcagua (*ä-kon-kä′gwä*). (1) Mountainous prov., Chile. Produces alfalfa and Mediterranean fruits. Cap. Valparaiso. Area, 7,279 sq. m.; pop. 450,000. (2) Extinct volcano in S. Andes; highest peak of New World (22,868 ft.).

Acqui (*ä′kwē*), cathedral tn., Piedmont, Italy, 28 m. N.W. of Genoa; warm sulphur springs. Pop. 16,000.

A′cre, port, N. Palestine; taken by Crusaders and retaken by Saracens in Crusades; unsuccessfully besieged by Napoleon (1799). Trade has passed to Beirut and Haifa. Pop. 6,500.

Ac′tium, promontory, Gulf of Arta, w. Greece. Octavian defeated Mark Antony here, 31 B.C., gaining control of Roman Empire.

Ac′ton, tn., Middlesex, England; w. suburb of London. Pop. 70,500.

Ada (*od′o*), tn., Yugoslavia, on R. Tisa; steamer port; cattle market. Pop. 12,000.

Adabazar′, tn., Asia Minor, Turkey, 75 m. E. of Scutari; linen and silk; trade centre. Pop. 83,500.

Adal′ia, or ANTALIA, port, s. Asia Minor, Turkey, at head of Gulf of Adalia. Exports timber, grain, cattle, horses; has coast trade; trade decreased after extension of Anatolian rys. Pop. 39,000.

Adamä′wa, fertile country, w. Africa, midway between Bight of Biafra and L. Chad; cotton, ground-nuts, ivory; divided between Britain and France.

Adams. (1) Tn., N.W. Massachusetts, U.S.A.; paper, cotton, woollens, silk. Pop. 14,000. (2) Mt., Cascade Range, Washington, U.S.A.; alt. 12,470 ft.

Adam's Bridge, ridge of sand and coral reef off N.W. Ceylon; length 30 m.; railway proposed between Ceylon and India.

Adam's Peak, mt., Ceylon (7,352 ft.); consists of granite; foot-like depression on summit ascribed by Mohammedans to Adam and by Buddhists to Buddha.

Adana (*ä'dä-na*). (1) Vilayet, S.E. Asia Minor, Turkey; unexploited minerals; cereals, cotton, wool, fruits. Area, 15,400 sq. m.; pop. 228,000. (2) Chief tn. of above, on Seihan riv.; railway centre. Pop. 73,000.

Ad'da, riv., Italy; flows through L. Como to R. Po; 150 m.

Addis Ababa (*ä'dis ä'bä-bä*), cap., Abyssinia, in Shoa prov.; terminus of rly. from Jibuti. Founded in 1892, and has merely local industries. Pop. (fluctuating according to troops quartered in town) *c.* 70,000.

Ad'dlestone, vil., Surrey, England, 1½ m. S.E. of Chertsey; site of new model village and park (war memorial). Pop. 7,800.

Ad'elaide, cap., S. Australia, on Gulf of St. Vincent. Founded in 1836. Has univ., government house, two cathedrals. Exports wheat, wine, wool, fruit, silver, copper. Pop. (with suburbs) 317,000.

Adelbod'en, health resort, Bernese Oberland, Switzerland, 19 m. S.W. of Interlaken; alt. 4,600 ft.; mineral springs.

Ad'elsberg. See POSTUMIA GROTTE.

A'den. (1) Brit. possession and fortified port, S.W. Arabia. Tn. in volcanic crater; important coaling, cable, and transhipment station. Imports coffee, cottons, grain, hides, coal, sugar, tobacco; Brit. since 1839; hinterland protectorate, 9,000 sq. m.; under the govt. of Bombay. Pop. (including Perim) 55,000. (2) GULF OF, between S. Arabia and Somaliland (500 m. by *c.* 170 m.).

Ader'no, tn., Sicily, Italy, at base of Mt. Etna, 22 m. by rail N.W. of Catania; Norman tower. Pop. 40,000.

Adige (*ä'dē-jä*), second most important riv. of Italy, rises in Rhætian Alps and enters Adriatic Sea, N. of mouth of R. Po. Length, 240 m. Chief avenue from Ital. plain through Trentino to Brenner Pass and Innsbrück.

Adiron'dacks, mt. group, N.E. New York, U.S.A. Many isolated peaks, loftiest Mt. Marcy (5,344 ft.); region contains L. Champlain and L. George; heavily forested; holiday resort. Adirondack Park includes a forest reserve (*c.* 2,000,000 ac.).

Ad'lington, urb. dist., N. Lancs, England, 6 m. N.E. of Wigan. Cotton spinning, calico printing, and bleaching. Pop. 4,200.

Admiralty Gulf, large inlet, Kimberley div., N.W. of W. Australia, with many islands. Port Warrender stands at its head.

Admiralty Island, isl., Alexander Archipelago, between Chichakov and Baranov Islands and mainland of Alaska; densely forested; coal and copper mines. Belongs to U.S.A.

Admiralty Islands, group of forty islands to N.E. of New Guinea. Largest, Manus. Coconuts; pearl fisheries. Included in Australian mandate of New Guinea. Pop. (Papuans) 13,800.

Ado'ni, tn., Madras, India, 64 m. N.E. of Bellary; one of chief cotton markets of Deccan. Pop. 30,500.

Adour (*ä-door'*), riv., France; rises in Pic du Midi de Bigorre, Pyrenees; drains N.W. slopes of Pyrenees to Bay of Biscay, 4 m. below Bayonne; length, 207 m.

Ad'ra, port, Almeria, S. Spain; exports lead, grapes, wine, esparto. Pop. 9,000.

Adramyti (*ä-drä-mē'tē*), tn., vilayet Brussa, Asia Minor, Turkey; on trade route to Panderma; wine and olive oil.

Ad'ria, tn., prov. Rovigo, Italy, between Rs. Adige and Po; formerly on coast, now 15 m. inland. Pop. 14,000.

Adriano'ple (Turkish *Edirne*), tn., Turkey in Europe, at confluence of Rs. Tunja and Maritsa, 137 m. W.N.W. of Constantinople by rail. Important commercial centre for silk, attar of roses, opium, wine, cereals, and tobacco. Pop. 35,000.

Adriatic Sea, arm of Mediterranean Sea, between Italy and the coasts of Yugoslavia and Albania. Extreme length, 450 m.; aver. breadth, 90 m. Tides are negligible, but navigation difficult for sailing ships by reason of *bora* (N.E. wind). Chief industry fishing, also sponge fishing. Chief ports, Brindisi, Ancona, and Venice; Trieste, Pola, and Fiume; Valona, Bar, Split, and Zara.

Ad'uwa, formerly ADOWA, tn., Tigré prov., Abyssinia, 145 m. N.E. of Gondar. Scene of defeat of Ital. army (March 1896). Pop. *c.* 5,000.

Adwick-le-Street (*ad'dik*), urb. dist., W. Riding, Yorks, England, 4 m. N.W. of Doncaster; 1 m. E. of (Roman) Ermine Street; collieries. Pop. 20,300.

Adzhar'ia, rep., Transcaucasia, U.S.S.R., on Black Sea; forests; maize, wheat, fruits, cotton, silk, tobacco. Chief tn., Batum. Area, 530 sq. m.; pop. 130,000.

Æge'an Sea, part of Mediterranean Sea between Greece (W.) and Asia Minor (E.), connected with Sea of Marmora by Dardanelles. Studded with islands, including the groups of the Cyclades (Greek) and Sporades (Italian); in N. Imbros and Tenedos are Turkish. All have fine climate and scenery.

Ægi'na, isl., Greece, 20 m. S. of the Piræus; many antiquities; sponge fisheries. Chief tn., Ægina.

Æo'lian Islands. See LIPARI ISLANDS.

Æto'lia, dist., N. Greece. Central plain agricultural; N. and E. mountainous (Kiona, 8,240 ft.); Ætolia, with Acarnania, forms dep. of modern Greece.

Afghanistan', country, S.W. Asia. Length from Herat frontier to Khaibar Pass, *c.* 600 m.; greatest breadth from N.E. to S.W., *c.* 700 m.; bounded on W. by Persia, N. by Turkmen, Uzbek, and Tadzhik reps., U.S.S.R., E. by tribes under Brit. influence and India, S. by Baluchistan. Main features are sand, rocks, hills, snow-topped mts.; surface rugged, much of it consisting of offshoots from Hindu Kush and other ranges to Sulaiman Mts.; plateaus between vary from 4,000 to 7,000 ft.; temp. depends on elevation; climate in higher districts very hot in summer, very severe in winter; rainfall slight. North drained by Oxus and tribs.; N.W. by Murghab and Hari-Rud; S. and S.W. by Helmand; E. by Kabul and Gomal. Fauna includes leopards, jackals, tigers, bears, gazelles. Valleys fertile; irrigation used; two harvests every year, yielding cereals, vegetables, and abundant fruit; castor-oil plant, madder, and asafœtida abound. Mineral resources await development. Fat-tailed sheep is most important animal; horses, camels, and goats reared. Chief industries are manufactures of silk, felt, carpets, woollen cloth, sheepskin coats, camel and goat hair fabrics. Exports: silk carpets, madder, gums, fruit and vegetables, grain, drugs, cattle, hides, tobacco. Imports: cotton goods, dyes, sugar, hardware, leather. Large transit trade from Persia, Bokhara, Turkestan, India, to Herat and Kabul; transport is by horses and camels; no good roads except Brit. military roads; no railways; no navigable rivers, but timber floated down-stream. Pop. Afghans, Tajiks, Hazaras, Chahar-Aimaks, Uzbegs; languages, Persian and Pushtu, the former being the court language; religion, Islam; education still in elementary state; Government is a constitutional monarchy with legislative and state assemblies, and a cabinet over which the king presides. Country is politically divided into five provs., Kabul, Afghan Turkistan, Herat, Kandahar, and Kataghan-Badakhshan, each under a governor. Chief towns: Kabul, Kandahar, Herat. Area, *c.* 250,000 sq. m.; pop. *c.* 8,000,000, of whom *c.* 2,200,000 are Afghans (Duranis and Ghilzais).

Afiun Qarahisar (*ä-fē-oon' kä-rä-hi-sär'*), tn., Brusa, Asia Minor, Turkey; opium. Pop. 20,000.

Africa, second largest continent of Old World, extends S. from Mediterranean Sea, and is almost bisected by equator; greatest length, *c.* 5,000 m.; greatest breadth, *c.* 4,500 m.; area, *c.* 11,500,000 sq. m. Africa approaches Europe at Strait of Gibraltar in N.W., and touches Asia at Isthmus of Suez in N.E. Off S.E. coast is large isl. Madagascar; Canaries off N.W. coast; coast-line singularly unbroken, length about 16,000 m.; principal inlets, Gulfs of Cabes and Sidra on N., Gulf of Guinea with Bights of Benin and Biafra on W. Land rises rapidly from coast; from fairly continuous outer rim of mountains greater part of surface spreads inwards in two tablelands, of which the southern has mean elevation of over 3,500 ft. and slopes down to northern, which has mean height of *c.* 1,300 ft.; latter in some parts falls still lower, part of N.E. Sahara being below sea-level. Higher plateau has number of ridges, and in equatorial regions are many craters of extinct volcanoes, such as Kilimanjaro (20,000 ft.) and Mt. Kenya (18,500). Chief mt. ranges near coast are Atlas on N. and Drakensberg on S.E. Along E. part of plateau are many large lakes: Rudolf, Albert, Albert Edward, Victoria, Tanganyika, Mweru, Bangweulu, Nyasa. N.E. is drained by Nile and tribs., S.W. by Zambezi, Shiré, Limpopo, etc.; principal W. coast rivers, Senegal, Gambia, Volta, Niger, Ogowe, Congo, Cuanza, Cunene, Orange.

Rainfall is slight except near equator and parts of coast; rainiest region, W. of Cameroon Mts.; interior exposed to dry winds, known variously as *sirocco, khamsin, harmattan*; tropical dists. unhealthy. Typical flora: date palm in Sahara; mangrove on coast; rubber trees; many orchids, and in S. heaths. Fauna includes the lion, leopard, panther, jackal, hyena, elephant, rhinoceros, hippopotamus, zebra, camel, buffalo, giraffe, antelope, baboon, gorilla, crocodile, python, ostrich, secretary bird, locust, and tsetse fly, many of which are peculiar to Africa.

Geologically, Africa is old, and its stability is disturbed neither by great earthquakes nor by volcanic eruptions. Slight earthquakes at times disturb the comparatively new Atlas regions, and volcanic eruptions the coast lands round the Bight of Biafra, and an eastern belt from Kilimanjaro to the Red Sea.

Political Divisions.—Within Brit. Empire are, in E. Africa, Somaliland, Anglo-Egyptian Sudan, Uganda, Kenya, Zanzibar, Nyasaland, and mandated Tanganyika Terr.; in W. Africa, Gambia, Sierra Leone, Gold Coast, Nigeria, and mandated Togoland and Cameroons; in S. Africa, Union of S. Africa, with mandated S.W. Africa, Basutoland, Bechuanaland, Swaziland, S. and N. Rhodesia; and islands of Ascension, St. Helena, Mauritius, Seychelles, etc.; total area, *c* 4,000,000 sq. m. France has Algeria, Fr. Somaliland, Fr. Equatorial Africa, Fr. W. Africa, Madagascar, Tunisia, and Protectorate in Morocco—in all *c.* 4,300,000 sq. m. Belgium has Belgian Congo—930,000 sq. m. Italy has Eritrea, Tripolitania, and Cyrenaica, and Italian Somaliland —*c.* 680,000 sq. m. Portugal has Angola, Port. E. Africa, and Portuguese Guinea—*c.* 788,000 sq. m. Spain has Rio de Oro and Muni River Settlement—*c.* 129,000 sq. m. Abyssinia (350,000 sq. m.), Liberia (43,000 sq. m.), and Egypt (350,000 sq. m.) are independent states. Total pop. *c.* 180,000,000.

Peoples.—Majority of inhabitants are Negroes, of whom two main groups occur—Negroes proper in N. half and Bantus in S. of continent. Negroes proper have many different languages, while Bantus all speak Bantu dialects. Other inhabitants include Bushmen,

Eastern Hamites, Libyans, Semites, while intermingling has resulted in large number of tribes of mixed race. Bushmen are brown nomadic race of hunters, and with the Hottentots, who are said to be racially akin to them, formerly inhabited Cape of Good Hope, but were driven N. to Kalahari desert; Libyans, or Berbers, white race, occupy Algeria and Morocco; and Semites, or Arabs, are found in E. and N.E. Semito-Hamites chiefly inhabit Abyssinia. Equatorial regions from Uganda to the Gabon are inhabited by pygmy people—dark brown race of hunters concerning whom little is known. Original African stocks are generally supposed to have been Negroes and Bushmen, of whom former probably had original home near the large lakes, while latter have been put down as primeval inhabitants of S. regions. Hamites apparently spread from Horn of Africa, and enforced emigration of Negroes, whose subsequent mingling with Bushmen probably produced Hottentots. Libyans coming from N. also intermingled with Negroes, which resulted in the Fulas. A most important migration was that of Zulu tribes toward N., chief tribes being Matabele and Angoni. Madagascar was early occupied by a Malayo-Indonesian race known as Hovas, who are still chief group of its population, others being Malagasy and Negroid tribes.

Africa long remained isolated from world trade, partly because there was no way of communicating with interior of continent, but also because of unhealthy districts round coasts and inactivity of natives. Of these drawbacks the first hardly exists any longer, and second has been greatly ameliorated. Progress of civilization has led to increase of trade. Africa's chief resources are: jungle products, such as rubber, oil, timber of various kinds, gums, and nuts; fruits; cultivated plants, such as coffee, cotton, sugar, cereals, and tobacco; ivory, hides, wool, ostrich feathers, and other animal products; and minerals, such as gold, diamonds, tin, copper, iron, antimony, phosphates, and lead. Means of communication have improved, and railways have been greatly extended. A trans-continental railway from Cape to Mediterranean is partly constructed. Telegraphic system is also well developed.

Ag'ades, tn., cap., Aïr (Asben), Sahara, Africa; important caravan centre. Pop. 8,000 (Tuaregs).

Agadir (*ä-gä-dēr'*), most southerly port, key to Morocco, N. Africa; on Atlantic Ocean; in French terr. Pop. *c.* 2,000.

Agaña (*ag-än'ya*), tn., cap., Guam I., Pacific Ocean; belongs to U.S.A. Pop. 7,000.

Agen (*ä-zhon'*), cathedral tn., France, 84 m. S.E. of Bordeaux; trade in poultry, prunes, brandy, wine, grain. Pop. 20,000.

Aggtelek (*og'tel-ek*), vil., N. Hungary, 94 m. N.E. of Budapest; stalactite caves. Pop. 600.

Agincourt (*ä-zhan-koor'*), vil., Pas de Calais, France; here Henry V. of England with small force, mostly archers, defeated French army (1415).

Agira (*ä-jē'ra*), tn., Sicily, 35 m. W. of Catania; fine marble in vicinity. Pop. 24,000.

Ag'ra, chief tn., Agra dist., United Provs., India, on R. Jumna. Industries: cotton mills, flour mills, carpets. On bank of river is the exquisite Taj Mahal, a mausoleum in white marble erected (1632) by Shah Jehan for his favourite wife. Pop. 185,500.

Agram. See ZAGREB.

Agrigentum. See GIRGENTI.

Aguadilla (*ä-gwäi-dēl'ya*), tn., Porto Rico, 65 m. W. of San Juan. Exports sugar and coffee. Pop. 17,000.

Aguascalientes (*äg'wäs-kal-yen'tes*). (1) State, central Mexico; cereals, stock raising; textiles. Area, 2,969 m.; pop. 108,000. (2) Cap. of above, 70 m. N.W. of Leon; hot springs; alt. 6,400 ft. Pop. 48,000.

Aguilar de la Frontera (*ä-gē-lär' dä lä fron-tä'rä*), tn., Andalusia, Spain, on the Cabra R., 27 m. S. of Cordoba;

wine, olives; dismantled Moorish castle. Pop. 15,000.

Aguilas (*ä'gē-las*), port, Murcia, Spain; exports esparto grass and iron ore. Pop. 17,000.

Agulhas (*ä-gool'yäs*), CAPE, most southerly point, Africa; stormy; dangerous for shipping; lighthouse (1849).

Ah'len, tn., Westphalia, Prussia, 17 m. S.S.E. of Münster; manufactures metals and enamels. Pop. 22,000.

Ahmadabad', tn., Bombay, India, N. of Gulf of Cambay; magnificent mosques; Jain temple; silk, gold, and cotton industries. Pop. 274,000.

Ahmadna'gar. (1) Dist., Bombay, India; cotton, cereals, indigo. Pop. 732,000. (2) Cap. of above, 125 m. E. of Bombay; mission station; cottons, carpets, saris (women's dresses); copper and brass vessels. Pop. 50,000.

Ahwaz', tn., Khuzistan, Persia, on Karun riv.; contains part of oil-pipe line from Abadan I. to Anglo-Persian oilfields. Pop. *c.* 15,000.

Aidin (*ī-dēn'*), tn., Asia Minor, Turkey, 60 m. S.E. of Smyrna; morocco leather, cotton, fruits; connected by rail with Smyrna (*c.* 70 m.). Pop. 70,000.

Aigues-Mortes (*āg-mort'*), tn., Gard, France, at W. edge of delta of R. Rhone, 3 m. from Mediterranean Sea; formerly a fortified seaport; harbour long silted up, hence name, 'dead waters'; centre of canals; fishing. Pop. 3,400.

Aigun (*ī'goon*), tn., Manchuria, on R. Amur; local trade in cattle, grain, and flour. Pop. 20,000.

Ailsa Craig, precipitous islet, Firth of Clyde, Scotland; alt. 1,114 ft.; lighthouse.

Ain (*ăn*). (1) Dep. of E. France; bisected by R. Ain; E. mountainous, W. flat. Hemp, vines, grain, sheep, poultry raised; cereals; stock raising; silk factories; forest industries. Cap. Bourg. Pop. 317,000. (2) Riv., France; rises Jura range; joins Rhone above Lyons.

Ain Sefra (*īn sef'ra*), terr., S. Algeria; traversed by Oran Rly. Pop. 174,000.

Aintab (*īn'tab*), Asia Minor, Turkey, 60 m. N. of Aleppo; bazaars; hides and morocco leather. Pop. 60,000.

Ain'tree, vil., Lancs, England, 5 m. N.E. of Liverpool; on its racecourse Grand National Steeplechase is run.

Air (*a-ēr'*), or ASBEN, Saharan dist., Niger Colony, French W. Africa; mts. rise to 5,000 ft. Caravan centre; dates, millet, indigo, and senna produced; inhabitants (Tuaregs) of mixed race. Cap. Agades.

Air'drie, mkt. tn., munic. burgh, Lanarkshire, Scotland, 11 m. E. of Glasgow; collieries, ironworks; first free library in Scotland (1856). Pop. 26,000.

Aire (*ār*), riv., W. Riding, Yorks, England; joins R. Ouse. Coal and manufacturing area.

Airedale, valley of R. Aire, Yorks, England; has ruins of Kirkstall Abbey, near Leeds.

Aisne (*ān*). (1) Riv., N. France, rises in the Argonne, dep. Meuse, and falls into R. Oise at Compiègne; connected by canals with other important rivs. of region; navigable to Condé; scene of three important battles during Great War; length, 175 m. (2) Dep., N. France; hilly in N.E.; remainder well-wooded plains and valleys. Agriculture highly developed; timber, chemicals, iron goods, sugar, brewing, textiles. Cap. Laon. Area, 2,866 sq. m.; pop. 489,000.

Aitutak'i, one of Cook Islands, S. Pacific; belongs to New Zealand; coconuts.

Aivali (*ä-ē-vä'lē*), port, Asia Minor, Turkey; opposite Mitylene I.; exports fish, wine, raisins. Pop. 17,000.

Aix (*āks*), tn., Bouches-du-Rhône, France, 18 m. N. of Marseilles; old cap. of Provence; thermal springs; olive oil, confectionery, flour. Pop. 23,500.

Aix-la-Chapelle. See AACHEN.

Aix-les-Bains (*āks-le-ban*), health resort, Savoie, France, 9 m. N. of Chambéry; near Lake Bourget; hot springs (alum and sulphur). Pop. 8,000.

Ajaccio (*ä-yät'chō*), cap., Corsica,

France, on Gulf of Ajaccio. Birthplace of Napoleon; winter resort. Exports wood, sardines, anchovies, wine, fruit. Pop. 21,000.

Ajmer (*aj-mēr'*), tn., Rajputana, India; cap. of Ajmer-Merwara; on slopes of Taragarh Hill; fortress. Mayo College for Rajput chiefs; cotton, salt, oil, opium. Pop. 114,000.

Ajmer'-Merwar'a, prov., India; cotton, millet, wheat, oil-seeds. Chief tn., Ajmer. Area, 2,599 sq. m.; pop. 448,000.

Akaba. See AQABA.

Akas'a, tn., coaling and transhipment station, R. Nun mouth, S. Nigeria; govt. engineering and repair shops; ground nuts, palm oil. Pop. 31,000.

Ak'ashi, tn. and summer resort, Honshu, Japan, 12 m. W. of Kobe; meridian regulates Japanese time. Pop. 35,000.

Akhaltsikh (*ä-chäl'tsēch*), tn., Georgian rep., U.S.S.R.; silver filigree work; silk, honey, wax. Pop. 15,000.

Ak-Hissar', tn., Asia Minor, Turkey, 58 m. N.E. of Smyrna; exports carpets, cereals, opium, cotton, dyes; anc. *Thyatira.* Pop. 48,000.

Akhmim, tn., Upper Egypt, on R. Nile; manufactures cotton goods. Pop. 28,000.

Akhtyrka (*ä-chtēr'kä*), tn., Ukraine rep., U.S.S.R., *c.* 70 m. N.W. of Kharkov; woollens, fruit, beet sugar. Pop. 30,000.

Akkerman. See CETATEA ALBA.

Akmolinsk'. (1) Prov., Kazak rep., U.S.S.R.; copper and coal; nomadic Kirghiz rear sheep, cattle, horses, goats, and camels. Area, 97,600 sq. m.; pop. 288,000. (2) Tn. in above, 280 m. S.S.W. of Omsk; caravan entrepôt. Pop. 10,000.

Ako'la. (1) Dist., Berar, India; cotton, cereals. Area, 4,111 sq. m.; pop. 800,000. (2) Tn. in above, 53 m. S.W. of Amraoti; cotton centre. Pop. 38,000.

Akreyri (*ak-rī'rē*), tn., N. Iceland; chief station of Iceland herring fishery; train-oil boileries. Pop. 3,000.

Ak'ron, city, Ohio, U.S.A., 35 m. S. by E. of Cleveland; largest rubber-manufacturing centre in world; corn mills; clay beds; flour and woollens. Pop. 254,000.

Aksu', city, W. Sinkiang, China; earthenware, copper, iron, leather goods; caravan centre. Pop. 20,000.

Aksum', formerly AXUM, anc. city, Tigré, N. Abyssinia; alt. 7,226 ft.; sacred city.

Ak'yab, port, Burma, on Bay of Bengal; third port of Burma; exports rice. Pop. 38,000.

Alabä'ma. (1) S. state, U.S.A.; bounded N. by Tennessee, E. by Georgia, W. by Mississippi, S. by Florida and Gulf of Mexico. Surface flat, except Appalachian Mts. in N.E.; soil of coastal plain sandy; farther N., rich black soil ('Black Prairie'), where cotton is grown. Chief rivs.: Alabama, Mobile, Tennessee; coast-line short; one good harbour, Mobile Bay. Climate varied, healthy; rainfall about 60 in. Chief industry, agriculture; cotton, maize, wheat, oats, potatoes, sugar, tobacco; chief minerals, iron, coal, gold, silver, lead; much timber; manufactures iron, steel, coke, cotton goods, fertilizers, turpentine, resin. Tuskegee Institute (for Negroes). Chief tns., Montgomery (cap.), Mobile, Birmingham. Area, 51,998 sq. m.; est. pop. 2,550,000 (40 per cent. Negroes). (2) Riv., U.S.A.; joins Tombigbee, forming Mobile R.

Alago'as, Atlantic state, Brazil; sugar, cotton, tobacco, rubber; cap. Maceio. Area, 11,028 sq. m.; pop. 1,117,000.

Alai Mountains (*Alai Tagh*), lofty mts., Central Asia, S.W. extension of Tian-Shan Mts.

Alais. See ALÈS.

Alajuela (*ä-lä-choo-äl'a*), prov. and tn., central Costa Rica; coffee, sugar. Pop. (tn.) 9,000, (prov.) 98,000.

Alame'da, tn., California, U.S.A., on San Francisco Bay; borax, potteries. Pop. 34,000.

Åland Islands (*ō'länd*), about three hundred islands, Gulf of Bothnia; eighty inhabited; cereals, cattle.

Islands now form a dep. of Finland. Area, 551 sq. m.; pop. 27,000.

Alapaevsk, tn., Ural Area, Russia, 80 m. N.E. of Sverdlovsk; iron and copper mines. Pop. 12,000.

Ala-shan. (1) Mts., Inner Mongolia; highest peak, 11,000 ft. (2) Or LITTLE GOBI, sandy desert, S. Mongolia; inhabitants, Mongols and Kalmucks.

Ala-Shehr (*al-a-shār'*), anc. city, Asia Minor, 105 m. by rail E. of Smyrna; mineral springs; trades in grain, tobacco, cottons. Pop. 33,000.

Alas'ka, peninsula, N. America, terr. of U.S.A.; bounded by Arctic Ocean on N., Arctic Ocean and Bering Str. on W., Pacific on S., Canada on E.; traversed by many mt. ranges (principal peaks, Mts. McKinley and Foraker); many active volcanoes; hot springs. Coast much indented; chief isls.: Aleutian and Kodiak Isls. in S.W., Alexander Archipelago in S.E.; first and third are remains of submerged mt. ranges; principal riv. Yukon; large forests. Climate is damp and very severe; fauna includes the moose, caribou, sable, otter, seal, wolf, bear, beaver, ermine, fox, mink; flora includes balsam, fir, cedar, hemlock, spruce. Fisheries, salmon canning; furs; gold, silver, tin, copper; large coal areas. Terr. sold by Russia to U.S.A., 1867, for £1,440,000; Alaskan-Canadian boundary dispute settled at London, 1903. Chief towns: Juneau (cap.), Ketchikan (anchorage), Sitka. Area, 590,884 sq. m.; pop. 55,000.

Alas'sio, tn., Liguria, Italy; in Italian Riviera; winter resort. Pop. 6,000.

Ala-tau, mt. range, Central Asia, S.E. of L. Balkash; chief peak, Khan Tengri (24,000 ft.).

Alat'ri, tn., Italy, 45 m. S.E. of Rome; tapestry and cloth. Pop. 15,000.

Alatyr (*ă-lă-tēr'*), tn., Chuvash rep., Russia, *c.* 130 m. S.W. of Kazan; milling, brewing; grain trade. Pop. 22,000.

Al'ava, prov., N. Spain; viticulture; cereals, timber, salt; cap. Vitoria. Area, 1,175 sq. m.; pop. 100,000.

Al'ba, tn., prov. Cuneo, Italy, 42 m. by rail S.E. of Turin; viticulture, sericulture. Pop. 14,000.

Albacete (*äl-bă-thă'ti*). (1) Prov., Murcia, Spain; cereals, fruit, sheep. Area, 5,737 sq. m.; pop. 315,000. (2) Cap. of above; trade in saffron and agricultural produce. Pop. 36,000.

Al'ba Iulia (*yool'yă*), formerly KARLSBURG or GYULA-FEHÉRVÁR, tn., Transylvania, Romania, on R. Mures; wine; union of Transylvania with Romania proclaimed here, 1918. Pop. 13,500.

Alba'nia, kingdom on E. shore of Adriatic Sea. Traversed by high mts.; coast plains fertile. Chief rivs.: Drin, Shkumbi, Viossa; Lakes Scutari and Okhrida on frontier. Climate extreme; fever on swampy coast lands: Wolves in all parts; game abundant; primitive cultivation; minerals undeveloped; forests of oak, beech, ash, etc.; cereals, tobacco, olives, oranges, vines, and mulberries; cattle raised; exports animal foods, fish, cereals, hides and skins.

Albanians are warlike race of highlanders, Ghegs in the N., Tosks in the S. They have retained their own language, of which Gheg and Tosk are principal dialects. Chief towns: Koritsa, Scutari, Tirana (cap.). Area (est.), 17,374 sq. m.; pop. (est.) 834,000.

Al'bany. (1) Tn., W. Australia, on King George Sound; importance declined with rise of Fremantle; whaling. Pop. 4,000. (2) Cap., New York state, U.S.A.; at head of large steamer navigation, Hudson R., and terminal point of the Erie Canal (opened 1825); formerly a fur-trading station, now a large manufacturing and distributing centre. Manufactures iron and brass goods, chemicals, textiles, paper. Pop. 127,000.

Albay. (1) Prov., S.E. Luzon, Philippines; manila hemp production; copra, sugar, rice, tobacco. Area, 997 sq. m.; pop. *c.* 250,000.

(2) Cap. of above; includes port of Legaspi. Pop. 53,000.

Albert. (1) (*al-ber'*) Small tn., Somme, France, on R. Ancre; suffered destruction in the Great War. (2) LAKE, in R. Nile basin, Uganda, Africa; 100 m. long, 20 m. wide; area, 1,640 sq. m. Receives Semliki R. from L. Edward in S.W., Victoria Nile in N.E., N. outlet, White Nile; navigable, except in S.; discovered by Sir Samuel Baker (1864).

Alber'ta, prov., W. Canada. Surface generally level in N. and S.E., mountainous in W. (Rockies); much of S. is prairie; chief rivs.: Peace, Athabasca, Saskatchewan; lakes: Lesser Slave, Claire, part of Athabasca; climate extreme; rainfall, 13 in. In N. are forests; S.W. is important ranching dist., with cattle, horses, and sheep; dairying. Wheat and other grains, fruits, and tobacco cultivated; 'dry farming'; alfalfa on irrigated lands; farms in Peace valley. Minerals include coal, petroleum, natural gas, asphalt, gold. Banff, in Canadian National Park, has hot springs. Chief tns., Edmonton (cap.), Calgary. Area, 255,285 sq. m.; pop. 608,000.

Albert Edward, LAKE. See EDWARD, LAKE.

Albertville. (1) Tn., Savoie, France, 50 m. N.E. of Grenoble; silver-lead mines, slate. Pop. 6,000. (2) Trading station, Belgian Congo, on W. of L. Tanganyika; rly. to Lualaba riv.

Albi, tn., Tarn, France, 48 m. N.E. of Toulouse; wheat, prunes, wines. Pop. 22,000.

Albrun Pass, Alpine bridle path (7,907 ft.), 17 m. N.E. of Simplon Tunnel; leads by Rs. Binn and Devero valleys from Switzerland into Italy.

Albuquerque (*ăl-boo-kerk'ā*), tn., New Mexico, U.S.A., on Rio Grande; wool, hides, timber; irrigation centre. Pop. 27,000.

Al'bury, tn., New South Wales; at head of navigation of R. Murray; sheep, fruit, cereals. Pop. 8,500.

Al'camo, tn., Sicily, Italy, 24 m. S.W. of Palermo; centre of fertile dist.; Saracen castle. Pop. 63,000.

Alcaraz (*ăl-kă-răth'*), mts., Spain; at head of basin of Guadalquivir; loftiest peak, 5,900 ft.; San Juan de Alcaraz copper mines in vicinity.

Alcazar de San Juan (*ăl-kă-thăr' de săn choo-ăn'*), tn., Spain, 92 m. by rail S.S.E. of Madrid; rly. jn.; soap, gunpowder factories; wine. Pop. 16,000.

Alcester (*aul'ster*), tn., Warwickshire, England, 15 m. S.W. of Warwick; site of Roman camp; cycles; agricultural implements. Pop. 2,300.

Alcira (*ăl-thē'ra*), tn., Spain, 22 m. S.W. of Valencia; silk, fruit, rice. Pop. 20,000.

Alcoy (*ăl-ko'ē*), tn., Spain, 34 m. N. of Alicante; textiles, agricultural machinery, cigarette paper. Pop. 37,000.

Aldborough, vil., Yorks, England, 7 m. S.E. of Ripon; on Watling Street; Roman remains. Pop. 600.

Aldeburgh or **Aldborough** (*auld'boru* or *aul'boru*), seapt., Suffolk, England; herring and lobster fishing; importance diminished since 17th cent. Pop. 2,500.

Al'derley Edge, urb. dist., Cheshire, England, 8 m. S.W. of Stockport; copper mines till 1879. Pop. 3,100.

Al'derney, most northerly of Channel Islands; separated from Normandy by Race of Alderney. Coast fringed with reefs—the Caskets; surface an open tableland; soil fertile, vegetable produce for early Fr. and Brit. markets grown. Alderney cattle once famous. Regular steamer communication between Alderney, Guernsey, and Cherbourg; harbour at Braye. Cap. St. Anne, near centre of isl. Area, 1,962 ac.; pop. 2,000.

Al'dershot, munic. bor., Hants, England, 35 m. S.W. of London; military camp established in 1855; permanent barracks erected in 1881. British Expeditionary Force (Aug. 1914) mobilized here. Pop. 34,300.

Alemtejo (*ă-lan-tă'zhō*), largest prov., Portugal; several mt. chains; rivs., Tagus, Guadiana. Cereals; stock raising; forests; copper and iron mines. Cap. Evora. Area, 9,219 sq. m.; pop. 502,000.

Alençon (*ä-lan-sōn'*), chief tn., Orne, N.W. France; woollens, linen; gave name to famous lace. Pop. 14,000.

Alep'po (Turkish *Haleb*), city, Syria, 70 m. S.E. of its port, Alexandretta; in fertile plain; important trade centre before discovery of sea route to India. Tobacco, wheat, hemp; manufactures silk and cotton stuffs. Rlys. to Damascus, Alexandretta, and Baghdad. Pop. *c.* 200,000.

Alès (*ä-lez'*), formerly ALAIS, tn., Gard, S. France, at base of Cevennes Mts.; silk market; coal and iron mines. Pop. 30,000.

Alessan'dria. (1) Prov., Piedmont, Italy; agricultural; silk. Area, 1,960 sq. m.; pop. 782,000. (2) Fort. tn., cap. of above, 48 m. S.E. of Turin; rly. jn.; linen, felt hats, macaroni. Pop. 85,000.

Ales'sio, port, Adriatic Sea, Albania, 17 m. S.E. of Scutari. Pop. 3,500.

Al'etsch, glacier, Switzerland, largest in Europe (12½ m. long), S. of Jungfrau.

Al'etschhorn, mt. peak, Bernese Oberland, Switzerland (13,773 ft.); first ascended 1859.

Aleutian Islands (*ä-loosh'i-an*), chain of small islands, Alaska, Pacific Ocean; extend over 1,000 m. towards Kamchatka from Alaska; many are volcanic; largest, Unimak, has two volcanoes; principal industries: fishing, hunting, sealing, fox farming; Unalaska is sealing and whaling centre. Pop. 1,000.

Alexander Archipelago (over 1,100 islands), off Alaska; chief islands, Baranov, Prince of Wales; belong to U.S.A.

Alexandretta (Turkish *Iskanderun*), tn., N. Syria; port for Aleppo; exports live-stock, textiles, tobacco, silk, and fruit. Pop. 15,000.

Alexandria. (1) Port, Egypt; built on peninsula between Mediterranean and Lake Mareotis, and on isthmus joining Pharos to mainland; fine harbour; floating dock; graving dock (opened 1905); torpedo station; good railway and telegraphic communication; handles 80 per cent. of entire Egyptian trade; exports cotton, wool, sugar, eggs; imports coal, textiles, machinery. Pop. 570,500. (2) Tn., Dumbartonshire, Scotland, on R. Leven; bleaching, dye works. Pop. 10,500. (3) Tn., Virginia, U.S.A., on Potomac riv.; fertilizers, silk, leather, shoes, bottles. Pop. 24,000.

Alexandropol. See LENINAKAN.

Alexan'drovsk. (1) Port, Murman coast, N. Russia; terminus of Murman rly.; ice-free throughout the year. (2) See ZAPOROZHE.

Alexan'drovsk - Grushev'ski, tn., North Caucasian Area, R.S.F.S.R., 50 m. N.E. of Rostov; in anthracite coal dist. Pop. 20,000.

Alexandrovsky, tn., Russia, 5 m. S.E. of Leningrad; cotton, glass, porcelain. Pop. 10,000.

Alföld (*ol'fēld*), the great central plain of Hungary; grain, fruit, wines.

Al'ford. (1) Vil., Aberdeenshire, Scotland, on R. Don, 29¼ m. N.W. of Aberdeen; centre of agricultural dist.; stone circle; Kildrummy Castle is 10 m. to W. Pop. 600. (2) Urb. dist., Lincs, England, 23¼ m. by rail N.E. of Boston; mkt. tn. Pop. 2,200.

Alfreton (*aul'fre-ton*), mkt. tn., Derbyshire, England, 14 m. N.N.E. of Derby; collieries, ironworks, potteries. Pop. 21,200.

Algar've, southmost prov., Portugal; mts. in N.; fertile and well cultivated in S.; fruit and fisheries. Area, 1,937 sq. m.; pop. 270,000.

Algeciras (*äl-cheth-ē'räs*), port, Spain, opposite Gibraltar (5 m.); whale and other fisheries; winter resort. Pop. 20,500.

Alge'ria, Fr. colony, N. Africa; bounded N. by Mediterranean, E. by Tunisia, S. by Sahara, W. by Morocco. Country divided by elevation and climatic conditions into three unequal parallel zones: (1) The Tell, undulating N. region (containing the Little Atlas) of forests and arable land; (2) The Steppe region of herbaceous vegetation and of pasture land diversified by ranges of mts.; (3) The Sahara (S. of Sahara Atlas), where agriculture is possible only by irrigation in oases. Coast, 690 m.; high and rocky. Rivs. nothing but torrents (*wadis*), frequently dried up; some dammed for irrigation; in steppes they form the *Shotts* of the plains, shallow lakes where snow and rain-water gather in winter. Climate, Mediterranean type; two seasons—dry and hot (summer), wet or cold (autumn, winter, spring). Great forests on the mt. slopes, containing oaks, cedars, junipers, and other trees. Cultivated plants include cereals—wheat, oats, and barley being grown in the Tell—flax, and tobacco; vines, olives, oranges, and other fruits cultivated, and various vegetables grown. Olive oil produced; important fisheries; horses, mules, cattle, and sheep raised in large numbers. Minerals include iron, lead, copper, zinc, phosphates, salt, petroleum, antimony, mercury. Among exports are sheep, wool, hides, cereals, cattle, horses, fruit, wines, olive oil, eggs, metals, phosphates, tobacco; imports textiles, petroleum, motor-cars, machinery, paper, coal, sugar, coffee. Rly. mileage is over 2,700; good postal and telegraphic communications. Chief seaports, Algiers (cap.), Bougie, Philippeville, Oran, Bona; largest inland tn., Constantine. Inhabitants include French, Jews, Moroccans, etc. Area, 847,500 sq. m.; pop. 6,000,000 (835,000 Europeans).

Alghero (*ăl-gă'rō*), port, Sardinia; coral fisheries; fruit; wine. Pop. 12,500.

Algiers (*al-jērz*), cap., Algeria, N. Africa; modern tn. along shore, anc. city on hill behind; important port, coaling station, and health resort; good harbour; exports grain, fruit, wool. Pop. 226,000.

Algo'a Bay, wide, shallow bay, S. Africa; Brit. emigrants landed here in 1820 and founded Port Elizabeth.

Alham'bra, tn., Los Angeles, California, U.S.A., at entrance to San Gabriel valley; mainly residential, but manufactures power appliances, electrical supplies, beeswax, and earthenware. Pop. 30,000.

Alican'te. (1) Prov., S.E. Spain; almonds, olives, oranges, grapes. Area, 2,185 sq. m.; pop. (prov.) 533,000. (2) Cap. of above, on Mediterranean Sea; exports wine, esparto grass, fruit. Pop. 68,500.

Al'ice, tn., Cape Prov., S. Africa, 88 m. W. by N. of East London by rail; tourist resort; it is near Lovedale mission station.

Alice Springs, administrative centre, Central Australia; on overland railway line; cattle station.

Aligarh (*ă-lē-gur'*), anc. tn., United Provinces, India, 75 m. S.E. of Delhi; Moslem univ. Pop. 67,000.

Aliquip'pa, tn., Pennsylvania, U.S.A., 20 m. N.W. of Pittsburgh; iron and steel industries. Pop. 27,000.

Aliwal' North, tn., Cape Prov., S. Africa, on Orange riv.; alt. 4,300 ft. Health resort; sulphur springs. Pop. 6,500.

Alkmaar', tn., Netherlands, 24 m. by rail N N.W. of Amsterdam; cheese trade centre; salt. Pop. 27,500.

Allahabad', cap., United Provinces, India, at confluence of Jumna with Ganges; great annual fair; centre of pilgrimage; rly. centre. Pop. (tn.) 157,500.

Alleghany (*ăl'i-gā-nē*) **Mountains.** See APPALACHIANS.

Al'legheny. (1) Part of Pittsburgh, Pennsylvania, U.S.A.; residential, manufacturing centre; iron, steel industries. (2) Riv., rises in W. of New York State, U.S.A., joins R. Monongahela at Pittsburgh, forming R. Ohio.

Al'len, LOUGH, between counties of Leitrim and Roscommon, I.F.S. R. Shannon navigable from here to sea. Length, 5 m.; breadth, *c.* 3 m.

Al'len, Bog of, group of morasses in cos. Kildare, Offaly, Leix, and West Meath, I.F.S.; area, *c.* 240,000 ac.

Allenstein, tn., E. Prussia, Germany, 64 m. S. of Königsberg; saw-mills, breweries, match factory. Pop. 38,000.

Al'lentown, city, Pennsylvania, U.S.A., 50 m. N.W. of Philadelphia; one of leading furniture and silk producers in U.S.A.; tobacco, machine-shop products. Pop. 92,000.

Allep'pey, tn., Travancore, s.w. India; commercial centre; good harbour; oil-mills; coffee, cardamoms. Pop. 32,000.

Allier (*ăl-yā'*). (1) Dep., central France; fertile; cereals, fruits; livestock; coal, iron; mineral springs. Chief tns., Moulins, Montluçon, and Vichy. Area, 2,849 sq. m.; pop. 370,000. (2) Riv., France; flows N. through Central Plateau to join Loire. Length, 270 m.

Al'loa, tn. and port, Clackmannanshire, Scotland, on R. Forth; yarn factories, breweries, distilleries, glass works; exports coal. Pop. 13,300.

Al'loway, vil., Ayrshire, Scotland, 2 m. s. of Ayr; birthplace of Robert Burns; cottage now a Burns Museum.

Al'ma, riv., Crimean Rep., Russia; enters Black Sea 17 m. w. of Sevastopol; scene of Franco-Brit. victory over Russians, 1854.

Alma Ata, or VERNI, tn., S.E. Kazak, U.S.S.R.; cattle breeding; bee keeping; vines and fruits. Pop. 45,000.

Almaden (*ăl-mă-*thăn'), tn., Estremadura, Spain, 48 m. s.w. of Ciudad Real in Sierra Morena Mts.; quicksilver mines worked for over two centuries; Moorish castle. Pop. 10,000.

Almelo (*al-mă-lō'*), tn., Overyssel, Netherlands; yarn, cotton goods; manufactures damask. Pop. 29,000.

Almeria (*ăl-me-rē'a*). (1) Prov., s. Spain; fruit, especially grapes; esparto; iron ore; chief rivs., Almeria, Almanzora, have fertile valleys. Area, 3,360 sq. m.; pop. 373,000. (2) Tn., cap. of above, on Mediterranean Sea; oil-fuel port; exports grapes, esparto; iron, lead. Pop. 51,000.

Almond. (1) Riv., Scotland; enters Firth of Forth at Cramond. (2) Riv., Perthshire, Scotland; enters Tay at Scone.

Almondbury (*ăm'bur-i, aum'bur-i,* or *ä'mond-bur-i*), tn., Yorks, England; forms S.E. part of Huddersfield. Pop. 15,500.

Almo'ra, tn., United Provinces, India, on slopes of Himalayas; alt. 5,400 ft.; health resort; orchards, tea. Pop. 8,500.

Alnmouth (*ăl'muth*), wat.-pl., Northumberland, England, at mouth of R. Aln, 4 m. S.E. of Alnwick.

Alnwick (*an'ik*), mkt. and co. tn., Northumberland, England. Alnwick Castle, seat of Percies since 1310. Brewing, tobacco; fishing-tackle. Pop. 6,900.

Al'ora, tn., Spain, 25 m. N.W. of Malaga by rail; oranges, lemons, olives; hot sulphur springs; mediæval ruins. Pop. 11,500.

Al'ost, tn., E. Flanders, Belgium; centre of hop trade; linen, silk, and cloth. Pop. 37,000.

Alpe'na, city, Michigan, U.S.A., on E. coast of Lake Huron; cement and paper factories; tanneries; lumber; mineral products. Pop. 12,000.

Alpes, BASSES. See BASSES-ALPES.

Alpes-Maritimes (*alp-mă-rē-tēm*), dep., S.E. France; sheep pasturage; olives, wines, fruits; health resorts, Nice, Cannes, Mentone. Area, 1,443 sq. m.; pop. 435,500.

Alps, crescent-shaped mt. system, extending from Gulf of Genoa to Vienna; total length, *c.* 700 m.; breadth, 30–160 m.; area, *c.* 80,000 sq. m.; topographically divided into (1) W. Alps (Col di Tenda to Simplon), including Maritime Alps, Cottian Alps, Dauphiné Alps, Graian Alps, chain of Mont Blanc, Pennine Alps; (2) Central Alps (Simplon to Reschen, Scheideck, and Stelvio), including Bernese Alps, N. Swiss Alps, Lepontine and Adula Alps, Tödi group, Rhætian Alps; (3) E. Alps, (Reschen, Scheideck, and Stelvio to the Semmering), including Ortler, Adamello, and Brenta groups, Limestone Alps of Bavaria, N. Tyrol and Salzburg, Central Tyrolese Alps, S. Tyrolese Alps (Dolomites), S.E. Alps (Carnic, Karawanken, and Julian Alps). Snow-line varies from 8,900 ft. on S. side to 9,200 ft. on N.; glaciers of upper valleys descend to 4,000–5,000 ft. above sea-level—Aletsch, 4,400 ft

Best-known peaks of Western Alps —Gran Paradiso (13,320 ft.), Mont Blanc (15,780), Dent du Midi (10,690), Matterhorn (14,775), Monte Rosa (15,215), Aletschhorn (13,770), Jungfrau (13,670), Mönch (13,460), and Finsteraarhorn (14,020).

Drained by Rhine and tributaries, Aar, Reuss, Limmat; Danube and tributaries, Iller, Lech, Isar, Inn; Po and tributaries, Dora Riparia, Ticino, Mincio, Adige; Rhone with Arve, Isère, Durance; and smaller streams flowing to Adriatic and Ligurian Sea.

Chief passes: Great St. Bernard, E. of Mont Blanc to Rhone; Mont Cenis, from R. Dora Riparia N.W. to Arc and Isère; Simplon, from Maggiore to Brieg; St. Gotthard, from Ticino to Upper Reuss valley; Brenner, from Adige to Innsbrück. There are railways crossing by Col dell' Altare; Mont Cenis, tunnel over 7½ m. long, opened 1871; Simplon, tunnel 12¼ m. long, opened 1906; St. Gotthard, tunnel over 9½ m. long, opened 1882; Arlberg, opened 1884; Brenner, opened 1867, series of twenty-seven tunnels; Semmering, opened 1853. Several non-snowy peaks have tourist railways up their slopes; the only snowy peak with one is Jungfrau. Highest villages, Juf (6,998 ft.) in Grisons, L'Ecot (6,713) in Savoy, St. Véran (6,726) in Dauphiné, Trepalle in Ital. Alps (6,788), Ober Gurgl (6,322) and Fend (6,211) in Tyrolese Alps; minerals abound in Austrian part of range, where coal, iron, lead, gold, silver, copper, and mercury are worked.

The distinctive Alpine plants include gentians, saxifrages, rhododendrons, primulas, edelweiss; general characteristics are dwarfish woody stems, large flowers, woolly texture. Fauna includes bouquetin or Alpine ibex, marmot, chamois, white hare, fox, lynx, wild-cat, wolf, bear; vultures, eagles, ptarmigan, grouse, etc., are found.

Alsace-Lorraine (*ăl-săs' lor-ān'*): Alsace, the most easterly region of France, stretches from the crest of the Vosges Mts. to the R. Rhine; Lorraine, which lies N.W. of Alsace, consists of a low plateau drained by the Saar (Sarre) in the E., and the Moselle in the W. Cereals, potatoes, sugar-beet, flax, tobacco, hemp, fruit, and wine are the principal products. Forests, all state-owned, occupy 30 per cent. of total area. Minerals—iron, coal, salt, and building stone—are concentrated in Lorraine. Potash deposits in Alsace extremely valuable. Chief industries of Lorraine are iron smelting and founding, and the manufacture of machinery; of Alsace, textiles, glass, porcelain, chemicals, and paper. There are 1,320 m. of railways and a number of canals—Rhine-Marne, the Rhine-Rhone, and the coal canal of the Saar (Fr. Sarre). The prov. of Alsace is divided into deps. of Haut-Rhin (chief tns., Mulhouse and Colmar), and Bas-Rhin (Strasbourg); Lorraine includes deps. of Moselle (Metz), Meurthe-et-Moselle (Nancy), Meuse (Bar-le-Duc), and Vosges (Epinal). Surrendered by France to Germany, 1871; restored to France after Great War. Alsace, area, 3,202 sq. m.; pop. 1,162,000. Lorraine, area, 9,150 sq. m.; pop. 1,786,000.

Alsager (*awl'sā-jer*), urb. dist., Cheshire, England, 5¼ m. E. of Crewe. Pop. 2,900.

Alsatia, old name for Alsace. It was also the name given to the Whitefriars dist., London, which, till 1697, was a debtors' sanctuary and haunt of thieves.

Alsen (*al'zen*), isl., Baltic Sea, in Little Belt; Dan. till 1864, then Prussian; returned to Denmark, 1920. Area, 120 sq. m.; pop. 25,000.

Alston (*aul'ston*), tn., Cumberland, England, in Pennine Mts.; limestone quarries. Pop. 3,000.

Altai Mountains (*al-tī'*), Central Asia. Altai proper and Greater Altai stretch from Gobi N.W. in two parallel ranges across Siberian frontier. Contains upper streams of Ob and Irtysh rivs. Northern Altai (highest peak, Byelukha, 14,890 ft.), to the N. of and parallel to first group. Altai consist of schists, granite, slate, carboniferous and Devonian deposits. Alpine and herbaceous plants; forests. In Russian Altai, copper, lead, zinc, silver, gold.

Altamaha', riv., Georgia, U.S.A., enters Atlantic Ocean; navigable for small vessels to Macon; length, 155 m.

Altamu'ra, tn., Apulia, S.E. Italy; wine; wool. Pop. 27,000.

Altdorf, cap., Uri, Switzerland, near S.E. end of L. Lucerne; alt. 1,516 ft.; associated with William Tell; large statue. Pop. 4,000.

Altenburg (*äl'ten-boorg*), tn., Thuringia, Germany, 23 m. S. of Leipzig; horse fairs; woollen yarn. Pop. 42,000.

Al'tendorf, suburb of Essen, Rhineland, Prussia.

Altmühl (*alt'mool*), riv., Bavaria, Germany; joins Danube W. of Regensburg; connected with R. Main by Ludwig's Canal; total length, 116 m.

Al'tofts, urb. dist., W. Riding, Yorks, England, 7 m. S.E. of Leeds; coal mining. Pop. 5,000.

Alton (*aul'ton*). (1) Tn., Hants, England, 15 m. N.E. of Winchester; corn markets. Pop. 6,200. (2) Tn., Illinois, U.S.A., on Mississippi R.; manufactures of machinery, glass, flour. Pop. 30,000.

Altona (*äl'tō-na*), tn., Schleswig-Holstein, Prussia; on R. Elbe, near Hamburg, and commercially incorporated with it; fine docks; ship repairing, brewing, ironfounding, flour milling, cotton, woollen, tobacco, leather, glass, and soap manufactures. Pop. 185,000.

Altoon'a, tn., Pennsylvania, U.S.A., 117 m. E. of Pittsburgh; in coalfield; centre of railway work. Pop. 82,000.

Altrincham (*aul'tring-am*), tn., Cheshire, England, 8 m. S.W. of Manchester by rail; linotype works, engineering, and market garden produce; aerodrome. Pop. 21,400.

Altyn-Tagh (*äl'tin-tach*), mts., northernmost range of Kunlun Mountains, Central Asia.

Al'va, tn., Clackmannanshire, Scotland, 3¼ m. N. of Alloa; manufactures serges and tartans. Pop. 3,800.

Al'verstoke, par., Hants, England, on Portsmouth Harbour; includes Gosport; several barracks. Pop. 33,600.

Alwar (*äl'wur*). (1) Indian state, Rajputana, India. Area, 3,185 sq. m.; pop. 702,000. (2) Cap. of above, 85 m. S.W. of Delhi; palaces. Pop. 45,000.

Alyth (*ä'lith*), mkt. tn., Perthshire, Scotland, 4½ m. E.N.E. of Blairgowrie; jute, wool. Pop. 1,700.

Amade'us Lake, shallow salt lake, S. and W. Australia; discovered by Giles (1872). Length, 200 m.

Am'ager, low, flat isl., off Zealand, Denmark; market garden of Copenhagen. Christianshavn is on W. side.

Amal'fi, port, Gulf of Salerno, Italy; devastated by inundations (1343), and by earthquake (1930). Now a tourist resort. Fisheries; macaroni, paper, soap. Pop. 7,000.

Aman'us (Turkish *Alma Dagh*), mt. range, N.W. Syria; caravan routes through passes.

Amara. See KUT-AL-IMARA.

Amaril'lo, tn., N. Texas, U.S.A.; rly. jn. and trade centre; oil refining, zinc smelting; creameries and grain elevators. Pop. 43,000.

Amasia (*ä-mä'sēa*), tn., Asia Minor, Turkey, on Yeshil Irmak riv.; rly. to Samsun, 50 m. distant, on Black Sea; silk, wine, fruit, salt. Pop. 61,000.

Amatitlan', tn., S. Guatemala, on lake of same name; hot springs near lake; cochineal. Pop. 40,000.

Amaton'galand, terr., E. coast, S. Africa; annexed to Natal (1897). Area, *c.* 600 sq. m.; pop. *c.* 13,500.

Am'azon, great riv. of Brazil, S. America; flows from Andes along equator to Atlantic Ocean; largest river of world in volume; area of basin 2,700,000 sq. m. (two-fifths S. America); head stream Alto Marañon (Peru), which issues from Lauricocha Lake (alt. 11,980 ft.). Numerous affluents form giant network of streams debouching into Atlantic at rate of 2,542,000 cub. ft. per second. Alto Marañon becomes navigable for small craft 2,700 m. from Atlantic. Ocean-going steamers penetrate to Iquitos (1,935 m. from mouth). On entering Brazil known as Solimos —tribs. Javary (550 m.), Judahy (400 m.), Jurua, and Purus, r. bk.; Putumayo (650 m.), Japura (930 m.), l. bk. At confluence of Negro (480 m.), on the l. bk., is Manaos. Below this, main stream known as Amazon. Joined (r. bk.) largest of tribs. Madeira. Other notable tribs.: Tapajoz, Xingu, and Tocantins (500 m.). Negro connected with Orinoco system. Madeira formed by Beni and Marmoré; Madeira-Marmoré railway facilitates transport of produce from Bolivia and Brazilian prov. of Matto Grasso. Tidal influence felt 400 m. upstream. In flood time enormous areas of surrounding country under water, thus fertilizing trees producing 'Para' rubber. Breadth at mouth, 200 m.; from 3 to 4 m. or more at 1,000 m. from ocean. Numerous marshy islands at mouth; largest Marajo (2,060 sq. m.). Total length of Amazon 4,000 m.; of waterways in system 30,000 m. Yellow and other fevers common; campaign against fever-bearing mosquito in progress. Produce of region: rubber, quinine, caffeine, cotton, indigo, nuts, sugar, cacao, coffee, tobacco. The river is said to contain a fresh-water replica of every salt-water fish. Turtles abound.

Amazo'nas. (1) State, Brazil; forest country produces rubber, timber, vegetable ivory, tropical fruits; grassy uplands support cattle. Manaos commercial centre. Area, 704,835 sq. m.; pop. 410,000. (2) Dep., Peru, in R. Amazon basin; rubber. Area, 13,943 sq. m.; pop. (est.) 80,000. (3) Terr., s. Venezuela; rubber, wild cacao; great part unexplored. Pop. *c*. 60,000.

Ambac'a, tn., Angola (Portuguese W. Africa); 140 m. E. by s. of Loanda by rail; centre of coffee-growing dist.

Ambal'a, tn., Punjab, India, on rly. between Delhi and Lahore; military cantonment; cotton ginning; flour mills. Pop. 76,500.

Ambat'o, tn., Ecuador, 80 m. s. of Quito; alt. 8,500 ft. Sugar, cereals, cochineal; boots, shoes, and cordage. Pop. 25,000.

Am'berg, tn., Bavaria, Germany, 35 m. E. of Nürnberg; coal and iron in vicinity; varied manufactures. Pop. 26,500.

Ambert (*on-bār'*), tn., dep. Puy de Dôme, France, 55 m. w. by s. of Lyons. Celebrated paper mills; also excellent cheese. Pop. 8,000.

Amble, seapt., Northumberland, England, at mouth of R. Coquet; coal exports; fish curing. Pop. 4,200.

Am'bleside, mkt. tn., Westmorland, England, 1 m. from head of L. Windermere. Centre for tours in Lake Dist. Pop. 2,300.

Amboi'na, most important isl. of Moluccas, Dutch E. Indies; produces ordinary tropical fruits and vegetables; cloves; copra; Amboina wood. Area, 386 sq. m.; pop. 115,000.

Ambriz', port, Angola (Portuguese W. Africa); *c*. 70 m. N. of Loanda. Exports sugar-cane, rubber, coffee, and copper. Pop. 3,000.

America, two continents (connected by isthmus), western hemisphere; comprises N., S., and Central America; total area, *c*. 16,000,000 sq. m.; total pop. *c*. 210,000,000; named after the navigator, Amerigo Vespucci, who followed up Columbus.

N. AMERICA is bounded N. by Arctic Ocean; N.E. by Smith Sound, Baffin Bay, Davis Strait; S.E. by Atlantic; s. by Gulf of Mexico and Central America; w. and s.w. by Bering Strait, Bering Sea, Pacific. Extreme length is *c*. 4,500 m.; width, *c*. 3,300 m.; area, *c*. 8,300,000 sq. m. Continent expands broadly in N. and tapers to the s. Coast-line is much indented. Surface consists of great lowland region in centre, drained by large rivers; in E. are highlands and in w. high mountain ranges. Principal mts. in w. are the Cordilleras, including the Rockies, and a parallel range known as Sierra Nevada in California and as Cascade range farther N. (chief peak of Rockies, Mt. McKinley, 20,300 ft.; of Sierra Nevada, Mt. Whitney, 14,900 ft.); and in E. Appalachian Mts. (highest peak, Mt. Mitchell, 6,700 ft.). Principal rivs. are St. Lawrence in E., Yukon, Fraser, Columbia, Colorado in W., Mississippi-Missouri, Peace-Mackenzie, Saskatchewan-Nelson draining central plains and flowing respectively to Gulf of Mexico, Arctic, and Hudson Bay. Chief lakes are Great Bear, Great Slave, Athabasca, Deer, Wollaston, Winnipeg, in Canada; Superior, Michigan, Huron, Erie, Ontario, between Canada and U.S.A.; Great Salt Lake in U.S.A. Chief islands are Newfoundland, Cape Breton, Anticosti, Prince Edward I., off E. coast of Canada; Vancouver, Queen Charlotte Is., Prince of Wales I., Aleutians, off W. coast; some of W. Indies in S.; Arctic archipelago.

Climate varies; has great extremes in centre. There are vast forests of pine, beech, oak, hickory, ash, sycamore, chestnut, and other trees; enormous quantities of wheat, maize, barley, potatoes, peas produced; many fruits cultivated; rice, sugar, coffee, cotton grown. Minerals include coal, iron, gold, silver, copper, lead, nickel, salt, petroleum.

Political divisions are Dominion of Canada, which includes all British North American possessions except Newfoundland, in N. half; United States of America and Mexico in S. half; Alaska in N.W. belongs to U.S.A. Pop. *c.* 130,000,000.

CENTRAL AMERICA unites N. and S. America; extreme length, *c.* 1,000 m.; breadth, 70 to over 300 m.; area, *c.* 210,000 sq. m.; bounded N. by Mexico, E. by Caribbean Sea, S. and W. by Pacific. Northern part is mountainous, with steep slope to Pacific, and tableland, intersected by valleys, sloping more gradually to Atlantic; narrow S. part is mountain from sea to sea. There are many volcanoes. The mountain barrier disappears in two places: first, at the Isthmus of Panama, where the Panama Canal connects the Atlantic with the Pacific; and also between Nicaragua and Costa Rica, where the R. San Juan and Lakes Nicaragua and Managua afford an easy passage from sea to sea. Political divisions are British Honduras in N.E. and the independent states of Guatemala, Honduras, Salvador, Nicaragua, Costa Rica, and Panama. Climate varies according to elevation; earthquakes frequent. In tropical belt, rubber, mahogany, cacao occur; coffee and grain are largely produced; other products are sarsaparilla, tortoiseshell, fruits, indigo, hides. The people are of Indian or mixed Span. and Ind. race. Pop. *c.* 5,500,000.

The WEST INDIES lie to the E. of Central America, between N. and S. America. They include Cuba and Haiti, which are independent reps., the Bahamas, Barbados, Trinidad, Jamaica, Leeward and Windward Islands, which belong to Britain.

SOUTH AMERICA is bounded N. by Caribbean Sea, N.E. by N. Atlantic, E.S.E. by S. Atlantic, W. by Pacific. Extreme length is *c.* 4,750 m.; breadth, *c.* 3,200 m.; area, 7,300,000 sq. m. Whole of W. side is occupied by the Andes, from the N. of which an offshoot curves round by the N. side of the Orinoco. Along the S. side of the lower Orinoco, and eastward, is the plateau of Guiana; and in E., between mouth of Amazon and Rio de la Plata, is plateau of Brazil. Rest of surface consists of great plains —wooded selvas and grassy llanos and pampas. N. is drained by Colombian Magdalena and Orinoco, N. centre by Amazon and its tributaries and Tocantins; extreme E. projection by San Francisco R.; S. centre by Paraguay, Parana, Uruguay, and their tribs. Coast-line little broken, except at river mouths and along S. part of W. side. Chief lake is Titicaca, in Bolivia and Peru.

Climate varies from tropical to temperate. There are enormous forests, those in tropical regions having magnificent trees and flowering plants. Fruits grown include oranges, pineapples, guavas, mangoes, bananas;

rubber, coffee, quassia, cinchona, tapioca, vanilla, indigo, cacao, sugar-cane also produced. Minerals include gold, silver, diamonds, copper, iron, tin.

Political divisions are the republics of Colombia, Venezuela, Ecuador, Brazil, Peru, Bolivia, Chile, Argentine Republic, Paraguay, Uruguay; colonies of British, Dutch, and French Guiana in N.E.; Falkland Islands in S.E. belong to Britain. Pop. *c.* 65,000,000.

Races.—Arctic regions of N. America are inhabited by Eskimos, a yellow race, who live chiefly by fishing and seal-hunting; they are short, fat, with black hair and brown skin. Their origin has not been authoritatively established. Aboriginal inhabitants of remainder of continent were Indians; these are generally tall and well developed, with black hair and high cheek-bones. These Amerinds are called 'Red Indians' from the copper-coloured skin of certain tribes. Best-known tribes are the Sioux in the W. plains, the Iroquois in Canada and elsewhere, the Araucanians and Patagonians in S. America. Aztecs of Mexico and Incas of Peru were civilized. In Mexico and Central America the people are chiefly creoles and half-breeds; in Brazil are large numbers of Negroes and mulattoes, while the S. American pampas are the home of a mixed race called the Gauchos. There are many Negroes in U.S.A. The European inhabitants of N. America are chiefly of Brit., Ger., and Scandinavian descent, those in S. America of Span., Port., and Italian descent.

Amersfoort (*ā'merz-fōrt*), tn., Holland, 11 m. N.E. of Utrecht; rly. jn.; cottons, woollens, leather, soap, beer, and tobacco. Pop. 36,000.

Am'ersham, tn. and par., Bucks, England, 26 m. W.N.W. of London; flour mills; breweries; chair and lace making industries. Pop. 4,500.

Amesbury (*āmz'ber-i*). (1) Tn. and par., Wilts, England, famous for large earthwork of Bronze or Neolithic age. Stonehenge 1½ m. distant. Sheep fairs. Pop. (par.) 1,530. (2) Tn., Massachusetts, U.S.A., 43 m. N. of Boston; cotton goods, motor-cars and accessories. Pop. 12,000.

Amha'ra. See ABYSSINIA.

Amherst (*ăm'erst*). (1) Tn., Massachusetts, U.S.A., 16 m. N. of Springfield; noted college; manufactures straw hats. Pop. 6,000. (2) Port, Nova Scotia, Canada; shipbuilding yards. Pop. 10,000. (3) Fishing vil., Burma, 32 m. S. of Moulmein. Pop. *c.* 3,500.

Amiens (*ă-mē-an'*), chief tn., Somme, France, on R. Somme; market gardens; manufactures linen, woollens, silks, velvets. Cathedral is one of finest Gothic buildings in Europe. Pop. 92,000.

Amiran'te Islands, coral group, 120 m. S.W. of Seychelles, by which they are administered; guano and phosphate deposits. Pop. *c.* 100.

Amlwch (*am'looch*), port and wat.-pl., Anglesey, N. Wales, 15 m. N.W. of Beaumaris; has some coasting trade. Pop. 2,600.

Am'manford, urb. dist., Carmarthenshire, Wales, 7 m. S. of Llandilo; coal mines; tin and oil works. Pop. 7,200.

Amoy, treaty port, Fukien, China; fine protected harbour; formerly great tea port; now exports bricks, fruits, china ware, and grass-cloth. Pop. 115,000.

Ampt'hill, urb. dist., Beds, England, 7 m. S. of Bedford. Sir Philip Sidney said to have written *Arcadia* at Houghton House (ruins in neighbourhood). Pop. 2,200.

Amrao'ti, tn., Berar, India, *c.* 80 m. W. of Nagpur; cotton mills and textile trade. Pop. 41,000.

Amrit'sar, city, Punjab, India, 32 m. E. of Lahore; religious cap. of Sikhs, and, next to Lahore, most flourishing city of Punjab. Manufactures Kashmir shawls, fine silks, and carpets. Pop. 160,500.

Am'sterdam. (1) Port, and commercial cap. of Holland; at mouth of Amstel; built on piles; intersected by canals; connected with North Sea by two canals (1825 and 1876). Busy and extensive harbour. Chief industries: diamond cutting, sugar refining, tobacco, cigars, shipbuilding, engineering. Exports: Dutch produce, butter, cheese. Pop. 735,000. (2) City, New York, U.S.A., 33 m. N.W. of Albany; manufactures woollen and knit goods. Pop. 35,000.

Amu Darya. See OXUS.

Amur (*ä-moor'*). (1) Prov., Far Eastern Area, U.S.S.R.; vast tracts uninhabited; mountainous; climate continental; gold mines; stock raising; fisheries. Chief tn., Blagovyeshchensk; administrative centre, Khabarovsk. Area, 95,000 sq. m.; pop. 394,000, chiefly Russians. (2) The 'Great River,' formed by junction of Shilka and Argun, forms part of boundary between U.S.S.R. and Manchuria. Navigable for light craft below Blagovyeshchensk. Chief tribs., r. bk., Sungari and Ussuri; enters sea at Nikolaievsk, opposite N. end of Sakhalin. Amur system affords 8,400 m. waterways navigable from May to October.

'An'a, tn., Iraq, on river Euphrates, 80 m. N.W. of Hit; agriculture, viticulture, and fruit growing; formerly chief Arab trading centre on Euphrates. Pop. *c.* 15,000.

Anacon'da, city, Montana, U.S.A., 26 m. N.W. of Butte; alt. 5,300 ft.; copper, zinc, manganese. Pop. 13,000.

Anadyr (*ä-nä-dēr'*), riv., Far Eastern Area, U.S.S.R.; rises in Stanavoi Mts., falls into Gulf of Anadyr; length, 500 m.; slow and shallow.

Anahuac (*ä-nä'wak*), central tableland of Mexico, from valley of Mexico to El Paso on Rio Grande del Norte; contains many *barrancas* or cañons. Alt. 7,500 ft.

Anamal'ai Hills, mt. range, Coimbatore dist., Madras, India, containing highest elevations (8,850 ft.) S. of Himalayas. Densely forested.

Anan'iev, tn., govt. Kherson, Ukraine, U.S.S.R., 100 m. N. of Odessa; centre of great wheat-growing dist. Pop. 20,000.

Anato'lia. See ASIA MINOR.

Anco'na. (1) Prov., Italy, in the Marches, between Central Apennines and Adriatic; silkworms reared, grain and fruit grown; sulphur mined. Area, 748 sq. m.; pop. 335,000. (2) Tn., cap. of prov., on Adriatic, 123 m. from Venice; fine harbour; sugar refining; shipbuilding; exports tartar, hides, silk, asphalt. Pop. 66,500.

Ancre (*änkr*), small riv., trib. of R. Somme, N. France; rises in chalk down 4 m. S. of Bapaume, and flows past Albert to R. Somme, 10 m. E. of Amiens.

An'crum, vil., Roxburghshire, Scotland, 3½ m. N.W. of Jedburgh; *Ancrum Moor,* 2 m. N.W., scene of battle in which English defeated by Scots (1545). Pop. 900.

Andalusia (*än-dä-loo'shē-ä*) (Spanish *Andalucia*), largest of anc. S. divs. of Spain, divided into Upper and Lower; now includes provs. of Almeria, Cadiz, Cordoba, Granada, Huelva, Jaen, Malaga, and Seville. Watered by Guadalquivir; mountainous in N. and S., elsewhere very fertile and productive. Chief tns.: Seville, Malaga, Granada, Cadiz. Produces sherry, silk, fruit; copper, lead.

Andaman' and Nic'obar Islands, two groups of islands (200) forming one province of British India, 600 m. from mouth of Hugli, in Bay of Bengal. Hilly and well-wooded. Chief harbour, Port Blair. Natives negroid, of low stature and civilization. Islands were convict settlement of Indian Government, but transport ceased in 1921. In 1926 convicts numbered 7,963, of whom more than half were on ticket-of-leave and were working to support themselves. Islands are rich in timber, including marblewood. Tea, coffee, rice, sugar-cane, and maize are cultivated. Area, 2,508 sq. m.

Andenne (*on-den'*), tn., prov. Namur, Belgium, on R. Meuse, 11 m. E. of Namur; in zinc, iron, lead, and coal mining dist.; manufactures paper and pottery. Pop. 8,000.

An'derlecht, tn., Belgium; S.W.

suburb of Brussels; cotton mills and dyeworks. Famous for subterranean church of St. Guy.

An'dermatt, vil., upper valley of R. Reuss, Uri, Switzerland (alt. 4,738 ft.); chief military station of St. Gotthard Pass. Winter health resort. Pop. 1,000.

An'dernach, tn., Rhineland, Prussia, on R. Rhine, 11 m. N.W. of Coblenz. Trade in millstones and tufa. Pop. 11,000.

An'derson. (1) Tn., Indiana, U.S.A., 40 m. N.E. of Indianapolis; iron, steel, brass, paper. Pop. 40,000. (2) Tn., S. Carolina, U.S.A., 120 m. N.W. of Columbia; cotton manufactures. Pop. 11,000.

Andes (*ăn'dēz*), mt. system extending along W. side of S. America from Isthmus of Panama and mouth of Orinoco to Tierra del Fuego. In middle section, two main chains; elsewhere three. Total length of system, 4,000 m. In Ecuador, eighteen giant peaks are over 15,000 ft. (Chimborazo, 20,498); highest peak, Aconcagua (22,868 ft.), ascended by Rankin in 1902; to the N. of 20° S., breadth exceeds 500 m. Lake Titicaca (alt. 12,000 ft.) has area of 3,300 sq. m. Many volcanoes still active. Minerals: gold, silver, copper, iron, manganese, tin, sodium nitrate, borax, and quicksilver. Richest metal-bearing states are Peru and Bolivia; latter contains famous silver mt. of Potosi. In 1910 Andes tunnelled and Argentine and Chilean rlys. linked up by Uspallata tunnel (*c.* 2 m. long; alt. 10,500 ft.). Rly. from Buenos Aires to Bolivia connects with lines to Antofagasta and Arica in Chile and to Mollendo in Peru (*via* steamer on Lake Titicaca).

Andijan', tn., prov. Ferghana, Uzbek rep., U.S.S.R., on l. bk. of Sir Darya (alt. 1,500 ft.); terminus of branch of Transcaspian Rly. from Bokhara (completed 1899). Famous for its gardens; grows and manufactures cotton. Pop. 74,000.

Andor'ra, small Pyrenean semi-independent state on Franco-Spanish frontier, in a high valley (3,000 ft.) among peaks rising to 10,000 ft. Pays annual tax of about £40 to Spain. There are six chief villages. Life of people of primitive simplicity. Cattle rearing, horse breeding, vines and tobacco; smuggling between France and Spain a regular industry. Cap. Andorra. Area, 191 sq. m.; pop. 5,500.

An'dover. (1) Bor., Hants, England, 27 m. N. of Southampton; ironworks; malting; Royal Air Force Staff College. Pop. 9,700. (2) Tn., Massachusetts, U.S.A., 10 m. E. of Lowell; woollen and rubber goods. Pop. 10,000.

An'dria, tn., Apulia, S. Italy; has large trade in almonds. Pop. 60,000.

An'dros, largest of Bahama Is., W. Indies; all settlements on E. coast. Sponge collecting; sisal hemp culture.

Andujar (*ăn-doo'har*), tn., prov. Jaen, Spain, on R. Guadalquivir; flour, oil, wax candles, and porous water-coolers. Pop. 18,000.

Angara', riv., Siberian Area, U.S.S.R.; traverses Lake Baikal; exit S.W. side; trib. of Yenisei. Length, 1,300 m.

Angermanland (*ong'er-măn-lănd*), beautiful dist. on Gulf of Bothnia, Sweden; formerly a prov., now in govt. of Westernorrland. Agriculture, forestry, stock raising, and mining.

Angers (*on-zhā'*), chief tn., Maine-et-Loire, France; agricultural centre, textiles, ironware; slate quarries near. Pop. 78,000.

Anglesey or ANGLESEA, isl. and co., Wales, N.W. of mainland, from which it is separated by Menai Strait, which is crossed by two bridges. Low plateau, monotonous and treeless; copper, lead, marble, asbestos, limestone, potter's clay; Holyhead, port for Ireland. Area, 276 sq. m.; pop. 49,000.

Anglo-Egyptian Sudan. See under SUDAN.

Angmagsalik, small vil., most northerly important Eskimo settlement, near Arctic Circle, E. coast Greenland.

Ang'mering-on-Sea, garden city,

Sussex, England, 5 m. S. of Arundel. Pop. 1,100.

Ango'la, or PORTUGUESE W. AFRICA, Portuguese colony; bounded by Belgian Congo on N. and N.E., N. Rhodesia on E., Bechuanaland and S.W. Africa on S., and Atlantic on W. Extensive mt. range in N. forming watershed between Atlantic-flowing and Congo-flowing rivers. S. is great plateau (alt. 5,000–6,500 ft., highest peak in Lovile Mts., 7,800 ft.); colony well watered; chief riv. Kwanza (520 m., navigable 200 m. up); interior cool and dry; malarial in low-lying parts. Natural resources chiefly vegetable, but also copper, iron, malachite, petroleum, salt, diamonds, and gold. Exports rubber, bees-wax, oil, palm kernels, palm oil, sugar, maize, coffee, coconuts, and diamonds. Total length of rlys. open, 818 m.; others proposed to link up with Central African Rlys. Loanda, cap.; chief ports: Ambriz, Benguella, Mossamedes, and Lobito. Area, 500,000 sq. m.; pop., chiefly Bantu-Negro, *c.* 4,000,000.

Ango'niland, plateau, central Nyasaland, Africa; average alt. 4,000 ft.; inhabited by pastoral Angoni; few white settlers.

Angora (*ăng'go-ra*) (Turkish *Ankara*). (1) Inland vilayet, central Asia Minor, Turkey, 200 m. E.S.E. of Constantinople. Watered by Sakaria, Kizil Irmak, and tribs.; three-fourths under cultivation; wheat, barley, rice, and fruit. Staple export, mohair, silky fleece of white Angora goat (Angora wool); silver and copper mines; hot springs. Pop. 405,000. (2) City in above vilayet, cap. of Turkey since 1924; mohair cloth manufactures; honey, fruit. Pop. 108,000.

Angostu'ra. See CIUDAD BOLIVAR.

Angoulême (*on-goo-lām'*), cap., dep. Charente, France, on l. bk. of R. Charente; headquarters of cognac trade; paper-making. Pop. 32,000.

Angra do Heroismo (*ăn-gră' dō ă-rō-ēs'mo*), cap., Azores, on S. coast of Terceira I.; exposed harbour; exports wine, cheese, honey, grain, and flax. Pop. 10,000.

Angra Pequeña. See LÜDERITZ.

Anguilla, or LITTLE SNAKE I., most northerly of Lesser Antilles, Brit. W. Indies; cattle; cotton, phosphates. Area, 35 sq. m.; pop. 4,000.

An'gus (formerly FORFARSHIRE), maritime and agricultural co., E. Scotland; bounded by Kincardine and Aberdeen on N., North Sea on E., Firth of Tay on S., and Perthshire on W.; high lands in N. separated from Sidlaw Hills by Strathmore; between Sidlaws and Firth of Tay is Carse of Gowrie; cattle and sheep; barley, fruit; flax and jute manufactured. Chief tns.: Dundee, Arbroath, Montrose, Forfar (county town). Area, 873 sq. m.; pop. 270,200.

An'halt, Free State, Germany, nearly surrounded by Saxony; N. part mainly agricultural; smaller W. part rich in minerals. Beetroot, sugar, brewing, distilling. Cap. Dessau. Area, 888 sq. m.; pop. 351,000.

Anhwei, or NGANHUI, prov., China; lat. 32° N. cuts it into two parts; S. drained by Yangtze Kiang. Wheat, millet, and beans grown in N.; S. is probably richest rice and tea region of China; large inter-prov. trade; rly. system well developed in the N., but only road and river in S. Cap. Anking. Area, 54,826 sq. m.; pop. *c.* 20,000,000.

Anjou', former countship, France, now forms most of Maine-et-Loire and part of Mayenne, Sarthe, Indre-et-Loire; cap. was Angers.

An'king, cap., prov. Anhwei, China; on l. bk. Yangtze Kiang; provincial mint. Pop. 40,000.

Anko'ber, tn., prov. Shoa, Abyssinia, formerly cap. of prov.; important caravan centre. Pop. 3,000.

Anko'le, S.W. dist., Uganda Protectorate, Africa; mountainous (5,000 ft.); iron ore; W. fertile and cultivated.

An'naberg, tn., Saxony, Germany, on Erzgebirge (alt. 1,894 ft.), 20 m. S. of Chemnitz. Chief seat of Ger. lace making; haberdashery. Pop. 18,500.

Annabon. See ANNOBON.

Annam', Fr. protectorate, E. Indo-China, between Tongking and Cochin-

China; long narrow dist., area 39,758 sq. m.; mountainous except along coast. Rainy season September to March. People of Mongolian race. Extensive rice-fields on coast; sugar-cane near Tourane; silkworms; iron-wood, teak, dyewoods, lacquer on hills; minerals include coal, iron, gold, silver. Tourane Bay is best harbour; cap. Hué. Pop. 5,172,000.

An′nan, royal burgh and port, Dumfriesshire, Scotland, on R. Annan; local industries fishing and tanning. Pop. 3,400.

Annap′olis, cap., Maryland, U.S.A.; excellent harbour; oyster canning. Pop. 11,500.

Annapolis Royal, tn., on arm of Bay of Fundy, Nova Scotia, Canada; formerly cap. of prov. Annapolis valley is famed for its apple orchards. Pop. 1,000.

Ann Ar′bor, city, Michigan, U.S.A., on Huron R., 38 m. w. of Detroit; makes motor lorries, agricultural implements, pianos. Pop. 27,000.

Annecy (*an-sē′*), chief tn., Haute-Savoie, France, on beautiful Lake of Annecy; much frequented in summer; bell foundry; paper mills; textiles. Pop. 15,500.

An′nen, tn., Westphalia, Prussia, 6 m. s.w. of Dortmund; coal mines and foundries. Pop. 18,000.

Ann′field Main, urb. dist., N. Durham, England, 7 m. w. of Chester-le-Street; coal mining. Pop. 15,900.

An′niston, city, N.E. Alabama, U.S.A.; in productive coal and iron dist.; chemical products; cotton goods. Pop. 22,000.

Anniviers (*ä-nē-vyā′*), VAL D′, beautiful valley, Valais, Switzerland, with head of Zinal Glacier, notable peaks, a deep limestone gorge, and fine waterfalls.

An′nobon, isl., Gulf of Guinea, Africa; belongs to Spain; volcanic mts. Area, 6¾ sq. m.; pop. *c.* 2,000.

Annonay′, tn., Ardèche, France, 50 m. s. of Lyons; paper, leather, silk goods. Pop. 13,500.

Ansdell, vil., Lancs, England, 1¼ m. w. of Lytham; seaside resort.

Anso′nia, tn., New Haven, Connecticut, U.S.A., 12 m. N.W. of New Haven; clocks, brass and copper goods. Pop. 20,000.

Ans′pach, tn., Bavaria, 25 m. s.w. of Nürnberg; machinery; weaving. Pop. 22,000.

Anstruther. See KILRENNY AND ANSTRUTHER.

Antananarivo (*-rē′vo*), cap., Madagascar, Africa; alt. *c.* 5,000 ft.; connected by rail with port of Tamatave. Pop. *c.* 90,000.

Antarc′tic Regions, area around S. Pole and within Antarctic Circle (66° 30′ s. lat.); so far as known include a plateau continent called Antarctica (alt. *c.* 10,000 ft.; area, over 5,000,000 sq. m.); surrounded by ice barrier, which prevents easy access by sea. Enclosing seas consist of s. portions of Atlantic, Indian, and Pacific Oceans, sometimes termed S. or Antarctic Ocean; the whole region is divided for convenience into four quadrants—Enderby, s. of Africa; Victoria, s. of Australia; Ross, s. of Pacific Ocean; and Weddell, s. of S. America. In each quadrant small parts of coast have been mapped: in Victoria an outline is drawn to within 85° s. lat.; in Weddell a submarine ridge is supposed to link S. America with Graham Land and S. Shetlands by S. Orkneys, Sandwich Group, and S. Georgia. Continent ice-covered, with many glaciers; active volcanoes, *e.g.* Erebus in Victoria quadrant (alt. 13,300 ft.); coal found; subject to intense cold (lowest temperature recorded, − 77° F.) and snow blizzards; rain unknown; no flowering plants or land mammals; penguins, skuas, and snow petrels; whales and seals in surrounding seas. S. Magnetic Pole (72° 25′ s., 155° 16′ E.) discovered in Shackleton's expedition, 1904; S. Pole reached by Amundsen (Dec. 1911) and Capt. Scott (Jan. 1912); Byrd flew over S. Pole in 1929.

Antequera (*än-tā-kā′ra*), tn., Spain, 27 m. N. of Malaga; sugar, woollen, tanning, and silk industries. Pop. 32,000.

Antibes (*on-tēb′*), tn. and health resort, French Riviera, 12 m. s.w. of Nice; oranges, olives, and flowers for perfume manufacture. Pop. 13,000.

Antioos′ti, isl., Gulf of St. Lawrence, Canada, 140 m. by 27½ m.; low-lying and sterile; timber; fishing. Pop. 250.

Antigua (*an-tē′gwa*). (1) Isl. and seat of government, Leeward Islands, Brit. W. Indies. Barbuda and Redonda are dependencies. Suffers from hurricanes; no rivers and few springs, but soil fertile. Staple product sugar; sea-island cotton, limes, onions, and coconuts also grown. Cap. St. John's. Area, 108 sq. m.; pop. 30,000. (2) Tn., Guatemala, 23 m. s.w. of Guatemala city; alt. 5,314 ft.; coffee plantations. Pop. 20,000.

Antilles. See West Indies.

An′tioch (modern *Antakiyah*), tn., Syria, on R. Orontes; on main route into Asia, hence early became centre of wealth and luxury; tobacco, olives, maize, cotton; soap and silk manufactures. Pop. *c.* 30,000.

Antioquia (*ăn-tē-ok-ē′a*), inland dep., Colombia, S. America, one of wealthiest and most populous in republic; traversed by Andes; alt. 8,400 ft.; tropical and subtropical products, chiefly maize, coffee, sugar, and fruits; gold and silver; Panama hats are made. Cap. Medellin. Area, 22,752 sq. m.; pop. 824,000.

Antip′odes Islands, isolated group of rocky islands, s.e. of Stewart I., New Zealand; uninhabited; so called as being the land nearest antipodes of London (London, 51° 30′ n.; 0° 5′ w.; Antipodes Is., 49° 41′ s.; 178° 43′ w.).

Antisä′na, snow-clad, inactive volcanic peak, Andes, Ecuador, 35 m. e. of Quito (alt. 19,300 ft.).

Anti-Taurus. See Taurus.

Anti′vari. See Bar.

Antofagas′ta. (1) Port, n. Chile; exports nitrates, copper, borate of lime, silver, and salt. Pop. 52,000. (2) Largest prov. of Chile; in Atacama Desert; mineral deposits. Area, 46,518 sq. m.; pop. 172,500.

An′trim. (1) Co., N. Ireland. Surface is basaltic plateau, eastern half hilly; numerous peat bogs in s.w.; Lough Neagh in s.w.; Giant's Causeway, remarkable basaltic cliffs, on n. Chief riv., Bann. Climate temperate; produces flax, cereals; cattle, sheep, pigs; iron, rock-salt, bauxite. Industries: linen manufactures, fisheries, distilling. Largest tn., Belfast. Area, 1,098 sq. m.; pop. (excluding Belfast co. bor.) 192,000. (2) Mkt. tn., cap. of above; linen, paper. Pop. 2,000.

Antung′, port, Manchuria, at mouth of Yalu riv.; exports silk, beans, and timber. Pop. 72,500.

Ant′werp (French *Anvers*). (1) Prov., Belgium; surface level; grain, flax. Area, 1,093 sq. m.; pop. 1,138,000. (2) Fortified city, port, and cap. of above; chief commercial city of Belgium, on R. Schelde; excellent harbour; extensive quays; dry docks. Chief industries: shipbuilding, sugar, textiles, lace, petroleum, tobacco, distilling, diamond cutting; exports: glass, coal, chemicals, iron, steel, cotton, drugs. Pop. 300,000.

Anzin (*ăn-zăn*), tn., Nord, France, on R. Schelde; suburb of Valenciennes; chief coal-mining centre of France; glass works, machinery. Pop. 15,000.

Aomor′i, port, extreme n. of Honshu, Japan; salmon, sharks' fins, and variegated lacquer. Pop. 60,000.

Aos′ta, tn., n.w. Piedmont, Italy; birthplace of Anselm. Pop. 8,500. *Val d' Aosta,* Piedmontese Alpine valley of great beauty.

Aparri′, port, Cagayan prov., Luzon, Philippines; only safe port on n. side of island; tobacco. Pop. 21,000.

Ap′atin, tn., n. Yugoslavia, on R. Danube; manufactures rope, madder, and silk. Pop. 15,000.

Apeldoorn, tn., Gelderland, Holland, 11 m. n.w. of Deventer; manufactures paper. Pop. 57,000.

Ap′ennines, mt. range, Italy, extending s. from Alps through Italy and Sicily; average height *c.* 4,000 ft., sinking in the N. to 3,500 ft., and rising in centre to about 7,000 ft. Range is crossed by several rlys. at heights of from 1,500 to 2,000 ft. Rivs. rising in Apennines are Arno, Tiber, etc. Marble is found at Carrara, etc.; lower slopes are heavily forested.

Apenrä'de. See AABENRAA.

Ap'ia, seapt., Upolu, Samoan Islands; exports copra and cocoa beans; wireless station. R. L. Stevenson resided (1900–4) at Vailima.

Ap'lerbeck, tn., Westphalia, Prussia, 4 m. S.E. of Dortmund; coal and iron mining, ironfounding. Pop. 11,000.

Apol'da, tn., Germany, 9 m. E.N.E. of Weimar; bell foundries; hosiery; preserved foods. Pop. 25,500.

Appală'chians, mt. system, U.S.A., extending over 1,500 m. from N. to S. along Atlantic coast; divided by Hudson R., L. Champlain, and Richelieu R. into two unequal groups—Green Mts. and White Mts. to N., Alleghany Mts. and Blue Mts. to S. Highest point, Mount Mitchell (6,711 ft.) in Blue Ridge. Appalachian valley divides system lengthwise in S. Rich in coal, iron, petroleum, and natural gas; forests. Traversed by several railways; easiest through route by Hudson and Mohawk valleys.

Appenzell (*ă-pent-zel'*), canton, N.E. Switzerland; divided (1597) into two half-cantons—Inner Rhoden (cap. Appenzell), pastoral; and Outer Rhoden (cap. Trogen), industrial. Embroidery, cotton and silk manufactures. Pop. of Inner Rhoden (72 sq. m.), 15,000; of Outer Rhoden (93 sq. m.), 55,500.

Ap'pin, dist. and vil., Argyllshire, Scotland, E. of Loch Linnhe; slate and granite quarries.

Ap'pleby, county tn., Westmorland, England, 13 m. S.E. of Penrith; holiday resort. Pop. 1,600.

Ap'pleton, city, Wisconsin, U.S.A., on Lake Winnebago; paper making. Pop. 25,000.

Aprice'na, tn., Apulia, Italy; marble quarries, 23 m. N. of Foggia; much of dist. is malarial. Pop. 8,000.

Apsheron', peninsula, Azerbaijan, extending into Caspian Sea; petroleum wells.

Apulia (*ă-poo'lēa*), dep., S. Italy; in the N. a plain on which sheep, cattle, and horses are raised; in the S. a limestone plateau where wheat (used in the manufacture of macaroni), barley, maize, and pulses are grown; olive oil, wine, and fruits also products; marble is quarried in Monte Gargano. Chief ports: Brindisi, Bari, and Taranto. Area, 7,376 sq. m.; pop. 2,300,000.

Apure (*ă-poo'rā*), trib. of Orinoco, Venezuela; joins main river below San Fernando. Navigable for over 600 m.

Apurimac (*ă-poo-ri-măk'*). (1) Riv., joining Ucayali, Peru; swift current. (2) Dep., S. Peru; sugar-cane. Area, 8,187 sq. m.; pop. 280,000.

Aqaba (*ă'kă-bă*). (1) Gulf forming E. arm of N. end of Red Sea. (2) Tn., near head of gulf.

Aquila or AQUILA DEGLI ABRUZZI (*ă'kwēlă del'ye ăbroo'tsē*). (1) Apennine prov., dep. Abruzzi and Molise, E. Italy; cereals, fruits, flax, and hemp produced. Area, 1,945 sq. m.; pop. 326,000. (2) Cap. of above, 55 m. N.E. of Rome; summer resort; saffron, lace. Pop. 56,000.

Aquitaine (*ăk-wi-tān'*), corrupted later to GUIENNE, old prov., France, between R. Garonne and Pyrenees.

Arabgir', or ARABKIR, tn., Asia Minor, Turkey, 140 m. S.S.E. of Trebizond; fruit, silks and cottons. Pop. 22,000.

Ara'bia, peninsula, S.W. Asia, between Persian Gulf and Gulf of Oman on E. and Red Sea on W.; united to Africa by Isthmus of Suez; length, *c.* 1,500 m.; average breadth, *c.* 800 m. Surface plateau with gradual decline from W. to E.; this plateau rises from elevation of 2,500 ft. in N. to over 7,000 ft. in S.W., and is bounded by mt. ranges in S. and W.; between mts. and sea is strip of low fertile land which continues along practically whole of W. coast and about 400 m. along S. coast. N. part of Arabia includes Syrian Desert and Great Nefud

Desert; central Arabia is mainly steppe interspersed with fertile tracts; in W. is Hejaz, in the centre is Nejd. S. Arabia includes Asir and Yemen on W. coast, Hadhramaut and Aden on S. coast, Oman on E. coast. Climate generally is very dry and hot; in plains heat is excessive, in mt. ranges of Yemen and Hadhramaut temperature is more moderate, and in Nejd great cold occurs in winter. Rainy season generally lasts from June till Sept. Simoom, a hot desert wind, blows in N. from interior towards coast.

Divisions.—Hejaz and Nejd (kingdom); Yemen (ruled by an imam); Oman (ruled by sultan); Koweit and Hadhramaut (partly under British influence); Aden and Bahrein (British protectorate).

Arabia has wide stretches of grass, which afford excellent pasture for horses, for which country has long been famed. Large numbers of camels, sheep, goats, and oxen are raised. Vegetable products are dates, coffee, cereals, fruits, spices, drugs, gums, resin, sugar, cotton. Minerals include iron, lead, copper, coal, precious stones. There are few manufactures; coarse linens and woollens made by Bedouin women. Trade is carried on chiefly by caravans, which bring quantities of merchandise both for internal use and to distribute among pilgrims; exports coffee, hides, wool, dates, figs, spices, drugs. Communications are chiefly by sea or caravan, but a railway is laid from Damascus to Medina and surveyed to Mecca and Jidda, and motor transport is employed. Chief seaports: Muscat, on Gulf of Oman; Jidda and Hodeida, on Red Sea; good harbour at Aden, on S. coast. Inhabitants are traditionally of the Arab and Ishmaelitic stocks; former represented by agricultural population round coast, latter by Bedouins of desert and central Arabia. In S. are many Jews. Principal religion is Mohammedanism; every year pilgrimage, or *haj*, is made to holy city, Mecca, by thousands of devotees. Area, *c.* 1,000,000 sq. m.; pop. *c.* 7,000,000.

Ara′bian Sea, N.W. portion of Indian Ocean, between India and 'horn' of Africa; branches are Gulf of Oman and Gulf of Aden; includes Socotra I., Kuria Muria Is., and Laccadive Is.

Aracaju (*ar-ak-a-zhoo′*), port, Brazil, 170 m. N.N.E. of Bahia; sugar, cloth, soap manufactures; exports cotton, hides and skins, coffee, cacao. Pop. 38,000.

Aracaty, or ARACATI (*ă-ră-kă-tē′*), port, N.E. Brazil; hides, cotton, rubber, fruit; regular steamer service with Pernambuco. Pop. 18,000.

Arad (*or′od*). (1) Tn., Romania, on r. bk. of R. Muresul (Maros); rly. centre; wine trade, corn, tobacco; cattle market. Pop. 79,000. (2) NEW ARAD, tn., Romania, opposite Arad. Pop. 6,000.

Arafu′ra Sea, between N. Australia and W. New Guinea; through it are important steamship routes.

Ar′agon, anc. kingdom, Spain; cap. Saragossa; now forms provs. of Huesca, Saragossa, and Teruel; forests on Pyrenees; irrigation works on R. Ebro; coal, iron, and other minerals. Area, 18,300 sq. m.; pop. 1,000,000.

Arago′na, tn., Sicily, 7 m. N. of Girgendi; important sulphur mines; mud volcano of Maccaluba. Pop. 14,000.

Araguaya (*ă-ră-gwi′ă*), riv., Brazil, trib. of Tocantins; lower course obstructed by rapids. Length, 1,080 m.

Arakan′. (1) Div., Lower Burma; rice, tobacco, timber; cap. Akyab. Area, 18,540 sq. m.; pop. 910,000. (2) Anc. cap. of above; ruins of fort and city wall; unhealthy situation led to decay.

Ar′al, SEA OF, inland sea, Asia; 'sea of islands'; variable level; shallow; fed by rivs. Oxus and Sir Darya; shores uninhabited; sturgeon, carp, herring fishing; drying up.

Ar′an, group of islands, Galway, W. Ireland; antiquarian and archæological interest; fishing. Area, 11,579 ac. Chief islands., Inishmore, Inishman, Inisheer.

Aranjuez (*ā-rän-choo-eth'*), tn., prov. Madrid, Spain; spring residence of Span. monarchs; market gardens. Pop. 14,000.

Ar'arat. (1) Double volcanic peak in Armenia (alts. 17,325, 12,840 ft.); peaks above the line of perpetual snow; source of rivs. Araxes and Euphrates; identification of Ararat with peak on which Ark rested (Gen. 8 : 4) is doubtful. (2) Tn., Ripon co., Victoria, Australia, 130 m. W.N.W. of Melbourne; wool and grain trade; alluvial gold mining; vineyards. Pop. 5,500.

Ar'as, Armenian riv.; rises S. of Erzerum, and flows 600 m. to Caspian Sea.

Arauca'nia, terr., Chile, S. America; now includes provs. of Arauco, Biobio, Malleco, and Cautin; land of Araucanian Indians.

Arau'co, prov. S. Chile; cereals, alfalfa, vegetables, and fruit. Cap. Lebu. Area, 2,189 sq. m.; pop. 60,500.

Aravalli Hills (*ā-rä-vul'lē*), mt. range extending for 300 m. N.E. from Bombay Presidency through Rajputana. Highest peak, Mt. Abu (5,650 ft.).

Arbroath (*är-brōth'*), old royal burgh and port, Angus, Scotland, 17 m. N.E. of Dundee; good tidal harbour; manufactures coarse linens, boots and shoes. Pop. 17,600.

Arcachon (*är-kä-shōn'*), health resort, France, 37 m. W.S.W. of Bordeaux; steam fishing fleet; oyster beds. Pop. 12,000.

Arca'dia, dep., Peloponnesus, Greece; basin surrounded by mts.; pastoral; chief tn., Tripolitza. Area, 2,020 sq. m.; pop. 166,000.

Archangel (*är-kān'jel*). (1) Prov., N. Russia, including Novaya Zemlya, Vaigach, Kolguev Is.; produces timber, hemp, flax, barley, rye; salt, mica, naphtha, lignite; salmon, herring, cod. Drained by Rs. Petchora, Mezen, Dvina, Onega. Katharina Harbour is ice-free. Area, 180,300 sq. m.; pop. 430,000. (2) Port of above; at mouth of riv. N. Dvina; timber; annual fish fair; ice-free May–Nov. Pop. 71,000.

Archipelago (*är-ki-pel'ag-ō*), (Gr., 'chief sea'), originally the island-studded Ægean Sea; now also applied to any group of islands.

Arcis-sur-Aube (*är-sē-soor-ōb'*), tn., Aube, France, on R. Aube; hosiery. Pop. 3,000.

Ar'cos de la Fronte'ra, tn., Cadiz, Spain, 20 m. N.E. of Jerez; so called because it stood on frontiers of the old Moorish kingdom of Granada. Pop. 16,000.

Arcot', tn., Madras, India, 65 m. W.S.W. of Madras; taken by Clive (1751). Pop. 11,000.

Arc'tic Regions, area around N. Pole and within Arctic Circle (66° 30' N. lat), but better defined as polar area beyond limit of tree growth; includes the Arctic Ocean, practically landlocked by Eurasia, N. America, and Greenland. The Arctic Ocean (area, 5,400,000 sq. m.), which surrounds N. Pole, is deepest in centre (over 2,000 fathoms), but shallow over a wide continental shelf where many islands occur. It communicates with the Atlantic Ocean between Greenland and Norway, where it is known as the Greenland Sea (2,000 fathoms), and between Greenland and Baffin Land by shallow Davis Strait; and with the Pacific Ocean through Bering Strait between Asia and N. America. Principal islands are Spitsbergen, Franz Josef Land, and Novaya Zemlya, which with Norway bound the shallow Barents Sea; to E. of Novaya Zemlya is Kara Sea (100 fathoms); farther E. are New Siberian Islands and Wrangel I.; off N. America is a vast arctic archipelago (Canadian). Arctic Ocean is largely ice-covered; much of it unexplored; salinity low; whale, seal, walrus, and other fisheries, esp. in shallow parts; polar bears. The arctic lands are practically uninhabited except by nomadic Lapps, Samoyedes, and Chukchees of Eurasia and Eskimos of N. America, who live on reindeer, musk-ox, walrus, and other arctic animals and fishes. Within these regions lay the historic routes of search for N.E. and N.W. Passages to

China, Japan, and India; N.E. Passage found by Nordenskiöld, 1879; N.W. Passage discovered by Sir John Franklin, 1845–46, but first traversed by Amundsen, 1906; during search for N.W. Passage Ross discovered N. Magnetic Pole (70° 30′ N. lat., 97° W. long.), 1831; N. Pole was reported as reached by Peary, 1909; in 1926 Byrd and Amundsen separately flew over the N. Pole.

Ardebil′, tn., Azerbaijan, N.W. Persia; warm mineral springs; dried fruits; carpets and rugs. Pop. *c.* 18,000.

Ardèche′, dep., France; occupied by Cevennes Mts.; bounded on E. by R. Rhone; drained by Ardèche R. Olives, vines, mulberries, silk; iron, coal, zinc, and lead. Chief tn., Privas. Pop. 290,000.

Ar′den, FOREST OF, wooded dist., N. Warwickshire; one of the largest of anc. Brit. forests, said to have extended from Severn to Trent.

Ardennes (*är-den′*). (1) Hilly dist., France and Belgium; beech and pine forests; agriculture, stock breeding. (2) Dep., N. France; hilly, forest country; crossed by Ardennes Canal joining Rs. Meuse and Aisne; iron, slates, sheep; woollen industry at Sedan. Chief tn., Mézières. Area, 2,028 sq. m.; pop. 297,500.

Ardmore, tn., S. Oklahoma, U.S.A.; cotton, coal mining; oil refineries. Pop. 15,000.

Ardnamur′chan. (1) Par. and vil., Argyllshire, Scotland. Pop. 1,500. (2) POINT, most westerly point of mainland of Scotland; lighthouse.

Ard′och, par. and vil., Perthshire, Scotland, 12 m. N.N.E. of Stirling; Roman camp. Pop. 900.

Ardrish′aig, vil., Argyllshire, Scotland, at S. end of Crinan Canal; summer resort. Pop. 1,000.

Ardros′san, port and wat.-pl., Ayrshire, Scotland; exp. coal to Ireland; shipbuilding, engineering. Pop. 6,900.

Ards′ley, urban dist., W. Riding, Yorks, England, 2 m. E. of Barnsley; coal mining and glass manufacture. Pop. 9,200.

Ard′straw, vil. and par., co. Tyrone, N. Ireland, 3 m. N.W. of Newton-Stewart; limestone, freestone, and clay slate. Pop. (par.) 8,100.

Arecibo (*ä-rä-sē′bō*), tn. and port, N. coast, Porto Rico, W. Indies; coffee, sugar; exposed, shallow roadstead. Pop. 11,000.

Ar′endal, tn., S. Norway, at mouth of R. Nid; good harbour; timber, wood pulp, aluminium. Pop. 10,300.

Areop′agus, hill, Athens (Mars Hill); alt. *c.* 370 ft.

Arequipa (*ä-rä-kē′pa*). (1) Dep., S. Peru; silver, copper, cotton, rice, sugar-cane; cattle and sheep breeding. Area, 21,947 sq. m.; est. pop. 360,000. (2) Cap. of above; alt. 7,600 ft.; ores, wools. Pop. 58,000.

Arezzo (*ä-ret′sō*). (1) Prov., Italy; cereals, wine. Area, 1,275 sq. m.; pop. 300,000. (2) Tn., cap. of above, 54 m. S.E. of Florence; silk, leather, pottery, and hats. Pop. 58,500.

Argä′o, tn., E. Sebu, Philippines; cocoa, rice, sugar; cotton. Pop. 40,000.

Argentan (*är-zhōn-tōn′*), tn., Orne, N. France, 22 m. N. of Alençon; gloves, lace, stained glass. Pop. 7,000.

Argenteuil (*är-zhon-tŭ′ē*), suburb of Paris, on r. bk. of Seine; watches and wine. Pop. 44,000.

Argentière (*är-zhon-tē-är′*), COL DE L', one of the S. Alpine passes (6,545 ft.), leading from Barcelonette in France to Cuneo in Italy.

Ar′gentine Republic (ARGENTINA), federal rep., S. America; length, *c.* 2,000 m.; width, *c.* 800 m.; bounded N. by Bolivia, N.E. by Paraguay, E. by Brazil, Uruguay, S. Atlantic, W. by Chile; includes E. part of Tierra del Fuego. Surface slopes gradually from foothills of Andes on W. towards E., and almost whole consists of great plains. Of flat ground, N. part (Gran Chaco) is densely wooded, central pampas portion has great stretches of treeless pasture, and S. portion (Patagonia) contains expanses of stony desert with patches of stunted thorn bush. Drainage of N. and centre is by Paraná-Paraguay R. (with tribs. Pilcomayo,

Bermejo, Salado), and Uruguay, which forms boundary with rep. of Uruguay; farther s. are rivs. Colorado, Negro, Chubut, Chico, and Santa Cruz; in interior numerous streams end in marshes. The Rio de la Plata (R. Plate) receives the waters of the rivs. Paraná and Uruguay. Rainfall over great part of the country is from 30 to 40 in., but diminishes in San Juan to *c.* 2 in. In N. are forests of hardwood, invaluable for railway sleepers, and quebracho, used in tanning; here are produced tobacco, jute, ramie, sugar, cotton, yerba maté, castor oil, fruits. In Andes regions are magnificent pine forests. In extreme s. seal hunting and ice collecting are carried on. There are many fibre-producing plants. Most economic minerals occur, but await development; oil is found. Agriculture and pasture are chief sources of wealth. Large numbers of sheep and cattle are raised; dairying important. Argentine is second wool-producing country in world. Horses, mules, asses, goats, and pigs also raised in large numbers. Chief crops are wheat, maize, linseed, oats, barley, alfalfa, rye; sugar-cane and fruits also cultivated. Exports, animals, wool, hides, chilled and frozen meat, butter, sugar, wheat, maize, etc. About one-third of import and one-sixth of export trade is with Great Britain. Language is Spanish. Chief tns., Buenos Aires (cap.), Rosario, Córdoba, La Plata, Tucumán. Area, 1,153,119 sq. m.; pop. *c.* 10,650,000.

Argenton-sur-Creuse (*ăr-zhon-tōn'-soor-krooz*), tn., Indre, France, 17 m. s. of Châteauroux; manufactures gloves, linen, and lace. Pop. 5,000.

Argonne (*ar-gon'*), FOREST OF, plateau of N.E. France, between R. Aisne and its trib. the Aire, is a long low ridge of clay, about 40 m. long and 8 m. wide. No other part of France is so thickly wooded (oak and beech), and in its deep recesses wolves still lurk; crossed by two main roads, and by rly. from W. to E.

Ar'gos, tn., E. Peloponnesus, Greece; acropolis, anc. theatre; modern town is straggling place. Pop. *c.* 10,000.

Argosto'li, port, cap. of Cephalonia, Ionian Islands, Greece. Shipbuilding and silk spinning. Exports currants and wine. Pop. 11,500.

Argun (*ar-goon'*), riv., forming boundary between Siberia and Manchuria, rises in Great Khingan Mts.; one of headstreams of R. Amur. Length, 440 m.; large portion navigable.

Argyll (*ar-gīl'*), co., W. Scotland; besides irregularly shaped part of mainland, includes Mull, Iona, Islay, Jura, and many other islands; surface mountainous; highest peak, Ben Cruachan; coast-line deeply indented by arms of sea—Loch Long, Loch Fyne, Loch Linnhe; chief inland lake, Loch Awe; Crinan Canal connects Ardrishaig with Crinan; fine moors and deer forests; Highland cattle bred, sheep largely raised; quarrying, fishing, distilling. Cap. Inveraray; largest tns., Campbeltown, Dunoon, Oban. Area, 3,165 sq. m.; pop. 63,000.

Ariano di Puglia (*ar-e-ä'no dē pool'ya*), tn., Italy, 47 m. N.E. of Naples; sulphur mines in Apennine Mts. Pop. 8,400.

Arica (*ar-ē'ka*), tn. and port, Tacna, s. Peru; exports copper and nitrates. Pop. 9,000.

Ariège (*ar-ē-āzh'*), dep., s. France; extends up N. slope of Pyrenees; forests, cereals, fruit; stock raising; iron, lead, copper, manganese. Chief tn., Foix. Area, 1,892 sq. m.; pop. 167,000.

Arizo'na, state, U.S.A., bounded N. by Nevada and Utah, E. by New Mexico, s. by Mexico, W. by California and Nevada. In N.E. is high plateau, in S.W. low-lying plains; has many short mountain ranges; highest points, Thomas Peak, Ord Peak. Chief rivs. are Colorado (lower part navigable) and its trib. Gila. Climate varies, hottest in s.; rainfall slight; irrigation required. Animals found are the coyote, wildcat, mountain lion. Flora includes cactus, fir, juniper.

Area of forests, about 20 per cent. of surface. Cattle, sheep, and horses raised; chief crops, cotton, wheat, maize; potatoes and apples grow in N., figs, grapes, oranges, lemons in S. Minerals include copper, lead, gold, silver, asbestos, zinc. Industries include copper refining, car construction, timber working, meat packing. Cap. Phœnix. Area, 113,810 sq. m.; pop. 474,000.

Arkansas (*ar'kan-saw*), state, U.S.A., bounded N. by Missouri, E. by R. Mississippi, S. by Louisiana, W. by Texas and Oklahoma. Hilly in N.W.; remainder mostly plain. Chief mts. are Boston range in N., Ouachita in S. Through centre flows Arkansas R., other important streams being Ouachita, White, Bartholomew, and Red rivs. Climate is healthy except in E., where swamps cause malaria.

Arkansas is an agricultural state; chief crops, maize, oats, rice, potatoes, hay, forage, cotton, tobacco. In N.W. many fruits are grown, including apples, peaches, grapes. Horses, mules, cattle, sheep, and pigs are raised. Trees include cotton-wood, hickory, red cedar; timber working is an important industry. Coal and petroleum are largely produced; other minerals include bauxite, manganese, lead, natural gas. Industries include cotton ginning, smelting, and printing. Cap. Little Rock. Area, 53,335 sq. m.; pop. 1,944,000.

Arkansas City, tn., Kansas, U.S.A., on Arkansas River, centre of important oil region; flour mills, foundries. Pop. 14,000.

Arkansas River, trib. of R. Mississippi, rises in high mts. of central Colorado. Length over 2,000 m.

Arklow (*ark'lō*), port and mkt. tn., Wicklow, I.F.S., on R. Avoca; explosives. Pop. 4,500.

Arl'berg, pass (5,912 ft.), Austrian Alps, connecting valleys of Rs. Rhine and Inn; carriage road superseded by rly. tunnel (6 m. 650 yds.).

Ar'lecdon and Friz'ington, urb. dist., Cumberland, England, 5 m. N.E. of Whitehaven; iron mining. Pop. 4,300.

Arles (*arl*), tn. and riv. port, Bouches-du-Rhône, France, on R. Rhone. Trade in corn, oil, wine; silk spinning. Pop. 16,300.

Ar'madale, tn., W. Lothian, Scotland, 3 m. W. of Bathgate; steel and brick industries. Pop. 4,900.

Armagh (*ar-mä'*). (1) Co., N. Ireland; chief rivs., Bann, Blackwater, Newry, Callan; hilly; potatoes, oats, fruit; linen industry. Area, 512 sq. m.; pop. 110,000. (2) Co. tn. of above; mkt. tn.; linen, leather, distilling industries; cathedral. Pop. 7,400.

Arme'nia, Socialist Soviet Republic, Transcaucasia, U.S.S.R. Bounded N. by Georgia, E. by Azerbaijan, S. and W. by Anatolia and rep. of Nakhichevan. Surface is series of pastoral plateaus from 3,000 to 12,000 ft. above sea-level; highest point, Mt. Ararat (17,325 ft.); drained by Rs. Euphrates, Kur, Aras, Tigris. Climate severe; cold N. winds; valleys have vineyards and orchards, and produce cotton, tobacco, rice, fruits, mulberry trees. Cattle rearing and forestry are important; copper is mined. Cap. Erivan. Area, 12,399 sq. m.; pop. 880,000.

Armentières (*ar-mon-tyār'*), tn., dep. Nord, France, on R. Lys, near the Belgian border; manufactures cloth and linen. Pop. 19,000.

Ar'midale, tn., N.E. New South Wales, Australia; gold, agriculture, and stock raising in vicinity. Pop. 5,800.

Arn'hem, tn., cap. Gelderland, Netherlands, on r. bk. of R. Rhine; important market; woollen goods and tobacco. Pop. 76,000.

Arnhem Land. See NORTHERN TERRITORY.

Ar'no, riv., Italy; rises in Central Apennines; enters Mediterranean (Gulf of Genoa). Length, 140 m.; navigable by barges to Florence.

Ar'nold, urb. dist., Notts, England, 4 m. N. of Nottingham; hosiery, lace; brewing, soap making. Pop. 14,500.

Arns'berg, tn., Westphalia, Prussia,

in R. Ruhr valley; rly. workshops; paper and cellulose. Pop. 11,700.

Arnside, vil., Westmorland, England, on Morecambe Bay, 5¾ m. N. of Carnforth; wat.-pl. Pop. 1,700.

Arnstadt (*arn'stat*), tn., Thuringia, Germany, 14 m. S. of Erfurt; chemicals, dyes; saline springs. Pop. 22,000.

Arnswalde (*arns'val-de*), tn., Brandenburg, Prussia, 41 m. S.E. of Stettin; machinery, brushes, bricks. Pop. 11,000.

Ar'ran, isl., Firth of Clyde, Scotland; chief vils., Brodick, Lamlash, Corrie, summer resorts; excellent fishing and game; surface mountainous—highest peak, Goatfell (2,877 ft.); rainfall heavy; produces oats, potatoes; exports cattle, fish, sheep, oats. Area, 165 sq. m.; pop. 8,300.

Arras, tn., cap. of dep. Pas-de-Calais, France, on R. Scarpe, 35 m. N.E. of Amiens and 120 m. N. of Paris; one of principal grain markets of France; oil and dye works; hosiery, beer; important rly. jn., and road centre. Scene of important battles during Great War. Pop. 26,000.

Ar'ta. (1) Cap., prov. Arta, Greece; cotton and woollen goods; trade in wine, tobacco, and cattle. Pop. 7,500. (2) GULF OF, arm of Ionian Sea, W. coast of Greece. (3) Tn., Majorca, Balearic Isles; coarse linen; dyeing. Pop. 5,800.

Artemovsk', formerly BAKHMUT, tn., Ukraine, U.S.S.R., 120 m. S.E. of Kharkov; rly. jn.; salt mines and salt springs; coal, iron, alabaster, and quicksilver. Pop. 37,000.

Ar'thur's Seat, hill dominating Edinburgh; of volcanic origin. Alt. 823 ft.

Artois (*ar-twa'*), former prov., N.E. France, now forming the greater part of dep. Pas-de-Calais. Artesian wells derive their name from this province. Chief tns., Arras, Bapaume, Béthune, Lens.

Aru Islands (*a-roo'*), group of nearly a hundred islands, Dutch E. Indies; heavily forested; bird skins, pearls, and tortoise-shell. Area, 3,244 sq. m.; pop. 18,000.

Ar'undel, munic. bor., Sussex, England, 11 m. E. of Chichester; mkt. tn. Pop. 2,500.

Arzamas', tn., Russia, 70 m. S. of Nijni-Novgorod; timber milling; tanneries, oil and tallow factories. Pop. 19,000.

Ascension, volcanic isl., S. Atlantic, 700 m. N.W. of St. Helena; 7½ m. by 6 m. Dry, healthy; turtles abound; phosphates and guano. Cap. George Town. Area, 34 sq. m.; pop. *c.* 300.

Asch (*ash*), tn., Czechoslovakia, in extreme W. of Bohemia; hosiery, dress stuffs, and lace. Pop. 22,000.

Aschaffenburg (*a-shaf'-fen-boorg*), tn., Bavaria, Germany, 26 m. S.E. of Frankfurt-on-Main. Paper and papier-mâché; leather, beer, chemicals. Pop. 34,000.

Aschersleben (*ash-ers-lā'ben*), tn., Saxony, Germany, 32 m. S.W. of Magdeburg; saline spring; chemicals, woollens, hardwares, and sugar. Pop. 29,000.

Ascoli Piceno (*as'kō-lē pē-chā'nō*). (1) Prov., Italy, in the Marches, sloping N.E. from the central Apennines to the Adriatic. Area, 805 sq. m.; pop. 265,200. (2) Tn., cap. of above, on Adriatic coast; majolica and paper. Pop. 36,400.

As'cot or **Ascot Heath,** racecourse, Berks, England, 6 m. S.W. of Windsor.

Ashanti (*ash-an'tē*), dependency, Gold Coast Colony, W. Africa. Surface covered with forest; cultivated land produces crops of maize, cocoa, coffee, and kola-nuts; gums, dye-woods, and timber are also important. Chief exports are cocoa, gold, and kola. Rubber is produced. The natives manufacture cotton goods, gold and silver work, earthenware. Chief tn., Kumasi. Area, 13,470 sq. m.; pop. 407,000.

Ash'bourne, mkt. tn., Derbyshire, England, 13 m. N.W. of Derby; angling centre; milk condensing; corset factories. Pop. 4,500.

Ash'burton. (1) Mkt. tn., Devon, England, 19 m. S.W. of Exeter; serges; paint factories; sawmills. Pop. 2,500. (2) Riv., W. Australia, rising in hills w. of the Great Sandy Desert; runs 400 m. to Indian Ocean at Onslow; not navigable.

Ash'by-de-la-Zouch (*zoosh*), mkt. tn., Leicestershire, England, 21 m. N.W. of Leicester; collieries. Pop. 5,100.

Asheville (*ash'vil*), city, w. N. Carolina, U.S.A.; sanatorium; leather, textiles, furniture. Pop. 50,000.

Ash'ford, mkt. tn., Kent, England, near R. Stour, 56 m. S.E. of London; breweries, tanneries, locomotive works; agricultural implements. Pop. 15,200.

Ash'ington, urb. dist., Northumberland, England, 4 m. E. of Morpeth; coal mines. Pop. 29,400.

Ash'land. (1) Tn., Wisconsin, U.S.A., on an arm of L. Superior; blast furnaces, iron and steel works; shipping trade. Pop. 11,000. (2) Tn., Kentucky, U.S.A., on R. Ohio; iron and steel, lumber, and leather. Pop. 29,000. (3) Tn., Ohio, U.S.A., 50 m. S.W. of Cleveland; grain trade; agricultural implements; poultry foods; aluminium wares. Pop. 11,000.

Ashqabad (*ash-ka-bad'*) tn., Turkmen Rep., U.S.S.R., on Trans-Caspian Rly.; tanneries, cotton and brick factories. Pop. 54,000.

Ashraf', tn., Persia, near S.E. corner of Caspian Sea; silk and cotton goods. Pop. *c.* 6,000.

Ashstead, vil., Surrey, England, 2 m. S.W. of Epsom. Pop. 3,250

Ashtab'ula ('fish river'), city, Ohio, U.S.A., 3 m. from L. Erie and 45 m. E. of Cleveland; ships iron ore and coal; manufactures agricultural implements, iron and steel goods, leather. Pop. 29,000.

Ash'ton-in-Mak'erfield, urb. dist., Lancs, England, 4 m. S. of Wigan; collieries; locks and tools. Pop. 20,500.

Ash'ton-under-Lyne, parl. and munic. bor., Lancs, England, 6½ m. E. of Manchester, on R. Tame; dyeing, silk and cotton spinning; coal mining; hats, machinery. Pop. 51,600.

A'sia, the largest continent; bounded N. by Arctic Ocean, E. by Pacific, S. by Indian Ocean, S.W. by Africa, W. by Europe; greatest length, 5,350 m.; breadth, *c.* 6,000 m. Coastline irregular; E. coast fringed by Sea of Okhotsk, with Kamchatka peninsula and Kuril Islands outside; Sea of Japan, with Jap. islands outside; Yellow and E. China Seas, with Luchu Islands outside; S. China Sea, with Philippines and Borneo outside. In S., Bay of Bengal and Arabian Sea are respectively E. and W. of India. E. Indies extend S.E. from mainland.

Relief.—In S.W. of continent is plateau called Pamir, where India, Afghanistan, U.S.S.R., and China meet, and whence great mt. chains run in all directions. Principal mt. system is Himalayas—highest point, Mt. Everest (29,140 ft.); chief range extends S.E. from Pamir to borders of China, there breaking into numerous ranges which traverse Burma and Malay Peninsula; Karakoram Mts. and Kunlun Mts. form the northern flank of system. Tien Shan Mts. extend N.E. from Pamir to Mongolia; further N., Altai and other ranges extend eastwards across N. Mongolia and E. Siberia towards Sea of Okhotsk, forming northern boundary of Desert of Gobi, eastern boundary of which is formed by Khingan Mts. Mt. ranges also extend from Pamir S.W. through India and Afghanistan, and W. towards Caspian Sea. Tableland of Tibet (alt. 10,000–17,000 ft.) lies N. of principal range of Himalayas, to S. of which is Ind. peninsula with tableland of Deccan (1,500–3,000 ft.). In S.W. is tableland of Arabia (2,500–7,000 ft.). Other plateaus are those of Iran, Armenia, and Asia Minor. Principal rivs. are Ob, Yenisei, and Lena in N.; Amur, Hoang-Ho, and Yangtze Kiang in E.; Mekong, Irrawaddy, Brahmaputra, Ganges, Indus in S.; Euphrates and Tigris in S.W.; Sir Darya and Oxus to Sea of Aral. Largest lakes are Caspian Sea (partly in Europe), Sea of Aral, Lake Balkhash, Lake Baikal, and Lob Nor. There are lowlands along western Caspian-Ob dist.; in Manchuria, China, Siam, Lower Burma; in curve formed by valleys of Ganges and Indus in N. India; and in valleys of Euphrates and Tigris.

Climate varies greatly. Around Verkhoyansk, in N. of E. Siberia, is coldest part of eastern hemisphere. Warmth gradually increases southward, the highest temperatures being experienced in S.W. Asia and India. Winds blow from different quarters, the most interesting and important and regular being the monsoons, which blow from N.E. from Oct. to March, and from S.W. from May to Oct. over S.E. Asia. Rainfall is great where high ground intercepts wet winds, but there are rainless stretches in centre and on plateau from Persia westwards.

Flora.—Vegetation varies according to climate, latitude, and altitude. Dwarf willows and birches occur in *tundra* districts, N. of Arctic Circle, where also mosses and lichens are found. Chief trees are pine, larch, birch in Siberia, coniferous trees on Himalayas, oak, teak, deodar, sandalwood, palm, in India and Malaya. Tropical flowers occur on lower Himalayan slopes, rhododendrons higher up. In Syria and Asia Minor flora is Mediterranean in character. Central Asia produces vines, olive, fig, apple, and other European fruit trees. Japan and China produce ordinary types of vegetation, including varieties of Alpine plants, while in S.E. occur many indigenous plants—sugar-cane, cotton, pepper, areca, sago, banana, and coconut palms growing wild here, as well as many fruit trees and drug- and rubber-producing plants. Bamboos are abundant in China and India. Cultivated plants include tea in Assam, Ceylon, China, Japan; coffee in Arabia, S. India; rice, maize, and cotton in monsoon lands. Date palms abound in oases.

Fauna includes the camel, yak, elephant, tiger, leopard, bear, wolf, Arctic fox, ermine, deer, marmot, monkey, some marsupials (in Malaya), the crocodile, python, rhinoceros, cheetah; pheasant, ptarmigan, guillemot.

Minerals.—Gold, precious stones, coal, iron; petroleum found in Caucasus, Burma, and Sumatra.

Peoples.—Inhabitants of Asia form over half population of world and belong to five different groups—Mongolian, Caucasian, Malayan, Dravidian, Negroid. Mongolians, numerically greatest, inhabit China, Japan, Tibet, N. Asia; Caucasians predominate in W. from Afghanistan to Asia Minor, and in India; Malayans in eastern peninsula and Eastern Archipelago; Dravidians in S. India and Ceylon; Negroid peoples in S.E. Asia and Philippine Islands. Other inhabitants are Russians, British, Jews, Arabs. Area, *c.* 17,000,000 sq. m. Total pop. over 1,000,000,000. See under individual countries.

Asia Mi'nor, or ANATOLIA, western peninsula, Asia, forming part of Turkish rep.; bounded N. by Black Sea, E. by Armenia and Persia, S. by Mediterranean Sea and Syria, W. by Bosporus, Sea of Marmara, Dardanelles, and Ægean Sea; coast-line broken in W. Central tableland, 3,000–6,000 ft., bounded by mt. ranges N. and S.; has salt lakes. Elsewhere are fertile riv. valleys and waste strips; in S. is Plain of Adana. Climate extreme on plateau, temperate on Mediterranean. Chief rivs., Kizil Irmak, Sakaria. Roads are practically unknown; traffic dependent on horses, camels, mules. Hill slopes of N. are covered with trees—walnut, box, oak, beech, plane, ash. There are many cattle, sheep, goats, horses. Cereals, tobacco, figs, fruits, opium are grown. Mineral wealth is believed to be abundant. Manufactures include silks, cottons, carpets, mohair, wine, soap, liquorice paste, sugar, copper utensils. Among imports are textiles, iron, coal, petroleum; among exports, grain, cotton, dried fruits, wine, oil, hides, mohair, tobacco, meerschaum. Area, 305,090 sq. m.; pop. 13,660,000. See also TURKEY.

As'kern, vil., W. Riding, Yorks,

England, 6¼ m. N. of Doncaster; medicinal springs. Pop. (par.) 3,730.

Asmar'a, tn., cap. of Eritrea, N.E. Africa; caravan and trading centre; gold mines in vicinity. Pop. 14,700.

Aspa'tria, urb. dist., Cumberland, England, 20 m. S.W. of Carlisle; coal mines in vicinity; agricultural college. Pop. 3,200.

Aspinwall. See COLON.

Aspull, urb. dist., Lancs, England, 3 m. N.E. of Wigan; coal mining; cotton spinning. Pop. 7,200.

Assam', British prov., in extreme N.E. of India. N. part lies along Brahamaputra valley, southern along Surma valley; between these two rivs. lies hill district; chief mts., Himalayas in the N., Assam hills in the S.; large amount of forest ground and fertile land. Mainly agricultural; produces about two-thirds of tea grown in India; rice, jute, and cotton; large deposits of coal; petroleum, iron, and limestone also worked; forests contain rubber trees, sal, and other hardwoods. Exports tea, jute, rice, timber, coal; imports woollen and cotton goods, salt, glass, earthenware, tobacco, opium, betel. Chief tn., Shillong. Area, 61,461 sq. m.; pop. 7,990,000.

Assin'iboine, riv. of Canada, trib. of Red Riv., which it joins at Winnipeg.

Assisi (*ä-sē'zē*), tn., Umbria, Italy, 15 m. by rail S.E. of Perugia; birthplace of St. Francis, 1182. Pop. 20,000.

Assiut. See ASYUT.

Assyr'ia, anc. country lying N. of Babylonia, now forming part of Iraq; named from Assur, its capital; became one of the most extensive empires of anc. world, comprising Babylonia, W. Media, Armenia, Syria, Palestine, and Egypt. Surface of country is high plain crossed by mts. and drained by R. Tigris and its tribs.

Asterabad'. (1) Prov., N.E. Persia; productive soil, but scanty population; rice, wheat. Area, 5,630 sq. m. (2) Cap. of above, 20 m. from Caspian Sea; trade in carpets, cotton, rice, salt. Pop. 9,000.

Asti, tn., episc. see, Italy, 27 m. S.E. of Turin; silk and famous wine. Pop. 25,000.

Ast'ley Bridge, vil., Lancs, England, 3 m. N. of Bolton; cotton spinning; orphanage. Pop. (dist.) 8,500.

As'ton, former munic. and parl. bor., Warwickshire, England, incorporated (1911) with Birmingham; motor works. Pop. 61,000.

Asto'ria, city, Oregon, U.S.A., on l. bk. of Columbia R.; lumber, flour, and salmon canning. Pop. 16,000.

Astrakhan (*as-tra-kan'*). (1) Prov., Russia, U.S.S.R., on Lower Volga. Fertile along R. Volga; cattle, salt, melons, and vegetables. Area, 11,193 sq. m.; pop. 516,700. (2) City, cap. of above, on l. bk. of R. Volga, 50 m. from its mouth; chief Caspian port. Exports: fish, caviare, petroleum, dyed wool of new-born lambs (astrakhan), water melons, wine, grain, salt, textiles. Univ. established, 1919. Pop. 176,000.

Asturias. See OVIEDO (1).

Asuncion (*ă-soon-thē-on'*), cap., Paraguay, S. America; port on Paraguay R.; trades in leather, tobacco, sugar. Pop. 103,800.

Aswan', tn., Upper Egypt, on r. bk. of R. Nile; cap. of prov. of same name; winter health resort and tourist centre; Aswan dam, 3½ m. above tn., pounds Nile waters into vast lake. Pop. 16,500.

Asyut'. (1) Prov., Upper Egypt. Area, 812 sq. m.; pop. 1,079,000. (2) Tn., cap. of prov., near l. bk. of R. Nile. Caravan centre; pottery, ivory work; below tn. is great barrage to regulate supply of irrigation water. Pop. 57,000.

Atacă'ma, prov., Chile, S. America, between Pacific and Argentine Rep. and provs. of Antofagasta and Coquimbo. Desert region in N. Rich in silver and copper, also gold, iron, nickel, salt, saltpetre, nitrates, borax, and guano (exports); cap. Copiapo. Area, 30,699 sq. m.; pop. 48,000.

At'bara, or BLACK NILE, riv., last trib. of R. Nile rising in Abyssinia; brings down highly fertilizing mud and causes annual floods of Nile. Length, 790 m.

Atch'ison, city, Kansas, U.S.A., on R. Missouri; flour, live-stock, lumber. Pop. 15,000.

Ates'sa, tn., Abruzzi, Italy, 24 m. S.E. of Chieti; woollen goods, sausages (*salami*). Pop. 11,000.

Ath (*ät*), tn., Hainault, Belgium, 18 m. E. of Tournai; iron and copper foundries, linen, lace, cutlery; long famous for annual fête. Pop. 10,400.

Athabas'ka. (1) Riv., Canada; rises in Alberta, E. of Mt. Hooker; flows N.E. to L. Athabaska after impeded course of 740 m. (2) LAKE, Alberta and Saskatchewan, Canada; area, 3,085 sq. m., having outlet in Slave R.

Ath'elney, vil. and par., Somerset, England, 9 m. N.E. of Taunton; slight mound in neighbourhood, formerly encircled by marsh, said to be Alfred's place of retreat (879); Alfred's jewel discovered in vicinity (1693).

Ath'enry, mkt. tn., Galway, I.F.S., 12 m. E. of Galway; cattle fairs. Pop. 800.

Ath'ens. (1) Cap. of Greece, situated on small stretch of flat ground N.W. of Gulf of Ægina, between rivs. Ilissus and Cephissus; 4½ m. by rail from its harbour at Piræus. Spinning of coarse cotton yarns, manufacture of coarse cotton cloths; distilling, tanning, and carpet making. Univ. Pop. 453,000. Ancient Athens was built on several low hills rising from Attic plain. Interest of old town lies chiefly in Acropolis, hill in centre of city. Summit was occupied by many of finest buildings of world, some of which are wonderfully preserved. Near centre is Parthenon, chief temple of goddess Athena. (2) City, Georgia, U.S.A., 73 m. N.E. of Atlanta; seat of Univ. of Georgia; cotton goods, cotton-seed oil, lumber. Pop. 21,000.

Ath'erstone, mkt. tn., N. Warwickshire, England; Bosworth Field is 8 m. to the N.E. Hat factories. Pop. 5,900.

Ath'erton, tn., Lancs, England, 5 m. S.S.W. of Bolton; collieries, cotton mills; iron foundries. Pop. 20,000.

Athlone', mkt. tn., Westmeath, I.F.S., on R. Shannon, 78 m. W. of Dublin; agricultural centre; woollen mills; salmon fishery. Pop. 7,500.

A'thol, tn., Massachusetts, U.S.A., 25 m. N.W. of Worcester; large boot, shoe, tool, and furniture factories. Pop. 9,600.

A'tholl, or ATHOLE, dist., N. Perthshire, Scotland, watered by Rs. Tay, Tilt, Tummel, and crossed by Grampian Mts.; glens are of great beauty; deer forests and grouse moors. Area, 450 sq. m.

Ath'os, peninsula, Macedonian coast, Greece; extends into Ægean Sea; connected with mainland by narrow strip of land; ends in conical peak, Mt. Athos (6,778 ft.); remarkable for religious establishments; monastic rep. since 1060; visited by many pilgrims.

Athy (*ath-ī'*), mkt. tn., Kildare, I.F.S., at junction of Barrow and Grand Canal; bricks and tiles. Pop. 3,500.

Atitlan (*a-tē-tlan'*), lake, volcano, and tn., Guatemala; lake in crater 24 m. long, 10 m. broad; alt. 4,700 ft.; depth 1,100 ft.; has no apparent outlet. Volcano near S. end, alt. 11,719 ft. Tn. on S. shore of lake; mineral springs; cotton spinning. Pop. 7,700.

Atlan'ta, cap. of Georgia, U.S.A.; educational centre—Atlanta Univ. (for Negroes); chief commercial centre of S.E. states; cotton and cotton goods, cotton-seed oil, paper, lumber products; agricultural implements; extensive publishing trade. Pop. 361,000.

Atlan'tic City, coast resort, New Jersey, U.S.A., 55 m. S.E. of Philadelphia; attracts 200,000–300,000 visitors weekly. Permanent pop. 66,000.

Atlan'tic Ocean, ocean separating Old from New World, Europe and Africa lying to E., N. and S. America to W.; opens northward into Arctic Ocean; spreads out southward into great Southern Ocean; extreme length *c.* 8,500 m. along part enclosed by land; greatest breadth, *c.* 5,000 m.; narrowest part, between Brazil and African coast, 1,800 m. Area, over 31,000,000 sq. m. Deepest point, 90 m. N. of Porto Rico, has depth of 4,662 fathoms. Bed crossed by number of telegraphic cables from E. to W. Relatively salter than other oceans. Chief commercial highway of world.

At'las Mountains, irregular series of mountain groups running along N. of Africa from Cape Ghir in Morocco to Cape Bon in Tunisia, distance of 1,500 m. Greatest height between 14,000 and 15,000 ft., is near W. end, S. of city of Morocco. The valleys are fertile and the hills are well forested.

Atrat'o, riv. Colombia, S. America, flowing into Gulf of Darien; length, 410 m.; navigable for 250 m.

At'tica, eastern div. anc. Greece, in form of triangle, one side of which is separated from Bœotia by mts., while other two are washed by Ægean Sea; chief rivs., Ilissus, Cephissus; chief mts., Cithæron and Parnes ranges. Surface consists of series of plains separated from each other by mountain ridges. Attica produces olives, grapes, figs. Cap. Athens. Area, 2,474 sq. m.; pop. 341,200.

At'tleboro, tn., Mass., U.S.A., 31 m. S.W. of Boston; cotton, jewellery, silverware. Pop. 22,000.

At'tleborough, par. and tn., Norfolk, England, 16 m. S.W. of Norwich; markets. Pop. (par.) 2,400.

Attock', tn. and fort, Punjab, India, at confluence of Kabul and Indus rivs., 47 m. by rail E. of Peshawar; bridge over Indus; military post; oil wells.

Aubagne (*ō-ban'y*), tn., Bouches-du-Rhône, S. France, 10 m. E. of Marseilles; earthenware. Pop. 6,800.

Aube (*ōb*), dep., Central France; watered by Rs. Seine and Aube; cereals, market produce, timber; horses reared. Chief tn., Troyes. Area, 2,326 sq. m.; pop. 238,200.

Aubenas (*ōb-nä'*), tn., Ardèche, S. France, on R. Ardèche, 20 m. S.W. of Privas; silk; coal and iron mining in vicinity. Pop. 4,200.

Aubervilliers (*ō-ber-vē-yä'*), tn., France, on R. Seine; suburb of Paris (N.N.W.); chemicals and perfumery. Pop. 48,000.

Aubin (*ō-ban'*), tn., Aveyron, S. France, 30 m. N.W. of Rodez; coal, iron, marble. Pop. 9,500.

Au'burn. (1) Tn., New York, U.S.A., 25 m. S.W. of Syracuse; shoes, woollens; cordage, agricultural implements; printing. Pop. 37,000. (2) Tn., Maine, U.S.A., 32 m. N. of Portland; boots, shoes, moccasins. Pop. 19,000.

Aubusson (*ō-bus-son'*), tn., Creuse, France, 42 m. N.E. of Limoges; carpet and tapestry factories. Pop. 6,000.

Auch (*ōsh*), chief tn., Gers, France, 43 m. W. of Toulouse; thread, cotton, and woollen goods; poultry, wine, brandy. Pop. 9,000.

Auchinleck (*auch-in-lek* or *af-flek'*), par. and vil., Ayrshire, Scotland, 4½ m. S.E. of Mauchline; coal and iron mines. Pop. (par.) 7,200.

Auchterarder (*auch-ter-ar'der*), burgh and mkt. tn., Perthshire, Scotland, 14 m. S.W. of Perth; wool weaving. Pop. 2,300.

Auck'land. (1) Provincial dist., North Island, New Zealand; goldfields; kauri gum; coal. Area, 25,364 sq. m.; pop. 425,000. (2) Largest city in New Zealand, cap. of above; two harbours; sawmills, shipbuilding, glass factories, sugar refinery. Univ. Pop. 206,800.

Auckland Islands, volcanic islands, Pacific Ocean, 180 m. S. of New Zealand, to which they belong; well forested; uninhabited. Area, 350 sq. m.

Aude (*ōd*). (1) Riv. S.W. France, enters Mediterranean Sea. Length, 140 m. (2) Maritime dep., France; maize, vines, fruit; slate, marble, salt, iron ore, manganese. Cap. Carcassonne. Area, 2,448 sq. m.; pop. 292,000.

Au'denshaw, urb. dist., Lancs, England, 5½ m. E. of Manchester; cotton. Pop. 8,500.

Aud'ley, urb. dist., Staffs, England, 4½ m. N.W. of Newcastle-under-Lyme; coal and ironstone. Pop. 13,600.

Aue (*ow'i*), tn., Saxony, Germany, 21 m. S.W. of Chemnitz; machinery, metal work. Pop. 21,300.

Augsburg (*owgz'boorg*), cathedral tn., Bavaria, Germany, 35 m. N.W. of Munich; cotton spinning and weaving mills; woollen and paper factories; breweries; chemicals, dye works. Pop. 166,000.

Augus'ta. (1) City, Georgia, U.S.A., on Savannah R.; winter resort; commercial centre; cotton, cotton-seed oil, chemical works, and foundries. Pop. 60,000. (2) Cap., Maine, U.S.A.; manufactures boots, shoes, cotton goods, paper; lumber; printing. Pop. 17,000. (3) Tn. and port, Syracuse, Sicily. Saltworks. Pop. 17,000.

Aumale (*ō-mal'*), tn., Seine-Inférieure, France, 37 m. N.E. of Rouen; cloth, leather, and steel. Pop. 2,400.

Aurangabad', tn., Hyderabad, Deccan, India, 170 m. N.E. of Bombay; embroidery, silverware, textiles. Pop. 37,000. Area of dist., 6,212 sq. m.; pop. 714,000.

Auray (*ō-rā*), tn., Morbihan, N.W. France, 11 m. W. of Vannes; leading centre of oyster culture; dairy produce and fruit. Pop. 6,500.

Aurillac (*ō-rē-yak'*), chief tn., Cantal, France; agricultural trade; wooden shoes, umbrellas. Pop. 14,000.

Auro'ra, city, Illinois, U.S.A., 38 m. W. of Chicago; foundries, machine shops, textile factories. Pop. 47,000.

Aussig (*ow'sig*). See USTI NAD LABEM.

Austerlitz (*ows'ter-lits*), tn., Moravia, Czechoslovakia, 15 m. S.E. of Brno; scene of Napoleon's victory over Austrians and Russians (1805). Pop. 3,600.

Au'stin. (1) Cap. of Texas, U.S.A., on r. bk. of Colorado R. Important seat of education; state univ. Flourishing agricultural centre; printing; flour, bricks, furniture. Pop. 53,000. (2) Tn., Minnesota, U.S.A., 90 m. S. of St. Paul; packing houses, chicken hatcheries. Pop. 12,000.

Australasia, popular term comprising region from Wallace's Line (Lombok I.) to New Zealand, and including Australia, New Guinea, New Britain, and other archipelagos.

Australia, Brit. Dominion, S. hemisphere, bounded N. by Arafura and Timor Seas, E. by S. Pacific, S.W. and N.W. by Indian Ocean; separated from Tasmania by Bass Strait. Coastline little indented; mts. mostly in E., where they extend from Cape York to Tasmania in Great Dividing Range, known in different places as New England and Liverpool Ranges, Blue Mts., Australian Alps, and Grampians; highest peak, Mt. Townshend (7,350 ft.), Australian Alps; across centre of continent are Coast, Macdonnell, and Flinders Ranges; in S.W. is Darling Range. There are no active volcanoes; there are tablelands on either side of Great Dividing Range, that on W. sloping to great central Upland Plains, which pass into Great Sandy and Victoria Deserts farther W. Lakes are Eyre, Torrens, Gairdner, Amadeus, Frome—all salt lakes—in S. Australia and Central Australia; Austin, Barlea, Cowcowing, in W. Australia. Principal rivs. are Victoria and Roper, in N. Australia; Flinders, Burdekin, Fitzroy, and Brisbane in Queensland; Hunter in New South Wales; Ashburton, Murchison, and Swan, in W. Australia; S.E. watered by Murray-Darling system, which drains Great Lowland Plain, entering sea on S. coast.

The *climate* generally is warm and dry; heat greatest in N. Rain in some parts torrential; often there are long droughts, disastrous to stock. In certain areas water from artesian wells is used for live-stock. For climate and production, Dividing Range is important, as it lies directly in path of S.E. Trades, and therefore drains moisture from rain-bearing winds blowing inland, with result that E. coast strip receives too much rain, central and W. dists. too little. The

S.W. strip receives westerly rains in winter. Rainfall is heaviest in N.

Australia has unique fauna, having great number of marsupial animals, among which kangaroos, wombats, and opossums may be mentioned as typical Australian mammals. Platypus and spiny ant-eater are peculiar to the continent. Many parrots occur, and emus, lyre-birds, and black swans are found. Temperate flora has adapted itself to resist drought.

Resources.—Vegetable productions may be divided into (1) tropical and subtropical forest and crops, in N. and part of E. Queensland coast; (2) forests and crops of temperate zone, in E. and S. coasts, except along Bight; (3) mountain forests of temperate zone, along Dividing Range; (4) evergreen bushes, in S.W. and both sides of Spencer Gulf; (5) pasture and scrub, on rest of country except deserts. There are many valuable trees—eucalyptus, blue gum, red gum, iron bark, stringy bark, acacia, cabbage palm, karri, jarrah, kangaroo grass, and salt-bush. Pasture is great source of wealth; sheep and cattle largely raised. Australia is greatest wool-producing country in world, Australian merino wool is longer in staple and heavier than any other; most goes to U.K. Cattle rearing has greatly developed recently, through spread of frozen-meat trade. Rabbits (introduced from Britain) have become a pest. Chief crops are wheat, hay, potatoes, maize, oats, barley. Grapes, bananas, and other fruits, sugar-cane, cotton, and tobacco are grown; wine industry is rapidly growing. Minerals include gold, silver, copper, lead, tin, coal, iron, manganese, antimony, cinnabar, rubies, sapphires. Coal is worked. Bulk of trade is carried on with Brit. Empire. Principal exports are wool, wheat, butter, beef and mutton, skins and hides, sugar and gold.

Communication.—Australia has regular communication with all countries. Rly. mileage is *c.* 28,000; lines run from Adelaide to Brisbane; from Brisbane, Rockhampton, and Townsville into interior; and from Perth to Geraldton and Albany. Transcontinental rly. was completed in 1917 from Port Augusta (S. Australia) to link up at Kalgoorlie with W. Australian line. Trans-Australian rly. from N. to S. is under construction. Airway routes are developing rapidly.

Australia consists of six original states, New South Wales, Victoria, Queensland, South Australia, Western Australia, with Northern Territory (now divided into North Australia and Central Australia); and island of Tasmania. Of these, New South Wales is oldest. In 1901 the states were all united in a federation called the Commonwealth of Australia.

The *people* are mainly British, favouring 'White Australia' policy. Aborigines, numbering *c.* 60,000, constitute a distinct race, and are sometimes regarded as lowest human family. Cap. Canberra. Area, 2,974,581 sq. m.; pop. 6,263,000.

Austra'lian Alps, broad plateau, S.E. Australia; part of Great Dividing Range; stretches N.E. from near Melbourne to Canberra; contains Mt. Kosciusko, highest mt. in Australia.

Aus'tria, inland republic, Europe; bounded N. by Germany and Czechoslovakia, E. by Hungary, S. by Yugoslavia and Italy, W. by Switzerland; divided into provs. of Burgenland, Lower Austria, Upper Austria, Salzburg, Styria, Carinthia, Tyrol, Vorarlberg, Liechtenstein. Surface is mountainous; Lower Austria is flat round Vienna; drained by R. Danube. There are small lakes in S.; mineral springs in N.W. Climate extreme. Animals include wild boar, chamois, bear, wolf, jackal, deer, golden eagles, herons. Much of surface is covered with forests. Austria produces wheat, oats, rye, potatoes, beet, hemp, rape, flax, hops, tobacco; horses, cattle, pigs, and sheep are raised; silkworms and bees are kept. Minerals include coal, lignite, graphite, salt, zinc, silver, iron, lead, quicksilver, copper. Industries include sugar making, manufacture of woollen, linen, silk, and cotton textiles, iron and steel, glass, beer. More than half population is engaged in agricultural pursuits; dairy farming important in Alpine districts; exports timber, furniture, chemicals, sugar, dairy produce; imports wool, cotton, silk, coal, wine, iron goods, rice. Country has over 4,000 m. of rlys. Most important waterways are R. Danube and tribs. Over 90 per cent. of people are German-speaking. Chief tns., Vienna (cap.), Graz, Linz. Area, 32,369 sq. m.; pop. 6,534,000.

Austria, LOWER, prov., Austria; part plain; crossed by R. Danube; industries and agriculture; chief city, Vienna. Area, 7,452 sq. m.; pop. 1,480,000.

Austria, UPPER, prov., Austria; drained by R. Danube; hilly; forests; salt and mineral springs; chief tn., Linz. Area, 4,626 sq. m.; pop. 876,000.

Austria-Hungary, former empire, Central Europe; territories included Empire of Austria, Kingdom of Hungary, and Provinces of Bosnia and Hercegovina. It was bounded N. by Germany and Russia, E. by Russia and Romania, S. by Romania, Serbia, Montenegro, W. by Germany, Switzerland, Italy.

Autun (*ō-tun'*), tn. and episc. see, dep. Saône-et-Loire, France, 43 m. S.W. of Dijon; leather, umbrellas, furniture; brewing. Pop. 11,500.

Auvergne (*ō-vārn'*), former prov., central France, now comprising deps. of Puy-de-Dôme and Cantal and N.W. portion of Haute-Loire.

Auxerre (*ō-zār'*), tn., cap. of Yonne dep., France. It stands in the midst of vineyards, and manufactures bricks, ochre, and iron goods. Pop. 18,500.

Auxonne (*ō-zon'* or *ōk-son'*), fort. tn., Côte d'Or, France, on l. bk. of R. Saône; trade in vegetables and market garden produce. Pop. 3,000.

Av'a, ruined city, Burma, India, on R. Irrawaddy, 10 m. S.W. of Mandalay; former capital.

Avallon (*a-va-lon'*), tn., Yonne, France, 34 m. S.E. of Auxerre; trade in leather, wine, wood, grain. Pop. 4,800.

Av'alon, peninsula at extreme S.E. of Newfoundland; fishing.

Avatcha (*a-vä'cha*). (1) Active volcano (1827, 1837, 1855), with double peak, Kamchatka, Asia. (2) See BERING ISLAND.

Avebury (*āv'ber-i*) or ABURY, vil., Wilts, England, 6 m. W. of Marlborough; anc. large stone circle. Pop. 525.

Aveiro (*a-vā'ē-rō*). (1) Dist., Beira, Portugal; good grazing ground; copper and lead mines. Area, 1,065 sq. m.; pop. 344,200. (2) Port, cap. of above, 35 m. S. of Oporto; sardines, salt, wine, fruit, and oil. Pop. 10,000.

Avellino (*a-vel-ē'no*), tn., Campania, Italy, 30 m. E. of Naples; hazel nuts; manufactures linen, paper, hats. Pop. 30,000.

Aver'nus, small lake near Naples; crater of extinct volcano.

Aver'sa, tn. and episc. see, Caserta, Italy, 10 m. N. of Naples; wine, hemp, cotton, furniture. Pop. 23,000.

Avesnes (*a-vān*), tn., dep. Nord, France, 24 m. S.E. of Valenciennes; wool-spinning. Pop. 4,600.

Aveyron (*a-vā-ron'*), dep., S. France. Chief rivs., Lot, Aveyron, and Tarn. Varied soil; potatoes, rye, oats, vines; sheep, cattle; Roquefort cheese; extensive forests; coal, zinc. Chief tn., Rodez. Area, 3,385 sq. m.; pop. 329,000.

Aviemore (*äve-mōr'*), vil., Inverness-shire, Scotland, near R. Spey, 12½ m. S.W. of Grantown-on-Spey; holiday resort. Pop. 650.

Avigliano, tn., Italy, 8 m. N.W. of Potenza; marble. Pop. of comm. 20,000.

Avignon (*a-vēn-yon'*) ('windy city'), chief tn. Vaucluse, France, on R. Rhône; residence of popes (1309–79); flour, oil, soap, chemicals, leather, madder. Pop. 52,000.

Avila (*ä'vē-la*). (1) Prov., Spain, S. of Valladolid; mountainous, centre and S.; merino wool, timber; jasper and marble; lower fertile tracts towards the N.; grain. Area, 3,042 sq m.; pop. 215,000. (2) Tn., cap. of above. Pop. 13,000.

Aviles (*ä-vē-lāz'*), port, Oviedo, N. Spain; fishing; exports coal. Pop. 15,000.

Avlona. See VALONA.

Avo'ca, or OVOCA, riv. and valley, co. Wicklow, I.F.S.; thickly wooded.

Av'ola, tn., prov. Syracuse, Sicily; wine, almonds, sugar. Pop. 16,500.

Avon (*ā'von*) ('river'). (1) EAST AVON, rises in Wilts, England; enters Eng. Channel at Christchurch. (2) LOWER AVON, rises in Cotswold Hills, Gloucestershire; flows into Bristol Channel at Avonmouth. (3) UPPER AVON, rises at Naseby, Northants; flows past Stratford; joins Severn below Tewkesbury. (4) Trib. of Clyde, Scotland. (5) Trib. of Spey, Banffshire, Scotland. (6) Trib. of Forth, Scotland.

A'vonmouth, tn., Gloucestershire, England, 6 m. N.W. of Bristol; docks; grain, provisions, meat. Pop. 3,000.

Avranches (*av-rānsh'*), tn., S.W. Manche, France; lace, salt, leather dressing; salmon fisheries. Pop. 6,200.

Avre, riv. of Picardy, trib. of Somme, France.

Awaji (*a-wä'jē*), isl., Japan, at E. entrance to Inland Sea; hilly; famous for pottery; tourist centre. Area, 218 sq. m.; pop. 170,000.

Awe (*aw*). (1) Freshwater loch, Argyllshire, Scotland; salmon and trout fishing. (2) Riv. flows from above loch through Pass of Brander to Loch Etive; salmon and sea trout.

Ax'holme, ISLE OF, dist., N.W. Lincolnshire, England; bounded by rivs. Trent, Idle, and Don; 17 m. long by 9 m. broad; formerly marshy; fertile; celery, flax, and various crops. Pop. 6,800.

Ax'minster, par. and mkt. tn., S.E. Devon, England; brush making; timber working. Famous carpet industry now transferred to Wilton. Pop. 2,300.

Axum'. See AKSUM.

Ay (*ī*), tn., Marne, France, 13 m. S. of Reims; in centre of Champagne dist. Pop. 7,200.

Aylesbury (*ālz'ber-e*), mkt. tn., Bucks, England; duck rearing, printing, motor-cars, condensed milk. Pop. 13,400.

Aylesford (*ālz'ford*), tn., and par., Kent, England, 3 m. N.W. of Maidstone; scene of battle between Britons and Saxons, in which Horsa fell (455). Pop. (par.) 3,100.

Aylesham (*ālz'ham*), tn., Kent, England; on coalfield N. of Dover. Pop. 2,000.

Ayr (*ār*), royal burgh, chief tn. of Ayrshire, Scotland; at mouth of R. Ayr; famous old bridge; associated with poet Burns; cattle markets; chief Scot. horse-racing centre; exports coal, iron; shipbuilding, engineering, sawmills. Pop. 36,800.

Ayrshire (*ār-shir*), co., S.W. Scotland; watered by Rs. Ayr, Stinchar, Doon, Irvine, Girvan; hilly districts in N. and S.; chief lake, Loch Doon; famous for early potatoes, dairy farming, cheese; coalfields, ironworks; fireclay, limestone, and honestone deposits; carpets, tweeds, cottons, chemicals, explosives, leather, tools, fisheries; chief ports, Ayr (chief tn.), Ardrossan, Girvan, Troon, Largs. Area, 1,132 sq. m.; pop. 285,200.

Ayuthia (*a-yoo'thi-a*), tn., Siam, 42 m. N. of Bangkok; great trade in rice. Pop. 12,000.

Azamgarh', tn., United Provinces, India, 52 m. N. of Benares; in fertile dist.; heavy crops of rice and sugar-cane. Pop. 15,000.

Azerbaijan (*az-er-bī-jan'*). (1) Mountainous prov., N.W. Persia, W. of Caspian Sea; grain, fruits, tobacco, and saffron; lead, copper, sulphur; cap. Tabriz. Area, 32,000 sq. m.; pop. 1,500,000. (2) Socialist Soviet Republic; stretches along the western shore of Caspian Sea; on N. is Dagestan; to W. are Georgia and Armenia. Industries are agriculture, cattle rearing; oil wells and refineries, salt, fisheries. Cap. Baku. Area, 32,686 sq. m.; pop. 2,313,000.

Azores (*a-zōrz'*), three groups of hilly

islands in Atlantic Ocean belonging to Portugal; about 900 m. w. of Portugal; extend over length of *c.* 400 m.; of volcanic origin, and have frequently suffered from earthquakes. Hot mineral springs occur. Climate is temperate. Largest isl. is São Miguel (41 by 9¼ m.); smallest, Corvo (4½ by 3 m.). Eastern group comprises Santa Maria, São Miguel, Formigas Rocks; central, Terceira, Graciosa, São Jorge, Pico, Fayal; western, Flores, Corvo. Azores produce wine, pineapples, oranges, bananas, grain, pulse, sweet potatoes, tobacco; industries include butter and cheese making, distilling, whale fishing. Best harbour is at Horta, Fayal I. Cap. Angra, in Terceira, 922 sq. m. Pop. 232,000.

Az'ov. (1) Tn., N. Caucasian Area, U.S.S.R., on l. bk. of R. Don; fisheries. Pop. 17,500. (2) SEA OF, connected with Black Sea, s. of Russia; very shallow; gradually silting up; valuable fisheries; caviare and isinglass.

Azuaga (*a-thoo-ă'ga*), tn., prov. Badajoz, Spain, 54 m. N.W. of Cordoba; woollen goods; live-stock market. Pop. 16,600.

Azuay (*ă-soo-ī'*), southern prov., Ecuador, S. America; cap. Cuenca; agriculture, cattle raising, and manufacture of straw hats. Area, 3,874 sq. m.; pop. 150,000.

Azul (*a-sool'*), tn., prov. Buenos Aires, Argentina; cattle and sheep. Pop. *c.* 8,000.

B

Ba'albek (anc. *Heliopolis*), tn., Lebanon, Syria, 40 m. E. of Beirut. Formerly a magnificent city; vast Roman remains; attracts tourists. Pop. *c.* 3,000.

Baanfu. See BATANG.

Babbacombe, eccles. dist. and coastal vil., Devon, England, 1½ m. N.E. of Torquay Seaside resort. Pop. 2,000.

Bab-el-Mandeb ('Gate of Tears'), strait, 14½ m. wide, uniting Red Sea and Indian Ocean.

Babuyan'es, volcanic island group, N. of Philippines. Products: tobacco, rice, maize. Pop. 10,000.

Bab'ylon ('gate of the god,') anc. tn. Iraq, on l. bk. of R. Euphrates, cap. of Babylonian Empire. Its hanging gardens, built in terrace form and supported on arches resting upon other arches, were one of the 'Seven Wonders of the World.'

Babylo'nia, anc. country of Mesopotamia, lying s. of Assyria; lowlying district; name taken from anc. cap., Babylon. The country is interesting chiefly through its entry into Bible history, and the antiquities it has yielded.

Bacau (*bă'kow*), tn., Romania, 52 m. s.w. of Jassy; petroleum springs. Pop. *c.* 28,000.

Baccarat (*bă-kă-ră'*), tn., Meurthe-et-Moselle, France, 30 m. S.E. of Nancy; glass factories. Pop. 7,300.

Bacchiglione (*bă-kēl-yō'nă*), riv., Italy; flowing to Adriatic. Towns on its banks are Padua and Vicenza. Length, 90 m.

Backergunge, or BAKARGANJ, dist. s. Bengal, India, in Ganges delta; three crops of rice annually; betel-nuts. Area, 3,490 sq. m. Pop. 2,624,000.

Back's River. See GREAT FISH RIVER (2).

Bacolod', tn., N.W. coast Negros I., Philippines. Sugar industry; productive fisheries. Pop. 19,000.

Bactria. See BALKH.

Ba'cup, munic. bor. and mkt. tn., E. Lancs, England, 16 m. N. of Manchester; cotton spinning, weaving, corn milling, and ironfounding. Pop. 20,600.

Badajoz (*bă-dă-hōth'*). (1) Prov.,

largest in Spain, bordering on Portugal. Stock raising; cereals, olives. Area, 8,451 sq. m.; pop. 706,000. (2) Cap. of above, on Guadiana R.; old cathedral, ruins of Moorish castle; foodstuffs, woollens, leather, and wax. Pop. 41,000.

Badakhshan', prov., N. Afghanistan, drained by R. Oxus and tribs. Salt, gold, iron, rubies, lapis lazuli. Cap. Faizabad. Area, 8,500 sq. m.; pop. *c.* 100,000.

Badalo'na, port, N.E. Spain, 6 m. N.E. of Barcelona. Wine and brandy; shipyards, glass, and chemical works. Pop. 29,000.

Baden (*bä'den*). (1) Rep. and component state of Germany, along E. bk. of R. Rhine. Surface in the E. is hilly, with the Odenwald in N., Black Forest in S.; in the W. is part of Rhine valley; extreme S.E. drained by R. Danube; rest drained by Rhine and tribs. Main and Neckar. About half of area is forested. Rhine dist. produces grain, tobacco, hemp, rape, chicory, hops; vines on hills, forests of pine, oak, beech, birch, ash in Black Forest; several districts noted for wine. Minerals include limestone, gypsum, salt, soda; many mineral springs. Manufactures: cottons, ribbons, paper, beet sugar, cigars, clocks, musical instruments, wooden ornaments, toys, chemicals. Chief tns., Mannheim, Karlsruhe, Freiburg, Pforzheim, Heidelberg. Area, 5,819 sq. m.; pop. 2,312,000. (2) Or BADEN-BADEN, cap. of above; is a beautifully situated health resort; mineral springs and baths; wood carving. Pop. 26,000. (3) Tn., Aargau, Switzerland, 13 m. N.W. of Zurich; famous for hot mineral springs since Roman times; for three centuries was seat of Swiss federal council; electrical engineering. Pop. 8,300. (4) Or BADEN BEI WIEN, spa and tn., Austria, 17 m. S. of Vienna; warm sulphur springs. Pop. 22,000.

Bad'enoch, extensive mountainous dist., S.E. Inverness-shire, Scotland; traversed by R. Spey; deer forests.

Bad Lands, rough and barren tracts, western U.S.A. The condition is due to the action of occasional rains and running water upon arid plateaus of soft, poorly cemented rock, *e.g.*, on White, Cheyenne, Lower Yellowstone, and Little Missouri Rivers.

Bad'minton, GREAT, par. and vil., Glos, England, 14 m. N.E. of Bristol; gives name to the game.

Badne'ra, tn., Berar, India, 90 m. W.S.W. of Nagpur; cotton manufactures. Pop. 11,000.

Bad'rinath, peak of Himalayas, United Provinces, India; alt. 23,210 ft.; shrine of Vishnu attracts 50,000 pilgrims annually.

Baena (*bä-ā'na*), tn., Cordoba, Spain, 43 m. N.W. of Granada; horse breeding, linen, olive oil. Pop. 18,000.

Baeza (*bä-ā-tha*), tn., Spain, 18 m. N.E. of Jaen; important Moorish city; univ. (1533). Pop. 15,000.

Baffin Bay, sea, W. of Greenland; whale and seal fishery; first explored by Baffin (1616).

Baffin Land, barren island, W. of Baffin Bay, Franklin, Canada; inhabited by a few Eskimos. Area, *c.* 236,000 sq. m.

Bagamo'yo, port, Tanganyika Terr., Africa, near mouth of navigable R. Ruwu; formerly an important caravan centre and starting-point of exploration. Pop. 5,200.

Baghdad. (1) Vilayet of Iraq (Mesopotamia), in basin of Rs. Euphrates and Tigris; alluvial plain, formerly one of the granaries of the world; dates, bitumen, naphtha, and petroleum; exports wool, carpets, mohair, skins; bituminous coal plentiful. Area, 54,450 sq. m.; pop. 1,360,000. (2) Cap. of Iraq, on R. Tigris, 340 m. from mouth of Shatt-al-Arab; on Baghdad Railway; important centre of air routes; caravan centre and emporium. Silk and other textiles, copper utensils, and leather goods are manufactured. Built on both banks of river (300 yds. wide, crossed by bridge of boats); modern city (eastern section) includes governor's palace, the European consulates, chief bazaars; western section is principal Persian quarter; city encircled and interspersed with groves and date palms; cosmopolitan pop. Baghdad reached height of its glory under Haroun-al-Raschid (9th cent.). Pop. about 250,000 (Mohammedans, 180,000; Jews, 50,000; Christians, 15,000).

Baghelkhand′, Agency of E. Central India; contains twelve states; largest Rewah (13,000 sq. m.); rich in minerals. Cap. Rewah, 72 m. s.w. of Allahabad. Area, 14,323 sq. m.; pop. 1,770,000.

Bagheria (*bä-gä-rē′a*), or BAGARIA, tn., Palermo, Sicily; formerly fashionable resort. Pop. 20,000.

Bagillt, eccles. dist. and vil., Flintshire, Wales, on R. Dee; lead working, coal mining; chemicals. Pop. (dist.) 4,000.

Bagir′mi, dist., Chad Colony, French Equatorial Africa; plateau (alt. 1,000 ft.) drained by Shari and tribs. Grain, cotton. Area, 25,000 sq. m.; pop. 154,000.

Bagnara (*ban-yä′ra*), tn., Reggio di Calabria, s. Italy; almost destroyed by earthquake (1908); dist. produces good wine. Pop. 11,100.

Bagnères (*ban-yer′*). (1) DE BIGORRE, tn., on R. Adour, Hautes-Pyrénées, France; one of chief health resorts of France; mineral springs; woollen goods. Pop. 7,300. (2) DE LUCHON, tn., Haute-Garonne, France; hot mineral springs. Pop. 3,700.

Bagni (*ban′yä*). (1) DI LUCCA, tn., Italy, 11 m. N. of Lucca; mineral springs. Pop. 15,000. (2) DI SAN GIULIANO, tn., 5 m. N.E. of Pisa, Italy; anc. mineral springs still used; textiles and soap. Pop. 21,000.

Bagno (*ban′yo*). (1) A RIPOLI, tn., 2 m. E. of Florence, Italy; many fine villas. Pop. 14,000. (2) IN ROMAGNA, tn., Italy, 35 m. E. of Florence; warm mineral springs. Pop. 9,600.

Bahä′mas, or LUCAYOS, chain of coral islands, W. Indies, N. of Cuba; belong to Britain; include 29 isls. and 660 islets, about 20 being inhabited. Largest are Andros, Great Abaco, Great Bahama, and Great Inagua I.; soil fertile. Products: maize, cotton, sisal hemp, pineapples, oranges, lemons, tomatoes, olives; sponges in surrounding seas; principal exports, sponges, tomatoes, sisal fibre. Islands were first land sighted by Columbus on his voyage of discovery; have belonged without interruption to Britain since 1783. Cap. Nassau, New Providence I. Area, 4,404 sq. m.; pop. *c.* 59,000 (mainly Negroes).

Bahaw′alpur, Indian state, Punjab, India; level and partly desert; silks, chintzes. Cap. Bahawalpur (pop. 18,000), on R. Sutlej. Area of state, 15,000 sq. m.; pop. 781,000.

Bahia (*ba-ē′a*). (1) Atlantic state of Brazil; occupies middle and N. São Francisco valley. Products: diamonds, sugar, cotton, coffee, cocoa, tobacco. Area, 204,340 sq. m.; pop. 3,859,000. (2) Or SÃO SALVADOR, cap. of above; important port of rep.; cocoa, tobacco, sugar, hides, and piassava (palm) fibre. Pop. 348,000.

Bahia Blanca (*ba-ē′a blank′a*), tn., Buenos Aires prov., Argentina; wool and grain; chief naval port of rep. Pop. 44,100.

Bahrein (*bar-ā′en*) **Islands**, group of islands, Persian Gulf, off Arabian coast. Under Brit. protection; principal island, Bahrein; cap. Manama; pearl fishing; coffee, dates. Pop. 100,000.

Bahr-el-Abiad (*bär-el-ab′yad*), or WHITE NILE. See NILE.

Bahr-el-Az′raq, or BLUE NILE. See NILE.

Bahr-el-Ghazāl′ ('river of the gazelles'), riv. Sudan, trib. of White Nile; gives name to dist. between Nile on E. and Darfur and Kordofan on N.

Baiæ (*bī′ā*), tn., Campania, Italy, 10 m. W. of Naples; favourite wat.-pl. of the Romans under late republic and empire.

Baiern, or BAYERN, Ger. name of BAVARIA.

Baikal (*bī′kāl*), lake, s. Siberia; largest fresh-water lake in Eurasia; area, 13,500 sq. m.; surface about 1,500 ft. above sea-level; average depth 900 ft.; frozen Dec. to May;

surrounded by mts.; Siberian Rly. passes round S. shore; salmon and sturgeon fisheries; discharges by lower Angara R. to Yenisei R.

Baildon, urb. dist., W. Riding, Yorks, England, 4 m. N. of Bradford; worsted weaving; chemical manufactures. Pop. 7,800.

Bailen (*bä-ēl-en'*) or BAYLEN, tn., Andalusia, S. Spain, 22 m. N. of Jaen; galena, glass. Pop. 9,000.

Baireuth. See BAYREUTH.

Bairnsdale, port, Victoria, Australia, 150 m. E. of Melbourne; grain, fruit, butter, leather; goldfields in vicinity. Pop. 3,400.

Baja (*bŏ'yŏ*), tn., S. Hungary, on Danube; fruit, grain, hogs; alcohol. Pop. 20,000.

Bajaur, terr., N.W. Frontier Province, India; chief tn., Nawagai, 50 m. N.N.W. of Peshawar. Area, *c.* 900 sq. m.; pop. *c.* 100,000 (almost entirely Pathans).

Bakarganj. See BACKERGUNGE.

Baker, city, Oregon, U.S.A., 240 m. E.S.E. of Portland; mining, wool, livestock, lumber, flour mills. Pop. 10,000.

Baker, MOUNT, active volcano, N.W. Washington, U.S.A.; height, 10,830 ft.

Baker Islands, coral islands, Pacific, on the equator; guano; under Brit. protection.

Bakersfield, city, California, U.S.A., 100 m. N.W. of Los Angeles; oil refineries, cotton, fruit; commercial air-port. Pop. 26,000.

Bakewell, anc. mkt. tn., Derbyshire, England, 10 m. S.E. of Buxton; chalybeate springs; zinc and marble in vicinity. Pop. 3,000.

Bakhchi-Sarai (*bak-chē-sä-rä'i*) ('garden palace'), tn., Crimea, U.S.S.R.; residence of khans (15th cent.–1783); morocco leather, cutlery. Pop. 10,000.

Bakhmut. See ARTEMOVSK.

Bakhtigan', or NIRIZ, salt lake, Fars, Persia. Area, 400 sq. m.

Bakony Wald (*bok'ony*), forested hills, Hungary, N. of Lake Balaton. Alt. 2,300 ft.

Baku', cap. Azerbaijan, U.S.S.R., on Caspian Sea; rich petroleum field; pipe-line to Batum (560 m.); univ. Pop. 453,000.

Bal'a. (1) Mkt. tn., Merionethshire, Wales, on Bala L.; flannel. Pop. 1,400. (2) LAKE, largest l. in Wales; 4 m. long by 1 m. wide; expansion of R. Dee.

Balaklav'a, port and health resort, Crimea, U.S.S.R. Scene of famous cavalry charges by Light Brigade and Heavy Brigade (1854).

Balasore. (1) Dist., Bihar and Orissa, India; rice. Area, 2,085 sq. m.; pop. 1,100,000. (2) Chief tn. and port of above. Pop. 17,000.

Bal'aton Lake, Hungary, largest lake in Central Europe; 50 m. long by from 2 to 7 m. broad; brackish water; abounds in fish.

Balbo'a, tn., Panama Canal zone; port of Panama; navy yard.

Balbrig'gan, port and mkt. tn., co. Dublin, I.F.S., 18 m. N. of Dublin; cotton, hosiery. Pop. 2,300.

Bal'dock, urb. dist., Herts, England, 4¾ m. N.E. of Hitchin; on (Roman) Icknield Way. Pop. 3,200.

Balear'ic Islands, group of islands off E. coast of Spain (largest, Majorca, Minorca, Iviza, and Formentera); belong to Spain. Minorca was a Brit. possession in 18th cent., but was restored to Spain (1803). The inhabitants were renowned slingers in anc. times. Chief products: swine, fruit, fish. Cap. Palma (Majorca). Area, 1,935 sq. m.; pop. 350,000.

Bal'i, or LITTLE JAVA, Dutch isl., E. of Java; mountainous and volcanic; fertile, well-cultivated; rice, cotton, coffee, copra, tobacco, fruits. Area, 2,100 sq. m.; pop. 960,000.

Baliuag (*bal-ē'wag*), tn., Luzon, Philippines, 25 m. N.W. of Manila; fibre goods, silk, bamboo hats. Pop. 18,000.

Balize. See BELIZE.

Balk'an Peninsula, easterly peninsula, S. Europe, includes Yugoslavia, Albania, Bulgaria, Turkey, and Greece. Rhodope plateau is core of peninsula; it is flanked by folds of Dinaric Alps, and Pindus Mts. on W., Balkans on

E.; valleys fertile. Climate is Mediterranean on coasts, extreme in interior. Chief rivers are Danube and tribs., Vardar and Maritza; lakes, Scutari and Ochrida. Pop. is very mixed; consequent hostility tends to incessant unrest. Area, *c.* 203,000 sq. m.; pop. *c.* 26,000,000.

Balkash′, LAKE. See BALKHASH.

Balkh (BACTRIA). (1) Anc. dist. of Bactria or Bactriana, N. Afghanistan, Central Asia; situated between Oxus R. and Hindu-Kush Mts.; fertile patches, but climate unhealthy. (2) Anc. city, S. of upper Oxus R., former cap. of above; at one time the rival of Nineveh and Babylon; is now much decayed in importance; silk.

Balkhash′, LAKE, Central Asia, *c.* 450 m. long and from 30 to 50 m. broad; no apparent outlet, but water fresh.

Ballachulish (*bă-lă-hoo′lish*), vil. on Loch Leven, Argyllshire, Scotland; slate quarries. Pop. 700.

Ballantrae′, par. and vil., Ayrshire, Scotland, at mouth of R. Stinchar; fish-curing. Pop. (par.) 1,300.

Ballarat′, city, Victoria, Australia, 70 m. W. of Melbourne; originally a gold-mining centre; 'Welcome Stranger' (largest of all gold nuggets) found here; now more important as agricultural and pastoral market; ironfounding, wool, flour milling; railway centre. Pop. 42,000.

Ballari. See BELLARY.

Ball′ater ('town on a sloping hill'), burgh and summer resort, W. Aberdeenshire, Scotland; rly. station for Balmoral. Pop. 1,200.

Ballina′, mkt. tn., co. Mayo, I.F.S., on Killala Bay; angling centre; salmon fishing; snuff and coarse linen. Pop. 4,900.

Ballinasloe′, mkt. tn., on borders of cos. Galway and Roscommon, I.F.S., on R. Suck; great horse and cattle fair (Oct.). Pop. 5,200.

Ballinrobe′, mkt. tn., co. Mayo, I.F.S., near L. Mask; angling centre; 13th cent. abbey (ruins). Pop. 1,300.

Ball′och, vil., Dumbartonshire, Scotland, at S. end of Loch Lomond (pier for lake steamers); adjoining is Loch Lomond Park, belonging to corporation of Glasgow.

Ballycastle, mkt. tn., co. Antrim, N. Ireland, opposite Rathlin I.; bathing resort; golf links; 5 m. E. is Fair Head. Pop. 2,000.

Ballyclare, mkt. tn., co. Antrim, N. Ireland, 11 m. S.W. of Larne; paper mills, bleaching greens. Pop. 3,400.

Ballymē′na, tn., co. Antrim, N. Ireland, 11 m. N. of Antrim; second of the 'linen' towns of Antrim. Pop. 11,900.

Ballymoney, mkt. tn., co. Antrim, N. Ireland; agricultural centre; linen trade. Pop. 3,200.

Ballymote, mkt. tn., E. Sligo, I.F.S.; agricultural centre; carriage building; remains of monastery (in which *Book of Ballymote* was written before A.D. 1400). Pop. 750.

Ballyshannon, mkt. tn., co. Donegal, I.F.S., on both banks of the Erne; salmon fisheries; near is Bundoran, a rising wat.-pl., and Belleek, famous for pottery. Pop. 2,100.

Balmain, tn., New South Wales, Australia; suburb of Sydney; sawmills, iron foundries. Pop. 40,000.

Balme (*bām*), COL DE, pass of Rhone valley between Chamonix and Martigny; height over 7,000 ft.

Balmerino (*bal-mer-ē′no*), par. and vil., Fife, Scotland, on Firth of Tay; ruined Cistercian abbey.

Balmor′al Castle, royal residence, Deeside, Aberdeenshire, Scotland, 9 m. W. of Ballater.

Balquhidder (*balwhid′er*), vil. and par., S.W. Perthshire, Scotland, at E. end of Loch Voil; Rob Roy's burial-place.

Balta, chief tn., Moldavian Rep., U.S.S.R., 120 m. N. by rail from Odessa; cattle, horses, grain. Pop. 24,000 (about three-fourths Jews).

Baltic Port, tn., Estonia, at entrance to Gulf of Finland; an ice-free port.

Baltic Provinces, formerly Russian provs., now forming republics of Estonia, Latvia, and Lithuania.

Baltic Sea, inland sea, N. Europe, surrounded by Denmark, Germany,

Lithuania, Latvia, Estonia, Russia, Finland, and Sweden; connected with North Sea by Sound, Great Belt, Little Belt, Cattegat, Skager Rack; in N. is Gulf of Bothnia, in E. Gulfs of Finland and Riga. Principal islands are: Åland Isls., belonging to Finland; the Danish isls. of Zealand, Fünen, Laaland, and Bornholm; Gottland and Oland, belonging to Sweden. Length, *c.* 950 m.; greatest width, *c.* 150 m.; area, *c.* 170,000 sq. m.; average depth, 20 fathoms; little tide, except at entrance; navigation dangerous; great part frozen in winter. Baltic Sea at Kiel and North Sea at mouth of Elbe were connected by canal (1895).

Bal'timore, city, Maryland, U.S.A., on Chesapeake Bay. Seat of Johns Hopkins Univ., law and medical faculties of Maryland Univ., a coll. for Negroes, and a medical coll.; Johns Hopkins Hospital; only port of great importance in Maryland; exports cereals, flour, cotton, tobacco, copper, meat; industries include fruit and vegetable canning, shipbuilding, manufacture of bricks, clothing, fertilizers, iron, steel. Pop. 806,000.

Baltistan', or LITTLE TIBET, dist., Kashmir, India; crossed by Karakoram Mts., which culminate in Mt. Godwin-Austen, over 28,000 ft.; drained by Indus. Cap. Skardo. Pop. *c.* 50,000.

Baluchistan (*baloochistan'*), country, S.W. Asia, between Afghanistan and Arabian Sea. Coast-line extends *c.* 600 m., but there are no good harbours. Considerable portion is under Brit. control, called *British Baluchistan,* in N.E.; whole is within Brit. sphere of influence. Surface generally consists of dry tablelands, but there are low-lying plains in E. Principal mts. are Sulaiman system in N., Kirthar range in E., Pab Hills in S., Makran coast range in S. Chief rivs.: Nari, Bolan, Badra, in E. Climate has extremes of cold and heat; rainfall slight. Fruits, cereals, and potatoes are grown; camels, horses, oxen, and cows kept. Minerals include coal, iron, lead, asbestos, chromite, salt, but are little worked. There are few manufactures; needlework, felts, pottery; exports dates. Inhabitants are chiefly of Pathan, Brahin, and Baluch races; Pathans found in directly administered districts, Brahins in middle, Baluchi in S. Cap. Kalat. Area, 134,638 sq. m.; pop. 800,000.

Bam, tn., Kerman, Persia, 180 m. N.E. of Bander Abbas; famous citadel; centre of dist. growing dates and henna. Pop. *c.* 13,000.

Bamangwato, native dist., S. Africa, in E. of Bechuanaland Protectorate; cap. Serowe. Pop. *c.* 35,000.

Bam'berg, tn., Bavaria, Germany, 35 m. N. of Nürnberg; Romanesque cathedral (1004), contains tomb of founder, Henry II.; manufactures cottons, rope, tobacco; famous market gardens in vicinity. Pop. 50,100.

Bam'bouk, or BAMBUK, hilly dist., French Sudan, W. Africa, in R. Senegal basin; cattle raising; gold, iron, ivory, fruits; climate unhealthy. Pop. (est.) 800,000.

Bam'burgh, or BAMBOROUGH, coast par. and vil., Northumberland, England, once Saxon royal burgh; popular resort; burial-place of Grace Darling; castle founded *c.* 547, stands on Whin Sill; restored by Lord Armstrong (1894). Pop. 700.

Bam'ian, mountainous valley (8,500 ft.), Afghanistan, 80 m. N.W. of Kabul; seat of Buddhist worship; two enormous idols (173 and 120 ft. high), carved out of rock which forms N. side of valley.

Bampton, tn., N. Devon, England, 7 m. N. of Tiverton; Exmoor ponies. Pop. 1,400.

Banat' ('frontier province'), former dist. Hungary, lying between Rs. Danube, Tisa, and Maros; divided by Peace Conference between Yugoslavia and Romania. Wheat, wine, minerals, silk. Area, 11,260 sq. m.; pop. *c.* 1,500,000.

Ban'bridge, mkt. tn., co. Down, N. Ireland, on R. Bann. Chief seat of county's linen manufacture; chemicals. Pop. 4,900.

Ban'bury, mkt. tn., N. Oxfordshire,

England; mentioned in Domesday Book; anc. cross, noted in nursery rhyme, destroyed by Puritans (1610); famous cakes; rope, leather. Pop. 14,000.

Banchory (*bank'or-e*), tn., Kincardineshire, Scotland, on R. Dee; sanatorium. Pop. 1,700.

Ban'da. (1) Dist., Allahabad, India; rice. Area, 3,060 sq. m.; pop. 657,000. (2) Cap. of above, 70 m. N. of Cawnpore; cotton market. Pop. 20,000.

Banda Islands, group of islands, Dutch E. Indies. Nutmegs, mace, cloves, cinnamon. Area, 20 sq. m.; pop. 10,000.

Ban'der Ab'bas, or BENDAR ABBAS, tn., port, Kerman, Persia, on Persian Gulf. Chief exports: dates, almonds, raisins, carpets, raw cotton, wool. Pop. *c.* 8,000.

Ban'der Lin'geh or LINGEH (*lin'je*), tn. and port, Persian Gulf; pearl fisheries; exports dried fruits. Pop. 8,000.

Ban'don. (1) Mkt. tn., co. Cork, I.F.S., on R. Bandon; agricultural centre; brewing, distilling, tanning. Pop. 2,800. (2) Riv., co. Cork, I.F.S., rises in Carberry Mts.; flows into Kinsale harbour. Length, *c.* 40 m.

Ban'dra, suburb of Bombay, India, on S.W. shore of Salsette I.; connected with Bombay by causeway and bridge; European residential place. Pop. 24,000.

Ban'dung, cap. of Preanger residency, Java, Dutch E. Indies, 75 m. S.E. of Batavia; quinine, and railway rolling stock factories. Pop. 170,000.

Banff (*bamf*). (1) Royal and parl. burgh, port and co. tn., mouth of R. Deveron, Banffshire, Scotland; fishing, shipbuilding, brewing and distilling. Pop. 3,500. (2) Tn., Alberta, Canada, on C.P. Rly., 80 m. W. of Calgary; in Rocky Mts. National Park; with grand mountain scenery; summer resort. Pop. 900.

Banffshire, co., N.E. Scotland, between Moray, Inverness, and Aberdeen. Agriculture important; oats, barley, wheat grown; cattle raised; industries include distilling, fisheries; granite and slate quarried; surface mountainous in S., low-lying in N.; well wooded; drained by Rs. Spey, Deveron, Avon, Fiddich; chief mt., Cairngorm (4,084 ft.). Cap. Banff. Area, *c.* 631 sq. m.; pop. 54,800.

Bangalōre', city, cap. of Mysore, India; consists of native city ($2\frac{1}{2}$ sq. m. in area) and Brit. 'assignment' ($12\frac{1}{2}$ sq. m.), the latter forming the largest military cantonment in S. India; climate healthy; silks, cottons, carpets; palace of the Maharajah. Pop. 237,500.

Bangkok', cap. and chief port of Siam, on both bks. of R. Menam, 20 m. from Gulf of Siam; covers area of over 10 sq. m. Royal palace contains the famous emerald Buddha; univ. (1917); rice milling (over eighty factories), tea, saw milling, boat building, engineering; chief exports, rice and teak. Pop. 452,000.

Ban'gor. (1) City and port, Carnarvonshire, N. Wales, at N. entrance to Menai Strait; exports slate; cathedral; Univ. College. Pop. 11,000. (2) Par., urban dist., and port, co. Down, N. Ireland, on Belfast Lough; fishing and muslin embroidery; sea-bathing resort. Pop. of urb. dist., 13,300. (3) Tn., Maine, U.S.A., on Penobscot R.; lumber, boots and shoes, clothing, paper mills. Pop. 29,000.

Bangweu'lu, or BEMBA, shallow lake formed by head-streams of Congo, Northern Rhodesia; alt. 3,765 ft.; area (much of it marsh), 1,600 sq. m. (doubled during rains); discovered by Livingstone (1868).

Banjaluka (*ban-yă-loo'ka*), tn., Yugoslavia, 90 m. N.W. Sarajevo; tobacco, gunpowder; hot springs. Pop. 18,000.

Banjermas'in ('saline garden'), tn., cap. of Dutch S. and E. Borneo, on S. coast of Borneo; built on piles; gold dust, coal, wax, rattan, gums, and resins. Pop. *c.* 70,000.

Bank'a, or BANGKA, isl., Dutch E. Indies; 138 m. long, 62 m. broad;

hilly; important tin mines; fishing. Area, 4,460 sq. m.; pop. 160,000.

Bank'ura. (1) Dist., Burdwan div., Bengal, India; flat and well-watered, but liable to drought and flood; has silk, cotton, and shellac manufactures. Area, 2,621 sq. m.; pop. 1,020,000. (2) Cap. of above, 90 m. N.W. of Calcutta; manufactures silk and cotton. Pop. 25,000.

Bann, riv., N. Ireland, rises in Mourne Mts., and flows through Lough Neagh to the Atlantic; salmon fisheries; length 90 m.

Ban'nockburn, tn., Stirlingshire, Scotland, 2 m. S.E. of Stirling; manufactures tweeds, tartans, and carpets; has coal mines and tanneries. Pop. 4,000. Here Robert the Bruce disastrously defeated English under Edward II. (June 24, 1314), and thus secured independence of Scotland. Traditional Bore Stone marks site.

Ban'stead, vil., Surrey, England, 3 m. E. of Epsom, on N. Downs (alt. *c.* 520 ft.); centre of hunting. Pop. (par.) 7,350.

Banswar'a, Indian state, S. Rajputana, India; more than half of state is jungle; agriculture is backward. Cap. Banswara, 60 m. S.E. of Udaipur. Area, 1,946 sq. m.; pop. 190,000.

Bant'am, residency, extreme W. of Java, Dutch E. Indies; rice, rubber. Area, 3,053 sq. m.; pop. 918,000.

Bant'ry. (1) Port, co. Cork, I.F.S.; tourist resort; fishing. Pop. 2,700. (2) BAY, one of best anchorages in S.W. of Ireland.

Bar (1) or ANTIVARI (*an-tē'va-rē*), tn., with port of same name 3 m. distant, Yugoslavia; on Adriatic Sea; tobacco; olive oil; fishing. Pop. 2,000. (2) Tn., W. Ukraine, U.S.S.R., 50 m. N.E. Kamenets Podolskiy; grain; leather dressing, distilling. Pop. 9,400.

Bara Banki. (1) Dist., United Provinces, India; rice, wheat, sugar, opium. Area, 1,758 sq. m.; pop. 1,030,000. (2) Tn. of above, 17 m. N.E. of Lucknow; cotton, sugar. Pop. 3,000.

Barab'a Steppe, immense stoneless region, Siberia, between Rs. Ob and Irtish; forests in N.; grain in fertile areas. Area, 100,000 sq. m.

Baracal'do, river port, Biscay, N.E. Spain; iron and steel works. Pop. 27,000.

Baraco'a, port, N.E. Cuba; exports bananas and coconuts. Pop. 5,200.

Barada. See ABANA.

Baran'ov, isl., Alexander Archipelago, Alaska; coal, gold; fur; fishing and canning industries. Pop. 1,400.

Barbace'na, tn., Minas Geraes, Brazil, 130 m. N. of Rio de Janeiro; agriculture, cheese; gold mining. Alt. 3,500 ft. Pop. 6,000.

Barbaco'as, tn., Colombia, S. America, 130 m. N.E. of Quito; gold mining. Pop. 6,000.

Barbados (*bar-bā'dos*), isl., Brit. W. Indies; most E. of W. Indies; mostly of coral formation; extremely fertile; sugar-cane cultivation and sugar manufacture; sugar, molasses, rum, raw cotton exported; invigorating climate; health resort. Cap. is Bridgetown. Area, 166 sq. m.; pop. 168,000.

Bar'bary, former name for region of N. Africa; inhabited by Berbers; includes Morocco, Algeria, Tunisia, Tripoli, and Barca. Barbary pirates were the corsairs of these coasts.

Bar'berton. (1) Dist. and tn., Transvaal, S. Africa, 180 m. E. of Pretoria; goldfields and asbestos mining; cotton, and citrus fruits. White pop. 1,100. (2) Tn., Ohio, U.S.A., 7 m. S.W. of Akron; manufactures motor tyres and matches. Pop. 24,000.

Barbu'da, isl., Leeward group, Brit. W. Indies; dependency of Antigua; coral formation; sea island cotton; cattle, horses, mules, and asses are reared. Area, 62 sq. m.; pop. 900.

Barca. See BARKA.

Barcellona (*bar-che-lō'na*), tn., Messina, Sicily; silk industries; sulphur baths. Pop. (comm.) 25,000.

Barcelona (*bar-thā-lō'na*). (1) Maritime prov., N.E. Spain; mts. rich in iron; wine, oil, fruit, cork; woollens, cottons. Area, 2,969 sq. m.; pop.

1,426,000. (2) Cap. of above, on Mediterranean Sea; first commercial centre and second port of Spain; good harbour; univ.; noble cathedral; cotton manufactures and engineering works; soap and glycerine factories, tanneries; chief exports, almonds, olive oil, wines, cork. Pop. 760,000.

Bard'sey ('Bards' I.'), isl., co. Carnarvon, Wales, legendary last retreat of Welsh bards; farming and fishing. Pop. 60.

Barèges (*ba-rāzh'*), vil., Hautes-Pyrénées, France, 13 m. s. of Bagnères-de-Bigorre; summer resort; sulphurous springs; alt. 4,040 ft.

Bareilly (*ba-rā'li*), or BARELI, tn. United Provinces, India; college; manufactures bamboo furniture; military station. Scene of fighting during Mutiny of 1857. Pop. 129,400.

Bar'ents. (1) Isl., Spitsbergen group, in Arctic regions; named after Dutch navigator; highest point, 1,998 ft. (2) SEA, between Spitsbergen and Novaya Zemlya; shallow; pack ice, fogs, in N.; cod, haddock, and plaice fisheries.

Barfleur (*bar-fler*), port, bathing resort, France, on Eng. Channel, 16 m. E. of Cherbourg; *White Ship* wrecked outside harbour (1120). Pop. 1,100.

Barfrush', tn., Persia; near Caspian Sea; commercial centre; bazaars; cottons, silks, fruits. Pop. 30,000.

Bar Harbor, vil., Maine, U.S.A., on Mt. Desert I.; fashionable summer resort. Pop. 3,700.

Bari. (1) Prov., Apulia, s. Italy; fruit; salt industry; cattle and sheep pasturing. Area, 1,990 sq. m.; pop. 924,000. (2) Port and archiepisc. see, cap. of above; cathedral; iron foundry; olive oil, soap; trade in wine, fruit. Pop. 110,000.

Baring'o. (1) Dist., Kenya, Africa; grain. (2) Lake in dist.; alt. 3,300 ft., 18 m. long, 10 m. wide; first visited by Joseph Thomson (1883).

Bar'isal, tn., Bengal, India; on Barisal R., 120 m. E. of Calcutta; centre of river trade. Pop. 27,000.

Bar'ka, or BARCA (anc. *Cyrenaica*), former Turkish vilayet, N. Africa; annexed by Italy, 1912; now Cyrenaica.

Bar'king, mkt. tn. and urb. dist., Essex, England, E. suburb of London. Norman church; chemical works. Pop. 51,300.

Bar'kly East. (1) Sheep-farming dist., Cape Province, S. Africa, lying due s. of Basutoland. (2) Cap. of above; elevation nearly 6,000 ft. Pop., dist. 8,000; tn. 1,638.

Bar'kly West. (1) Dist., Griqualand W., S. Africa. (2) Cap. of above; diamonds. Pop. 2,000.

Bar-le-Duc, chief tn., Meuse, France; preserves, cotton, hosiery, machinery. Pop. 14,000.

Barlet'ta, port, Bari, s. Italy; good harbour; centre of wine trade. Pop. 50,000.

Bar'men, manufacturing tn., dist. Düsseldorf, Prussia; ribbon weaving, button making, dyeing, calico printing. Pop. 187,000.

Bar'mouth, tn., Merioneth, Wales, on beautiful Mawddach estuary; summer resort and wat.-pl. Pop. 2,500.

Bar'nard Castle, mkt. tn., co. Durham, England; on l. bk. of R. Tees; ruins of Castle Barnard; birthplace of John Baliol; flax thread. Pop. 3,900.

Barnaul (*bar-na-ool'*), tn., Siberia, on R. Ob; butter, bacon, wax, honey; smelting furnaces. Pop. 74,000.

Bar'nes, urb. dist., N. Surrey, England, on R. Thames, 7 m. s.w. of London; was residence of Fielding, Cowley, and Handel. Pop. 42,400.

Bar'net, tn., Herts, England, 10 m. N. of London; residential dist.; part of Greater London; cattle fairs; paper and metal works. Pop. 14,700.

Barnoldswick (*bar-nōld'z-wik*), urb. dist., W. Riding, Yorks, England, 8 m. s.w. of Skipton; cotton manufacture. Pop. 11,900.

Barn'sley, co. bor. and mkt. tn., W. Riding, Yorks, England; coalfields, iron, steel, glass. Pop. 71,500.

Barn'staple, port and par., N. Devon, England, on R. Taw; lace, gloves, and pottery (Barum ware). Pop. 14,700.

Barn'wood, vil., Glos, England, 2 m. E. of Gloucester, of which it is a suburb; on (Roman) Ermine Street; asylums. Pop. (par.) 1,350.

Baro'da. (1) Indian state, Gujarat and Kathiawar, Bombay, India; produces food grains, cotton, sugar, tobacco, and opium (state monopoly). Area, 8,099 sq. m.; pop. 2,126,600. (2) Cap. of above state; has many palaces and Hindu temples. Pop. 94,700.

Barot'seland, dist., most W. section of N. Rhodesia; inhabited by Bantu race, who make wicker-work. Area, *c.* 180,000 sq. m.

Barquisime'to, cap., prov. Lara, Venezuela, 150 m. W. of Caracas; wheat, coffee, cocoa, sugar, beans, and fibre. Pop. 23,000.

Bar'ra, isl. and par. including several other islands, Outer Hebrides, Scotland; fisheries. Pop. 2,300.

Barrackpore, tn., Bengal, India, 15 m. N. of Calcutta; military cantonment. Pop. 38,000.

Barranquilla (*bar-an-kēl'-ya*), port on R. Magdalena, Colombia, S. America; cotton, coffee, tobacco, bananas. Pop. 81,000.

Barre, tn., Vermont, U.S.A., 6 m. S.E. of Montpelier; numerous granite quarries in vicinity; tombstones, quarry machinery, tools. Pop. 4,000.

Barrhead, tn., Renfrewshire, Scotland, 3½ m. S.E. of Paisley; shawl and calico weaving; iron and brass working; and sanitary appliances. Pop. 12,300.

Barrie, tn. on L. Simcoe, Ontario, Canada; boat building; leather goods, woollens; rly. centre. Pop. 7,000.

Barrier Reef. See GREAT BARRIER REEF.

Barrow, riv., Leinster, I.F.S., joins Suir, forming as its estuary Waterford Harbour. Length, 119 m.

Bar'rowford, urb. dist., Lancs, England, 5 m. N.N.E. of Burnley; cotton manufacture. Pop. 5,300.

Bar'row-in-Fur'ness, co. bor., port, and manufacturing centre, Lancs, England. Huge steel and iron works, engineering shops, foundries, jute and flax factories, paper and pulp works. Great shipbuilding and naval armament works. Pop. 66,400.

Bar'ry. (1) Port, Glamorgan, S. Wales; important outlet for S. Wales coalfield. Pop. 38,900. (2) Coast par. and vil., Angus, Scotland. Training ground for artillery and Territorial forces. Pop. 4,900.

Bar'si, tn., Bombay, India, 120 m. E. of Poona; cotton and oil-seeds. Pop. 22,000.

Bar-sur-Aube (*-ōb*), tn., dep. Aube, France, 34 m. E. of Troyes; weaving; wine, brandy. Pop. 4,500.

Bart'fa, or BARTFELD, tn., Saros, Czechoslovakia, 80 m. S.E. of Cracow; chalybeate waters. Pop. 7,600.

Bar'ton-on-Hum'ber, urb. dist. and mkt. tn., Lincs, England; pottery, bricks, rope, sailcloth. Pop. 6,300.

Bar'ton-on-Sea, vil., S. Hants, England, 5½ m. S.W. of Lymington; holiday resort. Pop. 1,300.

Bar'ton-upon-Ir'well, par. and vil., Lancs, England, 5½ m. W. of Manchester; here the Bridgewater Canal is carried over the Manchester Ship Canal by a large swing-bridge. Pop. 4,000.

Barvas, par., N. Lewis, Scotland; lochs and streams abound in fish. Area, 152 sq. m.; pop. 7,000.

Bar'well, vil., Leicestershire, England, 2 m. N.E. of Hinckley; boots and shoes. Pop. 3,500.

Basel. See BASLE.

Bashahr, Indian hill-state, Punjab, India, E. of R. Sutlej; under Brit. administration; has valuable forests. Area, 3,820 sq. m.; pop. 100,000.

Ba'shan, extensive region, anc. Palestine, E. of Lake of Galilee; fertile tableland; famous for oak forests and cattle. Alt. 2,000 ft.

Bash'kir Republic, rep. in E. of European Russia. Consists mainly of plateau land and densely wooded slopes of Ural Mts. Gold, copper, coal; agriculture. Chief tn., Ufa. Area, *c.* 60,000 sq. m.; pop. 2,741,000.

Basilicat'a, dep., S. Italy, including

provs. of Matera and Potenza; fertile in places; malarial coast; grain, vineyards, olive oil. Area, 3,855 sq. m.; pop. 469,000.

Ba'singstoke, munic. bor. and mkt. tn., N. Hants, England. Agricultural centre; manufactures farming implements. Pop. 13,900.

Basle (*bäl*) or **Basel.** (1) Canton in N.W. Switzerland; consists of Rural (agriculture, forest, vineyards) and Urban Basle. Area, 177 sq. m.; pop. 235,000. (2) Frontier tn., cap. of above; divided by R. Rhine into Great (residential and professional) and Little (chemical and ribbon works) Basle; univ.; important river port. Pop. 141,700.

Basque Provinces (*bask*), dist., N.E. Spain, on Bay of Biscay; comprising three provinces, Vizcaya, Guipuzcoa, and Alava; traversed by Pyrenees; iron mining. Area, 2,739 sq. m.; pop. 811,400.

Bas'ra, BASSORA, or BUSSORAH, tn. and chief port of Iraq, 70 m. up Shatt-al-Arab, at head of Persian Gulf; on Baghdad Rly. and Europe-India air line; famous as place from which Sindbad the Sailor set sail; centre of trade in dates. Pop. 85,000.

Bas Rhin. See ALSACE-LORRAINE.

Bas'sa, dist., N. Nigeria; forests, rubber trees; southern part unexplored. Area, *c.* 7,000 sq. m.; pop. *c.* 205,000.

Bas'sam, tn. and port, Ivory Coast, French W. Africa; ivory, gold dust, palm oil. Pop. 2,500.

Bassan'o, tn., Venetia, Italy, on R. Brenta; wine, olives, asparagus; straw hats, silk; printing and manufacture of majolica. Pop. 10,100.

Bassein (*bă-sān'*), tn. and river port, Burma, on R. Bassein; centre for rice trade. Pop. 43,000.

Bas'senthwaite. (1) Lake, Cumberland, England, expansion of R. Derwent, N. of Derwent Water; fishing; length 4 m., breadth ¾ m.; alt. 223 ft. (2) Par., on W. of lake, 7½ m. N.W. of Keswick. Pop. 450.

Basses-Alpes (*bas-alp*), dep. S.E. France; mountainous; good pastures; olive grows in lower valleys; fruits, wine. Chief tn., Digne. Area, 2,697 sq. m.; pop. 88,300.

Basses-Pyrénées (*bas-pē-rā-nā*), dep., S.W. France. Pyrenees occupy southern portion, elevation increasing W. to E.; many passes; extensive forests; N. and E. terr. consists of pastures and fertile valleys; mineral springs; sheep, cattle; maize. Pau (chief tn.) and Biarritz are health resorts. Area, 2,977 sq. m.; pop. 415,000.

Bassora. See BASRA.

Bass Rock, THE, volcanic islet, entrance of Firth of Forth, Scotland; 350 ft. high; circumference, 1 m.; area, 7 ac.; served as prison for Covenanters; last Brit place held by Jacobites against William III. (1691–94); resort of solan goose; lighthouse on S. side.

Bass Strait separates Tasmania from Victoria, Australia; breadth, 140 m.

Bast'ar, Indian state, S. Central Provs., India; high flat plateau; some mountains; dense forests; jungles inhabited by aboriginal tribe; timber, tanning, and dyeing barks. Chief tn., Jagdalpur. Area, 13,062 sq. m.; pop. 464,000.

Basti, tn. and dist., United Provs., India, 110 m. E. of Lucknow; level, well-watered plain producing rice, wheat, barley. Area, 2,792 sq. m.; pop. (dist.) 1,846,000, (tn.) 17,700.

Bastia (*bas-tē'a*), port, N.E. Corsica; fishing; fruit. Pop. 34,000.

Basu'toland, or LESUTO, Brit. crown colony, S. Africa; bounded by Orange Free State on N. and W., Cape Prov. on S., Natal on E. and N.E.; surface is part of rugged plateau, *c.* 5,000 ft. above sea-level, and has mts. crossing it, including Maluti ranges and Drakensberg; principal rivs., Orange, Caledon; healthy climate. Inhabitants are of Bantu stock, majority Basutos proper, with admixture of other tribes. Basutoland is a native reserve. Productions include great quantities of cereals, wool, and mohair; cattle, ponies, and sheep raised for export. Cap. is Maseru. Area, 11,716 sq. m.; pop. 496,000 (including 1,600 whites).

Batal'a, tn., Punjab, India, 55 m. N.E. of Lahore; cotton, silk, leather. Pop. 26,000.

Batang', or BAANFU, frontier tn., cap. of Si-K'ang div., on border of Tibet; important depot on Lhasa trade route.

Batan'gas, prov. and port, Luzon, Philippines, 65 m. s. of Manila; sugar, corn; horses, cattle. Prov., area, 1,108 sq. m.; pop. 258,000; tn., 41,000.

Batā'via. (1) Residency, Java, Dutch E. Indies; includes some adjacent islands; N. half, flat; S. half, mountainous; soil fertile; rice, coffee, tea, coconuts, rubber. Area, 11,979 sq. m.; pop. 1,224,000. (2) Port, N. coast, Java; cap. and chief commercial city, Dutch E. Indies; mixed population; coffee, rice, sugar, rubber, pepper, tea, quinine. Pop. 290,000. (3) Tn., New York, U.S.A., 32 m. S.W. of Rochester; agricultural machinery. Pop. 16,000.

Bath. (1) Wat.-pl. and largest tn., Somerset, England, 12 m. S.E. of Bristol; on R. Avon; the Roman *Aquæ Solis*; its hot saline and chalybeate springs were known to Romans from 1st cent.; contains Roman baths and other antiquities. Pop. 68,800. (2) Tn., Maine, U.S.A., on Kennebec R., 30 m. N.E. of Portland; shipbuilding, engineering. Pop. 9,000.

Bath'gate, tn., W. Lothian, Scotland, 19 m. from Edinburgh; minerals, distilling, engineering. Pop. 10,100.

Bath'urst. (1) Tn., New South Wales, Australia, 100 m. N.W. of Sydney; gold, silver; brewing; boots and shoes. Pop. 9,000. (2) Cap., Gambia, W. Africa; groundnuts. Pop. 9,000. (3) Tn., Cape Province, S. Africa, 80 m. N.E. of Port Elizabeth; pineapples, oranges. Pop. (white) 250.

Baticalo'a, cap. of E. prov., Ceylon; rice and coconuts. Pop. 10,000.

Batley, tn., W. Riding, Yorks, England, 8 m. S.W. of Leeds; heavy woollens, shoddy. Pop. 34,600.

Baton Rouge (*bat'on roozh*), city, Louisiana, U.S.A., on R. Mississippi; state cap.; univ.; cotton-seed products, lumber; sugar, and rice mills; oil refining. Pop. 31,000.

Bat'tenberg, tn., Hessen-Nassau, Prussia, on Eder trib. of R. Weser, *c.* 70 m. E. of Cologne. Battenberg family married into British royal family, and in 1917 gave up its German titles, changing its name to Mountbatten.

Battersea, metropolitan bor., S.W. London; fine park; factories and foundries. Pop. 159,500.

Bat'tle, urb. dist., Sussex, England, formerly Senlac; received name from battle of Hastings (1066). Pop. 3,500.

Battle Creek, city, Michigan, U.S.A., 115 m. W. of Detroit; manufactures health foods; machinery. Pop. 43,000.

Battleford, tn., Saskatchewan, Canada, 77 m. N.W. of Saskatoon; agricultural centre. Pop. 1,300.

Batum', fort. tn. and port in Transcaucasia, U.S.S.R.; on Black Sea; exports oil, raw silk, oil-cake. Pop. 46,000.

Bau'ang, tn., Luzon, Philippines, 5 m. N.W. of Batangas; hats, mats, and baskets of palm fibre. Pop. 28,000.

Bau'chi ('land of slaves'), region N. Nigeria, British W. Africa; the larger portion N.W. to S.E. occupied by belt of highlands; tin mines; plateaus forming S.W. of prov. fertile, and grow grain, cotton, indigo. Pop. *c.* 1,000,000.

Bautzen (*bowt'sen*), tn., Saxony, Germany; on R. Spree; many industries; machinery, woollen goods, leather. Pop. 40,300.

Bava'ria, or BAYERN, rep. of Germany occupying the E. side of S. Germany. Bavaria has detached portion called Palatinate or Rhenish Bavaria, W. of R. Rhine, N. of Alsace. Surface along boundaries is generally hilly; chief ranges, those of Alps in s. (highest peak, Zugspitze, 9,700 ft.); Frankenwald, Fichtelgebirge, and Rhongebirge in N.; Böhmerwald in N.E.; Haardt Mts. in Palatinate. Palatinate is drained by R. Rhine and tribs., s. of Bavaria proper by R. Danube with tribs. Isar and Inn, N. by R. Main; principal lakes Ammer See, Starnberger See, Walchen See. Over half area is cultivated; chief crops are rye, oats, potatoes, wheat; hops, sugar-beet, tobacco, vines; one-sixth of surface under grass; cattle and sheep largely raised, dairy farming carried on; one-third of area under timber—oak, beech, pine; chief forest districts are along Alps, in s., in Franconia and Palatinate. Chief minerals are salt, coal, iron, graphite, lithographic stone; mineral springs abound. Most important manufacture is beer; other industries are pencil making, manufacture of glass, porcelain, sugar, toys, chemicals, jewellery, mathematical instruments. Cap. Munich. Area, 29,334 sq. m.; pop. 7,380,000.

Baw'try, mkt. tn., W.R., Yorks, England, 9 m. S.E. of Doncaster; on (Roman) Ermine Street. Pop. 1,500.

Bay City, tn., Michigan, U.S.A., on Saginaw R.; extensive fisheries; beet-sugar, chicory, cigars, chemicals, cement. Pop. 47,000.

Bayern. See BAVARIA.

Bayeux (*ba-yu'*), tn., Calvados, France, 7 m. from Eng. Channel; cathedral; lace, linen, pottery. Bayeux Tapestry (231 ft. long, 20 in. wide), preserved in Bayeux Museum. Pop. 6,500.

Bay Islands, group in Caribbean Sea, N. of Honduras; ceded by Britain to Honduras, 1859; bananas, pineapples, and coconuts. Pop. 4,000.

Bayonne (*ba-yon'*). (1) Fortified tn., Basses-Pyrénées, France, 4 m. from Bay of Biscay; 13th cent. cathedral; leather, chocolate, hams. Pop. 28,000. (2) City, New Jersey, U.S.A., adjoins Jersey City; chemicals and petroleum refining; copper and nickel articles. Pop. 86,000.

Bayreuth (*bī-royt*), or BAIREUTH, tn., Upper Franconia, Bavaria, 45 m. N.E. of Nürnberg; noted musical festivals in Wagner Theatre; woollen, linen, and cotton goods; marble works. Pop. 35,000.

Bayswater, residential dist., London; was source of many springs.

Bayu'da Steppe, vast desert of stony hills and thickets, Anglo-Egyptian Sudan.

Baza (*bă'tha*), tn., Spain, 55 m. N.E. of Granada; agricultural centre; linen, hempen goods, pottery; mineral springs. Pop. 16,000.

Beach'ley, vil., Gloucestershire, England, 2 m. S.E. of Chepstow; southern extremity of Offa's Dyke; salmon fishing.

Beachy Head, headland, s. coast of Sussex, England; perpendicular chalk cliff, projecting into Eng. Channel, 570 ft. high.

Beaconsfield (*bek'ons-fēld*). (1) Tn. and par., Bucks, England; ribbons; residential suburb of London. Pop. 4,800. (2) Suburb, Kimberley, Cape Prov., S. Africa; diamond mines. Pop. 20,300. (3) Tn., Tasmania; centre of richest goldfield in island.

Beaminster (*bĕ'min-ster*), mkt. tn., Dorset, England, 6 m. N. of Bridport; cheese factories. Pop. 1,500.

Bear Lake, GREAT. See GREAT BEAR LAKE.

Bears'den. See KILPATRICK (1).

Be'as. One of the five rivs. of Punjab, India (*Hyphasis* of Greeks); joins R. Sutlej; length, 295 m.

Beath, par., Fife, Scotland. Cowdenbeath (in the par.) is the centre of the largest coalfield in the country. Area, 6,343 ac.; pop. 25,000.

Beat'tock, vil., Dumfriesshire, Scotland; rly. jn. Beattock Summit, on L.M.S. Rly., 1,014 ft. high.

Beauce (*bōs*). (1) Dist., Eure-et-Loir and Loir-et-Cher, France; wheat, clover, sheep. Area, 2,800 sq. m. (2) Dist., Quebec, Canada. Pop. 51,400.

Beaufort (*bō'fort*). (1) Tn., N. Carolina, U.S.A., 17 m. s.w. of Cape Hatteras; summer resort; fisheries. Pop. 3,000. (2) Tn., S. Carolina, U.S.A., 45 m. s.w. of Charleston;

winter resort; fertilizers; lumber; canned vegetables; turtle farms in vicinity. Pop. 4,100.

Beaufort West, tn. and dist., Cape Prov., S. Africa, 339 m. by rail N.W. of Cape Town; health resort; sheep farming. Pop. (dist.) *c.* 10,000; (tn.) 6,300.

Beaulieu (*bū'li*), par., Hants, England, 6 m. N. of Lymington; abbey (1204). Pop. 800.

Beauly (*bū'li*), vil., Inverness-shire, Scotland, at head of Beauly Firth; ruined priory; fishing; school of forestry. Pop. 900.

Beauly Firth, a division of Moray Firth, S. of Black Isle, Ross-shire.

Beaumaris (*bū-mar'is*), mkt. tn., Anglesey, Wales; ruins of 13th cent. castle; summer resort. Pop. 1,700.

Beaumont (*bō'mont*), city, Texas, U.S.A., on Neches R., 80 m. N.E. of Houston; lumber centre; very rich oilfields. Pop. 57,000.

Beaune (*bōn*), tn., dep. Côte d'Or, France, 23 m. S. of Dijon; famous wines; manufactures casks and agricultural machinery. Pop. 11,000.

Beauvais (*bō-vā'*), tn., cap. of Oise, France; fine incomplete Gothic cathedral; Gobelin tapestry; textiles. Pop. 17,000.

Beaver Falls, bor., Pennsylvania, U.S.A., 30 m. N.W. of Pittsburgh; extensive implement manufactures; porcelain, tiles. Pop. 13,000.

Bea'war, tn., Rajputana, India, 33 m. S.W. of Rajputana; important centre of cotton trade; many mills. Pop. 22,000.

Beb'ington and Brom'borough, urb. dist., Cheshire, England, 3 m. S. of Birkenhead; contains model village of Port Sunlight. Pop. 26,700.

Beccles (*bek'lz*), mkt. tn., Suffolk, England, 8 m. W. of Lowestoft; printing works, maltings; agricultural implements. Pop. 6,500.

Bechuanaland (*betch-oo-an'a-*), dist., Brit. S. Africa, between Zambezi and Orange Rivs., and between S.W. Africa on the W. and Transvaal on the E. Southern part, as far N. as R. Molopo, was incorporated with Cape Colony in 1895; rest of district, extending to Victoria Falls on Zambezi, is a protectorate. Surface is part of great central plateau, with elevation of *c.* 4,000 ft. Produces maize, millet; great herds of cattle. Rainfall scanty, but wells and irrigation might render soil very fertile. Gold occurs in places. Seat of administration of Protectorate is at Mafeking, in Cape Province. Area of Cape part, 51,254 sq. m.; pop. 99,500 (including 15,000 whites). Area of Protectorate, *c.* 275,000 sq. m.; pop. 153,000.

Beck'enham, urb. dist., par., and tn., Kent, England, 7 m. S.E. of London; part of Greater London; residential district. Pop. 43,800.

Beckerek, VELIKI (*bech-ke'r-ek, ve-l-i-kē*), formerly NAGY BECSKEREK, tn., Yugoslavia, 40 m. N. of Belgrade; extensive trade in grain. Pop. 32,000.

Beddgelert (*beth-gel'ert*), ('Gelert's grave'), par. and vil., Carnarvonshire, Wales, 11 m. S.E. of Carnarvon; tourist summer resort; slate quarries. Scene of traditional story of Llewellyn's dog. Pop. (par.) 1,200.

Beddington and Wallington, urb. dist., Surrey, England, 2 m. W. of Croydon. In Beddington is beautiful anc. church. Pop. 26,200.

Bed'ford. (1) Munic. bor. and co. tn., Beds, England, on R. Ouse; grammar school, founded by Edward VI. (1552); statue and relics of John Bunyan; agricultural implements, engineering, lace. Pop. 40,100. (2) City, Indiana, U.S.A., 70 m. S. by W. of Indianapolis; stone quarries. Pop. 13,000.

Bedfordshire, or BEDS, co., England, bordering on Huntingdon, Northampton, Buckingham, Hertford, Cambridge; about 36 m. long, 21 broad; mainly consists of fertile clayey plain, undulating and well-wooded, watered by R. Ouse and tribs., and bounded on S. by Dunstable and Luton Downs, continuations of Chiltern Hills. Co. is partly devoted to sheep grazing, partly to market gardening, partly to corn growing; manufactures: agricultural machinery, straw plaiting, pillow lace; produces phosphate of lime and fuller's earth; co. tn., Bedford; ten mkt. tns. Area, 480 sq. m.; pop. 220,500.

Bed'lington, tn., Northumberland, England, on R. Blyth; coal, iron, nails, chains. Pop. 27,300.

Bed'loe's Island, or LIBERTY ISLAND, New York harbour, U.S.A.; on it stands Bartholdi's statue of Liberty, presented by France to America.

Beds. See BEDFORDSHIRE.

Bedwas and Machen, urb. dist., Monmouthshire, England, 8 m. w. of Newport; collieries; rly. workshops. Pop. 9,200.

Bed'wellty, urb. dist., Monmouthshire, England, 16 m. N.W. of Newport; collieries; ironworks. Pop. 30,100.

Bed'worth, tn., Warwickshire, England, 5 m. N. of Coventry; coal, iron; ribbons, silk. Pop. 12,100.

Bedzin (*ban'jin*), or BENDZIN, tn., Poland, 40 m. W.N.W. of Cracow; iron, coal, and zinc mines. Pop. 42,000.

Beech'worth, tn., Victoria, Australia, 22 m. S.W. of Albury; gold mining, tanning, coach building. Pop. *c.* 8,000.

Beersheba (*bē'er-shē'ba*), vil., Palestine; region mentioned in O.T. as residence of Abraham and site of famous wells; its position in extreme S. of Judah gave rise to phrase 'from Dan to Beersheba'—*i.e.*, all Israel.

Bee'ston, par. and tn., Notts, England, 3 m. S.W. of Nottingham; silk, hosiery, lace, automobiles, cycles. Pop. 16,000.

Behar. See BIHAR.

Behei'ra, prov., Lower Egypt, in R. Nile delta; cotton. Cap. Damanhur. Area, 1,639 sq. m.; pop. 977,000.

Beira (*bā'ē-ra*). (1) Prov., Portugal; between rivs. Douro and Tagus; crossed by Serra da Estrella; forest; heath with fertile plain; cereals, fruit, sheep farming; olives; salt from coastal lagoons. Area, 9,200 sq. m.; pop. 1,598,000. (2) Dist., Port. E. Africa; rubber and coconut trees. (3) Port, cap. of (2) above; exports sugar, rubber, cotton, ivory; gateway to Mashonaland; rly. communication with Cape Town via Bulawayo; rly. to the R. Zambezi (1922) serves Nyasaland. Pop. 17,000 (2,100 whites).

Beirut (*bī'root*), port, Syria; silk goods, gold and silver thread; fruits, hides, wool; entrepôt for exports and imports of central Syria. Anc. Phœnician town of Berytus. Pop. 80,000.

Beith (*bēth*), tn., Ayrshire, Scotland, 19 m. S.W. of Glasgow; important coal-mining dist.; linen thread, leather work. Pop. 6,300.

Beja (*bā'zha*). (1) Dist., Alemtejo prov., S. Portugal; grain, fruit; cattle, pigs. Area, 3,958 sq. m.; pop. 200,600. (2) Chief town of above; manufactures pottery, cloth, olive oil. Pop. 10,500.

Békés (*bā'kesh*). (1) Co., Hungary, bordering on Romania. (2) BÉKÉS-GYULA, cap. of co.; frontier tn.; cattle, corn, wine. Pop. 27,000. (3) BÉKÉS-CSABA (*-chā'bo*), tn., Békés co., Hungary, 10 m. W.N.W. of (2); milling, hemp weaving; important rly. jn. Pop. 43,000. (4) BÉKÉS, tn., Békés co., Hungary, 12 m. N.W. of (2); formerly an imperial free town. Pop. 25,000.

Belem. See PARÁ (2).

Belfast, cap. Northern Ireland; port and great commercial centre of Ulster, on Belfast Lough, 12 m. from Irish Sea; headquarters of linen trade in U.K.; great shipbuilding yards. Industries include distilling, brewing, ironfounding, bacon curing, making of rope, sailcloth, aerated waters; harbour very large and safe; Prot. and R.C. cathedrals; univ. Public buildings include magnificent city hall, Parliament buildings, Ulster Hall, free library, museum. Pop. 415,000.

Belfast Lough (*loch*), inlet on east coast of N. Ireland; 12 m. long.

Belfort (*bel-for'*). (1) TERRITORY OF, dep., E. France; cereals, potatoes, machinery, brewing. Area, 235 sq. m.; pop. 94,000. (2) Fort. tn. in above; important strategical position near Swiss frontier; industries include cotton spinning, brewing, wire drawing, locomotives, machinery. Pop. 36,400.

Belgaum (*bel-goum'*). (1) Dist., s. Bombay, India; cereals, rice, cotton. Area, 4,611 sq. m.; pop. 953,000. (2) Tn. in above, 50 m. N.E. of Goa; cotton mills; soap and pottery works. Pop. 48,000.

Belgian Congo. See CONGO, BELGIAN.

Belgium (*bel'jum*), kingdom, Europe, bounded N. by Netherlands, E. by Netherlands, Prussia, and Luxembourg, S. and S.W. by France, N.W. by North Sea; length, *c.* 170 m.; width, *c.* 108 m. Surface is flat and low-lying except in S.E., where Ardennes rise to 2,000 ft.; coast districts, in some places below sea-level, protected by sand-dunes and dykes; along Dutch border is marshy tract called Campine, with woodland and good agricultural ground; drained by Rs. Schelde and Meuse (Maas), with tribs.—of former, Lys, Dender, Durme, Rupel; of latter, Sambre and Ourthe. Climate resembles that of S. of England. Rs. Schelde and Maas are navigable; many canals. Forests cover about one-sixth of surface, and about two-thirds are cultivated; chief crops, wheat, rye, oats, barley, potatoes, beet, hemp, flax, tobacco, hops, chicory, madder. Horses are bred; honey is produced, silkworms reared. Minerals include coal, iron, lead, zinc, copper, manganese, E. and S.E. districts being rich in ores. The coalfield, practically co-extensive with industrial region, crosses country from French frontier near Valenciennes to the German frontier near Aix-la-Chapelle. Deposits also exist in Campine. Belgium is pre-eminently a manufacturing country, and has many important industrial towns, while Antwerp is one of the greatest shipping and manufacturing centres in N. Europe. Metal manufactures are valuable and numerous, including machinery, firearms, cannon, wire, gold, silver, tin, brass, and copper goods. Other industries are linens, lace, woollens, carpets, cottons, silk, velvet, hosiery, glass, paper, leather, gloves, sugar, brewing, distilling, fisheries. Chief manufacturing towns besides Antwerp are Liége, Brussels, Ghent. Exports include sugar, glass, cottons, linens, woollens, fruit, flour, oils, coal, coke, grain, chemicals, iron, steel, machinery, diamonds, rubber goods. Brussels, Louvain, Ghent, and Liége have univs. Cap. Brussels. Area, 11,755 sq. m.; pop. 7,466,000.

Belgrade' ('white castle') (BEOGRAD), cap. of Yugoslavia; at confluence of Rs. Danube and Sava; has cathedral, royal palace, univ., national museum and library; tobacco, woollen, chocolate factories; brewing, boots, soap, preserved meats. Pop. 250,000.

Belize (*bel-ēz'*), cap. and port, Brit. Honduras, Central America; exports mahogany, dyewoods; bananas, coconuts, tortoiseshell, turtles. Pop. 13,000.

Bellagio (*bel-äj'ō*), tn., Italy, on L. Como; summer resort. Pop. 1,100.

Bellahous'ton, s.w. suburb of Glasgow, in par. of Govan, Lanarkshire, Scotland.

Bellaire, city, Ohio, U.S.A., on Ohio R., 3 m. s. of Wheeling; iron, steel, limestone, farming implements, stoves, glass. Pop. 13,000.

Bellar'y, or BALLARI. (1) Dist., Madras, India, in Deccan, between Hyderabad and Mysore; produces cereals, pulse, cotton, and oil-seeds. Area, 5,710 sq. m.; pop. 862,000. (2) Cap. of above; cotton; military station. Pop. 39,800.

Belleek', par. and vil., N.W. Fermanagh, N. Ireland, on R. Erne; fine porcelain. Pop. 1,300.

Belle-Ile-en-Mer (*bel-ēl'ān-mār*), isl., Morbihan, France, in Bay of Biscay; pilchard fisheries. Area, 33 sq. m.; pop. 6,700.

Belle Isle (*bel-īl'*). (1) Rocky isl., off N. coast of Newfoundland; two lighthouses; original home of Newfoundland dog. (2) STRAIT, between

Labrador and Newfoundland; 9 miles wide at narrowest part; navigation dangerous owing to floating ice and fogs.

Belle'ville. (1) City, Illinois, U.S.A., 14 m. S.E. of St. Louis; brewing, iron-founding; manufactures shoes, flour, stoves, hosiery. Pop. 28,000. (2) City and port, on Bay of Quinte, L. Ontario, Canada; mills, foundries, kilns. Pop. 12,000. (3) Tn., New Jersey, U.S.A., suburb of Newark; chemicals, wire cloth, hats. Pop. 27,000.

Bellingham (*bel'in-jam*), city, Washington, U.S.A., on Puget Sound; fine landlocked harbour; tulips and hyacinths; sawmills, paper mills, salmon canneries. Pop. 31,000.

Bellinzona (*bel-ēn-tsō'na*), cap. Ticino, Switzerland, 12 m. N.E. of L. Maggiore. Important transit trade with Italy. Pop. 11,600.

Bell Island, isl., Conception Bay, Newfoundland; valuable iron mines.

Bello Horizon'te, cap. Minas Geraes, Brazil, 220 m. N.N.W. of Rio de Janeiro; gold mines in neighbourhood. Pop. 56,000.

Bell Rock, or INCHCAPE ROCK, reef off Angus coast, Scotland; entirely submerged to depth of 12–16 ft. at high tide; 2 ac. exposed at ebb; lighthouse built by Robert Stevenson (1807–11).

Bellshill, tn., Lanarkshire, Scotland, 11 m. S.E. of Glasgow; centre of coal mining, steel and iron working. Pop. (including Mossend) 16,700.

Bellu'no, tn. and episc. see, prov. of same name, N. Italy, 50 m. N. of Venice; cathedral; silk mills. Pop. 30,000.

Beloit'. (1) City, Wisconsin, U.S.A., on S. boundary; college; manufactures agricultural machinery, knives, shoes. Pop. 21,000. (2) City, Kansas, U.S.A., on Solomon R., 190 m. W. of Kansas City; flour milling; agricultural produce; live-stock; limestone quarries. Pop. 3,000.

Bel'per, urb. dist. and mkt. tn., Derbyshire, England, 7 m. N. of Derby; seat of cotton trade; engineering and iron works; manufactures hosiery and lace. Pop. 13,000.

Belt, GREAT, str. between Zealand and Fünen, Denmark; navigation difficult because of shoals and winter ice. Length, 40 m.; breadth, 10–20 m.

Belt, LITTLE, str. between Jutland and Fünen, Denmark. Length, 30 m.; breadth, 1–12 m.

Bem'bridge, vil., Isle of Wight, Hants, England, on E. coast. Pop. (par.) 1,975.

Benā'res, or KASI, city, United Provinces, India, on R. Ganges; labyrinth of narrow streets; many temples, mosques, shrines, palaces; notable buildings are mosque of Aurungzebe and Golden Temple and old observatory. From remotest ages Benares has been Hindu holy city, and centre of Brahminical learning; annually visited by innumerable pilgrims who come to bathe in sacred river; remarkable river front; burning ghats where cremation is practised; commercial centre, with manufactures of brocade, gold filigree, silver, lacquered toys. Pop. 198,000.

Benbec'ula, isl., Outer Hebrides, Scotland; fishing. Area, 36 sq. m.; pop. 1,300.

Ben Cru'achan, mt., 3,690 ft., Argyllshire, Scotland, between L. Awe and L. Etive; huge granite mass.

Bender. See TUGHINA.

Bender Abbas. See BANDER ABBAS.

Ben'digo, formerly SANDHURST, tn., Victoria, Australia, 75 m. N.N.W. of Melbourne; is a gold-mining centre and manufactures bricks; fruit market. Pop. 34,000.

Bendzin. See BEDZIN.

Beneven'to. (1) Mountainous and agricultural prov., Italy. Area, 999 sq. m.; pop. 300,000. (2) Cap. of above, 32 m. N.E. of Naples; Roman triumphal arch (A.D. 115); cathedral (built 12th to 13th cent.); leather, parchment, plated goods. Pop. 34,000.

Bengal', presidency, India; includes deltas of Ganges and Brahmaputra and alluvial plains along their courses;

bounded N. by Sikkim, Bhutan, E. by Assam, Upper Burma, W. by Bihar and Orissa, S. by Bay of Bengal. Heavy rainfall and moist, warm atmosphere make production enormous; mainly rice, but also pulse, jute, opium, sugar-cane, oil-seeds, tobacco, tea, cinchona, spices, timber; great mineral wealth —coal, iron, saltpetre; manufactures jute fabrics, gunny bags, cottons, silk, canvas, muslin, and pack-thread; good communications by rail and river. Cap. Calcutta; hot weather cap., Darjeeling. Area, 76,843 sq. m.; pop. 47,000,000.

Bengal, BAY OF, northern extension of Indian Ocean; excellent harbours on E.; length, 1,200 m. N. to S.

Benghā'zi, port, Cyrenaica, N. Africa; exports cereals. Pop. 32,000.

Benguella (*ben-gä'la*), SÃO FELIPE DE, port and cap. of dist. of same name, Port. W. Africa; sulphur, rubber, wax; founded in 1617. Pop. 3,000.

Beni (EL BENI). (1) Dep., N. Bolivia, S. America; rubber, pasture for cattle. Area, 95,354 sq. m.; pop. 26,000. (2) Riv., Bolivia, flows through fertile and mineral-bearing country; joins Mamoré R., feeder of R. Madeira, trib. of Amazon.

Benin'. (1) Dist., W. Africa, part of S. Nigeria; exports large quantities of palm oil, kernels, rubber, mahogany. Area (approx.), 3,750 sq. m.; pop. 84,000. (2) Tn., cap. of above; for long seat of slave trade. Pop. 15,000. (3) Riv., Benin dist., enters Atlantic; navigable to Sapele; length, 70 m. (4) BIGHT OF, div. of Gulf of Guinea.

Beni-Suef (*bā-nē-swāf*). (1) Prov., Upper Egypt. Area, 423 sq. m.; pop. 508,000. (2) Tn., cap. of above, on R. Nile, 64 m. S. of Cairo; carpets; has cotton mills and quarries of alabaster. Pop. 40,000.

Ben Law'ers, mt., Perthshire, Scotland, rises from N. shore of Loch Tay. Alt. 3,984 ft.

Ben Le'di, mt., 2,875 ft., S. Perthshire, Scotland; referred to by Scott in *The Lady of the Lake.*

Ben Lo'mond, mt., 3,192 ft., N.W. Stirlingshire, Scotland; on E. side of Loch Lomond; mica, slate, granite, and quartzite.

Ben Macdhui (*ben mik-doo'e*), ('hill of the black sow'), 4,296 ft., W. Aberdeenshire, Scotland.

Ben Nev'is, mt., S.W. Inverness-shire, Scotland, 4,406 ft. high; highest mt. in Brit. Isles; station of Scottish Meteorological Society up to 1904; pierced by tunnel 15 m. long conveying water power from Loch Treig to aluminium works near Fort William.

Ben Rhydding (*rid'ding*), vil., W. Riding, Yorks, England, 1 m. E. of Ilkley; hydropathic (alt. 500 ft.). Pop. 1,500.

Bent'ley with Ark'sey, urb. dist., W. Riding, Yorks, England, on R. Don, 2 m. N. of Doncaster. Pop. 16,500.

Benue (*ben'we*), principal trib. of R. Niger, W. Africa; length, 800 m.

Ben Venue', mt., 2,393 ft., S.W. Perthshire, Scotland, overlooking Trossachs, at S. end of Loch Katrine.

Ben Voirlich (*vor'lich*), mt., 3,224 ft., S. Perthshire, Scotland, S. of Loch Earn; mentioned in Scott's *Lady of the Lake.*

Ben Wyvis (*wiv'is*), mt., 3,429 ft., E. Ross and Cromarty, Scotland.

Beograd. See BELGRADE.

Berar', dist. central India, united to Central Provs. for purposes of administration; mostly a valley in basin of R. Tapti; chief crop cotton; also millet, wheat, oil-seeds; held on perpetual lease from Nizam of Hyderabad. Area, 18,000 sq. m.; pop. 3,000,000.

Beraun. See BEROUN.

Ber'ber, prov. and tn., Anglo-Egyptian Sudan, r. bk. of R. Nile; commercial centre; cotton. Pop. of prov. 88,000; tn. *c.* 10,000.

Berbera (*ber-bä'ra*), chief port and tn., Brit. Somaliland, N.E. Africa; annual fair of inland tribes, Oct. till April; exports gums, resin, skins. Pop. 10,000.

Berbice (*ber-bēs'*). (1) Riv., Brit. Guiana, S. America, navigable for 50 m. New Amsterdam stands at its mouth. (2) Dist. drained by above; sugar, timber, tropical fruits. Area, *c.* 21,000 sq. m.; pop. 60,000.

Berck, wat.-pl., Pas-de-Calais, N. France; fisheries and boat building. Pop. 10,000.

Berdichev (*ber-de-chef'*), town, Ukraine, U.S.S.R., 90 m. S.W. of Kiev; tobacco, soap, leather, bricks. Pop. 56,000.

Berdyansk', or BERDIANSK, ice-free port, Sea of Azov, Ukraine, U.S.S.R.; exports wheat, barley, hemp, wool, skins. Pop. 26,000.

Berehaven, tn. and roadstead, N. shore of Bantry Bay, I.F.S. Pop. *c.* 2,000.

Berezina (*bā-res'i-na*), riv., Russia, U.S.S.R.; trib. of R. Dnieper. Length, 350 m.

Berezovsk (*bā-rā-zofsk'*), tn., Ural Area, U.S.S.R., on trib. of R. Ob, 400 m. N. of Tobolsk; gold mines; leather and wooden articles. Pop. 8,000.

Ber'gama (anc. *Pergamos*), tn., Anatolia, Asia Minor, 46 m. N. of Smyrna; parchment invented here; leather. Pop. *c.* 6,000.

Bergamo (*bār'ga-mō*), tn., N. Italy, 30 m. N.E. of Milan; silks, cottons, hats. Pop. 84,000.

Ber'gedorf, tn., Hamburg, Germany, on R. Elbe, 10 m. S.E. of Hamburg; market gardens; leather, glass, enamel. Pop. 18,000.

Ber'gen, port and fort. tn. at head of Byfjord, Norway; second largest tn.; principal shipowning centre; tourist centre; exports fish and fish products, hides, butter. Pop. 91,500.

Ber'gen-op-Zoom, tn., N. Brabant, Holland, 20 m. N. of Antwerp; sugar-beet industry; oyster culture. Pop. 21,000.

Bergerac (*bār-zhrak*), tn., Dordogne, France, on R. Dordogne; grains, wine, salmon, chestnuts. Pop. 11,000.

Berhampore', munic. tn., Bengal, India, 105 m. N. of Calcutta; college; first act of Indian Mutiny here. Pop. 26,000.

Berhampur, munic. tn., N.E. Madras, India, 25 m. S.W. of Chilka L.; tussore silk, rice, leather. Pop. 32,000.

Bering Island (*bā'ring*), or AVATCHA, isl., Asia, in Bering Sea, E. of Kamchatka; belongs to Russia. Barren and treeless. Area, 615 sq. m.; pop., including the neighbouring Copper I., 650.

Bering Sea, between N. America and Asia, is connected with Arctic Ocean by Bering Strait (36 m. wide; 30 fathoms deep); important seal fisheries.

Berislav', tn., Ukraine, U.S.S.R., on R. Dnieper; important trade in corn and wood. Pop. 12,000.

Berja (*ber'ha*), tn., Spain, 27 m. W. of Almeria; lead mines. Pop. 11,000.

Berk'eley (*bark'li*) ('birch field'). (1) Par. and vil., Gloucestershire, England, 15 m. S.W. of Gloucester; birthplace of Jenner, pioneer of vaccination; cheese. Pop. 800. (2) City, California, U.S.A., on San Francisco Bay; seat of California (state) Univ.; gloves, furniture, machinery, chemicals. Pop. 82,000.

Berk'hampstead, or GREAT BERKHAMPSTEAD, mkt. tn. and urb. dist., Herts, England, 26 m. N.W. of London; manufacture of straw hats, chemicals, turned woodware. Pop. 8,100.

Berk'shire (*bark'*), or BERKS, inland co., England, separated from Buckinghamshire and Oxfordshire by R. Thames; borders also on Hampshire, Surrey, and Wiltshire. Generally undulating and moderately well wooded; principal hills are Berkshire Downs, or White Horse Hills, with Cumnor Hurst in N.W. and Inkpen Beacon near S.W. boundary. It is watered by Rs. Thames, Ock, Kennet, Cole, Lambourn, and Pang. Two-thirds of area is under cultivation, oats being the chief crop; dairying and grazing also successfully engaged in. There are biscuit factories, seed warehouses, and nurseries (Reading); iron foundries, engineering works, boat building, carpet and clothing factories. Windsor Castle and Frogmore are in county. Chief natural curiosity is the great 'White Horse,' nearly 400 ft. in length, cut on chalk hillside in Vale of

Ock. Chief tns., Reading (co. tn.) and Windsor. Area, 725 sq. m.; pop. 311,100.

Ber'lad, tn., Romania, 60 m. N. of Galatz; candles and soap; annual horse fair. Pop. 25,000.

Berlin'. (1) Largest city and cap. of Prussia and of Germany, on R. Spree. Height is *c.* 100 ft. above sea; site level; well laid out; the R. Spree divides city into two parts; on its r. bk. are oldest parts, Old Berlin, with the Rathaus, and Old Kölln, with royal palace, on an island. Seventy-five per cent. of buildings are modern; principal old building is Kloster Kirch. Principal street is famous Unter den Linden, over a mile long, formed by three avenues of lime trees; it contains numerous public buildings, government offices and statues, and claims to be finest street in Europe. Here also are the new Reichstag building and a royal palace; univ. is foremost in Germany; near it is the Royal Library. There are many bridges over river.

Berlin's geographical situation in centre of N. Prussia and of waterways covering dist. between Rs. Elbe and Oder, and at crossing of lines of communication between Brandenburg, Silesia, Saxony, Hanover, Mecklenburg, and Pomerania, is commercially advantageous. Great manufacturing city; produces woollens, cottons, porcelains, earthenware, machinery, metal goods, beer, paper, gold, silver, and bronze work, hardware. Berlin is a great publishing centre and is the hub of the German rly. system. Pop. 4,024,000. (2) Ontario, Canada. See KITCHENER. (3) City, New Hampshire, U.S.A., 90 m. N. of Concord; pulp, paper, lumber. Pop. 16,000. (4) City, Wisconsin, U.S.A., 20 m. S.W. of Oshkosh; dairy produce; granite quarries. Pop. 4,000.

Bermejo (*ber-mē'ho*), riv., flowing S.E. through Argentine Chaco to join Paraguay R. Length, 1,300 m.

Ber'mondsey, metropolitan bor. of London; centre of leather industry. Pop. 111,500.

Bermū'das, Brit. crown colony, consisting of 360 small islands (*c.* 20 inhabited) in N. Atlantic, 600 m. E. of Cape Hatteras; oldest colonial representative government in British Empire; principal islands, Main I. and St. George; health resort; early vegetables. Cap. Hamilton. Area of islands, 19 sq. m.; pop. 30,800.

Bermu'dez, asphalt lake (2 sq. m.), Venezuela.

Bern'burg, tn., Anhalt, Germany, on R. Saale, 25 m. S. of Magdeburg; lead smelting; chemicals; agricultural machinery; market gardening. Pop. 34,000.

Berne. (1) Canton, Switzerland; most populous and second largest in area; contains Bernese Oberland in S.; fertile valleys; grain and cattle; cheese; watch making, wood carving. Area, 2,657 sq. m.; pop. 699,000. (2) Cap. of Switzerland and of above, situated on rocky peninsula, almost surrounded by R. Aar; commands magnificent Alpine views of Bernese Oberland; univ., museum; textiles, musical boxes; chocolate. Pop. 109,000.

Bernese Oberland, highland district of Berne, Switzerland; occupied by Bernese Alps, which culminate in Finsteraarhorn, Jungfrau, and Aletschhorn; among chief passes are Jungfraujoch, Gemmi, Lauithor, Mönchjoch. Region includes summer resorts of Grindelwald, Interlaken, Meiringen, and great glaciers of Ober- and Unter-Grindelwald.

Bernina Alps. See RHÆTIAN ALPS.

Bernina Pass (*ber-nē'na*), (7,645 ft.), Swiss pass; running S.E. from St. Moritz in Upper Engadine to Valtellina; hospice on summit.

Bernina Piz, loftiest summit (13,304 ft.) of Bernina Alps; first climbed in 1850. See RHÆTIAN ALPS.

Beroun (*ber-ōn'*), tn., Bohemia, Czechoslovakia, 16 m. S.W. of Prague; textiles, sugar refining, brewing; cement. Pop. 11,500.

Bertino'ro, tn., Emilia, Italy, 18 m. S. of Ravenna; vineyards, mineral springs. Pop. 8,800.

Ber′vie, or INVERBERVIE, royal burgh and port, Kincardineshire, Scotland; flax spinning. Pop. 1,000.

Berwick, NORTH. See NORTH BERWICK.

Berwickshire (*ber′ik-*), co., S.E. Scotland; Lammermoors in N. are chief hills; Tweed is most important river, for 21 m. forming S. boundary; also watered by Leader, Whiteadder, and other affluents of Tweed; fertile productive dist.; many varieties of soil; agriculture principal industry; sheep and cattle largely raised; important fisheries; manufactures include paper, woollens, blankets. Co. tn., Duns. Area, 457 sq. m.; pop. 26,600.

Berwick-upon-Tweed, walled mkt. tn., England, on N. side of mouth of R. Tweed; since 1885 included in Northumberland; remains of castle and fortifications; new bridge over river opened in 1928; salmon and sea fisheries; coal and grain. Pop. 12,300.

Ber′wyn, tn., Cook, Illinois, U.S.A.; 9 m. W. of Chicago, of which it is a residential suburb. Pop. 47,000.

Besançon (*be-zän-sön*), chief tn., Doubs, E. France; fortress; univ., observatory; watch making and artificial silk manufactures. Pop. 58,000.

Bes′kid Mountains, a range of the Carpathians, now forming frontier between Czechoslovakia and Poland; crossed by Budapest and Breslau Rly. over Jablunka Pass, also by Munkacs and Lemberg Rly. over Beskid Pass.

Bessarabia (*bes-sa-rā′bi-a*), prov., Romania, lying between the rivs. Dniester and Pruth; N. occupied by spurs of Carpathians, but W. flat and fertile, where agriculture is main occupation—maize, wheat, wine, plums; higher ground covered with wood; in low ground cattle are bred; manufactures include leather, soap, and iron goods; marble quarries. Area, 17,146 sq. m.; pop. 2,345,000.

Bess′brook, tn., co. Armagh, N. Ireland, 2 m. N.W. of Newry; flax spinning. Pop. 2,800.

Bes′semer, city, Alabama, U.S.A., 12 m. S.W. of Birmingham; blast furnaces, foundries, rolling and planing mills. Pop. *c.* 40,000.

Beth′any ('house of dates'), vil., Palestine, at foot of Mount of Olives; mentioned in N.T. as home of Martha, Mary, and Lazarus. Modern tn., El Azariyeh.

Beth′el ('house of God'), an anc. sanctuary of Israel (probably modern Beitin, 12 m. N. of Jerusalem); mentioned in O.T. in connection with Abraham, Jacob, and as resting-place of Ark.

Bethes′da, tn., Carnarvonshire, Wales, 4 m. S.E. of Bangor; slate quarries. Pop. 4,500.

Beth′lehem ('house of bread'). (1) Vil. (modern Beit-Lahm), Palestine, 5 m. S. of Jerusalem; birthplace of David and afterwards of Christ (Matt. 2 : 1–6); church of the Nativity—probably the oldest Christian church in the world. (2) City, Pennsylvania, U.S.A., 50 m. N.W. of Philadelphia; univ.; iron and steel works, silk mills. Pop. 58,000.

Beth′nal Green, eastern metropolitan bor., London; headquarters of costermongers; museum. Pop. 108,200.

Bethsai′da. (1) Tn., Palestine, E. of R. Jordan; scene of two of Christ's miracles. (2) Tn., W. of R. Jordan, birthplace of Philip, Andrew, and Peter (Mark 6 : 45).

Béthune (*bā-toon′*), tn., dep. Pas-de-Calais, France, 20 m. W.S.W. of Lille, in the centre of a rich coalfield; connected with La Bassée and Lille by canal; oil, tanning, salt; earthenware and casks. Centre of much fighting in Great War. Pop. 19,000.

Bettws-y-Coed (*bet′oos-i-koyd′*), urb. dist., Carnarvonshire, Wales, 13 m. S. of Conway; artist and tourist resort. Pop. 900.

Betul′, dist., Central Provinces, India; plateau surrounded by belt of hilly forest country; R. Tapti flows through S. portion; wheat, pulses, oil-seeds; teak. Area, 3,826 sq. m.; pop. 364,000.

Beuthen (*boi-ten*), frontier tn., S.E. Prussian Silesia, Germany; lead, zinc, chemicals, machinery. Pop. 63,000.

Beveland (*bā'vi-land*), two islands, Zeeland, Holland; S. Beveland is bisected by canal and connected with mainland and Walcheren by rly. embankments. Aggregate area, 120 sq. m.

Bev'erley, mkt. tn., near Hull, E. Riding, Yorks; leather, agricultural implements, cloth weaving, chemicals. Pop. 14,000.

Bev'erly, port, Massachusetts Bay, U.S.A., 2 m. N. of Salem; boots and shoes; machinery; market gardening. Pop. 27,000.

Bewd'ley, mkt. tn., Worcestershire, England, 3 m. W.S.W. of Kidderminster; horn goods. Pop. 2,900.

Bex'hill, munic. bor., Sussex, England, 5 m. S.W. of Hastings; popular wat.-pl. Pop. 21,200.

Bex'ley, urban dist., Kent, England, 13 m. S.E. of London; part of Greater London; machinery and chemicals. Pop. 32,900.

Beybazar', tn., Turkey, 65 m. W. of Angora; rice, cotton, fruits. Pop. 21,000.

Beyrout. See BEIRUT.

Beziers (*bā-zē-ā'*), tn., dep. Hérault, France, 8 m. from Gulf of Lions; red wines, brandy; manure, chemicals. Pop. 66,000.

Bezwä'da, tn., Madras, India, on R. Kistna; important road, rail, and canal meeting-place; rice mills, cotton factories. Pop. 44,000.

Bhagalpur'. (1) Div., Bihar and Orissa, India. Area, 18,613 sq. m.; pop. 7,887,000. (2) Central dist. in above; rice, maize, wheat, oil-seeds, cotton. Area, 4,226 sq. m.; pop. 2,034,000. (3) Chief tn. of above dist., on R. Ganges; Mohammedan shrines and interesting Jain temples; agricultural produce; silk weaving. Pop. 69,000.

Bhamo'. (1) Dist., Upper Burma; in basin of R. Irrawaddy; rich teak forests. Area, 4,416 sq. m.; pop. *c.* 80,000. (2) Chief tn. of above dist.; highest point of Irrawaddy navigation, Pop. 7,700.

Bhandar'a. (1) Dist., Nagpur div., Central Provinces, India; rice, wheat, oil-seeds, bamboo, tobacco. Area, 3,623 sq. m.; pop. 718,000. (2) Chief tn. of above dist., 30 m. E. of Nagpur; brass working and cotton cloth. Pop. 14,000.

Bharatpur (*bhurt'pōr*). (1) Indian state, Rajputana, India, on border of United Provs.; cotton cloth, ironware, glass. Area, 1,982 sq. m.; pop. 496,000. (2) Cap. of above, 30 m. W. of Agra.

Bhaunagar (*bow-nug'er*). (1) Indian state, Bombay, India, in Kathiawar Pen.; grain, cotton, salt. Area, 2,860 sq. m.; pop. 426,000. (2) Chief tn. and port of above, on Gulf of Cambay; iron and tile works; exports cotton. Pop. 59,000.

Bhir, dist., N.W. Hyderabad, India; wheat, cotton, linseed, sugar. Chief tn., Bhir, 190 m. E. of Bombay. Area, 4,460 sq. m.; pop. 400,000.

Bhiwani (*be-won'ē*), tn., Hissar dist., Punjab, India, 70 m. W. of Delhi; metal working; cotton goods. Pop. 33,000.

Bhopal'. (1) Largest Indian state in Central India Agency; next to Hyderabad, most important Mohammedan state in India. Hilly tableland. Area, 6,902 sq. m.; pop. 692,000. (2) City, cap. of above state, 180 m. N.W. of Nagpur; weaving and printing of cotton cloth, jewellery. Pop. 45,000.

Bhor, Indian state, Bombay Presidency, India; rice. Chief tn., Bhor, 25 m. S. of Poona. Area, 925 sq. m.; pop. 130,000.

Bhuj, cap. of Indian state of Cutch, N.W. India; silver work. Pop. 19,000.

Bhutan', independent state under Brit. protection, E. Himalayas; is bounded N. and E. by Tibet, S. by Brit. India, W. by Sikkim and Chumbi Valley (belonging to Tibet). Surface is mountainous; watered by various tribs. of Brahmaputra. Climate varies according to elevation. Bhutan has extensive forests, and produces maize, wheat, rice, millet, and mustard; manufactures strong cloth, mats and baskets, swords. Inhabitants are chiefly Bhutias, racially allied to Tibetans. Chief tns., Punakha (cap.) and Tasichozong. Area, *c.* 18,000 sq. m.; pop. *c.* 300,000.

Biaf'ra, BIGHT OF, a large and deep indentation on W. coast of Africa, between mouth of R. Niger and Cape Lopez (400 m.).

Bialystok (*bya-wis'tok*). (1) County, Poland, bordering on E. Prussia and Lithuania; well-watered, sandy plain with extensive coniferous forests; chief crops, potatoes, rye, oats, flax. Area, 12,597 sq. m.; pop. 1,303,000. (2) Tn., cap. of above, 110 m. N.E. of Warsaw; woollen factories; boots and shoes. Pop. 76,800.

Biarritz (*bē-ar-rēts*), tn., Basses-Pyrénées, France, on Bay of Biscay; fashionable winter and summer seaside resort. Pop. 18,400.

Bicester (*bis'ter*), urb. dist., Oxfordshire, England, 12 m. N.N.E. of Oxford; lace, sacking; cattle fairs; hunting centre. Pop. 3,100.

Bidasso'a, small riv., N. Spain; lower course forms part of frontier with France.

Bid'deford, city, Maine, U.S.A., 17 m. S.W. of Portland; has cotton, woollen, and lumber mills, receiving water power from falls of Saco R.; granite. Pop. 18,000.

Bid'dulph, urb. dist., N. Staffs, England, 3 m. S.E. of Congleton; ironworks, collieries; cloth. Pop. 8,300.

Bid'eford, par. and port, N. Devon, England; potteries, shipbuilding, sail lofts, etc. Pop. 8,800.

Bieb'rich, tn., Hesse-Nassau, Prussia, on R. Rhine, 3 m. S. of Wiesbaden; cement, aniline dyes. Pop. 21,000.

Biel (*bēl*). See BIENNE.

Bielaya-Tserkov (*bē-ā-la'ya-tser-kof'*), tn., Ukraine, U.S.S.R.; on trib. of R. Dnieper, 150 m. E.S.E. of Kiev; important annual fairs; trade in cattle, beer, grain. Pop. 54,000.

Bielefeld (*bē'le-felt*), tn., Westphalia, Prussia, 27 m. S.E. of Osnabruck; centre of linen industry; damask, silk, sewing machines, engines, motor-cars; bleaching fields. Pop. 86,000.

Bielgorod (*bē-āl'go-rod*), tn., Kursk, Russia, 50 m. N. of Kharkov; famous annual fairs; soap, candle, brick making; bee keeping. Pop. 22,000.

Bielitz (*bē-lētz*), tn., Poland, 46 m. S.W. of Cracow; manufactures woollen goods, linen, jute, machinery. Pop. 18,600.

Bielopol (*bē-yā'lo-pol*), tn., Russia, 120 m. N.W. of Kharkov; distilling, tanning, brick making. Pop. 16,000.

Bienne (*bē-en*), tn., Berne, Switzerland, on lake of same name, 16 m. N.W. of Berne; important watch factories; museum, rich in antiquities. Pop. 37,000.

Bier'ley, NORTH, par., W. Riding, Yorks, England, 2 m. S.E. of Bradford; coal mines; iron works. Pop. 16,000

Biesbosch (*bēs'bosch*), dist., Netherlands, *c.* 6 m. E. of Dordrecht; agglomeration of islands, waterways, and marshes; result of bursting of dam in Maas (1421); most of land reclaimed by dykes; intersected by artificial channel, and connected with North Sea by two waterways. Area, 77 sq. m.

Big'gar, par. and tn., Lanarkshire, Scotland, 8 m. S.E. of Carstairs; cattle and horse fairs. Pop. of town, 1,300.

Big'garsberg Mountains, in Natal, S. Africa; branch of Drakensberg Mts.; highest peak, Indumeni (7,200 ft.).

Big'gleswade, urb. dist., Beds, England, 9 m. S.E. of Bedford; corn trade; market gardening. Pop. 5,800.

Bihar' and Oriss'a, prov., E. India; bounded N. by Nepal, E. by Bengal, S. by Bay of Bengal and Madras, W. by Central Provs. and United Provs.; drained mainly by R. Ganges, in S. by R. Mahanadi; contains N.E. extremity of Deccan, with rich coalfields, iron, copper, and mica; remainder of prov. agricultural; rice, wheat, maize, pulses, sugar-cane, tobacco; principal industry, iron and steel manufacture at Jamshedpur. Prov. separated from Bengal in 1912; cap. Patna. Area, 111,809 sq. m.; pop. 38,000,000.

Bij'apur. (1) Dist., S. Bombay, India; rainfall irregular; cotton and wheat. Area, 5,669 sq. m.; pop. 797,000. (2) Tn., in above dist., 50 m. s. of Sholapur; cotton ginning; trade in grain and cattle. Pop. 27,600.

Bijä'war, Indian state, Central India; well-forested; barley, grain; iron ore. Area, 973 sq. m.; pop. 112,000. Chief tn., Bijawar, 105 m. N.N.W. of Jubbulpore. Pop. 6,000.

Bijnor', dist., United Provinces, India; sugar-cane grown; sugar manufacture. Area, 1,791 sq. m.; pop. 740,200. Cap. Bijnor, 35 m. N.E. of Meerut; sugar. Pop. 18,000.

Bikaner (*be-kan-er'*). (1) Indian state, Rajputana, India; mostly sandy and waterless; frequent famines; camels, horses, and sheep reared; woollen shawls, carpets, leather work. Area, 23,315 sq. m.; pop. 660,000. (2) Cap. of above, 130 m. N.W. of Ajmer. Pop. 69,000.

Bilaspur', tn., Central Provinces, India, 16 m. S.E. of Jubbulpore; silk weaving, cotton cloth manufacture. Pop. 24,000.

Bilbao (*bēl-bä'ō*), tn., principal port, N. Spain; centre of great mining dist.; iron, copper ores. Pop. 148,000.

Billericay (*bil-er-ik'i*), mkt. tn., s. Essex, England, 8 m. s. of Chelmsford. Pop. 1,500.

Bill'ingham, urb. dist., Durham, England, 2 m. N. of Stockton; anc. church. Pop. 18,000.

Bil'lings, city, Montana, U.S.A., on Yellowstone R.; cattle and sheep raising; beet sugar. Pop. 16,000.

Bil'lingsgate, old river-gate and wharf, now fish-market of London.

Bil'lingshurst, vil., w. Sussex, England, 6 m. s.w. of Horsham. Pop. 1,875.

Bil'liton, isl., Dutch East Indies; between Banka and Borneo; tin deposits; coconuts, sago; trepang, tortoises, edible birds' nests; copra and gum exported. Area, 1,873 sq. m.; pop. 69,000.

Bil'oxi, tn., Mississippi, U.S.A., on Gulf of Mexico, 75 m. N.E. of New Orleans; summer and winter resort; important fisheries; oysters, crabs, turtles. Pop. 15,000.

Bil'ston, urb. dist., par., and mkt. tn., Staffs, England, 2½ m. S.E. of Wolverhampton; iron smelting and founding; engineering; coal mines; grindstones. Pop. 31,200.

Bingen (*bĕng'ăn*), tn., Hesse, Germany, on l. bk. of R. Rhine; wine, leather; tourist resort; in middle of river stands the famous 'Mouse Tower.' Pop. 9,100.

Bingerville (*băn-zhă-vēl*), tn., Ivory Coast, W. Africa; cap. and administrative seat of the colony.

Bing'hamton, tn., New York, U.S.A., on Susquehanna R., 140 m. N.W. of New York; shoes, cigars; iron and steel goods; patent medicine. Pop. 77,000.

Bing'ley, mkt. tn., W. Riding, Yorks, England, 5 m. N.W. of Bradford; woollens and metal working. Pop. 20,600.

Bio-Bio (*bē'o-bē'o*). (1) Prov., Chile, S. America; mountainous and forested; agriculture, timber. Cap. Los Angeles, 60 m. S.E. of Concepcion. Area, 5,353 sq. m.; pop. 107,000. (2) Riv., Chile; length, 220 m.; navigable 100 m.

Birbhum (*bēr'boom*), dist., Bengal, India; dry climate; healthy; rice, sugar-cane grown; manufactures cotton, silk. Cap. Suri, 105 m. N.N.W. of Calcutta. Area, 1,752 sq. m.; pop. 847,000.

Birch'ington, par. and vil., N.E. Kent, England, 3½ m. w. of Margate; fashionable seaside resort; D. G. Rossetti, poet and painter, died here (1882). Pop. (par.) 3,500.

Birkenfeld (*bēr'ken-felt*), detached province of Oldenburg, Germany, in s. of Rhineland, Prussia; hilly, well-wooded; agriculture; ironstone and slate quarries. Cap. Birkenfeld. Area, 312 sq. m.; pop. 56,000.

Birk'enhead, co. bor. and port, Cheshire, England; has ferry, and tunnels under Mersey connecting it with Liverpool; large shipbuilding works, iron foundries, breweries, flour mills; splendid docks (water area 165 ac.); exports coal; enormous cattle and meat trade. Pop. 147,900.

Bir'mingham. (1) City, Warwickshire, England, with suburbs extending into Staffordshire and Worcestershire; the greatest Midland manufacturing town, 97½ m. S.E. of Liverpool, 112 m. by rail N.W. of London. Town irregularly laid out; some fine streets and public buildings near centre, including town hall, art gallery, and council house. Univ. was established in 1900, and there are a technical school, a school of art, and a grammar school founded and endowed by Edward VI.; several large hospitals and charitable institutions. Manufactures include all kinds of metal work, especially in brass; founding, rolling, stamping, plating, drawing; making of machinery, iron roofs, girders, gasometers; steam, gas, and hydraulic engines; railway plant, motor-cars, tyres, rubber goods; electric apparatus, tools, guns, rifles, bells, electroplate, watches, clocks, table glass, chemicals, ammunition, swords, jewellery, coins, buttons, buckles, lamps, toys, pins, steel pens, nails, screws, locks. Rlys. run in all directions; canals to Severn, Thames, Mersey, and through Potteries to Trent. Pop. 1,002,400. (2) City, Alabama, U.S.A.; important iron and steel manufactures; cotton; chemicals; centre of agricultural trade. Pop. 258,000.

Bir'nam, vil. and hill, near Dunkeld, Perthshire, Scotland; frequented by tourists. Pop. 700.

Birr, or PARSONSTOWN, urb. dist., Offaly co. (King's co.), I.F.S.; Birr Castle houses famous Rosse telescope. Brewing. Pop. 3,400.

Bir'stall, urb. dist., W. Riding, Yorks, England, 3 m. N.N.W. of Dewsbury; woollens, shoddy, carpets, rugs. Pop. 7,200.

Birt'ley, par. and vil., Durham, England, 5¼ m. S.E. of Gateshead; coal mining; clay and stone quarries. Pop. (par.) 11,300.

Bis'bee, tn., S.E. Arizona, U.S.A., 7 m. from frontier of Mexico; copper mined in great quantity; silver, gold, lead, zinc. Pop. 18,000.

Bis'cay. (1) Or VIZCAYA, prov., N. Spain; mainly hilly; drained by Rs. Cadagua and Ibaizabal; much forest and coarse pasture; little agriculture. Produces iron ore, live-stock, maize, fruit. Cap. Bilbao. Area, 836 sq. m.; pop. 444,000. (2) BAY OF, bay of Atlantic Ocean; formed by coasts of France and Spain; shores rocky and inhospitable; subject to severe storms.

Bish'op Auck'land, urb. dist., Durham, England, 9 m. S.W. of Durham; collieries and iron works in vicinity. Pop. 12,300.

Bish'op's Stort'ford, mkt. tn., Herts, England, 11 m. N.E. of Hertford; has maltings and breweries. Pop. 9,500.

Bishop's Waltham, tn., Hants, England, 9 m. S.E. of Winchester; ruins of Waltham Palace (1135) lie to S.W. Pop. 4,600.

Bis'kra, tn. and oasis, Algeria, Africa, 200 m. S.E. of Algiers; comprises number of small villages, separated by olive groves and date palms; genial winter climate; popular resort. Pop., tn. 9,400; oasis, 16,500.

Bis'ley, vil., N.W. Surrey, England, 6 m. from Aldershot; its common is meeting-place of the National Rifle Association.

Bismarck, cap. of N. Dakota, U.S.A., on l. bk. of R. Missouri; dairy produce, flour milling. Pop. 11,000.

Bismarck Archipelago. See NEW BRITAIN (1).

Bismarck Mountains, a N.W. to S.E. range in S.W. of Territory of New Guinea; some peaks are perpetually ice-capped. Gold has been found in the range.

Bissag'os Islands, archipelago of about thirty volcanic isls. off Senegambia, W. Africa, belonging to Portugal. Largest of group is Orango.

Bitche (*bĕch*), (German BITSCH), tn., Moselle, France, at N. base of Vosges, 49 m. by rail N.W. of Strasbourg; citadel 250 ft. above tn.; shoes, watches; in German terr. 1871–1918. Pop. 2,500.

Bit'lis, vilayet and tn., E. Turkey, 110 m. S.S.E. of Erzerum; sulphur springs; fruit; manufactures red cotton cloth. Pop. of vilayet, 90,000.

Bitolj (*bē'tolzh*), formerly MONASTIR, tn., Yugoslavia (Serbia), 137 m. by rail W.N.W. of Salonika; tanneries; manufacture of carpets, ribbons, stockings; important trading centre for cereals and hides. Pop. 28,400.

Biton'to, tn. and episc. see, Apulia, S.E. Italy, 9 m. W. of Bari. Wine and olive oil are produced. Pop. 32,000.

Bit'ter Lakes, GREAT and SMALL, 6 m. N. of Suez, Egypt. The two lakes form about 23 m. of the Suez Canal.

Biwa (*bē'wa*), LAKE, S. Honshu, Japan, 30 m. N.E. of Osaka, largest in Japan. Area, 180 sq. m.

Bizerta (*bē-zār'ta*), port, Tunisia, N. Africa; fisheries; coaling and naval station. Pop. 21,000.

Björneborg. See PORI.

Black'burn, parl., munic., and co. bor., Lancs, England; centre of Lancashire cotton spinning and weaving; birthplace of Hargreaves, who invented spinning-jenny (1764). Pop. 122,700.

Black Country, Eng mining and manufacturing district in S. Staffs, stretching from Birmingham to Wolverhampton in one direction, and Walsall to Dudley in another.

Black Earth Area, CENTRAL, administrative unit, Russia, U.S.S.R. Established by Soviet Govt. in 1928. Productive plain; rye, millet, oats, summer wheat, potatoes, hemp, sunflower seed, sugar-beet. Cap. Voronezh. Area, 78,000 sq. m.; pop. 11,600,000.

Black Forest, or SCHWARZWALD, mountainous dist., Baden and Würtemberg, Germany, east of R. Rhine; highest peak, Fieldenberg, 4,900 ft.; extensive forests; picturesque scenery; tourist resort; cattle, clocks, toys. Area, 1,844 sq. m.; pop. 596,000.

Blackheath, a common now 267 ac. in extent, partly in bor. of Greenwich and partly in Lewisham, London; at one time noted haunt of highwaymen.

Black Hills, mts. in S. Dakota and Wyoming, U.S.A.; highest peak, Harney (7,216 ft.); gold and silver mines; fine grazing. Area, *c.* 6,000 sq. m.

Black Isle, peninsula (20 m. by 12 m.), Ross and Cromarty, between Beauly and Moray Firths and Cromarty Firth, Scotland; agriculture, quarrying, fisheries.

Black'pool, munic. and co. bor., and popular wat.-pl., Lancs, England, 46 m. N. of Liverpool; excellent sands and beautiful promenade; winter gardens. Pop. 101,500.

Black Rock, urb. dist., Dublin, I.F.S., on Dublin Bay; residential quarter. Pop. 10,000.

Blackrod, urb. dist., Lancs, England, 6 m. W. of Bolton; coal-mining. Pop. 4,000.

Black Sea, or EUXINE, land-locked sea, between Europe and Asia; area, 164,000 sq. m.; outlet to Mediterranean by Bosporus, Sea of Marmara, and Dardanelles; average depth, *c.* 3,900 ft.; shores low on N. and W.; good harbours except in N.; numerous inflowing rivers; surface waters fresher than ocean, bottom waters salt and lifeless; nearly always ice-free; chief ports, Varna, Odessa, Batum. Area, 164,000 sq. m.

Blackwater, name of some twenty rivers and eight villages in U.K.; frequent occurrence of name in Ireland due to dark-coloured bog water; most important of rivs. rises on borders of Cork and Kerry and flows into Youghal harbour; length, 100 m.

Blaenau Festiniog (*blen'ī fes-tin'i-og*), vil., Merioneth, Wales, 2½ m. N. of Festiniog; part of Festiniog urb. dist.; slate quarries.

Blaen'avon, urb. dist. and par., Monmouthshire, England, 5 m. N.W. of Pontypool; iron and steel manufactures; tinplate; coal mines. Pop. 11,100.

Blagovyeshchensk (*blago-vāsh'-chensk*), tn., E. Siberia, U.S.S.R., on l. bk. of R. Amur; river port; trades in gold, cattle, cereals; flour mills and ironworks. Pop. 61,200.

Blai'na or **Nantyglo and Blaina,** urb. dist., Monmouthshire, England, 3 m. N. of Abertillery; coal mines and blast furnaces. Pop. 13,200.

Blair A'tholl, or BLAIR ATHOLE, vil.

and par., N. Perthshire, Scotland, 3 m. N. of Pass of Killiecrankie; Blair Castle, seat of Duke of Atholl. Pop. of par. 1,800.

Blairgow'rie, tn., Perthshire, Scotland, on R. Ericht, 14 m. N. of Perth; fruit-growing centre; agricultural machinery; linen and jute mills. Includes Rattray. Pop. 4,700.

Blanc (*blon*), MONT, highest peak (15,782 ft.) of Alps, and, outside of some Caucasus peaks, the loftiest summit in Europe; on boundary of France and Italy; first ascended 1786.

Blanche, DENT. See DENT BLANCHE.

Bland'ford Forum, munic. bor. and mkt. tn., Dorsetshire, England, 16 m. N.E. of Dorchester; anc. earthworks and barrows in dist. Pop. 3,400.

Blankenberghe (*blank'en-ber-ge*), seaside resort, Belgium, 10 m. N.E. of Ostend; fisheries; golf links. Pop. 6,800.

Blankenburg (*blank'en-boorg*), wat.-pl., Brunswick, Germany, on N. slopes of Harz Mts., 37 m. S.W. of Magdeburg; market gardening. Pop. 12,000.

Blan'tyre ('warm retreat'). (1) Tn. and par., Lanarkshire, Scotland, 3 m. N.W. of Hamilton; coal; birthplace of Livingstone. Pop. 18,200. (2) Mission station, Nyasaland, Africa; named after Livingstone's birthplace; founded 1876; commercial centre.

Blar'ney, vil., co. Cork, I.F.S., 5 m. N.W. of Cork; in outer wall of Blarney Castle is the famous 'Blarney Stone.' Pop. 700.

Blay'don, urb. dist. and tn., Durham, England; on R. Tyne; coal mining; machinery, tools. Pop. 32,300.

Blenheim (*blen'im*). (1) Vil., Bavaria, near Danube, 30 m. N.E. of Ulm. Scene of Marlborough's victory, 1704. (2) Chief tn. of Marlborough, S. Island, New Zealand, near Cook Strait; rich agricultural and fruit district; gold in vicinity. Pop. 3,800.

Blet'chingley, par. and vil., Surrey, England, 3 m. E. of Redhill; its High Street is part of the Pilgrims' Way to Canterbury. Pop. (par.) 2,300.

Bletch'ley, urb. dist., N.E. Bucks, England, 1 m. W. of Fenny Stratford; rly. jn. Pop. 6,200.

Blida (*blē'da*), fort. tn., Algeria, N. Africa, 23 m. S.W. of Algiers; orange and flour trade. Pop. 25,000.

Block'ley, par. and vil., E. Worcs, England, 11½ m. S.E. of Evesham; in detached part of co. Pop. (par.) 1,800.

Bloemfontein (*bloom'fon-tīn*), cap., Orange Free State, Union of S. Africa; situated on a plain; elevation, 4,518 ft.; well built; large gardens; healthy climate; Grey Univ. Coll.; large live-stock fairs. Pop. 39,000 (whites 23,000).

Blois (*blwä*), anc. city, dep. Loir-et-Cher, France, on R. Loire; famous château, seat of Dukes of Orleans; wine, timber; boots, shoes; furniture. Pop. 19,000.

Bloom'field, tn., New Jersey, U.S.A., adjoining Newark; manufactures woollens, rubber goods, silks, paper. Pop. 38,000.

Bloom'ington. (1) City, Illinois, U.S.A., 60 m. N.E. of Springfield; coal mines; motor-cars; stationery. Pop. 31,000. (2) City, Indiana, U.S.A., 50 m. S.W. of Indianapolis; state univ.; large limestone quarries; furniture, gloves. Pop. 18,000.

Blox'wich, par. and vil., Staffs, England, 2½ m. N.W. of Walsall; coal and ironstone mines; ironworks. Pop. (par.) 15,000.

Bluefields, port, Nicaragua, on Caribbean Sea; bananas; lumber and cattle are exported. Pop. 7,200.

Blue Mountains. (1) Mt. range, New S. Wales, Australia. (2) Range, Oregon, U.S.A. (3) Ridge, E. Jamaica. (4) Range, Pennsylvania, U.S.A.

Blundellsands and Crosby, dist., Lancs, England, 6¼ m. N.W. of Liverpool; residential area. Pop. 4,000.

Blyth, port, Northumberland, England, 8 m. N. of Tynemouth; exports coal; shipbuilding; imports timber. Pop. 31,800.

Bob'rinets, tn., Ukraine, U.S.S.R.,

100 m. N. of Kherson; manufactures tobacco; flour mills. Pop. 15,000.

Bobruisk (*bo-broo'isk*), tn., White Russia, U.S.S.R., on r. bk. of Berezina R.; flour mills, foundries; river trade in grain, timber. Pop. 51,000.

Bo'cas del To'ro. (1) Prov., Panama; banana production; tropical agriculture; fishing. Pop. 22,000. (2) Cap. of above; exports bananas, coconuts. Pop. 10,000.

Bochnia (*bok'nya*), tn., Galicia, Poland, 22 m. E.S.E. of Cracow; salt and gypsum mines. Pop. 11,000.

Boch'olt, tn., Westphalia, Prussia, near Dutch frontier; woollens; machinery, iron foundries. Pop. 30,000.

Boch'um, tn., Westphalia, Prussia, in Ruhr coal basin; steel and iron works. Pop. 211,000.

Bodenbach. See PODMOKLY.

Bodensee. See CONSTANCE.

Bod'min, tn., Cornwall, England; agricultural trade; boots and serges; live-stock fairs. Pop. 5,500.

Bodö (*bo'de*), port, Nordland, Norway, on Saltenfjord; fish; eiderdown. Pop. 4,800.

Bœotia (*bē-ō'shi-a*), dist., ancient Greece, bounded by Phocis, Gulf of Corinth, Attica, and the Euripos; chief city was Thebes; chief riv., Cephissus; chief lake, Copais; plains bounded by mts.; Mt. Helicon in S.W. Bœotia with Attica now dep. of Greece. Pop. 793,800.

Boeroe. See BURU.

Bog'nor Regis, seaside resort, Sussex, England; fine sands. Pop. 13,500.

Bogodukhov (*bō-hō-doo'chof*), tn., Ukraine, U.S.S.R., 30 m. N.W. of Kharkov; mkt. gardens; tanning industry. Pop. 16,000.

Bogong', MOUNT, a summit (6,508 ft.) of Australian Alps, Victoria.

Bogorodsk (*bō-hō-rodsk'*), tn., Russia, U.S.S.R., 35 m. E. of Moscow; textile mills; chemicals. Pop. 35,000.

Bōgōta', cap., Colombia, S. America, on plateau 8,000 ft. above sea; cathedral, capitol, observatory, library, univ., and museum; subject to earthquakes. Pop. 166,000.

Bohē'mia, western part of Czechoslovakia; bounded N. and W. by Germany, S. by Austria, E. by Moravia. Surface is undulating plateau with slight northern slope, surrounded by mt. ranges, N.E. by Riesengebirge, N.W. by Erzgebirge, S.W. by Bohemian Forest, S.E. by Bohemian and Moravian Mts.; drained by R. Elbe and tribs., chief being Moldau, Iser, and Eger. Climate is genial in valleys, cold in higher districts. About one-third of surface forested; over half cultivated; chief crops: wheat, rye, barley, oats; flax, hops, fruit, beet produced. The chief mineral is lignite; black coal, iron ore, silver, gold, antimony, zinc, tin, graphite, lead, sulphur also produced; manufactures include sugar, woollens, carpets, cottons, linen, silk, gloves, glass, buttons, bottles, porcelain. There are mineral springs at Carlsbad, Marienbad, Sedlitz, etc. Bohemia imports agricultural machinery and road-rollers from U.K., tools from Germany. Cap. Prague (Praha). Area, 20,102 sq. m.; pop. 6,923,000.

Bohemian Forest, range of mts. between Bohemia and Bavaria; Mt. Arber (4,785 ft.) is chief peak; pine and beech forests; crossed by three rlys. and four roads.

Bohol', isl., Philippines, N. of Mindanao; coffee, sugar, rice. Area, 1,400 sq. m.; pop. 243,150.

Boise (*boi'zā*), cap. Idaho, U.S.A.; valuable mines; centre of well-irrigated dist. yielding fruit. Pop. 20,000.

Bois-le-Duc. See 'S HERTOGENBOSCH.

Bokhara. See BUKHARA.

Bokoto. See PESCADORES.

Boks'burg, tn., Transvaal, S. Africa, 12 m. E. of Johannesburg; gold and coal mining. Pop. 37,000 (whites, 12,100).

Bolan' Pass, narrow gorge leading N.W. from R. Indus valley to the highlands of Sarawan, Baluchistan; is traversed by military road and by rly. to Quetta. Length, 60 m.; summit attains 5,900 ft.

Bolbec', tn., dep. Seine-Inférieure,

France, 17 m. E. of Havre; spinning, weaving, and printing. Pop. 10,000.

Bolgrad′, tn., Bessarabia, Romania, at head of L. Yalpukh, 25 m. N. of Ismail; trade in grain; brick making; tallow factories. Pop. 13,000.

Bolivar (*bo-lē′vär*). (1) State, Venezuela, S. America; well-forested plains with many rivers; rubber, copaiba, balsam, tobacco; gold is found. Cap. Ciudad Bolivar. Area, over 90,000 sq. m.; pop. 75,000. (2) Prov., Ecuador, S. America; coffee, tobacco, cereals grown; mostly forest. Cap. Guarando, 100 m. s. of Quito. Area, 1,159 sq. m.; pop. 45,000. (3) Maritime dep., N. Colombia, S. America; densely wooded plains; little cultivation. Cap. Cartagena. Area, 22,320 sq. m.; pop. 457,000.

Boliv′ia, inland rep., S. America; bounded N. and E. by Brazil, s. by Paraguay and Argentina, w. by Chile and Peru. W. consists of plateaus lying between Andes and Cordillera Real to E.; of these, Oruro plateau (with Lakes Titicaca and Poopo) is 13,000 ft. above sea-level; southern part lower, a sandy or salt-covered desert; along N.E., hills sink rapidly, and on E. by series of terraces to northern and eastern plains; former drained by Rs. Beni and Mamore to R. Madeira, latter by R. Paraguay; other rivs. are Guaporé, Purus. Chief mts. are Bolivian Andes; there are many active volcanoes. Climate varies with altitude and exposure; higher plateaus have hot days, cold nights; lower plateaus and eastern terraces temperate; upper valleys subtropical; northern and eastern plains tropical; first two regions have wet and dry seasons; elsewhere rain falls all year round. Fauna includes great variety of monkeys, birds, and insects. Condors and humming-birds occur; wild animals include tapir, jaguar; rly. communications poor (*c.* 1,500 m.); Rs. Beni and Mamore are navigable; roads few and bad. Upper plateaus produce potatoes, barley; lower plateaus, wheat, maize; upper valleys, fruits; great plains have luxuriant tropical vegetation. There are grassy savannas in s., valuable timber in N.; rubber, copal, coffee, cocoa, coca, rice, cotton, cinchona, pineapples, bananas produced; cattle and sheep largely bred; vicuña, alpaca, llama, guanaco, chinchilla are valued for their skins and wool. Minerals include silver, copper, tin, lead, zinc, antimony, bismuth, wolfram, gold, salt, oil; many of these await development. Tin is the great source of wealth, silver coming next in importance. Chief imports are provisions, wines, spirits, textiles, hardware; exports, silver, rubber, tin, wool, hides, cattle, coffee, cocoa. Chief towns, La Paz (actual cap.), Cochabamba, Potosi, Sucre (nominal cap.), Oruro. Area, 514,155 sq. m.; pop. 2,975,000.

Bolkhov′, tn., Russia, 35 m. N. of Orel; trade in cattle, agricultural products; orchards. Pop. 18,000.

Boll′ington, urb. dist., Cheshire, England, 3 m. N. of Macclesfield; cotton manufacture. Pop. 5,000.

Bologna (*bō-lōn′yä*). (1) Prov., Italy, between R. Po and Apennines; wheat and maize largely grown. Area, 1,465, sq. m.; pop. 642,700. (2) Cap. of above; two leaning towers; univ. (11th cent.); great rly. centre; sausages, macaroni; sugar refining; rly. rolling stock. Pop. 240,000.

Bolse′na, lake, Italy, w. of R. Tiber, in centre of volcanic district; 1,000 ft. above sea-level; abounds in fish. Area, 71 sq. m.

Bol′sover, urb. dist., par., tn., Derbyshire, England, 5½ m. E. of Chesterfield; coal mines; magnesian limestone quarries. Pop. 11,800.

Bols′ward, tn., Friesland, Netherlands, 13 m. s.w. of Leeuwarden; cheese, butter. Pop. (comm.) 7,000.

Bolt Head, cape, s. Devonshire, England; alt. 420 ft.

Bol′ton. (1) Co. bor., Lancs, England; centre of cotton industry; manufactures muslins, velvet, paper, chemicals; iron foundries, sawmills; coal mines in neighbourhood; grammar school (1641). Pop. 177,300. (2) -UPON-DEARNE, urb. dist., W. Riding, Yorks, England, 7 m. w. of Doncaster; coal-mining. Pop. 14,200.

Bo'ma, port, and former cap. Belgian Congo, on r. bk. of R. Congo, 55 m. from mouth. Was a slave market. Pop. *c.* 3,000.

Bombay. (1) Presidency, British India; bounded N. by Baluchistan and Punjab, E. by Rajputana, Central India Agencies, Berar, Hyderabad, and Madras, S. by Mysore and Madras, W. by Arabian Sea; coast-line towards N. broken by Gulfs of Cutch and Cambay; Narbada R., flowing to latter, divides prov. into two parts, of which northern consists of Gujarat and great plain of Sind, southern of coastal strip along Arabian Sea and part of Deccan tableland; chief mountains are W. Ghats, Satpura range, and outliers of Aravalli Hills; rivs. Indus (which traverses Sind), Narbada, Tapti. Climate varies; high temp. in Sind plains; rainfall slight in N., moderate on tableland; heavy on coastal strip; wettest months, June to October; chief crops are wheat, cotton, millet, rice; other products are pulse, oil-seeds, sugar-cane, indigo, tobacco; principal industries, cotton manufacture, silk weaving, carpets, leather goods, pottery, brasswork; water-power from Western Ghats; minerals are scarce. Rly. mileage, principal lines, *c.* 6,000 m. Area (including feudatories and the dependency of Aden), 187,074 sq. m.; pop. 27,000,000. (2) Cap. of above, and second port of India, situated in S. of isl. of same name, lying off coast of prov. and connected with mainland by bridges and causeways. In N. is native town; in S., European garrison; natives are of many different races. Bombay has some fine buildings, including a univ., the Victoria railway terminus, Ragabai Tower, municipal offices, several colleges, and large hospitals; most important manufacturing town in India; has magnificent natural harbour, wet docks, and many dry docks; rly. communication with all parts of India; centre of cotton trade; other industries are dyeing, tanning, metal work, and the making of 'Bombay blackwood furniture'; great sea trade; exports: raw cotton, seeds, grain; imports: manufactured goods, metals, machinery. Pop. 1,176,000.

Bona. See BÔNE.

Bondy (*bon-dē'*), comm., Seine, France; environs of Paris; brewing; chemical manufactures. Pop. 7,500.

Bône, or BONA, port, Algeria, N. Africa; good harbour; manufactures tapestry and leather; exports phosphates, sheep, barley, esparto; imports manufactured articles. Pop. 52,000.

Bo'ness', or BORROWSTOUNNESS, port, West Lothian, Scotland, on S. shore of Firth of Forth; extensive harbour; large shipping trade; coal, iron, bricks, pottery; imports pit wood. Pop. 10,100.

Bon'hill, tn. and par., on R. Leven, Dumbartonshire, Scotland; has calico printing, bleaching, and dye works. Pop. (par.) 16,600.

Bo'ni, native state, S. Celebes, Dutch E. Indies; rice, tobacco; plaited goods. Area, 2,600 sq. m.; pop. *c.* 200,000.

Bonifacio (*bon-i-fäch'-yo*). (1) Port, Corsica, on peninsula in Strait of Bonifacio; olive oil; tobacco; cork-cutting; coasting trade. Pop. 2,300. (2) STRAIT OF, narrow, rocky, and difficult channel, some 7 m. wide, between Corsica and Sardinia.

Bonin Islands (*bo-nēn'*), or OGASAWARA JIMA, chain of twenty small volcanic islands, N. Pacific, between Japan and Marianas Islands; belong to Japan; cap. Port Lloyd, on Peel I., the largest of the chain; tropical vegetation; valuable timber. Turtles caught in large numbers. Pop. 5,000.

Bonn, tn., Rhenish Prussia, Germany, on l. bk. of R. Rhine; famous univ.; antiquarian museum and library; fine bridge across Rhine; manufactures stoneware. Pop, 90,200.

Bonny'. (1) Port, Nigeria; exports palm oil. Pop. *c.* 7,000. (2) Riv. on which above is situated; falls into Bight of Biafra; one of most easterly distributaries of R. Niger.

Bon'nyrigg and Lasswade', burgh, Midlothian, Scotland, 5 m. S. of Edinburgh; paper mills; carpets; coal mining. Pop. 4,500.

Boom, tn., Belgium, 9 m. S. of Antwerp; brick-kilns; tanning. Pop. 17,200.

Boone, city, Iowa, U.S.A., 38 m. N.W. of Des Moines; bricks, hosiery; coal and lumber exported. Pop. 12,000.

Boo'tle, co. bor., Lancs, England; continuous with Liverpool; chemicals; jute; engineering works; timber yards. Pop. 76,800.

Bop'pard, tn., Rhenish Prussia, on R. Rhine, 10 m. S. of Coblenz; fruit and wine; tourist centre. Pop. 6,500.

Borås (*bo'ros*), tn., Sweden, 45 m. E. of Göteborg; spinning and weaving. Pop. 35,000.

Bordeaux (*bŏr-dō'*), tn. and port, Gironde, France, on l. bk. of R. Garonne; in midst of great wine, fruit, grain, and timber-producing country; trading centre; exports wine, brandy, hides, wool, fish, fruits, potatoes, sugar, oil, resins; univ. Pop. 256,000.

Border Province or GRENZMARK POSEN-WESTPREUSSEN, prov. of Prussia. See GRENZMARK.

Bordighera (*bōr-di-gā'ra*), tn., Riviera, Italy, 2 m. N.E. of Nice; winter resort. Pop. 5,500.

Borgå. See PORVOO.

Bor'go Pass, mt. pass in Carpathians, near frontiers of Bukovina, Transylvania, and Romania.

Borkum, E. Frisian isl.; belongs to Prussia; low and sandy; summer resort. Area, 12 sq. m.; pop. 3,000.

Bor'neo, large isl., Malay Archipelago, immediately N. of Java; bounded E. by Celebes Sea, Macassar Strait; S. by Java Sea; W. and N.W. by China Sea; length, 830 m.; breadth, 600 m. About two-thirds of island in S.E. and S. belong to the Dutch, while N. and N.W. (states of N. Borneo, Brunei, and Sarawak) belong to Britain. Mountain ridge runs from N.E. to S.W., height ranging from 8,000 ft. in N.E. to 3,500 in S.W.; in extreme N., Kinabalu range reaches height of 13,700 ft.; interior mountainous, with rich river valleys and marshy plains; principal rivs., Barito, Kapuas; few lakes; coast is low and swampy. Best bays are in Brunei and Brit. N. Borneo. Rainfall is heavy. Forests produce ironwood, teak, sandalwood, ebony, indiarubber, sago, camphor, pepper, cloves, nutmegs, cinnamon, ginger, betel nuts, coconuts, gambier, bamboo, canes. Rice, sugar-cane, sago, tapioca, coffee, earthnuts, indigo, maize, hemp, cotton, tobacco, are cultivated; minerals, except coal, only in traces as yet. Edible birds' nests, trepang, pearls, and tortoise-shell are obtained. Exports are pepper, spices, drugs, timber, canes, gutta-percha, indiarubber, and many of above productions; imports general goods, clothing, machinery, hardware, opium, rice. Area, 289,860 sq. m.; pop. *c.* 3,000,000.

BRITISH NORTH BORNEO is mainly hilly; rubber, tobacco, pepper, gambier, sugar-cane, sago are cultivated; exports: rattans, nuts, edible birds' nests, rubber; minerals not developed. Chief tn., Sandakan. Area, 31,106 sq. m.; pop. 257,800.

DUTCH BORNEO, largest and most important part. (Products, etc., described under Borneo.) Chief tn., Bandjermasin. Area, over 200,000 sq. m.; pop. *c.* 2,000,000.

Born'holm, Dan. isl., Baltic Sea; kaolin, freestone; fisheries; flax, hemp, oats. Chief tn., Rönne. Area, 225 sq. m.; pop. 44,000.

Bornu (*bor-noo'*), state, Nigeria, Africa, W. and S. of Lake Chad; surface flat; branches of Komadugu R. flow to Lake Chad; climate very hot and unhealthy; produces indigo, maize, millet, cotton, ground-nuts; imports calico, sugar, salt. Chief tns., Kuka and Maidugari. Area, *c.* 50,000 sq. m.; pop. *c.* 4,000,000.

Borodino (*bor-ō-dē'nō*), vil., Russia, on trib. of Moskva R., 70 m. W. of

Moscow; French victory over Russians in 1812 led to fall of Moscow.

Bor'oughbridge, mkt. tn., W. Riding, Yorks, England, on R. Ure, 11 m. by rail N.E. of Harrogate; megalithic monuments. Pop. 800.

Borrome'an Islands, four small islands, Lake Maggiore, Italy; Isola Bella has an Italian 17th cent. baronial palace; Isola Madre, a botanical garden.

Borrowdale, picturesque valley, Cumberland, England, s. of Derwentwater; slate quarries.

Borrowstounness. See BO'NESS.

Bos'cobel, par., Shropshire, England, 6 m. N.E. of Shifnal; contains house where Charles II. hid after Worcester (1651).

Bosham (*boz'am*), vil. and par., w. Sussex, England, 3½ m. w. of Chichester; oyster beds; fishing. Pop. (par.) 1,560.

Bos'nia and Hercegovina (*her'tse-go-vi-na*), dist., Yugoslavia; Dinaric Alps run from N.W. to S.E., surface sloping thence N.E. to Sava basin, S.W. to Adriatic. Hercegovina, in S., is bare and rocky; Bosnia, to N., has mt. forests and fertile valleys; chief rivs., Save and its affluents; large part of surface wooded—lime, beech, oak, pine, larch. Great majority of population are engaged in agriculture; chief crops: tobacco, grain, fruits, beet, flax, hemp; cattle, sheep, swine, horses, mules are largely raised; wine is made; anthracite and iron ore mined. Exports include timber, fruit, coal, iron, chemicals, live-stock; imports include oils, coffee, wool, cottons, silk, rice, paper, leather, glass, hardware, machinery, soap. Cap. of Bosnia, Sarajevo; of Hercegovina, Mostar. Area, 19,768 sq. m.; pop. 1,890,000.

Bos'porus, or BOSPHORUS, strait (17 m. long and ½ m. to 2¾ m. wide) between Black Sea and Sea of Marmara.

Bos'ton. (1) Port and mkt. tn., Lincolnshire, England, on R. Witham; deep-sea fishing; manufacture of agricultural implements and oilcake. Pop. 16,600. (2) Port, cap. Massachusetts, U.S.A., on Boston Harbour, at mouth of Charles and Mystic rivs. Boston is a great rly. centre; number of lines of steamers ply regularly to foreign ports; has excellent harbour accommodation and a good system of street rlys. and subways. Chief industries: printing, textiles, boots and shoes, confectionery. Imports include wool and woollens, chemicals, iron and steel manufactures, wood, leather, fruit, fish, paper; exports provisions, live cattle, bread-stuffs, cottons, leather goods, wood, iron and steel manufactures, spirits; noted educational centre; has famous library, univ., medical school of Harvard University, fine arts school, etc. Pop. 787,000.

Botany Bay, bay and suburb of Sydney, New South Wales; received its name from the richness of its flora; original landing-place of convicts from Britain; now a popular seaside resort. Pop. 7,200.

Both'nia, GULF OF, northern arm of Baltic Sea. See BALTIC SEA.

Both'well, tn. and par., N. Lanarkshire, Scotland, 8 m. S.E. of Glasgow; coal mines and freestone quarries; iron and steel works. Pop. (par.) 60,900; (tn.) 3,500.

Botosani (*bo-to-shä'ni*), chief tn. of dist. of same name, Romania, 50 m. S.E. of Cernauti; starch and flour mills. Pop. 33,000.

Bot'trop, tn., Westphalia, Prussia, 6 m. N.W. of Essen; coal mines. Pop. 82,000.

Bouches-du-Rhône (*boosh-doo-rōn'*), dep. S.E. France, at mouth of R. Rhone; w. part consists of marshy plain (Camargue), which includes Rhone delta; E. part is hilly; wheat, oats, olive trees, vine, almonds, mulberry are cultivated. Industries: pottery, silk, soap. Chief tn., Marseilles. Area, 2,025 sq. m.; pop. 930,000.

Bougainville (*boo-gān-vēl'*), largest of Solomon Islands, Pacific Ocean; timber. Area, 3,500 sq. m.; pop. 46,000.

Bougie (*boo-zhē'*), port, Algeria; at one time greatest commercial centre

N. African coast; exports oils, wax, hides, wool. Pop. 16,000.

Bould'er. (1) Tn., Colorado, U.S.A., 30 m. N.W. of Denver; seat of Colorado Univ.; gold and silver; health resort. Pop. 11,000. (2) Tn., W. Australia, close to Kalgoorlie; largest gold-mining centre in W. Australia. Pop. 5,900.

Boulogne-sur-Mer or **Boulogne** (*boo-lōn'y-sur-mār'*), port, Pas-de-Calais, France, 130 m. N.N.W. of Paris, and connected with Folkestone by daily cross-Channel service; divided into Haute-Ville and Basse-Ville; harbour, recently enlarged, is great port for herring and cod fishing; cement, steel pens, ropes, chocolate, boots and shoes are made; exports raw silk, wine, brandy, fruit, potatoes, poultry; imports woven goods and machinery. Pop. 76,000.

Boulogne-sur-Seine (*boo-lōn'y-sur-sān'*), suburb of Paris, with 'Bois de Boulogne,' a famous pleasure ground and public park (2,158 ac.), containing zoo and racecourses of Longchamps and Auteuil. Pop. 68,000.

Bourbon, Isle. See Réunion.

Bourbonne-les-Bains (*boor-bon-lā-ban'*), tn. and health resort, in Haute-Marne, France, 30 m. s.w. of Chaumont; hot mineral springs; trade in timber, plaster. Pop. 2,600.

Bourg-en-Bresse (*boorg-an-bres'*), cap. Ain, France, 38 m. N.E. of Lyons; rly. jn.; copper ware, pottery, tallow; dist. famous for poultry. Pop. 16,000.

Bourges (*boorzh*), tn., cap. Cher, central France; govt. arsenal and gun foundry; breweries, leather, cutlery, biscuits; remains of Roman ramparts. Pop. 36,000.

Bourget (*boor-zhā'*), Lac du, largest lake in France, dep. Savoie; 758 ft. above sea-level; connected with R. Rhone by Canal de Savières. Area, 16 sq. m.

Bourget, Le, tn., outskirts of Paris; air-port for cross-Channel service.

Bourke, tn., New South Wales, Australia, on R. Darling; copper ore; trade in tinned meat; irrigation works. Pop. 2,600.

Bourne, urb. dist., s. Lincs, England, 9½ m. w. of Spalding; remains of castle, once residence of Hereward the Wake. Pop. 4,900.

Bournemouth (*bōrn'muth*), wat.-pl. and co. bor., English Channel, Hants, England; mild climate; beautiful scenery; pier over 1,200 ft. long. Pop. 116,800.

Bourn'ville, model vil., near Birmingham, England; site of Cadbury's chocolate works.

Boussa (*boos'a*), tn., N. Nigeria, W. Africa; Mungo Park drowned in R. Niger here (1806). Pop. 13,000.

Boussu (*boos-su'*), tn., Belgium, 7 m. w. of Mons; coal, iron, copper. Pop. 11,500.

Bov'ey Tra'cey (*buv'i*), vil. and par., s.E. Devon, England, 6 m. N.W. of Newton Abbot; lignite deposits; potteries. Pop. (par.) 2,800.

Bowdon (*bō'don*), urb. dist., Cheshire, England, 9 m. s.w. of Manchester, of which it is a residential suburb. Pop. 3,300.

Bowling Green. (1) City, Kentucky, U.S.A., 100 m. s.w. of Louisville; centre of oilfield; evaporated milk. Pop. 12,000. (2) City, Ohio, U.S.A., 20 m. s. of Toledo; oils and natural gas, machinery. Pop. 7,000.

Bowness-on-Windermere (*bō'nes*), par., Westmorland, England; tourist centre; pier for L. Windermere steamers. Pop. 3,800.

Boyaca (*bo-ya-kā'*), dep., Colombia, S. America; traversed by E. Cordilleras of Andes; forested; has richest emerald mine in world; minerals. Cap. Tunja, 80 m. N.E. of Bogotą. Area, 16,460 sq. m.; pop. (dep.) 657,000.

Boyle, mkt. tn., co. Roscommon, I.F.S., 28 m. S.E. of Sligo. Pop. 2,300.

Boyne, riv., I.F.S.; enters Irish Sea s. of Drogheda; length, 70 m. Scene of battle where William of Orange defeated James II. (1650).

Brabant'. (1) Mediæval duchy of Low Countries, corresponding to the modern prov. of North or Dutch Brabant and the Belgian provs. of Brabant and Antwerp. (2) Prov.,

Belgium, between Rs. Meuse and Schelde; industrial and agricultural; thickly populated; cap. Brussels. Area, 1,268 sq. m.; pop. 1,643,000. (3) NORTH, prov., southern Holland; surface flat; heathy and marshy tracts; agriculture and cattle rearing. Chief tn., s' Hertogenbosch. Area, 1,921 sq. m.; pop. 837,000.

Brac (*brach*), or BRAZZA, largest of Dalmatian islands, Yugoslavia, in Adriatic Sea; mountainous but fertile; wines, olives, figs, almonds; marble; fisheries. Area, *c.* 200 sq. m.; pop. 19,300.

Brackley, mkt. tn., Northants, England, on R. Ouse; brewing. Pop. 2,200.

Brack'nell, vil. and par., S.E. Berks, England, 4½ m. E. of Wokingham; in anc. Windsor Forest. Pop. (par). 3,500.

Brad'dock, bor., Pennsylvania, U.S.A., 10 m. S.E. of Pittsburgh; iron and steel manufactures. Pop. 46,000.

Brad'ford. (1) City, W. Riding, Yorks, England, 9 m. W. of Leeds; chief seat of woollen and worsted manufacture; important wool market; silks and velvets also made; good rly. communication; connected with Humber and Liverpool by canal; coal and iron mines, stone quarries in vicinity; engineering. Pop. 298,000. (2) City, Pennsylvania, U.S.A., near N. boundary; oil-wells, machinery. Pop. 17,000.

Bradford-on-Avon, mkt. tn., Wilts, England; rubber industries and bathstone quarries; famous for woollens. Pop. 4,700.

Braemar', par., vil., S.W. Aberdeenshire, Scotland, alt. 1,100 ft.; health resort; bracing climate; Ben Macdhui near by. Pop. of par., 1,000.

Brag'a. (1) Dist., N.W. Portugal; largely pastoral. Area, 1,040 sq. m.; pop. 376,000. (2) Archiepisc. see, cap. of above; cutlery, firearms, felt hats. Pop. 22,000.

Bragan'ça, or BRAGAN'ZA. (1) Dist., N.E. Portugal; agriculture; rearing of silkworms; silk manufactures. Area, 2,513 sq. m.; pop. 170,000. (2) City, episc. see, cap. of above; silk, velvet. Pop. 5,800.

Brahmapu'tra ('son of Brahma'), riv., Asia, rising E. of Lake Manasarowar, on tableland N. of the Himalayas in W. Tibet, close to head-waters of Rs. Sutlej and Indus; has course eastward of *c.* 1,000 m., as Tsangpo, then turns S.E., through Himalayas, and flows through Assam to join R. Ganges. Length, *c.* 1,800 m. (navigable about 800 m.); drainage area, over 361,000 sq. m.

Braila (*bra-ē'la*), tn., Romania, on l. bk. of R. Danube, 12 m. S.S.W. of Galatz, is principal port for the grain trade and has extensive docks; imports coal. Pop. 66,000.

Brain'tree. (1) Mkt. tn., Essex, England, 14 m. W. of Colchester; engineering; silk, crêpe. Pop. 8,900. (2) Tn., Massachusetts, U.S.A., 10 m. S.E. of Boston; leather, shoes, carpets, rubber goods. Pop. 16,000.

Bramhall. See HAZEL GROVE AND BRAMHALL.

Bramp'ton. (1) Mkt. tn., Cumberland, England, 9 m. N.E. of Carlisle; antiquities. Pop. 2,500. (2) Tn., Ontario, Canada, 20 m. W. of Toronto; flour, pumps, gas pipes. Pop. 3,500.

Bran'denburg. (1) Prov. of Prussia, Germany; sandy plain with fertile districts; watered by Rs. Elbe and Oder; numerous lakes; fruit, flax, barley, rye, hemp, tobacco; chalk, alum; sheep rearing; cap. Berlin. Area, 15,072 sq. m. Pop. 2,600,000. (2) Tn. in above, 37 m. W.S.W. of Berlin; on R. Havel; cloth, tinplate, bicycles. Pop. 59,000.

Bran'don. (1) Mkt. tn., Suffolk, England, on R. Little Ouse, on border of Norfolk; flint working in vicinity. Pop. 2,400. (2) City, Manitoba, Canada, 130 m. W. of Winnipeg; flour mills; brickworks. Pop. 16,000.

Brandon and Byshottles, urb. dist., Durham, England, 3 m. S.W. of Durham; coal-mining. Pop. 17,100.

Brant'ford, city, Ontario, Canada, on Grand R., 25 m. S.W. of Hamilton; ploughs, bicycles, railway material. Pop. 29,500.

Bras d'Or (*brădor*), almost land-locked, tideless gulf, Cape Breton I., Nova Scotia, Canada; divided into Bras d'Or and Little Bras d'Or Lakes, connected by Grand Narrows (bridged by Canadian National Rly.); ship canal connects s. end of Lake Bras d'Or with St. Peter's Bay; lumbering on its shores; productive fisheries.

Brasov (*bră-shov*), or KRONSTADT, tn., Transylvania, Romania, 85 m. N.N.W. of Bucharest; cloth, leather, cement, candles. Pop. 40,000.

Bratislava, formerly PRESSBURG, or POZSONY, tn., Czechoslovakia, on R. Danube, 35 m. E. of Vienna; chief river port and rly. centre of Czechoslovakia; centre of wheat and wine growing dist.; weaving, furniture, chemicals, tobacco, spirits; important annual Orient fair; univ. Pop. 93,000.

Braunsberg (*browmz'berg*), tn. and port, E. Prussia, 38 m. s.w. of Königsberg; some shipping trade; breweries and tanyards. Pop. 14,000.

Braun'ton, vil. and par., N.W. Devon, England, at mouth of R. Taw, 5¾ m. N.W. of Barnstaple; lighthouse and lifeboat station. Pop. (par.) 2,650.

Bray (1) (Irish, *Bri Chualann*), urb. dist., mkt. tn., and wat.-pl., cos. Wicklow and Dublin, I.F.S.; known as 'Irish Brighton'; brewing, fishing. Pop. 8,600. (2) Vil. and par., Berkshire, on R. Thames; referred to in ballad 'The Vicar of Bray.' Pop. of par., 3,800.

Brazil' ('red dyewood'). (1) Republic, occupying nearly half of the S. American continent; extreme length, 2,695 m.; breadth, 2,691 m. Brazil is bounded N. by Venezuela, Brit., Dutch, and French Guiana; N.E. and S.E. by Atlantic Ocean; s.w. by Uruguay, Argentina, Paraguay, Bolivia; w. by Peru, Colombia. In basin of R. Amazon are the tropical forests called *selvas*; s.w. is in Rs. Parana-Paraguay basin; both it and Amazon basin have large amount of unhealthy, low-lying, and swampy land; E. and S.E. occupied by great plateau, with open prairie lands called *campos*; average elevation of plateau over 3,000 ft.; there is a higher tableland cut by deep valleys, having appearance of series of mt. ranges, some reaching height of over 7,000 ft.; these, running parallel with Atlantic, render communication with interior very difficult; large part of country still unexplored. Chief tribs. of R. Amazon are Japura, Rio Negro from N., Jurua, Purus, Madeira, Tapajos, Xingu from s. R. Tocantins flows northward, entering sea near mouths of R. Amazon; and San Francisco R. cuts across eastern ranges, entering sea between Maceio and Aracaju; Paraguay, Taquary, and Parana drain s.; Madeira and rivs. E. of it, and Parana and tribs., flow through tableland and hills, and have many falls and rapids. There are few lakes. Climate varies, with elevation from tropical to temperate.

Flora includes cabinet woods, rubber, palms, mimosa, bombax, lianas, grasses, ferns, orchids, cypresses, acacias, myrtles, coffee, cacao, tobacco, and many other valuable trees and plants. Fauna includes many kinds of birds, butterflies, snakes, monkeys, deer, bats, opossums, jaguars, pumas, sloths, armadillos, rodents. Timber and other vegetation of great tropical forests along Amazon and elsewhere are most valuable, including rubber, fibre plants, nuts, furniture woods, dye woods, drug plants. Cultivated products include coffee, sugar-cane, tobacco, cotton, maté, rubber, balata, cassava, cinchona, cocoa, vines. In s. inland provs. are raised great herds of cattle. Minerals are abundant but undeveloped, except gold; in s. are beds of coal, lignite, bituminous schist, peat; silver, lead, iron, copper, manganese, quicksilver also occur; diamonds are found in Minas Geraes, Bahia, São Paulo, Matto Grosso; other deposits are saltpetre, rock salt, mineral oil, china clay. Brazil is largely agricultural, with only a small proportion cultivated at present, but there are some industries, including cotton spinning and weaving, woollen manufactures, silk weaving, flour mills, fruit preserving, distilling, brewing. Exports: coffee, rubber, tobacco, sugar, cocoa, maté, gold, hides, cotton, oil-seeds. Chief tns. are Rio de Janeiro (cap.), São Paulo Santos, Bahia, and Pernambuco. Area, 3,285,318 sq. m.; pop. (est.) 36,871,000. (2) Tn., Indiana, U.S.A., 16 m. N.E. of Terre Haute; coal, clay; pig iron; consequent industries. Pop. 9,300.

Braz'os, riv., Texas, U.S.A.; formed by junction of Clear Fork and Salt Fork rivs.; enters Gulf of Mexico. Length, over 900 m.; navigable to Columbia (40 m. from mouth).

Brazza. See BRAC.

Braz'zaville, tn., Middle Congo Colony, Fr. Equatorial Africa, on Stanley Pool, R. Congo; headquarters of gov.-gen.; railhead. Pop. *c.* 5,000.

Breadal'bane, dist., Perthshire, Scotland, comprising many lofty peaks of the Grampians (highest, Ben Lawers, 3,984 ft.) and lochs. Area, 1,020 sq. m.

Brechin (*brĕch'in*), royal burgh, Angus, Scotland, on l. bk. of R. South Esk; 7¾ m. w. of Montrose; brown linen, and sailcloth; spinning, bleaching, distilling; 12th cent. cathedral (now parish church). Pop. 6,800.

Brec'kenridge, tn., Texas, U.S.A., 85 m. w. of Fort Worth; oil. Pop. 18,000.

Brec'on, or BRECKNOCK, mkt. tn. and co. tn., Breconshire, S. Wales, at the confluence of Rs. Honddu and Usk; lime; flannels, brewing, and tanning. Pop. 5,300.

Breconshire, or BRECKNOCKSHIRE, inland co., S. Wales, bounded by Radnor, Hereford, Monmouth, Glamorgan, Carmarthen, Cardigan; surface mountainous; highest peak, Pen-y-Fan; chief rivs., Wye, Usk; has several lakes and mineral springs. Breconshire produces wheat, oats, barley; timber, dairy produce; cattle and sheep raised; manufactures include woollens, leather, iron goods; minerals include coal, iron, limestone. Co. tn., Brecon. Area, 733 sq. m.; pop. 57,800.

Bre'da, tn., N. Brabant, Holland, at junction of Rs. Aa and Merk; carpets, linen, rope, soap; brewing. Treaty signed here between England and Holland, 1667. Pop. 43,400.

Bredbury and Romiley, urb. dist., N.E. Cheshire, England, 2 m. N.E. of Stockport; cotton manufacture. Pop. 10,900.

Bregenz (*brā'gents*), tn., summer resort, Austria, at S.E. angle of Lake Constance; silk industry; trade in foodstuffs. Pop. 13,000.

Brem'en. (1) Free state of Germany, in basin of lower R. Weser; cattle largely reared; market gardening and fishing. Area, 99 sq. m.; pop. 339,000. (2) City of Germany, cap. of above state, a Hanseatic town on both banks of R. Weser, next to Hamburg among ports of Germany; jute spinning, woollen and cotton goods, shipbuilding; iron foundries, rope making, petroleum refining, distilling, brewing, and sugar refining; great cotton market of Germany; large trade in tobacco and rice; emigration centre. Pop. 295,000.

Brem'erhaven, outport of Bremen (38 m. N.), Germany, at mouth of R. Weser; commodious and well-equipped harbour. Pop. 24,000.

Bren'ner Pass, mt. pass between Austria and Italy, 20 m. s. of Innsbrück; lowest of all the great Alpine passes (4,485 ft.); shortest route between Germany and Italy; railway constructed in 1864–67.

Bren'ta, riv., N. Italy, rises Tirol, enters Adriatic Sea. Length, 106 m.

Brent'ford and Chiswick, urb. dist. and mkt. tn., Middlesex, England; part of Greater London; soap, distilling, rubber industry; market gardens and fruit farms in vicinity. Pop. 62,600.

Brent'wood, mkt. tn., Essex, England, 11 m. s.w. of Chelmsford; breweries, brickworks. Pop. 7,200.

Brescia (*brā'sha*). (1) Prov., N. Italy, between Tyrol, Lake Garda, and R. Oglio; rice, maize, wine, and fruits; silk, machinery, and leather. Area, 1,823 sq. m. Pop. 652,000. (2) Tn., cap. of above, 9 m. from Lake Garda; woollens, linens, silks, stockings, iron and steel wares, small arms. Pop. 113,500.

Breslau (*brez'lou*), tn., Silesia, Prussia, on R. Oder; most important educational and commercial centre in E. Germany; univ. (1702); machinery, railway carriages; musical instruments, glass, beet sugar, chemical manures. Pop. 557,000.

Bres'say, isl. of Shetland group, 1 m. E. of Lerwick on Mainland; 6 m. long by 3 m. broad; slate and flagstones quarried. Pop. 600.

Brest, chief naval base and arsenal on Atlantic, N.W. France; sea approaches studded with rocks and islands; about 9,000 persons employed in arsenal; fisheries; candles, cork, hats, ropes, soap, and leather; exports vegetables, strawberries, and potatoes. Pop. 68,000.

Brest-Litovsk', fort. tn., Poland, on R. Bug; great rly. centre; grain, wood, cattle, tobacco. Here treaty was signed between Russia and Central Powers (1918). Pop. 29,000.

Bretagne. See BRITTANY.

Brewood (*brood*), tn. and par., Staffs, England, 8 m. N. of Wolverhampton; on canal to Liverpool. Pop. (par.) 2,600.

Briançon (*brē-an-son'*), tn. and fortress, Hautes-Alpes, S. France, at confluence of Rs. Durance and Guisane; highest town in France (4,335 ft.); silk. Pop. 2,800.

Briansk', tn., Russia, 75 m. N.W. of Orel; great annual fair; tallow; saw and flour mills; iron, machinery, glass, rope. Pop. 24,000.

Bridgend, mkt. tn., Glamorganshire, Wales, 20 m. W. of Cardiff; stone quarries; bricks, tiles; lime burning. Pop. 10,000.

Bridge of Allan, tn., Stirlingshire, Scotland, on Allan Water, 3 m. N.W. of Stirling; mineral springs; residential tn. Pop. 2,900.

Bridge of Weir, tn., Renfrewshire, Scotland, 6 m. W. of Paisley; residential dist.; calico printing and leather works. Quarrier's Homes in vicinity. Pop. 2,600.

Bridgeport, city, Connecticut, U.S.A., on Pequonnock Creek, Long Island Sound; sewing-machine works; cartridges, carriages, corsets, hardware, and ordnance; electrical machinery. Pop. 147,000.

Bridgeton, city, New Jersey, U.S.A., 37 m. S. of Philadelphia; pig iron and ore; machinery, nails, glass; canned fruit and vegetables. Pop. 16,000.

Bridgetown, port and cap., Barbados, Brit. W. Indies; open roadstead, but small inner harbour. Pop. 13,500.

Bridge'water, tn., Massachusetts, U.S.A., 26 m. S. of Boston; ironworks, brickyards; lumber, shoes. Pop. 9,000.

Bridg'north, munic. bor., Shropshire, England, on R. Severn; manufactures carpets and worsteds. Pop. 5,200.

Bridg'water, port, Somersetshire, England, on R. Parret, 12 m. from Bristol Channel; manufactures bathbricks; coasting trade. Pop. 17,100.

Brid'lington, munic. bor. and wat.-pl., E. Riding, Yorks, England; fine bay and good harbour. Pop. 19,700.

Brid'port, port, Dorsetshire, England; cordage, ropes, and sailcloth; fishing (mackerel). Pop. 5,900.

Brieg (*brēg*), tn., Silesia, Prussia, on l. bk. of R. Oder; textiles, metal-work soap; cattle markets. Pop. 27,000.

Brienz (*brē-ents*), vil., Berne, Switzerland, on L. Brienz; centre of wood-carving industry; tourist resort. Pop. 2,600.

Bri'erley Hill, urb. dist., Staffs, England, 2½ m. N.E. of Stourbridge; bottle-making, brick-works, potteries; chains and nails. Pop. 14,300.

Brig, or BRIGUE (*brēg*), tn., Valais, Switzerland, on R. Rhone at N. end of Simplon tunnel. Pop. 3,000.

Brigg, or GLANFORD BRIGG, mkt. tn., Lincs, England, 10 m. S. of Barton-on-Humber. Pop. 4,000.

Brig'ham, city, Utah, U.S.A., near N. shore of Great Salt Lake; agricultural centre; canned tomatoes, beet sugar. Pop. 5,000.

Brig'house, tn., W. Riding, Yorks, England, 4 m. N. of Huddersfield; woollens and worsteds, cotton, carpets; machinery and soap; flagstone quarries. Now includes Rastrick. Pop. 19,800.

Bright'lingsea, port, Essex, England, on estuary of R. Colne; oysters; yacht and boat building. Pop. 4,100.

Brigh'ton. (1) Co. bor., Sussex, England, 51 m. S. of London; on Eng. Channel; fashionable holiday resort; mild climate; magnificent promenade (3 m.); fisheries. Pop. 147,400. (2) Tn. and wat.-pl., Victoria, Australia, on Port Phillip Bay. Pop. *c.* 15,000.

Brignoles (*brēn-yōl'*), tn., Var, France, 35 m. E.N.E. of Marseilles; marble quarry; wine, olives, fruits. Pop. 4,500.

Brigue. See BRIG.

Brindaban', tn., United Provinces, India, near r. bk. of R. Jumna, 35 m. N.W. of Agra; place of pilgrimage; calico printing. Pop. 18,400.

Brindisi (*brin'dē-zē*), port and archiepisc. see, Lecce, S.E. Italy; only really good harbour between Venice and extremity of S.E. Italy on Adriatic; exports figs, wine, olive oil, coral, and silk; imports coal. Pop. 41,000.

Brionian Islands (*brē-o'nē-an*), group of twelve small islands in Adriatic Sea, N.W. of the harbour of Pola, Istria; quarries; Brione (largest), bathing resort.

Brioude (*brē-ood'*), tn., Haute-Loire, France, 50 m. W.S.W. of St. Etienne; alt. 1,467 ft.; wine, wood, corn; market gardening. Pop. 4,500.

Bris'bane, port, cap. of Queensland, Australia, on riv. of same name, 25 m. from mouth in Moreton Bay; river navigable up to city for ocean-going steamers; shipping trade concentrated in S. Brisbane (dry dock); univ. of Queensland opened here, 1911; preserved and frozen meats, fruit, hides and skins, wool, tallow, and pastoral produce. Pop., with suburbs (10 m. radius), 295,400.

Bris'tol. (1) City, England, in Gloucestershire and Somersetshire, at junction of Rs. Frome and Avon; important port, with good dock accommodation; large trade with U.S.A., Canada, W. Indies, and other parts of empire; exports coal, salt, tinplates, machinery, cottons, chemical products; imports bananas, provisions, tobacco, timber, grain, oils, marbles, ores. Factories produce chocolate, sugar, leather, chemicals, beer, sailcloth. Univ. (1909). Pop. 396,900. (2) Tn., Tennessee, U.S.A., joined with (3) city, Virginia; rly. centre; flour, tobacco, cheese, and butter. Pop. 22,000. (4) Bor., Pennsylvania, U.S.A., on Delaware R.; cottons and woollens; makes carpets, wallpaper, chemicals, and leather. Pop. 12,000. (5) Port, Rhode I., U.S.A.; famous yacht-building centre; rubber and woollen goods. Pop. 12,000. (6) Tn., Connecticut, U.S.A., 15 m. S.W. of Hartford; clocks; foundries, machine shops, and engine works. Pop. 28,000.

Bristol Channel, arm of Atlantic, extending from mouth of R. Severn to St. George's Channel, separating S. Wales from S.W. counties of England; noted tidal bores; important fisheries.

Bris'tow, tn., Oklahoma, U.S.A., 65 m. N.E. of Oklahoma City; oil; glassworks. Pop. 15,000.

British Central Africa. Term formerly used to denote all Brit. territory in Central Africa (as distinguished from Brit. East, Brit. West, and Brit. South Africa)—viz., Nyasaland and that part of Rhodesia N. of the Zambezi.

British Colum'bia, prov., Dominion of Canada; mostly between Rocky Mts. and Pacific; includes Vancouver and Queen Charlotte Islands. The surface is very mountainous, the Rockies reaching a height of 13,068 ft. in Mount Robson. To the W. of the Rockies are the Selkirk and Gold Ranges, which rise to 11,000 ft.; Cascade or Coast Range, rising to 10,000 ft. Chief rivs. are Columbia, Fraser, Thompson, Peace. Climate varies; mild near coast, dry and hot in S. interior, severe winters in N.; heavily wooded; important commercial trees are Douglas fir, maple, yellow cypress, red and yellow cedar, white spruce; much pastoral and agricultural land. Chief industries are lumbering, mining, fruit growing, ranching, fishing, canning, fur sealing; very rich in minerals; gold is worked at Cariboo and Kootenay; coal, silver, lead, copper are also mined; the working of cinnabar, platinum, gypsum, asbestos, plumbago has begun. Cap., Victoria, on Vancouver I.; other tns., Vancouver and New Westminster, on mainland. Area, 355,855 sq. m. Pop. 525,000.

British East Africa, Brit. terr. in E. Central Africa, comprising (1) Kenya Colony and Protectorate. (2) Uganda Protectorate. (3) Zanzibar Protectorate.

British Empire, the unofficial but popular and convenient term for the aggregation of territory under the Brit. crown. These territories are officially classified as follows: (1) Self-governing dominions: (*a*) Canada, New Zealand, Union of S. Africa, Irish Free State, Newfoundland; (*b*) Australian Commonwealth and its six component states. (2) Southern Rhodesia, with responsible government, subject to certain powers with regard to native administration reserved to High Commissioner for South Africa. (3) Malta, with responsible government for internal affairs. (4) Colonies without responsible government: (*a*) with elected House of Assembly and nominated Legislative Council—Bahamas, Barbados, Bermudas; (*b*) with partly elected Legislative Council (without official majority)—British Guiana, Ceylon, Cyprus; (*c*) with partly elected Legislative Council (with official majority)—Fiji, Grenada, Jamaica, Kenya, Leeward Islands, Mauritius, Nigeria, St. Lucia, St. Vincent, Sierra Leone, Straits Settlements, Trinidad; (*d*) colonies and protectorates with Legislative Council nominated by crown—British Honduras, Falkland Islands, Gambia, Gold Coast, Hong Kong, Northern Rhodesia, Nyasaland Protectorate, Seychelles, Uganda Protectorate; (*e*) colonies and protectorates with no Legislative Council—Ashanti, Basutoland, Bechuanaland Protectorate, Gibraltar, Northern Territories of Gold Coast, St. Helena, Somaliland, Swaziland; (*f*) islands under Western Pacific High Commissioner. (5) Mandated Territories. The following ex-German colonies are held by mandate from the League of Nations: part of Togo, Cameroons, and Ger. E. Africa; island of Nauru (S. Pacific); Ger. S.W. Africa (held by Union of S. Africa); Ger. Samoan Islands (held by New Zealand); all Ger. possessions s. of equator except those mentioned above (held by Commonwealth of Australia). The Anglo-Egyptian Sudan is held jointly by Egypt and Britain; the New Hebrides by France and Britain. The extraordinary growth of the empire between 1837 and the present time may be judged from the fact that in the former year the extent of Brit. territory was under 5,000,000 sq. m., and its population less than 200,000,000, about 30,000,000 being whites. Its area now exceeds 13,313,000 sq. m., or about one-fourth of the land surface of the world, and its pop. over 456,000,000 (over 66,000,000 whites)—at least one-fourth of the world's inhabitants.

British Guiana (*gē-ā'na*), Brit. colony, S. America, bordering on Caribbean Sea; surface rises from flat, swampy coast (below sea-level in parts) to Guiana highlands; chief rivs., Essequibo, Berbice, Demerara, Corentyne; climate not unhealthy; products are sugar, rice, coffee, coconuts, balata and rubber, timber, bauxite; 97 m. of railway; cap. Georgetown. Area, 89,480 sq. m. Pop. 308,000.

British Hondu'ras, crown colony, E. coast of Central America, on Caribbean Sea, between Mexican state of Yucatan and Guatemala. The N. is low and full of swamps; S. is mountainous. Staple products are mahogany, logwood, bananas, cacao, plantains. Climate generally damp and hot, but not unhealthy. Cap. and chief port is Belize. Area, 8,598 sq. m.; pop. 49,000.

British Isles, THE, archipelago on the continental shelf W. of the continent of Europe; separated from Continent by North Sea, Strait of Dover, and the English Channel; consist of two large islands and some 5,000 small islands and islets. The largest isl. is Great Britain (England and Wales, Scotland); the other large island is Ireland (Northern Ireland and Irish Free State). Among single islands are Isle of Man, Angelsey, and Isle of Wight; amongst the groups are Orkney and Shetland Islands (to N.) and Hebrides (to W. of Scotland); Scilly Islands (S.W. of England). The Channel Islands, geographically French, belong to Britain. Total area, 120,882 sq. m.; pop. 49,000,000.

British North Borneo. See BORNEO.

British West Indies. See WEST INDIES.

Brit'on Ferry, tn., Glamorganshire, Wales, 7 m. E. of Swansea; extensive steel and iron works. Pop. 9,100.

Brit'tany, or BRETAGNE, former prov., France, now the deps. Ille-et-Vilaine, Côtes-du-Nord, Finistère, Morbihan, and Loire-Inférieure; peninsula bounded N. by Eng. Channel, W. by Atlantic, S. by Bay of Biscay; coast deeply indented; surface mountainous; fishing and farming are the main industries. Area, 13,643 sq. m.; pop. 3,063,000.

Brive (*brēv*), or BRIVE-LA-GAILLARDE, tn., Corrèze, France, on R. Corrèze, trib. of R. Dordogne, in fertile, picturesque district, producing early vegetables, truffles, wine, *pâté de fois gras*. Pop. 20,000.

Brix'ham, port and mkt. tn., on Tor Bay, Devonshire, England; important trawling centre; some coasting trade. Pop. 8,100.

Brix'ton, dist. of S. London; in metropolitan bor. of Lambeth. Pop. 76,000.

Brno (*bur'no*) or BRÜNN, tn., cap. of Moravia, Czechoslovakia; woollen factories; machinery, brewing, distilling. Pop. 222,000.

Broach. (1) Dist., Gujarat, Bombay, India; broad alluvial plain of Lower Narbada; cotton, wheat. Area, 1,468 sq. m.; pop. 307,700. (2) Chief tn. of above, 35 m. N. of Surat; cotton factories. Pop. 43,000.

Broad Arrow, tn., W. Australia, 24 m. N.W. of Kalgoorlie; centre of goldfields. Pop. of dist. 3,000.

Broads, THE, series of picturesque shallow fresh-water lakes in Norfolk (mainly) and in Suffolk, largest being Hickling (400 ac.); 200 m. of navigable water in dist.; famous for yachting, fishing, and fowling.

Broadstairs, eccles. par. and wat.-pl., Isle of Thanet, Kent, England. Pop. 12,700.

Broad'way, par. and vil., S.E. Worcs, England, 5 m. S.E. of Evesham; at base of Cotswold Hills; artists' resort. Pop. (par.) 1,860.

Brock'en, central summit of Harz Mts., N Germany; alt. 3,733 ft.

Brock'enhurst, par. and vil., S.W. Hants, England, 4 m. N. of Lymington; in New Forest. Pop. (par.) 2,160.

Brock'ton, city, Massachusetts, U.S.A., 20 m. S. of Boston; large shoe factories; machinery, tools. Pop. 64,000.

Brock'ville, riv. port, Ontario, Canada, on St. Lawrence R., 60 m. S. of Ottawa; farming implements; motor boats; edge tools. Pop. 10,000.

Brod, tn., Slavonia, Yugoslavia, on R. Sava; riv. port; corn, wine, fruit, wood. Pop. 10,600.

Brod'ick, par. and tn., Isl. of Arran, Buteshire, Scotland; seaside resort. Pop. of par. 1,760.

Broken Hill. (1) Tn., in W. of New South Wales, Australia, in rich silver-mining dist.; zinc. Pop. 24,000. (2) Tn., N. Rhodesia, 320 m. N.E. of Livingstone; centre of rich mining dist.

Bromberg. See BYDGOSZCZ.

Brom'ley, mkt. tn., Kent, England;

residential centre for Londoners; part of Greater London. Pop. 45,300.

Broms'grove, mkt. tn., Worcestershire, England, 12 m. s.w. of Birmingham; nails and buttons. Pop. 9,500.

Brom'yard, urb. dist., N.E. Herefordshire, England, 11 m. S.E. of Leominster; Norman church. Pop. 1,600.

Bronx, THE, most northerly of the five boroughs comprising New York city, U.S.A. Area, 39½ sq. m.; pop. 732,000.

Brook'lands, noted motor track, w. Surrey, England, 1 m. s. of Weybridge.

Brook'line, tn., Massachusetts, U.S.A.; residential suburb of Boston. Pop. 47,000.

Brook'lyn, bor. of New York city, western end of Long Island and connected with mainland by bridges; favourite residential quarter; U.S. navy yard; important trading and manufacturing centre; flour mills, sugar refineries, brass works, and breweries. Pop. 2,018,000.

Broome, port, Dampier Land, N.W. coast, W. Australia; pearl fishing. Pop. 900.

Broseley, tn., Shropshire, England; pottery; part of Wenlock famous for clay tobacco pipes. Pop. 3,000.

Broughty Ferry (*braw'te*), par. and tn., Angus, Scotland, on Firth of Tay; part of city of Dundee; wat.-pl. Pop. 5,300.

Brown, MOUNT, peak, Rocky Mts., Canada, near source of Rs. Fraser and Columbia: alt. 9,055 ft.

Brown'hills, urb. dist., Staffs, England, 6 m. w. of Lichfield; important coal-mining centre. Pop. 18,400.

Browns'ville, city and riv. port, Texas, U.S.A., near mouth of Rio Grande; important market for livestock, sugar-cane, grape fruit, vegetables. Pop. 18,000.

Brox'burn, tn., W. Lothian, Scotland, 10½ m. w. of Edinburgh; coal mines; centre of shale-oil industry. Pop. 8,300.

Bruay (*broo-ā'*), tn., Pas-de-Calais, France, 5 m. s.w. of Bethune; in rich coal-mining district. Pop. 31,000.

Bruchsal (*brooch'säl*), tn., Baden, Germany, 14 m. N.E. of Karlsruhe; tobacco, paper, machinery, beer. Pop. 16,000.

Bruges (*broozh*), city, cap. of Flanders, Belgium, 63 m. N.W. of Brussels and 8 m. inland from North Sea; connected by ship canal with Zeebrugge; famous belfry, 353 ft. high; chief industry, lace making. Pop. 52,000.

Brunei (*broo-nī'*), state, Brit. protectorate, N.W. Borneo; exports sago, wild rubber, hides and horns; oil is found. Chief tn., Brunei. Area, *c.* 2,500 sq. m. Pop., state, 25,500; tn. 12,000.

Brün'ig Pass (3,396 ft.), pass leading from Bernese Oberland to Unterwalden, Switzerland.

Brünn. See BRNO.

Brunsbüttel (*broonz'boo-tel*), tn. and port, Schleswig-Holstein, Germany; w. terminus of the North Sea–Baltic canal. Pop. 7,800.

Bruns'wick. (1) or BRAUNSCHWEIG, Republic of Germany; Harz Mts. in s.; rivs., Ocker, Weser, navigable; beech, fir, pine, oak forests; coal, iron, agriculture, and cattle rearing important; sugar and chemicals principal manufactures. Area, 1,418 sq. m. Pop. 502,000. (2) Cap. of above; industries include printing, jute spinning, manufacture of chemicals, machinery, sugar. Pop. 147,000. (3) City, S.E. Georgia, U.S.A.; seaside resort; resin, turpentine, lumber products. Pop. 20,000. (4) Tn., Maine, U.S.A., 20 m. N.E. of Portland; paper, pulp, cotton mills. Pop. 8,000.

Brunswick, NEW. See NEW BRUNSWICK.

Brusa or BURSA (*broo'sa*), tn., Asia Minor, 25 m. from Sea of Marmara; silk, cotton, carpets; iron and sulphur springs. Pop. 61,000.

Brus'sels, or BRUXELLES, cap. of Belgium, prov. of Brabant; centre of canal and rly. system; industries: lace, carpets, furniture, bronzes, woollens, cottons, automobiles, leather goods; chief exports: glass, sugar, coal, candles. Modern town is well laid out, has fine lime-planted boulevards separating it from suburbs, and avenues connecting it with parks and *bois*. Important buildings are town hall, magnificent palais de justice, royal palace, houses of Parliament, three fine old churches, art and natural history museums, univ.; centre of art and music. Pop. (Greater Brussels) 815,200.

Bruton, mkt. tn., S.E. Somerset, England, 10½ m. S.W. of Frome; educational centre; annual cattle show. Pop. 1,725.

Brüx. See MOST.

Brynmawr (*brin-maur'*) ('great hill'), tn., Breconshire, Wales, 8 m. W. of Abergavenny; extensive ironworks; coal mining. Pop. 7,200.

Bucaramanga (*boo-ka-ra-man'ga*), tn., Colombia, S. America, 185 m. N.N.E. of Bogota; important coffee centre; tobacco, cocoa, cotton; gold, silver, iron; manufactures cigars and cigarettes. Pop. 30,000.

Buch'an (*bŭch'an*), dist. of N.E. Scotland, now included in Banffshire and Aberdeenshire; coast-line bold, rocky. Chief tns., Peterhead, Fraserburgh.

Buchan Ness, rocky peninsula, Aberdeenshire, Scotland; most easterly point of Scotland.

Bucharest (*boo-ka-rest'*), tn., cap. of Romania, situated in Wallachian plain and traversed by Dimbovitza R. Climate extreme; state univ.; great educational centre. Trade in wheat, maize, timber, petroleum. Varied industries. Pop. *c.* 800,000.

Buch'holz, tn., Saxony, Germany, 18 m. S. of Chemnitz; school of lace making; cardboard boxes. Pop. 9,700.

Buck'fastleigh, urb. dist., S. Devon, England, 6¾ m. N.W. of Totnes; woollen factories; restored Saxon abbey. Pop. 2,400.

Buckhaven, tn., Fife, Scotland, on Firth of Forth; forms a burgh with Methil and Innerleven; colliery trade, engineering, flax spinning. Pop. 17,600.

Buckhurst Hill, urb. dist., Essex, England, 10 m. N.E. of London; residential dist.; part of Greater London. Pop. 5,500.

Buck'ie, fishing tn., Banffshire, Scotland, on Moray Firth; sawmills, distillery; rope and sail yards. Pop. 8,700.

Buck'ingham, munic. bor., N. Bucks, England; agricultural centre; condensed-milk factory, corn mills. Pop. 3,100.

Buckinghamshire, or BUCKS, co., England; bounded N. by Northampton, E. by Bedford, Hertford, Middlesex, S. by Berkshire, W. by Oxford; surface generally undulating; in S. are Chiltern Hills, which are well wooded, especially with beeches; in centre is Vale of Aylesbury, a dist. noted for dairy produce, ducks, and sheep; drained by R. Thames, which bounds co. on S., and by Rs. Ouse, Colne, Thame; there are no large towns; manufactures unimportant, include straw-hats, wooden chairs, thread lace, paper. Famous school, Eton, is near southern boundary. Cap. Aylesbury. Area, 749 sq. m.; pop. 271,600.

Buckley, urb. dist., Flint, Wales, 2 m. E. of Mold; coal mining; earthenware. Pop. 6,900.

Budapest (*boo-da-pesht'*), cap., kingdom of Hungary; consists of two tns., Buda and Pest, on opposite banks of R. Danube. Buda (or Ofen) is principal seat of government. Pest is commercial centre, but contains houses of parliament and univ. Budapest contains many mineral springs, and some splendid baths. Industries include flour milling, tanning, brewing, distilling, manufacture of tobacco and leather goods; trade carried on in corn, wine, spirits, cattle. Pop. 1,005,000.

Budaun (*boo'da-oon*). (1) Dist., United Provinces, India; level and fertile; rice, sugar-cane, poppy. Area, 2,014 sq. m.; pop. 975,300. (2) Chief tn. of above dist., 27 m. S.W. of Bareilly. Pop. 39,000.

Bud'don Ness, sandy promontory,

Angus, Scotland; military camp is in vicinity.

Bude, or BUDE HAVEN, eccles. dist. and small port, N. Cornwall, England; rising seaside resort. Pop. (including Stratton) 3,800.

Budejovice (*bood'ye-yo-vit-se*), formerly BUDWEIS, town, s. Bohemia, Czechoslovakia; lead pencils, porcelain, chemicals, beer. Pop. 44,000.

Bud'leigh Salt'erton, urb. dist., E. Devon, England, 4½ m. E. of Exmouth; wat.-pl.; fishing. Pop. 3,200.

Buenos Aires (*bwā'nōs ī-rās*). (1) Prov., Argentina, S. America; surface is treeless plain, crossed by many streams and dotted with lakes; chief industry, sheep and cattle raising; produces cereals, tobacco, fruits; exports butter, wool, wheat, jerked beef; cap. La Plata. Area, 117,777 sq. m. Pop. (not including town of Buenos Aires) 2,899,000. (2) Cap. and chief port of Argentina, and largest city in southern hemisphere, on r. bk. of La Plata R.; terminus of many rlys.; great manufacturing tn., and centre of inland trade; manufactures cloth, carpets, furniture, cigars, boots, shoes; city regularly laid out, with fine squares and parks. Pop. (est.) 2,030,700.

Buer (*boor*), tn., Westphalia, Prussia, 9 m. N. of Essen; coal mining. Pop. 99,000.

Buf'falo, city and port, New York state, U.S.A., at E. end of Lake Erie; terminus of Erie Canal, and a great trading and rly. centre; manufactures iron and steel, flour, grain, and meat products. Grain, flour, live-stock, coal, and lumber are chief articles of commerce. Industries include meat packing, oil refining, brewing, distilling, car and ship building, manufacture of leather, tobacco, clothing; has fine harbour; univ. Pop. 573,000.

Bug (*boog*). (1) Western or Polish Bug, trib. of R. Vistula, rises in E. Galicia, and enters R. Vistula 23 m. N.W. of Warsaw; 450 m.; navigable from Brest. (2) Southern or Black Sea Bug, rises in Volhynia and flows S.E. to Nikolaiev, where it forms an estuary joining the R. Dnieper; 450 m.; navigable from Nikolaiev to the sea (50 m.).

Builth (*bilth*), mkt. tn., Breconshire, Wales, on R. Wye; chalybeate and sulphur springs. Pop. 1,700.

Buitenzorg (*boi'ten-zorg*), tn., health resort, Batavia, Java; famous botanical gardens and institute. Pop. 46,000.

Bujalance (*boo-ha-lan'thā*), town, Spain, 24 m. E. of Cordova; centre of agricultural trade; tanneries, woollen goods. Pop. 11,000.

Bukhara (*booch-är'a*). (1) Part of Uzbek rep., U.S.S.R. Rivs. are Oxus, Zarafshan, Surkhab; soil barren, except where irrigated from rivs. W. is hot and dry, with flat surface, fertile through irrigation; produces pasture for stock; cotton, vines; middle is plateau, producing fruits and pistachios; E. is mountainous, valleys yielding cereals, mulberries; sheep, goats, camels, horses, asses raised; silkworms reared. Minerals include salt, sulphur, alum. Area, 83,000 sq. m. Pop. over 1,000,000. (2) Tn., cap. of above, on Transcaspian Rly.; textiles; chief commercial tn. of Central Asia. Pop. 71,000.

Bukovina (*boo-kō-vē'na*) ('beech land'), prov. of Romania; great part occupied by Carpathian Mts.; fertile, extensive forests; cattle, grain, wool, agricultural produce; cap. Cernauti. Area, 4,030 sq. m.; pop. 800,000.

Bulair', ISTHMUS OF, neck of land 5 m. wide between Gulf of Saros (Ægean Sea) and Sea of Marmara, connecting Gallipoli peninsula with mainland of Thrace.

Bulandshahr (*boo-lund-shär'*). (1) Dist., United Provinces, India; fertile plain; canal irrigation; wheat, maize, barley; cotton and sugar-cane. Area, 1,904 sq. m.; pop. 1,066,000. (2) Cap. of above, 40 m. S.E. of Delhi; artistic wood carving. Pop. 19,500.

Bulawayo (*boo-lă-wä'yō*) ('place of the killing'), largest town and most important commercial centre, Southern Rhodesia, S. Africa; gold mining; observatory. White pop. 7,650.

Buldä'na, dist., Berar, India; partly forested; wheat, cotton in fertile valleys; chief tn., Buldana, 190 m. W.S.W. of Nagpur. Area, 3,662 sq. m.; pop. 699,000.

Bul'ford, par. and vil., Wilts, England, on R. Avon, 2 m. N.E. of Amesbury; military camp. Pop. (par.) 3,800.

Bulga'ria, kingdom, Balkan Peninsula, S.E. Europe; bounded N. by R. Danube, E. by Black Sea, S. by Macedonia and Thrace, W. by Yugoslavia. Drained by R. Maritsa and affluents of R. Danube; crossed by Balkans and Rhodope Mts. In N. between Tirnova and Rustchuk are grass-covered plains. Country is almost entirely agricultural, about two-thirds of population engaged on land. Wheat, the principal product, is largely exported; wine, tobacco, silk also produced. Minerals include coal, lead, copper, zinc, aluminium. Chief manufactures are attar of roses (at Kazanlik), tobacco, flour; fisheries in Danube and Black Sea; exports, cereals, live-stock, attar of roses, rice, silk, wine, tobacco, eggs, skins; railway mileage, 1,651. Chief tns., Sofia (cap.), Philippopolis, Varna and Rustchuk (ports), Slivno. Area, 39,814 sq. m.; pop. 5,483,000.

Bul'li. (1) Coast tn., New South Wales, Australia, 40 m. S. of Sydney; coal-mining dist.; exports steam coal. Pop. 1,400. (2) Pass (1,000 ft.) in Illawarra Mts., leading inland from town.

Bun'bury, port, Wellington, W. Australia, 90 m. S. of Fremantle; outlet for timber, coal, wheat, fruit; holiday resort. Pop. 5,600.

Buncrä'na, mkt. tn. and wat.-pl., Tirconaill (Donegal), I.F.S., on Lough Swilly; agricultural centre; linen; salmon and sea fisheries. Pop. 2,300.

Bundaberg', port, Burnett R., Queensland, Australia, 52 m. N.W. of Maryborough; sugar factories, timber. Pop. 11,000.

Bundelkhand', Agency E. Central India, comprising over twenty Indian states; hilly, with level country in N.E.; has unexploited mineral wealth; generally level country. Area, 10,118 sq. m.; pop. 1,375,300.

Bundi (*boon'dē*). (1) Indian state, Rajputana, India, 100 m. S.E. of Ajmer; maize, wheat, opium; limestone for building. Area, 2,200 sq. m.; pop. 187,000. (2) Cap. of above. Pop. 19,300.

Bundo'ran, vil., wat.-pl., S.W. Tirconaill (Donegal), I.F.S., Ireland; bracing climate; barytes mines in vicinity; pop. 1,300.

Bungay, urb. dist., N.E. Suffolk, England; printing works. Pop. 3,100.

Bunzlau (*boonts'lou*), tn., Silesia, Prussia, 25 m. W. of Liegnitz; woollens, linens, brown stoneware pottery. Pop. 18,000.

Bur'dekin, riv., Queensland, Australia; Charters Towers on its banks; drains sugar-growing country.

Burdwan. (1) Dist., Bengal, India, along r. bk. of R. Hooghly; flat, well-watered plain; silk weaving; indigo; coalfields, ironworks. Area, 2,703 sq. m.; pop. 1,439,000. (2) Tn., cap. of above, 55 m. N.W. of Calcutta; palace of maharajah; tombs and temples. Pop. 35,000.

Burg (*boorg*), tn., Prussian Saxony, Germany, 14 m. N.E. of Magdeburg; cloth, boots; asphalt, starch. Pop. 24,300.

Burgas (*boor-gas'*), port, Bulgaria, on Black Sea; exports grain, wool, butter. Pop. 31,000.

Bur'gess Hill, urb. dist., E. Sussex, England, 9 m. N. of Brighton; brickyards; potteries. Pop. 6,000.

Burgos (*boor'gos*). (1) Prov., N. Spain; E., mountainous; W., part of old Castile tableland; well forested; poor soil; vines, merino sheep. Area, 5,480 sq. m.; pop. 342,000. (2) Tn., cap. of above prov., 80 m. S. of Santander; leather, cloth, hosiery. Pop. 33,000.

Bur'gundy, anc. prov. of E. France; historic cap., Dijon. Soil is fertile; famous for wines and agricultural produce.

Burhanpur (*boor-han-poor'*), tn., Central Provinces, India, on R. Tapti, on border of Bombay; cottons, silks, gold and silver thread. Pop. 36,000.

Buriat Mongol Republic (*boo'rē-at*), rep. of U.S.S.R., E. of L. Baikal, Asia; horses and cattle; rye, wheat, barley; iron, manganese. Chief tn., Verkhne-Udinsk. Area, 167,600 sq. m.; pop. 522,000.

Burley-in-Wharfdale, urb. dist., W. Riding, Yorks, England, 8 m. N. of Bradford; worsted manufacture. Pop. 4,000.

Bur'lington. (1) City, S.E. Iowa, U.S.A., on Mississippi R.; rly. centre; machinery, furniture. Pop. 27,000. (2) City and lake port, Vermont, U.S.A., on L. Champlain; lumber centre; packing boxes, refrigerators, spools and bobbins. Pop. 23,000. (3) City and river port, New Jersey, U.S.A., 18 m. N.E. of Philadelphia, on Delaware R.; iron pipes, typewriter ribbons, carbon paper. Pop. 13,000.

Bur'ma, large prov. in E. of Indian Empire, *c.* 1,200 m. in extreme length, *c.* 600 in breadth; bounded N. by China, E. by China, Fr. Indo-China, and Siam, S. by Bay of Bengal, W. by Bay of Bengal, Bengal, Manipur, Assam; includes Upper and Lower Burma. Surface is mountainous, with vast forests of teak and bamboo; river plains or deltas at river mouths are only flat parts, and are flooded in wet season; principal mts. are the Patkoi Hills in N., the Kachin, Shan, and Karen Hills in E., Pegu Yoma and Arakan Yoma; chief rivs., Irrawaddy, Sittang, Salween; climate trying; huge rainfall up country. Rice is largely cultivated in both Upper and Lower Burma, and is chief export. Teak, oil tree, ironwood, and palms are among valuable trees, and many fruits are grown, including bananas, pineapples, guavas. Tobacco, tea, cotton, sesamum, beans are cultivated; many varieties of precious stones found; rich ruby mines in upper district beyond Mandalay; sapphires and other gems, jade. Minerals include silver, zinc, copper, tin, petroleum. All these are exported, also rice, teak, bamboo, cotton, hides, wax, ivory, gum, rubber, oil. People display skill in silver repoussé work, wood carving, lacquer work, silk weaving; imports, European manufactured goods. Chief tns., Rangoon (cap.), Mandalay (native cap.). Area, 262,732 sq. m.; pop. 13,212,200.

Bur'nett, riv., Queensland, Australia, enters Pacific at Bundaberg.

Burn'ham, par. and vil., S.E. Bucks, England, 2½ m. E. of Maidenhead; agriculture; brickyards; Burnham Beeches, part of anc. forest, now open to public. Pop. (par.) 4,115.

Burn'ham-on-Crouch, wat.-pl., Essex, England, 11¾ m. S.E. of Maldon; boat building. Pop. 3,400.

Burn'ham-on-Sea, urb. dist., W. Somerset, England, on Bridgwater Bay; holiday resort; fishing. Pop. 5,100.

Burn'ley, mkt. tn., parl. and co. bor., E. Lancs, England, 29 m. N. of Manchester; extensive cotton weaving, ironfounding, loom making, and coal mining. Pop. 98,300.

Burntisland (*burnt-ī'land*), royal and munic. burgh, Fife, Scotland, on Firth of Forth; ferry port; coal exporting, shipbuilding. Pop. 5,400.

Burriana (*boor-re-ä'na*), port, Spain, 33 m. N. of Valencia; oranges, grain, wine, oil, melons. Pop. 14,000.

Burry Port, urb. dist., Carmarthen, Wales, on Burry Inlet; seapt.; copper works. Pop. 5,800.

Bursa. See BRUSA.

Burslem. See STOKE-UPON-TRENT.

Burton Latimer, urb. dist., Northants, England, 2½ m. S.E. of Kettering; iron ores. Pop. 3,600.

Bur'ton-upon-Trent, munic. and co. bor., Staffs, England, on R. Trent; Eng. metropolis of brewing; engineering, coopering. Pop. 49,500.

Buru (*boo'roo*), or BOEROE, isl., Moluccas, Dutch E. Indies; mountainous and well forested; vegetable oil. Area, 3,400 sq. m.; pop. *c.* 20,000.

Burujird (*boo-roo-jērd*), tn., Persia, 70 m. S.S.E. of Hamadan; cottons and carpets. Pop. 22,000.

Bury (*ber'i*), mkt. tn. and co. bor., Lancs, England, on R. Irwell; cotton spinning and weaving, also bleaching, dyeing, and print works; machinery. Pop. 56,200.

Bury St. Ed'munds, mkt. tn., w. Suffolk, England; agricultural implements; cattle and corn markets. Edmund, King of E. Anglia, martyred here, 870. Pop. 16,700.

Bush'ey, urb. dist., s.w. Herts, England, 1¾ m. s.e. of Watford; Herkomer Art School. Pop. 11,200.

Bushire (*boo-shēr'*), port, Persia, on Persian Gulf; on sandy peninsula; exports opium, carpets, dates, hides; iron. Pop. 20,000.

Bussorah. See Basra.

Bute (*būt*). (1) Isl., Firth of Clyde, Scotland; separated from Argyllshire by Kyles of Bute; coast rocky, numerous bays; undulating interior; several small lochs; popular holiday resort; excellent crops; cattle and sheep; fisheries; quarries; chief tn., Rothesay. Area, 49 sq. m.; pop. 19,000. (2) Co., Scotland, comprising islands of Bute, Arran, and Cumbraes. Capital, Rothesay. Area, 220 sq. m.; pop. 18,800.

But'ler, tn., Pennsylvania, U.S.A., 28 m. n. of Pittsburgh; oil and natural gas; glass, steel, motor tyres. Pop. 27,000.

Butte (*būt*), tn., Montana, U.S.A., 50 m. s.w. of Helena; mining centre; copper, lead, gold, silver. Pop. 40,000.

Bux'ton, tn., Peak dist., Derbyshire, England; near head of Wye valley; celebrated mineral springs and natural hot baths. Pop. 15,400.

Buzau (*boo-tsou'*), tn., Romania, on r. bk. of R. Buzau, 60 m. n.e. of Bucharest; important rly. centre and market for grain, timber, and petroleum. Pop. 32,000.

Bydgoszcz (*bid'goshch*), or Bromberg, tn., Poland, 65 m. n.e. of Poznan; agricultural centre, timber. Pop. 88,000.

By'fleet, par. and vil., n.w. Surrey, England, 2¼ m. s. of Weybridge; brewing. Pop. (par.) 4,170.

By'ker, eccles. par., Northumberland, England; in co. bor. of Newcastle; lead, chemicals, glass, pottery. Pop. 60,000.

C

Cab'ra, tn., Spain, 30 m. s.e. of Cordoba; manufactures bricks and pottery. Pop. 15,000.

Cabre'ra, one of Balearic Islands in Mediterranean Sea. Area, 8 sq. m.

Caccamo (*kä-chä'mo*), tn., Sicily, 22 m. s.e. of Palermo; commands fine view; agate, beryl, jasper. Pop. 12,000.

Caceres (*ka-thā'-rāz*). (1) Prov., w. Spain, intersected by R. Tagus. Products: n., cereals, fruit, olive oil; s., pigs, sheep; most backward prov. of Spain. Area, 7,667 sq. m.; pop. 410,000. (2) Cap. of above. Pop. 24,000.

Cachar (*kat-shar'*), dist., Surma valley, Assam, India, between Sylhet on e. and Manipur on w.; rich vegetation. Products: tea, rice, petroleum. Area, 3,654 sq. m.; pop. 527,000.

Cad'der, par. and vil., Lanarkshire, Scotland, on Forth and Clyde Canal; scene of Wallace's betrayal (1305). Pop. (par.) 15,800.

Cadenab'bia, vil., health resort, on w. shore of Lake Como; contains Villa Carlotta (1747), with sculptures by Thorwaldsen and Canova.

Cader Idris ('the chair of Idris'), mt. peak, Merionethshire, Wales, 4 m. s.w. of Dolgelly; precipices, fine views. Alt. 2,929 ft.

Cadiz (*ka-thēth'*; Eng. *kā'dis*). (1) Prov., s. Spain, bordering on Atlantic and Strait of Gibraltar; mountainous; well watered; one of richest and busiest parts of country; supplies the world with sherry. Area, 2,834 sq. m.; pop. (est.) 548,000. (2) Cap. of above, on peninsula, 95 m. by rail s.s.w. of Seville; suffers from defective communication with mainland; exports valued at over £1,000,000 annually; wine, salt, corks, tunny fish, olives, and olive oil; graving dock; naval station; varied manufactures. Pop. 76,800.

Cad'oxton, par. and tn., Glamorganshire, Wales, 7 m. s.w. of Cardiff; coal mines and tinplate works. Pop. 19,300.

Caen (*kon*), chief tn., Calvados, France, on R. Orne; anc. cap. of Lower Normandy; univ. founded by Henry VI. of England; castle and church founded by William the Conqueror; lace, leather, gloves, timber, chemicals. Pop. 46,800.

Caerle'on, vil., Monmouthshire, England, on R. Usk, 3 m. N.E. of Newport; many Roman remains; associated in legend with King Arthur. Pop. 2,300.

Caerphil'ly, mkt. tn., Glamorganshire, Wales, 7 m. N.W. of Cardiff; collieries; noted for its cheese; ruins of fine castle with leaning tower. Pop. 35,800.

Cagayan'. (1) Prov., N.E. Luzon, Philippines; very fertile, heavily wooded; tobacco. Area, 5,291 sq. m.; pop. 155,000. (2) Cap., Misamis prov., N.W. Mindanao I., Philippines, on riv. near coast; gold. Pop. 7,000.

Cagliari (*kal-yä're*). (1) Prov., Italy, covering S. half of the island of Sardinia; zinc and lead mining (Iglesias dist.). Area, 5,184 sq. m. (2) Cap. of above prov. and of Sardinia, on S. coast of isl.; good harbour; exports lead, zinc, and salt; wine in vicinity. Pop. 57,200.

Caher (*kär*), or CAHIR, tn., Tipperary, I.F.S., on R. Suir; agricultural prod.; remains of monastery; stalactite caverns in neighbourhood. Pop. 1,700.

Cahors (*kä-or'*), tn., cap., dep. Lot, France, on R. Lot, trib. of R. Garonne; on rocky peninsula; riv. here crossed by finest mediæval fortified bridge in France; prod. wine, nuts, truffles. Pop. 10,200.

Caicos (*kī'kos*) **and Turks Islands,** group S. of Bahamas, Brit. W. Indies; under government of Jamaica; thirty small islands; eight inhabited; salt, sisal fibre, sponges, and turtle-shell; climate hot but healthy. Area, 165 sq. m.; pop. 5,600.

Caiman. See CAYMAN.

Cains'cross, par., Glos, England, 1 m. W. of Stroud; makes clothing. Pop. 2,400.

Cairns, seapt., Trinity Bay, N.E. coast of Queensland, Australia; excellent harbour; outlet for mineral fields of Chillagoe and Herberton; prod. sugar, tropical fruits, beef. Pop 9,000.

Cairo. (1) (*kī'ro*) Cap., Egypt, on R. Nile, 12 m. from apex of delta; joined by rail with Port Said (147 m.) and with Alexandria (130 m.); contains 260 mosques; magnificent mausoleums and tombs; univ. El-Azhar, chief univ. of Mohammedan world; many fine public buildings; native city fast disappearing to make way for hotels, offices, and shops; three railway stations, and three bridges across Nile; electric trams and lighting; suburbs contain large and increasing European pop. Inhabitants include Turks, Berbers, Copts, Arabs, Abyssinians, Jews, and Nubians; manufactures cotton, paper, silk goods, leather. Pop. 1,065,000. (2) (*kā'ro*) City, Illinois, U.S.A., at confluence of Mississippi and Ohio; much riv. commerce; manufactures lumber products, leather goods. Pop. 14,000.

Caist'er-on-Sea, vil., Norfolk, England, 3 m. N. of Yarmouth; holiday resort; ruins of 15th cent. castle; wireless station. Pop. 2,150.

Caith'ness, co., N.E. extremity of Scotland, bounded E. and S.E. by North Sea, W. by Sutherland, and on N. by Atlantic; mostly barren and treeless moors; mountainous in S. (Morven, 2,313 ft.; Scaraben, 2,054 ft.); watered by Wick, Forss, and Thurso rivs.; many lochs; precipitous coast with 'stacks'; climate wet and windy; oats, barley, turnips, potatoes; breeding of high-class pedigree horses and cattle; tweeds, ropes, agricultural implements, whisky, flagstone pavements; fisheries. Chief towns, Wick and Thurso. Area, 687 sq. m.; pop. 25,700.

Cajamarca (*kä-ha-mar'ka*), city, cap. of prov., N. Peru; woollens and cottons; silver mining and cattle raising. Pop. (city) 12,000.

Calabar', dist., Guinea Coast, W. Africa, now part of Nigeria, extending on E. to borders of Cameroons; includes ports of Calabar, formerly Old Calabar (with native quarter, Duke Town), on Cross R., and New Calabar, *c.* 100 m. to W., on New Calabar R.; exp. palm oil, kernels, ivory, rubber; missionary station. Pop. (Calabar tn.) *c.* 50,000.

Cala'bria, terr. div., S. Italy, peninsula between Gulf of Taranto and Tyrrhenian Sea; covered by extensions of Apennines; heavily forested in centre; fertile valleys and plains yielding grain, rice, fruits, flax; minerals include marble, salt, copper, gypsum; tunny and anchovy fisheries; volcanic; suffered from disastrous earthquakes in 1783, 1905, 1907, and 1908. Largest tn., Reggio di Calabria. Area, 5,819 sq. m.; pop. 1,500,000.

Calahor'ra, city and episc. see, Logrono, Old Castile, 70 m. N.W. of Saragossa; birthplace Quintilian; cathedral great place of pilgrimage; dist. fertile; fruit, vegetables, and wine. Pop. 10,700.

Calais (*kal'i*), tn., Pas-de-Calais, France, 21 m. E.S.E. of Dover; chief port for passenger traffic between England and the Continent; harbour accessible to vessels of largest size; old town on island hemmed in by canal and harbour basins, which cut it off from manufacturing quarter of St. Pierre de Calais; chief manufacture is lace; fishing centre. Pop. 60,900.

Calarasi (*ka-la-rä'shi*), tn. and riv. port, Jalomitsa, Romania, on l. bk. of Borcea arm of Danube, opposite Silistria; in fenlands on railway between Bucharest and Constanta; wheat, linseed, hemp, timber. Pop. *c.* 13,000.

Calatayud' ('castle of Ayub,' its Moorish founder), city, Spain, 46 m. S.W. of Saragossa, on main railway to Madrid; lower and upper (Moorish) towns; interesting churches; castle on rocky eminence; birthplace of Martial; dist. fertile. Pop. 12,000.

Calbä'yog, tn., Samar I., E. Philippines; has steamboat connection with Manila; hemp and extensive fishing, Pop. 25,300.

Calbe. See KALBE.

Calcut'ta, cap., Bengal, largest city of India, on l. bk. of Hugli, 85 m. from sea. To S.W. of city proper is Fort William; site of original fort occupied by post office; between the Hugli and Chauringhi Road is the Maidan, a large open space with racecourse, Eden gardens, cricket grounds, and numerous statues of Anglo-Indian notabilities. East of the Maidan is the European quarter. Many important buildings, including Government House, St. Paul's Cathedral, the Victoria Memorial, town hall, Dalhousie Institute, and Bengal Secretariat and University. Near post office is site of Black Hole of Calcutta. To N. extends native city, with narrow, crowded streets. City linked with industrial suburb of Howrah by swing bridges. On r. bk. of river are famous botanical gardens. Calcutta monopolizes export trade of Ganges and Brahmaputra valley, and is the great distributing centre for imports. Exp. jute, tea, hides, skins, oil-seeds, grains and pulses, raw cotton, lac, coal, raw silk, saltpetre, and oils. Docks extend ten miles. Industries may be gauged from exports. Monsoon climate; temp. of hot weather averages 85° F. Average rainfall of 60 in. falls in 118 days. Bulk of inhabitants Hindus, but large numbers of Mohammedans. Pop., with suburbs, 1,327,000. Cap. of India down to 1912, when superseded by Delhi.

Calder (*kawl'der*). (1) EAST, vil., Midlothian, Scotland, 11 m. S.W. of Edinburgh; shale mines and oilworks. Pop. of par. of Kirknewton and East Calder, 3,000. (2) MID, 12 m. S.W. of

Edinburgh, in midst of rich shale oil-field. Pop. 3,200. (3) WEST, 16 m. W.S.W. of Edinburgh; has grown with development of oil shale and coal seams. Pop. 7,800.

Cal'edon. (1) Dist. and tn., s.w. Cape Province, S. Africa; rising health resort. Chief prod. of dist., wool and grain. Pop. (tn.) *c.* 2,500. (2) Trib. of Orange R., forming the boundary between Basutoland and Orange Free State.

Caledo'nia, Roman name for that part of Scotland to the N. of the Roman wall between the Firths of Forth and Clyde. The conventional poetic name for Scotland.

Caledonian Canal, waterway, in counties Inverness and Argyll, joining Lochs Dochfour, Ness, Oich, Lochy, and connecting North Sea with Atlantic Ocean; 60½ m.; used by fishing fleets; favourite tourist route.

Cal'gary, chief city of s. Alberta, Canada, on Bow and Elbow rivers, and on C.P.R.; alt. 3,380 ft.; commercial and industrial centre of a large dist.; irrigation necessary; progressive and rapidly growing town; station of Royal Canadian Mounted Police, and of Hudson's Bay Co.; rly. workshops, lumber mills, tanneries. Pop. 65,300.

Cali (*ka-lē'*), tn., Colombia, S. America, on R. Cauca, *c.* 200 m. s.w. of Bogota; copper and coal mines in neighbourhood, and iron smelted; quinine and much agriculture. Pop. *c.* 45,000.

Calibo (*ka-lē'vō*), tn., Panay I., Philippines, 25 m. W. by N. of Capiz; cotton and abaca fabrics. Pop. 15,000.

Cal'icut, seapt. tn., w. Madras, Brit. India; gave its name to calico; chief exports, coffee, spices, and timber. Pop. 82,400.

Califor'nia, state, U.S.A., on Pacific coast; bounded N. by Oregon, E. by Nevada, Arizona, s. by Mexico, and W. by Pacific. Surface generally consists of two great mountain systems, the Sierra Nevada in the E. and the Coast Range along the coast, running lengthwise through state, with broad valley between them. In s. the Tehachapi range unites the two great systems. The central valley, remarkable for beauty, and called the Great Valley of California, is over 500 m. long and from 40 to 60 m. wide. It is drained by the Sacramento and the San Joaquin, which flow respectively through the N. and S., and, uniting, enter Suisun Bay to N. of San Francisco. The famous Yosemite Valley breaks through the E. branch of the Sierra Nevada. In the s. are depressed desert regions. Climate generally resembles that of the Mediterranean; rainfall decreases from N. to S. Gold, quicksilver, lead, silver, copper, iron, antimony, chromium are found in considerable quantities; petroleum abounds, but there is little coal. Agricultural wealth is remarkable, though in places irrigation is necessary; wheat and barley extensively cultivated; grapes, oranges, lemons, olives, citrons, peaches, pears, cherries, apricots, and other fruits largely produced; sugar-beet, cotton, tobacco, hops also cultivated. There are immense forests, with fir, cedar, pine, and other trees; and lumbering is an important industry. Sheep and cattle raised; silk produced; fisheries important. Industries include canning of fruits and vegetables, meat packing, flour milling, brewing, dairying, distilling, shipbuilding, tanning; exports, fresh, dried, and canned fruit, cereals, timber, wool, sugar, mineral products, petroleum, tobacco. California is connected with eastern states by four railways. Chief towns are San Francisco, Los Angeles, Oakland, Sacramento (cap.), San Diego, Pasadena, San José, Alameda. Area, 158,297 sq. m. (2,645 sq. m. being water); pop. 3,427,000.

California, LOWER, peninsula, a terr. of Mexico, between Gulf of California and Pacific Ocean; mountainous; water and vegetation scarce, but valleys produce cotton, maize, and wheat; horses and cattle reared; gold and silver mining and pearl-oyster fishing. Chief town, La Paz. Area, 55,654 sq. m.; pop. 62,900.

Cal'lander, mkt. tn., Perthshire, Scotland, on both banks of the Teith; centre for Trossachs and a residential town. Pop. 1,600.

Callao (*kalyä'ō*), chief port, Peru, S. America, 7 m. w. of Lima; docks and floating dock; starting-point for Oroya Rly.; exports sugar, cotton, wool, hides, copper, silver. Pop. 35,000.

Cal'lernish, vil. and dist., Uig, Lewis, Scotland; fine Druidical remains.

Calne (*kän*), munic. bor. and mkt. tn., Wiltshire, England, 6 m. E.S.E. of Chippenham; residence of W. Saxon monarchy, 10th cent.; bacon-curing industry. Pop. 3,500.

Cal'shot, seaplane station, Hants, England, on projecting tongue of land at w. of entrance to Southampton Water, 7 m. S.S.E. of Southampton.

Caltagirone (*kal-ta-jir-ō'nä*), tn., episc. see, Catania, Sicily; built on two hills (2,015 ft.) linked by bridge; pottery and artistic statuettes. Pop. 30,800.

Caltanissetta (*kal-ta-nē-sä'ta*). (1) Prov., Italy, in middle of Sicily; sulphur mines from which 500,000 tons exported annually; cereals, wine, olives. Area, 814 sq. m.; pop. 247,400. (2) Episc. see and cap. of above; centre of Sicilian sulphur industry; technical and mining school. Pop. 46,400.

Caluire et Cuire (*kal-wēr ā kwēr*), tn., Rhône, France, on Saône; copper and bronze foundries. Pop. 12,600.

Calumpit (*ka-loom-pēt'*), tn., Bulacan, Luzon, Philippines; in fertile region producing rice and sugar. Pop. 14,800.

Calvados', dep. of Normandy, France, between estuary of Seine on E. and Cotentin on w.; is famous for its pastures; cattle, sheep, and horses; large export trade in dairy produce and cider; fisheries; textiles; seaside resorts. Cap. Caen. Area, 2,197 sq. m.; pop. 390,500.

Calverley (*kä'verli* or *kauv'li*), urb. dist., W. Riding, Yorks, England, 4 m. N.E. of Bradford; woollen manufacture. Pop. 3,700.

Cal'vi, fortified tn. and harbour, N.W. coast of Corsica, France; nearest port of isl. to France (109 m. from Antibes); fishing. Pop. 2,500.

Cam, riv., Cambridgeshire, England, formerly known as Granta, rises near Ashwell (Herts), passes Cambridge, and joins Great Ouse (3½ m. s. of Ely). Length, 40 m.

Camagüey (*kä-mä'gwā*), or PUERTO PRINCIPE. (1) Prov. of Cuba; chief industries, cattle raising and sugar planting. Area, 10,064 sq. m.; pop. 258,700. (2) Cap. of above. Pop. 46,600.

Camargue, LA (*ka-marg'*), isl., France, Rhone delta; marshy, alluvial plains; cereals; vineyards; cattle and sheep rearing; reclamation proceeding.

Cambay'. (1) GULF OF, between peninsula of Kathiawar and mainland of Bombay; very high and swift tides; depth decreasing. (2) Indian state, Bombay, India, at head of Gulf of Cambay. Area, 350 sq. m.; pop. 71,800. (3) Port and chief town of above, on Gulf of Cambay; declined since silting up of gulf; agate and cornelian ornaments. Pop. 27,300.

Cam'berley, dist., Surrey, England, 2½ m. s.w. of Bagshot; part of urb. dist. of Frimley and Camberley; military college. Pop. of urb. dist. 16,500.

Cam'berwell, metropolitan and parl. bor., S.E. London; chiefly residential; includes Dulwich; S. London Fine Art Gallery; large parks. Pop. 251,400.

Cambo'dia, kingdom and Fr. protectorate, Indo-China, Asia, bounded N. by Laos and Siam, w. by Siam, E. by Annam, s. by Cochin-China and Gulf of Siam. Mainly alluvial plain of Lower Mekong and upper part of delta of that river; Tonle-sap ('great lake') is regulator for Mekong; has important fisheries. Beyond plain, country traversed by outlying ranges of Pnom-Dongrek; coast low with fringe of islands. Monsoon climate; in dry season temp. averages 77° to 80° F.; soil remarkably fertile; chief prod., rice, coffee, sugar-cane, pepper, cinnamon, tobacco, indigo, and sugar; cotton industry growing. Iron is only mineral worked. Staple industry fishing. Ruled by native king under Fr. protection. Cap. Pnom Penh. Area, 67,550 sq. m.; pop. 2,535,200.

Cam'borne, mkt. tn., Cornwall, England, 3 m. s.w. of Redruth; tin and copper mines. Pop. 14,200.

Cambrai', tn., Nord, France, on R. Schelde; important junction on main line of Northern Rly.; linen fabrics (cambrics), also copper working, brewing, distilling, tanning, and soap; seat of archbishop. Pop. 24,800.

Cam'bria, Lat. name for Wales, derived from the Celtic Cymru; originally applied to both Wales and Cymric kingdom of Strathclyde; now restricted to the principality.

Cām'bridge. (1) Munic. and parl. bor., Cambridgeshire, England, on R. Cam. Famous as univ. town. Cambridge Univ. became important early in 13th cent.; obtained papal recognition in 1231. Comprises 17 colleges; in addition there are two women's colleges, Girton and Newnham. Pop. 66,800. (2) City, Massachusetts, U.S.A., opposite Boston; seat of Harvard Univ. (1636), Harvard Observatory, Radcliffe Coll., and Prot. Episc. Divinity School; also important industrial interests. Pop. 114,000. (3) Tn., Maryland, U.S.A., on E. shore of Chesapeake Bay; oyster and herring fisheries. Pop. 7,500. (4) Tn., Ohio, U.S.A., 76 m. E. of Columbus; manufactures pottery and glass. Pop. 13,100.

Cam'bridgeshire, inland co., England, bounded N. by Lincoln, E. by Norfolk and Suffolk, S. by Essex and Hertford, and W. by Bedford, Huntingdon, and Northampton. For administrative purposes the northern part forms a separate county, known as the Isle of Ely. Surface is generally flat, except in S.; fen country in N. Chief rivers are Ouse, Cam, Nen, and Lark; intersected by canals. Chiefly an agricultural co., producing wheat, oats, barley, and potatoes; dairy farming is carried on in S.E. Chief tns., Cambridge (cap.), Newmarket, Wisbech, and Ely. Area, 864 sq. m.; pop. 217,700.

Cambuslang', tn. and par., l. bk. Clyde; residential suburb of Glasgow; contains one of largest steel works in kingdom; coal mining. Pop. (par.) 26,100.

Cambusneth'an, par. and vil., Mid-Lanarkshire, Scotland, 1½ m. N.E. of Wishaw; coal and iron; birthplace of Lockhart, Scott's biographer. Pop. (par.) 36,700.

Cam'den, city, New Jersey, U.S.A., on l. bk. of Delaware, opposite Philadelphia; large commercial and manufacturing centre; iron foundries, chemical and glass works, etc.; shipbuilding. Pop. 117,000.

Camerino (*ka-mā-rē'nō*), tn., episc. see, Italy, 40 m. s.w. of Ancona; seat of 'free' univ. (founded 1727) with 500 students. Pop. 12,000.

Cameroons', former German colony Kamerun, W. Africa, bounded W. by Atlantic, N.W. by Nigeria, N. by L. Chad, E. by Fr. Equatorial Africa. Surface generally is plateau with low-lying coastal strip; highest towards W. Mt. Cameroon is an isolated volcanic mass. Area is drained by Sanaga and other rivs. to sea, by Shari to L. Chad, by Sanga to Congo. Coffee, cocoa, tobacco, rice, manioc, yams, and cotton are grown; rubber, palm kernels and oil, ivory, cocoa, copra, and kola nuts are exported; gold and iron are found. From 1884 to 1919 it was a German Protectorate; now divided by mandate of the League of Nations between France and Britain; the share of the latter, British Cameroons, forms part of Nigeria. Area, *c.* 34,236 sq. m.; pop. 687,000. Chief tns., Victoria and Buea. French Cameroons, included in French Equatorial Africa. Area, 166,489 sq. m.; pop. 1,878,000. Chief tns., Duala and Yaunde.

Campagna di Roma (*kam-pan'ya*), marshy plain surrounding Rome; length *c.* 90 m., breadth 25 to 40 m.; almost entirely volcanic; traversed by Tiber; barely one-tenth cultivated because of malaria; used for winter pasturage of sheep; drainage and reclamation, planting of eucalyptus, extinction of mosquito pest, are in progress.

Campa'nia, territorial div. of Italy (comprising provinces of Avellino, Benevento, Naples, and Salerno); dense agricultural pop.; portion drained by R. Volturno richly fertile; Falernian wines; sulphur. Area, 5,276 sq. m.; pop. 3,254,000.

Cam'pbellton, tn., New Brunswick, Canada, on shore of upper Chaleur Bay; lumbering, fishing, paper-making. Pop. 6,500.

Campbeltown (*kam'bel-ton*), tn., port, royal burgh, Argyllshire, Scotland, in S. Kintyre; shipbuilding; whisky distilling; fisheries. Pop. 6,300.

Campeche (*kam-pĕ'che*), or CAMPEACHY. (1) State, Yucatan, Mexico, consists of 18,089 sq. m. of low, unhealthy land, producing rice, cotton, tobacco, and logwood (campeachy wood). Pop. 76,400. (2) Tn., seapt., and cap. of above, with harbour not suited to large vessels; exports logwood, hemp, cordage, wax, hides, cocoa, and salt; cigars. Pop. 16,900. (3) BAY OF, S.E. part of Gulf of Mexico to the W. of Yucatan peninsula.

Cam'perdown, stretch of dunes in N. Holland, *c.* 25 m. N. of Haarlem, off which Admiral Duncan won victory over the Dutch under de Winter (Oct. 1799).

Campobas'so. (1) Prov., central Italy, forming part of Abruzzi and Molise; sheep and cattle rearing; wheat, maize, wine, olives, hemp; cutlery, paper, hats, and silk. Area, 1,783 sq. m.; pop. 355,300. (2) Cap. of above; cutlery; museum with Samnite weapons. Pop. 16,300.

Campobel'lo. (1) Tn., Girgenti, Sicily; has sulphur mines. Pop. 12,000. (2) Tn., Trapani, Sicily; huge stone quarries. Pop. 10,000. (3) Island, Bay of Fundy, New Brunswick, at the entrance to Passamaquoddy Bay; 8 m. long; summer resort. Pop. *c.* 1,200.

Campos (*kam'poosh*). (1) Tn., state of Rio de Janeiro, Brazil, connected with Rio de Janeiro by the Leopoldina Railway; well laid out; exports sugar and coffee. Pop. *c.* 48,000.

Campulung', cap., dep. Muscel, Romania, at foot of outlying Carpathian hills, 80 m. N.W. of Bucharest; summer resort; first cap. of Wallachia. Pop. 18,500.

Ca'naan ('low lands'), name applied first to coast regions of Palestine and dist. drained by R. Jordan; later given to whole of Palestine W. of Jordan.

Can'ada, British overseas Dominion, covering all northern half of North America except Alaska and Newfoundland; includes Arctic archipelago in N. and N.E., stretching towards Pole; bounded N. by Arctic Ocean, E. by Atlantic and Newfoundland, S. by U.S., W. by Alaska and Pacific Ocean.

The E. coast is broken up by Hudson Strait and Bay, James Bay, Gulf of St. Lawrence, Bay of Fundy; importance of first three as harbours lessened by ice in winter, of last by height of tides and strength of tidal currents; W. coast much broken, fringed with islands, providing good, well-sheltered harbours; N. coast commercially useless on account of latitude; S.E. is cut up by chain of great lakes—greatest fresh-water area in world; largest are Lakes Superior and Huron.

Along E. coast, in Labrador, Cape Breton I., and Nova Scotia, are low hills, while S.E. of St. Lawrence basin is bounded by northern extension of Appalachians, with height of *c.* 4,000 ft. Along N.W. of St. Lawrence basin, of Great Lakes, and of their northern feeders, stretch Laurentian Plateau and Laurentian Range, with heights of from 1,000 to 3,000 ft. From N.N.W. to S.S.E., towards Pacific coast, run Rocky Mountains and parallel Selkirk and Cascade Ranges, with great intervening valleys and with average height of *c.* 8,000 ft.; highest peaks, Mts. St. Elias (18,000 ft.), Logan (19,850 ft.), Robson (13,000 ft.). Between Laurentian Range, N. of Lake

Superior, and foothills of Rockies, is enormous stretch of fertile prairie land, important for wheat growing and stock rearing; districts E. and W. of this are in many parts densely wooded. The N. is partly plateau, partly plain, valuable for minerals and fur-bearing animals. The great northern and north-eastern stretch drained by Upper Yukon, Mackenzie, Athabasca, Peace, Coppermine, Great Fish or Back's rivs., flowing to Arctic; Churchill, Nelson, Albany, entering Hudson Bay; E., S., and centre drained by St. Lawrence and its tributaries (Ottawa, etc.), Red R., Assiniboine, Saskatchewan; S.W. by Fraser and upper waters of the Columbia. Climate varies greatly; is generally one of extremes. Temp. in centre ranges from 44° to 88° F.; rainfall sufficient practically everywhere. Extreme length *c.* 2,100 m., width 3,600 m.

There are many sources of wealth. Central district is one of the great wheat areas of the world. Cattle rearing, fruit growing, dairying, are important industries; has great quantities of timber; extensive fisheries—lobster, salmon, cod, halibut; mineral deposits are valuable, including gold, coal, copper, nickel, silver, petroleum, asbestos, lead, zinc, iron. Exports include lumber, cheese, cattle, wheat, flour, bacon, fish, apples, skins, furs, sheep, butter, eggs, beef, paper, wood pulp, leather. Railway mileage in 1927 was 40,572, and is rapidly extending; Canadian Pacific Rly., running from Halifax to Vancouver, not counting innumerable branches, has a length of 2,885 m.; the Canadian National Rlys., formed by amalgamation of several companies, include two other transcontinental lines from the Atlantic ports in the E. to Vancouver and Prince Rupert in the W. Besides navigable rivers and great lakes, there is fine system of canals; shipping is of great importance.

The Dominion was formed by confederation between 1867 and 1873 of all the Brit. N. Amer. colonial possessions except Newfoundland and coast strip of Labrador between Hudson Strait and Gulf of St. Lawrence forming part of that colony. There are now nine provinces (Nova Scotia, New Brunswick, Prince Edward I., Quebec, Ontario, Manitoba, Saskatchewan, Alberta, and Brit. Columbia) and the Terr. of Yukon and N.W. Territories (Franklin, Keewatin, and Mackenzie). There are 22 universities. Inhabitants include Brit., Fr., and other European nationalities, Indians, and Chinese. Cap. Ottawa; largest tn., Montreal. Area, 3,684,723; pop. 9,934,000.

Cana'dian River, rises near Raton in New Mexico, U.S.A., and flows through Texas and Oklahoma; joins Arkansas R. at Tamaha. Length, 900 m.

Canal Zone, strip of land, 47 m. long by 10 m. wide, extending 5 m. on either side of the Panama Canal from the Atlantic to the Pacific Ocean; bought from Panama (1904) by U.S. for £2,000,000 and annual rental of £50,000. By Panama Act government of the zone vested in several departments all under direction of a governor (first governor, Col. G. W. Goethals, builder of the canal). U.S. have drained swamps, dealt with sewage, and effectively screened all government buildings from mosquitoes, and by so doing have so greatly reduced malaria and other diseases that health rate of zone compares favourably with that of U.S.

Cañar (*kan-yar*), prov., tableland of Ecuador, S. America; agriculture and manufacture of Panama hats; numerous Inca remains. Area, 1,520 sq. m.; pop. 74,000.

Cana'ry Islands, group of volcanic islands belonging to Spain, off N.W. coast of Africa, 62 m. from mainland. There are seven large islands, La Palma, Hierro, Gomera, Teneriffe, Grand Canary, Fuerteventura, Lanzarote. Climate is delightful; lowest temperature 48°, highest 95° F.; rainfall moderate; favourite place of residence for invalids. Islands produce onions, fruits (bananas, etc.), cochineal, wine, tobacco, vegetables; all exported. Imports include cottons, woollens, coal, flour, machinery, timber, hardware, etc. Great conical peak of Teneriffe (12,198 ft.) is visible 140 m. off. Chief town is Las Palmas, Grand Canary. Area, 2,807 sq. m.; pop. *c.* 530,000.

Canberra (*kan'ber-a*), cap. in course of construction for Commonwealth of Australia, on branch of Murrumbidgee R., 150 m. s.w. from Sydney and 75 m. from coast; operations begun 1913; foundation stone laid by Prince of Wales in course of Australian tour (1920). First session in new Parliament House held at Canberra May 9, 1927, which became from that date seat of Australian government. Area, 940 sq. m., including 28 sq. m. at Jervis Bay, its port.

Can'dia, largest town of Crete, on small artificial harbour (much silted); trades in island produce, chiefly olive oil and raisins; ruins of Cnossus 3 m. distant. Pop. 25,000 (Greek, with a few Moslems, Jews, etc.). See CRETE.

Can'don, tn., S. Ilocos, Luzon, Philippines; second largest town in prov.; large trade in indigo, rice, and tobacco; cotton, silk, and woollen goods. Pop. 20,000.

Candy. See KANDY.

Canea (*ka-nē'a*), cap. of Crete, on N. coast; cramped by Venetian walls; European quarter 1 m. E.; small artificial harbour (much silted); prod. soap and oil. Pop. 27,600.

Cangas de Tineo (*kang'-gas dā tē-nā'o*), tn., N. Spain, 38 m. s.w. of Oviedo; woollen and linen industries; leather and pottery. Pop. 23,000.

Canicatti (*ka-nē-kat'ē*), tn., Girgenti, Sicily, 15 m. N.E. of Girgenti; sulphur mines. Pop. 25,000.

Cannanore', or KANANUR, seapt., N.W. Madras, India; exports grain, timber, and coconuts. Pop. 27,700.

Cannes (*kan*), health resort, Alpes-Maritimes, Riviera, France, 20 m. s.w. of Nice; sheltered and equable climate; popularized by Lord Brougham, who settled here (1836); many Brit. visitors; perfume distilling. Pop. 36,800.

Can'nock, urb. dist., Staffordshire, England; tile making, edge tools, coal mining. Pop. 34,600. *Cannock Chase*, between Lichfield and Stafford, formerly wooded dist. devoted to hunting; now a heath, with coal measures and ironstone below the coal.

Cannstatt (*kän-shtät'*), or KANNSTATT, tn., Würtemberg, Germany, on Neckar, near Stuttgart; hot saline springs; railway plant; electrical machinery; chemicals. Pop. *c.* 27,000.

Can'onbie, vil., Dumfriesshire, Scotland, on R. Esk, 6 m. S.E. of Langholm; coal mines; quarries; remains of priory. Pop. 1,840.

Cañon City (*kan'-yon*), tn., Colorado, U.S.A., at mouth of Grand Cañon of the Arkansas; copper, petroleum, iron, limestone, coal; large zinc-lead smelting works; hot mineral springs and mild climate make it a health resort. Pop. 6,000.

Can'so, STRAIT OF, strait between Nova Scotia and Cape Breton I., connects Chedabucto Bay with Gulf of St. Lawrence (17 m. long, average breadth 2½ m.); only used by coasting vessels.

Canta'brian Mountains, range to the w. of the Pyrenees, extending over 300 m. across the N. of Spain; its highest peak is Peña Vieja (8,743 ft.); richest coal supplies of Spain; crossed by three railways.

Cantagal'lo, tn., Rio de Janeiro, Brazil, 100 m. N.E. of Rio de Janeiro; staple products are coffee and sugar. Pop. 30,000.

Cantal (*kan-tal'*), dep., Central France, s. portion of Auvergne, derives name from huge volcanic mass occupying centre (Plomb du Cantal, 6,100 ft.); rivers Dordogne and Truyère flow from this N. and w.; prod. rye, buckwheat, potatoes and chestnuts, butter and Roquefort cheese. Natural beauties and mineral springs attract many tourists. Coal, antimony, and marble are found. Cap.

Aurillac, 270 m. s. of Paris. Area, 2,229 sq. m.; pop. 197,000.

Can'terbury. (1) City, Kent, eccles. metropolis of England, a dignity which it has enjoyed since St. Augustine first settled there (597); on riv. Stour; cathedral on site of anc. monastery, completed about 1495; magnificent doubly cruciform edifice, fine examples of Norman and later styles; outstanding historical figure connected with cathedral is Becket (St. Thomas of Canterbury), whose shrine was place of pilgrimage for centuries. Pop. 24,500. (2) Provincial dist. in centre of South Island, New Zealand. Canterbury Plains occupy 3,900 sq. m.; chief wheat and sheep dist. of the Dominion; exports pastoral products. Cap. Christchurch; N. port, Lyttelton; S. Timaru. Area, 13,858 sq. m.; pop. 213,000.

Canton'. (1) Cap. of Kwangtung prov., 90 m. up Canton R.; one of the largest and most populous cities of China; there are now old and new cities, western suburbs, island of Honam, and foreign concessions in Shamien and Fati; has perhaps the largest water pop. of any city; sampans and small craft abode of the Tanka, large-footed race who spend whole lives on water; city lies low and suffers from floods; large and varied industries. Exports silk, leather, matting, tea, tobacco; imports cotton goods, metals, rice, sugar. Shipping trade at Whampoa, 12 m. down Canton R. Pop. (est.) 900,000. (2) City, Ohio, U.S.A., 50 m. S. of Cleveland; chief products are engines, cars, bridges, mill and agricultural machinery, clay, limestone, coal. Pop. 106,000. (3) RIVER or PEARL RIVER, formed by the union of the West (Si), North (Pe), and East (Tung) rivs., Kwangtung, China. Where it narrows are Bogue Forts (taken by British, 1841 and 1856). Whole country to N. very fertile (rice), and intersected by canals and waterways.

Canvey Island, isl., Essex, England, at mouth of R. Thames; holiday resort. Pop. of urb. dist. 3,500.

Cao-bang (*kā-ō-bang'*). (1) Dist., Tongking, French Indo-China; mountainous; tin, galena, and iron ore; forests. Area, 3,000 sq. m.; pop. *c.* 70,000. (2) Cap. of above, 72 m. N.N.W. of Langson. Pop. *c.* 6,000.

Cape Bret'on, island, Nova Scotia, Canada; separated from mainland by Strait of Canso; cut in two by Bras d'Or Lakes and a ship canal; produces grain, timber, coal, salt, marble, limestone, granite; agricultural and lumber products and important fisheries; iron and steel manufactures; shipbuilding; connected with mainland by Canadian National Railway ferry. Chief city, Sydney. Area, 3,120 sq. m.; pop. 130,000.

Cape Coast. See GOLD COAST.

Cape Cod, hook-shaped peninsula, Massachusetts, U.S.A.; cranberry culture; fishing; summer resorts. Cape Cod Canal, 8 m. long, connects Barnstaple Bay with Buzzard's Bay, lessening distance between Boston and New York by 70 m.

Cape Colony. See CAPE OF GOOD HOPE (2).

Cape of Good Hope. (1) Promontory, S. Africa; first sighted by Diaz (1486); called 'Cape of Storms'; rechristened by King of Portugal; has a lighthouse. (2) PROVINCE OF THE, formerly CAPE COLONY, part of Union of S. Africa forming extreme S. of African continent, bounded N. by S.W. Africa and Bechuanaland protectorates, N.E. by Transvaal, Orange Free State, Basutoland, Natal, S.E. and S. by Southern Ocean, and W. by Atlantic Ocean. Running parallel with coast, and about 150 m. distant from it, is series of mountains known by various names of Drakensberg, Stormberg, Sneeuwberg, Nieuwveld, Roggeveld, and Kamiesberg Mountains, with elevations of 6,000 to 11,000 ft. From coast surface rises by three terraces divided by subsidiary mountain ranges, large part of third terrace being occupied by Great Karroo, a long, treeless plateau, with bare table-topped hills, sloping from 4,000 ft. on

W. to 3,000 on E., and covered with scrubby karroo bush. The Little Karroo, or second terrace, resembles Great Karroo, and both have great fertility under irrigation. Coast terrace and hilly country in E. have grassy plains and woodlands. To N. of great range of mountains surface slopes to valley of Orange River, and plateau of interior beyond. Eastern part of province has rainfall 25 to 28 in.; centre, S. coast, and Little Karroo, 9 to 25 in.; Great Karroo and country N. and N.W. of it, 9 in. or less. No large river except Orange, which rises in mountains in E. Western districts have winter rains, and eastern summer rains. Mean temperature ranges from 51° to 79° F.

Resources.—Chief source of wealth is diamond mines, centre being at Kimberley in Griqualand W.; rich copper deposits in Namaqualand; manganese and tin near Cape Town; iron, zinc, lead. Sheep and Angora goats are reared in large numbers, producing great quantities of wool and mohair; cattle, horses, mules, donkeys bred; ostrich farming carried on, but now of less importance. Maize, millet, wheat, barley are cultivated; grapes, peaches, apricots, nectarines, figs, oranges, olives, pineapples, bananas, tomatoes, and other fruits and vegetables grown; wine, brandy, and raisins produced; manufactures unimportant; exports include diamonds, wool, mohair, ostrich feathers, copper ore, raw hides, maize; imports include clothing, iron, coal, textiles, hardware, cutlery, tools, provisions, liquors. Irrigation has made some progress. Railway mileage is *c.* 5,000.

Inhabitants include Dutch, English, and other European nationalities; in western districts are greatest number of Dutch, in eastern of English. The Boers are descended from early Dutch colonists and Huguenot exiles from France. Natives include Bantus or Kaffirs, Hottentots, Bushmen, Griquas, etc. Many of Bantus are people of fine physique; Hottentots are short, and Bushmen are lowest S. African race. There are also numbers of Indians and Malays, and of 'coloured' people (*i.e.* half-castes). Chief religion of whites is Protestantism (Dutch Reformed Church, Anglican, Presbyterian, etc.). Education is obligatory for European children.

Cape Colony was united with Natal, Transvaal, and Orange River Colony in 1910, as the Union of S. Africa; and became the Province of the Cape of Good Hope. The English and Dutch languages are both official. Cape Town is cap. of prov. and also seat of Union Parliament. Area, 276,966 sq. m.; pop. 2,782,719, of whom 650,609 are white.

Cape Race forms the S.E. extremity of Newfoundland; lighthouse.

Capernaum (*ka-per'nā-um*), scene of large part of ministry of our Lord Jesus Christ, and called 'his own city'; on N. shore of the Sea of Galilee; identified with Tell Hum, one building of which is said to be synagogue in which Christ preached.

Cape to Cairo Railway, a project originally conceived by Cecil J. Rhodes for great trunk line running from Cape Town at S. of continent to Cairo in N. Direct distance is 5,700 m., and as there are some 2,000 m. of waterways, this leaves about 4,000 m. to be covered by rail. The direct railway route from Cape Town runs as far N. as Bukama in the Belgian Congo, while from Cairo the railway runs S. as far as Sennar on the Blue Nile, some 100 m. from Khartoum. Between Khartoum and Bukama the journey is made partly by steamer, partly by road, and partly by rail, the following being the chief places passed: Rejaf, Stanleyville, Ponthierville, Kindu, and Congolo. This route follows a fixed time-table.

It is also possible to travel from Cape Town to Cairo entirely on British territory by taking the following route: Cape Town to Broken Hill in N.W. Rhodesia by train; thence by road to S. end of L. Tanganyika; by steamer to Kigoma at N. end of lake;

by rail through Tabora to Mwanza on L. Victoria; by steamer to Kampala at N. end of lake, and thence by road to Rejaf; thence down the White Nile by steamer to Khartoum, and so by rail to Cairo.

Cape Town, mother city of S. Africa, cap. of prov. of Cape of Good Hope, and seat of legislature of Union of S. Africa; beautifully situated on Table Bay, at foot of Table Mountain; many fine suburbs; also excellent harbour and docks. Notable buildings include old Dutch castle, government house, Houses of Parliament, museum, library, several colleges; mosques; observatory; seat of Anglican and R.C. bishops, and of univ.; exports wool, diamonds, fruit, gold, wine, ivory, hides, skins; imports textiles, hardware, general goods. Inhabitants include Europeans, natives, coloured people (half-castes), Malays, and Indians. Pop. 225,300 (126,700 whites).

Cape Verde, most westerly cape, Africa.

Cape Verde Islands, group 320 m. W. of Cape Verde, belonging to Portugal. Windward group includes Santo Antão, São Vicente, Santa Luzia, São Nicolão, Boa Vista, and Sal; Leeward group, Maio, São Thiago, Fogo, and Brava. Area, 1,475 sq. m.; volcanic; some islands arid, others with abundant rainfall, very fertile; largest island, São Thiago. Chief prod., coffee, castor oil, sisal, mustard, and brandy. Pop. 131,100.

Cap Haitien (*hä'tē-en*), tn., republic of Haiti, W. Indies, 85 m. N. of Port-au-Prince; good harbour; large export trade. Pop. (est.) 22,000.

Capiz (*kä'pēth*). (1) Province, Panay, Philippines, N. coast of the Visayan Sea; semicircular range of mountains encloses low and fertile plain watered by large and navigable R. Capiz; sugar, corn, rice, indigo; cattle and horses; gold and iron. Area, 1,661 sq. m.; pop. 283,900. (2) Tn., cap. of above prov., on l. bk. of Capiz; port of call; rice. Pop. 22,000.

Cap Martin (*cap mar-tan'*), headland, Alpes Maritimes, France, 2 m. from Mentone; pine forest; select winter resort.

Caprera (*ka-prä'ra*), ('goat island'), isl. off N.E. coast of Sardinia; residence of Garibaldi from 1854 to death (1882).

Capri (*kap'rē*), isl., S. side of Gulf of Naples, Italy; precipitous coasts; two towns, Capri and Ana Capri, connected by flight of 784 steps and carriage road; lovely scenery (notably Blue Grotto, rediscovered in 1826); attracts many visitors; fruits, wine, olive oil; fishing; good harbour; imperial Roman residence. Area, 5¾ sq. m.; pop. 7,000.

Cap'ua, tn. and archiepis. see, Italy, 20 m. N. of Naples; has 11th cent. cathedral, greatly modernized. Anc. city, 2 m. S.S.E., was once a rival of Rome and long famous for its luxury. Pop. 10,000.

Carabo'bo, dep., N. Venezuela, S. America; thickly populated in centre and S.W.; coffee, cacao, sugar; cattle and hides are exported from Puerto Cabello. Cap. Valencia. Area, 2,984 sq. m.; pop. 147,000.

Caracas (*ka-rak'as*), cap. of Venezuela, S. America, 8 m. S. of its port, La Guaira (by railway, 22½ m.); seat of archbishop; federal palace, univ., cathedral, museum, theatre, and Yellow House (residence of president); has suffered severely from earthquakes; exports coffee, cacao, tobacco. Pop. 135,200.

Carapegua (*kä-rä-pä-gwä'*), tn., Paraguay, S. America, 38 m. S.E. of Asuncion; district produces tobacco, sugar, and cotton. Pop. 12,000.

Caravä'ca, tn., S.E. Spain, 40 m. W.N.W. of Murcia; considerable industrial centre, though lacking railway communication; ironworks and tanneries; jasper quarries. Pop. 16,000.

Carberry Hill, hill, Scotland, 8 m. S.E. of Edinburgh; alt. 400 ft.; here Queen Mary surrendered to Confederate lords (1567); a monument marks the spot. On ridge to N.E. battle of Pinkie was fought (1547).

Car'bondale, city, Pennsylvania, U.S.A., 12 m. N.E. of Scranton; active coal-mining city (anthracite). Pop. 18,600.

Carcagente (*kar-ka-hān'tā*), tn., E. Spain, 25 m. S. of Valencia; dist. fertile; has mulberry and orange groves; rice; silk and linen fabrics. Pop. 13,800.

Car'car, tn., Cebu I., Philippines; active coast trade and fisheries; sugar-cane. Pop. 37,400.

Carcassonne (*kar-ka-son'*), (anc. *Carcaso*), cap. of Aude, S. France; lower town, well built and prosperous, on l. bk. of R. Aude; the upper town (Cité), on hill opposite, is the most perfectly preserved specimen in Europe of a mediæval fortress town; restored (1855–79); double rampart; 54 towers; two fortified gates; wine market; agricultural implements, etc. Pop. 28,900.

Cardenas (*kar-dā'nas*), tn. and port, Matanzas, N. Cuba; well built; has bronze statue of Columbus; export trade in sugar, tobacco, asphalt; good steamer service. Pop. 34,100.

Car'diff, parl. bor. and seapt., on Taff, Glamorgan, Wales. Among outstanding features are several parks, including Cathays Park, in which is Univ. College (one of three colleges of univ. of Wales); magnificent new town hall, munic. buildings, and law courts; offices of Central Board of Education for Wales, borough technical schools, and Baptist theological coll. Great manufacturing and trading centre; exports enormous quantities of coal, also iron, tinplate, etc.; industries include shipbuilding, smelting, iron and steel works, brewing, manufacture of chemicals; imports ores, provisions, live cattle, esparto; has large cold-storage accommodation and magnificent docks. Pop. 223,600.

Car'digan, co. tn. and seapt., Cardiganshire, S. Wales, on riv. Teifi; tile and brick making; ruins of Cardigan Castle. Pop. 3,300.

Car'diganshire, county, S. Wales; bounded by Merioneth, Montgomery, Radnor, Brecknock, Carmarthen, Pembroke, and Cardigan Bay; surface generally mountainous, except along coast; highest peak, Plinlimmon; chief rivers, Teifi, Aeron, Rheidol, Ystwith. Soil is chiefly sandy or peaty loam; produces barley, oats, wheat, and other crops; many cattle and sheep raised; minerals include lead, zinc, copper, slate; manufactures gloves, woollens; chief towns, Cardigan (co. tn.), Aberystwith, Lampeter. Area, 692 sq. m.; pop. 55,200.

Car'dross, vil., Dumbartonshire, Scotland, on N. shore of Clyde; here Robert the Bruce died (June 7, 1329).

Card'well, tn., Queensland, Australia, on Rockingham Bay; good harbour; preserved meat and sauces; exports cedar. Pop. 3,500.

Carei (*kar-ē'i*), formerly NAGY KAROLY, tn., N.W. Romania, near Hungarian border; sawmills; cotton, linen, and tobacco manufactures. Pop. *c.* 15,000.

Car'fin, vil., Lanarkshire, Scotland, 2 m. N.E. of Motherwell; coal mining; grotto a place of pilgrimage ('Scottish Lourdes'). Pop. 2,200.

Caribbean Sea (*kar-i-bē'an*), between Antilles and Central and S. America; connected by Strait of Yucatan with Gulf of Mexico; formed by subsidence of earth's crust. Area, 7,500 sq. m.; maximum depth, 2,844 fathoms.

Car'ibbee Islands, or LESSER ANTILLES, chain of islands E. of Caribbean Sea; portion of W. Indies; extends from Saba on N. to Grenada on S.

Carigara (*ka-rē-gā'ra*), tn. and port, N. Leyte, Philippines; hemp exported. Pop. 17,500.

Carini (*ka-rē'nē*), tn., Palermo, Sicily; mediæval Gothic castle, also ruins of anc. town. Pop. 14,200.

Carin'thia, prov., S. Austria; mountainous; watered by R. Drava; Alpine lakes; mineral springs; produces lead and iron ores; manufactures iron and steel goods, machinery, rails; rye, oats, and wheat grown; horses, cattle, and sheep raised. Cap. Klagenfurt. Area, 3,680 sq. m.; pop. 370,800.

Car'isbrooke, tn., Isle of Wight, England, 1 m. S.W. of Newport; mediæval stronghold; castle, now in ruins, was prison of Charles I. (1647–48). Pop. 4,700.

Car'lingford. (1) Tn., seapt., Louth, I.F.S.; fisheries, especially oysters. Pop. 547. (2) LOUGH, inlet between Louth and Down, Ireland; entrance rocky; shoals.

Carlisle (*kar-lil'*). (1) Co. tn., Cumberland, England; important railway centre; seat of bishop; fine cathedral; iron foundries; textiles. Pop. 57,100. (2) Bor., Pennsylvania, U.S.A., 17 m. S.W. of Harrisburg; seat of Dickinson Methodist Coll. (1783); bombarded by Confederates (July 1863); manufactures boots and shoes, and railway cars; mineral springs in vicinity. Pop. 10,900.

Car'low. (1) Co., Leinster, I.F.S.; bounded Wicklow, Wexford, Kilkenny, Leix, and Kildare; mountainous in S.E.; chief rivs. Barrow and Slaney; chiefly agricultural; dairy farming; corn, flour, butter; 12th cent. cathedral at St. Lazerian. Area, 265 sq. m.; pop. 34,500. (2) Munic. bor., cap. of above, on R. Barrow; brewing, flour milling, dairy produce. Pop. 7,200.

Carls'bad, tn. and wat.-pl., N.W. Bohemia, Czechoslovakia; fashionable resort, noted for mineral springs, of which most remarkable is Sprudel; this has numerous orifices and temp. of 164° F.; mineral waters and Carlsbad salts are largely exported. Pop 14,800.

Carlscro'na. See KARLSKRONA.

Carlsruhe'. See KARLSRUHE.

Carl'ton, urb. dist. and par., Notts, England, 3½ m. N.E. of Nottingham; lace and hosiery. Pop. 22,300.

Carluke', tn., Lanarkshire, Scotland, 5½ m. N.W. of Lanark; coal and iron; fruit growing and jam making. Pop. 5,400.

Carmar'then, co. tn. and port, Carmarthenshire, Wales, on R. Towy; anc. *Maridunum*; old castle now forms county jail; slates, tinplate; salmon fisheries. Pop. 10,300.

Carmar'thenshire, co., S. Wales; is bounded N. by Cardiganshire, E. and S.E. by Brecon and Glamorganshire, S. by Carmarthen Bay and Burry Inlet, and W. by Pembrokeshire. Surface generally mountainous; highest peak, Carmarthen Van (2,632 ft.); chief river, Towy; produces oats, barley; dairy farming carried on; horses, sheep, and cattle raised; coal and lead mining; iron foundries and smelting; tinplate; co. tn., Carmarthen. Area, 919 sq. m.; pop. 179,100.

Car'mel, MT., mountain ridge, Palestine; runs N.W. from the neighbourhood of Samaria and ends in a bold promontory S. of the Bay of Acre; luxuriantly wooded, and regarded from time immemorial as sacred; scene of deeds of Elijah and Elisha.

Carmo'na, tn., Spain, 20 m. E.N.E. of Seville; Roman and Moorish remains; products include olives, oil, wine, grain, fruit, and cattle. Pop. 22,100.

Carnac', vil., Morbihan, N.W. France, 15 m. S.E. of Lorient; remarkable on account of number of prehistoric stone monuments in its neighbourhood. The monoliths, of granite, are arranged in avenues, and vary in height from 3 to 18 ft.

Carnar'von, parl. and munic. bor. and seapt., cap. of Carnarvonshire, N. Wales; castle founded by Edward I. (1284); birthplace of Edward II.; Princes of Wales were formerly invested in its castle (now a mere shell), the ceremony being revived in 1911, at the investiture of Edward, Prince of Wales; exports slate and copper ore. Tourist centre for Snowdon dist. Pop. 8,500.

Carnarvonshire, co., N. Wales; bounded by Irish Sea, Denbigh, Merioneth, Cardigan Bay, Carnarvon Bay, Menai Strait; surface mountainous; in centre is Snowdon (3,560 ft.); watered by R. Conway and smaller streams; produces oats, barley; cattle and sheep raised; minerals, slate, lead, zinc. Co. tn., Carnarvon. Area, 572 sq. m.; pop. 120,800.

Carnat'ic, old subdivision of India,

on Coromandel coast; now part of Madras Presidency; scene of great struggle for supremacy in India between France and Britain in 18th cent.; formed dominions of Nawabs of Arcot, and was conquered by Britain in 1783, being formally annexed to Brit. Empire in 1801.

Carnedd Dafydd, Carnedd Llewelyn. See SNOWDON.

Carneg'ie, bor., Pennsylvania, U.S.A., 5 m. S.W. of Pittsburgh; steel and iron works. Pop. 13,000.

Carn'forth, urb. dist., N. Lancs, England, 6½ m. N. of Lancaster; iron smelting; rly. jn. Pop. 3,200.

Carnic Alps. See ALPS.

Carnio'la, former Austrian crown land, now N.W. part of Yugoslavia; climate severe in higher parts, but generally mild; valuable forests; quicksilver; iron, lignite found; household weaving of linen and lace. Chief tn., Ljubljana. Area, 3,845 sq. m.; pop. *c.* 530,000.

Carnoustie (*kar-noos'ti*), coast tn., Angus, Scotland; summer resort; fine golf links. Pop. 4,800.

Carn'wath, vil. and par., Lanarkshire, Scotland, 3 m. N.E. of Carstairs; coal and shale mining. Pop. (vil.) 960.

Caroli'na, or CAROLINAS, old Brit. colony in N. America, established by grant of Charles II. in 1663, and afterwards divided into the states of N. and S. Carolina (constituted an independent state in 1776). See NORTH CAROLINA and SOUTH CAROLINA.

Car'oline Islands, archipelago, Pacific Ocean, between New Guinea and the Marianas Islands, consisting of about 500 small islands, of which Babelthouap, Yap, Truk, and Ponape are most important; these are volcanic, most of others coral; climate temperate; chief product, copra. Mandated to Japan since the Great War. Area, *c.* 400 sq. m.; pop. *c.* 36,000.

Carpa'thian Mountains, great mt. range of S.E. Europe, in Czechoslovakia, Hungary, and Romania; length, *c.* 880 m.; form watershed between Black Sea and Baltic; chief ranges are Transylvanian Alps, Central and Little Carpathians, White Mts., Beskids; highest peak, Gerlsdorfer Spitze, in Hohe Tatra (8,787 ft.); covered with timber—oak, beech, fir—up to 4,000 ft.; rich in minerals—coal, silver, copper, lead, iron, salt, petroleum; geological formation chiefly granite, crystallines, and sandstone; numerous small tarns in Central Carpathians; crossed by many passes, including Jablunka and Rothenthurm (Turnul Ros) passes.

Carpenta'ria, GULF OF, large gulf, N. Australia; contains many islands; E. coast discovered by Dutch (1606).

Carpentras (*kar-pon-trä'*), tn., Vaucluse, S. France, 14 m. N.E of Avignon; walled, with four gates; trade in fruit, preserves; felt hats, silk; very rich city in Roman times. Pop. 8,400.

Carpi (*kar'pē*), tn., episc. see, Emilia, N. Italy, 9 m. N. of Modena; two cathedrals; Renaissance church; silk industries. Pop. 30,700.

Carrara (*ka-rä'ra*), tn., Italy, near E. coast of Gulf of Genoa; famous quarries of marble, mostly white, but also black, yellow, and green. Pop. 52,700.

Carriacou (*kar-re-a-koo'*), largest of the Grenadines, Windward Islands, Brit. W. Indies; building stone; cotton; oyster fishery. Area, 6,913 ac.; pop. 7,100.

Car'rick, southernmost div., Ayrshire, Scotland; anc. regality of county; Prince of Wales is also Earl of Carrick.

Carrickfer'gus, seaport, Belfast Lough, Antrim, N. Ireland; 12th cent. castle; landing place of William III. (1690); flax, linen, and cotton; oyster fisheries. Pop. 4,700.

Carrickmacross', mkt. tn., Monaghan, I.F.S., 13 m. W. of Dundalk; agricultural trade; lace manufacture. Pop. 2,000.

Carrick-on-Shannon, mkt. tn., cap., Leitrim, I.F.S.; mkt. for grain and dairy produce. Pop. 1,000.

Carrick-on-Suir, mkt. tn., Tipperary, I.F.S., on l. bk. of Suir; agricultural produce; woollens, linens; slate. Pop. 4,700.

Carron. See FALKIRK.

Carsebreck, pond, S.E. Perthshire, Scotland, 11 m. N.N.E. of Stirling; famous for annual bonspiel of Royal Caledonian Curling Club.

Carse of Gowrie, rich alluvial tract, N. bk. of R. Tay, Perthshire and Angus, Scotland; noted fruit dist.

Car'shalton, urb. dist., Surrey, England, 3 m. W. of Croydon; ironworks; cocoa, pencils. Pop. 28,800.

Car'so (Austrian *Karst*), limestone plateau, Italy, S. of Gorizia, extending behind Trieste and continuing S. almost to the Adriatic Sea; level plain and a low windswept tableland strewn with limestone boulders, seamed with deep fissures and covered with rough scrub and great masses of scree; scene of much fighting between Italians and Austrians during Great War.

Car'son City, cap. of Nevada, U.S.A.; gold, silver. Pop 1,600.

Carstairs', par. and vil., Lanarkshire, Scotland, 27½ m. S.W. of Edinburgh; rly. jn. Pop. (par.) 1,800.

Cartagena (*kar-ta-hä'na*). (1) Seaport, Murcia, S.E. Spain; naval arsenal; exports metal ores, metals, fruits, esparto grass. Pop. 97,000. (2) Seapt., Colombia, S. America, on Caribbean Sea; burned by Drake (1585); exports include rubber, hides, skins, gold and silver. Pop. 68,000.

Cartä'go. (1) Tn., Costa Rica, Central America, at foot of volcano Irazu; coffee, bananas, fruits. Pop. 16,200. (2) Tn., Colombia, S. America, 140 m. W. of Bogota; cacao, coffee, tobacco. Pop. *c.* 20,000.

Car'ter Bar, road summit, Cheviot Hills, between Roxburghshire and Northumberland; important in pre-railway times, now used mainly for motor traffic. Alt. 1,371 ft.

Car'thage, famous anc. city, N. Africa, situated N. of Tunis on peninsula jutting into Mediterranean.

Carupano (*ka-roo'pa-nō*), seapt., Venezuela, S. America, 65 m. E.N.E. of Cumana; commercial centre; cacao, sugar, timber. Pop. 11,000.

Carvin (*kar-van'*), tn., Pas-de-Calais, France, 10 m. S.S.W. of Lille; distilleries, coal mines, brass foundries. Pop. 11,000.

Casablan'ca, second city of Morocco, on Atlantic E. coast; one of the most important seaports of N. Africa; exports hides, wool, grain. Pop. 107,000.

Casale Montferrato (*ka-zä'lā mon-fer-rä'tō*), tn., episc. see, Alessandria, Italy, 38 m. E. of Turin; anc. Romanesque cathedral; cement works; syrup from juice of reed. Pop. 34,000.

Ca'sas Gran'des, vil., Mexico, 120 m. S.W. of El Paso (New Mexico); remarkable for aboriginal ruins.

Cascade' Mountains, mt. range, extending northwards through Oregon and Washington into Brit. Columbia; principal peaks about 14,000 ft.; numerous extinct volcanoes; heavily and extensively wooded; traversed by Fraser, Columbia, and Klamath rivers; name derived from cascades formed by Columbia R. in cutting through range.

Caserta (*kā-ser'tā*), tn., episc. see, Italy, 17 m. N.E. of Naples; cathedral and palace; silk works. Pop. 35,200.

Cash'el, city, Tipperary, I.F.S.; seat of R.C. archbishop and Prot. bishop; many interesting ruins, comprising 12th cent. cathedral, castle, chapel, round tower, anc. cross, exist on 'Rock of Cashel.' Pop. 3,000.

Cashmere. See KASHMIR.

Casoria (*ka-zō'rē-a*), tn., Italy, 6 m. N. of Naples; wine and silk culture. Pop. (comm.) 13,000.

Cas'pe, tn., Spain, on R. Ebro, 50 M. S.E. of Saragossa; sulphur baths in vicinity; oil, silk. Pop. *c.* 8,000.

Cas'per, largest city, Wyoming, U.S.A., on N. Platte R.; important oil-refining centre; chief prod. are petroleum, wool, sheep, and cattle. Pop. 23,300.

Cas'pian Sea, lying between Europe and Asia, and surrounded E., W., and

N. by Russia and S. by Persia; is largest inland sea or salt lake in the world; length, 760 m.; breadth, 130 to 300 m.; area, 170,000 sq. m. It is 90 ft. below sea-level, is tideless, has no outlet; shallow in N. (3 to 12 fathoms), deeper in S. (420 to 516 fathoms); northern part frozen in winter; receives waters of Volga, Ural, Emba, Kur, Terek, Atrek, Gürgen, Sefid-Rud, Aras, and other rivers; is believed to have been formerly connected with Sea of Aral; valuable fisheries—sturgeon, salmon, perch, carp, etc.; important export of caviare and isinglass; canals connecting upper waters of Volga with Lake Ladoga and the Southern Dvina give through communication to Baltic Sea; schemes for connecting Caspian with Sea of Azov and Black Sea not yet materialized; seal hunting is carried on in N.; transport trade in petroleum. Chief port, Astrakhan.

Cassaba, or KASSABA (*ka-sä'ba*), tn., Asia Minor, 35 m. E. of Smyrna; cotton, melons exported. Pop. 31,000.

Cas'sel, or KASSEL, cap., Hesse-Nassau, Prussia, on R. Fulda, trib. of Weser; has old palace of electoral princes; museum built (1769), which has fine library; newer part of town regularly laid out with wide streets; important industrial centre; manufactures include machinery, mathematical instruments, textiles, ironware. Pop. 171,500.

Castelbuono (*kas-tel-boo-ō'nō*), tn., Palermo, Sicily; has mineral springs. Pop. 11,000.

Castellammare del Golfo (*kas-tel-a-mä'rā del golf'ō*), tn., Trapani, Sicily; olive oil, anchovies, wine. Pop. 21,000.

Castellammare di Stabia (*kas-tel-a-mä'rā di stä'bia*), tn., Campania, Italy, on Bay of Naples; mineral springs; popular resort. Pop. 39,200.

Castellon de la Plana (*kas-tel-yon'*). (1) Maritime prov., Valencia, E. Spain; surface mountainous; plain bordering the coast; fisheries; fruit growing; linens, hempen fabrics. Area, 2,495 sq. m.; pop. 307,000. (2) Industrial tn., cap. of above; porcelain, leather, silk, flax goods of all kinds; watered artificially by Moorish aqueduct. Pop. 34,500.

Castelveträ'no, tn., Sicily, 22 m. S.E. of Marsala; wine, cotton, silk, flax. Pop. 25,000.

Castile (*käs-tēl'*), anc. kingdom, central Spain, stretching S. from Bay of Biscay and including upper basins of Douro, Tagus, and Guadiana rivs.; plateau (average alt. 2,500 ft.); climate extreme; much of surface is arid; sheep; wheat in riv. basins; Old Castile includes provs. of Santander, Palencia, Burgos, Lagroño, Valladolid, Soria, Segovia, and Avila; New Castile includes Madrid, Guadalajara, Toledo, Cuenca, and Ciudad-Real provs. The marriage of Isabella of Castile with Ferdinand of Aragon united Spain (1479); Castilian is literary language of Spain. Area, 53,307 sq. m.; pop. *c.* 4,500,000.

Castlebar', tn., cap., co. Mayo, I.F.S.; linen goods; agricultural produce. Pop. 4,300.

Castleca'ry, hamlet, Stirlingshire, Scotland, 6 m. W. of Falkirk; station on Antonine's wall; deposits of silica and fireclay.

Castle Ca'ry, tn., Somerset, England, 12 m. N.E. of Yeovil; horsehair and twine factories. Pop. *c.* 1,700.

Castle Don'ington, par. and tn., Leicestershire, England, 11 m. S.W. of Nottingham; manufactures hosiery and silk. Pop. (par.) 2,700.

Castle Douglas (*dŭg'las*), mkt. tn., Kirkcudbrightshire, Scotland, 4 m. W. of Dalbeattie; manufactures agricultural implements; sheep and cattle markets. Pop. 3,000.

Castleford, urb. dist. and par., W. Riding, Yorkshire, England, 10 m. S.E. of Leeds; glass, chemicals, coal mining. Pop. 21,800.

Castleisland, tn., Kerry, I.F.S., 12 m. S.E. of Tralee; agricultural centre. Pop. 1,300.

Castleknock, par. and vil., co. Dublin, I.F.S., 4 m. N.W. of Dublin; former vice-regal lodge in parish.

Cas'tlemaine, tn., Victoria, Australia, 65 m. N.W. of Melbourne; gold mines were the second worked in Victoria; wine and fruit. Pop. *c.* 7,000.

Cas'tleton, par., vil., Derbyshire, England, 10 m. N.E. of Buxton; ruins of Castle of the Peak (see Scott's *Peveril of the Peak*); fluorspar mines. Pop. 650.

Cas'tletown, tn., Isle of Man; cap. till 1862; anc. castle; public school. Pop. 1,900.

Castres (*kastr*), tn., dep. Tarn, France, 40 m. E. of Toulouse; famous 16th cent. Huguenot stronghold; soap, earthenware, leather goods. Pop. 20,800.

Castries (*käs-trē'*), port, cap. of St. Lucia, W. Indies; sugar. Brit. naval station; the harbour is one of finest in the W. Indies. Pop. 5,900.

Cas'tro del Ri'o, tn., Andalusia, Spain, 22 m. S.E. of Cordoba; textiles; Moorish castle. Pop. 11,900.

Castrogiovanni (*kas-trō-jō-van'ē*), tn. and episc. see, central Sicily, anc. *Enna*; was seat of worship of Demeter (Ceres), chief deity of anc. Sicily; rock salt. Pop. 26,400.

Castro Urdiales (*kas-tro oor-di-ä'les*), fishing port, Santander, N. Spain; exports iron ore and tinned sardines. Pop. 11,800.

Castrovillari (*kas-trō-vil-lä'rē*), tn., Calabria, Italy, 35 m. N. of Cosenza; anc. Norman castle; cheese; wine. Pop. *c.* 11,000.

Catalo'nia, former principality and province, N.E. Spain, now comprising Barcelona, Tarragona, Lerida, and Gerona; surface mountainous and wooded; watered by numerous streams; these, together with a good system of artificial irrigation, render Catalonia chief manufacturing and agricultural region of Spain; called the 'Lancashire of Spain'; produces cereals; cotton, silk, and woollen goods manufactured; coal, copper, zinc, lead, tin. Chief tn., Barcelona. Area, 12,427 sq. m.; pop. 2,345,000.

Catamar'ca. (1) Andean prov., Argentine Republic; mountainous, with fertile valleys; gold, silver, copper, lead, iron; maize, wheat, tobacco, cotton. Area, 36,800 sq. m.; pop. *c.* 120,000. (2) Tn., cap. of above, 230 m. N.W. of Cordoba; cathedral; exports flour, wine. Pop. 13,300.

Cata'nia. (1) Prov. of Italy, occupies middle of E. side of Sicily. Mount Etna fills N.E. quarter, and S. of it is fertile plain of Catania, drained by R. Simeto. Behind these two regions country is mountainous. Produces wheat, olives, wine, oranges, lemons, etc.; sulphur, silk, etc. Area, 1,379 sq. m. Pop. 784,000. (2) Tn. and seaport, cap. of above; cathedral dating from Norman times; rebuilt in 1693, after earthquake; observatory, univ., Roman remains; former Benedictine monastery. Manufactures of textiles; dye works; frequently suffered from earthquakes and eruptions of Etna. Pop. 263,000.

Catanzar'o. (1) Prov., Calabria, S. Italy; mountainous; forested; cattle grazing; wine, fruits; silk, velvet. Area, 2,034 sq. m.; pop. 514,100. (2) Tn., episc. see, cap. of above; suffered severely from earthquakes (1783, 1905, 1907); silk, velvet, and woollen fabrics. Pop. 34,300.

Cat'erham and Warlingham, urb. dist., Surrey, England, 7 m. S. of Croydon; Guards' camp in vicinity. Pop. 19,500.

Cath'cart, par., Renfrewshire and Lanarkshire, Scotland; residential suburb of Glasgow; engineering, paper works; battle of Langside fought near Cathcart Castle. Pop. 46,300.

Cats'kill, group of mts. of Appalachian system, New York, U.S.A.; well timbered; precipices, ravines, streams, waterfalls; popular resort; scene of Rip van Winkle's adventures.

Cat'taro. See KOTOR.

Cattegat. See KATTEGAT.

Cat'terick, vil., N. Riding, Yorks, England, on R. Swale, $4\frac{1}{2}$ m. S.E. of Richmond; Roman station on Watling Street; military camp during Great War; race meetings. Pop. 600.

Cauca (*kow'ka*), riv., Colombia, S. America; most important trib. of R. Magdalena, joins main river near Tacaloa; beautiful valley; mineral and agricultural wealth. Length, *c.* 700 m.

Caucasia (*kŏkā'zha*), general name for a part of the former Russian Empire, s. of and including the Caucasus Mts.; territorial changes followed Russian revolution and Great War; republics have been established in Georgia, Azerbaijan, Daghestan, and Armenia, and various terrs. of U.S.S.R. have been formed.

Caucasus (*kŏ'kaz-us*), lofty range of mts., Russia, extending from Taman peninsula, between Sea of Azov and Black Sea, to Caspian Sea; total length, 940 m.; forms boundary between Europe and Asia. Highest peaks are Mt. Elbruz (18,465 ft.), Koshtantau (16,875 ft.), Kasbek (16,545 ft.). Range consists of a core of granite and gneiss, flanked by clay slates. Some of highest peaks are volcanic in origin, but there are no active volcanoes, though earthquakes are frequent. The Little Caucasus in Armenia is connected with main range by short Suram range.

Caudebec en Caux (*kōd-bek ăn kō*), tn. and riv. port, Seine-Inférieure, France, on Seine, 27 m. W.N.W. by rail from Rouen; 15th and 16th cent. church; old-world streets. Pop. 2,000.

Causses (*kōs*), series of limestone plateaus near head-waters of R. Tarn, s. France. Surface pits, subterranean streams, and stalactite caverns abound.

Cauterets (*ko-te-rā'*), picturesque health resort, Hautes-Pyrénées, France, 18 m. s.w. of Bagnères de Bigorre; mineral springs. Pop. 1,000.

Cautin', prov., s. Chile; E. part occupied by cordillera of Andes (active volcano, Llaimas, 9,800 ft.); fruits, cereals, forests. Cap. Temuco, 80 m. N.E. of Valdivia; chief port, Tolten. Area, 6,381 sq. m.; pop. 193,600.

Cau'very, riv., s. India, rises in W. Ghats, flows S.E. through Mysore and Madras, enters Bay of Bengal; forms large delta which is extensively irrigated; falls are used to supply electric power; total length, over 400 m.

Cav'a dei Tirre'ni, tn., episc. see, Italy, 6 m. N.W. of Salerno; health resort; silk, woollens, linen, and cotton; Benedictine monastery (1025), famous for its archives, in vil. of Corpo di Cava near by. Pop. 26,700.

Cav'an. (1) Co., Ulster, I.F.S.; bounded by Fermanagh, Monaghan, Meath, Westmeath, Longford, and Leitrim; surface undulating; N.W. mountainous; rivs. Annalee, Blackwater, Erne, Woodford; mineral springs; agriculture; distilling. Area, 730 sq. m.; pop. 82,500. (2) Chief tn. of above; ruins of 14th cent. abbey. Pop. 3,000.

Cavite (*ka-vē'tā*), cap., prov. Cavite, Luzon, Philippines, 8 m. s.w. of Manila; chief naval station of archipelago; fortified; dry dock; situated in fertile region, producing rice, sugar, copra, cacao, and coffee. Pop. 22,200.

Caw'dor, vil., Nairnshire, Scotland, 5½ m. s.w. of Nairn; scene of traditional murder of King Duncan by Macbeth (1040).

Cawnpore, chief tn., Cawnpore dist., United Provinces, India, on Ganges; important railway centre; military station; memorial gardens and church commemorate massacre of Europeans by Nana Sahib, July 1857; manufactures cotton, leather, and woollen goods, and has a large trade in grain. Pop. 216,500.

Caxias (*kă-shē-ăsh'*), tn., Maranhão, N.E. Brazil, on riv. Itapicuru; cotton and rice. Pop. 25,000.

Cayenne', seapt. and cap., Fr. Guiana, S. America; official centre of Fr. penal settlement; fortified harbour; chief exp., phosphates, hides, cacao, cloves, and gold. Pop. 14,000.

Cayey (*kī-ā'*), tn., Porto Rico, W. Indies, on slopes of Cayey Mts., 30 m. s. by w. of San Juan; summer resort; tobacco and coffee. Pop. 5,800.

Cayman Islands (*kī'man*), three islands, Grand Cayman, Little Cayman, and Cayman Perac, Caribbean Sea, N.W. of and under government of Jamaica; discovered by Columbus; turtles; phosphates; coconuts. Pop. 5,300.

Ceará (*thā-a-rä'*). (1) State, N. Brazil; has Serra Grande and Serra Araripe in W.; climate healthy but hot; droughts occur; prod. include coffee, cotton, sugar, wax, rubber, and hides; cattle raised. Area, 57,356 sq. m.; pop. 1,319,000. (2) Or FORTALEZA, cap. of above state, on Atlantic Ocean; principal commercial centre and seaport, though sand bar hampers approach; large trade with Pernambuco in produce of state; well laid out. Pop. 78,500.

Cebu'. See SEBU.

Cedar Rapids, city, Iowa, U.S.A., 110 m. E.N.E. of Des Moines; products include 'Quaker oats,' meat products, agricultural machinery, starch, lumber. Pop. 56,000.

Cefalu (*chā-fä-loo'*), tn., episc. see, Palermo, Sicily; 12th cent. cathedral, with mosaics and cloisters; remains of Roman walls and Norman castle; sardine fishing. Pop. 13,200.

Ceglie (*chāl'yā*), tn., Apulia, Italy, 19 m. N.E. of Taranto; beautiful position; trade in grain, oil, and fruit. Pop. *c.* 20,000.

Cehegin (*thā-ā-hēn'*), tn., Murcia, Spain, 55 m. N.W. of Cartagena; wine, olive oil, hemp, honey, esparto grass (for paper); black marble quarries. Pop. 13,700.

Celaya (*sā-lä'ya*), tn., Guanajuato, Mexico, *c.* 150 m. N.W. of Mexico City; important silver mines in neighbourhood; carpets; saddlery. Pop. *c.* 26,000.

Celebes (*sel-ē'-bez*), isl., Dutch E. Indies, separated from Borneo by Strait of Macassar; great length of coast-line; inhabitants mainly belong to Malayo-Polynesian stock; isl. is traversed by volcanic range; has many lakes; proximity to sea makes climate endurable; wealthiest of Dutch E. Indies; much virgin soil; exports nutmeg, mace, copra, rattans, waxes, gums and resins, ores and hides, dry and salt fish, bêche-de-mer, mother-of-pearl, and tortoiseshell; chief tn. is Macassar. Area, 72,679 sq. m.; pop. 3,438,000.

Celje. See CILLI.

Celle (*tsel'le*), formerly also ZELLE, tn., Hanover, Prussia, 23 m. by rail N.E. of Hanover; residence of Dukes of Brunswick-Lüneburg (1369–1705); ducal castle; library with precious MSS.; prod. include printing ink, biscuits, umbrellas. Pop. 25,500.

Cenis (*sen-ē'*), MT., peak of Alps, between France and Italy; the pass is 6,700 ft. high, and over it a road was constructed by Napoleon. Near Mt. Cenis pass is tunnel over 7 m. long.

Central America. See under AMERICA; also BRITISH HONDURAS; COSTA RICA; GUATEMALA; HONDURAS; NICARAGUA; PANAMA; and SALVADOR.

Central Australia. See NORTHERN TERRITORY.

Central Falls, city, Rhode Isl., U.S.A., on Blackstone R., 6 m. N. of Providence; manufactures cotton. Pop. 26,000.

Central India, country occupied by Indian states grouped under political officer in charge of Central India Agency; divided into two parts by narrow strip of United Provinces; bounded N. by Rajputana, United Provinces, E. by Chota-Nagpur, S. by Central Provinces, W. by Bombay; comprises about seventy Indian states, of which Indore, Rewa, Bhopal, and Gwalior are most important treaty states; large part of surface rugged; drained by Ken, Narbada, Son, and other streams; chief mts., Vindhyas, Kaimur Hills; greater part covered by very fertile soil; cotton, opium, food grains. Cap. Indore. Area, 51,531 sq. m.; pop. 6,000,000.

Central Provinces and Berar, prov., British India; bounded N. by Central India and Chota-Nagpur, E. by Bihar and Orissa, Madras, S. by Hyderabad, W. by Bombay. Surface generally is upland, with two tracts of plain; chief ranges, Satpura, Maikal, drained by

Narbada, Tapti, Mahanadi, Indravati, Wardha, and other streams; climate mainly hot; rainy season, June to Sept.; numerous irrigation works; Berar has ample rainfall; rice, cotton, millet, wheat, oil-seeds; minerals include coal, manganese; manufactures cottons. Great majority of inhabitants are Hindus; other religions, Mohammedanism, Christianity. Chief towns, Nagpur, Jubbulpore. Area, 131,052 sq. m.; pop. 13,912,700.

Centuripe (*chen-too-rē'pe*), or CENTORBI, tn., Catania, E. Sicily; Greek and Roman antiquities; sulphur mines. Pop. 13,900.

Ce'os, ZEA, or TZIA, isl., Cyclades, Ægean Sea; 15 m. long by 8 m. broad; centre culminates in Mt. Elias (1,864 ft.); lemons, citrons, olives, wine, and honey.

Cephalo'nia, one of Ionian Islands, W. Greece; area, 290 sq. m.; surface mountainous; highest peak, Elato or Monte Negro (5,315 ft.); cap. Argostoli; prod. currants, olive oil, wine, grain, pulse. Pop. 71,200.

Ceram', or SERANG, isl. of Dutch E. Indies, in Molucca group, forming part of residency of Amboina; little is known of interior, which is scantily populated; coast is inhabited by immigrant Malays; chief prod. sago. Area, 6,600 sq. m.; pop. *c.* 100,000.

Cerignola (*chā-rē-nyō'la*), tn., episc. see, Italy, 22 m. S.E. of Foggia; rebuilt after earthquake in 1733; agricultural trade. Pop. 36,000.

Cerigo. See CYTHERA.

Cernauti (*cher-ne-ootsi'*), formerly CZERNOWITZ, cap. of Bukovina, Romania, on R. Pruth; seat of Greek archbishop; active trade in agricultural produce. Pop. 115,000.

Cernavoda (*cher-nă-vō'da*), vil., Dobruja, Romania, on E. bank of Danube where railway crosses marshy river region by the famous Carol Bridge (total length, including causeway, viaducts, approaches, etc., 12 m.), the only bridge between Belgrade and Black Sea; point of great strategic importance.

Cerro de Pasco (*ther'ō dā pas'cō*), tn., cap., Junin, Peru; alt. 14,270 ft.; one of most famous mining centres of the country; silver, copper, coal, and lead; copper smelting in one of world's largest metallurgical plants. Connected with Lima by Oroya Rly. Pop. *c.* 15,000.

Cesena (*chā-sā'na*), tn., episc. see, Forli, Italy, 17 m. N.W. of Rimini; cathedral; Capuchin church with masterpiece of Guercino; fine palaces; sulphur, wine, hemp, and silk. Pop. (comm.) 54,000.

Cetatea Alba (*che-tat'ya al'ba*), formerly AKKERMAN, tn., Romania, on R. Dniester, *c.* 10 m. from Black Sea; trade in wine, salt, wool, and fruit. Pop. 33,600.

Cetinje (*tset-tēn'yā*), cap., Montenegro, Yugoslavia; little more than a village; on narrow plateau (alt. 2,000 ft.) under shadow of Black Mountain; port Kotor. Pop. 5,500.

Cette (*set*), tn., Hérault, France; most important seapt. on Mediterranean after Marseilles; on broad, deep canal, which connects Canal du Midi with Rhone; wine trade; chemicals; oyster and anchovy fisheries; sea bathing; anc. *Setion.* Pop. 35,400.

Ceuta (*the-oo'tā*), fortified Spanish seapt. at E. end of Moroccan peninsula, jutting out towards Gibraltar (14 m. distant); anc. *Abyla*, one of Pillars of Hercules; free port; now military and convict station; 15th cent. cathedral. Administered as part of prov. of Cadiz. Pop. *c.* 37,000.

Cévennes (*se-ven'*), mt. range, S.E. France, stretching N.E. to S.W. for 330 m., forming S. and E. fringe of the central plateau; forms watershed between basins of Loire and Rhone; separates two climates, two vegetations, and two national types; chief heights, Mézenc (5,753 ft.) and Lozère (5,584 ft.); minerals include coal, iron, zinc, manganese; mineral springs; large forests and extensive grazing-grounds.

Ceylon', isl. and Brit. crown colony at S. extremity of India; consists largely of undulating plains, but S. part is mountainous in interior; extreme length, 272 m.; width, 137 m.; separated from India by Gulf of Manaar and Palk Strait, but closely connected by Adam's Bridge, over which it has been decided to carry railway. Highest mountains are Pedrotallagala (8,296 ft.) and Adam's Peak. Ceylon is drained by Mahaweli Ganga, which flows N.E., entering sea near Trincomali. Climate is tropical and healthy except on coast; chief prod. tea, copra, rubber, cocoa, cardamoms, cinnamon, tobacco. Chief towns are Colombo (cap.), Galle, Jaffna, Kandy, Nuwara Eliya. Area, 25,332 sq. m.; pop. 4,504,500.

Chablis (*shab-lē'*), tn., Yonne, N. central France, 10 m. E. of Auxerre; renowned white wines. Pop. 1,900.

Chä'co. (1) Terr., N. Argentine Republic, consisting of part of Gran Chaco lying S. of the Bermejo R. Only recently opened up to industry proper; cattle breeding is carried on; timber is exported and tannin is extracted from the quebracho trees which flourish in the forests; cap. Resistencia. Area, 52,741 sq. m.; pop. 46,300. (2) **Chaco,** EL GRAN. See GRAN CHACO.

Chad, large lake of Central Sudan, Africa; alt. 800 ft.; varies in extent according to season and is gradually drying up; depth of open water varies from 3 ft. in N.W. to over 20 in S.; receives Shari from S.E. and numerous other streams; shores are swampy and difficult of access; there are numerous islands.

Chad'derton, urb. dist., S.E. Lancashire, England, in parl. bor. of Oldham; cotton and chemical manufactures, engineering works and coal mines. Pop. 27,500.

Chaffarinas (*chaf-ar-ē'nāz*), or ZAFFARINES, group of three Span. islets, N. of Morocco, Africa; fortified.

Chä'gos Archipelago, British group of coral islands, Indian Ocean, S. of Maldive Islands; dependency of Mauritius; coconut oil manufactured.

Chalcis (*kal'sis*), or EGRIPO, chief tn., isl. of Eubœa, E. Greece, on Strait of Euripus; flourishing town and colonizing centre in anc. times; belonged successively to Athenians, Macedonians, Romans, and Turks; suffered from earthquake (1894). Pop. *c.* 16,000.

Chal'font St. Giles, vil., Buckinghamshire, England, 16 m. S.E. of Aylesbury; here Milton wrote parts of *Paradise Lost* and *Paradise Regained.* Pop. 2,100.

Chal'grove, vil., Oxfordshire, England, 10 m. S.E. of Oxford; in a skirmish here (1643) Hampden was killed. Pop. 360.

Châlons-sur-Marne (*shä-lon-soor-marn*), chief tn., dep. Marne, France, *c.* 100 m. E. of Paris and 25 m. S.S.E. of Reims, on r. bk. of the canalized Marne; narrow streets, fine boulevards, and park of 19 ac.; see of bishop; 13th to 17th cent. cathedral, with remarkable stained-glass windows; fine library, museum, school of arts and trades; principal industry is brewing, and there is great trade in champagne, grain, and hemp. Pop. 26,000.

Chalon-sur-Saône (*-sōn*), tn., Saône-et-Loire, France, on R. Saône, 64 m. N. of Lyons; tiles, iron goods, hats, gloves, glass; 14th cent. church. Pop. 28,400.

Chaman', tn., Baluchistan, on Afghan frontier; terminus of Indian North-Western Railway, through Quetta.

Chamba (*chum'ba*), Indian hill state, Punjab, India; chief rivers, Ravi and Chandra; rich in minerals, but little worked; agriculture, grazing; rice, maize, millet; cap. Chamba, 100 m. N.E. of Amritsar. Area, 3,216 sq. m.; pop. 141,900.

Chambal (*chum'bal*), riv., Central India, trib. of Jumna; rises in Vindhya Mts. Length, 650 m.

Chambersburg, bor., Pennsylvania, U.S.A., 46 m. S.W. of Harrisburg; machine shops, foundries, breweries; woollens. Pop. 13,200.

Chambéry (*shan-bā-rē'*), tn., cap., Savoie, S.E. France; archiepiscopal see; silk-gauze, lace, leather, hats. Pop. 19,500.

Chambon-Feugerolles, Le (*shan-bōn'foo-zhe-rōl'*), tn., Loire, France, 4 m. s.w. of St. Etienne; coal-mining centre; small-arms, railway material, screws and bolts. Pop. *c.* 12,000.

Chamonix (*sha-mo-nē'*), mt. valley and vil., Haute-Savoie, France, at foot of Mt. Blanc; seven glaciers, including Mer de Glace; tourist resort. Pop. (vil.) 1,360.

Champagne (*shon-păn'ye*), old prov., France, now included chiefly in Marne, Ardennes, Haute-Marne, Aube. Surface largely consists of chalk downs; in N. and E. are vineyards producing champagne wines.

Champaign (*sham-pān'*), city, Illinois, U.S.A., 125 m. s.w. of Chicago; railway workshops, foundries; industrial univ. Pop. 20,000.

Champar'an, dist., Bihar and Orissa, India, in N.W. corner of Orissa; mainly agricultural; saltpetre refineries; malarious endemic diseases prevail. Area, 3,531 sq. m.; pop. 1,940,800.

Champlain (*sham-plān'*), a lake between states of New York and Vermont, U.S.A.; area, *c.* 600 sq. m.; numerous affluents; contains about fifty islands; navigable for largest vessels; drains N. by Richelieu R. into St. Lawrence; communicates with Hudson R. by Champlain Canal; through traffic mainly in lumber and coal.

Chan'da, dist., Nagpur div., Central Provinces, India; grains, cotton, silk; live-stock; timber; coal and iron. Chief tn., Chanda, 80 m. s. of Nagpur. Area, 9,312 sq. m.; pop. (tn.) 23,000.

Chan'dausi, tn., United Provinces, India, 27 m. s. of Moradabad; cotton, sugar, hemp; important railway junction. Pop. *c.* 27,000.

Chandernagore (*chund-er-nug'-er*), or Chandarnagar, tn., on Hugli, Bengal, India; Fr. possession and settlement; manufactures cotton cloth; formerly rival of Calcutta, but now of no commercial importance. Pop. (settlement) 25,800.

Chang-chow, walled city, prov. Fukien, China, 20 m. w. of Amoy; centre of silk trade. Pop. (est.) 1,000,000.

Chang-chun, commercially Kwanchengtze, tn., Kirin, Manchuria, 170 m. N.E. of Moukden; Japan controls (since 1905) railway from here to Port Arthur Pop. *c.* 60,000.

Chang-sha, cap., Hunan, s. China; trades in antimony, tea, rice, coal. Pop. *c.* 535,000.

Channel Islands, or Iles Normandes, Brit. islands in Eng. Channel, off coast of Normandy; largest are Jersey, Guernsey, Alderney, Sark, Herm; produce large quantities of fruit, flowers, and vegetables, exported to England; important cod, lobster, and oyster fisheries; famous for cattle, each island having its particular strain; climate mild and sunny. The islands are favourite summer resort; they are surrounded by reefs on which many shipwrecks have taken place. Jersey and Guernsey (the latter including Alderney and Sark) are each administered according to their own laws, and have local copper coinage. Taxes and customs duties are very low. People are of Norman stock. Official language is French, but English is used for business and is taught in schools. Each island has its own local dialect. Area, 75 sq. m.; pop. 93,100.

Chantabun', cap. of div. of same name, Siam, on E. of Gulf of Siam; trades in pepper, cardamoms, rubies, sapphires. Pop. *c.* 5,000.

Chantă'da, tn., Lugo, N.W. Spain, 44 m. E. of Pontevedra; grain, fibres, dairy produce; tiles. Pop. 13,500.

Chantilly (*shon-tē-yē*), tn., Oise, France, 25 m. N. of Paris; many historic associations; formerly celebrated for manufacture of lace; its château is a magnificent specimen of Renaissance architecture and contains a valuable library and collection of pictures. Chantilly is a horse-racing centre, and the Prix du Jockey Club (the Fr. Derby) is run in May. Pop. 5,100.

Chao-chow, city, Kwangtung, China, 25 m. N. of Swatow; exports sugar, oranges, and vegetables; railway to Swatow.

Chap'el End, vil., N.E. Warwickshire, England, 2 m. N.W. of Nuneaton; collieries. Pop. 2,000.

Chapel-en-le-Frith, mkt. tn., Derbyshire, England, 5 m. N. of Buxton; paper-making and wadding mills; also bleach-works. Pop. 5,300.

Chap'ra, or CHUPRA, chief tn., Saran dist., Bihar and Orissa, India, near junction of Gogra and Ganges, 32 m. N.W. of Patna; indigo; has declined in importance, but is still a busy industrial town. Pop. *c.* 47,000.

Chard, mkt. tn., Somersetshire, England, 13 m. S.E. of Taunton; lace and woollen goods. Pop. 4,100.

Charente (*sha-ront'*). (1) Riv., France; enters Bay of Biscay below Rochefort; navigable as far as Angoulême. (2) Inland dep., France; traversed by riv. Charente; surface undulating, wooded hills, sandy plains; limestone and granite quarries; exports potatoes, cognac, and stone; chief town, Angoulême. Area, 2,305 sq. m.; pop. 312,800.

Charente-Inférieure, dep., W. coast, France, includes the islands of Ré and Oléron; well cultivated; good pastures; exports brandy and salt; oyster and pilchard fisheries; chief tn., La Rochelle. Area, 2,791 sq. m.; pop. 417,800.

Charenton-le-Pont (*sha-ron-ton'le-pon*), suburb of Paris, France; manufactures porcelain, artificial flowers. Charenton, on account of its lunatic asylum, is French equivalent of Eng. 'Bedlam.' Pop. 20,300.

Charkhar'i, Indian state and tn., Bundelkhand, E. Central India; town exports grain, cotton, linseed. Pop. (state) 123,400; (tn.) 9,600.

Charleroi. (1) (*shär-le-rwa'*) Tn., Hainaut, Belgium, on Sambre; collieries, iron foundries; glass, hardware. Pop. 27,400. (2) (*shär'le-roi*) Bor., Pennsylvania, U.S.A., 22 m. S.S.E. of Pittsburgh; prod. steel and glass. Pop. 11,500.

Charleston. (1) Seapt., S. Carolina, U.S.A., situated on point of land between Cooper and Ashley rivers, which, uniting, form fine harbour; naval station, military and musical academies, and a medical coll. Seat of Catholic bishop; important commercial centre; manufactures include fertilizers, clothing; exports cotton, rice, lumber, phosphates. Pop. 62,000. (2) Cap., W. Virginia, U.S.A.; important industrial centre producing coal, salt; hardware, lumber. Pop. 60,000.

Charleville', tn., Ardennes, France, on R. Meuse, opposite Mézières; manufactures iron goods and bricks. Pop. 21,700.

Charlotte', city, N. Carolina, U.S.A., 130 m. S.W. of Raleigh; rly. jn.; seat of univ. for Negroes; manufactures cotton and machinery. Pop. 83,000.

Charlotte' Amal'ie, now ST. THOMAS, port, St. Thomas, U.S. Virgin Islands, W. Indies. Pop. 6,400.

Charlot'tenburg, tn., Prussia; since 1920 part of Berlin; has royal palace; famous technical coll.; manufactures china, beer, machinery.

Char'lottesville, city, Virginia, U.S.A., 67 m. N.W. of Richmond; seat of Univ. of Virginia, founded by Thomas Jefferson; manufactures iron, lumber, flour, cigars, textiles. Pop. 10,700.

Char'lottetown, cap., Prince Edward I., Canada; fine harbour; has woollen factory, iron foundry, shipyards, and extensive and important fisheries. Pop. 10,800.

Charlton Kings, urb. dist., Glos, England, suburb of Cheltenham. Pop. 4,800.

Charn'wood Forest, rocky, undulating region, largely treeless, N. Leicestershire, rising to elevation of 912 ft.; granite quarries.

Char'ters Towers, tn., Queensland, Australia, 65 m. S.W. of its port Townsville; gold mines. Pop. 9,350.

Chartres (*shar'tr*), tn., Eure-et-Loir, France, 55 m. S.W. of Paris; seat of bishop; cathedral of Notre Dame is one of the most magnificent in France; corn market; industries include flour milling, brewing, distilling, and tanning. Pop. 20,700.

Châteaudun (*shä-tō-dun'*), tn., Eure-et-Loir, France, 28 m. s. of Chartres; has mediæval castle; manufactures flour, leather, jewellery, and machinery. Pop. 5,800.

Châteauroux (*shä-tō-roo'*), chief tn., Indre, France, on R. Indre, 60 m. S.E. of Tours; prod. textiles, machinery, and tobacco; famous castle. Pop. 22,200.

Château-Thierry (*shä-tō-tē-ā-rē'*), tn., Aisne, France, 59 m. E.N.E. of Paris, on rising ground on r. bk. of Marne; statue of La Fontaine, a native; manufactures musical and mathematical instruments. Pop. 7,200.

Châtelet (*shät-lā'*), tn., Hainaut, Belgium; 4 m. E. of Charleroi; coal mines, hardware factories, pottery. Pop. *c.* 13,000.

Châtellerault (*shä-tel-e-rō'*), tn., Vienne, France, 40 m. s. of Tours; cutlery, small-arms. Pop. 13,200.

Chat'ham. (1) Port and munic. and parl. bor., on Medway, Kent, England, adjoining Rochester, Brompton, and Gillingham; has important fortifications, and immense dockyards covering over 500 ac. and extending over 3 m. Important buildings are the arsenal, military and naval barracks, and hospitals; chief industries are shipbuilding, timber cutting, and brick making. Pop. 43,000. (2) Tn., port, New Brunswick, Canada, on Miramichi R.; lumber trade and fisheries; foundries. Pop. 4,500. (3) City, port, Ontario, Canada, on R. Thames, 10 m. from L. Erie; iron goods, machinery; large export trade in agricultural produce. Pop. 13,200.

Chat'ham Islands, Brit. group in S. Pacific Ocean, E. of New Zealand; consist of three islands (Chatham, the largest, 38 m. long) and several rocky islets; dependency of New Zealand; total area, 375 sq. m.; coasts rocky; surface hilly, undulating, fertile; stock rearing and export of wool. Pop. 560 (290 Maoris).

Chattanoo'ga, tn., Tennessee, U.S.A., on Tennessee R.; important railway centre and manufacturing town; has cotton mills, foundries, steel works, blast furnaces; manufactures include carriages, furniture, bricks, tiles, chemicals, and there is an extensive trade in lumber, grain, and coal. Scene of much fighting in American Civil War. Pop. 120,000.

Chat'teris, mkt. tn., Cambridgeshire, England, 10 m. N.W. of Ely; breweries, engineering and rope-making works; corn and roots. Pop. 5,200.

Chaumont (*shō-mon'*), chief tn., Haute-Marne, France, on R. Marne; chief industries, glove making, leather dressing. Pop. 12,900.

Chauny (*shō-nē'*), tn., Aisne, France, on r. bk. of the Oise; stands on main rly. line from Paris to Brussels; chemical and glass works. Pop. 9,000.

Chautauqua (*shaw-tawk'wa*), vil., summer resort, on Lake Chautauqua, w. New York, U.S.A.; centre of a great religious, educational, and social movement. Institution grounds cover 165 ac. Pop. 4,000.

Chaux-de-Fonds (*shō-de-fōn'*), LA, tn., Switzerland, 9 m. N.W. of Neuchâtel; centre of watch-making industry. Pop. 37,700.

Chav'es, tn., N. Portugal, near Spanish frontier; famous for hot saline springs; anc. *Aquæ Flaviæ*; silk, linen. Pop. 6,800.

Chead'le. (1) Tn., Cheshire, England, 3 m. s.w. of Stockport; printing and bleaching works. Pop. (with Gatley) 18,500. (2) Mkt. tn., Staffordshire, England, 13 m. N.E. of Stafford; coal mines; silk mills. Pop. 6,200.

Cheam. See SUTTON AND CHEAM.

Cheb (*keb*), formerly EGER, tn., Czechoslovakia, in extreme N.W. of Bohemia; contains ruined citadel; industries include brewing, textiles, and machinery. Pop. 27,500.

Ched'dar, vil., Somersetshire, England, 15 m. s.w. of Bristol; famed for its cliffs and caves; cheese. Pop. 2,000.

Chedu'ba, or MAN-AUNG, isl., coast of Arakan, Lower Burma; petroleum wells; rice and tobacco form the chief crops. Area, 220 sq. m.; pop. *c.* 30,000.

Chefoo′, known to Chinese as YEN-TAI, port, Shantung, China, at entrance to Gulf of Pohai; exports silk, groundnuts, soya beans, fruit. Pop. *c.* 93,000.

Chekiang′, maritime prov., China; hilly, fertile; silk, tea, and cotton are the chief exports; principal cities, Hangchow and Ning-po. Area, 36,670 sq. m.; pop. 22,000,000.

Chelmno (*kelm′nō*), tn., Poland, on R. Vistula; oil mills; trade in agricultural produce. Pop. 11,000.

Chelms′ford, co. tn., Essex, England; has grammar school, founded by Edward VI.; industries, electrical engineering, manufacture of motor-cars; trade in agricultural produce; its corn and cattle markets are among largest in county. Pop. 26,500.

Chel′sea. (1) Bor., London, England; on riv. Thames, communicating with Battersea by three bridges; residence of numerous celebrities, including Sir Thomas More, Katherine Parr, Walpole, Swift, Leigh Hunt, Carlyle, Turner, Rossetti, Whistler; formerly famous for porcelain; most notable building is Chelsea Royal Hospital, for invalid soldiers, designed by Wren. Pop. 59,000. (2) City, Massachusetts, U.S.A., suburb of Boston; iron, textile, and rubber goods. Pop. 45,000.

Chel′tenham, inland wat.-pl. and mkt. tn., on Chelt, Gloucestershire, England; mineral springs discovered (1716); has medicinal baths, winter gardens, parks, public school, and other educational institutions. Pop. 49,400.

Chelyabinsk′, town, Ural Area, Russia; corn trade; tanneries and distilleries; junction of rly. line from Leningrad via Perm and from Moscow via Samara; hence the gate of Siberia; centre of trade for Ural mining towns. Pop. 59,200.

Chem′nitz, tn., Saxony, Germany; one of the leading industrial commercial centres; has important locomotive and engineering works; manufactures fine cottons and woollens. Pop. 331,600.

Chemulp′ho, seapt., Korea; treaty port, opened 1883; exports soya beans, rice, hides; the Russo-Jap. War began here (1904). Pop. 53,700.

Chenab′, one of the 'five rivers,' Punjab, India; rises in Kashmir Mts., and with Jhelum, Ravi, and Sutlej joins Indus at Mithankot. Chenab Canal, largest and most profitable perennial canal in India, led to settlement of colony in formerly arid Rechna Doab, between Ravi and Chenab rivers.

Cheng-tu′, cap. of Szechwan, China; in centre of rich plain; silk, rice, fruit. Pop. (est.) 500,000.

Chepping Wycombe. See WYCOMBE.

Chep′stow, riv. port and mkt. tn., Monmouthshire, England, on r. bk. of Wye; ruins of 11th cent. castle; iron foundry, salmon fisheries; spring tides rise to height of 48 ft. Pop. 4,300.

Chequers (*chek′ers*), seat, Bucks, England, 2½ m. s.w. of Wendover. Gifted (1921) by Lord and Lady Lee of Fareham as official country residence of Prime Minister.

Cher (*shār*). (1) Riv., France, trib. of R. Loire; 200 m.; navigable for boats from Vierzon. (2) Dep., central France; generally flat, with low wooded hills; wheat, oats, wine; iron mines; porcelain. Chief tn., Bourges. Area, 2,819 sq. m.; pop. 298,400.

Cherbourg (*sher-boor′*), seaport, Manche, France, on N. coast of Cotentin peninsula; magnificent breakwater over two miles in length; has extensive docks and arsenal; chief importance is derived from its naval and commercial harbours; chief industries, shipbuilding, rope making, sugar refining, fishing and sawmilling; chief exports, stone; dairy and poultry produce. Pop. 43,700.

Cheribon′. (1) Prov., N. Java, Dutch E. Indies, producing sugar, coffee, rice, tea. Area, 2,620 sq. m.; pop. 1,006,000. (2) Seapt. tn., in above; exports sugar and coffee. Pop. 33,000.

Cher'iton, urb. dist., Kent, England, on coast 2 m. w. of Folkestone; wat.-pl. Pop. 8,100.

Cherkä'sy, tn., Ukraine, U.S.S.R., on Dnieper; sugar, tobacco; busy river port. Pop. 38,500.

Chernigov'. (1) Co., N. Ukraine, U.S.S.R.; plain, watered by Rs. Dnieper and Desna; climate is severe and soil is unfavourable to agriculture; main products are lumber, tan, leather goods. Area, 4,274 sq. m. (2) Cap. of above; leather goods and flour milling; two cathedrals. Pop. 34,300.

Cherrapunji (*cher'ra-poon'jē*), vil., Khasi Hills, Assam, India, 25 m. s. of Shillong; mean annual rainfall about 500 in., the heaviest known in the world. In 1861, 905 in. fell (366 in. in July).

Cherso (*ker'so*). (1) Isl., Gulf of Quernero, Adriatic Sea; belongs to Italy; long, narrow, mountainous; wine, fruits; sheep. Area, 150 sq. m.; pop. *c.* 8,000. (2) Seapt. and chief tn. of above; fishing, boat building. Pop. *c.* 4,000.

Chert'sey, urb. dist., Surrey, England, 23 m. s.w. of London; agricultural produce. Pop. 17,100.

Ches'apeake, bay, Atlantic coast, U.S.A.; receives rivers Susquehanna, Potomac, James, etc.; famous for oysters and wild fowl.

Chesham (*ches'am*), urb. dist., Bucks, England, on R. Chess, 5 m. s.w. of Berkhampstead; boots and brushes; wooden wares; brickfields. Pop. 8,800.

Chesh'ire, co., N.W. England. Bounded by Lancs, Yorks, Derby, Staffs, Salop, Denbigh, and Flint. Greater part of surface is undulating plain, with fine woods and number of small lakes; watered by Mersey, Dee, and other rivers; soil generally fertile; market gardening and dairying carried on, cheese largely produced; manufactures textiles and chemicals; shipbuilding, fisheries. Minerals include salt, coal. Canal systems of great importance include Manchester Ship Canal, Shropshire Union, and the Grand Trunk or Trent and Mersey. The county is well served with railways. Chief towns are Chester (cap.), Birkenhead, Macclesfield, Stockport, Crewe. Area, 1,028 sq. m.; pop. 1,087,500.

Cheshunt (*ches'unt*), urb. dist., on Lea, Hertfordshire, England, 16 m. N. of London by rail; nursery and market gardening. Pop. 14,700.

Ches'il Bank, remarkable ridge of sand and pebbles on coast of Dorsetshire, connecting Isle of Portland with mainland.

Ches'ter. (1) City, cap. of Cheshire, England, on R. Dee; canal port, great railway centre; surrounded by anc. walls; old Gothic cathedral (11th cent.); many old timbered houses; Gothic town hall; several public parks; racecourse ('Roodee'). Ironworks and breweries; manufactures of cheese, leather, gloves, boots, shoes. Pop. 41,000. (2) City, Pennsylvania, U.S.A., on the Delaware; military coll.; shipyard, lumber, and textiles. Pop. 41,400.

Ches'terfield, mkt. tn. and munic. bor., Derbyshire, England; Gothic church of All Saints and St. Mary contains anc. monuments, and has remarkable twisted spire, 230 ft. high; industries include making of fishing tackle, hosiery, cotton, machinery. Pop. 64,100.

Ches'ter-le-Street, tn., Durham, England, 6 m. N. of Durham; collieries, ironworks. Pop. 16,600.

Ches'terton, vil., on N. bank of the Cam, forming N.E. suburb of Cambridge, England; boat building and tile manufacture. Pop. 11,600.

Chev'iot Hills, range of rounded grassy hills forming border between England and Scotland; extending 35 m. N.E. to s.w.; highest point, 2,676 ft.; numerous ruins and border 'peels'; famed for valuable breed of sheep.

Cheyenne (*shī-en'*), cap. of Wyoming, U.S.A.; important railway terminus; centre of cattle industry of N.W.; railway works. Pop. 13,200.

Chhattisgarh (*chut-is-gār*), eastern div., Central Provinces, India; comprises the districts of Raipur, Bilaspur, and Drug. Area, 22,050 sq. m.; pop. 3,382,000.

Chhindwā'ra. (1) Dist. in Narbada div. of Central Provinces, India. Area, 4,630 sq. m.; pop. *c.* 491,000. (2) Tn. of above dist., 65 m. N. of Nagpur; market town with local industries in pottery and cotton hand-weaving. Pop. 13,400.

Chianti (*kē-an'tē*), mountain group of the Apennines, Upper Tuscany, Italy; vineyards supply well-known red wine of the same name.

Chiapas (*kē-ā'pas*), Pacific state, Mexico; mountainous; immense forests; chief products, dye and cabinet woods, cattle, hides, coffee, and rubber. Cap. Tuxtla-Gutierrez. Area, 27,222 sq. m.; pop. 456,400.

Chiavari (*kē-ā'vä-rē*), tn., Liguria, Italy, 24 m. E.S.E. of Genoa; manufactures chairs, lace, and silk. Pop. 12,500.

Chicago (*shi-kaw'gō*), city, Illinois, U.S.A.; at S.W. end of Lake Michigan, on small river Chicago; second largest city in U.S.A.; regularly laid out, with wide streets crossing each other at right angles; many fine parks, which almost surround city; some fine public buildings, including town hall, art institute, museum, library, auditorium, R.C. and Prot. cathedrals. One of busiest commercial centres in world, increasing in wealth and population. Natural advantages of situation, railway and waterway facilities, and enterprise and keen commercial spirit of its merchants, have made it what it is. Trade in grain, flour, and pork is enormous, surpassing anything else of kind in world; there are factories and workshops connected with hog and beef packing, soap, rolling mills, foundries, machinery, wagons, agricultural implements, cars, bridges, tanneries, boot making, electric supplies, jewellery, furniture, pianos, breweries, tobacco, clothing, furs, printing, bakeries, coffee and spice mills, all turning out products of large value. Rapid development was chiefly due to construction of Illinois and Michigan Canal and development of lake trade; in 1837 the town had about 4,000 inhabitants; pop. (1930) 3,375,000.

Chich'ester, city and munic. bor., Sussex, England, between S. Downs and an inlet of the Eng. Channel; has old octagonal market cross and remains of ancient walls; Holy Trinity Cathedral (dating from 11th cent.) has a detached belfry and contains interesting relics. No outstanding industries, but wooden ware, coal, timber, corn, flour, and malt are produced. Pop. 13,900.

Chick'asha, tn., Oklahoma, U.S.A., 40 m. S.W. of Oklahoma; trade centre for corn, cotton, live-stock. Pop. 14,000.

Chiclä'na, tn., Spain, 10 m. S.E. of Cadiz; mineral springs; centre of fruit and vine-growing district. Pop. 12,000.

Chic'opee, town, Massachusetts, U.S.A., at confluence of Chicopee and Connecticut rivs., 4 m. N. of Springfield; manufactures cotton, hardware, firearms, carpets, and automobiles. Pop. 44,000.

Chicoutimi (*shē-koo-tē-mē'*), chief tn., Chicoutimi co., Quebec, Canada, *c.* 230 m. N. of Quebec city; centre for lumber, pulp, and paper industries; great hydro-electric station. Pop. 8,900.

Chidam'baram, tn., Madras, India, 40 m. S. of Pondicherry; famous for great Hindu temple; visited by large numbers of pilgrims. Pop. 22,500.

Chieng-mai (*shē-eng-mī'*), trading tn., N. Siam; terminus of rly. from Bangkok; founded 11th cent.; walls and fortifications now in ruins; centre of teak trade. Pop. *c.* 30,000.

Chieri (*kē-ā'rē*), tn., episc. see, Piedmont, Italy, 8 m. S.E. of Turin; Gothic cathedral; manufactures silks and cottons. Pop. 13,600.

Chieti (*kē-ā'tē*). (1) Prov., Abruzzi, central Italy; barren mountainous region with low, fertile coast belt;

prod. include wheat, olives, wine, flax, tobacco, textiles, hats, leather goods; fishing, preparation of salt. Area, 1,001 sq. m.; pop. 333,600. (2) Cap. of above; archiepiscopal see; manufactures woollens, hats, soap. Pop. 17,900.

Chignecto (*shig-nek'tō*), bay, forming N.E. branch of Bay of Fundy, between Nova Scotia and New Brunswick, Canada.

Chig'well, par. and vil., Essex, England, 13 m. N.E. of London; in 'King's Head Inn' is room where Dickens wrote part of *Barnaby Rudge*. Pop. (par.) 2,900.

Chihli. (1) Prov., China. See HOPEH. (2) GULF OF. See POHAI.

Chihuahua (*chē-wä'wa*). (1) State, N. Mexico; hot, dry climate; in E., large tracts devoid of vegetation; traversed in W. by Sierra Madre, which form fruitful valleys of good pasture; primarily cattle country—great meat-raising dist. of Mexico; rich in minerals, gold and silver mining being principal industry. Area, 90,036 sq. m.; pop. 401,600. (2) City, cap. of above; mining; manufactures cotton and woollen goods. Pop. 37,100.

Chilas (*chē'las*), vil. and fort on R. Indus, Kashmir, India; strategic importance; commands direct route to Gilgit from Punjab.

Chile, or CHILI (*chi-lē'*), republic, S. America, lying along W. coast between main chain of Andes and Pacific; greatest length, 2,661 m.; breadth varies from 60 to 273 m.; bounded N. by Peru, E. by Bolivia and Argentina. Surface generally falls from E. to W., and also from N. to S., Andes being higher in N. than in S.; average height of Andes about 9,000 ft.—highest peak, Aconcagua (22,868 ft.). Many of these mountains are dormant or subdormant volcanoes. From E. to W. there are the Andes, a central valley tableland, the Coast Cordillera, and a coastal strip; the Andes slope down as they pass southward and finally dip under sea so that the Coast Cordillera to the W. takes the form of a chain of islands parallel to southern third of coast and curving S. round Tierra del Fuego. Juan Fernandez I., W. of Valparaiso, belongs to Chile. Owing to wide range of latitude climate is very varied; desert of Atacama in N. is practically rainless; but further S., in the region of the westerly winds, rainfall gradually increases and is adequate. Temperature is low, considering latitude, owing to influence of Humboldt Current; chief rivers are Maipu, Biobio, Loa, Copiapo, and Valdivia, providing a large amount of potential water-power. Soil of valleys in central provinces is very fertile; over half population engaged in agriculture, producing wheat and other cereals, rearing sheep and cattle, growing vines, oranges, figs, olives, and other fruits, and producing silk. In S. and islands are dense forests; in N. are enormous deposits of nitrates, which are great source of wealth. Other minerals of importance include copper, silver, manganese, gold, cobalt, iron, coal. Industries include copper smelting, sugar refining, tanning, manufacture of soap, candles, chemicals, boots, shoes, textiles. Chief exports are copper, nitrates, iodine, guano, wool, borax, and meat. Transandine Rly. brings Santiago within 36 hours of Buenos Aires. Chile is well provided with telegraphic communications. Chief towns are Santiago and Valparaiso. Area, 290,084 sq. m.; pop. 3,753,800.

Chil'koot (or CHILCOOT) **Pass,** a difficult pass over Coast Range of Rocky Mts., N. America, between Alaska and Yukon; highest point, 3,502 ft.; for some time one of the principal routes to the Yukon goldfields; open during most of year.

Chillan (*chēl-yän'*), tn., Chile, 55 m. N.E. of Concepcion; trade in cattle, grain, hand-made lace; hot sulphur springs. Pop. 30,900.

Chillicothe (*chil-i-koth'ē*). (1) City, Ohio, U.S.A., 45 m. S. of Columbus; rly. workshops, furniture, paper, leather. Pop. 15,800. (2) City,

Missouri, U.S.A., 70 m. N.E. of Kansas; coal, timber, and live-stock. Pop. 6,800.

Chiloe (*chē-lō-ā'*), southern prov., Chile, including large island of same name off coast, and about sixty smaller islands; cap. Puerto Montt. Area, *c.* 37,000 sq. m.; pop. *c.* 247,500.

Chil'tern Hills, low range of chalk downs crossing Buckinghamshire and Oxfordshire, England; highest peak, Wendover Hill, 905 ft.

Chil'vers Coton, suburb of Nuneaton, Warwickshire, England; coal mines; brick and tile works. Pop. 12,770.

Chimborazo (*chim-bō-rä'zō*). (1) Prov., Ecuador, S. America; sulphur. Area, 2,989 sq. m.; pop. 125,000. (2) Extinct craterless volcano in the Andes, Ecuador; alt. 20,498 ft.; snow-capped; several glaciers; first ascended by Whymper (1879–80).

Chim'kent, tn., Sir Darya prov., Kazak Rep., U.S.S.R., 70 m. N.N.E. of Tashkent; health resort; manufactures cotton, tobacco, flour. Pop. 21,700.

China, republic, eastern Asia; bounded N. by Siberia; E. by Korea, Yellow Sea, China Sea; S. by Fr. Indo-China, India; W. by Afghanistan and Turkestan; includes China Proper (with Manchuria), Mongolia, Tibet, and Sinkiang. Greater China is traversed by two folded mountain systems which stretch from Pamir plateau. To N.E. the Tien-Shan extend to the Khingan Mts. of Manchuria; S. of Taklamakan and Gobi Deserts the Kunlun Mts. continue into Honan as the Chin-ling-shan and Fu-niu-shan, while in W. Kansu the branch is the Nan-shan. Mts. of Shantung, forming a peninsula between the Gulf of Pohai and the Yellow Sea, are an isolated system. There are numerous other ranges. In products and climate the Kunlun Mts. divide N. from S. China. In the E. there is a great alluvial plain which covers over 200,000 sq. m. and supports an enormous population. Principal rivers are Yangtze Kiang, Hwang-Ho, and Si-kiang. There are numerous canals, including the Grand Canal, which crosses plain from Hangchow to Tientsin (850 m.). There are many lakes, chief of which are Tungting, Po-yang, and Tai-hu. As a defence against northern tribes the Great Wall, length *c.* 1,500 m., was completed in 214 B.C. The climate varies greatly from S. to N., and from coast to interior; it is generally monsoon in type with rain between April and Sept. Temperature in N. ranges from 23° to 80° F. at Peking, in S. from 60° to 85° F.; excessive dryness characterizes interior. Many parts of the country are extremely fertile, particularly the loess region of the N., the red basin of Szechwan, and the river valleys. Extensive forests are rare, but bamboo is of prime importance, while the camphor tree, maple, ebony, etc., are found, as is also the mulberry (for silkworms). Fish ranks with rice as staple food. China is very rich in minerals, possessing enormous coalfields which could make it one of the first coal-producing countries in the world; iron, copper, antimony, tin, zinc are also worked. Chinese are, however, primarily an agricultural people. Chief crops are rice, wheat, barley, millet, buckwheat, maize, soya bean in the N., and rice, cotton, indigo, sugar in S. Area under opium poppy is decreasing Pigs are reared everywhere. China produces much silk, but Chinese manufactures of silks and embroideries, porcelains, paper, lacquer ware, cotton, etc., are still largely carried on by manual labour; modern sugar refineries have been set up at Hong Kong, Swatow, and Amoy; iron and steel works at Han-yang, and many flour, rice, and oil mills. About fifty treaty ports and twenty-five other places are open to international trade. Chief exports are silk and manufactures, beans and bean cakes, tea, cotton, skins, and hides, sesamum seeds, tin, etc.

Most populous provs. are Szechwan and Kwangtung. Over sixty races or tribes are represented in republic and dependencies, comprising Chinese, Manchus, Mongols, Tibetans, etc. Present cap. Nanking; former cap. Peking (until 1928). Area (est.) 4,279,170 sq. m.; pop. (est.) 440,000,000.

Chinan. See TSINAN.

Chinande'ga, tn., w. Nicaragua, Central America; bananas, sugar-cane, and cotton are cultivated; mining is carried on. Pop. 14,400.

China Sea, part of Pacific Ocean, stretching from Korea to Malay Peninsula; two sections linked by Straits of Formosa—N. China Sea, including Eastern and Yellow Seas, and S. China Sea, from Formosa to Singapore. The sea is subject to typhoons in summer; it is rich in fish.

Chinde (*shēn'dā*), seapt., Portuguese E. Africa, at mouth of Chinde R.; only navigable mouth of Zambezi; chief port for Zambezi valley, and also serving Nyasaland.

Chindwin'. (1) Two districts (Upper and Lower), Sagaing div., Upper Burma; mountainous; valuable teak forests; extensive coalfields; rice cultivated. Areas, 16,037 and 3,480 sq. m.; pops. 186,900 and 342,900. (2) Riv., flowing through above; principal trib. of Irrawaddy; navigable over 400 m. during certain seasons of the year for steamers.

Ching'ford, urban dist., Essex, England, near Epping Forest; tourist resort. Pop. 22,100.

Ching'leput. (1) Dist., surrounding city of Madras, India; generally flat; soil poor; badly watered; suffered from famine; cotton and silk weaving. Area, 2,824 sq. m.; pop. 1,500,000. (2) Tn. in above, 30 m. s. of Madras; manufactures pottery. Pop. 11,800.

Chinkiang, city and treaty port, Kiang-su, China; on Yangtze, 160 m. above Shanghai; important commercial centre; chiefly acts as distributor of imported goods; trade is suffering through gradual silting up of harbour. Pop. *c.* 115,000.

Chinon (*shē-non'*), tn., Indre-et-Loire, France, 26 m. s.w. of Tours; trade in basket and rope manufactures; famous castle where Joan of Arc had first interview with Charles VII. Pop. 4,170.

Chinwangtao', treaty port, Hopeh, China; recently constructed harbour; exports coal; only ice-free port on w. shore of Gulf of Pohai. Pop. *c.* 5,000.

Chioggia (*kē-oj'e-a*), seapt., episc. see, Venezia, Italy; has ancient corn market (1322); fishing and coasting trade. Pop. 36,100.

Chios, KHIOS, or SCIO (*kī'os* or *kē'os*), Greek isl., Ægean Sea, off w. coast, Asia Minor; mountainous; subject to earthquakes; fine climate; fertile and well cultivated; antimony mines and marble quarries. Wine, figs, and gum mastic are chief exports. Chief tn., Chios, is by tradition birthplace of Homer. Area, *c.* 300 sq. m.; pop. (isl.) 75,700.

Chip'penham, mkt. tn., munic. bor., Wiltshire, England, 20 m. E. of Bristol; chief industries are ironfounding, boot making, bacon curing. Pop. 8,500.

Chip'pewa Falls, city, Wisconsin, U.S.A., 83 m. E. of St. Paul; lumber; flour and woollen mills; breweries. Pop. 9,000.

Chip'ping Nor'ton, munic. bor., Oxfordshire, England, 16 m. N.W. of Oxford; woollens, horsecloths, gloves. Pop. 3,500.

Chirk, par. and vil., Denbighshire, Wales, 9 m. s. of Wrexham; coal mines; paper. Pop. (par.) 3,000.

Chisinau (*kish-in-ow'*), formerly KISHINEV, tn., Bessarabia, N.E. Romania; centre of trade in grain, wine, tobacco, tallow, wool and hides; manufactures include brandy, leather, soap. Pop. 190,000.

Chis'lehurst, urban dist., Kent, England, 11 m. S.E. of London; mansion, Camden Place, was residence of Napoleon III., who died here (1873), and of Empress Eugénie (1871–80); residential dist. Pop. 9,900.

Chiswick. See BRENTFORD AND CHISWICK.

Chita (*chē'ta*), tn., Far Eastern Area, U.S.S.R.; at head of navigation of Amur system; important entrepôt of trade; administrative and commercial centre; exports furs, cattle, hides, tallow. Pop. 57,700.

Chitaldroog. (1) Dist., N. Mysore, India; poor soil; scanty rainfall; subject to periodic droughts and famine; cotton, rice. Area, 4,022 sq. m.; pop. 574,200. (2) Tn., administrative centre of above; cotton cloth. Pop. 8,500.

Chitral, small Indian state, s. of Hindu Kush Mts., N.W. Frontier Prov., Brit. India, occupies fertile valley of Chitral R.; cap. Chitral; is of great strategical importance, as it commands principal passes over the Hindu Kush. Area, *c.* 4,500 sq. m.; pop. *c.* 35,000.

Chittagong. (1) Maritime dist., Bengal, India, extending from Bay of Bengal to Lushai Hills. Area, 2,497 sq. m.; pop. 1,611,000. (2) Chief tn. of above; important trading centre; terminus of Assam–Bengal railway and chief port for Assam; exports jute, rice, tea, hides; mineral oil. Pop. 36,000.

Chittoor, tn., Madras, India, 80 m. w. of Madras; chief tn. of dist. of same name; Hyder Ali died here (1782). Pop. 17,900.

Chiusi (*kē-ooz'ē*), tn., episc. see, Tuscany, Italy, 37 m. S.E. of Siena; collection of Etruscan antiquities; 12th cent. cathedral. Pop. (comm.) 6,740.

Chivasso (*kē-vas'ō*), tn., episc. see, Italy, 12 m. N.E. of Turin; trade in cattle, corn, and silk; important fortress in Middle Ages. Pop. (comm.) 10,900.

Chobe (*chō'bā*), riv., S. Africa; rises in Angola; large r. bk. tributary of Zambezi; basin is forested and very fertile. Length, *c.* 600 m.; discovered by Livingstone (1851).

Choisy-le-Roi (*shwa-zē-le-rwa'*), tn., Seine, France, 7 m. S.E. of Paris; porcelain, earthenware, felt hats, gloves, etc. Pop. 15,900.

Chojnice (*koi-nē'tse*), formerly KONITZ, tn., Poland, 81 m. s. of Danzig; brushes, bricks, electrical works. Pop. 11,000.

Cholet (*shō-lā*), tn., Maine-et-Loire, France, 32 m. s.w. of Angers; linen manufactures; important agricultural centre. Pop. 17,900.

Cholon (*shō-lon'*), tn., Cochin China, French Indo-China, 4 m. s.w. of Saigon; commercial centre; extensive rice trade. Pop. *c.* 200,000.

Cholu'la, anc. tn., Puebla, Mexico, 6 m. w. of Puebla; remarkable pyramidal temple (177 ft. high and 1,423 ft. on E. side of base), dedicated to the god Quetzalcoatl. Pop. 6,300.

Chomutov (*ko'mū-tof*), formerly KOMOTAU, tn., Bohemia, Czechoslovakia, 50 m. N.W. of Prague; lignite mines; textiles, paper; distilleries, breweries, and rly. workshops. Pop. 21,000.

Chor'ley, munic. bor., Lancashire, England, 9 m. S.E. of Preston; cotton manufactures; coal mines and metal working. Pop. 30,800.

Chor'leywood, urb. dist., Hants, England, 18 m. N.W. of London; residential dist. Pop. 3,300.

Chor'lu, tn., European Turkey, 60 m. w. by N. of Constantinople; manufactures carpets. Pop. *c.* 10,000.

Chosen (*chō-sen*). See KOREA.

Cho'ta Nag'pur, div., central Bihar and Orissa, comprising, in addition to the Brit. districts, several tributary states; mountainous; forest-covered; rich in minerals; other chief productions are rice, lace, and tussore silk. Area, 27,065 sq. m.; pop. 5,653,000.

Christ'church. (1) Tn., Hampshire, England, at junction of Rs. Avon and Stour; famous church dating from 1095. Pop. 9,200. (2) City, Canterbury, South I., New Zealand; bishop's see; cathedral, government museum; manufactures boots; iron and agricultural implement works. Centre of rich agricultural district. Pop. (with suburbs) 122,000.

Christiania. See OSLO.

Chris'tiansand, fortified seapt., on fiord of Skagerrak, Norway, *c.* 170 m.

s.w. of Oslo; exports timber and fish. Pop. 16,500.

Christmas Island. (1) Brit. isl., Pacific Ocean, near equator, s. of Hawaii; discovered by Captain Cook, who celebrated Christmas here (1777); largest atoll in Pacific. (2) Isl., Indian Ocean, s. of Java; included in Straits Settlements (1900); exports phosphate of lime. Area, *c.* 62 sq. m.; pop. 1,160.

Chrudim (*chrood'yim*), tn., Bohemia, Czechoslovakia, 60 m. E. of Prague; manufactures agricultural implements; industries include manufacture of sugar, spirits, beer, and flour. Pop. 13,100.

Chuanchow, seapt., Fukien, China; centre of rice growing. Pop. *c.* 200,000.

Chubut (*choo-boot'*), terr., s. Argentine Republic; cattle breeding; cap. Rawson. Area, 93,427 sq. m.; pop. 32,900.

Chud'leigh, mkt. tn., S.E. Devon, England, on R. Teign, 14¾ m. by rail s.w. of Exeter; ruins of Bishop of Exeter's palace (1080). Pop. 2,000.

Chumbi Valley, Tibetan valley, Himalaya Mts., between Sikkim and Bhutan; main route from Bengal to Lhasa; by this route Sir F. Younghusband entered Tibet (1904). Elevation, 9,500 ft.

Chungking, commercial cap., prov. Szechwan, China, on Yangtze Kiang; treaty port; great entrepôt; exports include opium, silk, wax, beans, sugar; imports manufactured goods and machinery. Pop. *c.* 623,000.

Chuquisaca (*choo-ke-sä'ka*), dep., Bolivia, S. America; produces petroleum; grazing is carried on, and sheep, cattle, and llamas are raised; cereals are grown; cap. Sucre. Area, 36,132 sq. m.; pop. *c.* 242,000.

Chur, or COIRE, chief tn., Grisons, E. Switzerland; tourist resort; rich in antiquities; bishop's see. Pop. 15,600.

Church, urb. dist., S.E. Lancs, England, 4 m. E. of Blackburn; coal; print and dye works; chemicals. Pop. 6,200.

Church'ill. (1) Riv., Saskatchewan and Manitoba, Canada; flows through system of interconnected lakes; impeded by rapids; enters Hudson Bay. Length, 900 m. (2) Formerly FORT CHURCHILL, at mouth of Churchill R.; a station of Hudson's Bay Co., Manitoba, Canada; northern terminus of Hudson Bay Rly., on Hudson Bay.

Church Stret'ton, urb. dist., Salop, England, 12¾ m. by rail s.w. of Shrewsbury; fine scenery. Pop. 1,700.

Chu'san Archipelago, group of islands off N.E. coast, China; chief products, tea, rice, tobacco, camphor, fish; largest island, Chusan.

Chuvash', rep., central Russia; R. Volga flows through N. portion; traversed by Trans-Siberian Rly. from Moscow; extreme climate; forests in s.; chief crop, oats; cattle and poultry products exported; chief tn., Cheboksari, 125 m. E. of Nijni-Novgorod. Area, 7,107 sq. m.; pop. 895,000.

Cicero (*sis'erō*), tn., Illinois, U.S.A., 7 m. w. of Chicago; manufactures electrical apparatus, engines, pumps, enamelled ware. Pop. 66,000.

Cienfuegos (*thē-ān-fu-ā'gōs*), tn., s. Cuba; magnificent landlocked harbour; centre of sugar trade. Pop. 73,500.

Cieszyn. See TESCHEN (2).

Cieza (*thē-ā'tha*), tn., S.E. Spain, 24 m. N.W. of Murcia; flour and paper mills; and produces wines, esparto grass, grain. Pop. 13,700.

Cilli, or CELJE (*sel'ye*), tn., Slavonia, Yugoslavia, 38 m. N.E. of Ljubljana; coal mines; zinc-smelting furnaces; museum contains Roman remains. Pop. 7,700.

Cincinnat'i, second largest tn. of Ohio, U.S.A., on N. bank of Ohio R.; has important public buildings; archiepiscopal see of R.C. church and episcopal see of Prot. church; univ. (1873) is the only munic. univ. in U.S.A.; fine system of parks; important trading, railway, and industrial centre. Chief industries are transport of grain and trade in pork; manufactures include making of clothes, furniture, leather, shoes, tobacco, cutlery, saddlery, carriages; large river and canal traffic. Pop. 449,000.

Cinque Ports (*sank*), old name given to the five ports of Hastings, Romney, Hythe, Dover, and Sandwich; to these Winchelsea and Rye were added in the reign of Henry III. and other small places incorporated, the whole forming a jurisdiction for the defence of the coast of Kent and Sussex.

Cin'tra, tn., Estremadura, Portugal, 14 m. N.W. of Lisbon; beautifully situated; contains Moorish relics; by Convention of Cintra (1808) Napoleon undertook to evacuate Portugal. Pop. 7,100.

Circas'sia, region, W. Caucasus, part of North Caucausian Area, Russia; lies between Kuban R. and Black Sea; mountainous; Circassians are noted for their beauty, and are Mohammedans.

Cirencester (*sīr-en-ses'ter* or *sis'-et-er*), mkt. tn., Gloucester, England, 15 m. S.E. of Gloucester; 15th cent. church with three-storeyed porch; agricultural industries; contains Royal Agricultural Coll. Pop. 7,200.

Città di Castello (*chit'a dē kas-tel'o*), tn., episc. see, Italy, on R. Tiber, 26 m. N. of Perugia; mineral springs in vicinity; fine Renaissance buildings. Pop. 30,000.

Città Vecchia (*chit'ta vek'ke-a*), fort. city, Malta; bishop's see; cathedral. Pop. *c.* 6,000.

Ciudad Bolivar (*thē-oo-dad' bō-lē'-vār*), formerly ANGOSTURA, tn., cap. of Bolivar, Venezuela; commercial centre of Orinoco basin; trades in rubber, cattle, tobacco, coffee. Pop. *c.* 15,000.

Ciudad Porfirio Diaz (*thē-oo-dad' por-fē'ri-ō dē'as*). See PIEDRAS NEGRAS.

Ciudad Real (*thē-oo-dad' rā-al*). (1) Prov., Spain; intersected by riv. Guadiana; climate extreme; prod. grain, vegetables, wine; sheep, goats, and mules are reared. Area, 7,620 sq. m.; pop. 427,400. (2) Cap. of above; episc. see; market for cereals, oil, and wine of surrounding district. Pop. 19,000.

Ciudad Rodrigo (*thē-oo-dad' rō-drē'gō*), tn., Spain, near Portuguese frontier; trades in cereals, charcoal; manufactures soap, leather, linen, woollens; famous for siege during Peninsular War. Pop. 8,700.

Cividale del Friuli (*chē-vē-dāl'ā del frē-oo'lē*), tn., episc. see, Venetia, Italy, 10 m. N.E. of Udine; cathedral with baptistery (8th cent.); bridge (15th cent.); museum of antiquities; linen and cotton manufactures. Pop. 11,400.

Civita Vecchia (*chē'vē-tā vek'e-a*), seapt. tn., bathing-place, episc. see, Rome, Italy; cement works; sulphur springs and remains of Roman baths. Pop. 23,300.

Clackman'nan, co. tn., on Black Devon R., Clackmannanshire, Scotland; anc. market cross; ruins of Clackmannan Tower, once seat of Bruces; yarn mill; coal and ironstone mines; sandstone quarries. Pop. 2,600.

Clackman'nanshire, smallest co., Scotland; lies between Ochil Hills and Forth; bounded by Perth, Kinross, Fife, and Stirling; surface partly flat (carse), partly undulating and hilly; soil is fertile and well cultivated; uplands afford excellent pasturage; is rich in minerals, coal being extensively mined; woollen manufactures, distilleries, shipbuilding yards, and bottle and glass works. Chief towns, Alloa, Clackmannan (co. tn.), Alva, Dollar, Tillicoultry. Area, 55 sq. m.; pop. 31,900.

Clac'ton-on-Sea, urban dist., wat.-pl., Essex, England, 12 m. S.E. of Colchester. Pop. 15,900.

Clap'ham. (1) Parl. division, eccles. par., and part of civil par. of Wandsworth bor., S.W. London; residential suburb. Clapham Common is public park of 220 ac. Clapham Junction, which does not serve Clapham, is a great rly. centre. (2) Vil. and par., Yorkshire, England, 16 m. E.N.E. of

Lancaster; tourist centre; Ingleborough Cave, with stalactites, in vicinity. Pop. (par.) 600.

Clare, co., Munster, I.F.S.; bounded N. by Galway, E. by Tipperary, S. by Shannon estuary, W. by Atlantic; surface generally hilly, with some level tracts; bogs in W.; tracts of rich loam on banks of Shannon and Fergus; chief lake, Lough Derg, on eastern boundary; coast precipitous and much indented; chief islands, Aran Isles; important fisheries round coast, especially oysters; sheep and cattle raised; no important manufactures; agriculture neglected, except oats, potatoes. Minerals include iron, manganese, lead; mineral springs occur in several places. There are many old fortified castles. Chief tn., Ennis. Area, 1,230 sq. m.; pop. 95,000.

Clarks'burg, tn., West Virginia, U.S.A., on R. West Fork, 90 m. N.E. of Charleston; in mining and agricultural area; glass, pottery, tinplate, bricks, tiles, machinery are produced. Pop. 29,000.

Clay Cross, urb. dist., N.E. Derbyshire, England, 4 m. S. of Chesterfield; coal and iron mines. Pop. 8,500.

Clayton-le-Moors, urb. dist., S.E. Lancs, England, 4½ m. N.E. of Blackburn; calico-printing, cotton, machinery, soap. Pop. 7,900.

Cleat'or Moor, tn., Cumberland, England, 4 m. S.E. of Whitehaven; iron mining and engineering works. Pop. 6,600.

Cle'burne, tn., Texas, U.S.A., 25 m. S. of Fort Worth; large railway workshops; flour mills; a shipping point for live-stock, cotton, and grain. Pop. 11,000.

Cleck'heaton, tn., W. Riding, Yorkshire, England, 5 m. S.E. of Bradford; staple industries are manufacture of woollen and flannel goods. Pop. 12,500.

Clee'thorpes, tn. and wat.-pl., Lincolnshire, England, 2 m. S.E. of Grimsby. Pop. 28,600.

Clerk'enwell, northern par. in bor. of Finsbury, London, England; centre of watch making and jewellery.

Clermont-Ferrand (*klăr-mon' ferrăn*), chief tn., Puy-de-Dôme, central France; bishop's see; has famous mineral springs. Chief manufactures, preserves, semolina, chemicals, rubber goods; important grain and cattle market. Pop. 101,500.

Clermont-l'Hérault (*klăr-mon-lă-rō'*), tn., Hérault, S. France, 20 m. W. of Montpellier; woollen manufacture, tanning and leather dressing. Pop. 5,000.

Cleve, or KLEVE (Fr. *Clèves*), tn., Rhenish Prussia, Germany, about 2 m. from l. bk. of R. Rhine; manufactures boots, shoes, machinery, tobacco; mineral wells; growing summer resort. Cap. of former duchy of same name. Pop. 20,000.

Cleve'don, urb. dist., N.E. Somersetshire, England; seaside resort. Pop. 7,000.

Cleve'land. (1) Parl. dist., N.E. Yorkshire, England; chiefly moorland; crossed by Cleveland Hills, which are famous for exceedingly rich deposits of iron ore; numerous blast furnaces, supplying about one-third of the total pig-iron for Great Britain; fine breed of horses. Area, 420 sq. m. (2) City, Ohio, U.S.A., on S. shore of Lake Erie, and on Cuyahoga R., which forms inner harbour; northern terminus of Ohio Canal; great railway centre. Cleveland is chief centre in U.S.A. for iron ore; great lumber and coal trade; iron manufacture in all branches; petroleum refineries, meat-packing establishments, manufacture of clothing, paint, chemicals. Pop. 900,000.

Cleve'land Heights, town, Ohio, U.S.A.; adjoins Cleveland, of which it is a residential suburb. Pop. 50,000.

Cleve'leys, tn., Lancs, England, 4 m. N. of Blackpool; seaside resort. Pop. 2,920.

Cleves. See CLEVE.

Clif'ton, W. suburb of Bristol, Gloucestershire, England; mineral springs; Roman relics; famous public school; suspension bridge over Avon gorge. (2) Tn., New Jersey, U.S.A., close to tn. of Passaic; manufactures include woollens, leather belting, steel goods, chemicals. Pop. 46,000.

Clin'ton. (1) City, E. Iowa, U.S.A., on Mississippi R.; seat of Wartburg Coll.; numerous mills; furniture and structural ironwork. Pop. 26,000. (2) Tn., Massachusetts, U.S.A., 15 m. N.N.E. of Worcester; prod. machinery, carpets, ginghams. Pop. 12,000.

Clith'eroe, munic. bor. and mkt. tn., Lancashire, England, 34 m. N. of Manchester; remains of 12th cent. castle; 16th cent. grammar school; cotton and paper mills. Pop. 12,000.

Clonakil'ty, seapt., mkt. tn., co. Cork, I.F.S., on Clonakilty Bay; breweries, corn mills, yarn. Pop. 2,800.

Clones, mkt. tn., W. Monaghan, I.F.S.; corn mills and agricultural trade; interesting ruins. Pop. 2,400.

Clonmacnoise', par., Offaly co., I.F.S., on R. Shannon; seat of religion and learning in anc. times; many remarkable antiquities. Pop. 700.

Clonmel', munic. bor., mkt. tn., co. Tipperary, I.F.S., on R. Suir; brewing, tanning; exports corn, cattle, provisions, butter. Pop. 9,000.

Clovel'ly, vil., N. Devon, England, 11 m. S.W. of Bideford; on cliff, 400 ft. high; fishing; famed for picturesque scenery. Pop. 600.

Cluj (*klŭẓh*), formerly KOLOZSVAR or KLAUSENBURG, tn., Transylvania, Romania; cap. of dep. of same name; intellectual centre of Transylvania; industries include making of textiles, paper, sugar, soap, earthenware. Pop. 110,000.

Clu'ny, tn., Saône-et-Loire, France, 12 m. N.W. of Macon; famous Benedictine Abbey (founded 910), now in ruins; great seat of learning, 11th and 12th cents.; paper, pottery, leather. Pop. 3,300.

Clu'tha, riv., S.E. Otago, South Island, New Zealand (named after R. Clyde, Scotland); drains Lakes Hawea, Wanaka, and Wakatipu; alluvial deposits rich in gold; length, 154 m.

Clwyd, riv., Denbighshire, N. Wales, flows through picturesque valley for 31 m., and enters Irish Sea at Rhyl.

Clyde (anc. *Clutha*), riv., W. of Scotland; rises in S. borders of Lanarkshire; enters Firth of Clyde at Dumbarton; navigable for liners up to Glasgow; of great commercial importance, and principal shipbuilding centre in world; has celebrated falls, near Lanark, where there are hydro-electric power stations; valley famous for 'Clydesdale' horses; orchards; iron and coal fields; about one-third of population of Scotland found in its basin. Length, 105 m.; drainage area, 1,481 sq. m.

Clydebank, police and munic. burgh, Dumbartonshire, Scotland; extensive shipbuilding and engineering works; manufacture of sewing-machines. Pop. 47,000.

Coahuila (*kō-a-wē'la*), northern state, Mexico, adjoining Texas; rich in minerals; coal, copper, silver, and gold; agricultural products include cotton, Indian corn, wheat, and beans. Chief tn., Saltillo, in S.E. of state. Area, 63,786 sq. m.; pop. 393,500.

Coal'brookdale, eccles. dist. and vil., Shropshire, England, 4 m. S. of Wellington; iron, brick, and tile works; iron bridge across Severn here. Pop. 1,400.

Coal'ville, tn., Leicestershire, England, 5 m. S.E. of Ashby-de-la-Zouche; extensive coalfields; tile and brick making; iron foundries and brick works. Pop. 21,900.

Coast Range. See ROCKY MTS.

Coatbridge, munic. burgh, tn., Lanarkshire, Scotland; centre of most important coal and iron dist. in Scotland; blast furnaces, tube works, boiler works, etc.; brick and tile works; technical school. Pop. 43,100.

Coates'ville, city, Pennsylvania, U.S.A., 35 m. W. of Philadelphia; industrial centre; iron, steel, brass foundries; silk mills. Pop. 15,000.

Coats Land, part of Antarctica, on E. shore of Weddell Sea.

Co'balt, tn., Ontario, Canada, *c.* 330 m. N. of Toronto; centre of rich silver district; also produces cobalt, arsenic, and nickel. Pop. 4,400.

Coban', tn., Guatemala, Central America, 60 m. N. of Guatemala City; centre of coffee trade. Pop. *c.* 23,000.

Co'bar, municipality, post tn., New South Wales, Australia, 350 m. N.W. of Sydney; large copper mines in neighbourhood; gold and silver; also an important pastoral centre. Pop. *c.* 1,500.

Cobh (*kōv*), formerly QUEENSTOWN, tn., seaport, and port of call, co. Cork, I.F.S.; situated on Great Island, Cork Harbour; is port of call for U.S.A. mail steamers; naval docks. Pop. 7,100.

Cob'ham, or CHURCH COBHAM, par. and vil., Surrey, England, on R. Mole, 6½ m. W. of Epsom; in wooded country; sawmills. Pop. (par.) 5,100.

Coblenz (*kō'blents*), fortified town, cap. of Rhine Province, Prussia, Germany, at confluence of Rs. Rhine and Moselle; contains many fine buildings; centre of wine trade, and manufactures pianos, paper, machinery, and chemicals. Pop. 58,200.

Co'bourg, tn., Ontario, Canada, on Lake Ontario; woollen mills, carpet factories, foundries. Pop. 5,300.

Co'burg, manufacturing tn., N. Bavaria, Germany; many fine buildings and monuments, including statue of Prince Albert, erected by Queen Victoria (1865); important trade in cattle; manufactures include machinery, glass, and porcelain; there are iron foundries and sawmills. Pop. 24,700.

Cocanā'da, tn. and seapt., Madras, India, N. of R. Godavari delta; chief exports, cotton, oil-seeds, and rice. Pop. 53,300.

Cochabamba (*kō-cha-bam'ba*). (1) Dep. of Bolivia, S. America; products include dyewoods, timber, wheat, maize, sugar, cocoa, and coffee, and the precious metals. Area, 25,288 sq. m.; pop. *c.* 650,000. (2) Cap. of above, 130 m. S.E. of La Paz; manufactures include cotton and woollen goods, leather, and earthenware; railway development is adding to its importance. Pop. 43,000.

Cochin (*ko-chĕn'*). (1) Indian state, Madras, India, between Malabar and Travancore, a small portion of S.W. angle bordering Arabian Sea; surface generally occupies sloping plains; watered by numerous rivers forming series of shallow lagoons, subject in wet seasons to sudden floods; communication chiefly by boat; teak forests; rice, coconuts; cap. Ernakulam. Area, 1,418 sq. m.; pop. 979,000. (2) Seapt. tn., Malabar dist., Madras, India; first European fort built in India (1503); shipbuilding; exports coconut oil, coir, and tea. Pop. 20,600.

Cochin-China, colony, French Indo-China, bounded N. by Cambodia and Annam, S.E. by S. China Sea, W. by Gulf of Siam; surface mainly broad plain; mountainous in N.; watered by Mekong, Donnai, and other rivers; monsoon climate; chief prod. are rice, rubber, maize, cotton, fruits; river and coast fisheries. Majority of inhabitants are Annamese; religion, Buddhism; cap. Saigon. Area, 26,476 sq. m.; pop. 4,002,000.

Cocken'zie and Port Seton, combined police burgh in par. of Tranent, E. Lothian, Scotland, on Firth of Forth; fishing and coal mining. Pop. 2,500.

Cock'ermouth, mkt. tn., Cumberland, England, 23 m. S.W. of Carlisle; anc. castle (14th or 15th cent.); Wordsworth's birthplace; extensive coal mines in vicinity. Pop. 4,800.

Co'cos, isl., Pacific Ocean, off W. coast of S. America, to N. of Galapagos Islands; reputed site of pirates' buried treasure.

Co'cos (or KEELING) **Islands,** group of twenty-three atolls, Indian Ocean, 581 m. W. of Java; under Brit. protection since 1857; politically part of Singapore; copra, coconuts. Pop. *c.* 800.

Cof'feyville, city, S.E. Kansas, U.S.A., near border of Oklahoma; oil, zinc, bricks, flour; important shipping point for grain. Pop. 16,200.

Cog'geshall, tn., Essex, England, 6 m. E. of Braintree; ruins of priory; silk and velvet. Pop. 2,600.

Cognac (*kōn-yak'*), tn., Charente, W. France, on R. Charente; viticulture and manufacture of 'cognac'; cooperage, bottle works. Pop. 16,500.

Cohoes (*kō-hōz'*), city, New York, U.S.A., 9 m. N. of Albany; manufactures knitted goods from cotton, wool, worsted; paper mills, foundries. Pop. 23,000.

Coimbatore (*kō-im-bă-tōr'*). (1) Dist., Madras, India; flat country hemmed in by mountains on N., W., and S.; drained by Cauvery and feeders; pulses, tobacco, coffee; large forests with valuable timber. Area, 7,225 sq. m.; pop. 2,220,000. (2) Cap. of above, 80 m. S.E. of Calicut; cotton spinning, coffee, sugar. Pop. 65,800.

Coimbra (*kō-ēm'bra*). (1) Dist., Beira, Portugal. Area, 1,508 sq. m.; pop. 353,100. (2) Cap. of above, on R. Mondego; former cap. of Portugal; cathedral; important for its university, the only one in the country. Pop. 20,800.

Coin (*ko-ēn'*), tn., Malaga, S. Spain, 20 m. S.W. of Malaga; marble quarries; fruit. Pop. 11,600.

Coire (*kwar*). See CHUR.

Colchagua (*kol-chăg'wa*), prov., Chile, S. America; cap. San Fernando, 83 m. S. of Santiago; stock raising and mining are the chief industries; wheat, fruit, wine are exported. Area, 3,851 sq. m.; pop. 166,300.

Col'chester, mkt. tn. and riv. port, Essex, England, on R. Colne; castle—largest specimen of Norman architecture in England; remains of Augustinian Priory of St. Botolph; many churches; grammar school (founded 1539); market for oyster fisheries and agricultural produce, annual 'oyster feast.' Pop. 48,600.

Cold'stream, par. and police burgh, Berwickshire, Scotland, on R. Tweed; 'Coldstream Guards' raised here (1650) by General Monck; fishing centre; formerly matrimonial haven for runaway couples. Pop. (par.) 1,200.

Cole'ford, urb. dist., Glos, England, 4½ m. E.S.E. of Monmouth; on border of Forest of Dean; coal mines. Pop. 2,800.

Coleraine (*kōl-rān'*), port and mkt. tn., co. Londonderry, N. Ireland, on R. Bann; extensive linen industry, distilling, fisheries (salmon and eel). Pop. 8,100.

Coles'hill, mkt. tn., Warwickshire, England, on R. Cole, 8½ m. E. of Birmingham; Home for poor children. Pop. 3,250.

Colima (*ko-lē'ma*). (1) Small mountainous state, Mexico, on Pacific coast; on N. frontier is active Volcan de Colima (12,750 ft.); sugar, rice, maize, coffee; copper. Area, 2,272 sq. m.; pop. 91,800. (2) Tn., cap. of above; cotton, cigarettes; commercial centre. Pop. 28,300.

Coll, isl., Argyllshire, Scotland; one of Inner Hebrides, W. of Mull; dairy farming, sheep rearing; harbour at Arinangour. Pop. 400.

Col'lingwood. (1) Tn., Victoria, Australia; suburb of Melbourne; tanneries, breweries. Pop. *c.* 35,000. (2) Tn., Ontario, Canada, 90 m. N.W. of Toronto; shipbuilding yards and steel works. Pop. 5,900.

Col'mar, tn., Haut-Rhin, E. France; textile industries; bleaching and brewing; vineyards. Pop. 38,700.

Colne (*kōn*). (1) Munic. bor. and mkt. tn., Lancashire, England, 5 m. N.N.E. of Burnley; cotton. Pop. 23,800. (2) Riv., Essex, England; oyster fisheries.

Cologne (*ko-lōn'*), or KOLN, tn., Rhine Prov., Prussia, on R. Rhine; one of principal western fortresses of Germany. From its position at head of Rhine navigation for seagoing vessels, as centre of rail and river systems, and being near rich coal and iron field, Cologne has great commercial importance; archiepiscopal see; has magnificent Gothic cathedral, several other fine churches, and other interesting buildings; manufactures include cottons, woollens, beet sugar, chemicals, spirits of wine, eau-de-Cologne, tobacco, machinery, chocolate, carriages, porcelain, soap. Pop. 698,300.

Colombes (*ko-lonb'*), tn., Seine, France, 3 m. N.W. of Paris; petroleum refineries; manufactures vinegar and measuring instruments. Pop. 42,300

Colom'bia, republic, S. America; bounded N. by Caribbean Sea; E. by Venezuela, Brazil; S. by Peru, Ecuador; W. by Pacific, Panama. Extreme length, 1,050 m.; width, 860 m. From Pasto in S.W. corner three Cordilleran ranges spread out northwards, like ribs of fan. Main ranges are Western, Central, and Eastern Cordilleras; intervening valleys drained by Cauca and Magdalena rivers. These valleys are richly wooded. Unhealthy, swampy plains or llanos in E. are drained by head-waters of Orinoco. Climate varies greatly, ranging from tropical to arctic conditions according to elevation; rainy season, Oct. to Dec.; dry season, Dec. to Feb. Most of inhabitants live on plateaus, which are treeless but well-watered prairies, of which those of Antioquia and Bogotá are most important. The country is subject to earthquakes. Agricultural products include coffee, tobacco, cotton; cocoa, sugar, vegetable ivory, dyewoods, wheat and maize. On llanos in E. cattle are reared. Country is rich in minerals, gold, coal, copper, lead, platinum, cinnabar, petroleum, emeralds, and manganese being the chief; there are valuable pearl fisheries along coast. Manufactures include textiles, cigars, cigarettes, but are as yet little developed. Chief exports, coffee, hides, bananas, gold, platinum. Cap. Bogotá, standing 8,700 ft. above sea-level. Area, 440,846 sq. m.; pop. 5,855,000.

Colom'bo, cap. and principal seapt., Ceylon, on W. side of isl.; extensive trade; great entrepôt; magnificent artificial harbour; port of call for Eastern steamers; coaling station; seat of Anglican and R.C. bishops; many fine buildings; fresh-water lake. Pop. 244,100.

Colon (*kō-lon'*), or ASPINWALL, seaport, Panama; spacious harbour; Atlantic terminus of Panama Canal and Panama Rly. American control of sanitation has made Colon one of healthiest tropical cities in the world. Pop. *c.* 33,000.

Col'onsay and **Or'onsay,** two islands, Inner Hebrides, Argyllshire, Scotland; former is traditional landing-place of St. Columba (563); sheep rearing. Pop. 284.

Colorä'do. (1) W. central state of U.S.A., bounded N. by Wyoming and Nebraska; E. by Nebraska, Kansas; S. by Oklahoma, New Mexico; W. by Utah. Surface shows two natural divisions—great plains in E., mountains in W., where Rocky Mts. cross the state in several ranges; highest peaks—Mt. Elbert, Mt. Harvard, Pike's Peak, all over 14,000 ft. Chief rivers are Grand in W., Arkansas and S. Platte in E. Climate varies with elevation; generally healthy; rainfall slight. Colorado is pre-eminently a mining country; produces immense quantities of gold and silver; large deposits of lead, zinc, iron ore, copper, anthracite, and bituminous coal; also produces petroleum, bismuth, mica, tungsten, and radium. Mineral springs occur in various places. Agriculture has improved since development of system of irrigation; wheat, oats, maize, barley, potatoes, hay produced; fruits and vegetables grown; sugar-beet is largely cultivated. Horses, cattle, sheep, and pigs raised in considerable numbers. Industries include metal smelting and refining, meat packing, flour milling, brewing, dairying, manufacture of machinery, cars, beet-sugar. Cap. Denver. Area, 103,948 sq. m.; pop. (est.) 1,090,000. (2) River of south-western U.S.A., formed by union of Green and Grand rivers; flows S.W. through dry tableland and southern part of Utah into Arizona; afterwards separates Arizona on E. from Nevada and California on W.; enters Gulf of California; course forms several remarkable cañons of great depth; Grand Cañon of the Colorado (attaining depth of 6,000 ft.) extends over 200 m. in length, 8 to 10 m. in breadth—total length of riv., *c.* 1,800 m. (3) Riv., Texas, U.S.A.; 650 m. long; flows roughly S.E. and enters Gulf of Mexico. (4) Riv., Argentina, S. America; rises in Andes and flows generally S.E. to Atlantic.

Colora'do Springs, city, on E. side Rocky Mts., Colorado, U.S.A.; fashionable summer and health resort; pleasant climate; Manitou mineral springs in vicinity; smelters, and reduction mills. Pop. 33,000.

Colum'bia. (1) City, S. Carolina, U.S.A.; cap. of state; at head of navigation of Congaree R.; seat of univ. of S. Carolina; various colleges; cotton mills, ironworks. Pop. 50,000. (2) City, Missouri, U.S.A., 26 m. N. of Jefferson City; seat of univ. of Missouri; lumber, flour. Pop. 10,400. (3) Tn., Pennsylvania, U.S.A., 70 m. W. of Philadelphia; trading and shipping centre. Pop. 10,800. (4) Tn., Tennessee, U.S.A., 36 m. S. of Nashville; live-stock; textiles. Pop. 5,500.

Columbia, BRITISH. See BRITISH COLUMBIA.

Columbia, DISTRICT OF. See WASHINGTON (2).

Columbia River, or OREGON, large riv., N. America, 1,400 m. long; rises in Brit. Columbia, on W. slope of Rocky Mts.; flows first N.W., then turns S. and passes into United States, S.W., through Washington; forms part of N. boundary of Oregon and Washington; enters Pacific; principal affluents, Clark's Fork and Snake R.; navigable for sea-going vessels to 100 m. from its mouth; by the construction of canals for the avoidance of numerous falls and rapids river steamer traffic will be further developed; salmon fisheries are very important.

Colum'bus. (1) Cap. of Ohio, U.S.A., on Scioto R.; important commercial and industrial centre; trades in grain, live-stock, wool, coal, iron; manufactures include carriages, machinery, shoes, soap. Pop. 289,000. (2) Tn., Georgia, U.S.A., on border of Alabama; cotton goods and machinery. Pop. 43,000. (3) City, Mississippi, U.S.A., near border of Alabama; cotton, cotton-seed oil, and dairy produce. Pop. 10,500. (4) City, Indiana, U.S.A., 40 m. S.S.E. of Indianapolis; tanneries; agricultural implements; furniture. Pop. 10,000.

Col'wyn Bay, urban dist., wat.-pl., Denbighshire, Wales; fine promenade. Pop. 20,900.

Comayagua (*kō-mī-ăg'wa*), tn., Honduras, Central America; cathedral; has much declined within the last hundred years. In 1827 pop. was 18,000, now it is only *c.* 7,000.

Combe Martin (*koom*), par. and vil., N. Devon, England, 6 m. E. of Ilfracombe; market gardens. Pop. (par.) 2,000.

Comines (*kō-mēn'*), or COMMINES, frontier tn., Flanders; divided by Lys R. into two parts, Belgian and French; textiles. Pop. (Belgian) *c.* 7,000; (Fr.) *c.* 6,000.

Comiso (*kō'mē-sō*), tn., S.E. Sicily, 8 m. W. of Ragusa; pottery, cotton, soap. Pop. *c.* 25,000.

Commentry (*kom-mon-trē'*), tn., Allier, central France, 7 m. S.E. Montluçon; centre of rich coalfield; ironworks, foundries. Pop. 7,200.

Co'mo. (1) Lake, Lombardy, Italy, at foot of Alps; beautiful scenery; tourist resort; exposed to sudden and violent storms. Length, 35 m.; area, 55½ sq. m. (2) City, cap., prov. Como, Lombardy, Italy, at S.W. extremity of Lake Como; bishop's see; many fine old buildings and Roman relics; district rich in orange groves and olives; manufactures silk, satin, velvet, gloves. Pop. 48,100.

Comorin', CAPE, southern extremity, India; temple of goddess Kanniyambal on headland.

Com'oro Islands, volcanic archipelago, Mozambique Channel, E. Africa; French colony ranking as prov. of Madagascar; principal islands, Great

Comoro, Anjuan, Mayotta, and Mohéli; mountainous; loftiest heights, 8,500 ft.; fertile soil; inhabitants, Arabs, Malagasy, Negroes; religion, Mohammedan; coconut palm oil; export hides, cane sugar, vanilla, and copra; turtle fishing. Area, *c.* 800 sq. m.; pop. 119,300.

Compiègne (*kon-pē-ān'*), tn., Oise, France, *c.* 50 m. N.N.E. of Paris; formerly fortified; favourite residence of Fr. kings; summer resort; royal palace, now used as museum of antiquities; canvas, rope making, boat building, and copper and iron founding are chief industries. Compiègne Forest (30,000 acres), formerly favourite hunting ground, now magnificent recreation park. Pop. 14,400.

Concarneau (*kon-kär-nō'*), seapt., Finistère, N.W. France; sardine and mackerel fisheries; resort of artists. Pop. 5,700.

Concepcion (*kon-sep-sē-ōn'*). (1) Prov., Chile, S. America; immense fertile plains; coal mines; chief prod. are wheat, flour, wine, cattle, wool, and timber. Area, 3,313 sq. m.; pop. 246,700. (2) Tn., episc. see, cap. of above; important manufacturing and trading centre; chief industries are flour milling, distilling, and brewing; frequently destroyed by earthquakes. Pop. 64,000. (3) Or VILLA CONCEPCION, city, Paraguay, on Paraguay R.; chief centre for export of yerba maté tea. Pop. *c.* 11,000.

Con'cord. (1) Tn., cap., New Hampshire, U.S.A.; famous granite quarries; machinery, textiles, printing and publishing. Pop. 25,000. (2) City, N. Carolina, U.S.A., 20 m. N.E. of Charlotte; cotton and textiles. Pop. 12,000. (3) Tn., Massachusetts, U.S.A., 18 m. N.E. of Boston; scene of first fight in Amer. War of Independence; famous literary centre; textiles. Pop. 7,000.

Concor'dia, tn., Argentina, on Uruguay R., with port 2 m. lower down; exports meat, hides. Pop. 20,100.

Conegliano (*kon-āl-yä'nō*), town, Venetia, Italy, 30 m. N. of Venice; wine, silk. Pop. 15,000.

Co'ney Island, popular seaside resort, at entrance to New York Harbour, at s.w. extremity of Long Island.

Cong'leton, munic. bor. and mkt. tn., Cheshire, England, 11 m. N.E. of Crewe; silk; cotton weaving; iron and brass foundries. Pop. 12,900.

Cong'o, largest river of Africa, formed by union of two streams, the Luapula, which issues from Lake Bangweulu and flows through Lake Mweru, and the Lukuga from Lake Tanganyika. The united waters, known as Lualaba, flow N. to Nyangwe, after which the name Congo is given to the river. Congo then flows N. as far as equator, when it curves to N.W. as far as 2° N., after which it turns S.W., entering sea at Banana; length, *c.* 3,000 m.; drains area of *c.* 1,425,000 sq. m. Principal tributaries are Aruwimi from E., Ubangi from N., Lomami and Kasai from S. Kasai, the chief southern trib., has numerous affluents, and joins Congo near Ngato. From its mouth the Congo is navigable for ocean steamers to Matadi (*c.* 100 m.); from Matadi to Stanley Pool (*c.* 200 m.) rapids make navigation impossible, but a railway has been constructed for the transit of goods and passengers; from Stanley Pool to Stanley Falls (*c.* 1,600 m.) navigable for boats of 4 ft. draught.

Congo, BELGIAN, Belgian colony, comprising practically basin of riv. Congo, and small part of basin of Upper Nile, Africa; bounded by French Equatorial Africa, Sudan, Uganda, Tanganyika Terr., N. Rhodesia, and Angola. Surface generally a depression, which not improbably was formerly occupied by inland sea; great part covered by trackless primeval forests, and surrounded by highlands and hills; chief lakes are Leopold II., Tumba, in W.; Tanganyika, Mweru, on E. boundary. Climate is tropical. There are many tropical fruits; chief products are rubber, palm oil, coffee, tobacco, maize, rice, corn, cacao, and ivory; cattle are bred. Minerals are important, and include copper in Katanga dist., gold, iron, and tin. By a railway line passing through Bukama, Kambwe, and Elisabethville, which connects with the N. terminus of the Rhodesian railways, Katanga is brought into direct communication with Cape Town and with Beira, to which latter port the Katanga copper is sent. Principal exports are rubber, ivory, palm oil, copal, gold, copper, diamonds, tin, and cotton. Communications include the Congo and its tributaries, which are navigable to an extent of 5,500 m. There is a railway mileage of *c.* 2,200 m. Chief settlements are Boma, Banana, Leopoldville (cap.), Matadi, Stanleyville, Coquilhatville, and Elisabethville. Area, *c.* 918,000 sq. m.; pop. 8,520,000, of which about 20,700 are white.

Con'isbrough, urb. dist. and par., W. Riding, Yorkshire, England, on R. Don, 5 m. s.w. of Doncaster; in a colliery district. Pop. 18,200.

Con'iston. (1) Vil., Lancashire, England, at head of Coniston Water; tourist centre; slate quarries near. Pop. 1,100. (2) CONISTON WATER, lake, Lancashire, England, in Lake District. The mountain, Coniston Old Man, lies to w. of head of lake.

Conjeeveram', tn., Madras, India, 40 m. s.w. of Madras city; one of most sacred cities of India; several large temples, numerous pagodas; silk and cotton weaving. Pop. 61,400.

Con'nah's Quay, urb. dist., Flint, Wales, 3¼ m. s.E. of Flint; seaport. Pop. 6,000.

Con'naught, or CONNACHT, w. prov., I.F.S., comprising counties of Mayo, Galway, Leitrim, Roscommon, and Sligo; mountainous in w.; principal riv., Shannon; fine scenery; sheep rearing, agriculture, and fishing; formerly Irish kingdom ruled by O'Connors; divided into counties about 1580. Area, 6,611 sq. m.; pop. 552,900.

Connecticut (*kon-et'i-kut*). (1) New England state, U.S.A.; bounded N. by Massachusetts, E. by Rhode I., S. by Long I. Sound, w. by New York. Surface generally consists of three river valleys, Connecticut flowing through middle of state, Thames through E., and Housatonic through w. In E. and w. are hilly districts. Climate is temperate. Average annual rainfall, 50 in. River valleys are fertile, especially that of Connecticut R.; produce maize, rye, oats, potatoes, wheat, buckwheat, and great quantities of hay; tobacco largely cultivated; fruits produced, including apples, peaches; horses, cattle, sheep, and pigs raised; dairying carried on; fine lobster and oyster fisheries along coast. Minerals include brownstone, iron ore, tungsten, nickel, lime, cobalt, trap-rock. Mineral springs occur in various places. Connecticut is great industrial state, manufacturing cottons, woollens, silks, paper, machinery, clocks, brass goods, rubber articles, hosiery, leather, etc.; watch making at Waterbury, firearms and machinery at Bridgeport, hats at Danbury. Chief towns are Hartford (cap.), New Haven, Bridgeport. Area, 4,965 sq. m.; pop. 1,380,600. (2) River, New England, U.S.A., rises extreme N. of New Hampshire, flows S., forming boundary between New Hampshire and Vermont; enters Long I. Sound at Saybrook. Length, 345 m.

Con'nellsville, tn., Pennsylvania, U.S.A., 37 m. S.E. of Pittsburgh; largest coke industries in U.S.A.; manufactures machinery and motor-cars. Pop. 13,800.

Connemä'ra, dist., w. Galway, I.F.S.; mainly mountain and lough; wild, romantic scenery; building stone and (Connemara) marble quarried.

Con'sett, urban dist., Durham, England, 12 m. s.w. of Newcastle; iron and steel works; coal mines. Pop. 12,300.

Con'stance. See KONSTANZ.

Con'stance, LAKE (Ger. *Bodensee*), expansion of Rhine, between Switzerland, Austria, and Germany; glacial origin; shores hilly and picturesque; remains of prehistoric dwellings. Area, *c.* 208 sq. m.

Constanta (*con-stant'sa*), seapt., Black Sea, Romania; owes its importance to its being Romania's chief outlet to the Black Sea; main exports are oil and cereals; mineral springs in the neighbourhood. Pop. 65,000.

Constan'tia, dist., Cape of Good Hope, Africa, adjoining Cape Town; noted for excellence of wines it produces; originally Dutch wine farm (1680); government experimental wine farm; fruit.

Constantine', tn., N. Algeria; situated on rocky hill, with ravines surrounding it on three sides; episc. see; has citadel, mosques, bey's palace; manufactures woollens, leather goods; centre of wheat trade. Pop. 88,500 (41,500 Europeans).

Constantino'ple (Turkish *Istambul*), tn., European Turkey; built on several hills; beautifully situated; surrounded on three sides by water: Sea of Marmara and Bosporus on S. and E.; and on N.E. side the Golden Horn separates city proper from Galata-Pera, the centre for business and for the Christian European community, forming a safe, spacious, and deep harbour, about five miles long and half a mile broad, bridged at two points. Scutari, on Asiatic side of Bosporus, is reckoned a suburb of Constantinople. The city proper lies to the S., and contains most of the finest buildings—*e.g.* the Mosque of St. Sophia, the interior of which, with its dome, marbles, and mosaics, is of marvellous beauty. There are in all 800 mosques. In extreme S.E. stands the old Serai, within whose high walls were the divan and harem of former sultans, and whose famous gate (Sublime Porte) gave its name to the sultan's government. Till 1924 the capital of Turkey. Streets are mostly ill-paved and crooked; houses are low and small, and business is transacted in bazaars. Pop. 673,000.

Constanza. See CONSTANTA.

Conversan'o, tn., Apulia, Italy, 16 m. S. of Bari; episc. see; has cathedral (11th cent.); castle. Pop. *c.* 15,000.

Con'way. (1) Mkt. tn. and seapt., mouth of riv. Conway, Carnarvonshire, Wales; surrounded by high walls with battlements and towers; river crossed by fine bridges; Conway Castle (built by Edward I., 1284) is famous ruin. Pop. 8,800. (2) Riv. on which above is situated; navigable for small vessels for 10 m.; vale of Conway is favourite resort of artists.

Cooch Behar'. (1) Indian state, Bengal, India; near Himalayas; fertile and well cultivated; chief prod. are rice, jute, and tobacco. Area, 1,318 sq. m.; pop. 592,500. (2) Cap. of above, 270 m. N. by E. of Calcutta. Pop. 11,400.

Cook Islands, group in Pacific Ocean, lat. 20° S., long. 160° W.; principal islands are Rarotonga, Mangaia, Aitutaki, Atiu; dependency of New Zealand since 1901; coffee, fruits, coconuts. Area, 150 sq. m.; pop. 7,500.

Cooks'town, mkt. tn., Tyrone, N. Ireland; manufactures linen; trades in agricultural produce. Pop. 3,600.

Cook'town, seapt., on Endeavour riv., N. Queensland, Australia; gold and tin mines; pearl shell, turtle, and bêche-de-mer fisheries.

Coolgar'die, tn., W. Australia, 300 m. E. of Perth; gold first discovered here in 1888; now relatively unimportant as a gold-mining centre. Pop. *c.* 2,000.

Coorg, prov., Brit. India; bounded N. and E. by Mysore, S. and W. by Madras. Surface mountainous; mostly covered by forests; crossed by W. Ghats; abundant rainfall; watered by Cauvery and its affluents. Coorg produces coffee, rice, rubber, tea, and sandalwoods. Cap. Mercara. Area, 1,582 sq. m.; pop. 163,800.

Copenha'gen, cap. of Denmark; situated on E. shore of Zealand, with suburb Christianshavn, on island of Amager, connected at two places. The channel between Copenhagen and Slottsholm I. forms a spacious harbour and great naval station. Portion of town, cut off by canals, forms Castle I., or Slottsholm, with many fine public buildings, including royal palace of Christiansborg, govt. buildings, univ. (1479), royal library, Thorwaldsen Museum. Most important commercial city of Denmark; its trade increased as the result of part of the port being made a free harbour in 1894; chief industries are shipbuilding and metal working; chief exports, butter, bacon, corn. A train ferry connects the city with Malmö in Sweden. Pop. 731,000.

Copiapo′, tn., Chile, on riv. of same name, 380 m. N. of Valparaiso; smelting works; exports gold, silver, and copper ore. Pop. 9,800.

Cop′permine, river, Canada; rises in Lake Providence, flows N.W., and enters Coronation Gulf, in Arctic Ocean; not navigable because of rapids. Length, 300–400 m.

Coquilhat′ville, tn., Belgian Congo, on R. Congo; cap. of Equator Province.

Coquimbo (*kō-kēm′bō*), seapt. and prov., Chile, 200 m. N. of Valparaiso; chief industry, copper mining and smelting; exports copper, manganese, cattle, and hides; has cathedral. Pop. (tn.) 15,400; (prov.) 160,200.

Corä′to, city, Apulia, Italy, 25 m. W. of Bari; centre of agricultural dist. Pop. 49,000.

Corbeil (*kor-bā′ē*), tn., Seine-et-Oise, France, on R. Seine, 17 m. S. of Paris; has important flour mills, printing and paper works. Pop. 11,000.

Cor′bridge, mkt. tn., Northumberland, England, on R. Tyne, 3½ m. E. of Hexham; Roman remains. Pop. 2,400.

Cor′doba. (1) Prov., Andalusia, Spain, on S. slopes of Sierra Morena; traversed by Guadalquivir; plains produce fruit, wine, olives, grain; cattle and horses on slopes; coal, silver, zinc mined. Area, 5,300 sq. m.; pop. 565,200. (2) Cap. of above prov., on R. Guadalquivir; with Moorish walls, 8th cent. bridge, and magnificent 8th cent. mosque, now a Christian cathedral; remains of Moorish palace; famed for silversmith's work; manufactures textiles; distilling and brewing. Pop. 73,700. (3) Prov., Argentine Republic; wooded mts. in N., pampa in S.; cattle rearing; copper, lead, and gold mining carried on to very limited extent. Area, 66,912 sq. m.; pop. 735,500. (4) Cap. of above prov., *c.* 400 m. N.W. of Buenos Aires; centre of wheat area; flour mills, shoe factory; trades in wool. Pop. 135,000. (5) Tn., Mexico, 55 m. S.W. of Vera Cruz; has cotton and woollen manufactures; trades in tobacco, coffee, and sugar. Pop. 10,300.

Corfe Castle, tn., Isle of Purbeck, Dorsetshire, England, on rly. to Swanage; ruined castle. Pop. 1,400.

Corfu′. (1) One of Ionian Islands, Greece, off W. coast; divided into three districts by mountain ranges; highest point, 3,000 ft.; beautiful scenery; exports oranges, wine, olive oil, grapes. Length, 40 m.; breadth, 20 m. Area, 270 sq. m.; pop. 106,200. (2) Seapt. on E. coast of above; good harbour. Pop. 32,200.

Cor′inth. (1) Anc. and modern city, on Gulf of Corinth, Greece. New Corinth has arisen since destruction of old town by earthquake (1858); lies some 3 m. distant from anc. site, but, notwithstanding completion of Isthmian Canal (1893), has regained little of Corinth's historic prosperity and splendour; exports currants, oil, silk, and cereals. Pop. *c.* 6,000. (2) Gulf of Corinth or Lepanto separates Hellas from Morea; shores fertile, but liable to earthquakes; scene of many battles. (3) Isthmus of Corinth separates Gulf of Corinth from Gulf of Ægina; connects Morea with Attica; ship canal (opened 1893). The ruins include the Isthmian Wall and the temple of Poseidon.

Corinto (*ko-rēn′tō*), seapt., Nicaragua, on Pacific coast; greater part of Nicaragua's foreign trade passes through the town; chief exports are coffee, sugar, hides, dyewoods, and cattle. Pop. *c.* 3,000.

Cork. (1) Co., Munster, I.F.S.; largest in Ireland; bounded by

Kerry, Limerick, Tipperary, and Waterford; generally hilly—in the W. mountainous and boggy, and in the E. rich and fertile. Mountain ranges divide Cork into parallel basins through which flow the rivers Blackwater, Lee, and Bandon. The coast, which is exceedingly indented, and is about 250 m. long, has many beautiful bays. Large number of islands off the coast, the most notable being Cape Clear I., most southerly point of Ireland. Dairy farming is extensively carried on. Minerals little worked. Most important manufactures are leather, tweeds, whisky, and beer. Principal towns are Cork (chief tn.), Cobh (Queenstown), Kinsale, and Youghal. Area, 2,880 sq. m.; pop. 365,700. (2) Cap. of above, on R. Lee, at head of Cork Harbour; railway centre; univ. coll.; dairy and agricultural school; industries are manufactures of motor-cars, tanning, distilling, brewing, ironfounding, woollens; exports butter, provisions, livestock, hides, eggs, etc. Pop. 78,500. (3) CORK HARBOUR, landlocked natural harbour at mouth of R. Lee; Cobh (Queenstown) is on Great I.; Spike I. is fortified.

Corleone (*kor-lā-ō'nā*), tn., Sicily, 25 m. S.S.W. of Palermo; two mediæval fortresses; mineral springs. Pop. 15,300.

Corner Brook, tn., W. coast, Newfoundland; near mouth of Humber riv. and on rly.; paper mills worked by power from Grand L. Pop. 2,000.

Cor'ning, city, New York state, U.S.A., 75 m. S.S.E. of Rochester; centre of region producing dairy products and tobacco; manufactures include brick, terracotta, and glass. Pop. 16,000.

Corn'wall. (1) Co., S.W. England; great promontory, bounded N. and N.W. by Atlantic, E. by Devon, S. by Eng. Channel; contains Lizard Point, most S. point of England, and Land's End, most W.; 25 m. W. by S. lie Scilly Islands, included in co. In W. are broken and picturesque hills and tors. The Tamar, Fowey, Fal, and Camel are most important rivers. Coast is almost entirely rockbound, with unsurpassed cliff scenery. Over 70 per cent. of land is under crops and grass, chief crop oats; large numbers of cattle reared; market gardening in Penzance district. Formerly famous for tin, but few mines are now worked. Copper mines now practically abandoned; radium obtained from pitchblende at St. Ives; kaolin worked; granite and slate quarried; important fisheries and brisk coasting trade. Exceedingly rich in prehistoric antiquities. Cromlechs called *quoits* are the largest and most important known; monoliths, circles, avenues of stone, hut-dwellings, caves, cliff-castles, hill-castles, and ancient Christian crosses also found. Co. tn., Bodmin; principal ports are Falmouth, Penzance, and Hayle. Area, 1,356 sq. m.; pop. 318,000. (2) Port, Ontario, Canada, on St. Lawrence R.; manufactures woollen goods, cotton, pulp, paper, and flour. Pop. 12,500.

Coroman'del Coast, name formerly given to part of E. seaboard of India, on W. shore of Bay of Bengal.

Corpus Christi, tn., S.E. Texas, U.S.A., at mouth of R. Nueces; fish, oysters, and vegetables, as well as cotton, are exported. Pop. 28,000.

Corrèze (*kor-āz'*), dep., S.W. France; forms part of old prov. Limousin; surface hilly and mountainous; chief rivers, Dordogne, Vezère, and Corrèze; soil poor; climate variable; chief products are coal, iron, granite, wine, and timber; cereals are also grown and cattle raised; chief tn., Tulle. Area, 2,272 sq. m.; pop. 269,300.

Cor'rib, LOUGH, W. Ireland, in cos. of Galway and Mayo; drains by riv. Corrib to Galway Bay; length, 27 m.; extreme breadth, 7 m.

Corrientes (*kor-ē-ent'es*). (1) Prov., Argentine Republic, S. America, between rivers Paraná and Uruguay; forms vast plain; northern districts largely covered by swamps and lagoons; exports include timber, cotton, tobacco, oranges, rice, sugar, cattle, and horses. Area, 33,535 sq. m.; pop. *c.* 421,000. (2) Cap. of above, on R. Paraná; port and commercial town. Pop. *c.* 35,000.

Cor'sham, or CORSHAM REGIS, mkt. tn., Wilts, England, 4¼ m. s.w. of Chippenham; quarries. Pop. 4,500.

Cor'sica (Fr. *Corse*), isl., Mediterranean Sea, belonging to, and dep. of, France; over 100 m. long and 50 m. broad; E. coast is exceedingly regular, but w. deeply indented; interior mountainous; chief summit is Cinto (8,881 ft.), in N.W. A large plain, fertile but marshy, extends from E. coast to foot of mts. Immense tracts of splendid forests, notably of chestnut trees and olives. Higher up are Alpine pastures with many sheep and goats. Most important agricultural products are olives, wines, fruits (notably lemons), and potatoes; important fisheries, also coral fishing; minerals include lead, copper, and antimony; granite and marble. Climate is salubrious, except on E. coast, where plain is malarious. Cap. is Ajaccio; other ports, Bastia and Calvi. Pop. is almost entirely Italian. Area, 3,367 sq. m.; pop. 289,900.

Cort'land, city, New York, U.S.A., 30 m. s. of Syracuse; manufactures include stoves, wire, wirecloth, and netting. Pop. 13,300.

Corun'na (or *Kor-oon'ya*). (1) Prov., N.W. Spain; bounded N. and w. by Atlantic Ocean; dist. is mountainous, but generally fertile; extensive fisheries; chief exports, farm produce, fish. Area, 3,051 sq. m.; pop. 708,600. (2) Cap. of above prov.; seapt.; has two old churches, two hospitals, arsenal, barracks, cigar factory; exports cattle, vegetables, sardines. Scene of Sir John Moore's repulse of the French and his death (1809). Pop. 62,000.

Cor'wen, mkt. tn., on R. Dee, Merionethshire, Wales; slate quarries near. Pop. 2,700.

Cos, or STANKO, isl., Ægean Sea, w. of Asia Minor; surface partly mountainous, partly fertile and well cultivated; fine climate. Exports wine and raisins, melons, and other fruits; ceded to Italy by Treaty of Lausanne (1923). Chief town, Cos (pop. 10,000), on N.E. coast. Area, 115 sq. m.; pop. 16,100.

Cose'ley (*kōz'le*), suburb of Wolverhampton, Staffordshire, England; coal and iron mines in neighbourhood. Pop. 25,100.

Cosenza (*kō-sent'sa*), tn., archiepisc. see, Calabria, s.w. Italy; Gothic cathedral and ruined castle; iron and steel works; trades in wine, oil, silk. Pop. (com.) 32,600.

Coshoc'ton, city, Ohio, U.S.A., 68 m. E.N.E. of Columbus; trade centre for agricultural produce; manufactures paper, glass. Pop. 11,000.

Costa Rica (*kōs'ta rē'ka*), republic of Central America, stretching from sea to sea, and bounded by Nicaragua and Panama. The country is generally mountainous, with many volcanoes; earthquakes frequent; coast is flat, with dense forest lands on Atlantic slopes. Principal products are coffee and bananas. Other exports include cocoa, tropical woods, and hides. New rubber plantations are proving productive. Gold is mined in places; silver, copper, and other metals also found. Cap. San José. Area, *c.* 23,000 sq. m.; pop. 471,500.

Côte d'Azur (*kōt däz-oor'*, 'the azure coast'), shores of Riviera, S.E. France; includes many tourist resorts. See RIVIERA.

Côte-d'Or (*kōt-dor*), dep., E. central France; surface elevated and well wooded in N.; Côte-d'Or Mts. in s.; chief rivers, Seine and Saône; good pastures; important vineyards give the dep. its name, 'Golden Hillside'; famous Burgundy wines produced; fertile valleys and plains; chief industries, sheep and cattle rearing; iron and steel; chief tn., Dijon. Area, 3,391 sq. m.; pop. 328,900.

Cotentin (*kō-ton-tan*), peninsula, France, projecting into Eng. Channel; fertile and good pasture ground for cattle; butter; part of department of La Manche; chief town, Cherbourg.

Côtes-du-Nord (*kōt-doo-nor'*), dep., France, bordering Eng. Channel; part of anc. prov. of Brittany; traversed by chain of hills, running S.E. to N.W.; coast much indented; rivers short and navigable; climate humid; good pastures; chief occupations, fishing and linen manufacture; coast region produces wheat, hemp, flax; iron, slate, lime, freestone mined; chief tn., St. Brieuc. Area, 2,786 sq.m.; pop. 552,800.

Cöthen, or KÖTHEN (*koo'ten*), tn., Anhalt, Germany, 34 m. N.N.W. of Leipzig; ironfounding, manufacture of machinery; sugar and chemical works. Pop. 26,800.

Cotopax'i, an active volcano, Andes, Ecuador, S. America; loftiest active volcano in world (*c.* 19,600 ft.); frequent eruptions; first ascent by Reiss (1872); Whymper first to reach crater (1880).

Cotrone (*ko-trō'nā*), seapt., episc. see, Calabria, s. Italy, 30 m. N.E. of Catanzaro; cathedral, old castle; anc. *Croton.* Pop. *c.* 10,000.

Cots'wold Hills, range, Gloucestershire, England, extending s.w. to N.E. for upwards of 50 m., separating basin of Lower Severn from the sources of Thames; oolitic; highest point, Cleeve Cloud (1,134 ft.); well-wooded valleys; was long famous for breed of sheep now scarce.

Cottbus. See KOTTBUS.

Cot'tian Alps, name given to part of Alps between Maritime Alps and Graian Alps; highest peak is Monte Viso (12,609 ft.); railway crosses chain by Mont Cenis Tunnel.

Cott'ingham, urb. dist., E. Riding, Yorks, England, 4 m. N.W. of Hull; contains Hull waterworks. Pop. 6,200.

Coulommiers (*koo-lom-ē-ā'*), tn., Seine-et-Marne, France, 45 m. E. of Paris; industries, printing and tanning; cheese. Pop. 5,300.

Couls'don and Pur'ley, urb. dist., Surrey, England, 5 m. s. of Croydon. Pop. 37,700.

Council Bluffs, city, Iowa, U.S.A., on Missouri R.; important shipping, railway, and industrial centre; manufactures agricultural implements, paper, machinery. Pop. 42,000.

Coupar-Angus (*koop'er*), mkt. tn., Perthshire, Scotland, 16 m. N.E. of Perth; ruins of 12th cent. Cistercian abbey; fruit farming, linen. Pop. 1,800.

Courbevoie (*koorb-vwā'*), industrial suburb of Paris, France; bleaching; manufactures drugs and biscuits. Pop. 47,500.

Courcelles (*koor-sel'*), tn., Hainaut, Belgium, 5 m. N.W. of Charleroi; coal and iron. Pop. *c.* 15,500.

Courtrai (*koor-trā'*), (Flem. *Kortrijk*), tn., w. Flanders, Belgium, on the Lys, 27 m. by rail s.w. of Ghent; famous for its table linens and lace. Pop. 37,900.

Coutances (*koo-tans'*), tn., episc. see, Manche, France, 40 m. s. of Cherbourg; fine Gothic cathedral; 14th cent. aqueduct; black lace, woollens, leather; trade in cattle and horses. Pop. 5,700.

Cov'entry (*kuv'-*), city, mkt. tn., Warwickshire, England; ruined abbey; noted since Middle Ages for wool and dyeing trade; important centre for manufacture of motor-cars and bicycles; ribbons, watches, ironfounding. Area, 4,147 ac.; pop. 167,000.

Covilhã (*kō-vil-yan'*), tn., Portugal, on E. slope of Serra da Estrella; mineral baths and springs in neighbourhood; manufactures coarse cloth, used by peasantry. Pop. 14,000.

Covington (*kuv'-*), city, Kentucky, U.S.A., on R. Ohio, opposite Cincinnati; famous suspension bridge across Ohio; furniture, machinery, leather, tobacco. Pop. 65,000.

Cow'al, peninsular district, Argyllshire, Scotland, between Firth of Clyde and Loch Fyne; mountainous in N.; fertile valleys in S.; noted coaching road; chief tn., Dunoon.

Cow'bridge, munic. bor., mkt. tn., Glamorganshire, Wales, 10 m. w. of Cardiff; wholly dependent on agriculture; good markets and cattle fairs. Pop. 1,000.

Cowdenbeath', police burgh, s. Fife, Scotland; centre of coal-mining industry. Pop. 12,700.

Cowes, seapt., wat.-pl., Isle of Wight, England; headquarters of Royal Yacht Club; celebrated regattas. Osborne House, former royal residence, presented to nation by Edward VII. as convalescent home for officers. Pop. (including E. Cowes) 14,800.

Cracow (*krä'kow*), fort. city, on Vistula, Poland; intellectual and art centre of Poland. Notable buildings include Gothic cathedral, where Polish kings were crowned and buried; royal castle; univ. (founded 1364); chief industries, machinery, chemicals, tobacco, agricultural implements. Pop. 181,700.

Crad'ock, tn., Cape Province, S. Africa, 130 m. N. of Port Elizabeth; wool. Pop. 6,800.

Crail, coast tn., E. Fife, Scotland; summer resort; lobster and crab fishing. Pop. 1,100.

Craiova (*krä-yō'vä*), or KRAJOVA, tn., Romania; chief commercial tn. w. of Bucharest; trade in cereals, cattle, fish, and timber. Pop. 70,000.

Cram'lington, urb. dist., Northumberland, England, 8 m. N. of Newcastle; coal mining. Pop. 8,200.

Cran'brook, mkt. tn., Kent, England, 12 m. E. of Tunbridge Wells; chief industries, hop growing and farming; grammar school (16th cent.). Pop. 3,800.

Cran'ley, or CRANLEIGH, par. and vil., Surrey, England, 8 m. S.E. of Guildford; formerly manufactured iron from local ore. Pop. (par.) 4,000.

Crans'ton, tn., Rhode I., U.S.A., adjoining Providence; includes several cotton manufacturing villages; extensive market gardening. Pop. 44,000.

Cranwell, par. and vil., Lincs, England, 4 m. N.W. of Sleaford; Cadet College for Air Force. Pop. (par.) 2,190.

Craw'fordsville, city, Indiana, U.S.A., 40 m. N.W. of Indianapolis; centre for important stock-raising area; manufactures machinery, wagons, carriages, etc. Pop. 10,100.

Craw'ley, par. and vil., Sussex, England, 7 m. N.E. of Horsham. Pop. (par.) 4,745.

Crayford, urb. dist., Kent, England, 8 m. S.E. of Greenwich; part of Greater London. Pop. 15,900.

Cred'iton, mkt. tn., near junction of Creedy and Yeo, Devonshire, England, 7 m. N.W. of Exeter; confectionery; large cattle fair. Pop. 3,500.

Cree'town, tn., small port, Kirkcudbrightshire, Scotland; granite quarries; dist. scene of part of Scott's *Guy Mannering*. Pop. 750.

Crefeld, or KREFELD, tn., Rhineland, Prussia; principal seat in Germany of silk and velvet manufacture; famous technical weaving school. Pop. 130,000.

Creil (*krä-ē'*), tn., river port, Oise, France, *c.* 30 m. N. of Paris; iron and machinery; railway works. Pop. 10,300.

Crema (*krā'mä*), tn., episc. see, Lombardy, N. Italy, 22 m. N.W. of Cremona; cathedral; centre of rich agricultural district; bell-casting industry. Pop. 11,900.

Cremo'na, tn., episc. see, cap. of Cremona prov., N. Italy, on R. Po; numerous old churches and palaces; manufactures silk, cotton, and musical instruments; famous violins by Amati, Stradivarius, and Guarneri were made here. Pop. 59,000.

Cres'wick, tn., Victoria, Australia, 86 m. N.W. of Melbourne; gold mines; agriculture. Pop. *c.* 3,700.

Crete, large Greek island in E. Mediterranean; most southerly part of Europe; length, 160 m.; breadth, 7 to 30 m. Coast is much indented and has good harbours—Suda Bay in N. and Kali Limenes in S. Four ranges run from E. to W.; Mt. Ida (8,070 ft.) lies in centre. The valleys are fertile under irrigation; rivers are often dry. Climate is delightful, the heat being tempered by sea breezes. Chief products are olive oil, wine of inferior quality, goats'-milk cheese, silk, leather, and fruits;

trade mostly with Turkey and Greece. Archæological discoveries at the palace of Knossos in E. Crete prove the existence of an advanced civilization as early as 3,400 B.C. Chief tn., Candia. Area, 3,300 sq. m.; pop. 386,400.

Creuse (*krooz*), dep., central France; chief river, Creuse; surface hilly; climate cold and damp; soil poor, except in valleys, where leading industry is the rearing of cattle, horses, and sheep; coal found; principal products, rye, buckwheat, chestnuts, potatoes, fruit. Chief tn., Guéret. Area, 2,164 sq. m.; pop. 219,100.

Creusot (*krooz-ō'*), or CREUZOT, LE, tn., Saône-et-Loire, France, *c.* 55 m. s.w. of Dijon; centre of coal and iron area; ironworks (1837) among largest in Europe; producing guns, armour-plate, locomotives, and machinery. Pop. 24,200.

Crevillente (*krā-vēl-yen'tā*), town, S.E. Spain, 20 m. s.w. of Alicante; famed for melons. Pop. 11,200.

Crewe (*kroo*), munic. bor., Cheshire, England; important railway junction; has extensive railway workshops. Pop. 46,100.

Crewkerne (*kroo'kurn*), mkt. tn., Somersetshire, England, 8 m. s.w. of Yeovil; manufactures sailcloth, webbing, and twine. Pop. 3,500.

Criccieth (*krik'yeth*), wat.-pl., s. Carnarvonshire, Wales; Welsh home of Mr. Lloyd George. Pop. 1,400.

Crick'lade, mkt. tn., on R. Thames, Wiltshire, England; agricultural produce. Pop. 1,400.

Crieff, mkt. tn., summer resort, on riv. Earn, Perthshire, Scotland; manufactures woollen goods; Drummond Castle, famous for beauty of its gardens, is in neighbourhood. Pop. 5,500.

Crim'ea, peninsula, rep. U.S.S.R., between Black Sea and Sea of Azov, joined to mainland by isthmus of Perekop; Balaklava and Sevastopol have good harbours; Theodosia is ice-free. Crimea is divided into two regions by the Salgir, its largest river; in N. pastureland; in S. mountains, forests, and health resorts; here Crimean War (1854–56) was fought. Prod. include grain, tobacco, wines, and fruit. Area, *c.* 10,000 sq. m.; pop. 700,000.

Crimmitzschau, or KRIMMITSCHAU (*kri-mit'show*), tn., Saxony, Germany, on R. Pleisse, 24 m. w. of Chemnitz; manufacture of machinery, buckskin; wool spinning. Pop. 27,100.

Crin'an Canal, across peninsula of Kintyre, Argyllshire, Scotland; between Ardrishaig and Crinan; constructed 1793–1801; takes vessels of 200 tons.

Croatia-Slavonia (*krō-ā'-sha-sla-vō'-ni-a*), dist. of Yugoslavia; bounded by Adriatic on s.w., and separated from Hungary on N.E. by rivers Drava and Danube; mountainous, with plains in N.E. There are extensive marshes. Area is intersected by the riv. Sava. Earthquakes are frequent in Zagreb district. Soil is fertile; staple crops are wheat, maize, pulse, potatoes, flax, hemp, tobacco. Wine is largely produced. Timber is an important product. Swine are reared in the oak forests of Slavonia; and cattle, sheep, and horses are bred. Agriculture is the main industry. Cotton and beautiful silk fabrics are produced. Cap. Zagreb (Agram). Area, 16,418 sq. m.; pop. 2,700,000.

Crom'arty. (1) Port, Ross and Cromarty, on Cromarty Firth, Scotland; the birthplace of Hugh Miller, geologist; fisheries; important naval base during Great War. Pop. 800. (2) Former co., Scotland, now joined with Ross to form the co. Ross and Cromarty. (3) FIRTH, opening into Moray Firth; accommodates the largest vessels; two hills, 'Sutors of Cromarty' (400-500 ft. high; *c.* 1,500 yds. apart), guard entrance.

Cro'mer, wat.-pl., Norfolk, England; crab fishing; has repeatedly suffered from encroachments of sea; Old Cromer now under the sea. Pop. 4,200.

Cromp'ton, township, Lancashire, England, 2 m. N. of Oldham; cotton mills; colliery. Pop. 14,800.

Crook, urb. dist., Durham, England, 6 m. N.W. of Bishop Auckland; coal mines. Pop. 11,700.

Cros'by, or GREAT CROSBY, coast tn., Lancashire, England, 6 m. N.W. of Liverpool; Merchant Taylors' schools for boys and girls respectively. Pop. 18,300.

Cross River, W. Africa; rises in Cameroons Mts.; enters Bight of Biafra; in last 60 m. flows through dense mango swamps; length, 500 m.

Crow'borough, par. and vil., Sussex, England, 7 m. N.E. of Uckfield. Pop. (par.) 6,000.

Crow'land, or CROYLAND, par. and mkt. tn., Lincolnshire, England, 8 m. N.E. of Peterborough; contains Benedictine abbey founded 8th cent., portion remaining is now used as parish church; curious Gothic triangular bridge for foot-passengers (14th cent.). Pop. 2,700.

Crowle, urb. dist., N. Lincs, England, 6 m. E. of Thorne; flax grown. Pop. 2,800.

Crow'thorne, par. and vil., Berks, England, 2½ m. S.E. of Wokingham; par. contains Wellington College and Broadmoor Lunatic Asylum. Pop. (par.) 4,000.

Croy'don, co. bor., Surrey, England, part of Greater London; chiefly residential; handsome parish church and public buildings; air port; breweries; clock factory and bell foundry. Pop. 233,100.

Cru'den Bay, summer resort, Aberdeenshire, Scotland, S. of Buchan Ness; golfing centre. Pop. 2,600.

Csaba. See under BÉKÉS.

Cu'ba, republic and largest of W. Indian islands, at entrance to Gulf of Mexico; 730 m. long; breadth, 20–90 m.; coast-line, *c.* 2,000 m., exceedingly dangerous for shipping owing to banks and reefs. There are numerous excellent harbours—notably Havana. In the Sierra Maestra Mts. Monte Tarquino rises 8,397 ft. These mts. are densely wooded, and contain copper, iron, and other minerals. The w. is mostly low-lying plain land. The largest river is the Cauto (250 m. long). The climate of Cuba is more temperate than that of other W. Indian islands, and healthy in highlands of the interior. During coldest months (Dec. and Jan.) the temp. seldom falls below 50° F., and during July and Aug. 83° is about the maximum. The rainy season lasts from May to Oct. Desolating hurricanes are frequent. Large tracts of forest are rich in mahogany, cedar, ebony, and other kinds of timber. A considerable portion of the island is devoted to cattle breeding. About half the cultivated land consists of sugar plantations, sugar being the most important product. Tobacco is the second largest product. Other products are sisal hemp, maize, coffee, cotton, cacao, and tropical fruits. Only industries of importance are cigar making and sugar manufacture. Chief trade is with U.S.A. Chief towns are Havana (cap.), Santiago, and Camagüey. Two-thirds of inhabitants are whites (mostly of Span. descent). Area, 44,164 sq. m.; pop. 3,579,500.

Cuckfield (*kook'fēld*), urb. dist., Sussex, England, 14 m. N. of Brighton; fine views over Downs. Pop. 2,100.

Cuddalore', chief tn., S. Arcot, Madras, India, 20 m. S. of Pondicherry; chief exports are grain, sugar, oil-seeds, cotton goods. Pop. 50,500.

Cud'dapah. (1) Dist., Madras, India; very unhealthy; watered by Pennar and tributaries; chief prod. are millet, rice, melons, and cotton; muslin manufactured. Area, 5,918 sq. m.; pop. 887,900. (2) Tn., cap. of above, 135 m. N.W. of Madras; exports cotton. Pop. 19,500.

Cud'worth, urb. dist., W. Riding, Yorks, England, 3 m. N.E. of Barnsley. Coal mining. Pop. 9,400.

Cuenca (*kwen'ka*). (1) Inland prov., Spain, lying to W. of Valencia; mainly mountainous, valleys, forests; suffers from drought; main occupation of people is raising of sheep, goats, and mules; forests produce pinewood; coal and salt are mined; agriculture is very backward. Area, *c.* 6,636 sq.

m.; pop. 281,600. (2) City, cap. of above, 100 m. N.W. of Valencia; Gothic cathedral; trades in timber, and manufactures furniture, pottery, leather, and paper. Pop. 12,800. (3) City, S. Ecuador, S. America; cathedral, university; sugar refineries, woollen goods, and pottery. Pop. *c.* 30,000.

Cuevas de Vera (*kwāv'as dā vā'ra*), tn., S.E. Spain, on R. Almanzora, 43 m. N.E. of Almeria; dist. rich in silver mines; saltpetre; chief market for agricultural produce of dist. Pop. 20,400.

Culebra (*koo-lā'bra*). (1) Isl., W. Indies, between Porto Rico and St. Thomas; good harbour; U.S.A. naval base. Pop. 800. (2) Station, Panama; Culebra (Gaillard) Cut offered great difficulties in construction of canal.

Cul'len, royal and munic. burgh, Banffshire, Scotland, on Moray Firth; fishing centre; rope and sail making. Pop. 1,700.

Cullera (*kool-yār'ā*), seapt., Spain, 22 m. S. of Valencia; walled town; ruined Moorish citadel; exports grain, fruit. Pop. 13,100.

Cul'linan, tn., Transvaal, S. Africa, 24 m. E. of Pretoria; centre of diamond-mining dist. The famous Cullinan Diamond was bought by the Transvaal Government and presented to Edward VII., stones cut from it being used in the British sceptre and crown. Pop. *c.* 11,800.

Cullo'den, moor, 6 m. N.E. of Inverness, Scotland, scene of defeat of Prince Charles Edward by Duke of Cumberland (April 16, 1746); also called Drummossie Muir; fine examples of stone circles on neighbouring plain of Clava.

Cullomp'ton, or COLLUMPTON, mkt. tn., Devon, England, on R. Culm, 12½ m. N.E. of Exeter; blankets and serges; paper mills. Pop. 2,735.

Culross (*koo'ros*), royal burgh, par., Fife, Scotland, 6 m. W. of Dunfermline, on Firth of Forth; formerly important export of coal and salt, now mainly a holiday resort; has remains of Cistercian abbey (1217). Pop. (par.) 4,100; (burgh) 500.

Cumana (*koo-ma-nā'*), city and port, Venezuela; subject to earthquakes; products include coffee, cacao, sugar, tobacco, rum. Pop. 18,700.

Cum'berland. (1) Co., N.W. England, bordered by Scotland and Solway Firth in N. The centre is hilly; the W. and N.W. low and flat. The S.E. comprises part of the 'Lake District,' the largest lakes being Ullswater, Derwentwater, Bassenthwaite, Thirlemere, Buttermere, Wastwater, Ennerdale. Chief mts. are Scafell Pike (3,210 ft.), Scafell (3,162), Helvellyn (3,118), Skiddaw (3,053), Bow Fell (2,960), Cross Fell (2,929). The most important rivers are Eden, Esk, and Derwent; numerous waterfalls of great beauty. The climate is wet and variable, specially from July to Oct. Dairy farming very important; large numbers of sheep and cattle reared; oats produced; coal extensively worked; red hæmatite iron ore mined, and iron and steel manufactured; limestone, granite, slate, zinc, lead found; shipbuilding; fisheries. Chief towns are Carlisle (co. tn.), Cockermouth, Whitehaven, Workington, Maryport, Wigton, Penrith, and Keswick. Area, 1,520 sq. m.; pop. 262,900. (2) City, W. Maryland, U.S.A., on Potomac R.; bituminous coal; iron, steel works; important rly. jn. Pop. 38,000. (3) Tn., Rhode Island, U.S.A., on N.E. border of Massachusetts; coal mines; cotton manufactures. Pop. 10,300.

Cum'braes, THE, two islands, Firth of Clyde, Scotland, between island of Bute and Ayrshire; form parish of co. of Bute. Great Cumbrae has circumference of 10½ m.; only town, Millport, summer resort. Little Cumbrae has area about 1 sq. m.; lighthouse. Pop. (par.) 5,900.

Cum'nock. (1) NEW, par. and vil., Ayrshire, Scotland, 4½ m. S.E. of Old Cumnock; coal mining; limestone and potter's clay. Pop. (par.) 6,400. (2) OLD, par. and mkt. tn., 14 m. E. of Ayr; coal mining and agricultural machinery. Pop. (par.) 5,600.

Cundinamarca (*koon-dē-na-mär'ka*), dep., Colombia, S. America, lying between Rs. Orinoco and Magdalena; w. traversed by Andes (highest point, 15,780 ft.); llanos in E. feed large number of cattle; coffee, sugar, cocoa, tobacco; salt, copper, coal mines. Cap. Bogota. Area, 8,046 sq. m.; pop. 812,000.

Cuneo (*koo'nā-ō*). (1) Prov., N. Italy; bounded w. and s. by Cottian and Maritime Alps; cattle breeding; cereals, fruit, silk, marble, iron; mineral springs. Area, 2,870 sq. m.; pop. 624,000. (2) Tn. and episc. see, cap. of above, 65 m. w. of Genoa; cathedral (restored); 12th cent. church; silk, cotton, paper manufactures. Pop. 31,000.

Cupar (*koop'er*), or CUPAR-FIFE, co. tn., royal burgh, Fife, Scotland; agricultural centre, large trade in grain; beet-sugar factory; flax spinning and malting. Interesting historical buildings in dist. Pop. 4,600.

Curaçao, or CURAÇOA (*koo-rä-sä'ō* or *koo-rä-sō'ä*), isl., Dutch W. Indies, in Caribbean Sea, off N. coast of Venezuela; surrounded by coral reefs; oil refining; salt, phosphates, and cattle exported. Chief tn., Willemstad. Area, 210 sq. m.; pop. 41,000.

Curico (*koo-ri-kō'*). (1) Prov., Chile; copper, gold mines; very fertile; produces cereals, fruit, wine; cattle grazing. Area, 3,045 sq. m.; pop. 108,000. (2) Tn., cap. of above, 116 m. s. of Santiago. Pop. 16,000.

Curityba (*koo-rē-tē'bä*), tn., cap. of Paraná, Brazil, 225 m. s.w. of S. Paulo; prepares yerba maté tea; match factories; porcelain works. Alt. *c.* 3,000 ft. Pop. 37,000.

Curragh (*kur'rach*), common, Kildare, I.F.S., 26 m. s.w. of Dublin; famous racecourse; was training centre for troops during Great War.

Curzola (*koor-dzō'lä*). (1) Isl., Adriatic Sea, Yugoslavia; mountainous, well-wooded, produces much fruit; has limestone quarries. Area, 100 sq. m.; pop. 28,000. (2) Seapt., cap. of above; fortified; cathedral, and Franciscan monastery (15th cent.); boat building. Pop. 7,000.

Cutch, Indian state, Western India States Agency, India, forming peninsula in N.W. Bombay; is largely barren, rocky; wheat, barley, cotton in fertile tracts; embroidery, silver-work; frequent earthquakes; governed by Indian ruler under British protection. Chief tn., Bhuj. Area, 7,616 sq. m.; pop. 484,500. N. and E. lies the Runn of Cutch, which is flooded half the year, and converts Cutch into an island. When not flooded, the Runn is mostly a desert covered with a deposit of salt.

Cut'tack, city, cap. of Cuttack dist., S.E. Bihar and Orissa, India, at apex to delta of Màhanadi; situation gives it military and commercial importance; famous for gold and silver filigree work; produces rice. Pop. 51,000. Area of dist., 3,654 sq. m.; pop. 2,064,700.

Cuxhaven (*kooks-häf'en*), seapt. tn., Hamburg, Germany, on w. side of mouth of Elbe. Great harbour works were constructed (1891–96) capable of berthing largest ocean steamers, and Cuxhaven became the port of the Hamburg-Amerika line. Cuxhaven is a free port, has a fishing industry, imports coal, brick, and timber. Pop. 17,600.

Cuyaba (*koo-yä'ba*), tn., cap. of Matto Grosso, Brazil, S. America, on Cuyaba R., trib. of R. Paraguay; cathedral; arsenal; seat of bishopric, and important military centre. Pop. 14,300.

Cuzco (*koos'kō*). (1) Dep., s. Peru, largely mountainous; agriculture, stock breeding, and, to a lesser degree, mining, though the district is rich in minerals. Area, 55,716 sq. m.; pop. *c.* 700,000. (2) City, Peru, cap. of above, in valley of Andes, 360 m. S.E. of Lima; founded by Manco Capac (11th cent.); anc. cap. of the Incas; site of famous Temple of the Sun; has remains of gigantic fortress and other Inca architecture; taken by Pizarro (1533); bishop's see; cathedral, univ.; manufactures cotton and woollen goods, gold and silver articles. Pop. *c.* 37,000.

Cyclades (*sik'la-dēs*), group of Greek islands in Ægean Sea; of volcanic origin; generally mountainous; mostly fertile; among principal are Syra, Andros, Paros, Delos, Melos, Tinos, Myconos, Naxos, Thera, Ceos; export emery, iron ore, wine, tobacco. Area, *c.* 1,042 sq. m.; pop. 129,700.

Cyprus (*sī'prus*), third largest isl. in Mediterranean; a British Crown Colony; 60 m. w. of Syria, 44 m. s. of Asia Minor; length, 140 m.; breadth, 30 to 60 m. In N. are two ranges of mts., and one in s., with Mt. Troödos (6,406 ft.). In the centre is a low-lying fertile plain. Rivers are generally dry channels; torrents after heavy rains (Nov.–May) and snow melting. Irrigation is effected by wells and a canal. Climate is good, except in hot season, when fever is prevalent in low-lying regions. Forests formerly yielded much material for shipbuilding, but have almost entirely vanished; climate and soil have suffered accordingly. Cyprus was famed of old for copper, which derived its name from this island, and copper is still mined. Salt is mined and procured by evaporation. Most important products are wheat, barley, locust beans, cotton, silk, flax, tobacco, wool, gypsum, fruits, sponges, and large quantities of wine. Splendid mules are bred. The principal towns are Nicosia (cap.), Larnaca, Limasol, Famagusta. Area, 3,584 sq. m.; pop. 311,000.

Cyrenaica (*sir-en-ā'ikă*), dist., Italian Libya, N. Africa, between Tripolitania and Egypt; mainly desert; chief oasis, Kufra; cattle, sheep, and camels raised; barley; coastal fisheries (sponges, tunny); salt pans; settlement possible on coast; rly. mileage, 100. Cap. Benghazi. Area, *c.* 285,000; pop. *c.* 200,000.

Cythera (*sith'er-a*), (modern *Cerigo*), most southerly of Ionian Islands, s. of Laconia, Greece; in anc. times had magnificent temple to Aphrodite; surface mostly rocky and mountainous; produces wheat, grapes, olives, cotton; sheep and goat rearing; cap. Capsali.

Czechoslovakia (*chek'o-slō-văk'i-a*), inland republic, central Europe; comprises Bohemia, Moravia, part of Silesia, Slovakia, and Ruthenia; frontiers are Bohemian Forest in s.w., Erzgebirge in N.W., Riesengebirge, Sudetes Mts., and Carpathians in N., R. Danube in s.; surface mountainous with fertile valleys; drained by Elbe and tribs., and March; climate generally continental; industries include agriculture, mining (especially coal), lumbering, brewing and distilling, sugar refining, calicoes, woollens, chemicals, porcelain, glass; chief crops, wheat, rye, barley, oats, potatoes, sugar beet, maize. Cap. is Prague. Area, 54,207 sq. m.; pop. 13,613,200.

Czernowitz. See CERNAUTI.

Czestochowa (*chans-tō-kō'va*), tn., Poland, *c.* 120 m. s.w. of Warsaw; place of pilgrimage; manufactures cotton yarns, cloth, and paper. Pop. 80,600.

D

Dabrowa Gornicza (*dōn-brō'va gurnē'cha*), tn., Poland, 38 m. N.W. of Cracow, on coalfield adjoining Prussian Silesia. Pop. 42,000.

Dacca. (1) Dist., Bengal, India, an alluvial plain intersected by rivs. and canals; jute and rice. Area, 2,723 sq. m.; pop. 3,126,000. (2) Chief tn. of above, 150 m. N.E. of Calcutta; second city of Bengal; great jute centre; fine muslin; gold and silver utensils, filigree, carving of shells; univ. Pop. 120,000.

Dagenham', par. and vil., Essex,

England, 3 m. E. of Barking; motor works; bricks and tiles. Pop. 89,400.

Daghestan (*dä-ge-stän'*), republic, Russia, on W. shore of Caspian Sea; mountainous; rivs. Sulak, Samur, and Terek (to the Caspian); extreme climate; people mainly Lesghians, Tatars, and Georgians; cattle and sheep; cotton, tobacco, fruit, silkworms; copper, salt, sulphur. Cap. Makhach-Kala. Area, 22,000 sq. m.; pop. 788,000.

Dag'ö. See HIIUMAA.

Dagupan', tn., Luzon, Philippines, on Lingayen Bay; makes wooden shoes; exp. salt. Pop. 22,500.

Daho'mey, French colony, Guinea coast, W. Africa; Nigeria on E., Togoland on W.; moist, hot; palm kernels and palm oil. Chief tn., Porto Novo; chief port, Kotonu, from which rly. to R. Niger. Area, 41,000 sq. m.; pop. *c.* 1,000,000 Negroes.

Dairen (*dī'ren*), port, Liaotung pen., Manchuria, on land leased to Japan; fishing; salt; exports soya beans. Pop. 300,000.

Dakar', cap. of French W. Africa; port in Senegal; most westerly port of Africa; naval station; submarine cable to Brest; outlet for Senegal and adjoining region. Pop. 34,000.

Dako'ta, N. and S. See NORTH DAKOTA and SOUTH DAKOTA.

Dalbeat'tie, tn., Kirkcudbrightshire, Scotland; granite quarries and polishing works. Pop. 3,000.

Dalecarlia (*dä-le-kar'li-a*), former prov., central Sweden, drained by R. Dal; iron ore.

Dalkeith', mkt. tn., Midlothian, Scotland, at junction of N. and S. Esk; brush factories, brass works. Pop. 7,500.

Dal'key, wat.-pl., on Irish Sea, co. Dublin, I.F.S. Pop. 4,150.

Dallas, city, E. Texas, U.S.A.; important rly. centre in rich cotton, corn, wheat, alfalfa, and fruit dist.; oil fields; lumber, meat-packing, cotton, cotton-seed oil, and other industries. Pop. 260,000.

Dalma'tia, coast dist., Yugoslavia; narrow, mountainous country with numerous islands on N.E. coast of Adriatic Sea; breadth, 2–40 m.; mountain ranges include W. chains of Dinaric Alps and Karst plateaus; indented coast. Climate sub-tropical. Mostly pasture-land and woods, producing timber, wine, olive oil; shipbuilding in some islands; iron, lignite, asphalt, and salt; maize, rye, barley, fruits; makes Maraschino liqueur; famous lace school in Split. Inhabitants are mostly Serbo-Croats and Italians. Chief ports, Kotor and Split. Area, 4,916 sq. m.; pop. 622,000.

Dalmel'lington, vil., Ayrshire, Scotland, on R. Doon; ironworks and collieries. Pop. 3,500.

Dalmen'y, par. and vil., W. Lothian, Scotland; station for Forth Bridge; oilworks. Pop. (par.) 5,000.

Dalry'. (1) Tn., Ayrshire, Scotland, 6 m. N.E. of Ardrossan; manufactures tweed and hosiery; coal and iron mines in vicinity; limestone. Pop. 4,800. (2) Par. and vil., Kirkcudbrightshire, 16 m. N.W. of Castle Douglas; holiday resort. Pop. (vil.) 540.

Dal'ton, city, N.W. Georgia, U.S.A., in iron and manganese dist.; lumber, textiles, canned goods. Pop. 8,000.

Dal'ton-in-Fur'ness, mkt. tn., Lancs, England; Furness Abbey 1½ m. distant; iron ore and limestone. Pop. 10,300.

Daman, or DAMAUN, Portuguese port, Gulf of Cambay, Bombay, India; teak forests; cotton weaving; salt; fisheries. Area, 150 sq. m.; pop. 49,000.

Damanhur', tn., Egypt, 38 m. E.S.E. of Alexandria; commercial centre; cotton factories. Pop. 48,000.

Damar'aland, central prov., Terr. of S.W. Africa; extends from Atlantic Ocean inland to Kalahari Desert; mountainous; copper; stock raising; contains Windhoek, cap. of Terr., and port of Walfish Bay.

Damas'cus, city, cap. of Syria; situated on R. Barada, surrounded by orchards at base of Anti-Lebanon Mts.; probably the oldest city in the world still inhabited; streets are narrow, and houses ruinous; great caravan and railway centre; manufactures embroidered goods, inlaid and metal work, jewellery; chief imports, woollens, raw cottons, silks, tobacco, sugar, petroleum, and leather. Pop. 170,000.

Damiet'ta, riv. port, Lower Egypt, on E. distributary of Nile; cottons; pottery; gave name to dimity; eclipsed by Port Said. Pop. 35,000.

Danä'o, tn., Cebu I., Philippines; rice, sugar, copra, cocoa; coal mines in vicinity. Pop. 23,000.

Dan'bury, city, Connecticut, U.S.A., 60 m. N.N.E. of New York; manufactures hats, paper, silk, and silverware. Pop. 22,000.

Dannemo'ra, ironfield, Sweden, 25 m. N. by E. of Uppsala; ore needs no reducing agents; worked since 1579.

Dan'ube (German *Donau*), second largest riv. of Europe and chief highway of commerce for central Europe, drains *c.* 320,000 sq. m.; total length, 1,725 m.; rises in Black Forest; course generally eastwards; flows through Germany, Austria; between Czechoslovakia and Hungary; through Hungary, Yugoslavia; between Romania and Bulgaria, and through Romania into Black Sea through vast delta; has innumerable tribs., including Lech, Isar, Inn, Morava (March), Drava, Tisa, Sava, Morava, Seret, Prut. Chief tns. on banks are Vienna, Bratislava, Budapest, Belgrade. Danube is navigable from Ulm to Black Sea, and is open to all nations; shipping enters at Sulina mouth (greatly improved by European Commission of the Danube, instituted 1856); famous Iron Gates rapids long hindered navigation. Danube is connected with Rhine by Ludwigs Canal (1844) in process of great enlargement, since 1921, with Elbe by Vltava (Moldau) and Mühl canals.

Danville. (1) City, Virginia, U.S.A., on border of N. Carolina; cotton and tobacco factories. Pop. 22,000. (2) City, Illinois, U.S.A., 120 m. S. of Chicago; centre of coal mining; rly. carriages, lumber, textiles, flour, bricks, and glass. Pop. 37,000.

Danzig (*dänt'sĕch*), Free City with port, fortress, and naval station, 3 m. from Baltic, W. of E. Prussia. Mottlau, trib. of R. Vistula, flows in two branches through the town; trade more than doubled between 1884 and 1909, due to deepening of river and creation of free port at Neufahrwasser; shipbuilding; sugar refining; distilling, brewing, liqueurs; iron and machine works, ordnance factories; tobacco, cigars, bricks, and cutting of amber. Imports coal, chemical products, herrings, petroleum, iron, and earthenware. Exports wood, sugar, grain, flour, molasses, and oilcake. Peace Conference of Paris in 1919 decided that Danzig should be a free city under the League of Nations. It is a member of the Polish customs administration. Area, 754 sq. m.; pop. 390,000; of city proper, 230,000.

Darbhanga', tn., Bihar and Orissa, India, 60 m. N.E. of Patna; group of villages round maharajah's palace; large bazaars; rice, oil-seeds, food grains, sugar, saltpetre, and tobacco. Pop. 54,000.

Dardanelles' (*-elz'*) (anc. *Hellespont*), long, narrow strait connecting Ægean Sea with Sea of Marmara; length, 45 m.; width varies from 5 m. to less than 1 m.; on N.W. is peninsula of Gallipoli, on S.E. Asia Minor; entrance from Ægean Sea 2 m. wide; from this point Asiatic shore curves in crescent shape, while European shore is almost straight, to the 'Narrows' between Chanak (Asiatic side) and Kilid Bahr (European shore); navigation is dangerous; vast strategic importance; fortified since 1460; opened to Russian merchantmen in 1774; demilitarized since Great War.

Dar-es-Salaam' ('harbour of peace'), port and cap., Tanganyika Territory, Africa, 50 m. S. of Zanzibar; starting-point of Central Rly. through Tabora to Kigoma; overland telegraph via Ujiji with S. Africa; submarine cable with Zanzibar; handles half of trade of Terr. Pop. 25,000.

Dar'field, urb. dist., W. Riding, Yorks, England, 5 m. E.S.E. of Barnsley; coal mining; noted church. Pop. 5,300.

Darfur', w. prov., Anglo-Egyptian Sudan, Africa; administered by its hereditary sultan; a sandy steppe-like plateau; fertile valleys; gum arabic, wheat, millet, cotton, sesame, and tobacco; cattle raising most important. Cap. El Fasher. Pop. 1,000,000.

Dar'gai, hill station, N.W. Frontier Province, India; terminus station of Malakand Rly.

Darial', gorge, in Caucasus, E. of Mt. Kasbek, on Georgian military road; chief pass across Caucasus from early times; traversed by the river Terek; alt. *c.* 5,000 ft.

Darien. See PANAMA.

Darjee'ling, tn., dist. of same name, Bengal, India, 300 m. N. of Calcutta, on Himalayas; alt. 7,200 ft.; hot weather residence of Bengal govt.; mountain scenery unrivalled, including Kinchinjunga and Everest; tea. Pop. 23,000.

Dar'laston, part of parl. bor. of Wednesbury, s. Staffs, England, 9 m. from Birmingham; coal and ironstone; blast furnaces, steel works, and hardware (nuts and bolts). Pop. 19,700.

Dar'ley, NORTH, urb. dist., N. Derbyshire, England, 2½ m. N.W. of Matlock; holiday resort; lead mining. Pop. 4,100.

Dar'ling, riv., E. Australia; flows from Dividing Range between Queensland and New South Wales to join R. Murray at Wentworth on borders of Victoria; length, 1,160 m.; variable in volume according to season; in good season navigable to Bourke.

Darling Downs, tableland, S.E. Queensland; excellent grazing country; tin and silver. Chief tn., Toowomba. Area, 25,000 sq. m.

Darling Range, scarped mts., E. of Perth, W. Australia; 400 m. long; greatest alt. 1,500 ft.

Dar'lington, parl. and munic. bor., s. Durham, England; rapid growth began in 1825 with opening of Stockton and Darlington Rly.; engine factories; worsted spinning; iron and brass foundries. Pop. 72,100.

Darm'stadt, cap. of Hesse-Darmstadt, Germany, 17 m. s. of Frankfurt-on-Main; old and new tns. enclosed by walls; centre of applied art; iron foundries and boiler factories, machine shops, and chemical works. Pop. 90,000.

Dart, riv., rising in Dartmoor, Devon, England; flows 36 m. to English Channel at Dartmouth; summer steamers; fine scenery.

Dart'ford, mkt. tn., on R. Darent, Kent, England; lies between Woolwich and Gravesend; powder and paper mills; engineering, chemical, and cement works. Pop. 28,900.

Dart'moor, plateau, s.w. Devon, England; average alt. 1,500 ft.; numerous granite hills (tors) fantastically weathered; highest points, High Willhays (2,039 ft.), Yes Tor (2,028 ft.); streams form deep picturesque valleys (cleaves); fine scenery on Dart, Bovey, Teign, Taw, Okement, and Tavy; convict prison at Princetown; *c.* 22 m. long (N. to S.) by *c.* 20 m. broad (E. to W.).

Dart'mouth. (1) Munic. bor. and port, s. Devonshire, England, on w. side of Dart estuary, opposite Kingswear; Royal Naval College on a hill above the town; yachting centre. Pop. 6,700. (2) Tn., Nova Scotia, Canada, on Halifax Harbour opposite Halifax; foundries, tanneries, oilworks, rope walks, and sugar refineries. Pop. 8,000.

Dar'ton, urb. dist., W. Riding, Yorks, England, 3 m. N.W. of Barnsley; coal mining; nail making. Pop. 12,600.

Daru (*dä'roo*), port, Papua, Brit. New Guinea, on isl. at w. of entrance to Fly R.; recruiting centre for Torres Strait pearl-shell fishery.

Dar'vel, burgh, Ayrshire, Scotland, 9 m. E. of Kilmarnock; curtains, carpets, lace, muslin. Pop. 3,200.

Dar'wen, tn., Lancs, England, 3 m. S.S.E. of Blackburn; cotton and paper mills, blast furnaces, iron and brass foundries, paper-staining and glazed-brick works; flagstone quarries. Pop. 36,000.

Dar'win, formerly PALMERSTON, cap., Terr. of N. Australia, on Port Darwin, s. of Melville I.; mail station; rly. to interior; overland telegraph to Adelaide; pearl-shell and other fisheries, cattle. Pop. *c.* 1,000.

Dat'chet, residential tn., Bucks, England, on R. Thames, 2 m. E. of Windsor; angling. Pop. 2,400.

Dau'gavpils, or DVINSK, tn., Latvia, on S. Dvina R., 115 m. S.E. of Riga; rly. jn.; military centre; timber industries. Pop. 41,000.

Dauphiné (*dō-fē-nā'*), former prov., France; between Alps (E.), Rhone (W. and N.), and Provence (S.); cap. Grenoble.

Dav'enport, city, Iowa, U.S.A., on Mississippi R.; leading commercial city of state; agricultural implements. Pop. 61,000.

Dav'entry (or *dān'trĭ*), munic. bor. and mkt. tn., Northants, England, 12 m. W. of Northampton; high-power wireless station; boot and shoe industry. Pop. 3,600.

Da'vis Strait, between Greenland and Baffin Land; connects the Atlantic with Baffin Bay; minimum breadth 200 m.; whale-fishing industry, now declined.

Dav'os, two vils. (Platz and Dörfli), Swiss canton of Grisons, 15 m. E. of Chur; alt. 5,100 ft.; well adapted for consumptive patients. Pop. 10,000.

Daw'ley, urb. dist., Salop, England, 4 m. S.E. of Wellington; coal and iron. Pop. 7,400.

Daw'lish, urb. dist. and seaside resort, S. Devonshire, England; sheltered situation. Pop. 4,600.

Daw'son, mining town, Yukon, Canada, at junction of Klondike R. with Yukon R.; founded (1896) after the gold rush; metal works and saw-mills. Pop. *c.* 1,000

Dax, tn., Landes, S.W. France, on R. Adour; hot sulphur springs; mud baths; resins, wool, wood, and honey; asphalt, rock salt, and iron ore. Pop. 10,000.

Daylesford (*dālz'ford*), tn., Victoria, Australia, 55 m. N.W. of Melbourne; gold mining, alluvial and quartz; wheat. Pop. 5,000.

Day'ton, city, Ohio, U.S.A., 45 m. N.N.E. of Cincinnati; electrical machinery; aeroplanes; contains works of the National Cash Register Co. Pop. 200,000.

Dayto'na Beach, city, E. Florida, U.S.A.; winter resort; racing course for motor vehicles on beach. Pop. 10,000.

D.C., contraction for District of Columbia. See WASHINGTON (2).

De Aar, tn., Cape of Good Hope prov., Union of S. Africa, 500 m. N.E. of Cape Town; important rly. jn.; alt. 4,079 ft. Pop. 5,000.

Dead Sea, lake, S. Palestine, occupying a depression 47 m. long by 9½ m. wide, into which R. Jordan flows, lowest and largest of three lakes in rift-valley of Jordan, and fed by that river; has no outlet; mean level 1,292 ft. below level of Mediterranean (lowest level of any known water); greatest depth (N. end), 1,310 ft.; water contains *c.* 25 per cent. of salt (five times that of the ocean); water has unusual buoyancy; human body floats on surface; poisonous to animal life; bitumen floats on the water.

Deal, port and munic. bor., Kent, England; between coast and Goodwin Sands are the Downs; Walmer Castle, residence of the Warden of the Cinque ports; Walmer (continuous with Deal on the S.) contains extensive barracks and a naval and military hospital. Pop. 13,700.

Dean, FOREST OF, hilly dist. between Severn and Wye, W. Gloucestershire, England; coal and iron mines; stone quarries; 20 m. long, 10 m. broad.

Dear'born, tn., Michigan, U.S.A., 10 m. W. of Detroit, on R. Rouge; residential suburb of Detroit. Pop. 50,000.

Deauville (*dō-vēl*), fashionable wat.-pl., on English Channel, France,

10 m. s. of Havre; racecourse; international regatta. Pop. 5,000.

De'bar, tn., Yugoslavia, near point where Black Drin riv. enters Albania; cattle; maize, tobacco. Pop. 7,500.

Debreczen (*deb'ret-sen*), tn., Hungary, 143 m. E. by rail of Budapest; rly. jn.; noted Protestant theological centre; univ.; large annual fairs; cattle; grain. Pop. 108,000.

Deca'tur. (1) City, Illinois, U.S.A., 38 m. E. of Springfield; iron-foundry products; railway workshops; coal, live-stock, and agricultural produce. Pop. 58,000. (2) City, N. Alabama, U.S.A., 75 m. N. of Birmingham; steel works, lumber mills; cotton and silk industries. Pop. 15,000.

Decazeville (*dĕ-käz-vēl*), tn., Aveyron, s. France, 21 m. N.W. of Rodez; coal and iron. Pop. 12,000.

Dec'can, name applied to the whole peninsula of India s. of Vindhya Mts., between Bay of Bengal on E. and Arabian Sea on W.; sometimes limited to that portion of the table-land lying between rivs. Narbada and Kistna.

Decin (*dye'chēn*), formerly TETSCHEN, tn., Czechoslovakia, on r. bk. of R. Elbe, 50 m. N. of Prague; riv. port; chemicals, paper, textiles. Pop. 12,000.

Dede-Agatch (*dā-dā-ä-gätch'*), officially known as ALEXANDROUPOLIS, port, W. Thrace, Greece, on Gulf of Enos; serves Bulgaria and Adrianople; exports grain, timber. Pop. 13,000.

Dee. (1) Riv. of England and Wales, flows into and from Bala Lake, Merionethshire; traverses vale of Llangollen; nearly encircles city of Chester; thereafter canalized for 7 m.; estuary greatly impeded by sandbanks; length, 80 m. (2) Riv., Aberdeenshire and Kincardineshire, Scotland; one of the finest salmon rivers in Britain; rises in Cairngorm Mts. and enters North Sea at Aberdeen, passing Braemar, Balmoral Castle, and Ballater; supplies Aberdeen with water. (3) Riv., Kirkcudbrightshire, Scotland; issues from Loch Dee and flows to Solway Firth; good salmon river.

Dehra (*dā-rä'*), chief tn., Dehra Dun dist., United Provinces, India, 75 m. E. of Ambala; contains the Indian Forest School and Military College. Pop. 38,000.

Dehra Dun, dist., United Provinces, India; dun or valley between Siwalik Hills on s. and Himalayas on N., extending from Jumna valley on W. to Ganges valley on E.; fertile and well wooded, with many tea gardens. Chief tn., Dehra. Area, 1,193 sq. m.; pop. 215,000.

Deir ez-Zor (*dār ez-zōr*), tn., cap. of Zor Sanjak, Syria, on r. bk. of Euphrates, crossed here by modern stone bridge; on motor route between Damascus and Baghdad. Pop. *c.* 10,000.

Dej (*dezh*), tn., N.W. Romania, on R. Somesul (Szamos); vines; salt mines near; linen weaving. Pop. 11,500.

Delago'a Bay, inlet of Indian Ocean, Mozambique, E. Africa; receives Tembe, Umbelusi, and Usutu rivs.; s. part, sheltered by Inyak peninsula and isl., forms harbour of Port Melville; principal port, Lourenço Marques; rlys. from port to Transvaal and Swaziland; was first port of call by Portuguese ships on return from Goa, hence its name.

Del'atyn, tn., s. Poland, on R. Prut, 65 m. W.N.W. of Cernauti (Czernowitz); medicinal springs and baths. Pop. 49,000.

Del'aware. (1) Atlantic state, U.S.A., situated on peninsula formed by Chesapeake Bay and Delaware R.; bounded N. by Pennsylvania, W. and s. by Maryland, E. by Delaware R. and bay; shores sandy and marshy, with many creeks and bays; some parts reclaimed from sea by dykes. The N. beautiful, fertile dist., with rolling hills and deep valleys. The s. is almost flat, and some parts swampy. Rivs., small but navigable, include Brandywine; canal connects Delaware R. with Chesapeake Bay; principal harbours, Wilmington, Newcastle, and Lewes. State is chiefly agricultural; fruits (especially peaches and strawberries) and grain; market gardening, dairy farming, stock raising, and oyster fishing carried on; forests supply fine timber; manufactures include iron and steel products, ships, leather goods, cottons, flour, and paper. Cap. Dover. Area, 2,370 sq. m., of which 405 sq. m. water; pop. 223,000. (2) City, Ohio, U.S.A., 23 m. N. of Columbus; railway workshops; iron foundries; mineral springs. Pop. 9,000.

Delaware River, E. U.S.A., 410 m. long; rises in Catskill Mts. and flows into Delaware Bay. Chief tn. on its banks, Philadelphia.

Delft, tn., S. Holland, Holland, 5 m. S.E. of The Hague; in 17th and 18th centuries famous for faïence pottery—'Delft ware'; now 'New Delft' is made; chemicals; tobacco. Pop. 49,500.

Delfts'haven, or DELFSHAVEN, S.W. suburb of Rotterdam (q.v.).

Delhi (*del'i*), cap. of Brit. India; imperial enclave (557 sq. m.), Meerut dist., United Provinces, India, on r. bk. of Jumna; surrounded by wall 5¼ m. in circumference. 'The Ridge' with its monuments and the battered Kashmir gate recall incidents in Indian Mutiny. At Delhi Durbar (Dec. 1911) King-Emperor George V. laid foundation stone of new cap.; new government buildings are already established; bazaars famous for shawls, precious stones, gold and silver ware; important centre of wheat trade; has many cotton mills. Pop. 305,000.

Delitzsch (*de-lĕch'*), tn., Prussian Saxony, Germany, 16 m. E. of Halle; tobacco, cigars, hosiery, and beer; market gardening; coal mines in dist. Pop. 15,000.

Del'menhorst, tn., Oldenburg, Germany, 8 m. W. of Bremen; jute spinning, linoleum, woollens. Pop. 24,500.

Delphi (*del'fī*), small tn., Greece, near Gulf of Corinth; famous for oracle of Apollo, in charge of Pythian priestess; situated on steep slope on S. side of Mt. Parnassus; shut in on S. by mts.; important excavations by Fr. archæologists since 1891.

Demavend', peak, Elburz Mts., Persia, *c.* 60 m. N.E. of Tehran; extinct volcano; alt. 17,930 ft.; sulphur and pumice.

Dembe'a, prov., Amhara, Abyssinia, along N. shore of L. Tana; filigree silver and leather work; oxen reared. For L. Dembea, see TANA.

Demerä'ra. (1) Co. of Brit. Guiana, S. America, between Essequibo and Demerara rivs.; exports sugar, molasses, rum, and timber. Pop. *c.* 170,000. (2) Riv., Brit. Guiana, rising in Maccari Mts. and flowing to Atlantic; length, 170 m.

Demmin (*dem-ēn'*), tn., Pomerania, Prussia, 72 m. N.W. of Stettin; iron foundries; textiles; probably oldest tn. in Pomerania. Pop. 13,000.

Denain (*dĕ-ñan'*), mining tn., Nord, France, 8 m. S.W. of Valenciennes; coal mines; ironworks; glass. Pop. 24,500.

Denbigh (*den'bi*), munic. bor., co. tn., Denbighshire, N. Wales; timber, shoes; slate, flagstone, and lime quarries. Pop. 7,200.

Denbighshire, maritime co., Wales; Irish Sea on N., R. Conway forming W. and Dee part of E. boundary; surface partly mountainous, divided into several fertile valleys; greater part of lower ground produces oats, barley, turnips; uplands form pasturage; dairy produce; coal, lead, slate, limestone, and freestone; collieries and extensive ironworks; woollen manufactures; co. tn., Denbigh; other tns., Wrexham, Ruthin. Area, 665 sq. m.; pop. 157,600.

Denia (*dă-nē'ă*), tn. and port, Alicante, Spain, on Mediterranean; Moorish remains; woollen and linen; exports fruit and vegetables; fishing. Pop. 13,000.

Denil'iquin, tn., Riverina, New South Wales, Australia, near border of Victoria; distributing centre for surrounding sheep stations. Pop. 3,000.

Den'ison, city, Texas, U.S.A., 70 m.

N. by E. of Dallas, near Red R.; cotton, flour, and lumber mills. Pop. 14,000.

Deniz'li, tn., Smyrna vilayet, Asia Minor, Turkey, 80 m. E. of Aidin; leather curing and cotton manufactures. Pop. 35,000.

Den'mark, kingdom, N. Europe; partly mainland, partly archipelago; mainland part, Jutland, is N. part of the long peninsula extending N. of Germany, between North and Baltic seas; divided from Norway by Skagerrak, from Sweden by Kattegat and Sound. The larger islands are Zealand and Fünen, the smaller Langeland, Laaland, Falster, Möen, and, 90 m. to the E., Bornholm. The surface is generally low, and in places is protected by dykes; many lakes. The climate is temperate and damp; about half of the country is in pasture, most of the remaining available land being arable; chief crops, oats, barley, potatoes, wheat, rye, sugar beet; beech flourishes better than anywhere else in Europe; large fisheries. Industries include distilling, brewing, sugar refining, and margarine making; principal exports are butter, eggs, pork, bacon, besides sheep, hides, wool, cereals, fish, margarine. The enormous amount of dairy produce is obtained largely by co-operation and scientific methods of manufacture. Imports include coal, manufactured goods, and raw products. On shallow W. coast is rapidly-growing port of Esbjerg; the more important ports are on the E.; there are 3,219 m. of rly. (largely owned by the state) connected by steamboats or in winter by iceboats.

The Faroes are an integral part of Denmark, whose only colonial possession is Greenland.

Chief tns. are Copenhagen (cap.), Aarhus, Odense, Aalborg. Area, 16,568 sq. m.; pop. 3,435,000.

Den'ny, tn., Stirlingshire, Scotland, 12 m. S. of Stirling; coal, ironstone, chemicals, paper. Pop. (with Dunipace) 5,500.

Dent Blanche (*don blansh*), mt. peak, Valais, Switzerland, in Pennine Alps; alt. 13,415 ft.

Dent du Midi (*don du mē-dē*), a summit of Swiss Alps, in Rhone valley, near French frontier; alt. 10,700 ft.

Den'ton, tn., Lancs, England, 5 m. S.E. of Manchester; felt and silk hats; coal mines and ironworks in vicinity. Pop. 17,400.

D'Entrecasteaux Islands. See under NEW GUINEA.

Den'ver, cap., Colorado, U.S.A., on S. Platte R.; alt. 5,200 ft.; centre of important mining area and of ranching and irrigated agricultural dist.; cattle and sheep stockyards; lead, copper, iron, gold, and silver smelting. Pop. 288,000.

Deptford (*det'ford*), metropolitan and parl. bor., Greater London, 4 m. E. of St. Paul's; royal dockyard founded by Henry VIII. was filled up, and became in 1871 a foreign cattle market; Peter the Great worked in dockyard; Royal Naval Victualling Yard; timber trade; engineering. Pop. 106,900.

Dera Ghazi Khan (*dä'rä gä-zē' kän*), cap. of dist. of same name, Punjab, India, near r. bk. of Indus; silk, brass vessels, and ivory bangles; grain, cotton, and indigo exported. Area of dist., 5,300 sq. m.; pop. (tn.) 25,000, (dist.) 470,000.

Dera Ismail Khan (*dä'rä ēs-mä-ēl' kän*), cap. of dist. of same name, at S. extremity of N.W. Frontier Prov., India, on R. Indus; inlaid woodwork. Area of dist., 3,403 sq. m.; pop. (tn.) 40,000, (dist.) 261,000.

Derbent', or DERBEND, tn., Dagestan, U.S.S.R., on W. coast of Caspian Sea; textile factories; exports madder, fruit, silk, and cotton. Pop. 25,000.

Derby (*där'bi*), co. tn., Derbyshire, England; important rly. centre; L.M.S. rly. works; first successful silk mill in kingdom (1717); china manufacture began in 1750; modern industries, chenille, cotton, and lace goods, elastic web, 'Crown Derby' china, and articles in fluor-spar and marble; motor-cars. Pop. 142,400.

Der'byshire, co., England; bounded N. by Yorks, E. by Notts, S. by Leicestershire and Staffs, W. by Staffs and Cheshire. In N. is grand and rugged scenery of the Peak dist., where Pennine Range culminates in the Peak; sheep farming is practised; wide moorlands in N.W.; E. surface is gently undulating, and S. mostly flat, with good crops of wheat and barley, and large dairy farms. Co. abounds in picturesque scenery; valleys of Derwent and Wye especially beautiful; many caves in limestone region; other rivs. are Trent, Dove, and Dane. Co. yields limestone, lead, zinc, and has important collieries, chiefly in E. Manufactures include silk, cotton, elastic web, porcelain, and lace. Chief tns. are Derby (cap.), Chesterfield, Glossop, Ilkeston, Ashbourne; Matlock, Buxton, and Bakewell are inland wat.-places. Area, 1,030 sq. m.; pop. 757,300.

Dereham (*dēr'hăm*), mkt. tn., Norfolk, England, 15 m. W.N.W. of Norwich; agricultural implements. Pop. 5,700.

Derg. (1) Lough, Tipperary, Galway, and Clare, I.F.S.; an expansion of R. Shannon; length, 24 m.; average width, 2 m.; beautiful islands. (2) Lough, S. Donegal, I.F.S.; 3 m. by 2½ m.; studded with islands and rocks; resort of pilgrims since Middle Ages.

Derna', port, Cyrenaica, Italian Libya, N. Africa; only tn. of importance between Alexandria and Benghazi; open roadstead; trades in fruit, hides, and wool; caravan trade. Pop. *c.* 10,000.

Der'went. (1) Riv. of Cumberland, England, drains Derwentwater and Bassenthwaite, and enters Irish Sea at Workington; length, 38 m. (2) Riv. of Yorks, England; rises in Yorkshire Wolds; joins Ouse at Barmby-on-the-Marsh; navigable as far as Malton; length, 70 m. (3) Riv. of Derbyshire, England, rises N. of the Peak, and flows past Buxton, Belper, and Derby to R. Trent; it and its trib. the Wye are famed for their beauty; length, 60 m. (4) Riv., Tasmania; issues from Lake St. Clair and flows into Storm Bay, forming the estuary on which Hobart stands; length, 130 m.

Der'wentwater, lake, Cumberland, England; an oval expansion of the Derwent at N. end of Borrowdale; considered by many the most beautiful of Eng. lakes; area, 2 sq. m.; several small islands; 'floating island' of decayed vegetation appears at intervals.

Des'borough, urb. dist., Northants, England, 5 m. S.E. of Market Harborough; boot and shoe manufacture; iron ore. Pop. 4,400.

Des Moines (*dē moin'*), cap. and largest city, Iowa, U.S.A., on Des Moines R.; rly. centre; in coal dist.; printing and publishing; foundry and machine-shop products. Pop. 142,000.

Dessau (*des'ou*), cap., Anhalt, Germany, on R. Mulde, near its confluence with R. Elbe; sugar refining; chemicals; textiles. Pop. 71,500.

Det'mold, cap., Lippe-Detmold, Germany, on E. slope of Teutoburger Forest; 47 m. S.W. of Hanover; linen weaving, tanning, brewing; marble quarrying. Pop. 16,000.

Detroit'. (1) Cap., Michigan, U.S.A., on Detroit R., connected by tunnel and train ferries with Windsor, Ontario; important rly. centre; ranks next to New York and Chicago in value of its manufactures; owes its rapid rise to increasing production of motor-cars; excellent harbour, with extensive docks; largest exporting tn. on Great Lakes; grain, lumber; motor-cars; aircraft; shipbuilding; foundry and machine-shop products, slaughtering and meat-packing. Pop. 1,574,000. (2) Riv., Michigan, U.S.A., connecting Lake St. Clair with L. Erie; length, 25 m.; carries more shipping than any other waterway in the world; navigable for *c.* eight months in the year.

Det'tingen, vil., Bavaria, Germany, on R. Main, 17 m. S.E. of Frankfurt; here George II. defeated French (1743).

Deux-Sèvres (*doo-sāvr*), dep., w. France; formed of parts of old prov. of Poitou; textiles; agriculture; vineyards; coal, marble, granite; chief tn., Niort. Area, 2,337 sq. m.; pop. 310,000.

Dev'enter, tn., Overyssel, Holland, on R. Ijssel; carpet factories. Pop. 35,000.

Devil's Island, French Guiana. See ILE DU DIABLE.

Devi'zes, mkt. tn., Wilts, England, on Kennet and Avon Canal; corn exchange; grain trade; makes agricultural implements. Pop. 6,100.

Dev'on, co., s.w. England; bounded N. by Bristol Channel, w. by Cornwall, s. by English Channel, E. by Dorset and Somerset; coast (especially N.) bold and rugged, with fine rock scenery; inland surface hilly and uneven; Dartmoor in s.; Exmoor in N.; less elevated parts fertile and well cultivated; South Hams especially rich in orchards; riv. valleys beautiful and well-wooded; one of the chief cattle and sheep raising counties; hardy ponies on Dartmoor and Exmoor; cider and clotted cream; pilchard and other fisheries; copper, tin, manganese, granite, slate, marble, and potters' clay. Chief rivs. (Exe, Dart, Tamar, Teign, Taw, Torridge, and Plym) rise mostly in Dartmoor and abound in trout. Torquay, Sidmouth, and Teignmouth are health resorts, on account of mild climate in s. Other tns. are Exeter (cap.), Plymouth, Tiverton, Barnstaple, Dartmouth, and Tavistock. Area, 2,605 sq. m.; pop. 732,900.

Dev'onport. (1) Munic. and parl. bor., Devonshire, England, part of Plymouth; most westerly of the 'Three Towns' (Plymouth, E. Stonehouse, and Devonport—one town since 1914), at head of Plymouth Sound; on E. shore of Tamar estuary; royal dockyard; important naval and military station. Pop. 70,500. (2) Tn. on mouth of R. Mersey, Tasmania; third port of island. Pop. 3,500.

Dews'bury, munic. and parl. bor., W. Riding, Yorks, England, on R. Calder, 8 m. s. of Leeds; heavy woollen cloths, blankets, druggets, rugs; dye works; glass-houses; iron foundries. Pop. 54,300.

Dhanushkodi, tn., Madras, India, on isl. at entrance to Palk Strait; ferry port for passenger traffic from India to Ceylon.

Dhar. (1) Indian state, Central India; grain and cotton are exported. Area, 1,778 sq. m.; pop. 230,500. (2) Cap. of above, 45 m. s.w. of Indore; centre of grain trade. Pop. 16,000.

Dharm'sala, hill station, and headquarters of Kangra dist., Punjab, India, 100 m. N.E. of Amritsar; sanatorium; alt. 6,000 ft.; imposing scenery. Pop. 5,000.

Dhar'war, dist., Bombay, India; cotton ginned and manufactured; gold mines. Cap. Dharwar, 70 m. E. of Goa. Area, 4,600 sq. m.; pop. 1,037,000.

Dholpur'. (1) Indian state, Rajputana, India; crossed in s.w. by range of sandstone hills much quarried for local building and export purposes. Area, 1,155 sq. m.; pop. 230,000. (2) Cap. of above, 34 m. s. of Agra by rail; cattle and horse fair (Oct.). Pop. 16,500.

Dhran'gadra. (1) Indian state, Kathiawar, India; cotton and grain; salt. Area, 1,167 sq. m.; pop. *c.* 100,000. (2) Cap. of above, 75 m. w. of Ahmadabad; brass vessels, cloth and pottery. Pop. 18,000.

Dhulia (*doo'lē-ă*), tn., Khandesh dist., Bombay, India, 120 m. E. of Surat; important trade in cotton and linseed; cotton and woollen cloth. Pop. 31,000.

Diakovo. See DJAKOVO.

Diamantina (*dē-ă-măn-tē'nă*), tn., Minas Geraes, Brazil, 340 m. N. of Rio de Janeiro; diamond fields; agricultural dist.; manufactures cotton, leather, and cheese; diamond cutting. Pop. 15,000.

Diarbek'r. (1) Vilayet, Asia Minor, Turkey; traversed by upper Tigris; mountainous; stock raising; fruit; copper; galena; inhabitants mainly nomads. Area, 14,480 sq. m.; pop. 195,000. (2) Cap. of above, at head of navigation of R. Tigris; citadel on rock 1,950 ft. high; morocco leather, filigree work, cotton, silk, mohair, copper ore, sheep and goat skins. Pop. 98,000 (Turks, Kurds, Arabs, Armenians).

Dibrugarh (*dē-broo-gur'*), tn., headquarters of Lakhimpur dist., Assam, India; terminus of rail and steamer communication along Brahmaputra from Calcutta; coal mines. Pop. 16,000.

Die'denhofen. See THIONVILLE.

Dieppe (*dē-ep'*), port, Seine-Inférieure, France, on English Channel, 38 m. N. of Rouen; fashionable wat.-pl.; daily sailings between Dieppe and Newhaven (64 m.); harbour safe and deep; active foreign trade; important fisheries; shipbuilding; oil refining; machinery. Pop. 24,000.

Digne (*dēn'yi*), chief tn., Basses-Alpes, France, 70 m. N.E. of Marseilles; preserved fruits, honey, wax. Pop. 4,370.

Dijon (*dē-zhōn'*), tn., Côte-d'Or, France, 196 m. S.E. of Paris; important rly. jn.; strongly fortified; great wine trade; state tobacco factory; breweries, distilleries, textile works. Pop. 76,000.

Dinan (*dē-non'*), tn., Côtes-du-Nord, France, on l. bk. of R. Rance, 15 m. S. of St. Malo; noted for its mediæval houses and ramparts; tourist centre; leather, earthenware, cider. Pop. 9,000.

Dinant (*dē-non*), historic tn., prov. Namur, Belgium, on r. bk. of the Meuse, at the base of limestone cliffs on which stands a dismantled citadel; summer resort. Pop. 7,000.

Dinapore', tn. and cantonment, Patna dist., Bihar and Orissa, India, on r. bk. of Ganges; oil presses and printing works. Pop. *c.* 31,000.

Dinard (*dē-när'*), tn., Ille-et-Vilaine, France; opposite St. Malo; chief wat.-pl. of Brittany. Pop. 8,000.

Dinar'ic Alps, connecting link between Julian Alps and mountain system of W. Balkans, stretch along E. shore of Adriatic Sea for 400 m. between Dalmatia and Bosnia. Highest peaks, Dinara (5,940 ft.) and Oryen (6,230 ft.).

Din'digul, tn., Madura dist., Madras, India, 25 m. S. of Trichinopoly; cigars, cotton, coffee, cardamoms. Pop. 31,000.

Dindings', THE, narrow strip of Brit. terr. along the coast of Perak, with off-lying Pangkor I., Malay Peninsula; included in Penang (Straits Settlements).

Dingle. (1) Port and mkt. tn., Kerry, I.F.S., on Dingle Bay; fishing (mackerel) centre; exports butter and fish. Pop. 2,000. (2) BAY, inlet in W. of Kerry, extends 24 m. inland and is 18 m. wide at entrance; famous for cliff scenery.

Ding'wall, mkt. tn. and royal burgh, Ross and Cromarty, Scotland, on Cromarty Firth; agricultural centre. Pop. 2,600.

Diredawa (*dē-rē-dă'wa*), tn., Abyssinia, about 25 m. N. of Harar, of which it is the station; linked with Jibuti, French Somaliland (190 m.), and Addis Ababa by rly.; rly. workshops, soap factory. Pop. 30,000.

Dirschau. See TCZEW.

Dis'ko, large isl. off W. coast of Greenland, in Baffin Bay; Godhavn, in S., is seat of govt. of N. Greenland, and a rendezvous for whalers. Area, 3,200 sq. m.

Diss, mkt. tn., Norfolk, England, on R. Waveney; agricultural implement works. Pop. 3,400.

Dis'tington, par. and vil., Cumberland, England, 4½ m. N. of Whitehaven; coal mining. Pop. 2,100.

Dit'tersbach, tn., Silesia, Germany, 42 m. S.W. of Breslau; coal mining and chemicals. Pop. 15,000.

Diu (*dē-oo'*), isl. and tn., S. extremity of Kathiawar peninsula, India; belong to Portugal. Area, 20 sq. m.; pop. 14,000.

Dizful', tn., Khuzistan, Persia, 32 m. N.W. of Shushtar; indigo; reed pens. Pop. 15,000.

Djakovo (*dyă'kō-vō*), tn., Yugoslavia, 80 m. E. of Cetinje; agricultural produce. Pop. 8,000.

Dnepropetrovsk', formerly EKATERINOSLAV, tn., Ukraine, U.S.S.R., on r. bk. of R. Dnieper; ironworks; flour mills; coal, iron, and manganese in vicinity. Pop. 188,000.

Dnieper (*nē'pĕr* or *dnyep'er*), riv., Ukraine, U.S.S.R.; rises in N. of Smolensk prov., flows generally S. into Black Sea at Kherson (ice-free for *c.* 277 days); length, *c.* 1,400 m.; navigable to Dorogobuzh; engineering works have overcome rapids to large extent; chief tribs., Berezina, Pripet, Desna; important fisheries.

Dniester (*nēs'tĕr* or *dnyes'ter*), riv. between Ukraine and Romanian Bessarabia, rises in N.E. Carpathians (Czechoslovakia), and flows S.E. past Yampol rapids to enter Black Sea through a shallow lagoon on which is Cetatea Alba; fisheries; length, over 850 m.; drainage area, *c.* 30,000 sq. m.; traffic mainly in cereals and timber.

Do'ab, Ind. name for a tract of country between two rivs.; particularly land between Ganges and Jumna.

Dö'beln, tn., Saxony, Germany, 30 m. N.W. of Dresden; cloth; morocco leather; agricultural implements. Pop. 23,000.

Dobruja, region between lower Danube and Black Sea; mostly marshes and steppes; area, 9,000 sq. m.; chief port, Constanta, connected by rly. with Bucharest across famous Cernavoda bridge. Pop. *c.* 700,000.

Dodec'anese, group of twelve islands in E. Mediterranean, N.E. of Crete; belong to Italy. Area, 455 sq. m.; pop. *c.* 80,000.

Dod'worth, urb. dist., W. Riding, Yorks, England, 2 m. S.W. of Barnsley; coal mining. Pop. 4,200.

Dog'ger Bank, extensive shoal, North Sea, 60 m. E. of N. England; sea depths vary from 6 to 20 fathoms; important fisheries.

Dogs, ISLE OF, peninsula, S.E. London, England; formed by bend of R. Thames opposite Greenwich; has Millwall docks and shipbuilding yards.

Dôle (*dōl*), chief tn., Jura, France, on R. Doubs; wine; copper; iron foundries; agricultural implements. Pop. 15,000.

Dolgelly (*dol-geth'li*), mkt. tn., cap., Merionethshire, Wales; flannels, tweeds; lead, iron, and some gold found in vicinity; tourist resort. Pop. 2,300.

Dol'lar, par. and tn., Clackmannanshire, Scotland; coal and sandstone; extensive bleachfields. Pop. (tn.) 1,500.

Dol'omites, THE, group of limestone mts., S. Tirolese Alps, N.E. Italy; principal peak, Marmolata (*c.* 11,000 ft.); dist. much frequented by tourists; peaks assume fantastic forms.

Dolon Nor, tn., Mongolia, China, 160 m. N. of Peking; many Buddhist temples and ruins; manufactures iron and brass idols, bells, and vases. Pop. *c.* 30,000.

Dominica (*dom-in-ē'ka* or *dom-in'i-ka*), isl., Leeward group, Brit. W. Indies; surface mountainous; well covered with timber; fertile valleys, watered by numerous streams; of volcanic origin; contains sulphurous and thermal springs and famous 'Boiling Lake'; exports mainly limes, also coconuts, cocoa, oils, fruit. Cap. Roseau; principal harbour, Portsmouth, on St. Rupert's Bay on N.W. coast. Area, 305 sq. m.; pop. 41,000.

Dominican Republic. See SANTO DOMINGO.

Do'mo d'Os'sola, frontier tn., Piedmont, Italy, near R. Toce, *c.* 20 m. W. of upper part of L. Maggiore; tourist centre. Pop. 6,000.

Domrémy-la-Pucelle (*don-rā-mē' lā pu-sel'*), vil., Vosges, France, on R. Meuse; birthplace of Joan of Arc. Pop. 200.

Don. (1) Riv., Russia; rises in Lake Ivan, flows generally S. through N. Caucasian Area, enters Sea of Azov, forming delta 130 sq. m. in extent; length, 1,325 m.; important fisheries; navigable to Voronezh; in upper course connected with Volga by canal. (2) Riv., Aberdeenshire, Scotland; enters North Sea near Old Aberdeen; salmon fishing; length, 82 m.

Donaghadee′, port, seaside resort, co. Down, N. Ireland; flax mills; farm produce exported. Pop. 2,500.

Donau. See DANUBE.

Donauwörth (*dō′nou-voort*), tn., Bavaria, Germany, at confluence of Wörnitz with Danube; machinery; sawmills; breweries; trades in agricultural produce. Pop. 5,000.

Don Benito (*ben-ē′to*), tn., Spain, 60 m. E. of Badajoz; fruit and vegetable culture; woollens; wines. Pop. 21,000.

Don′caster, mkt. tn., W. Riding, Yorkshire, England, on R. Don; celebrated for annual race-meeting (St. Leger), dating from 1776; locomotive and carriage works of L.N.E. Rly.; breweries; large agricultural trade; great corn market; agricultural implements manufactured. Pop. 63,300.

Don Cossacks, former terr., Russia, in valley of Lower Don; now part of N. Caucasian Area; almost wholly steppe; elevated in N. and W.; soil very fertile; mineral products—iron, salt, gypsum; agriculture, cattle breeding, fishing, are important; extensive vineyards; ironworks, tobacco factories. Area, 63,532 sq. m.; pop. 4,013,400.

Donegal, or TIRCONAILL. (1) Co., N.W. I.F.S.; chief inlet, Lough Swilly; includes Aran I.; surface mainly barren mountain land with bogs and lakes; granite, marble; linen, woollens, muslin; fisheries; cap. Lifford. Area, 1,865 sq. m.; pop. 152,500. (2) Mkt. tn. and port of Donegal co., on Donegal Bay; homespun tweeds. Pop. 1,300.

Don′gola. (1) Prov., Anglo-Egyptian Sudan, Africa; extends along both banks of R. Nile; Wadi el Kab (*c.* 60 m.) also has good arable land; much desert; chief grain crops, durra and barley; dates extensively cultivated; cotton; fine horses bred; cap. Merowé. Area, *c.* 141,000 sq. m.; pop. *c.* 60,000. (2) NEW, tn. of above prov., on l. bk. of R. Nile, above third cataract; superseded Old Dongola (now a ruined city), 75 m. farther up the Nile; agricultural and trading centre. Pop. 15,000.

Doon, LOCH, Ayrshire, Scotland, 3 m. S. of Dalmellington; 6 m. long by ¾ m. broad; has five islands; R. Doon, immortalized by Burns, flows from loch into Firth of Clyde (27 m.), 2 m. S. of Ayr.

Dor′chester. (1) Co. tn. of Dorset, on R. Frome, England; centre of agricultural dist.; breweries. Pop. 10,000. (2) Vil., 9 m. S.E. of Oxford, with a fine abbey church. Pop. 900.

Dordogne (*dōr-don′ye*). (1) Navigable riv., S.W. France; rises on Puy-de-Saucy; flows W. to join estuary of Garonne; length, 300 m. (2) Dep., S.W. France; drained by R. Dordogne; surface in N. mainly sterile plateaus; large area is forest, with fertile valleys (agriculture, fruit growing); live-stock; minerals; wine; truffles. Chief tn., Périgueux. Area, 3,550 sq. m.; pop. 392,500.

Dor′drecht, or DORT, tn., S. Holland, 11 m. S.E. of Rotterdam; resort of artists; sawmills; shipbuilding; sugar refining. Pop. 55,000.

Dor′king, urb. dist. and mkt. tn., Surrey, England, 6 m. W. of Reigate; flour; lime; gives name to breed of poultry. Pop. 10,100.

Dor′noch, royal burgh, co. tn., Sutherlandshire, Scotland, on Dornoch Firth; holiday resort; excellent beach; dry, bracing climate. Pop. 700.

Doroho′i, or DOROGOI, tn., Moldavia, Romania, 33 m. S.E. of Cernauti; timber; farm produce; great annual fair. Pop. 13,000.

Dorpat. See TARTU.

Dor′setshire, or DORSET, maritime co., S.W. England; bounded N. by Wilts, N.W. by Somerset, W. by Devon, S. by English Channel, E. by Hants; surface hilly; fine chalk-cliff scenery on coast; special features are Poole harbour, Purbeck Isle (a peninsula), St. Alban's Head, Isle of Portland (connected with mainland by Chesil Bank), Portland harbour of refuge (a naval station); chalk hills or downs afford pasture for sheep; soil rich and well cultivated, particularly in Vale of Blackmore; orchards and dairy farms; quarries in Purbeck and Portland supply building stone, marble, pipeclay; manufactures paper, flax, hemp, silk, pottery; coast fisheries. Principal tns., Dorchester (co. tn.), Bridport, Poole, Weymouth, Swanage, Wareham, Shaftesbury. Area, 978 sq. m.; pop. 239,300.

Dortmund (*dort'moont*), tn., Westphalia, Prussia, on R. Emscher; extensive coalfields; iron and steel works; breweries; trade in corn and wood. Pop. 320,500.

Douai (*doo-ā'*), or DOUAY, tn., dep. Nord, France, on R. Scarpe, 17 m. S. of Lille; coal mining; iron and engineering works, ordnance works; glass; chemicals; sugar refineries; breweries; wool, paper, and leather factories. Here the 'Douai' Bible was prepared. Pop. 25,500.

Douarnenez' (*doo-ar-ni-nā'*), tn., on Douarnenez Bay, S. of Brest harbour, France; coasting trade; sardine fishing and preserving. Pop. 11,000.

Douay. See DOUAI.

Doubs (*doob*). (1) Riv., E. France; rises in Jura Mts., flows N.E., joins Saône at Verdun-sur-le-Doubs; length, 260 m. (2) Dep., E. France; watered by Doubs and affluents; traversed by Jura Mts.; good mountain pastures; dairy farming; plains produce wheat, oats, vines, and fruits; chief industries, watch making, ironfounding, brandy distilling; cap. Besançon. Area, 2,052 sq. m.; pop. 297,000.

Douglas (*dŭg'las*). (1) Port and wat.-pl., cap. of Isle of Man; fine landing pier; contains House of Keys, meeting-place of Manx Legislature. Pop. 28,000. (2) Par., vil., Lanarkshire, Scotland, 11 m. S.W. of Lanark; remains of Sir Walter Scott's 'Castle Dangerous.' Pop. (par.) 3,000.

Doullens (*doo-lon'*), tn., Somme, France, 20 m. N. of Amiens; trades in phosphates; cotton, leather, and paper industries. Pop. 4,000.

Dour'o, riv., Spain and Portugal; flows generally W. and falls into Atlantic at Oporto; navigable for 90 m.; in Portugal flows through one of richest wine-producing regions in world; length, *c.* 485 m.

Dove (*dŭv*), riv., Derbyshire and Staffs, England; rises S.W. of Buxton; enters Trent at Newton Solney; trout fishing; romantic scenery.

Do'ver. (1) Port and munic. bor., S.E. Kent, England, on Strait of Dover; chief port for passenger and mail traffic with Continent; was one of the Cinque Ports; Shakespeare's Cliff (350 ft.) on the W. pierced by rly. connecting Dover with Folkestone; Admiralty Pier (length, 780 yds., completed in 1871); commercial harbour (1901); Prince of Wales's Pier; great artificial naval harbour (1909); now commercial, modern residential town; popular wat.-pl. Pop. 41,100. (2) City, New Hampshire, U.S.A., 10 m. N.W. of Portsmouth; abundant water-power; cotton, woollen, and silk mills; machinery, shoes, lumber. Pop. 13,000.

Do'ver, STRAIT OF (Fr. *Pas de Calais*), channel connecting North Sea with English Channel, extending from Dungeness and Cape Grisnez to S. Foreland and Calais, 22 m.; breadth between Dover and Calais, *c.* 21 m.

Do'vercourt, seaside resort, Essex, England; at estuary of Stour, immediately S.W. of Harwich; chalybeate spring. Pop. 8,000.

Down, mar. co., N. Ireland; bounded N. by Antrim, W. by Armagh, S. by Carlingford Lough, E. by Irish Sea; N. hilly and fertile; in S. are Mourne Mts. and much wsate land; chief rivs., Lagan and Bann; Lagan valley richest in cultivation; stock raising and dairy farming; fisheries; breweries; manufactures linen; principal tns., Downpatrick (co. tn.), Newry, Banbridge, Bangor. Area, 951 sq. m.; pop. 210,000.

Downham, or DOWNHAM MARKET, mkt. tn., Norfolk, England, on R. Ouse; tin-ware manufacture; flour mills; horse and cattle fairs; market gardening. Pop. 2,500.

Downpat'rick, mkt. tn., co. Down, N. Ireland; linen, soap, brewing, tanning. Pop. 3,100.

Downs. (1) Roadstead, off E. coast of Kent, England, between N. and S. Foreland; protected by Goodwin Sands. (2) Two ranges of chalk hills, S.E. England; N. Downs extend W. to E. from Hampshire through Surrey and Kent to Dover cliffs; S. Downs, in Hampshire and Sussex, terminate at Beachy Head; the two ranges enclose the Weald.

Down'ton, par. and tn., S. Wilts, England, on R. Avon; brick making, lime burning, tanning, paper making, and willow-basket industry. Pop. (par.) 2,000.

Drak'ensberg, mt. chain, S. Africa, between Orange Free State and Natal, extending for 500 m. from Great Fish R. to Olifants R.; culminates in Mont-aux-Sources (10,763 ft.); numerous passes; De Beers and Van Reenen's Passes (5,000 ft.) are crossed by rlys. connecting Orange Free State and Natal.

Dram'men, tn., on riv. of same name, Norway, 33 m. S.W. of Oslo; rly. jn.; sawmills; shipbuilding yards; exports timber, wood-pulp, paper. Pop. 26,000.

Drā'va, r. bk. trib. of R. Danube; rises in Tirol, Austria; flows E. through Klagenfurt area and N. portion of Yugoslavia, then S.E., forming boundary between Yugoslavia and Hungary; length, 450 m.

Drente (*drent*), prov. Holland; E. of Zuider Zee; surface a sandy plateau of bleak moorland; chief tn., Assen; potatoes, rye; pigs. Area, 1,030 sq. m.; pop. 223,000.

Dres'den, cap., Saxony, Germany, on R. Elbe; Altstadt (old tn.) on l. bk., Neustadt (new tn.) on r. bk., connected by fine bridges; educational, sport, and tourist centre; within easy reach of beautiful Saxon Switzerland; important rly. jn.; manufactures china, pianos, sewing machines, leather wares, chemical products, scientific instruments; great riv. trade. Pop. 619,000.

Dreux (*droo*), tn., Eure-et-Loir, France, 27 m. N.N.W. of Chartres by rail; boots and shoes. Pop. 9,500.

Drif'field, GREAT, mkt. tn., E. Riding, Yorks, England, 18 m. N. of Hull; chief tn. of the Wolds; agricultural centre; oilcake. Pop. 5,900.

Drighlington (*drig'lington* or *dril'ington*), urb. dist., W. Riding, Yorks, England, 5 m. S.E. of Bradford; woollen and worsted manufacture. Pop. 4,100.

Drogheda (*drō'hed-a*), port, mkt. tn., munic. bor., Louth, I.F.S.; on R. Boyne; milling, brewing, iron casting, tanning; linen and cotton; salmon fishing; trades chiefly with Liverpool and Glasgow. Pop. 12,700.

Drohobycz (*drō'hō-bĕch*), tn., Poland, 40 m. S.W. of Lwow; centre of large oilfield; oil-refining. Pop. 27,000.

Droitwich (*droit'ich*), munic. bor., mkt. tn., Worcestershire, England, 5 m. N.E. of Worcester; one of oldest centres of salt manufacture in England; brine springs; brine baths for rheumatic affections or dyspepsia. Pop. 4,600.

Drôme (*drōm*), dep., S.E. France; traversed by Isère, Drôme, and other tribs. of R. Rhone; surface mountainous; E. and S. partly forested; valley of Rhone fertile; wheat, olives, fruit, and wine; minerals include iron and lignite; silkworm rearing; flour milling; textiles; cap. Valence. Area, 2,532 sq. m.; pop. 264,000.

Dromore', mkt. tn., co. Down, N. Ireland, on upper Lagan; linen manufacture. Pop. 2,400.

Dron'field, tn., Derbyshire, England, 5 m. S. of Sheffield; iron industry the staple trade; foundries, hardware, edged tool factories; coal. Pop. 4,500.

Droyls'den, urb. dist., Lancs, England, E. suburb of Manchester; cotton mills, calico printing, chemical and dye works. Pop. 13,300.

Drum'mondville, tn., E. Townships, Quebec, Canada, 45 m. N.E. of Montreal; woollens. Pop. 6,000.

Dry'burgh Abbey, monastic ruin, Berwickshire, Scotland, on R. Tweed, 4½ m. S.E. of Melrose; building dates from 1140, and was finally destroyed in Hertford's raid, 1545; tombs of Sir Walter Scott (1832) and Earl Haig (1928) in N. transept; abbey gifted to nation (1918) by Lord Glenconner.

Dual'a, port, French Cameroons, W. Africa; rly. to Yaunde.

Dub'bo, tn., New South Wales, Australia, on Macquarie R., 180 m. N.W. of Sydney; sawmills, factories, and tanneries; coal and copper found near. Pop. 5,000.

Dub'lin. (1) Co., Leinster, I.F.S.; bounded N. and W. by Meath and Kildare, S. by Wicklow, E. by Irish Sea; part of central limestone plain of Ireland; mountainous in S.; chief riv., Liffey; nearly half of total area under grass, over one-third under crops; oats, potatoes; live-stock; Grand and Royal canals traverse co.; rural pop. is densest in Ireland; chief tns. are Dublin (cap.), Rathmines, Pembroke, and Kingstown. Area, 358 sq. m.; pop. (including metropolis), 506,000. (2) Or BAILE ÂTHA CLIATH, city, port, parl. bor., and cap. of I.F.S.; at mouth of R. Liffey on Dublin Bay; principal suburbs are Kingstown, Pembroke, Rathmines, Clontarf, Dalkey, and Killiney; R. Liffey crossed by twelve bridges; banks lined with quays; near mouth of riv. are extensive docks; centre of entrepôt trade; manufactures porter, whisky, and poplin; has foundries, shipbuilding yards, and a considerable export trade in whisky, porter, and agricultural produce. Pop. 419,000.

Dubois (*doo-boiz'*), city, Pennsylvania, U.S.A., 75 m. N.E. of Pittsburgh; foundries, lumber, leather, flour. Pop. 14,000.

Dubrov'nik, formerly RAGUSA, port, Dalmatia, Yugoslavia, on Adriatic Sea; fruit, liqueurs, cheese, silk; oil refining; metal work. Pop. 8,500.

Dubuque (*doo-book'*), city, Iowa, U.S.A., on R. Mississippi; manufactures of machinery; pork packing. Pop. 42,000.

Duchcov (*dook'tsof*), tn., N.W. Bohemia, Czechoslovakia, 5 m. S.W. of Teplice; lignite in dist.; glass, pottery, sugar. Pop. 15,000.

Dud'ley, mkt. tn., in part of Worcestershire enclosed in Staffs, England; in midst of 'Black Country'; important seat of hardware trade; motor-cars, iron and brass founding, glass. Pop. 59,600.

Dudweiler (*dood'vī-lĕr*), tn., Saar Dist.; coal mines, ironworks. Pop. 21,600.

Duf'field, par. and tn., Derbyshire, England, on R. Derwent, 4 m. N. of Derby; a place of great antiquity. Pop. 2,000.

Duff'town, tn., Banffshire, Scotland; distilleries, lime works. Pop. 1,500.

Du'isburg, tn., Rhineland, Prussia, at confluence of Ruhr with R. Rhine; riv.-port; exports coal; chemicals, brass goods, sugar, textiles. Since 1905 includes Meiderich. Pop. 275,000.

Dukeries, dist. of Sherwood Forest, Notts, England; so called from ducal mansions in neighbourhood.

Duke Town. See CALABAR.

Du'kinfield, tn., Cheshire, England, 4 m. E. of Manchester; collieries; cotton; iron, brick, and tile works. Pop. 19,300.

Dulcigno. See ULCINJ.

Dül'ken, tn., Rhineland, Prussia; 11 m. S.W. of Crefeld; iron foundries; textiles. Pop. 15,500.

Duluth', city, Minnesota, U.S.A., at W. end of L. Superior; head of navigation on Great Lakes; terminus of several rlys.; fine natural harbour; dockyards; trade in grain, iron ore, lumber; iron and steel manufactures; stockyards. Pop. 101,000.

Dulwich (*dŭl'ich*), suburb of London, in bor. of Camberwell; famous college. Pop. 61,300.

Dumaguete (*doo-mä-gā'tā*), tn., cap. of Negros, Philippines, on Tañon Strait; centre of rich agricultural dist. Pop. 16,500.

Dumbar'ton, co. tn., parl. and royal burgh and port, Dumbartonshire, Scotland, on Firth of Clyde; shipbuilding yards; famous old castle. Pop. 21,500.

Dumbar'tonshire, co., Firth of Clyde, Scotland; N. dist. round Lochs Lomond and Long is mountainous; central region less wild; s. dist., with Clyde seaboard, Vale of Leven, and main portion of co., rich and pleasantly varied; sheep farming; industries include cotton works, calico printing, bleaching, dyeing, paper making, shipbuilding, fisheries, coal mining; chief tns., Dumbarton (co. tn.), Clydebank, Helensburgh. Area, 246 sq. m.; pop. 147,800.

Dumfries', tn., royal and parl. burgh, Dumfriesshire, Scotland, on R. Nith; includes Maxwelltown; cattle markets; manufactures woollens, tweeds, and hosiery; saw mills. Pop. 22,800.

Dumfries'shire, border co., Scotland; bounded on s. by Solway Firth; mts. include Hart Fell (2,651 ft.), Queensberry (2,285 ft.), Blacklorg (2,231 ft.); N. region constitutes part of Southern Uplands; s. region drained by rivs. Nith, Annan, and Esk; co. agricultural and pastoral; commerce mostly conducted through Dumfries; chief tns., Dumfries (co. tn.), Annan, Lockerbie, Langholm, Moffat. Area, 1,078 sq. m.; pop. 81,100.

Düna. See DVINA, SOUTHERN.

Dunbar', port, E. Lothian, Scotland; potatoes exported; agricultural implements, rope making and brewing; holiday resort. Pop. 3,800.

Dunblane', tn., s. Perthshire, Scotland, on R. Allan; cathedral; mineral spring; wool and worsted works; holiday resort. Pop. 2,700.

Dun'cansby Head, cape, Caithness, Scotland; N.E. extremity of mainland; 1¾ m. E. of John o' Groat's House.

Dundalk (*dŭn-dawk'*). (1) Port, Louth, I.F.S., at mouth of Castleton R.; locomotive works; breweries and distilleries; shipbuilding yards; flax and jute spinning; fishing; dairy produce. Pop. 14,000. (2) BAY, shallow inlet of Irish Sea on which above is situated; oyster beds.

Dundas', tn., Ontario, Canada, at w. end of Lake Ontario; leather, paper, textiles. Pop. 5,000.

Dundee'. (1) Royal burgh, port, and third Scottish city, on Firth of Tay, Angus, Scotland; staple industry, jute manufacture; other manufactures, hemp and flax goods, linoleum, machinery, preserves, and confectionery; shipbuilding; extensive fisheries; harbour with fine docks; Tay Bridge (2 m. 73 yds.) over riv. Pop. 175,600. (2) Tn., Natal, S. Africa, 40 m. N.E. of Ladysmith; coal mining; alt. 4,098 ft. Pop. 4,000 (whites, 1,800).

Dundon'ald, coast par. and vil., Ayrshire, Scotland, 5 m. s.w. of Kilmarnock; coal mines and sandstone quarries. Pop. (par.) 18,400.

Dune'din, tn., South Island, New Zealand; cap. of Otago prov.; at head of Otago harbour; founded and called after Edinburgh by Scottish settlers (1848); exports wool, dairy produce, and frozen meat; has rly. workshops. Pop. 85,000.

Dunferm'line, royal and parl. burgh, Fife, Scotland; birthplace of Andrew Carnegie, who gave (1903) £500,000 for town's benefit; seat of damask linen trade; rubber works; coalfields; burgh includes Rosyth, on Firth of Forth. Pop. 35,000.

Dungan'non, mkt. tn., Tyrone, N. Ireland; linen, fire-bricks, earthenware; workable coal in vicinity. Pop. 3,800.

Dungarpur'. (1) Indian state, Rajputana, India; agriculture. Area, 1,447 sq. m.; pop. 190,000. (2) Cap. of above, 50 m. s. Udaipur; makes articles from local greenstone and from teak. Pop. 7,500.

Dungar'van, port, tn., co. Waterford, I.F.S., 28 m. w.s.w. of Waterford; brewing, woollens. Pop. 5,200.

Dungeness (*dŭnj-nes'*), low shingly headland, s. extremity of Kent, England; lighthouse.

Dunkeld', tn., Perthshire, Scotland, on R. Tay at entrance to Strathmore; cathedral; fishing and tourist resort. Pop. 1,000.

Dun'kirk. (1) (French *Dunkerque*) Port, Nord, France, on Strait of Dover; third Fr. port; large artificial harbour; extensive and varied manufactures and exports, and important fisheries; shipbuilding. Pop. 31,000. (2) Port, New York state, U.S.A., on L. Erie; extensive lake trade; iron and lumber manufactures. Pop. 20,000.

Dun Laoghaire (*lē'ri*). See KINGSTOWN.

Dunmore', tn., Pennsylvania, U.S.A., adjoining Scranton; anthracite coalfields; silk. Pop. 25,000.

Dunmow'. (1) GREAT, mkt. tn. and par., Essex, England, on R. Chelmer. Pop. (par.) 2,500. (2) LITTLE, vil., 2 m. E. of Great Dunmow; custom of 'Dunmow Flitch' originated here. Pop. 300.

Dunoon', wat.-pl., Argyllshire, Scotland, on Firth of Clyde; remains of ancient castle. Pop. 8,800.

Duns, co. tn., Berwickshire, Scotland; market; blankets. Pop. 1,800.

Dunsink', hill, Dublin, I.F.S., 4 m. N.W. of Dublin; 310 ft. high; observatory of Trinity College on summit.

Dun'stable, mkt. tn., S. Beds, England; printing, engineering. Pop. 9,000.

Dun'ster, mkt. tn., Somersetshire, England, 2 m. S.E. of Minehead; fine Norman castle. Pop. 700.

Duntocher (*dŭn-toch'ĕr*), tn., Dumbartonshire, Scotland, 9 m. N.W. of Glasgow; Roman remains. Pop. 3,500.

Dunwich (*dŭn-ich*), wat.-pl., E. Suffolk, England; anc. capital of E. Anglia; some fishing. Pop. *c.* 200.

Duquesne (*doo-kān'*), city, Pennsylvania, U.S.A., 9 m. S.E. of Pittsburgh; steelworks. Pop. 19,000.

Durance (*du-rons'*), riv., France, rises in Alps and falls into Rhone below Avignon; rapid current; valuable for irrigation; length, *c.* 220 m.

Duran'go. (1) Inland state, N.W. Mexico; crossed by Sierra Madre Mts.; climate dry and healthy; soil very fertile; few streams; silver, gold, copper, iron; wheat, tobacco, fruits, sugar-cane. Area, 42,272 sq. m.; pop. 337,000. (2) Cap. of above, 130 m. N.E. of Mazatlan, on Pacific coast; mt. of high-grade iron ore to N.W. Pop. 39,000.

Durazzo (*doo-rät'sō*), port, Albania; exports grain, olive oil, sheep. Pop. *c.* 10,000.

Dur'ban, formerly PORT NATAL, chief port and largest tn., Natal, S. Africa; harbour with projecting 'Bluff'; beautifully laid-out city; Berea, handsome suburb; much of Transvaal and Orange Free State trade passes through town; many industries; coaling port; whale and other fisheries; exports maize, wool, wattle bark, hides, skins, Angora wool. Pop. 187,000 (70,000 whites; as many Asiatics).

Düren, tn., Rhineland, Prussia, 23 m. S.W. of Cologne; textiles, sugar, steel, and paper; military barracks. Pop. 37,000.

Durham (*dŭr'am*). (1) Co., England; bounded N. by Northumberland, W. by Westmorland and Cumberland, S. by Yorks, E. by North Sea; in W. are branches of Pennine Range where chief rivers (Derwent, Tees, Wear) rise, and stretches of bare moorland rich in minerals; in E. are fertile and well-wooded valleys where celebrated cattle are reared; coal mines are among most productive in England; co. also produces limestone, slate, black marble, lead, zinc, firestone, and ironstone; chief industry shipbuilding, especially on R. Tyne; manufactures include iron, glass, chemicals, salt, and earthenware; chief tns., Durham, Sunderland, Darlington, Gateshead, S. Shields, Stockton, E. and W. Hartlepool, and Jarrow. Area, 1,014 sq. m.; pop. 1,486,000. (2) Co. tn. of above, parl. and munic. bor.; almost surrounded by R. Wear. Cathedral and university. Manufactures include ironware, carpets, and mustard; coal mines in neighbourhood. Pop. 16,200. (3) City, N. Carolina, U.S.A., 20 m. N.W. of Raleigh; tobacco factories; cotton and hosiery mills. Pop. 52,000.

Durlach (*door'läch*), tn., Baden, Germany, 2½ m. E. Karlsruhe; manufactures vinegar, chicory, tobacco, machinery; mineral baths. Pop. 15,000.

Durs'ley, mkt. tn., Gloucester, England, 13 m. S.W. of Gloucester; manufactures pins, cycles, dairy appliances, agricultural implements, and twine. Pop. 3,000.

Düs'seldorf, tn., Rhineland, Prussia; busy river port on Rhine; important rly. jn.; manufactures iron, chemicals, pianos, cotton, paper, glass. Pop. 430,000.

Dutch Borneo. See BORNEO.

Dutch East Indies. See EAST INDIES.

Dvina (*dvē'na*). (1) NORTHERN DVINA, riv., Russia; has origin in two head-streams in Vologda; enters White Sea by wide estuary, 25 m. below Archangel; length, *c.* 780 m., of which over 350 m. navigable for about 174 days; connected by canal with Neva and Volga. (2) SOUTHERN DVINA (Ger. *Düna*), riv., Russia and Latvia; rises near sources of Volga and Dnieper, flows S.W. to Vitebsk, then N.W. past Daugavpils to Gulf of Riga; length, *c.* 650 m.; small vessels ascend to Vitebsk; mouth frozen Dec. to March.

Dvinsk. See DAUGAVPILS.

Dyetskoye Selo' (*dyets'ko*), tn., European Russia; 15 m. S. of Leningrad; health resort; former imperial palaces, etc., now educational and medical establishments for children. Pop. 19,500.

Dyiarbekir. See DIARBEKR.

Dysart (*di'zart*), port, Fife, Scotland, on Firth of Forth; linens, woollens; exports coal. Pop. 4,600.

E

Eaglehawk', tn., Victoria, Australia, 4½ m. from Bendigo by tram-rail; gold mining. Pop. 4,800.

Eagle Pass, tn., S.W. Texas, U.S.A., on Rio Grande; fodder crops and onions. Pop. 5,800.

Ealing (*ē'ling*), munic. bor., W. suburb of London, 9 m. W. of St. Paul's Cathedral; wholly residential. Pop. 117,700.

Earlestown (*erls'ton*), par., urb. dist. Newton-in-Makerfield, Lancs, England, 5 m. N. of Warrington; engineering, and glass works; sugar refinery. Pop. 16,000.

Earl's Court, dist., Kensington, London; noted for exhibitions.

Earls'ton, par. and mkt. tn., Berwickshire, Scotland, on R. Leader, 4 m. N.E. of Melrose; fragment of old tower of Thomas the Rhymer, with whom vicinity is associated; woollen goods; cattle and sheep markets. Pop. of par. 1,600.

Earn (*ern*). (1) Loch, Perthshire, Scotland; 6 m. long, average width ¾ m. (2) Riv., Perthshire, issues from E. end of loch; joins R. Tay 6½ m. S.E. of Perth; salmon and trout.

Earsdon (*urz'don*), urb. dist., Northumberland, England, on coast 4 m. N.W. of N. Shields; coal mining. Pop. 13,100.

Easdale (*ēz'dāl*), isl., Firth of Lorn, Argyllshire, Scotland, 11 m. S.W. of Oban; slate quarries. Pop. 85.

Easingwold, tn. and par., N. Riding, Yorks, England, 13 m. N.W. of York; agricultural trade; Roman remains. Pop. (par.) 2,000.

East Barnet Valley, urb. dist., Herts, England, adjoining Barnet; part of Greater London; residential dist. Pop. 18,500.

East'bourne, munic. and co. bor., seaside resort, Sussex, England; fine sea-front and handsome parades; Beachy Head (575 ft.) shelters town on the S.W.; Roman antiquities; boat building, and some fishing. Pop. 57,400.

East Calder. See CALDER.

East Chicago (*she-kä'go*), city, Indiana, U.S.A., on L. Michigan, 17 m. S.E. of Chicago; port; iron and steel works; oil refineries. Pop. 55,000.

East Cleve'land, city, Ohio, U.S.A.; residential suburb of Cleveland. Pop. 40,000.

East Dere'ham, mkt. tn., Norfolk, England, 16 m. N.W. of Norwich; agricultural implements and silversmith's work. Pop. 5,600.

East'er Island, volcanic isl., Pacific Ocean, 2,000 m. from the coast of Chile, S. America; noted for remarkable stone images and ruins of stone houses with wooden tablets incised with picture writing in an unknown tongue. Area, 55 sq. m.; pop. 250.

Eastern Townships, dist., Quebec, Canada, between U.S. boundary and riv. St. Lawrence; comprising 12 cos.; traversed by W. ridges of Notre Dame Mts.; agriculture, dairying, and stock raising; asbestos and copper mined; maple-sugar industry. Founded by United Empire Loyalists, 1783. Chief tn., Sherbrooke.

East Grin'stead, mkt. tn., Sussex, England, 30 m. S. by E. of London; brewing, brick and tile making. Pop. 7,900.

East Ham, par. and co. bor., Essex, England, 6 m. E. of London; part of Greater London; chemicals. Pop. 142,500.

East Indies, or MALAY ARCHIPELAGO, the double chain of isls. extending from the S.E. corner of Asia to the N. extremity of Australia. On the Pacific side are the islands of Borneo, Celebes, Sula Islands, Buru, Halmahera, Amboina, Ceram, Waigeu, and New Guinea. The Sulu Islands and the Philippines are a northward extension of this chain. Next the Indian Ocean the chain includes Sumatra, Banka, Billiton, Java, Madura, Bali, Lombok, Sumbawa, Sumba, Flores, Timor, and the Tenimber, or Timor-Laut, Kei, and Aru groups. The Philippines and Holo Islands belong to U.S.A., the N. part of Borneo and the E. portions of New Guinea form part of Brit. Empire, the E. half of Timor is Portuguese; all the others form the Dutch E. Indies. Several of the islands (*e.g.* Java, Sumatra) are studded with active volcanoes. Their climate is hot; and it is also moist, for they fall within the influence of the monsoons. Products are of a tropical character—spices, fruits, coffee, sugar, cacao, rubber, indigo, tobacco, bamboo. The inhabitants are mostly of the Malay race. Area, *c.* 1,000,000 sq. m. Pop. over 60,000,000.

East'leigh and Bishopstoke, urb. dist., Hants, England, 5½ m. N.E. of Southampton; rly. jn. and rly. workshops. Pop. 18,300.

East Liverpool, city, Ohio, U.S.A., on Ohio R., 84 m. S.E. of Cleveland; great porcelain factories; brickyards, steelworks; rubber tyres. Pop. 25,000.

East London, port, and popular resort, Cape Prov., S. Africa, at mouth of Buffalo R.; chief exports, wool and mohair. Pop. 23,000.

East Lo'thian, formerly HADDINGTONSHIRE, maritime co. in S.E. of Scotland, bounded by Firth of Forth, North Sea, Berwickshire, and Midlothian. Lammermuir Hills rise in S.; highest point, 1,750 ft.; centre and N. mostly plain. Watered by R. Tyne. Chief industries are agriculture (cereals and potatoes), sheep farming, coal mining, and sea fishing. Co. tn., Haddington. Area, 267 sq. m.; pop. 47,400.

Eas'ton, city, Pennsylvania, U.S.A., on Delaware R., 60 m. N. of Philadelphia; in area rich in iron ore, brick clay, coal; produces steel, machinery, cement, furniture. Pop. 35,000.

East Orange, city, New Jersey, U.S.A., 12 m. W. of New York city; residential suburb; electrical apparatus; pharmaceutical supplies. Pop. 68,000.

East Prov'idence, tn., Rhode I., U.S.A., on Narragansett Bay and

Seekonk R.; chemicals; wire; oysters. Pop. 26,000.

East Prus'sia, detached prov., Prussia; bounded on N.W. by Baltic Sea, W. by terr. of Free City of Danzig, S. by Poland, N. and E. by Lithuania. Coast fringed with lagoons. Surface generally low, except in the S., which is traversed by a plateau containing numerous small lakes; about half of prov. is cultivated; oats, rye, potatoes, flax; horse and cattle breeding; coast region yields much amber; cap. Königsberg. Area, 1,304 sq. m.; pop. 2,256,000.

East St. Louis, city, Illinois, U.S.A., on Mississippi R., opposite St. Louis, with which it is connected by three bridges; great rly. centre; national stockyards just outside city limits; slaughtering and meat packing, machine shops, foundries; chemicals, glass bottles, petroleum products. Pop. 74,000.

Eastview, tn., Ontario, Canada; E. suburb of Ottawa. Pop. 5,730.

East Windsor, formerly FORD CITY, city, Ontario, Canada, on Detroit R., 2½ m. E. of Windsor, of which it is an industrial suburb. Pop. 15,000.

Eastwood, urb. dist., Notts, England, 9 m. N.W. of Nottingham; coal mining. Pop. 5,400.

Eat'on, Long. See LONG EATON.

Eat'on Soc'on, par. and vil., Beds, England, on R. Duse, near St. Neots; market gardening. Pop. (par.) 2,200.

Eau Claire (*ō klār*), city, N.W. Wisconsin, U.S.A., on the Chippewa R.; busy manufacturing and commercial city; exports lumber; makes paper, linen, furniture; fish hatchery. Pop. 26,000.

Ebbw Vale (*eb'oo*), urb. dist., Monmouthshire, England, 21 m. N.W. of Newport; coal and iron mines, iron and steel works. Pop. 31,700.

Eberbach (*ā'ber-bāch*), tn., Baden, Germany, on R. Neckar, 13 m. E. of Heidelberg; chemicals, cigars; trades in timber and wine. Pop. 7,000.

Eberswalde (*ā'bers-val-di*), tn., Brandenburg, Prussia, 27 m. N.E. of Berlin; ironworks; bricks; banknote paper. Pop. 29,500.

Ebingen (*ā'bing-en*), tn., Württemberg, Germany, 22 m. S. of Tübingen; textile manufactures and tanneries. Pop. 12,100.

E'bro, riv., Spain, rises on S. slope of the Cantabrian Mts., runs S.E. and E., and enters Mediterranean by a delta after course of 470 m.; only navigable for short distance; some progress in canalization.

Ecclefechan (*ek-el-fech'an*), vil., Dumfriesshire, Scotland, 5 m. N. of Annan; birthplace and burial-place of Thomas Carlyle. Pop. 800.

Eccles (*ek'elz*), munic. bor., Lancs, England, 4 m. W. of Manchester; gingham, cotton thread, silk, and fustian; engine works. Pop. 44,400.

Ec'clesfield, tn. and par., W. Riding, Yorks, England, 5 m. N. of Sheffield; cutlery and tools; collieries, ironworks, and paper mills. Pop. 23,000.

Echuca (*e-chu'ka*), tn. and riv. port, Victoria, Australia, on Murray R., 115 m. N. of Melbourne; centre of a wine-producing and pastoral dist.; important irrigation works. Pop. 5,000.

Ecija (*ā'thē-ha*), tn., Seville, Spain, on R. Genil, 48 m. N.E. of Seville; olive oil, soap, candles, wine, pottery. Pop. 30,000.

Eck'ington, par. and tn., Derbyshire, England, 7 m. S.E. of Sheffield; agricultural implements; large collieries. Pop. 12,600.

Ecuador (*ek-wa-dor'*), republic, N.W. of S. America, crossed by equator; bounded N. by Colombia, N.E., E., and S. by Peru, W. by Pacific Ocean. The exact boundary between Peru and Ecuador is still unsettled. The surface consists of a low-lying coastal region stretching inland to the foothills of the Cordillera; the mountains of the Andes, with plateaus 9,000 ft. above sea-level; and a vast plain covered with forests—Provincia del Oriente—sloping eastward from Andes. Many peaks of the Andes in Ecuador are active volcanoes; principal summits, Chimborazo (20,500 ft.), Cotopaxi (19,610 ft.). Ecuador is drained to E. of Andes by R. Amazon system; on W. are Daule, Vinces, Guayaquil, and other rivers flowing to Pacific. The Galapagos Islands, 730 m. off W. coast, belong to Ecuador. Climate is tropical in lowlands; in highlands there is an equable perpetual spring. In the E. there is heavy rain throughout the year; in W. and mountain plateaus there is hot rainy season from Dec. till May. Gold is found; silver, petroleum, copper, and other minerals exist. Vegetation is everywhere luxuriant; cocoa is at present the staple product; sugar and coffee are also cultivated; cereals, tropical fruits, tobacco, vegetables, and cotton are produced, and in vast forests are valuable medicinal and other plants—sarsaparilla, balsams, cinchona, vegetable ivory, rubber. The industries are unimportant: straw (Panama) hats, and woollens; flour mills, breweries, sugar works; chief exports are cocoa, coffee, ivory nuts, petroleum, minerals; chief imports, foodstuffs, textiles, machinery, hardware. Cap. Quito. Area, *c.* 150,000 sq. m.; pop. *c.* 2,000,000.

Edam (*ā-dam'*), tn., Holland, 13 m. N.N.E. of Amsterdam, on Zuider Zee; cheese making. Pop. 8,200.

E'den. (1) Riv., England; rises in the Pennines, Westmorland, flows through the beautiful valley of Mallerstang, and enters Solway Firth below Carlisle. Length, 65 m. (2) Riv., Fife, Scotland, flowing into St. Andrews Bay.

Edenbridge, mkt. tn. and par., Kent, England, 9 m. W. of Tonbridge. Pop. (par.) 2,900.

Edes'sa. See URFA.

Edfu (*ed'foo*), tn., Upper Egypt, on l. bk. of R. Nile, 50 m. S.E. of Thebes; has remains of Temple of Horus; earthenware manufacture. Pop. 20,000.

Edge'hill, hill ridge, S. Warwickshire, England, at base of Edge Hill, 3 m. S.E. of Kineton; scene of first battle of Civil War (1642).

Ed'inburgh, city, royal and munic. burgh, cap. of Scotland, on Firth of Forth; includes Leith, Portobello, Newhaven, Granton. Edinburgh is famed for its natural beauty, literary and romantic associations, and educational institutions. Its situation, its architecture, and its renown as a centre of learning have earned for the city the title of the 'Modern Athens.' Has famous Castle with Scottish National War Memorial; Palace of Holyroodhouse. Industries include printing, publishing, bookbinding, map making; insurance, banking, coal mining, brewing, distilling, rubber works, scientific instruments, paper making, fisheries. One of the greatest educational centres in the world; univ., founded 1582; great medical school. Pop. 439,000.

Leith is continuous with the city, and lies on the S. shore of the Firth of Forth; harbour works extensive. Industries: engineering, shipbuilding, flour milling, sugar refining, chemical manufactures, and saw milling. Chief imports: grain, flour, sugar, chemicals, esparto, and timber. Exports: coal, iron, petroleum, whisky, and paper. Although amalgamated with Edinburgh in 1920, the Port of Leith still retains its title.

Edirne. See ADRIANOPLE.

Ed'monton. (1) Tn., Middlesex, England, 7 m. N. of London; ammunition and varnish factories; brick works; market gardening. Pop. 77,700. (2) City, cap. of Alberta, Canada, at head of navigation of N. Saskatchewan R., 192 m. N. of Calgary; univ. with agricultural coll.; packing houses and creameries; centre of rich coal-mining and agricultural dist.; depot for fur trade. Pop. 65,200.

Edward, LAKE, Central Africa, in Uganda and Belgian Congo, is one of the great sources of the R. Nile; alt. 3,000 ft.; 44 m. long; 32 m. broad; connected with smaller L. George. Overflows to R. Nile by R. Ruchuru. Area, *c.* 820 sq. m.

Eecloo (*ā-klo'*), tn., E. Flanders,

Belgium, 11 m. N.W. of Ghent; textile industries. Pop. 13,300.

Eger (*ā'ger*), (1) or ERLAU, tn., Hungary, 90 m. N.E. of Budapest; wine, soap, candles, tobacco. Pop. 29,000. (2) See CHEB.

Eg'ham, tn., Surrey, England, on R. Thames, 4 m. S.E. of Windsor; has Royal Holloway Coll. for higher education of women, and Holloway Sanatorium. Pop. 15,900.

Egin (*ā'gin*), tn., Asiatic Turkey, on r. bk. of R. Euphrates; see of Armenian archbishop; orchards; cotton, silk, leather, wine. Pop. 23,000.

Egor'ievsk, tn., Russia, 60 m. S.E. of Moscow; dyes, cotton goods, buttons. Pop. 28,000.

Eg'remont. (1) Mkt. tn., Cumberland, England, 5 m. S.S.E. of Whitehaven; iron ore and limestone. Pop. 6,000. (2) Residential tn., Cheshire, England, 2 m. N.N.W. of Birkenhead; connected by ferry boat with Liverpool opposite. Pop. 16,000.

Egripo. See CHALCIS.

Egypt (*ē'jipt*), kingdom, N.E. Africa; extends from Mediterranean Sea to Anglo-Egyptian Sudan, a distance of 680 m.; bounded on W. by Libya and on E. by Red Sea; includes peninsula of Sinai. Egypt, 'the gift of the Nile,' is divided into Upper and Lower Egypt, and consists of two main features, the desert and the Nile. In Upper Egypt (*i.e.*, from Halfa to Beni Suef, *c.* 600 m.) mountains approach closely to the Nile; Lower Egypt is an alluvial plain deposited by the river. Below Cairo the river divides and enters the sea by two mouths, which enclose the famous Delta. S. part of Delta extremely fertile, N. part sandy and marshy. The sea-water lakes near the coast (Mareotis, Burlos, Menzaleh) are almost bays. Upper Egypt is undulating plateau sloping from E. to W. The chief oases in the Libyan desert are Siwa, Bahariya, Farafra, Dakhla, Kharga, and Selima, which stretch N. to S. They have been used immemorially by caravans. The Suez Canal connects the Mediterranean with the Red Sea. The Delta is not very healthy for Europeans, but the rainless, dry climate of the rest of the Nile valley has made it a health resort. In Upper Egypt the temperature sometimes rises to 140° F.; in Lower Egypt it varies from 50° to 60° F. in winter; and from 85° to 90° F. in summer. Snow occasionally falls on the highest mountains. The true Egyptian seasons are not, however, those of the sun, but of the Nile. See NILE. By the construction of dams and barrages perennial irrigation has been secured. Cotton, sugar, and rice are grown from March to Oct.; durra and vegetables, July to Oct.; wheat, barley, and other cereals, Nov. to May. More than half the native population is engaged in agriculture. Phosphates, petroleum, and manganese iron ore are the most important mineral products. Egypt exports cotton and cotton seeds, oilseed cake, eggs, manufactured tobacco, raw wool, hides, cane sugar, rice, henna, lentils, and tomatoes. Egyptian cigarettes are chiefly manufactured at Cairo and Alexandria, attar of roses at Cairo and in the towns of the Fayum, where there are large rose gardens; salt is obtained in large quantities from L. Mareotis.

The R. Nile, navigable throughout Egypt, is still the great thoroughfare for trade and travel, but there are 3,000 m. of railway, of which two-thirds are in the Delta. Caravan routes run in all directions.

There are about 12,000,000 Mohammedans, 860,000 Copts (native Christians), 200,000 Christians of various denominations, and 60,000 Jews. Racially the population is chiefly composed of an Arab element, a Turk. element, and a Coptic element. From 1882 to 1922 Egypt was under Brit. control, though nominally a Turk. prov. In 1923 it was made an independent state. Cap. Cairo. Area, *c.* 383,000 sq. m. (cultivated area is only *c.* 13,600 sq. m.); pop. 14,187,000.

Ehrenbreitstein (*ā-ren-brīt'stīn*), tn., Rhineland, Prussia, on R. Rhine, opposite Coblenz; known as 'the Gibraltar of the Rhine' on account of its strong fortifications. Pop. 3,000.

Eickel (*ī'kel*), tn., Westphalia, Prussia, 3 m. N.N.W. of Bochum; important coal mines. Pop. 33,500.

Eider (*ī'der*), riv., Schleswig-Holstein, Prussia, enters North Sea; tortuous course; connected with Baltic by Kiel Canal; length, *c.* 117 m.

Eigg (*ēg*), or EGG, isl., Inner Hebrides, Inverness-shire, Scotland; 6½ m. long by 4 m. broad; columnar cliffs. Pop. 190.

Eildon Hills (*ēl'don*), three peaks, Roxburghshire, Scotland, 1 m. from Melrose; highest peak, 1,327 ft.; near foot are remains of immense Roman encampment.

Eindhoven (*īnd'ho-ven*), tn., N. Brabant, Holland; textiles, tobacco, wireless apparatus, and electric bulbs. Pop. 69,000.

Eisenach (*ī'zen-a*ch), tn., N.W. Thuringia, Germany; near it is Wartburg, where Luther translated Bible; chemicals, woollens, pottery. Pop. 43,400.

Eisleben (*īs-lā'ben*), tn., Saxony, Prussia, 24 m. W. of Halle; Luther's birthplace; mining centre; machinery, cigars. Pop. 24,000.

Ekaterinburg. See SVERDLOVSK.

Ekaterinodar. See KRASNODAR.

Ekaterinoslav. See DNEPROPETROVSK.

El'ba, Italian isl., Mediterranean Sea off W. coast of Italy; mountainous; produces iron, marble, wine, fish; Napoleon banished here (1814–15). Area, 140 sq. m.; pop. 26,200.

Elbassan', tn., Albania, 65 m. W. of Monastir, on R. Skumbi; iron and copper wares. Pop. 16,000.

Elbe (*elb*), large riv., Germany, rises on Bohemian side of Riesengebirge; flows through Bohemia, then passes through the magnificent scenery of the 'Saxon Switzerland,' and through Prussia; 8 m. above Hamburg divides into several streams (which reunite at Blankenese), and enters North Sea at Cuxhaven. Chief tribs., Moldau, Eger, Schwarze-Elster, Mulde, Saale, Havel. Principal tns., Dresden, Hamburg, Magdeburg. Elbe is navigable as far as confluence of Moldau, Bohemia; connected with Baltic and Oder by canals; total length, 725 m., of which over 500 m. are navigable.

El'berfeld, tn., Rhineland, Prussia; chief seat in Germany of cotton, wool, silk, velvet manufactures; leather, and rubber goods, stained glass. Pop. 168,000.

Elbeuf (*el-boof'*), tn., Seine-Inférieure, France, on l. bk. of R. Seine, 12 m. S. by W. of Rouen; woollens. Pop. 17,300.

El'bing, port, E. Prussia, Germany; has one of the largest shipbuilding yards in Germany; textiles, leather; ironworks. Pop. 68,000.

Elbruz (*el-brooz'*), highest peak, Caucasus Mts., S.E. Europe; extinct volcano with two summits (alt. 18,470 ft. and 18,347 ft.); many glaciers.

Elburz (*el-boorz'*), mts., N. Persia, to S. of Caspian Sea; highest peak, Demavend (over 19,000 ft.); the northern slopes densely forested and well watered; chief pass, Kharzan.

Elche (*āl'chā*), tn., S.E. Spain, 14 m. S.W. of Alicante; famous palm groves; rope-soled shoes, oil, soap. Pop. 33,000.

El Dorä'do, tn., Arkansas, U.S.A., 27 m. S.S.E. of Camden; centre of important oilfield. Pop. 30,000.

Elephan'ta Isle, isl., in Bombay harbour, India; rock-cut Hindu temples; sheep and poultry rearing.

Elets (*yā-lets'*), tn., Russia, on R. Sasna, trib. of R. Don, 100 m. E.S.E. of Orel; iron foundries; tobacco; trade in cattle and cereals. Pop. 42,500.

El'gin. (1) Co. tn. and royal burgh, Moray, Scotland, on R. Lossie; has ruins of a fine cathedral; woollen mills, distilleries, sawmills, iron foundries. Pop. 8,800. (2) City, Illinois, U.S.A., 36 m. N.W. of Chicago; manufacture of watches; exports agricultural and dairy produce. Pop. 36,000.

Elginshire. See MORAY.

Elgon (*el-gōn'*), extinct volcano (over 14,000 ft.), Uganda, Africa, on border of Kenya; snow-capped; inhabited caves on s. face.

Elie (*ē'li*), coast tn. and summer resort, Fife, Scotland, on Firth of Forth; golf links. Pop. (with Earlsferry) 1,100.

Elisavetgrad. See ZINOVIEVSK.

Elisavetpol (*yă-lē-za-vet-pol'*). (1) Dist., Azerbaijan, U.S.S.R., extending from Caucasus to R. Aras; agriculture, carpet weaving, mining (copper, magnetic iron, cobalt). Cap. Gandzha. Area, 16,721 sq. m.; pop. 1,100,000. (2) See GANDZHA.

Eliz'abeth, city, New Jersey, U.S.A.; adjoins New York. Singer sewing machines; railway workshops; iron goods; oil refining; Princeton Univ. founded here. Pop. 115,000.

El Kantara, or QANTARA. See SUEZ CANAL.

Elk'hart, tn., Indiana, U.S.A., 80 m. E. of Chicago; manufactures paper, machinery, musical instruments. Pop. 33,000.

El'land, tn., W. Riding, Yorks, England, on R. Calder, 3 m. s. of Halifax; textile industries. Pop. 10,300.

Ellesmere (*elz'mĕr*). (1) Mkt. tn., Shropshire, England, 7 m. N.E. of Oswestry; agricultural centre; Ellesmere canal connects Rs. Mersey and Severn. Pop. 1,900. (2) Arctic region s. of Grinnell Land; barren and uninhabited.

Ellesmere Port and Whitby, urb. dist., Cheshire, England, 9 m. S.E. of Birkenhead; important port on Manchester Ship Canal. Pop. 18,900.

Ellice Islands (*el'les*), low coral islands, S. Pacific, N. of Fiji Is.; coconuts; form Brit. colony with Gilbert Is. Area, 14 sq. m.; pop. 3,600.

Ellichpur', tn., Berar, India, 35 m. N.W. of Amraoti; trade in cotton and forest produce. Pop. 24,000.

El'lis Island, small isl., New York harbour, U.S.A., 1 m. s.w. of Manhattan I.; since 1892 an important station for examination, etc., of immigrants.

Ellore (*el-ōr'*), inland tn., Madras, India, between mouths of R. Kistna and Godaveri; carpets, hosiery, cotton, rice, and oil mills. Pop. 45,000.

Elmina (*el-mē'na*), port, Gold Coast Colony, Brit. W. Africa; trade in palm oil, gold, ivory. Pop. 5,000.

Elmi'ra, city, New York, U.S.A., 80 m. S.E. of Rochester; railway centre; manufactures railway plant, agricultural implements, fire engines. Pop. 47,000.

El Obeid (*ō-bā-id'*), cap. Kordofan, Anglo-Egyptian Sudan, Africa; on extension of Cairo to Khartum railway; centre for gums, ivory, ostrich feathers. Pop. *c.* 17,000.

El Pas'o, city, Texas, U.S.A., on Rio Grande; smelting copper and lead ores; cotton factories; cattle products. Pop. 102,000.

Elsinore'. See HELSINGÖR.

Els'wick (*els'ik*), formerly township, now part of city of Newcastle-on-Tyne, England. Manufactures hydraulic machinery; gun making.

El'vas, fort. tn., Portugal, 10 m. W. of Badajoz; plums, olives. Pop. 11,700.

El Wad, tn., Sahara, Africa, 125 m. S.S.E. of Biskra; fine palm groves. Pop. 8,600.

El'wood, city, Indiana, U.S.A., 40 m. N.E. of Indianapolis; trade in grain and live-stock; tinplate and glass. Pop. 12,000.

Ely (*ē'li*), (1) ISLE OF, administrative co., N. part of Cambridgeshire, England. Area, 372 sq. m.; pop. 77,700. (2) Cap. of above, on R. Ouse; beautiful cathedral (11th cent.); numerous anc. buildings; isle was 'camp of refuge' of Saxons under Hereward the Wake; market gardens; beet-sugar factory. Pop. 8,400.

Elyr'ia, city, Ohio, U.S.A., 8 m. s. of L. Erie; motor-cars, hardware. Pop. 26,000.

Em'den, fort. port, Hanover, Prussia, near mouth of R. Ems; shipbuilding, herring fisheries; manufactures ropes, cement, chemicals. Pop. 28,000.

Emilia (*ā-mēl'ē-a*), territorial div. of

Italy, lying s. of R. Po.; it includes the provs. of Bologna, Ferrara, Forli, Modena, Parma, Piacenza, Ravenna, and Reggio; cereals, wine, fruits, rice, vegetables, sugar beet, flax. Area, 7,976 sq. m.; pop. 3,033,000.

Em'merich, tn., Rhineland, Prussia, on R. Rhine, near Dutch border; tobacco, chocolate, margarine, sugar; iron casting. Pop. 13,500.

Em'poli, tn., Florence, Italy, 20 m. W. of Florence; picture gallery; straw, cotton, and leather goods; pottery. Pop. 21,000.

Empo'ria, tn., Kansas, U.S.A., 52 m. s.w. of Topeka; trading centre of stock-raising and agricultural region; educational centre. Pop. 12,000.

Ems. (1) Wat.-pl., Hesse-Nassau, Prussia, Germany, on R. Lahn, 7 m. S.E. of Coblenz; thermal springs; silver and lead mining. Pop. 7,000. (2) Riv., Germany; flows N. through Westphalia and Hanover, entering North Sea by two mouths separated by I. of Borkum. Length, 200 m.

Ems'worth, port, Hants, England, on Sussex border; oysters. Pop. 2,500.

En'derby Land, desolate dist. in Antarctica, discovered by Captain John Biscoe (1831).

En'field, tn., Middlesex, England; part of Greater London; government small-arms factory; gave name to Enfield rifle. Pop. 67,900.

Engadine (*en-ga-dēn'*), upper valley of R. Inn, Grisons canton, Switzerland, amidst Alps; elevation, 4,000–6,000 ft.; great health centre in both summer and winter; fine scenery; contains Swiss National park. Chief tn., St. Moritz. Pop. 12,000.

Enghien (*on-gē-an'*), tn., Hainaut, Belgium, 18 m. s.w. of Brussels; lace, linen, and cotton manufactures. Pop. 5,000.

Eng'land, with Wales, is s. part of Great Britain. Greatest length, 420 m.; greatest breadth, 360 m. Coast line is *c.* 1,800 m. Separated from Scotland by Cheviot Hills and R. Tweed. Welsh boundary is the W. border of Eng. counties of Cheshire, Shropshire, Herefordshire, and Monmouthshire.

Deep bays on E. and W. coasts, with good harbours, cut into the country at nearly opposite points. On s. coast chief openings are Mounts Bay, Falmouth Harbour, Plymouth Sound, with Tor Bay, Weymouth Harbour, Poole Bay, and, between Hampshire and the Isle of Wight, the Solent and Spithead, with Southampton Water and Portsmouth Harbour running up into the land. Islands are Holy I. and Farne Islands (off Northumberland), the Isle of Wight (Hampshire), the Scilly Isles (Cornwall), Lundy Isle (Devon), Walney (Lancashire). The Channel Islands and Isle of Man do not form part of England.

A line of hills known as the Oolitic Escarpment runs from the Cleveland Hills, Yorks, s.w. to the Cotswold Hills; the part N.W. of this is of older geological character, and contains the mts. and coal measures of England. The mts. are: Pennine Chain, stretching s. from Cheviots to its s. culmination, the Peak, Derbyshire; Cumbrian mts. of Lake District (Scafell, 3,162 ft., Skiddaw, and Helvellyn are highest summits); Welsh or Cambrian Mts.; the s.w. mountains, comprising Exmoor and Dartmoor in Somerset, Devon, and Cornwall (chief heights, Dunkery Beacon, 1,707 ft., Yes Tor, 2,028 ft., and Brown Willy, 1,375 ft.), Mendip Hills, Somerset, Malvern Hills, Worcestershire, and Clee Hills and Wrekin, Shropshire. The newer S.E. portion of England contains Chalk Ridge, which runs s. from Flamborough Head as the York and Lincoln Wolds, E. Anglian Heights, Chiltern Hills, Marlborough Downs, to Salisbury Plain, from which North and South Downs extend E. to Dover Cliffs and Beachy Head respectively, and enclose district known as the Weald. This S.E. portion of England belongs structurally to Great Plain of Europe. Chief plains of England are Midland Plain, Plain of Lancashire and Cheshire, Vale of York, and Eastern Plain. The

Fens are a marshy district round the Wash; many of its towns, like Ely, were islands in Saxon times. A tract of clay known as the London Basin stretches from R. Thames along E. coast to N. of Norfolk, and round Portsmouth is another tract known as the Hampshire Basin. The Rs. Tyne, Wear, Tees, Ouse with most of its tribs., Trent and Witham, flow from E. slopes of Pennines into North Sea; the Rs. Lune, Ribble, and Mersey from W. slopes into Irish Sea. The two longest rivs. of England are the Severn and the Thames. Climate is temperate. Rainfall is abundant. Westerly winds with their warmth and moisture and the physical aspect of the country cause the western portions to have a higher (and more equable) temperature and greater humidity than the eastern parts.

The forty counties of England are: 1. (N.) Northumberland, Cumberland, Westmorland, Durham, Yorkshire, Lancashire; 2. (Midland) Derbyshire, Northamptonshire, Nottinghamshire, Staffordshire, Leicestershire, Rutlandshire, Warwickshire, Worcestershire, Oxfordshire, Buckinghamshire, Bedfordshire, Hertfordshire, Middlesex; 3. (W.) Cheshire, Shropshire, Herefordshire, Monmouthshire, Gloucestershire; 4. (E.) Lincolnshire, Norfolk, Cambridgeshire, Huntingdonshire, Suffolk, Essex; 5. (S.E.) Kent, Sussex, Surrey, Berkshire, Hampshire; 6. (S.W.) Dorsetshire, Devonshire, Cornwall, Wiltshire, Somersetshire. These are divided into fifty 'Administrative Counties.'

The railways are grouped into four systems—London, Midland and Scottish Railway; London and North-Eastern Railway; Great Western Railway; and Southern Railway; total mileage, 19,822. These groups radiate from London. There are 3,641 m. of canals.

England owes its industrial importance to coal. The coalfields belong almost entirely to the geological system of the N. and W. That of Northumberland and Durham has made the Tyne ports busy commercial centres; in this district, iron, steel, chemicals, machinery, and ships are manufactured. The Cumberland field supplies coal for iron and steel works at Barrow-in-Furness. The West Riding of Yorkshire is the chief wool-manufacturing area; Sheffield has cutlery industry. The S. Lancashire coalfield maintains the great cotton industry of Lancashire. The coalfields of N. and S. Staffordshire contain respectively the Potteries and the Black Country. The Potteries import china-clay from Cornwall and flint from Kent and Sussex. The Black Country, in the heart of the Midlands, has both coal and iron ore. The coalfields of the Forest of Dean, Gloucestershire, and of Bristol have decayed in importance since working of richest Brit. field, that of S. Wales. After coal, iron is the most important mineral product; it is found near the coal, and also in the Cleveland district of Yorkshire. Other minerals are tin (Cornwall), lead, gypsum, fireclays, china-clay, and salt. Lincoln, Leicester, and the N. and S. Downs are famous for sheep, Yorkshire and E. counties for horses; wheat is chiefly grown in S.E. counties; hops grow in S., especially Kent, and also in Herefordshire. Fruit, grown widely, abounds in Kent, Herefordshire (both called the 'garden of England'), and S.W. generally; cider is made in Devon and Somerset. Commerce is of the greatest importance. Chief ports are London, Liverpool, Cardiff, Hull, Newcastle, Bristol, and Southampton. Fishing is an important industry. Cap. London. Area, 50,874 sq. m.; pop. 37,790,000.

English Channel, narrow sea between England and France; connected with North Sea by Strait of Dover, its narrowest part (*c.* 21 m.), and also its shallowest (12 to 13 fathoms); stretching W., joins Atlantic between Scilly Isles and Cape Ushant. Length, *c.* 350 m. Eng. coast extends from Strait of Dover to Land's End. Only important river it receives is

Seine, from France. In English Channel are Isle of Wight and Channel Islands.

E'nid, city, Oklahoma, U.S.A., 42 m. N.W. of Guthrie; flour mills; ironworks; agricultural implements, tractors. Pop. 26,000.

En'nis, co. tn., Clare, I.F.S., 20 m. N.W. of Limerick; breweries, distilleries; flour mills. Pop. 5,500.

Enniscor'thy, mkt. tn., Wexford, I.F.S., on R. Slaney; flour mills, breweries; mineral waters; woollens. Pop. 5,500.

Enniskil'len, co. tn., Fermanagh, N. Ireland, on island between Upper and Lower Loughs Erne; flour mill; brewery; trade in corn. Pop. 4,900.

Enschede (*en-skā'de*), tn., Overijsel, Holland, near German boundary; cotton spinning and weaving. Pop. 49,500.

Entebbe (*en-teb'ā*), cap. Uganda, Africa, on N.W. shore of Lake Victoria; cotton ginning; fine botanic gardens. Pop. (white) 50.

Entre Minho e Douro, or MINHO, (*en'trā mēn'yo ā doo'rō*), prov., Portugal, between Rs. Minho and Douro; produces grain, fruits, wine, cattle, textiles. Chief tn., Oporto. Area, 2,790 sq. m.; pop. 1,304,000.

Entre Rios (*en'trā rē'ōs*), prov., Argentine Rep., S. America, between Paraná and Uruguay rivs.; well-watered, undulating plain; one-fifth forested; wheat, linseed, alfalfa; stock raising and vine growing. Chief tn., Parana. Area, 29,241 sq. m.; pop. 569,000.

Enzeli. See PAHLEVI.

Eperies. See PRESOV.

Epernay (*ā-per-nā'*), tn., Marne, France, on R. Marne; centre of champagne industry; rly. workshops. Pop. 19,000.

Epinal (*ā-pē-nal'*), chief tn., Vosges, France; fortress; cotton, weaving, and printing; embroidery, hats; has library with many valuable old MSS. Pop. 22,000.

Ep'ping, mkt. tn., Essex, England, 17 m. N.N.E. of London, on N. outskirts of Epping Forest; 5,600 ac. of forest preserved by City of London and open to public. Pop. 5,000.

Ep'som, mkt. tn., Surrey, England, 15 m. S.S.W. of London; medicinal springs. Epsom Downs have famous racecourse, where 'Derby' and 'Oaks' are run. Pop. 27,100.

Erfurt (*er'foort*), tn., Saxony, Prussia, on R. Gera, 65 m. S.W. of Leipzig; famous cathedral; flower seeds, flowers, and vegetables; dress stuffs; machinery; chemicals; brewing and dyeing. Pop. 136,000.

Er'icht, LOCH, lake between Perthshire and Inverness-shire, Scotland; well stocked with trout; length, 14 m. Dam in connection with hydro-electric scheme, where R. Ericht leaves the loch.

Erie (*ē'ri*). (1) Lake, N. America; one of the Great Lakes separating Canada from U.S.A.; length, 240 m.; breadth, 30 m. to 58 m.; area, 10,000 sq. m.; alt., 573 ft. (2) Canal, New York, U.S.A., connects L. Erie with Hudson R.; length, 340 m.; breadth, 150 ft.; depth, 12 ft. (3) City, Pennsylvania, U.S.A., on L. Erie; fine harbour; ironworks; machinery; asbestos products. Pop. 116,000.

Er'ith, tn., Kent, England, 5 m. E. of Woolwich; coal port; engineering and gun factories; gunpowder, oil, glue, and manure works. Pop. 32,800.

Eritrea (*ā-rē-trā'a*), Ital. colony on Red Sea, Africa; coast-line is *c.* 670 m. long, of coral formation, and with many islands. Interior consists of two regions—in N., part of Abyssinian plateau; in S., part of Afar country, large tracts of plain, mostly arid and often forming jungle of mimosa trees; principal rivs. enter salt basins. Water is scarce. Climate varies; on the coast, excessive heat; in valley-lands, more temperate; on plateau, cool. Good pearl fisheries; flax, tobacco, cereals, cotton; gold near Asmara. Inhabitants are largely nomadic, with flocks of sheep, cattle, camels, donkeys. Chief tns., Asmara (cap.) and Massawa. Area, 45,754 sq. m.; pop. 400,000.

Erivan'. (1) District, Armenia,

U.S.S.R., an elevated plain culminating in an extinct volcano, Alagoz (13,436 ft.); agriculture; famed for apricots and melons, and vineyards. Area, 1,985 sq. m.; pop. 176,000. (2) Cap. of above and of Armenia; machinery, wine, brandy, glycerine. Pop. 66,000.

Er'langen, tn., Bavaria, Germany, 11 m. N.W. of Nuremberg; breweries; manufactures electrical apparatus, gloves, paper, brushes. Pop. 30,000.

Erlau. See EGER.

Ermeland', region, E. Prussia, Germany, S. of Königsberg; centre of flax growing. Area, 1,650 sq. m.; pop. *c.* 240,000.

Ermelo', tn. and dist., Transvaal, S. Africa, 120 m. E.S.E. of Johannesburg; coal, gold; mealies. Pop. (tn.) 4,500.

Erne (*ern*). (1) Riv., Ireland; passes through two lakes of same name; enters Donegal Bay; cataract near mouth; length, *c.* 72 m. (2) UPPER LOUGH ERNE, shallow lake, Fermanagh, N. Ireland; rugged shores; numerous islets, 13 m. long. (3) LOWER LOUGH ERNE, lake, Fermanagh, N. Ireland, studded with islets; salmon and trout fishing; 18 m. long.

Erode, tn., Madras, India, on r. bk. of R. Cauvery; trade centre; cotton. Pop. 23,000.

Erzerum (*erdz-room'*). (1) Turkish vilayet, E. Asia Minor, formerly partly Armenian, occupying centre of the Armenian plateau, and containing sources of Rs. Euphrates, Choruk, and Aras (Araxes); agricultural and forest country, with iron, saline, and sulphur springs, salt, and lignite. Area, 19,600 sq. m.; pop. 270,000. (2) Tn., in above, at E. end of plain watered by R. Kara-Su (W. Euphrates), 6,000 ft. above the sea and frequently snowbound for six months in the year; horse-shoes, brasswork; salt works, tanneries. Pop. 78,000.

Erzgebirge (*erts'ge-bir-gi*), ('ore mountain'), mt. range between German Saxony and Bohemia (Czechoslovakia); highest peaks, Keilberg (4,062 ft.), Fichtelberg (3,950 ft.), Spitzberg (3,650 ft.); rich in minerals—tin, silver, lead, iron, copper; popular for winter sports.

Erzinjan', anc. tn. of Armenia, 85 m. s. of Trebizond and w. of Erzerum, situated 3,900 ft. above the sea; manufactures silk, cotton, and copper articles. Pop. 52,000.

Esbjerg (*es'byerg*), port, w. Jutland, Denmark; exports cattle, butter, bacon, fish, and eggs. Pop. 24,000.

Escanä'ba, city, Michigan, U.S.A.; shipping port of Lake Superior iron region; railway workshops; lumber products, chemicals. Pop. 13,200.

Eschwege (*esh'vā-gi*), tn., Hesse-Nassau, Prussia, on R. Werra, 28 m. S.E. of Cassel; textiles; tobacco factories; tanneries. Pop. 12,500.

Eschweiler (*esh'vī-ler*), tn., Rhineland, Prussia, 8 m. E.N.E. of Aachen; coal-mining and iron-working centre; zinc works; brewing. Pop. 26,000.

Esh'er and The Dittons, urb. dist., Surrey, England, on R. Mole; residential tn., part of Greater London; Sandown Park racecourse near by; associations with Cardinal Wolsey and Clive. Pop. 17,100.

Eshowe (*esh-ō'wā*), magisterial div., Zululand, Natal, S. Africa, 30 m. N. of mouth of Tugela R.; agricultural. Area, 736 sq. m.; pop. 34,000. Chief centre, Eshowe; asbestos mines.

Esk, four rivs., Scotland. (1) NORTH ESK, Angus; flows into North Sea; salmon and trout fishing; length, 29 m. (2) SOUTH ESK, Angus; flows into North Sea at Montrose; salmon and trout; length, 48 m. (3) Riv. formed by union of NORTH ESK and SOUTH ESK at Dalkeith, Midlothian; enters Firth of Forth at Musselburgh. (4) Riv. formed by union of BLACK ESK and WHITE ESK near Langholm; flows into Solway Firth near Gretna; salmon and trout fishing; length, 37 m.

Eskilstuna (*esh'il-stoo-na*), tn., Södermanland, Sweden, between Ls. Hjelmar and Malar; iron and steel industries; engineering. Pop. 31,000.

Eski-Shehr (*es'ki-shār*), ('old town'), tn. and vilayet, Turkey, Asia Minor,

130 m. w. of Angora; rly. centre; meerschaum; cereals, wool, hair. Pop. (vilayet) 154,000.

Esmeral'das, maritime prov., Ecuador, S. America; traversed by riv. of same name; cap. Esmeraldas, port, and centre of cacao and tobacco dist.; gold. Area, 5,465 sq. m.; pop. 20,000.

Es'na, tn. on l. bk. of R. Nile, Upper Egypt; barrage here; caravan centre; pottery. Pop. 16,000.

Espinal', tn., Colombia, S. America, 75 m. s.w. of Bogota; tobacco plantations and pottery works. Pop. 10,000.

Espi'rito San'to, mar. state, Brazil, S. America; surface flat in N., forested and mountainous in s.; sugar, cotton, coffee, cocoa, tobacco, and tropical fruits; cap. Victoria, 270 m. N.E. of Rio de Janeiro. Area, 17,248 sq. m.; pop. 587,500.

Esquimalt (*es-kwī'mawlt*), naval station, Vancouver I., Canada, adjoining Victoria; has naval yard and dry dock; salmon cannery. Pop. 5,000.

Esseg. See OSIJEK.

Es'sen, tn., Rhineland, Prussia; centre of Ruhr coalfield; large iron and steel works (including Krupp's); agricultural machinery, locomotives, cash registers; textiles, cigars; breweries; great rly. centre. Pop. 470,500.

Essequibo (*es-ā-kē'bō*), riv., Brit. Guiana, S. America; length, *c.* 600 m.; navigable 40 m.

Es'sex, mar. co., England, having on N. Cambridgeshire and Suffolk, on E. North Sea, on s. R. Thames, on w. Middlesex and Herts; long, flat coastline with shallow bays, occasionally fringed with marshland; inland, surface undulating, wooded; land sometimes inundated; contains Epping Forest. Chief rivs., Thames, Stour, Lea, Colne, Blackwater, and Roding; great grain-producing county important oyster fishing. Industries include powder works and breweries; important docks at Tilbury and Plaistow; Harwich has great continental traffic; co. manufactures agricultural implements and silk. Largest tns. are part of Greater London (East Ham, West Ham, Leyton, Walthamstow); other tns., Chelmsford (co. tn.), Southend, Colchester. Area, 1,530 sq. m.; pop. 1,755,200.

Esslingen (*es'ling-en*), tn., Württemberg, Germany, 9 m. S.E. of Stuttgart; famed for wines and fruit; manufactures include machinery and cottons. Pop. 41,000.

Estepona (*ās-tā-pō'na*), tn. and port, Malaga, s. Spain; fishing centre; fruit exported. Pop. 10,000.

Es'ton, urb. dist., N. Riding, Yorks, England, at foot of Cleveland Hills, 4 m. S.E. of Middlesbrough; blast furnaces, iron foundries, and ironstone quarries. Pop. 31,100.

Esto'nia, republic on E. shore of Baltic Sea, s. of Gulf of Finland; bounded by Russia on E. and Latvia on s.; surface flat; agriculture and dairy farming; chief crops, rye, oats, barley, potatoes; forests; produces textiles, cement, oil shale, matches, leather. Inhabitants mainly of Finnish race and Protestant. Cap. Tallinn. Area, 18,354 sq. m.; pop. 1,116,500.

Estra'da, LA, tn., Galicia, N.W. Spain, 18 m. N.N.E. of Pontevedra; agriculture, stock rearing; linen and paper manufactures. Pop. 25,000.

Estremadura (*es-trā-ma-doo'ra*) ('Land's End'). (1) Atlantic prov., Portugal; embraces dists. of Leiria, Lisbon, and Santarem; products, fruit, wine, fish, salt, fine lace. Area, 6,937 sq. m.; pop. 1,304,000. (2) Former prov. of w. Spain, divided into modern provs. of Badajoz and Caceres.

Esz'tergom, formerly GRAN, tn., Hungary, on r. bk. of R. Danube; mineral springs; cloth weaving, wine; cathedral; former cap. of Hungary. Pop. *c.* 20,000.

Etaples (*ē-tap'*), port and wat.-pl., Pas-de-Calais, France, 17 m. by rail s. of Boulogne; Brit. base hospitals in vicinity during Great War.

Ethiopia (*ē-the-o'pe-a*), ('land of the swarthy-faced'), name given by the ancients to an extensive tract of country on both sides of the Upper Nile. It corresponds to the modern

Nubia and Abyssinia. The cap. was Meroë, which was one of the principal trade centres of the anc. world.

Et'na, volcano, Sicily; height, *c.* 10,760 ft.; summit generally under snow; middle slopes wooded; soil at base fertile, producing fruits and vegetables; observatory situated *c.* 1,000 ft. below summit; last eruption 1928.

E'ton, tn., Bucks, England, on l. bk. of R. Thames, opposite Windsor; famous for college founded by Henry VI. (1440); beautiful old buildings, including quadrangles and chapel. Pop. 2,000.

Etruria (*et-roo're-a*), dist. of anc. Italy, probably including in early times N. Italy, between Alps and Tiber, but later reduced to dist. bounded by R. Arno, Apennine Mts., and R. Tiber. Formerly populated by Etruscans, a powerful people of whose history little is known.

Et'trick, riv., Selkirkshire, Scotland; rises in Capel Fell; flows N.E. to join Tweed, N.E. of Selkirk; chief trib., Yarrow. Length, 32 m.

Eubœa (*ū-bē'a*), largest isl. Grecian Archipelago; separated from E. mainland by channel, N.W. part of which was anciently called Eubœan Sea and narrowest part Euripus (*c.* 120 ft., and spanned by bridge). E. coast is steep and rocky, W. sloping gradually; interior wooded, fertile, mountainous; hot springs in N.; iron, coal, and marble in S. Principal products—corn, oil, and wine; minerals—black marble, lignite, and chrome ores. People mostly Greeks and Albanians. Chief tns., Carystos and Chalcis. Area, 1,460 sq. m.; pop. 154,000.

Euganean Hills (*u-gā'-ni-an*), volcanic hills, Lombardy, N. Italy, S.W. of Padua; several watering-places on slopes.

Eupato'ria, port, Crimean Rep., U.S.S.R.; machinery, chemicals, dried fish; exports cereals, salt. Pop. 23,000.

Eupen (*oi'pen*), tn., Belgium, 10 m. S. of Aachen; cloth and woollen industries; dye works; yarn-spinning mills. Ceded to Belgium after Great War. Pop. 13,500.

Euphrates (*ū-frā'tez*), largest riv. in W. Asia, called in O.T. 'the river' (Exod. 23 : 31) and 'the great river' (Deut. 1 : 7). Source, in Anatolia, consists of two branches, Kara-Su and Murad-Su; flows through mountainous region of Taurus; enters Syria, and at Abu Kamal flows into Iraq; is joined by R. Tigris at Kurna; united riv. called Shatt-al-Arab. Riv. in middle and lower courses flows through plains, deserts, and swamps, sparsely cultivated. In anc. times rich cultivated plain well watered by canals. Near Basra quantities of dates and rice are grown. Banks of riv. teem with anc. remains representing all periods; site of Babylon. Great floods take place, due to melting snows on mts. of upper course. Length, *c.* 1,800 m.; breadth varies greatly.

Eura'sia, name formed from Europe and Asia, applied to the great continental land mass which these two form.

Eure, dep., N. France; surface consists of plateaus with fertile valleys; drained by Rs. Eure and Seine; agriculture, orchards, stock raising; textiles; cap. Evreux. Area, 2,330 sq. m.; pop. 308,000.

Eure-et-Loir (*ūr-ā-lwar'*), dep., France, S. of Eure; flat in E.; W. hilly and forested; drained by Rs. Eure and Loir; granary of Seine basin; flour mills, textile factories, ironworks, cotton and paper mills. Cap. Chartres. Area, 2,291 sq. m.; pop. 255,000.

Eure'ka, tn., N. California, U.S.A., on Humboldt Bay; redwood lumber. Pop. 19,000.

Eur'ope, most W. and smallest continent of Old World. Extreme length (from Nordkyn on N. to S. of Greece) about 2,400 m., extreme width about 3,000 m. Bounded on N. by Arctic Ocean; E. by Ural Mts., Ural R., and Caspian Sea; S. by Caucasus Mts., Black Sea, Sea of Marmara, Ægean Sea, and Mediterranean Sea; W. by

Atlantic Ocean. Coast-line, about 48,000 m. in extent, is very much broken. It throws out the great south-pointing peninsulas of Scandinavia on the N., Iberian Peninsula, Italy, Balkans and Crimea on S., and north-pointing peninsula of Jutland. Brit. Isles are separated from mainland by the English Channel and North Sea, Iceland by Atlantic Ocean, Novaya Zemlya, Spitsbergen, etc., by Arctic Ocean. Except in Russia, no place is more than 300 m. from the sea. In N. traffic is interrupted in winter by the freezing of seas and waterways. Principal mts. radiate from the Alps. A great W. loop passes through the Apennines of Italy, Atlas of N. Africa, into Spain as the Sierra Nevada, and with the Pyrenees, a short branch, probably rejoins the Alps. To the E. the great Carpathian fold encircles the Hungarian plain before passing into the Balkan peninsula as the Balkan Mts., and by the Crimea into the Caucasus. Another fold, the Dinaric Alps, forms E. boundary of Adriatic Sea, becomes the Pindus range in Greece, and passes into Asia Minor. N. of this great system are the dissected plateaus of Spain, France, Bohemia, Scandinavia, and N. Scotland. About two-thirds of surface is a plain, of which greater part is under 600 ft. above sea-level. It begins in S. of England and extends through N. and E. of France, N.E. to tundras along Arctic Ocean, E. and S.E. to Caspian and Black Seas; along R. Danube, encircled by the Alps, Carpathians, and Balkans, are the plains of Hungary and Walachia. A considerable area around N. end of Caspian Sea is below sea-level. The Alps and Valdai Hills are the principal watersheds; from the former flow the Rs. Rhine (to North Sea), Rhone, Po, and Adige (to Mediterranean), and the Danube (to Black Sea); from the latter the N. Dvina (to White Sea), Volga (to Caspian), Don and Dnieper (to Black Sea), S. Dvina and Niemen (to Baltic).

Owing to Atlantic Drift Current along N.W., and the large amount of inland water, Europe has a more temperate yet more varied climate than any other continent. Extreme N. is arctic, the sheltered Mediterranean district sub-tropical. The S.W. winds bring abundant moisture and heat; nowhere is agriculture impossible owing to drought except in S.E. and in interior of Spain. As a rule, rainfall decreases and range of temperature increases from W. to E.

Flora and fauna vary from subarctic to sub-tropical. Indigenous animals include bear, wolf, elk, chamois, many species of deer, foxes, hares, and rabbits. The North Sea provides a valuable fishing ground for herring, cod, and mackerel, while tunny fishing is an important Mediterranean industry. Of native trees, fir, oak, apple, pear, and cherry are the most common. Central regions produce timber, fibres, cereals, and hardier fruits, the S. sub-tropical fruits, the N. the hardier cereals; good pasture in all parts.

The precious metals are not found in abundance, but there are rich veins of coal (chiefly in Britain, Belgium, France, Germany), iron (the same, with Sweden and Spain), copper (Sweden and Spain), lead (Spain), zinc (Germany), mercury (Spain and Austria), sulphur (Sicily), salt (Poland and England), and petroleum (Russia, Romania). Area, 3,750,000 sq. m. Pop. *c.* 500,000,000.

Euskirchen (*ois'kirch-en*), tn., Rhineland, Prussia, 10 m. W. of Bonn; cloth mills, tanneries, sugar and metal-ware factories. Pop. 15,000.

Euxine. See BLACK SEA.

Ev'anston, city, Illinois, U.S.A., on shore of Lake Michigan; residential suburb of Chicago. Pop. 62,000.

Ev'ansville, city, S.W. Indiana, U.S.A., on Ohio R.; one of largest hardwood markets in the world; coal mining; motor-cars, refrigerators, gas engines, agricultural implements. Pop. 103,000.

Ev'erest, MOUNT, peak, Himalayas, on frontiers of Nepal and Tibet, India;

highest measured mountain in world (over 29,000 ft.). Several climbing expeditions in recent years. In 1924 highest camp, 27,000 ft.; Messrs. Mallory and Irvine last seen at altitude reckoned by theodolite as 28,200 ft.

Ev′erett. (1) City, Massachusetts, U.S.A., a residential suburb of Boston; manufactures iron, steel, coke, and petroleum products. Pop. 48,000. (2) City, Washington, U.S.A., on Puget Sound; sawmills, iron smelting; canning of fish, fruit, and vegetables. Pop. 30,000.

Ev′erglades, swamp (140 m. by 50 m.) occupying most of s. portion of Florida peninsula, U.S.A.; contains Lake Okeechobee and numerous sluggish waterways. Now being drained.

Eves′ham, munic. bor. and mkt. tn., Worcestershire, England, on R. Avon, in Vale of Evesham; summer resort; orchards; market gardens; jam factories. Pop. 8,800.

Evo′ra, tn., archiepisc. see, cap. of dist. of Evora, Portugal, 72 m. E.S.E. of Lisbon; agricultural centre; copper and iron mines in vicinity. Pop. 16,000.

Evreux (*ā-vroo*), tn., episc. see, cap. of Eure dept., France, 30 m. S. of Rouen; iron foundries and glass works. Pop. 15,000.

Ew′ell, par. and tn., Surrey, England, 1½ m. N.E. of Epsom; residential town; pottery, brick and tile works. Pop. (par.) 4,200.

Exe, riv., England, flows through Somerset and Devon; enters Eng. Channel; trout fishing; navigable estuary; length, 54 m.

Ex′eter, co. tn., Devonshire, England, on R. Exe. Anc. city, believed to have been occupied by the Romans; famous cathedral. Manufactures agricultural implements, paper; brewing, ironfounding; important rly. centre. Exeter Ship Canal connects Exeter with estuary of riv. Pop. 66,000.

Ex′moor, high moorland on borders of Somerset and N. Devon, England; ponies, sheep, deer.

Ex′mouth, urb. dist., mkt. tn., and port, Devonshire, England, 10 m. S.S.E. of Exeter; fishing, brick making, and manufacture of Honiton lace. Pop. 14,600.

Eye (*ī*), munic. bor. and mkt. tn., Suffolk, England, 20 m. N. of Ipswich; brewing and ironworks. Pop. 1,700.

Eyemouth (*ī′mouth*), police burgh, Berwickshire, Scotland, at mouth of R. Eye, 8 m. N. by W. of Berwick; important fishing centre. Pop. 2,200.

Eyre (*īr*), LAKE, salt lake, S. Australia; in sandy waste known as 'Dead Heart of Australia'; in wet season fed by Warburton riv. and Cooper's Creek, in dry season a swamp; 38 ft. below sea-level.

F

Fabriano (*fäb-ri-ä′nō*), tn. and episc. see, Marches, Italy, 35 m. S.W. of Ancona; famous in 14th cent. for school of painting; paper mills. Pop. 25,200.

Facatativa (*fä′-kä-tä-tē′vä*), tn., Colombia, S. America, *c.* 20 m. N.W. of Bogota; in neighbourhood are interesting Indian carved stones; alt. 8,480 ft. Pop. *c.* 12,000.

Faenza (*fä-ent′sa*), tn. and episc. see, Emilia, Italy, 31 m. S.E. of Bologna; famous for glazed and painted pottery (faïence); silk manufactures. Pop. 22,400.

Faeroes, THE ('sheep islands') (*fā′rōs*), group of islands, North Sea, between Iceland and Shetland; belong to Denmark; 21 islands, of which 17 are inhabited; high and rugged, with broad inland terraces with sharp-pointed peaks (highest, 2,894 ft.); currents are dangerous, and storms frequent; chief industries are sheep farming, fishing, and wild-fowling. Cap. Thorshavn, in Strömö. Area, 540 sq. m.; pop. 22,800.

Fails'worth, urban dist., 4 m. N.E. of Manchester, Lancashire, England; cotton spinning, silk weaving, hat manufacture. Pop. 15,700.

Fair Head, rocky promontory, N. Ireland, in N. of co. Antrim; 636 ft. high.

Fair Isle ('sheep island'), rocky isl., Shetland, Scotland; 3 m. long by 2 m. broad; fishing and woollen hosiery.

Faiyum, El (*fi-yoom'*), prov., Egypt; fertile and well-watered by canals (especially Bahr Yusuf); in N. is L. Birket-el-Kerun; principal prods., fruit, cereals, rice, cotton, attar of roses. Area, *c.* 670 sq. m.; pop. 554,000. Chief tn., Medinet-el-Faiyum, 57 m. S.S.W. of Cairo (pop. 53,000).

Faizabad (*fiz-a-bad'*). (1) Cap. of Badakhshan, N.E. Afghanistan; is the chief cantonment for E. Afghanistan. (2) See FYZABAD.

Fa'kenham, par. and mkt. tn., Norfolk, England, 19 m. N.E. of King's Lynn. Pop. (par.) 3,000.

Falaise (*fa-läz'*), tn., Calvados, N. France, 20 m. S. of Caen; birthplace of William the Conqueror; cotton manufactures. Pop. 5,500.

Falkenstein (*fal'ken-stin*), tn., Saxony, Germany, 35 m. S.W. of Chemnitz; cotton goods, lace, window blinds; topazes found in neighbourhood. Pop. 16,000.

Falkirk (*fawl'kirk*), mkt. tn. and munic. burgh, Stirlingshire, Scotland; centre of agricultural and coal mining dist.; Carron, Falkirk, and Camelon ironworks, dating from 17th cent., now famous for fire-grates and stoves; other industries are brewing, distilling, brick and tile making, chemical manufactures. Pop. 36,600.

Falkland (*fawk'land*), tn. and royal burgh, Fife, Scotland, 8 m. S.W. of Cupar; linen and floorcloth manufactures; anc. palace. Pop. 800.

Falk'land Islands, British Crown Colony in S. Atlantic, 300 m. E. of Magellan Straits, consisting of E. Falkland (2,580 sq. m.), W. Falkland (2,038 sq. m.), and dependencies of S. Georgia (*c.* 1,000 sq. m.), S. Orkneys, S. Shetlands, Graham Land, Sandwich group; includes over 100 small islands. Coast is irregular, with many excellent harbours; many small rivers and lakes; climate bleak but healthy. Chief industry is sheep rearing; coaling station; wool, hides, tallow, whale oil exported. The islands are now the seat of the largest whaling business in the world. During the Great War naval battle of Falkland Islands (Dec. 1914) gave the Allies control of ocean trade routes. Cap. Stanley (E. Falkland). Total pop. *c.* 4,000.

Fall River, city and port, Massachusetts, U.S.A., 50 m. S. of Boston; has the most extensive cotton manufacture of U.S.A.; other industries are dyeing, brewing, ironfounding, oil refining, manufacture of machinery and silk; unrivalled facilities of water power and water transportation; line of steamers, the favourite means of travel between Boston and New York. Pop. 115,000.

Fal'mouth, munic. bor., seapt. and popular wat.-pl., Cornwall, England; fine harbour; docks and building yards; has important coasting trade and fishing industry. Pop 13,500.

Fal'ster, Danish isl., Baltic Sea; is very fertile; agriculture, fruit-growing, dairying; 30 m. long, 2–13 m. broad; chief town, Nykjöbing.

Fa'lun (*fä'loon*), tn., Kopparberg, Sweden, *c.* 150 m. N.W. of Stockholm; celebrated copper mine, worked since 13th cent.; iron, steel, wood pulp. Pop. 14,000.

Famagusta (*fä-mä-goos'ta*), seapt., Cyprus; exports wines, fruit, cotton, and potatoes; good harbour. Pop. 7,000.

Fanning Island, coral atoll, Pacific Ocean, near equator; is a station on Pacific cable route from Vancouver to Australia; guano and mother-of-pearl. Area, 15 sq. m.; pop. *c.* 400.

Fä'no, tn., episc. see, and seaside

resort, on Adriatic Sea, N. of Ancona, Italy; has Roman remains; first printing press with movable Arabic type was established here by Pope Julius II. (1514). Pop. (tn.) 12,000.

Far Eastern Area, Asiatic province of U.S.S.R., in N.E. Asia, stretching from the borders of Mongolia and Manchuria northwards to the Arctic Ocean, and bounded on the W. by the Yakutsk and Buriat-Mongol Soviet Republics. N. part of the island of Sakhalin included in the province. Area as yet little developed. Climate is very varied, the extreme north-eastern part lying within the Arctic belt. A great part of the area is mountainous, and in the Kamchatka peninsula there are volcanoes. The greater part is forest, and timber is one of the chief exports; furs form an important export of the region. Agricultural products, chiefly from the Amur district, include rice, cereals, soya beans, and fruits. Chief minerals are coal, gold, silver, zinc, lead, and iron. Chief tns., Vladivostok, Blagovyeshchensk, Khabarovsk, and Chita. Area, *c.* 1,138,259 sq. m. Pop. *c.* 1,843,000.

Fareham, mkt. tn., Hampshire, England, on Portsmouth Harbour; flour milling, tanning, earthenware. Pop. 11,600.

Far'go, city, N. Dakota, U.S.A., on Red River; large trade in grain and agricultural machinery; oil, flax, and flour mills. Pop. 29,000.

Faridkot'. (1) Sikh state, Punjab, India; surface level; fertile in E.; sandy in W. Area, 643 sq. m.; pop. 151,000. (2) Chief tn. of above, 65 m. S.W. of Amritsar; large grain trade. Pop. *c.* 12,000.

Faridpur'. (1) Dist., Bengal, India, in Ganges delta; fertile; rice, jute, sugar-cane. Area, 2,371 sq. m.; pop. 2,250,000. (2) Chief tn. of above, 120 m. N.E. of Calcutta; cloth and carpet weaving; brick making and oil pressing. Pop. 14,500.

Far'ingdon, GREAT, mkt. tn., par., Berkshire, England, 10 m. N.W. of London; centre of agricultural district; anc. church. Pop. (par.) 2,700.

Far'lington, par. and vil., Hants, England, on Langston Harbour, 43 m. N.E. of Portsmouth; reservoirs for Portsmouth dist. Pop. (par.) 2,000.

Farn'borough. (1) Urban dist., Hampshire, England; the parish includes Aldershot North Camp, and is a training centre for the Tank Corps and the Royal Air Force. Pop. 16,400. (2) Par. and vil., Kent, England, 4 m. S.E. of Bromley. Pop. (par.) 3,300.

Farne (or FERNE) **Islands,** group of 17 islands off Northumberland, England; naked basaltic rocks; dangerous to shipping; associated with heroism of Grace Darling. Area, 80 ac.

Farn'ham, urb. dist. and mkt. tn., Surrey, England, on R. Wey; residential town close to Aldershot camp; excellent hops grown. Pop. 18,300.

Farn'worth, tn., Lancashire, England; adjoins Bolton; cotton spinning and manufacture; machine and engineering works; coal mining. Pop. 28,700.

Faro (*fä'rō*). (1) Dist., S. Portugal; narrow, sandy coast strip; N. part of dist. mountainous; fruit, wine, fish. Area, 1,937 sq. m.; pop. 268,500. (2) Seapt., cap. of above; exports wine, fruit, cork, and baskets. Pop. 13,000.

Faroe (or FAEROE) **Islands.** See FAEROES, THE.

Farrukhabad'. (1) District, United Provinces, India; flat Gangetic plain noted for high standard of cultivation; wheat, barley, maize, rice, cotton. Area, 1,683 sq. m.; pop. 857,000. (2) Chief tn. of above, on R. Ganges, 90 m. N.W. of Lucknow; manufactures gold lace, brass and copper vessels. Pop. 51,500.

Fars, province on Persian Gulf, Persia; coast low and hot; interior mountainous (7,000–10,000 ft.), with long fertile valleys; many salt lakes. Produces corn, rice, fruits, tobacco, opium; cattle and sheep reared. Cap. Shiraz; Bushire is principal port. Area (est.) 60,000 sq. m.; pop. (est.) 750,000.

Fars'ley, urb. dist., W. Riding, Yorkshire, England, 4 m. N.E. of

Bradford; manufactures woollens and cloth. Pop. 6,200.

Fasä', tn., Fars, Persia, 180 m. E. of Bushire; silk, woollen, and cotton manufactures. Pop. *c.* 10,000.

Fasho'da. See KODOK.

Fast'net Rock, islet off S.W. coast of co. Cork, I.F.S.; lighthouse, with revolving light visible 18 m.

Fatehpur'. (1) Cap. of dist. of same name, United Provs., India, *c.* 70 m. N.W. of Allahabad; has trade in hides and grain; two fine mosques. Pop. 15,000. Area, dist., 1,642 sq. m.; pop. 652,500. (2) Fort. and residential tn., Rajputana, India; third largest town in state. Pop. *c.* 17,000.

Fatehpur' Sikri, tn., United Provs., India, 23 m. W. of Agra; former cap. of Mogul Empire, founded by Akbar (1570), now in ruins; modern town lies S.W. of anc. city. Pop. 5,500.

Fauld'house, par. and vil., W. Lothian, Scotland, 6 m. W. of W. Calder; coal and iron mines. Pop. 4,100.

Favä'ra, tn., Sicily, 4 m. E. of Girgenti; sulphur, alum, tourmaline and marble; 13th cent. château. Pop. 21,500.

Fav'ersham, mkt. tn. and seapt., N. Kent, England; has brewing, shipbuilding, oyster fishing, trade in timber, coal, and hops; manufactures bricks and gunpowder. Pop. 10,100.

Faw'ley, vil., Hants, England, on Southampton Water, 5½ m. S.S.E. of Southampton. Pop. 2,000.

Fayal (*fī-äl'*), one of the Azores islands; exports fruit. Chief tn., Horta. Pop. 19,000.

Fayum. See FAIYUM.

Fazogli (*fä-zog'lē*), dist., Anglo-Egyptian Sudan, traversed by Blue Nile; produces durra, tobacco. Gold is found. Pop. *c.* 500,000.

Featherstone, urb. dist., W. Riding, Yorks, England, 6 m. E. of Wakefield; has extensive coal mines. Pop. 15,000.

Fécamp (*fā-kon'*), port and wat.-pl., Seine-Inférieure, France, *c.* 25 m. N.N.E. of Havre; 'Bénédictine liqueur' is manufactured; metal founding, shipbuilding, and manufacture of fishing nets; centre for deep-sea fishing. Pop. 16,000.

Feck'enham, par. and vil., Worcestershire, England; 4½ m. S.W. of Redditch; manufactures needles, pins, and fish-hooks. Pop. (par.) 4,000.

Federated Malay States. See MALAY STATES.

Fehmarn (*fā'marn*), isl. of Prussia in Baltic Sea, between Holstein and Danish isl. of Laaland; stock raising and fishing. Chief tn., Burg. Area, *c.* 120 sq. m.; pop. *c.* 10,000.

Feilding, tn., North I., New Zealand, 85 m. N.E. of Wellington; in agricultural dist. Pop. 4,500.

Félegyháza (*fā-lej-häz'ō*), or KISKUN-FÉLEGYHÁZA, tn., Hungary, between rivers Danube and Tisa, 80 m. S.S.E. of Budapest; wine, fruit, tobacco, and agricultural produce. Pop. 37,000.

Fe'lixstowe, seaside resort, Suffolk, England, at mouth of Orwell; phosphate of lime is exported. Pop. 12,000.

Fel'ling, urb. dist., Durham, England; suburb of Gateshead; has paint and drug manufactures, shipbuilding, engineering, and coal mining. Pop. 27,000.

Felp'ham, seaside vil., Sussex, England, 1 m. N.E. of Bognor; Gothic church. Pop. 2,900.

Fel'stead or FELSTED, par. and vil., Essex, England, 9 m. N. of Chelmsford; has anc. public school which celebrated 350th anniversary in 1914. Pop. (par.) 2,100.

Feltham, urb. dist., Middlesex, England; part of Greater London; market gardens. Pop. 16,300.

Feltre (*fel'trā*), tn. and episc. see, Venetia, Italy, 45 m. N.N.W. of Venice, with cathedral, a palace (now a theatre), and remains of mediæval castle; trade in silk, wine, and oil. Pop. 19,000.

Fengtien. See LIAONING.

Fen'ny Strat'ford, par. and mkt. tn., Buckinghamshire, England, on old Roman Watling Street, 11 m. N.W. of Dunstable. Pop. 4,300.

Fens, flat, marshy tract of land round Wash, England, embracing parts of cos. of Lincoln, Northampton, Huntingdon, Cambridge, and Norfolk. Principal rivs., Great Ouse, Witham, Welland, Nen, and Cam. Considerable areas below level of spring tides are kept from flooding by embankments 10 to 15 ft. high. Water is raised and drained into rivers by steam pumps. Most successful attempt at drainage was Earl of Bedford's (17th cent.), in dist. called Bedford Level. The whole area now forms good agricultural and grazing land.

Fen'ton. See under STOKE-UPON-TRENT.

Ferentino (*fer-en-tēn'ō*), tn., episc. see, 48 m. S.E. of Rome, Italy; 12th cent. cathedral; remains of anc. wall; trade in wine and oil. Pop. (comm.) 15,500.

Ferghana (*fer-gä'na*). (1) Prov., Uzbek Republic, U.S.S.R., in valley of Sir Darya; fertile, well-watered plain, enclosed by mountains; mainly agricultural, producing large crops of grain, cotton, fruit; principal town is Khoqand. Area, *c.* 7,900 sq. m. (2) Tn. in above, formerly SKOBELEV or NEW MARGILAN, in Khoqand dist.; manufactures cotton. Pop. 12,000.

Fermanagh (*fer-man'a*), inland co., N. Ireland; almost divided into two parts by Upper and Lower Loughs Erne; surface generally hilly and undulating, mountainous in W., well wooded, several fertile vales; large tracts only suitable for stock rearing, dairy farming; limestone, iron, and marble found; principal industry agriculture; pottery works (Belleek); manufactures of coarse linen; chief town, Enniskillen. Area, 653 sq. m.; pop. 58,000.

Fermoy', tn., Cork, I.F.S.; market for agricultural produce; salmon fishing in river Blackwater. Pop. 4,500.

Fernan'do Po, Spanish isl., W. coast of Africa, in Bight of Biafra; of volcanic origin; coast steep, inland mountainous; principal peak, Mount Clarence (Span. *Pico de Santa Isabel*), 9,369 ft. Vegetation luxuriant; cocoa and palm oil are the chief exports. Cap. Santa Isabel. Area, 780 sq. m.; pop. 21,000.

Ferne Islands. See FARNE ISLANDS.

Fer'nie, tn., Brit. Columbia, Canada, 110 m. S.S.W. of Calgary; coal-mining centre. Pop. 4,500.

Ferozepore', cantonment, cap. Ferozepore dist., Punjab, India, 46 m. S.S.E. of Lahore; important centre of trade, especially in grain. Pop. 54,300. Dist. area, 4,286 sq. m.; pop. 1,098,000.

Ferrä'ra, city, archiepisc. see, cap. of Ferrara prov., N. Italy, 3½ m. S. of R. Po; cathedral and other fine churches; celebrated school of painting, 15th–16th cent.; birthplace of Ariosto, Tasso, and Guarini. Pop. 108,000.

Fer'ro, or HIERRO, most westerly of Canary Islands; in early times accounted most westerly of known lands; famous as first meridian chosen by Fr. scientists (1630). Area, 107 sq. m. Pop. 8,500.

Ferrol', city, prov. Corunna, N.W. Spain; has first-class arsenal, naval school, and modern dockyards; coaling station; manufactures chiefly connected with naval construction. Pop. 30,500.

Festiniog (*fest-in-i-og'*), urban dist., N. Merioneth, Wales; slate quarrying. Pop. 9,100.

Fetteres'so, coast par., Kincardine, Scotland, including part of Stonehaven; with ruins of anc. church of St. Caran and Fetteresso Castle. Pop. 5,700.

Feuerbach (*foi'er-bach*), tn., Württemberg, Germany, 2 m. N.W. of Stuttgart; manufactures chemicals. Pop. 21,000.

Fez (*fāz*), one of caps. of French Morocco; formerly cap. of Moorish kingdom; celebrated for centuries as a holy city; is surrounded by walls; has many fine mosques, univ., and the sultan's palace; commercial centre; active caravan trade; manufactures woollen, silk, and leather goods, gold and silver ware, carpets, olive oil. Pop. 81,500.

Fezzan′, Saharan prov., Italian Libya, Africa; barren plateaus; shallow valleys with fertile oases where grain, vegetables, and the principal food, dates, are grown; gentle slope to E.; climate very dry, but healthy, except for malaria; soda, obtained from salt lakes in N.W., only export trade. Cap. Murzuq. Pop. *c.* 65,000.

Fichtelgebirge (*fich′tel-ge-bir′gi*), mt. group, Bavaria, Germany; highest peak, Schneeberg (3,450 ft.); stretches from Bayreuth to frontier of Bohemia; great mineral wealth (iron, copper, lead); granite and marble quarries.

Ficks′burg, tn., Orange Free State, S. Africa, 100 m. E.N.E. of Bloemfontein; centre of fine agricultural and stock-raising region; extensive trade. Pop. 3,500.

Fiesole (*fē-ā′sō-lā*), tn. and episc. see, Italy, 3 m. N.E. of Florence; fine 11th cent. Tuscan-Roman cathedral and Etruscan and Roman remains; Fra Angelico was for a time prior of the Dominican convent; straw plaiting. Pop. (com.) 10,000.

Fife, mar. co. of E. Scotland, bounded on N. by Firth of Tay, S. by Firth of Forth. Co. is succession of undulating hills and small valleys. Highest hills are E. and W. Lomonds. Coal is extensively mined, and the co. is famous for linen (esp. Dunfermline) and linoleum (Kirkcaldy). Industries include iron founding, machine making, shipbuilding, distilling, brick and tile making, paper making, beet sugar manufacture, oilcake milling, aluminium production; and shipping and fishing are largely carried on. Chief ports, Kirkcaldy, Burntisland, and Methil. Agriculture is very highly developed, flax being largely grown. Historic centres are Dunfermline and St. Andrews; numerous popular watering-places and golf links. Co. tn., Cupar. Area, 504 sq. m.; pop. 276,300.

Figig, a walled oasis in S.E. Morocco; caravan rendezvous; contains about 200,000 date palms.

Figuéras (*fē-gār′as*), tn., Catalonia, N.E. Spain, 20 m. N. of Gerona; prominent in Peninsular War; cork, glass, soap, leather, and wine manufactures. Pop. 13,500.

Fiji (*fē′jē*), archipelago in Pacific Ocean, N. of New Zealand; about 250 islands, of which some 80 are inhabited, forming a British crown colony. Principal islands, Viti Levu, Vanua Levu, and Taviuni; larger islands of volcanic formation, and smaller of coral; vegetation luxuriant. Larger islands contain hills rising to 3,000 to 4,000 ft.; open, dry, undulating country, except certain rich tracts along coast of the two largest; many large rivers afford waterways to the rich lands on their banks; good climate. Exports include sugar, copra, bananas, molasses, and rubber. Vanua Batevu is a trading centre. Inhabitants of Melanesian-Polynesian stock, formerly cannibalistic and savage, are now mostly Christianized. Cap. Suva, on S.E. coast of Viti Levu. Area, 7,083 sq. m.; pop. *c.* 177,000.

Filey (*fī′lā*), wat.-pl., Yorks, England, 8 m. S.E. of Scarborough; consists of old town inhabited by fishermen and new town of villas and large boarding-houses; important fisheries. Pop. 3,700.

Finch′ley, N.W. dist. of Greater London, England, residential dist. Little now remains of Finchley Common, originally over 1,000 ac., where highwaymen used to lurk. Pop. 59,000.

Find′horn, salmon and trout river, Scotland. Rising in the Monadhliath Mts., it flows through counties of Inverness, Nairn, and Moray, entering the Moray Firth at the fishing village of the same name. Length, 70 m.

Find′lay, city, Ohio, U.S.A., 42 m. S. of Toledo; situated in oil and natural gas region; manufactures include machinery, glass, and rubber tyres. Pop. 17,000.

Finedon (*fīn′don*), urb. dist., Northants, England, 3 m. N. of Willingbrough; iron ore. Pop. 4,100.

Fingal's Cave. See STAFFA.

Finistère (*fē-nēs-tār′*), dep., N.W.

France; three peninsulas project to w.; very fertile; cereals, vegetables, fruit; flax; horses and cattle extensively reared; coal, granite, slate; important fisheries. Cap. Quimper. Area, 2,729 sq. m.; pop. 754,000.

Fin'land, rep., Europe; bounded on N. by Norway, w. by Sweden and Gulf of Bothnia, s. by Gulf of Finland, E. by Russia; includes large part of Lapland, with access to Arctic Ocean; coast much indented, and many small islands; interior contains wide expanses of forest, swamps, and innumerable lakes. Lake Saima, with natural outlet over Imatra Falls (finest in Europe), is the largest which is wholly in Finland; connected by canal (36 m.) with Gulf of Finland; highest mt., Haldefjall (4,126 ft.); principal rivers, Muonio, Kemi, Uleå, Kymmene. Climate is healthy; severely cold in winter, snow lying from Nov. to April; arctic in Lapland; summer hot and dry. Much pasture-land; chief crops, hay, oats, rye, barley, and potatoes. Wood is made into pulp for paper mills; granite of excellent quality is quarried. Important industries comprise iron and mechanical works, textiles, wood industries, paper, dairy produce, leather, chemicals. Principal towns are Helsinki (cap.), Turku, Tampere, Viipuri, Vaasa, Oulu. Area, 149,588 sq. m.; pop. *c.* 3,611,000.

Fin'land, GULF OF, shallow arm of Baltic Sea. Lakes Ladoga and Onega drain into it, hence water is but slightly salt; length, 260 m.

Fin'mark, most northerly prefecture of Norway; treeless, unsheltered plateau; alt., 1,600 ft.; is inhabited by nomadic Lapps; whale fisheries; cod-liver oil; potatoes and barley. Area, 18,591 sq. m.; pop. 44,500.

Fins'bury, parl. and metropolitan bor., London, England; industries include tobacco manufacture, printing, and the making of optical glass. Pop. 69,900.

Finsteraarhorn (*fin-ster-är'horn*), loftiest summit (14,026 ft.) of Bernese Oberland Alps, Switzerland.

Firminy (*fēr-mē-nē'*), tn., Loire, France, 8 m. s.w. of St. Etienne; coal-field in vicinity; manufactures iron and steel goods. Pop. 18,500.

Fish'guard, town, Pembrokeshire, Wales, at head of deep and sheltered bay; extensive harbour for G.W.R. route to Ireland (Rosslare, Wexford, 55 m.); large brickworks at Goodwick (twin town, pop. 2,300). Pop. 3,000.

Fitch'burg, city, Massachusetts, U.S.A., 45 m. W.N.W. of Boston; woollens, cotton, paper, and machinery. Pop. 41,000.

Fiume (*fē-oo'mā*), Ital. seapt. at head of Gulf of Quarnero, on the Adriatic, 70 m. by rail S.E. of Trieste, formerly chief port of Hungary; now cap. of the 'Free Zone of the Carnaro'; industrial suburb and harbour of Sushak is in Yugoslavia; principal buildings, cathedral and governor's palace; three harbours; exports include wood, rice, sugar, and petrol. Pop. of Fiume, 49,000, including Italians (22,000), and Croats or Southern Slavs, Magyars, and inhabitants of various nationalities.

Five Towns, name given to chief tns. in the Potteries, now amalgamated. See STOKE-UPON-TRENT.

Flam'borough Head, cape, Yorks, England, 18 m. S.E. of Scarborough, sheltering Bridlington Bay on N.; chalk cliff; lighthouse; between Head and Bridlington is old Brit. earthwork known as Dane's Dyke.

Flanders, the land of the Flemings, former name for modern Belgian provinces of E. and W. Flanders, part of Zeeland (Holland) and of N. France, which stretched along North Sea from Somme to Scheldt; name is now retained only in the Belgian provinces of East and West Flanders.

Flèche, LA (*la flāsh'*), tn., Sarthe, France, on R. Loire; military school; gloves, paper, and textiles. Pop. *c.* 10,000.

Fleet, urb. dist., Hants, England, 3 m. w. of Farnborough; residential tn. Pop. 4,500.

Fleet'wood, seapt. and wat.-pl.,

Lancashire, England, at mouth of R. Wyre; largest fishing port on w. coast; coasting and Irish trade; steamers to Belfast and Isle of Man; deep-sea fishing; saltworks; Rossall School in vicinity. Pop. 23,000.

Flens'burg, seapt., Schleswig-Holstein, Prussia, on Baltic Sea, 40 m. N.W. of Kiel; has coal trade, shipbuilding yards; manufactures sugar, paper, glass, and soap. Pop. 63,100.

Flers (*flăr*), tn., Orne, France, *c.* 40 m. s. of Caen; 16th cent. castle (now town hall); Norman church; cotton and linen manufactures; chemical works. Pop. 11,000.

Flint. (1) Munic. bor. and mkt. tn., Flintshire, Wales, on estuary of the Dee, 11½ m. N.W. of Chester; ruined castle of Edward I.; chemical works, paper mills. Pop. 7,600. (2) City, Michigan, U.S.A., 68 m. N.W. of Detroit; large lumber industry; second city in world for production of motor-cars; also manufactures woollens, flour, carriages. Pop. *c.* 156,000.

Flintshire, mar. co., N. Wales; bounded N. by Irish Sea, N.E. by Dee, E. by Cheshire, S. and W. by Denbighshire; detached portion Mælor lies a few miles S.E. Flintshire produces coal, limestone, zinc, lead, iron; agriculture and esp. stock rearing important; main rivers, Dee and Clwyd; famous for its wells. Chief towns, Mold (cap.), Flint, St. Asaph. Area, 255 sq. m.; pop. 112,800.

Flod'den, hill, near vil. of Branxton, Northumberland, England, 10 m. N.W. of Wooler; scene of battle (Sept. 9, 1513), in which Scots were defeated by English.

Flor'ence (Ital. *Firenze*). (1) Prov., central Italy; watered by the Arno and extending into Apennines on N.; fertile; wine, olive oil, silk. Cap. Florence. Area, 1,497 sq. m.; pop. 821,000. (2) Cap. of above, on Arno, in fertile valley among Apennines; world-famous for its art treasures, history, and natural beauty; abounds in wonderful mediæval and Renaissance buildings, rich picture galleries, fine statuary, gardens, etc. Among the most notable churches is the Duomo, with Campanile of Giotto, Baptistery, and Museum. Famous palaces include Palazzo Vecchio, Uffizi (picture and sculpture galleries containing many masterpieces), connected by Ponte Vecchio with Pitti Palace. Favourite tourist centre and residential resort for foreigners. Industries include straw plaiting, jewellery, porcelain, glass, mosaics, works of art, etc. Pop. 317,000.

Flores (*flō'rez*). (1) Most westerly isl. of the Azores; mountainous; well-watered and fertile; cereals and vines. Associated with the story of the *Revenge* (1591). Chief tns., Santa Cruz (cap.) and Lagens. Area, 57 sq. m.; pop. 6,600. (2) Isl., Dutch East Indies, S. of Celebes; very mountainous and volcanic; densely forested; rice, maize, and palms. Area, 8,870 sq. m.; pop. 433,000. (3) Department, S.W. Uruguay; cap. Trinidad. Area, 1,744 sq. m.; pop. 29,000.

Florianopolis (*flor-i-an-op'o-lis*), formerly DESTERRO, cap. of Santa Catharina, S. Brazil, on W. shore of Santa Catharina I., connected with mainland by bridge; small export trade. Pop. 20,000.

Flor'ida. (1) S.E. state, U.S.A., mostly a peninsula between Atlantic and Gulf of Mexico; bounded N. by Georgia and Alabama. Coast about 1,200 m. Many islands, including low islands or reefs called keys. Interior is low and flat; numerous lakes, largest being Okeechobee in S. (*c.* 1,250 sq. m.); many swamps; many mineral springs. St. John's is the most important navigable river. Climate sub-tropical, but cooled by sea breezes; subject to occasional severe frosts which destroy the orchard fruits; healthy climate makes Florida a favourite holiday winter resort. Soil sandy, and fertilized by heavy rains; great expanses of drained swamp now fertile land; fruit grows abundantly, esp. oranges and grape-fruit; other products are cotton, sugar, tobacco, potatoes, maize; there are also valuable timber forests. Industries comprise tobacco manufacture, lumber trade, manufacture of turpentine and rosin, and sugar-making; also valuable fisheries. Chief mineral products are phosphates, limestone, and fuller's earth. Chief towns: Tallahassee (cap.), Key West, Jacksonville, Pensacola, Tampa, Miami. Area, 58,666 sq. m. (of which 3,805 sq. m. is water); pop. 1,263,500 (of whom 401,700 are Negroes). (2) Dep., Uruguay, S. America; grassy plains and large herds of cattle; agriculture developing. Area, 4,673 sq. m.; pop. 88,000. (3) Cap. of above dep., 70 m. N. of Monte Video.

Flush'ing (Dutch, *Vlissingen*), fort. seapt., Holland, at mouth of Schelde, on s. coast of Walcheren; daily steamboat communication with Folkestone and Queenborough; summer resort. Pop. 22,000.

Fly River, largest river of New Guinea; rises in Victor Emanuel Mts. near centre of isl., and flows by large delta into Gulf of Papua; drains fertile plains; length, *c.* 600 m., 500 m. being navigable.

Fochabers (*foch'-a-bers*), vil. and tourist resort, Moray, Scotland, on R. Spey. Pop. 1,000.

Focsani (*fok-shan'i*), tn., Romania, 55 m. W.N.W. of Galatz; manufactures oil and soap. Pop. 28,000.

Foggia (*fō'ja*). (1) Prov., s. Italy, between Apennines and Adriatic Sea; except for promontory of Monte Gargano (3,460 ft.), belongs to treeless Apulian plain; pasturage for sheep. Area, 2,683 sq. m.; pop. 517,000. (2) Tn. and episc. see, cap. of above, 20 m. w. of Gulf of Manfredonia; important rly. jn. and centre of trade; Norman cathedral. Pop. (com.) 67,500.

Foles'hill, par. and vil., Warwickshire, England, 3 m. N. by E. of Coventry; coal and iron mines. Pop. (par.) 10,700.

Folkestone (*fōk'ston*), seapt. and wat.-pl., S.E. coast of Kent, England, 15 m. s. by E. of Canterbury; has steamer services to Boulogne and Flushing. Pop. 35,900.

Fond du Lac, city, Wisconsin, U.S.A., at head of Lake Winnebago; railway centre and workshops; in rich agricultural belt, with enormous output of cheese and butter; varied manufactures. Pop. 26,000.

Fonsagrada (*fon-sa-grad'a*), tn., Lugo, Spain, 75 m. E.N.E. of Santiago; agricultural centre; flour mills. Pop. 18,000.

Fonseca (*fōn-sä'ka*), BAY OF, inlet of Pacific Ocean, Central America; sheltered roadstead; numerous isls., Tigré, at entrance, having fine volcanic cone.

Fontainebleau (*fōn-tān-blō'*), town, Seine-et-Marne, France, 37 m. S.E. of Paris; surrounded by picturesque forest (65 sq. m.); favourite resort of Fr. landscape painters; magnificent palace, from Middle Ages one of chief residences of kings, emperors, and presidents of France; sandstone quarries; porcelain. Pop. 12,000.

Fontenoy (*fon-ten-oi'*), vil., Hainaut, Belgium, 5 m. S.E. of Tournai; site of fierce battle (1745).

Foochow', port and cap. of Fukien prov., S.E. China, on riv. Min; importance due originally to tea trade; trade of town now mainly in paper, foodstuffs, bamboo, soap, etc.; ocean steamers load and discharge at Pagoda anchorage, 9 m. away; cotton, silk, and porcelain are manufactured; was one of first five treaty ports opened by Treaty of Nanking (1843). Pop. (est.) 313,000.

Foots'cray. (1) Par., Sidcup urb. district, Kent, part of Greater London; fine woods, hop gardens, and fruit farms in vicinity; paper mills. Pop. 8,900. (2) Tn., Victoria, Australia, suburb of Melbourne; large bluestone quarries, from which most of Melbourne has been built.

Forbes, tn., New South Wales, Australia, 290 m. w. of Sydney, on the Lachlan R.; commercial and agricultural centre; wool scouring and meat freezing. Pop. 5,000.

Forcados (*for-sä'dozh*), tn., Nigeria,

c. 150 m. S.E. of Lagos, on one of the mouths of riv. Niger; one of principal ports of Nigeria.

Ford City. See EAST WINDSOR.

Ford'ingbridge, par. and mkt. tn., New Forest, Hampshire, England, on the Avon, 10 m. S. of Salisbury; Early English church. Pop. 3,400.

Foreland, NORTH AND SOUTH, two chalk headlands on coast of Kent, England, having Downs and Goodwin Sands off the coast between them; lighthouse on each headland.

Forest of Dean. See DEAN, FOREST OF.

Forez (*fō-rā'*), MONTS DU, mt. range, France; watershed between drainage areas of Rs. Loire and Allier; forested with pine and birch; highest point, Pierre-sur-Haute (5,380 ft.).

For'far, co. tn., royal burgh, Angus, Scotland, 13 m. N. by E. of Dundee; linen and jute manufacture; bleaching, tanning. Pop. 9,700.

Forfarshire. See ANGUS.

Forli (*fōr-lē'*), tn., and episc. see, cap. of prov. Forli, central Italy, at foot of Apennines, 40 m. by rail S.E. of Bologna; imposing palaces and fine churches; felt industry. Pop. 52,000.

Form'by, urb. dist., Lancashire, England, on coast 7 m. S.W. of Southport; cockles and shrimps; asparagus. Pop. 8,000.

Formia (*for'mē-a*), tn., prov. Rome, Italy, on Gulf of Gaeta; anc. tn. on Appian Way; was favourite seaside residence of Roman nobles, including Cicero. Pop. 9,500.

Formo'sa (1), or TAIWAN, Jap. isl., off coast of China, in China Sea. Mountainous chief summit, Mt. Morrison (14,720 ft.). Volcanoes in N. Plain stretching to W., with short mt. range presenting sheer cliff to Pacific. Two rivers, both called Tamsui Kai; hot springs numerous; mountains thickly wooded; country fertile, well cultivated, with tropical vegetation. Climate damp and hot; typhoons common. Peopled by aboriginals, who are uncivilized and fierce, Chinese traders, and Japanese. Products include rice, tea, sugar, camphor, jute. Active fisheries. Minerals: gold, silver, copper, petroleum, coal. Trade mostly with Japan. Chief exports are tea, sugar, camphor, and coal. Cap. Taihoku. Chief ports are Keelung and Ampin. Area, 13,892 sq. m.; pop. *c.* 4,000,000. (2) Terr., N.E. Argentine Republic, S. America; occupies forest-covered plain between rivers Paraguay, Pilcomayo, and Bermejo; principal occupation, timber cutting. Cap. Formosa, on Paraguay R. Area, 41,402 sq. m.; pop. 19,500.

For'res, mkt. town, royal burgh, Moray, Scotland, 12 m. W. by S. of Elgin; is sheltered and very healthy; distilleries and flour mills; woollens and chemicals. Pop. 4,200.

Forst, tn., Brandenburg, Prussia, 44 m. S. of Frankfurt-on-Oder; cloth manufacture, spinning, and dyeing. Pop. 36,000.

Fortaleza. See CEARÁ (2).

Fort Augustus, vil., Inverness-shire, Scotland, at S. extremity of Loch Ness, on Caledonian Canal, 33 m. S.W. of Inverness. Fort (built 1730) is now Benedictine coll., monastery, and hospice, ranking as an abbey. Pop. 660.

Fort Churchill. See CHURCHILL (2).

Fort de France (*for di frans*), formerly FORT ROYAL, cap. and commercial centre, Martinique, Fr. W. Indies; exports include rum, sugar, cocoa. Pop. 43,500.

Fort Dodge, city, Iowa, U.S.A., on Des Moines R.; large trade in grain, pottery, and cereal foods; quarries and coal mines in vicinity. Pop. 22,000.

Forteviot (*for-tē'vi-ot*), par. and vil., Perthshire, Scotland, on riv. Earn; site of anc. Pictish cap. Pop. 500.

Fort Garry. See WINNIPEG.

Fort George, fort, N.E. Inverness-shire, Scotland, 10 m. N.E. of Inverness; built 1748.

Forth, riv., Scotland; rises on N.E. side of Ben Lomond, flows eastward with many windings (links of Forth), and expands into Firth of Forth;

chief tribs., Teith, Allan, and Devon. *Firth of Forth,* an inlet of North Sea, extending from Alloa eastward about 50 m.; navigable for largest vessels to Queensferry, smaller vessels to Alloa; contains islands Inchkeith (fortified), Inchcolm, and Isle of May; has many good harbours; coaling ports; w. of Forth Bridge on Fife coast is former naval base of Rosyth; important fisheries.

Forth and Clyde Canal connects Firths of Forth and Clyde, Scotland, from Grangemouth on E. to Bowling, Dumbartonshire, on w.; *c.* 40 m. long, 10 ft. deep; reaches alt. of 156 ft. by twenty locks; completed 1791.

Fort Jameson, tn., N. Rhodesia, near borders of Nyasaland and Mozambique; formerly headquarters of administration of N.E. Rhodesia; has an increasing trade in cotton and tobacco; small white population.

Fort Johnston, tn., Nyasaland, on w. bk. of Shiré R.; trades in cotton and tobacco.

Fortrose, royal burgh and seapt., Ross-shire, Scotland, on Moray Firth, 7 m. N.N.E. of Inverness; agricultural centre; remains of cathedral; sea-bathing. Pop. 900.

Fort Royal. See FORT DE FRANCE.

Fort St. George. See MADRAS.

Fort Scott, city, Kansas, U.S.A., on Marmaton R., near border of Missouri; railway workshops and varied industries; exports corn, wheat, flax, cattle. Pop. 12,000.

Fort Smith, city, Arkansas, U.S.A., on Arkansas R.; manufactures wagons, furniture, and refrigerators; centre of cotton, corn, and potato dist. Pop. 31,000.

Fort Wayne, city, N.E. Indiana, U.S.A.; foundry and machine products, electrical instruments, knitting mills, and agricultural machinery. Pop. 115,000.

Fort William. (1) Tn., Inverness-shire, Scotland, at head of Loch Linnhe and at s. end of Caledonian Canal; aluminium works; tourist resort; starting-point for ascent of Ben Nevis; fort dismantled in 1860. Pop. 2,500. (2) City, Ontario, Canada, at head of navigation on Lake Superior; fine harbour; outlet for wheat of w. Canada; large grain elevators; workshops of C.P.R. Pop. 20,500.

Fort Worth, city, Texas, U.S.A., 170 m. N. of Austin; in a rich cotton and grain dist.; great railway centre; great trade in oil; meat packing. Pop. 161,000.

Fossä'no, tn., episc. see, Cuneo, Italy, 40 m. by rail s. of Turin; old walls; 14th cent. cathedral; silk, paper, leather. Pop. 18,500.

Fossombrone (*fos-om-brō'nā*), tn., episc. see, Pesaro and Urbino, Italy, 35 m. W.N.W. of Ancona; cathedral; silk; mineral springs. Pop. 10,500.

Fotheringhay (*foth'er-ing-gā*), par. and vil., Northamptonshire, England, 9 m. s.w. of Peterborough. Only a few fragments remain of the castle in which Mary Queen of Scots was imprisoned, tried, and beheaded (1587).

Fougères (*foo-zhār'*), tn., Ille-et-Vilaine, France, 23 m. E.S.E. of St. Malo; 11th cent. castle and 15th cent. hôtel de ville; boots and shoes, glass, sailcloth, flannel. Pop. 20,500.

Foula (*foo'la* or *fow'la*), isl., Shetland, 16 m. s.w. of Mainland (3 m. by 1½ m.); fishing station at Ham, on E. side. Pop. 150.

Fourmies (*foor-mē'*), tn., Nord, France, 40 m. by rail S.E. of Valenciennes; wool combing and spinning, glass works and iron foundries. Pop. 13,000.

Fouta Jalon (*foot'a jal'on*), plateau region, French Guinea, W. Africa. Area, *c.* 30,000 sq. m.; average alt., 4,000 ft.; contains headwaters of Niger, Senegal, Gambia; contains gold and iron; important towns are Tuba and Labi.

Fowey (*foy*), mkt. tn., port, and yachting resort, Cornwall, England, at mouth of Fowey R.; large harbour; pilchards, copper ore, china clay. Pop. 2,400.

Fox Channel, N. of Hudson Bay, Canada, bounded on w. by Melville Peninsula and Southampton I., and on E. by Baffin Land and Fox Land;

named after Luke Fox, who explored Hudson Bay in 1631.

Foy'ers, FALLS OF, two waterfalls, 40 ft. and 165 ft. respectively, on short riv. Foyers, about 1 m. from junction with Loch Ness on E. shore, Inverness-shire, Scotland; formerly most picturesque; now used to generate electricity for aluminium works.

Foyle, LOUGH, shallow lake-like estuary (15 m. long; aver. width, 7 m.) on riv. Foyle, N. coast of Ireland.

Fram'ingham, tn., Massachusetts, U.S.A., 20 m. W. by S. of Boston; rubber and leather goods; boots and shoes. Pop. 17,000.

Fram'lingham, mkt. tn., Suffolk, England, 18 m. N.E. of Ipswich; church contains monuments of Norfolk family. Pop. 2,500.

Francavil'la-Fontan'a, tn., Italy, 22 m. W. by S. of Brindisi; leather goods; wine and oil. Pop. 20,000.

France, rep. of W. Europe; includes isl. of Corsica; in N.E., France approaches within 21 m. of Eng. coast. Boundaries: Belgium, Luxembourg, Germany, Switzerland, Italy, Mediterranean Sea, Spain, Bay of Biscay, and Eng. Channel. Coast of Brittany is rocky and indented; farther E. are high chalk cliffs, farther S. flat and sandy; Mediterranean shore bordered by dunes and marshes W. of Rhone, but to E. of that river the Alps are close to the sea. The highlands of France lie mainly to the S. round the central plateau, which contains the Auvergne, Cévennes, Morvan, and La Marche. E. of this plateau are the Alps and Jura Mts.; W. are the Pyrenees. Between central plateau and Alpine and Pyrenean folded ranges (both barriers to communication) are easy routes of Rhone and Garonne valleys, connecting Mediterranean with northern plain. In E. are Vosges and W. extremity of Ardennes; in N.W. are heights of Brittany. Principal rivers: Seine (485 m.), flowing through the Paris Basin; Loire (634 m.), from central plateau to Bay of Biscay, with network of tributaries linked to other rivers by canals; Garonne (404 m.), flowing with Dordogne into R. Gironde, and joined from Toulouse to Mediterranean by Canal du Midi; Rhone (504 m.), from Alps, joined by slow-flowing Saône; and Rhine forming part of E. frontier. Climate of N. is like that of S. England, but becomes continental in centre and E.; mild, wet winters mark Mediterranean shorelands, where summers are relatively dry and hot. Rich soils and plentiful rains make France predominantly agricultural; wheat, rye, barley, oats, and potatoes are grown in N. and centre, sugar beet in N.E., flax and hemp in N.; vines grow best in Burgundy, Champagne, and round Bordeaux; silk is produced extensively in Rhone valley. Coal, iron, bauxite, pyrites, antimony, lead, and zinc are mined. Alsace-Lorraine is rich in potassium. Olive oil is prepared chiefly round Marseilles. Communications by road are excellent; six great railway companies—Nord, Est, Paris-Orleans, Paris-Lyons-Mediterranean, Midi, Alsace-Lorraine—and the État or State line give services to all parts; in 1928 the mileage was 25,947; all are to be electrified. Main canals are in N. and E., giving access to Belgium and the Rhine. Exports include silk and cotton textiles, iron and steel, chemicals, rubber goods, and wine. Cap. Paris. Area, 212,659 sq. m. Pop. 40,744,000; of these, 2,500,000 are foreigners, chiefly Italians, Belgians, Spaniards, and Germans.

Colonies and Dependencies. In Africa: Algeria, Tunis, Fr. West Africa, Fr. Equatorial Africa, Mayotte and Comoro Islands, Madagascar, Réunion, Fr. Somaliland, and a virtual protectorate over Morocco. In Asia: Fr. India, Fr. Indo-China. In Oceania: New Caledonia, with dependencies, Tahiti, and other Pacific islands. In America: French Guiana; Guadeloupe, Martinique; St. Pierre and Miquelon. Total area is 3,958,626 sq. m.; pop. 55,631,500.

France, ILE DE. See under ILE DE FRANCE.

Frank'enberg, tn., Saxony, 11 m. by rail N.N.E. of Chemnitz; woollens, cotton, silk, carpets. Pop. 14,000.

Frankenthal (*frank'en-tal*), town, Palatinate, Bavaria, Germany, 6 m. N.W. of Mannheim; engineering shops and bell foundries; agricultural implements. Pop. 25,000.

Frank'fort, city, N. Kentucky, U.S.A., on Kentucky R.; in agricultural and mining dist. famous for rearing thoroughbred horses; varied small manufactures. Pop. 10,000.

Frank'furt on Main, city, Hesse-Nassau, Prussia, on R. Main; great banking centre and leading Ger. rly. jn.; terminus of Rhine river traffic; has handsome modern streets, squares, and suburbs. Seat of univ., founded 1914. Industries are less prominent than trade, but include jewellery, soap, perfumery, chemicals, machinery, tapestry, waxcloth, carpets, tobacco, photographic and electrical apparatus. Pop. 466,500.

Frank'furt on Oder, tn., Brandenburg, Prussia, 50 m. S.E. of Berlin, on R. Oder; important commercial centre; three annual fairs; manufactures machinery, firearms, chemicals. Pop. 71,000.

Frank'lin, Provisional Dist., N.-W. Territories, Canada, comprising the islands from Banks I. in W. to Baffin Land in E.; mainly within Arctic Circle; fur-bearing animals numerous; inhabitants consist of a few Indians, Eskimos, and fur traders. Area, 554,000 sq. m.

Franz Josef Land (*frants yō'sef*), archipelago of some sixty islands, N. of Novaya Zemlya; *c.* 250 m. E. of Spitsbergen; glacier clad; discovered (1873) by Austro-Hungarian expedition; claimed by Russia (1929).

Frascati (*fras-kä'tē*), tn., summer resort, Rome prov., Italy, on N. slopes of Alban Hills; handsome villas of Roman nobility; Prince Charles Edward Stewart died here; famous wine. Pop. 11,000.

Fra'ser, riv., Brit. Columbia, formed by union of S. Fork and N. Fork; former rises in Mt. Brown, Rocky Mts., and at Fort George joins N. Fork, which rises in same mts.; enters Strait of Georgia at Vancouver after course of 750 m.; navigable as far as Yale (*c.* 100 m.). Salmon canneries on river.

Fra'serburgh, seaport, Aberdeenshire, Scotland, 47 m. N. by E. of Aberdeen; leading centre of herring fishery. Pop. 9,700.

Fray Bentos (*frī bent'ōs*), or INDEPENDENCIA, tn., Uruguay, cap. dep. Rio Negro, 170 m. N.W. of Montevideo; noted for meat extract. Pop. 5,000.

Fredericia (*fred-er-is'e-a*), seaport, Denmark, at N. entrance of Little Belt, on E. coast of Jutland; rly. jn.; steamship connection with Fünen; considerable shipping trade; railway works; manufactures tobacco and cotton goods. Pop. 18,500.

Fred'erick, city, Maryland, U.S.A., 42 m. N.W. of Washington; brush and canning factories, flour mills, tanneries; in a wheat dist. Pop. 11,000.

Fred'ericton, cap. New Brunswick, Canada, on St. John R., at head of navigation, 84 m. from sea; rly. jn.; seat of univ. of New Brunswick; large lumber trade; manufactures mill machinery and wooden ware. Pop. 8,000.

Fred'erikshavn, seaport, Denmark, on Kattegat, 36 m. N.E. of Aalborg; second best harbour on E. coast of Jutland; exports dairy produce and fish. Pop. 12,000.

Fredrikshald. See HALDEN.

Fred'rikstad, seaport, S. Norway, at mouth of R. Glommen; exports timber, stone, and bricks, and has railway workshops and shipbuilding. Pop. 14,500.

Free'town, cap. Sierra Leone, W. Africa; best harbour on W. coast of continent; coaling station; formerly 'the white man's grave,' now by sanitation and warfare on mosquitoes the old reproach has been removed; railway to Pendembu (227 m.). Pop. 44,000.

Freiberg (*frī'berg*), tn., Saxony, Germany, 20 m. E. of Chemnitz; centre of silver and lead mining; has important mining academy; manufactures woollen goods, ironware, and sugar. Pop. 35,000.

Freiburg (*frī'boorg*), (1) or FREIBURG-IM-BREISGAU, tn. and archiepisc. see, Baden, Germany, beautifully situated at foot of the Schlossberg (Black Forest), 39 m. by rail N.E. of Basle; streams from river flow through streets; fine buildings, including 12th-century cathedral, univ., and palaces of former grand-duke and archbishop; wine and timber; manufactures include buttons, tobacco, silk thread, and paper. Pop. 90,500. (2) See FRIBOURG.

Freising (*frīz'ing*), tn., Bavaria, Germany, 26 m. N.N.E. of Munich; iron foundries and manufactures of agricultural machinery and porcelain. Pop. 15,000.

Fre'mantle, tn., W. Australia, at mouth of Swan R.; seaport for Perth; first port of call in Australia for European mail steamers; soap, tin, leather; sawmills, ironfounding, and boat building; harbour enclosed by two large breakwaters. Pop. 29,000.

French Congo. See FRENCH EQUATORIAL AFRICA.

French Equatorial Africa, or FRENCH CONGO, Fr. terr. in W. Central Africa; enclosed by Gulf of Guinea, Nigeria, Fr. W. Africa, Anglo-Egyptian Sudan, Belgian Congo, and Port. Kabinda; it consists of Gabon Colony, Middle Congo, Ubangi-Shari Colony, and Chad Terr.; coast region swampy; climate unhealthy; immense forests with valuable wood. Chief rivers: Ogowe, Nyanga, Sanga, Gabon, Shari, Kuilu; communication mainly by rivers. Resources as yet undeveloped, but rubber, palm oil, coffee, cocoa, and cotton are produced. Ivory is an important export. Copper, zinc, and lead are found. Principal towns: Brazzaville (cap. Middle Congo), Libreville (cap. Gabon), Bangui (cap. Ubangi-Shari), Fort Lamy (cap. Chad Terr.), Loango (seapt.). Total area, 912,049 sq. m.; pop. 3,127,000.

French Guiana. See GUIANA.

French Guinea, colony Fr. W. Africa, between Portuguese Guinea and Sierra Leone; coast generally flat and low-lying; about 30 m. inland is Fouta Jalon plateau, edged by line of cliffs called the Susu hills. E. of this tableland country slopes to basin of the upper Niger, the greater part of which is in French Guinea. Climate is hot, moist, and unhealthy. Chief products and exports: rubber, palm oil, nuts, cattle, hides, and bananas; railway between Konakri and Niger at Kourassa, continued to Kankan. Konakri is cap. and principal port. Area, *c.* 92,640 sq. m.; pop. 2,186,000.

French India, five scattered provs. in India, Pondicherry, Karikal, Mahé, Yanaon, and Chandernagore. Combined area, 196 sq. m.; pop. 287,500. See separate articles.

French Indo-China embraces five states, Annam, Cambodia, Cochin-China, Tongking, and Laos, also Kwangchow-wan, leased from China. Chief exports are rice, rubber, fish, coal, pepper, cattle, and hides; zinc and tin are found. Cap. Hanoi. Area, *c.* 285,000 sq. m.; pop. *c.* 20,700,000. See articles on separate states.

French Sudan. See SUDAN.

French West Africa, general government uniting Fr. possessions in N.W. Africa; comprises Senegal, Mauritania, Upper Volta, French Sudan, Niger, French Guinea, Ivory Coast, Dahomey, and Circle of Dakar and dependencies; exports are fruits, oils, rubber, cotton, timber. Cap. Dakar, seat of gov.-gen. Area, *c.* 1,447,200 sq. m.; pop. *c.* 13,541,000.

French West Indies comprise the islands of Martinique, and Guadeloupe with its dependencies Marie Galante, Les Saintes Désirade, St. Bartholomew, and St. Martin (in part), all among the Lesser Antilles.

Freshwater, par. and bathing resort, S.W. coast, Isle of Wight;

Farringford House, residence of Tennyson, is near by. Pop. 3,400.

Fres'no, city, California, U.S.A., 160 m. S.E. of San Francisco; in fruit-growing and dairying region; oil and copper in vicinity. Pop. 53,000.

Fribourg (*frē-boor'*), or FREIBURG. (1) Canton, Switzerland, between the cantons of Berne, Vaud, and Neuchâtel; mainly pastoral and agricultural; manufactures cheese, watches, paper, and chocolate. Area, 644 sq. m.; pop. 143,000, mostly R.C. and French-speaking. (2) Cap. of above, 26 m. S.W. of Berne; seat of bishop and of R.C. univ. Pop. 20,000.

Friedrichshafen (*frēd'richs-hä-fen*), port and bathing resort, Württemberg, Germany, on E. shore of Lake Constance; machine shops, boat-building yards, zeppelin workshops. Pop. 11,500.

Friedrich-Wilhelmshafen. See MADANG.

Friendly Islands. See TONGA ISLANDS.

Fri'ern Bar'net, urb. dist., Middlesex, England, 3 m. S. of Barnet; part of Greater London; formerly contained a Friary of the Knights of St. John. Pop. 23,100.

Friesland (*frēs'land*), or VRIESLAND (anc. *Frisia*), prov., Holland, on N.E. of Zuider Zee; surface flat, part below level of sea; coasts protected by dikes; exports horses, cattle, dairy produce. Cap. Leeuwarden. Area, 1,249 sq. m.; pop. 403,500.

Frimley and Camberley. See CAMBERLEY.

Frin'ton-on-Sea, urb. dist., Essex, England, 1½ m. S. of Walton-on-the-Naze; wat.-pl. Pop. 2,200.

Fris'ian Islands, chain of islands in North Sea, between Zuider Zee and Jutland, made up of three groups—W. Frisian Islands, (Texel, Vlieland, Terschelling) belonging to Holland; E. Frisian Islands (Borkum, Juist, Norderney) belonging to Germany; and N. Frisian Islands (including Sylt, Föhr) divided between Germany and Denmark; chain is gradually being submerged through marine erosion.

Frod'sham, mkt. tn., Cheshire, England, at confluence of rivs. Weaver and Mersey, 10 m. N.E. of Chester; chemical works. Pop. 5,100.

Frome (*froom*), or FROME SELWOOD, mkt. tn., Somerset, England, on R. Frome, 12 m. S. of Bath; former extensive woollen trade now declining; metal works, brewing, printing, silk, tools, and wool-dressing cards. Pop. 10,700.

Fuca, JUAN DE (*foo'ka, whän de*), STRAIT OF, connecting Puget Sound with the Pacific, on N.W. coast of N. America; between state of Washington, U.S.A., and Vancouver, Brit. Columbia; average width, 15 m.; length, *c.* 100 m.

Fuente Ovejuna (*fwen'tā o-vā-hoon'a*) tn., Cordoba, Spain, 48 m. N.W. of Cordoba; honey largely produced in vicinity; cattle breeding; quarries and coal and lead mines. Pop. 15,500.

Fuenterrabia (*fwen-tā-ra-bē'a*), frontier town, N. Spain, at mouth of riv. Bidassoa; popular summer resort; fishing. Pop. 6,000.

Fuji-san', or FUJIYÁMA, highest, most beautiful, and best-known mountain of Japan, *c.* 60 m. W.S.W. of Tokyo; height, 12,395 ft.; a dormant volcano; visited by Japanese for worship; figures on Japanese works of art.

Fukien (*foo-kēn'*), mountainous and mar. prov. of S.E. China; poor sandy soil in valleys, but carefully cultivated and yielding abundant crops; watered by Min R. (N.), Lung R. (Amoy region), and head-waters of Han R. (S.); chief agricultural products include tea, rice, cotton, indigo, sugar, tobacco, and camphor; there is also a large trade in timber, especially fir, pine, and rosewood. Paper is manufactured from bamboo pulp. Minerals include coal, silver, and gold. Chief ports, Foochow (cap.) and Amoy (original treaty ports); imports mainly from Hong-Kong and Shanghai. Area, 46,320 sq. m.; pop. *c.* 13,158,000.

Fukui (*foo-koo'i*), tn., w. Honshu, Japan, on R. Ashiwa, 5 m. from sea; *c.* 200 m. w. of Tokyo. Paper and thin white silk. In volcanic dist., much exposed to earthquakes. Pop. 60,000.

Fukuoka (*foo-koo-o'ka*), town, Kyushu I., Japan, 90 m. N.N.E. of Nagasaki by rail; joined to Hakata; colossal bronze head of Buddha; silk manufactures. Pop. 146,000.

Fukushima (*foo-koo-shē'ma*), tn., Honshu, Japan, 150 m. N. of Tokyo; centre for raw silk and silkworms' eggs.

Fukuyama (*foo-koo-yä'ma*). (1) Formerly MATSUMAI, seapt., s. Hokkaido, Japan, 61 m. by rail s.w. of Hakodate; open roadstead; ruins of castle; temples. Pop. *c.* 15,000. (2) Tn., Honshu, Japan, on s. coast, 110 m. w. by s. of Kobe; temple with art treasures.

Fulda (*fool'dä*), tn. on R. Fulda, Hesse-Nassau, Prussia, 54 m. N.E. of Frankfort; has episc. palace; famous Benedictine abbey, founded in 744; most anc. seat of eccles. learning in Germany; textiles and iron goods. Pop. 30,000.

Ful'ham, suburb, London, on Thames; palace of bishops of London. Pop. 150,900.

Ful'ton, city, New York, U.S.A., 23 m. N.W. of Syracuse; woollens, flour, paper, cutlery. Pop. 13,000.

Fulwood, urb. dist., Lancs, England, suburb of Preston. Pop. 7,500.

Funchal (*foon-shal'*), seaport, cap. of Madeira Islands, on s. coast of Madeira; popular winter resort; a commercial centre; port of call for steamers. Pop. 21,000.

Fun'dy, BAY OF, inlet of N. Atlantic between New Brunswick and Nova Scotia, Canada; 145 m. long and 50 m. broad at s., narrowing to 30 m. at head, where it divides into Chignecto Bay and Minas Channel; highest 'bore' in world; tide rises at Chignecto to over 50 ft., with crest 3 to 6 ft. Chief harbours are St. Andrews and Saint John (New Brunswick), Digby and Annapolis (Nova Scotia).

Fünen (*fü'nen*), second largest Danish isl., between Kattegat and Baltic, separated from Zealand by Great Belt, and from Jutland by Little Belt; fruitful; well wooded; cereals and fine breed of cattle. Chief towns, Odense and Svendborg. Area, *c.* 1,100 sq. m.

Fünfkirchen. See PÉCS.

Furka Pass (*foor'ka*), saddle (7,992 ft.) separating upper Reuss valley from the valley of the Rhone, Switzerland, crossed by road from Andermatt; railway under construction which will pierce Furka by a tunnel (2,138 yds.).

Furneaux (or FLINDERS) **Islands** (*foor-nō'*), group in Bass Strait between Tasmania and Victoria, Australia; the chief is Flinders or Great Island (35 m. by 10 m.); mostly barren; named after Tobias Furneaux, who discovered them in 1773.

Furnes (*foorn*), tn., prov. W. Flanders, Belgium, 5 m. E. of French frontier, at the junction of several canals near North Sea; fête of Calvary celebrated on last Sunday of July each year. Pop. 8,000.

Fur'ness, detached dist. of N. Lancashire, England; hilly; N. portion part of Lake Dist.; s. portion a peninsula terminating at Piel. Between estuary of Duddon and Morecambe Bay is Walney I. Rich beds of hæmatite iron ore have led to rise of Barrow. *Furness Abbey,* now ruins, 2 m. N.E. of Barrow.

Fürstenwalde (*foors-ten-val'de*), tn., Brandenburg, Prussia, 28 m. E. of Berlin by rail; 14th cent. church; manufactures are important, including brewing, malting, wool combing, and cloth making; glass, chemicals, stoves; rich coalfields in vicinity. Pop. 23,500.

Fürth, tn., Bavaria, Germany, 5 m. N.W. of Nuremberg; manufactures picture-books, mirrors, lithographs, toys, bronze and gold-leaf articles. Pop. 74,000.

Fusan', port, Korea Bay, at S.E. tip of Korea, terminus of Seoul-Fusan railway. Exports include rice, raw silk, beans, and hides. Pop. 113,000 (41,000 Japanese).

Fushiki (*foo'shē-kē*), or FUSHIGI, seapt. on Toyama Bay, w. coast Honshu, Japan, 32 m. N.E. of Kanazawa; a special open port since 1889.

Fyne, LOCH, arm of Firth of Clyde, Scotland; breadth, 1 to 5 m.; length N. to S. over 50 m.; great variety of shore and mt. scenery; famous for its herrings.

Fyvie (*fī'vi*), par., Aberdeenshire, Scotland, 23 m. N.N.W. of Aberdeen; Fyvie Castle, seat of Lord Leith. Pop. 3,400.

Fyzabad'. (1) Dist., United Provs., India, lying between rivs. Gogra and Gumti; alluvial and well-wooded; exports rice, sugar, oil-seeds, cloth, and tobacco. Pop. 1,171,900. (2) Chief tn. in above; sugar-refining and agricultural produce; military cantonment. Pop. 56,600.

G

Gaba Tepe, headland, w. coast, Gallipoli, 5 m. from Maidos on Dardanelles; Australians and New Zealanders made famous landing on narrow beach *c.* 1 m. N. on April 25, 1915.

Ga'bes. See QABES.

Gablonz. See JABLONEC.

Gabon (*gä-bōn'*), maritime colony, French Equatorial Africa; resources undeveloped. Cap. Libreville, on R. Gabon estuary. Area, 104,320 sq. m.; pop. 390,000.

Gad'ag, or GARAG, tn., Dharwar dist., Bombay, India, 120 m. E. of Goa; large trade in raw cotton and cotton and silk fabrics. Pop. 41,500.

Gadames. See GHADAMES.

Gads'den, tn., Alabama, U.S.A., 57 m. N.E. of Birmingham; coal and iron in dist.; large steel plant; manufactures cotton, cotton-seed oil, cars. Pop. 15,000.

Gains'borough, mkt. tn. and port, Lincolnshire, England, on R. Trent, 15 m. N.W. of Lincoln; manufactures agricultural machinery; linseed and other oilcake mills; engineering; river trade. Pop. 18,700.

Gair'loch, sea-loch, w. Ross-shire, Scotland; length, 6 m.; breadth, 3 m.; gives its name to par. and vil. at head of loch.

Galapa'gos Islands (or *gal-ap'ag-os*), group of islands off w. coast of S. America belonging to Ecuador; largest isl., Albemarle, is *c.* 75 m. long; dense vegetation in S., covered with lava in N.; numerous volcanoes, some still active; tortoises now few in number; guano exported. Area, 2,868 sq. m.; pop. *c.* 500.

Galashiels', municipal burgh, Selkirkshire, Scotland, on Gala Water, 33½ m. S.E. of Edinburgh; important centre of Scottish woollen industry; specializes in tweeds; hosiery and boot making. Pop. 13,100.

Galatz', riv. port, Moldavia, Romania, on l. bk. of Danube, 10 m. above junction with Prut; iron, copper, candle, and soap industries; petroleum refineries; exports grain, meal, and timber; seat of Danube Commission. Pop. 154,000.

Gales'burg, city, Illinois, U.S.A., 45 m. N.W. of Peoria; rly. workshops; motor-cars, engines, typewriters; grain and coal in dist. Pop. 29,000.

Galicia (*gä-lish'ē-a*). (1) Part of Poland, on N. side of the Carpathians, bounded on N.W. by the Vistula, and in E. drained by Upper Dniester and Prut; fine pasture and arable land, and immense forests. (2) Anc. kingdom, N.W. Spain; divided into provs. of Corunna, Lugo, Orense, and Pontevedra; surface generally mountainous; climate mild; has many good harbours; principal river, Minho; lead, tin, copper, iron; agriculture backward; chief exports: timber, cattle, sardines; largest tn., Corunna. Area, *c.* 11,250 sq. m.; pop. 2,125,000.

Gal'ilee. (1) Part of Palestine, bounded N. by Syria, E. by R. Jordan, S. by Samaria and Mt. Carmel, W. by Mediterranean; length, *c.* 50 m.; breadth, 30 m.; chief interest lies in its being the cradle of Christianity; now a centre of Jewish Settlements. Area, *c.* 1,600 sq. m. (2) SEA OF, lake, N. Palestine; length, 13 m.; 680 ft. below sea-level, situated at bottom of volcanic basin; R. Jordan flows through the lake; W. side has good vegetation, but N. and E. are bare and rocky.

Gallarate (*găl-a-ră'tă*), tn., Lombardy, Italy, 25 m. N.W. of Milan by rail; cotton and linen factories. Pop. 10,000.

Galle (*gäl*), or POINT DE GALLE, port, S.W. Ceylon; formerly chief port of isl.; exports tea and coconut oil. Pop. 39,000.

Gallipoli, peninsula, Turkey, between Gulf of Xeros (Seres) and Strait of Dardanelles; 53 m. in length, and varying in width from 12 to 2 or 3 m.; mostly a mass of rocky ridges, covered with dense scrub; little cultivation and few villages; strip of level ground around Suvla Bay; in S. peak of Achi Baba (730 ft.). Scene of famous but unsuccessful Allied campaign during Great War.

Gal'loway. (1) Dist., S.W. Scotland, comprises shires of Wigtown and Kirkcudbright. Gives its name to a breed of cattle. (2) MULL OF, promontory, Wigtownshire, Scotland; at extremity of Rhinns of Galloway, most S. point of Scotland. (3) RHINNS OF. See RHINNS (1).

Gal'ston, tn., Ayrshire, Scotland, on R. Irvine; coal in vicinity; lace and hosiery. Pop. 4,600.

Galt, tn., Ontario, Canada, 25 m. W. by N. of Hamilton; founded by Scottish novelist, John Galt; flour and iron. Pop. 13,500.

Gal'veston, port and city, Texas, U.S.A., on Galveston I., Gulf of Mexico; connected by rly. and causeway with mainland; has large foundries, mills, and machine shops; principal cotton port of U.S.A. Pop. 53,000.

Gal'way. (1) Maritime co., Connaught, I.F.S.; coast-line broken; co. includes Lough Corrib and part of Lough Mask; in W. lies wild and mountainous dist. of Connemara; flat and marshy in E.; chief rivs. are Shannon (forming S. boundary), Black, and Suck; Slieve Aughty mts. in S.; Twelve Pins (2,395 ft.) in W.; valuable fisheries; marble, granite; has seven round towers and many monastic ruins. Co. tn., Galway. Area, 2,293 sq. m.; pop. 169,500. (2) Port, cap. of above; good harbour; fisheries; exp. agricultural produce, wool, marble. Pop. 14,200.

Gam'bia. (1) Riv., W. Africa; rises in Fouta Jalon, flows generally W., through Gambia to Atlantic at Bathurst; length, 1,000 m.; navigable for 200 m. (2) British crown colony and protectorate, W. Africa; consists of a narrow strip of country on both banks of R. Gambia, from its mouth to Yarbatenda, *c.* 250 m. inland; country flat and marshy; climate fairly healthy; chief exports, ground nuts, hides and skins, palm kernels; cable communication from Bathurst to St. Vincent and Sierra Leone; no rlys. Cap. Bathurst. Area, 4,134 sq. m. (colony, 4 sq. m.); pop. 210,500.

Gand'zha, formerly ELISABETPOL, cap. Elisabetpol dist., town, Azerbaijan, U.S.S.R., 190 m. W. of Baku; vineyards; textiles; copper, manganese. Pop. 55,500.

Ganges (*găn'jēz*), greatest and most sacred river of India; rises in Himalayas under name of Bhagirathi, and at junction with Alaknanda takes name of Ganges; flows generally S.E., and enters Bay of Bengal by one of largest deltas in world; most important distributaries, Hooghly, on W., Meghna on E.; length of main stream, 1,540 m., greater part of which is navigable; drains over 400,000 sq. m., mostly remarkably fertile and densely populated; chief tribs., Son,

Jumna, Ramgunga, Gumti, Gogra, Gandak, Jamuna, and Kosi; on its banks are many great cities, including Calcutta, Patna, Benares, Allahabad, Cawnpore. See also SUNDARBANS.

Ganjam', dist., extreme N.E. Madras Presidency, India; traversed by E. Ghats; fertile plains and valleys; is well watered; agriculture; salt. Cap. Berhampur. Area, 4,800 sq. m.; pop. 1,836,000.

Gap. (1) Chief tn., Hautes-Alpes, S.E. France; marble, hats, textiles, sawmills. Pop. 7,000. (2) CANAL, or CANAL DU DRAC, irrigation canal connecting the Drac and Durance rivs., S.E. France; completed in 1888; with branches, has total length of 445 m.

Garag. See GADAG.

Gard (*gär*), dep., S. France; on Mediterranean; surface slopes towards Rhone and Mediterranean, with numerous lakes and marshes on coast; chief rivs., Gard and Vidourle; rich in coal, iron, lead; olives and chestnuts extensively grown; important vineyards; silkworm rearing. Chief tn., Nîmes. Area, 2,270 sq. m.; pop. 403,000.

Gar'da, LAKE OF, N. Italy, between Lombardy and Venetia; drained by Mincio at S.E. end into river Po; studded with islands in midst of beautiful scenery; favourite health resort. Area *c.* 143 sq. m.

Gard'ner, town, Massachusetts, U.S.A., 25 m. N.N.W. of Worcester; one of leading centres for manufacture of chairs; other industries, toys, baby carriages, furniture, silverware, machinery. Pop. 17,000.

Gareloch (*gär'loch*), arm of Firth of Clyde, Scotland; runs N.W. from Helensburgh; good anchorage, where ships adjust compasses; summer resorts, Rhu, Shandon, Garelochhead, Clynder, and Roseneath, on its shores. Length, 7 m.; average breadth, 1 m.

Gar'field, tn., New Jersey, U.S.A., on Passaic R., 10 m. N. of Newark; woollen and worsted mills. Pop. 30,000.

Garhwal (*gŭr-whäl'*), dist., United Provinces, India, on S. slope of the Himalayas; adjoins Simla dist.; mountainous and densely forested; chief rivs., Alaknanda and other headstreams of Ganges; exp. grain and coarse cloth; trades with Tibet. Area, 5,612 sq. m.; pop. 485,000.

Garo' Hills, mountainous dist., W. Assam, India, bounded by R. Brahmaputra on W.; heavily forested. Area, 3,140 sq. m.; pop. 180,000.

Garonne (*gă-ron'*), riv., S.W. France, rises in Pyrenees, flows N.N.W., enters Bay of Biscay; length, 430 m.; navigable to Toulouse; chief tribs., Save, Gers, Baïse, Tarn, Lot, Dordogne.

Gar'ston, port, Liverpool bor., Lancs, England, on Mersey; docks; iron and copper works. Pop. 29,000.

Garut', dist., W. Java, Dutch E. Indies; tea, rubber, cinchona; health resort (alt. 2,300 ft.). Pop. 22,500.

Ga'ry, city, Indiana, U.S.A., on Lake Michigan; great steel and tinplate works. Pop. 101,000.

Gaspé (*găs'pā*), peninsula and dist., E. Quebec prov., Canada, between R. St. Lawrence on N. and Bay of Chaleur on S.; fisheries are richest in America. Area, 4,550 sq. m.; pop. 40,500, mostly fishermen.

Gasto'nia, city, N. Carolina, U.S.A., near boundary of S. Carolina, 20 m. W. of Charlotte; cotton mills; textile machinery. Pop. 13,000.

Gat'china. See TROTSK.

Gates'head, tn., Durham, England, on R. Tyne, opposite Newcastle, and connected with it by several bridges; locomotive depot; extensive ironworks; glass and chemical works; grindstone quarries; coal mines in vicinity. Pop. 122,400.

Gatoom'a, tn., S. Rhodesia; *c.* 100 m. S.W. of Salisbury; centre of rich gold field; aerodrome. Pop. (whites) 650.

Gauhati (*gou-hă'tē*), tn., Assam, India, on R. Brahmaputra; exp. cotton, silk, lac to Calcutta. Pop. 16,500.

Gävle, or GEFLE (*yäv'le*), port, Sweden, on inlet of Gulf of Bothnia; exp. timber, wood-pulp, iron and steel; manufactures sail-cloth, textiles, and tobacco; shipbuilding. Pop. 39,500.

Gaw'ler, tn., S. Australia, 25 m. N.E. of Adelaide; foundries, flour mills. Pop. 2,000.

Gaya (*gī'a*). (1) Dist., Bihar and Orissa, India; consists of a level and richly fertile plain; mica mines; chief river, Son. Area, 4,712 sq. m.; pop. 2,153,000. (2) Tn., India, cap. of above, 57 m. S. of Patna; centre of pilgrimage; silk and cotton manufactures. Pop. 68,000.

Ga'za, tn. and port, S. Palestine; commercial centre; coarse cloth; trades in wheat, barley, wool. Pop. 17,500.

Ga'zaland, dist., Portuguese E. Africa; watered by R. Limpopo; fertile in lower parts; sugar-cane, rice, maize; supplies labour for Transvaal mines.

Gdynia (*gdin'ya*), port, Poland, 12 m. N. of Danzig; canal to R. Vistula; exp. timber, coal, dairy produce, sugar. Pop. 40,000.

Géant, COL DU (*zhā'on*), glacier pass (11,060 ft.) in Alps; leads from Chamonix to Courmayeur; on N.E. is Aiguille du Géant (13,170 ft.).

Gebweiler (*gāb'vīl-er*). See GUEBWILLER.

Geelong (*jē-long'*), port, Victoria, Australia, 45 m. by rail S.W. of Melbourne; woollen mills; flour mills, salt works, tanneries. Pop. 39,000.

Geestemunde (*gās-tĕ-moon'de*), port, Hanover, Prussia, at mouth of R. Weser; deep-sea fisheries; included in Wesermünde. Pop. 30,000.

Gefle. See GÄVLE.

Geislingen (*gīs'ling-en*), tn., Württemberg, Germany, 38 m. by rail E.S.E. of Stuttgart; ivory and wood carving; iron and glass works; machinery. Pop. 14,000.

Gel'derland, prov., Holland, S.E. of Zuider Zee; surface more hilly than most of Dutch provs.; traversed by Waal, Rhine, Ysel, Maas; soil very fertile along riv. banks. Chief crops: cereals, flax, tobacco; cattle rearing; brick making; paper and cotton industries. Cap. Arnhem. Area, 1,941 sq. m.; pop. 812,000.

Gelligaer (*geth-lĭ-gīr'*), urb. dist., Glamorganshire, Wales, 14 m. N. of Cardiff; several collieries near. Pop. 41,000.

Gellivara (*yel-lē-vä'ra*), tn., N. Sweden, 43 m. N. of Arctic Circle; extensive iron-ore mines. Pop. 12,000.

Gelsenkirchen (*gel'zen-kēr-chen*), tn., Westphalia, Prussia, 6 m. E. of Essen; coal mining; steel, soap, glass, chemicals. Pop. 207,500.

Gem'mi Pass, Alpine route (7,641 ft.) connecting Swiss cantons Berne and Valais; steep descent to Leukerbad on S. side.

Gene'va (Fr. *Genève*). (1) Canton, Switzerland; market gardens, orchards, vineyards; watch making and jewellery. Area, 108 sq. m.; pop. 166,000. (2) Cap. of above, at S.W. end. Geneva is overlooked by Jura and Alps; R. Rhone, issuing from lake, flows through city; tn. a great commercial, industrial, and educational centre and favourite resort of foreigners; chief industries, watch making, jewellery, diamond cutting, enamelling, musical boxes, scientific instruments, and cutlery; headquarters of the League of Nations. Pop. 128,500. (3) LAKE OF, or LAC LEMAN, largest lake of Switzerland, bordering Haute-Savoie, France, and cantons Geneva, Vaud, and Valais; traversed by Rhone; length, 40 m.; greatest breadth, 8½ m.; alt., 1,230 ft. Rhone silt is continually diminishing its area; many famous resorts round shores. (4) City, New York, U.S.A., 40 m. S.E. of Rochester; state agricultural experiment station; manufactures razors, lenses, marine engines. Pop. 15,000.

Gen'oa (Italian, *Genova*), strongly fortified port and commercial city, Italy, on Gulf of Genoa; situated in Riviera; many palaces; shipbuilding, silk and velvet, cabinet-making, motor-cars, filigree work, damask, lace, embroidery, candied fruit, leather, macaroni. Pop. 316,500.

Gentilly (*zhŏn-tē′yē*), suburb of Paris, France, 2½ m. S. of Notre Dame; quarries, brick works, chemical works. Pop. 10,000.

George′town. (1) Cap. of Brit. Guiana, at mouth of Demerara R.; climate unhealthy; ships sugar, gold, diamonds, timber, balata, cocoa, coffee; good harbour. Pop. 60,000. (2) Part of Washington, cap. of U.S.A.; manufacturing dist.; trades in coal, tobacco, grain. (3) City, S. Carolina, U.S.A., 56 m. N.E. of Charleston; exp. cotton, rice, pinewood, fish, and turpentine. Pop. 5,000.

George Town, cap., Penang I., Straits Settlements. Pop. 27,000.

Geor′gia. (1) S. State, U.S.A., bounded by Tennessee and N. Carolina on N., S. Carolina and Atlantic Ocean on E., Florida on S., and Alabama on W. In N. and W. Appalachian Mts. rise to *c.* 5,000 ft. Principal rivs., Apalachicola (navigable *c.* 300 m.), flowing into Gulf of Mexico; Savannah and Altamaha (navigable *c.* 300 m.), flowing into Atlantic. Climate mild and, except in lowlands and swamp regions in S., agreeable and healthy. Game plentiful; alligators numerous in rivs.; *c.* 70 per cent. of country is farm land, largely worked by Negroes; state is large producer of cotton and greatest grower of sea-island cotton; corn and wheat are cultivated in N. regions; rice near the coast; sugar-cane; tobacco; much fruit—oranges, melons, grapes, pineapples, peaches, and bananas; pine forests; fisheries. Chief industries, cotton and woollen manufactures; iron and steel trades; lumber, timber planing, flour and grist milling. Cap. Atlanta; chief port Savannah; other cities are Augusta, Macon, and Columbus. Area, 59,265 sq. m. (of which 540 sq. m. are water); pop. 3,200,000. (2) Rep., U.S.S.R., between Caucasus Mts. and Armenia; rly. from Poti to Baku (in Azerbaijan); chief crops, wheat, barley, maize, rice, cotton, tobacco; Mediterranean fruits; silk; forests; large manganese deposits. Cap. Tiflis. Area, 26,381 sq. m.; pop. 2,667,000.

Geor′gian Bay, N.E. div. of Lake Huron, Ontario, Canada; waterway has been proposed to connect the bay with St. Lawrence, by way of French R., L. Nipissing, and Ottawa R.

Gera (*gā′ra*), tn., Thuringia, Germany, 45 m. S.S.W. of Leipzig; woollens, musical instruments, leather, printing; lignite mines. Pop. 81,000.

Ger′aldton, port on Champion Bay, W. Australia; outlet for Murchison goldfield; exp. gold, copper, wool, lead, and sandalwood. Pop. 4,000.

Gérardmer (*zhā-rär-mār′*), mkt. tn., and health resort, Vosges, France, 33 m. by rail E.S.E. of Epinal; famed for Gérome cheese; manufactures linen and woollen goods. Pop. 4,000.

German Vol′ga, rep., S.E. Russia; drained by R. Volga; extreme climate; scanty rainfall; barley, maize, rye, millet, sunflower seeds; sawmills and flour mills; tobacco factories; settled by German colonists (1760). Cap. Pokrovsk, on R. Volga, opposite Saratov. Area, 10,327 sq. m.; pop. 571,000.

Ger′many (DEUTSCHES REICH), rep., Central Europe, comprising seventeen states; bounded on N. by North Sea, Denmark, and Baltic Sea; on E. by Lithuania and Poland, which, with Free City of Danzig, separate E. Prussia from the rest of Germany; on S. by Czechoslovakia, Austria, and Switzerland; on W. by France, Luxembourg, Belgium, and Holland. The N. forms part of great European plain, the S. generally is hilly; important rivs. flowing N. are the Pregel in E. Prussia; Oder, with Warthe trib., to Baltic Sea; Elbe and Weser, to North Sea; middle course of Rhine, with Main, Ruhr, etc., of special value; Danube, rising in Black Forest; large fresh-water lagoons (*haffs*), at mouths of Niemen and Oder; North Sea coast fringed with sandbanks and chain of islands; Baltic coast higher, with chalk cliffs. Climate varies from equable in N.W. to extreme in E.;

rainfall moderate except on highlands; lakes and large rivs. of N. frozen in winter; Baltic ports sometimes closed by ice. Agriculture is chief occupation on plain; rye, wheat, barley, oats, and potatoes are principal crops; hops in Bavaria, rape in Prussia, flax, and tobacco; most important root crop is sugar-beet in dist. W. of Magdeburg; scientific agriculture is intensively practised; fruit, especially grapes, succeed best on hill slopes of middle Rhine; many large forests.

The most important mineral products are coal, iron, and zinc. Coal is mined round Aachen, in Ruhr valley, in Saar basin (at present occupied by France), in Saxony, and in Silesia; lignite abundant; iron ore deposits in the hilly ground where Westphalia, Rhineland, and Hesse-Nassau meet, in Silesia, and in Saxony; other minerals, zinc, lead, tin, silver, bismuth, antimony, nickel, cobalt, and copper; rock salt abundant; amber obtained on Baltic coasts.

Germany has large textile manufactures in the Ruhr basin, where woollens and silks predominate, in Silesia (woollens), in Saxony (cottons); shipbuilding and marine engineering are important at ports, especially Stettin; other industries include clockmaking (Black Forest), porcelain (Meissen), making of pianos and scientific instruments; chemical industries centre in Westphalia and Saxony. Largest exports are manufactured goods of all sorts. Communications (rlys., navigable waterways, and canals) are the best in Europe. Cap. Berlin. Area (including Saar dist.) 181,723 sq. m.; pop. (including Saar dist.) 63,180,000.

Ger'miston, tn., Transvaal, S. Africa, 9 m. E. of Johannesburg; important rly. jn.; gold-mining centre. Pop. 50,000, including 20,500 whites.

Gerona (*hā-rō'nā*). (1) Maritime prov., N.E. Spain, on Mediterranean Sea; wine, timber, cork; textiles; coal mines and mineral springs; fishing. Area, 2,264 sq. m.; pop. 326,000. (2) Cap. of above; manufactures paper, textiles, and cork. Pop. 18,000.

Ger'rard's Cross, par. and vil., Bucks, England, 3 m. S.E. of Beaconsfield; residential dist. Pop. (par.) 2,500.

Gers (*zhār*), dep., S.W. France; surface hilly, partly covered with wood and heath; chief rivs., Adour and tribs. of Garonne; live-stock and poultry; wheat, maize, oats; large area under vines; brandy and wine. Chief tn., Auch. Area, 2,428 sq. m.; pop. 196,500.

Gett'ysburg, bor., Pennsylvania, U.S.A., 36 m. S.W. of Harrisburg; iron mines; granite quarries in vicinity; manufactures furniture, bricks; scene of decisive battle in American Civil War (1863); battlefield now a public park. Pop. 4,500.

Gevelsberg (*gā'fels-berg*), tn., Westphalia, Prussia, 9 m. N.E. of Barmen; small ironworks. Pop. 21,000.

Gezira (*je-zē'ra*), THE, dist., Anglo-Egyptian Sudan, between Blue Nile and White Nile; irrigated by Sennar Dam at Makwar, 170 m. S. of Khartoum; grows cotton.

Ghadam'es, tn. and oasis, Italian Libya, N. Africa, *c.* 300 m. S.W. of Tripoli; caravan routes converge on tn.; oasis produces dates, figs, and apricots. Pop. *c.* 7,000.

Ghardaia (*gar-dī'a*), oasis tn., Sahara, Algeria, 300 m. S. by E. of Algiers; caravan trade in oil, dates, ostrich feathers, and pottery. Pop. 11,000.

Ghat, oasis and tn., Fezzan, Libya, N. Africa, in Sahara desert; sandy plain with date-palms; alt. 2,400 ft.; caravan resting-place.

Ghats (*gauts*), two mt. ranges, enclosing Deccan, India; border E. and W. shores, uniting near Cape Comorin. W. Ghats extend N. to Tapti valley (1,000 m.); precipitous and unbroken line of gneiss rocks; highest peaks, 8,000 ft. in S.; principal passes, Palghat in S., Thal Ghat and Bor Ghat near Bombay. E. Ghats, in Madras Presidency; average alt., 1,500 ft.;

broken by Godavari, Kistna, and Cauvery rivs. Both ranges have health resorts.

Ghazipur'. (1) Dist., United Provs., India, in alluvial plain of Ganges; rice, barley, sugar-cane; one of hottest and dampest dists. in India. Area, 1,392 sq. m.; pop. 832,500. (2) Chief tn. of above, 44 m. E. of Benares; rose-water and attar of roses manufactured. Pop. 25,000.

Ghazni (*ghuz'nē*), famous city, Afghanistan; situated on high tableland (7,500 ft.) on direct road between Kabul and Kandahar; intensely cold in winter; trades in madder, wool, skins, and fruit. Pop. fluctuates with seasons, but rarely exceeds 8,000.

Gheel (*gāl*), tn., Antwerp, Belgium; noted colony for insane persons. Pop. 18,000.

Ghent (*gent*), (Fr. *Gand*), city, Flanders, Belgium, at confluence of Schelde and Lys, 32 m. N.W. of Brussels; broken up by canal into about forty islands; commerce considerable, and has increased since extension of docks and ship-canal to Terneuzen; chief industries, woollens, linen, cotton, lace manufacture, leather work, horticulture; paper mills, iron foundries, and engine factories. Pop. 163,000.

Ghizeh. See GIZA.

Giant's Castle, summit of Drakensberg range, Union of S. Africa, on frontier of Natal and Basutoland. Alt. 9,650 ft.

Giant's Causeway, group of columnar basaltic rocks on N. coast of Antrim, N. Ireland; there are *c.* 40,000 five or six sided columns.

Giaveno (*ja-vā'nō*), tn., Turin, N. Italy, 17 m. W. of Turin; cotton and jute factories. Pop. 12,000.

Gibral'tar, rocky peninsula and Brit. crown colony, S. Spain, at most S. point of Andalusia, separated from Africa by Strait of Gibraltar, *c.* 16 m. wide; commands the Mediterranean gateway; connected with Spain by sandy isthmus *c.* 1¾ m. long and ½ m. wide, middle part being neutral ground; rock rises almost precipitously 1,400 ft., with exception of W. side on Bay of Gibraltar; length, 3 m. from N. to S.; breadth, ¾ m.; area, 1⅞ sq. m.; tn. lies on W. side, with extensive barracks; cable station; powerful lighthouse on Europa Point (the S. extremity). Gibraltar is a strongly fortified naval base and coaling station; climate hot, but not unhealthy. Pop. 21,000.

Giessen (*gē'sen*), tn., N.W. Hesse, Germany; manufactures machinery, rubber, chemicals, leather. Pop. 34,000.

Giff'nock, vil., Renfrewshire, Scotland, 5 m. by rail S.W. of Glasgow; residential dist.; sandstone quarries. Pop. 3,300.

Gifu (*gē'foo*), tn., central Honshu, Japan, 20 m. N. of Nagoya; silk; paper wares. Pop. 82,000.

Gijon (*hē-hōn'*), port, Oviedo, Spain, on Bay of Biscay; one of best roadsteads on Spanish coast; manufactures tobacco, earthenware, glass; coal mining; blast furnaces and petroleum refineries; exp. minerals and fruit. Pop. 58,000.

Gilan', prov., N. Persia, on S.W. Caspian Sea; forests; rice and fruits on coast; tobacco, silk; cap., Resht. Area, *c.* 5,000 sq. m.; pop. *c.* 200,000.

Gil'bert Islands, archipelago, Pacific Ocean, on equator; form Brit. colony with Ellice Islands; coral reefs or atolls; barren except for coconut palms. Area, 166 sq. m.; pop. 30,000 (264 Europeans).

Gil'dersome, urb. dist., W. Riding, Yorks, England, 5 m. S.W. of Leeds; founded by Dutch settlers (1571) and so named 'Home of the Gelders'; woollens. Pop. 3,000.

Gil'ead, region, Palestine, E. of Jordan; great beauty and fertility; mountainous; average alt. 2,500 ft.

Gil'git, outlying prov., extreme N.W. of India, under sovereignty of Kashmir; embraces part of basin of R. Gilgit; mountainous country, intersected by narrow valleys and with numerous glaciers and ice-fields; separated from Chinese frontier by mt. range; people are of mixed race, speaking different languages; agriculture is chief occupation; hill-station of Gilgit stands *c.* 4,890 ft. above sea-level. Area, *c.* 25,000 sq. m.; pop. *c.* 60,000.

Gil'lingham. (1) Munic. bor., Kent, England, on R. Medway; famous cherry orchards; extensive torpedo factory and brick and cement works. Pop. 61,000. (2) Mkt. tn., N. Dorset, England, 4 m. W. of Shaftesbury; famous 'pen-pits,' probably prehistoric dwellings. Pop. 3,500.

Gilly (*zhē-yē'*), tn., Hainaut, Belgium, adjoining Charleroi; coal mines; oil and nail works. Pop. 24,500.

Gilolo. See HALMAHERA.

Gioja del Colle (*jō'ya del kol'ā*), tn., Apulia, S. Italy, 22 m. S. of Bari; trade in wine, oil, almonds, wool; cattle fairs. Pop. 22,000.

Gipps'land, dist., S.E. Victoria, Australia, S. of Australian Alps; mountainous in N. and E.; farming and cattle grazing in S. and W.; gold, coal. Area, 13,900 sq. m.

Girga (*gēr'gā*), or GIRGEH, tn., Upper Egypt, on R. Nile, 90 m. S.E. of Asyut; excellent pottery. Pop. 20,000.

Girgenti (*jēr-jen'tē*), formerly AGRIGENTUM, tn., S. Sicily, Italy, now assuming name AGRIGENTO; sulphur mining. Pop. 25,000.

Gironde (*zhē-rōnd'*). (1) Estuary of united Rs. Garonne and Dordogne; largest in France; navigable for large vessels to Pauillac; obstructed by sandbanks. Length, 44 m. (2) Maritime dep., S.W. France; chief rivs., Dordogne and Garonne; surface generally flat, W. portion along sea coast consisting of sandy dunes planted with pines, and interspersed with lagoons, from which salt is obtained; extensive vineyards; some grain, vegetable, and fruit growing; chief product, wine. Chief tn., Bordeaux. Area, 4,140 sq. m.; pop. 828,000.

Gir'ton, par. and vil., 3 m. N.W. of Cambridge, England, with college for higher education of women. Pop. (par.) 650.

Gir'van, port, Ayrshire, Scotland; summer resort; excellent bathing. Pop. 5,300.

Gis'borne, port, Poverty Bay, North Island, New Zealand; Captain Cook landed here in 1769; centre of agricultural and pastoral region. Pop. 15,000.

Gisors (*zhē-zor'*), tn., Eure, France, 44 m. N.W. of Paris; cloth, leather, linen, and felt. Pop. 5,000.

Giugliano (*jool-yä'nō*), tn., Italy, 6 m. N.W. of Naples; fruit and grain. Pop. 19,000.

Giurgiu (*joor'joo*), tn., Romania; river port on R. Danube; exports timber and grain. Pop. 25,000.

Givet (*zhē-vā'*), tn., Ardennes, France, on R. Meuse; tanneries. Pop. 6,000.

Givors (*zhē-vōr'*), town, Rhône, France, on R. Rhone; engineering, glass; manufactures hats and silk; coal mines. Pop. 14,000.

Giza, or GHIZEH (*gē'za*), tn., Lower Egypt, Africa, on R. Nile, 3 m. S. of Cairo; 5 m. W. are the Pyramids; Sphinx and ruins of Memphis in vicinity; bridges over Nile. Pop. 11,000.

Glace Bay (*gläs*), port, Cape Breton I., Nova Scotia, Canada; coalfields; steel works; wireless station. Pop. 17,000.

Glad'bach. (1) Or BERGISCH-GLADBACH, tn., Rhineland, Prussia, 8 m. by rail N.E. of Cologne; iron and steel, paper, sawmills. Pop. 18,000. (2) Or MÜNCHEN-GLADBACH, tn., Rhineland, Prussia, 16 m. W.S.W. of Düsseldorf; cotton, calico printing, iron, silk, boots, bricks. Pop. 115,000.

Glamis (*gläms*), vil., Angus, Scotland, 5½ m. S.W. of Forfar; castle. Pop. 1,100.

Glamor'ganshire, most southerly co., Wales, bounded N. by Brecon and Carmarthen, E. by Monmouth, S. by Bristol Channel, W. by Carmarthen; enormous mineral productions; N. is rugged mountainous region, with rich coalfields; in S. are fertile wooded valleys; magnificent cliff scenery on coast; rivs. Rhymney, Taff, Tawe, Neath, flow into Bristol Channel; sheep and ponies reared; dairy farming, fishing; anthracite, coking coal, ironstone, and limestone produced; tin, copper, and lead smelted; machines, chemicals, tools, paper; iron, steel, and zinc works; chief tns. include Cardiff (co. tn.), Swansea, Merthyr Tydfil, Rhondda, and Aberdare. Area, 813 sq. m.; pop. 1,225,700.

Glä'rus, canton, central Switzerland; surface mountainous, rising in S. Tödi Mts.; traversed by R. Linth; chiefly pastoral; sheep and cattle rearing, cheese making; cotton manufactures. Cap. Glarus, 33 m. S.E. of Zurich. Area, 264 sq. m.; pop. (canton) 34,500; tn., 5,000.

Glas'gow, city, Lanarkshire, Scotland, situated on both bks. of R. Clyde, *c.* 22 m. from estuary; second city in Brit. Isles; includes Govan, Partick, Pollokshaws, and adjoining dists.; owes much of its prosperity and progress to its favourable position and proximity to rich fields of coal and ironstone; harbour extends from Glasgow Bridge to junction of Kelvin and Clyde, with 8 m. of quays; Clyde lined for many miles with shipbuilding yards and engineering works. Shipbuilding is the great industry—vessels of every type being built. Iron-founding of vast importance; manufactures of steam tubes, boilers, locomotives, machinery; muslin and other textiles; chemical, paper, glass, and china works; spinning, dyeing, brewing, and many other industries. Pop. 1,088,400.

Glasnev'in, part of Dublin city, I.F.S.; famous botanic garden; burial-place of many noted Irishmen.

Glas'tonbury, munic. bor., Somersetshire, England, 5 m. S.W. of Wells; tradition has it that Joseph of Arimathea brought here Holy Grail and founded first Christian church in Britain; also associated with King Arthur. Ruins of 8th cent. abbey. Manufactures include mats, gloves, pottery. Pop. 4,500.

Glatz, tn., Silesia, Prussia, 50 m. S.S.W. of Breslau; machinery, textiles. Pop. 17,000.

Glauchau (*glouch'ou*), tn., Saxony, Germany, 17 m. W. of Chemnitz; manufactures woollen materials, calicoes, dyes, flour, and beer; calico printing. Pop. 27,500.

Gleiwitz (*glī'vits*), tn., Silesia, Prussia, 43 m. S.E. of Oppeln; mining centre; iron foundries; glassworks; chemicals. Pop. 82,000.

Glenalmond (*glen-ă'mond*), vil., Perthshire, Scotland, on R. Almond, 8 m. N.E. of Crieff; seat of Trinity College public school.

Glencoe (*glen-kō'*). (1) Deep valley, N. Argyllshire, Scotland; scene of massacre of MacDonalds (Feb. 1692). (2) Tn., N.W. Natal, S. Africa, 6 m. W. of Dundee; rly. jn. White pop. 1,000.

Glen'dale, tn., California, U.S.A.; residential suburb of Los Angeles; manufactures pottery. Pop. 63,000.

Glendalough (*glen-dal'-u*), valley, Wicklow, I.F.S., 7 m. W. of Wicklow; celebrated for picturesque scenery and ecclesiastical ruins.

Glenelg', wat.-pl., on Holdfast Bay, S. Australia, 6 m. S.S.W. of Adelaide. Here (1836) S. Australia was proclaimed a Brit. colony.

Glenfin'nan, hamlet, Inverness-shire, Scotland, at head of Loch Shiel, 17 m. by rail W. of Fort William; monument erected (1815) on spot where Prince Charlie unfurled his banner in 1745.

Glengar'iff, or GLENGARRIFF, vil., on Glengariff harbour, Bantry Bay, co. Cork, I.F.S.; tourist resort.

Glenliv'et, valley, Banffshire, Scotland, 10 m. S.W. of Dufftown; distillery. Pop. 1,100.

Glenmore', valley, Inverness-shire, Scotland; through Lochs Lochy, Oich, and Ness runs Caledonian Canal, connecting Atlantic Ocean with North Sea.

Glenroy', valley, Inverness-shire, Scotland, 13 m. N.E. of Fort William; famous for three natural terraces, *parallel roads* (at levels of 1,155, 1,077, 862 ft.), successive shore-lines of anc. lake.

Glens Falls, city, New York, U.S.A., on Hudson R.; lumber, paper, and linen manufactures. Pop. 17,000.

Glogau (*glō'gou*), tn., Silesia, Prussia, on R. Oder; wool market; lithographic works, sugar, starch. Pop. 26,000.

Glom'men, largest riv. of Norway; flows generally s. and enters Oslo Fjord; navigable for short distance; much timber floated down it; length, 350 m.

Glos'sop, mkt. tn., Derbyshire, England, 13 m. S.E. of Manchester; cotton, woollen, and paper manufactures. Pop. 19,500.

Gloucester (*glos'ter*). (1) City and port, cap. of Gloucestershire, England, on R. Severn; connected with Sharpness by Gloucester and Berkeley Canal (16½ m.); shipbuilding, foundries, chemical works. Pop. 52,900. (2) City and port, Massachusetts, U.S.A.; excellent harbour; chief seat of cod, mackerel, and halibut fisheries in U.S.A.; granite; summer resort. Pop. 24,000.

Gloucestershire, or GLOS, co., England; bounded N. by Herefordshire, Worcestershire, and Warwickshire, E. by Oxfordshire, S. by Berks, Wilts, Somerset, W. by estuary of Severn and Monmouthshire. Surface is varied, with three distinct features: E., Cotswold Hills; centre, rich, fertile valleys of Severn and other rivs.; W., Forest of Dean; rivs. include Avon, Lower Avon, Wye, and Thames; extensive canal system. Sheep farming carried on in hills; in valleys pastureland, orchards, woods, and dairy farms celebrated for Gloucester cheese; in W. are coalfields of Forest of Dean and Bristol; other minerals, iron, ochre, building stone, freestone, and quartz; manufactures, woollens, cottons, silk, gloves, glass, hardware; salmon fisheries in Severn. Chief tns.: Gloucester (cap.), Cheltenham, Stroud, and part of Bristol. Area, 1,259 sq. m.; pop. 785,700.

Glov'ersville, city, New York, U.S.A., 45 m. N.W. of Albany; glove-making and leather-finishing factories. Pop. 23,500.

Glyncorrwg (*glin-kor'oog*), urban dist., Glamorgan, Wales, 10 m. N.E. of Port Talbot; coal, iron. Pop 10,200.

Gmünd, tn., Württemberg, Germany, 30 m. E.N.E. of Stuttgart; gold and silver jewellery. Pop. 20,500.

Gniez'no, formerly GNESEN, tn., Poland, 30 m. E.N.E. of Poznan (Posen); linens and woollens. Pop. 26,000.

Go'a. (1) Portuguese terr., W. coast India, S. of Bombay, extends 60 m. along Indian Ocean; surface hilly; forests; many rivs.; manganese; exp. salt, spices, fruit, coconuts, copra. Area, 1,461 sq. m.; pop. 532,000. (2) NEW GOA, or PANGIM, cap. of above, on R. Mandavi; harbour; experimental agricultural station. Pop. 7,500.

Gobi (*gō'bē*), also called SHAMO (sandy desert), and HAN-HAI (dry sea), Chinese name for desert stretching from Pamirs on W. to Great Khingan Mts. on E., and from Altai, Sayan, and Yablonoi Mts. on N. to most northerly ranges of Kunlun Mts. on S.; *c.* 600 m. from N. to S., and over 1,000 m. from S.W. to N.E.; alt. between 3,000 and 5,000 ft. In some parts are grassy steppes, masses of rocks and crags, and salt lakes; forests, good water, abundant vegetation, and some animal life are found in part known as Ordos. Climate has great extremes, with rapid changes; shifting sands have buried large extent of once cultivated country, and many discoveries of buried tns. have been made; principal caravan routes lead from Kalgan (on Chinese frontier) to Urga, from Soochow to Hami, and from Hami to Peking. Area over 300,000 sq. m.

God'alming, tn., Surrey, England, 34 m. S.W. of London; paper, leather, gloves, hosiery; Charterhouse School. Pop. 10,400.

Godä'vari. (1) Riv., Deccan, India; rises in W. Ghats, flows S.E., and enters Bay of Bengal by the seven mouths of its great delta; 900 m. long; one of twelve sacred rivers of India. (2) Dist., Madras, India, includes delta of Godavari R.; forests in

N.W.; rice, oil-seeds, tobacco, sugar-cane; graphite. Cap. and port, Cocanada. Area, 2,545 sq. m.; pop. 1,500,000.

Goderich (*gōd'rich*), port, Ontario, Canada, on L. Huron; salt industry; lake fisheries; manufactures boilers and machinery. Pop. 4,500.

Go'desberg, tn., Rhineland, Prussia, on R. Rhine, 4 m. S. of Bonn; mineral springs; summer resort. Pop. 20,500.

God'havn. See DISKO I.

Godh'ra, tn., Bombay, India, 52 m. by rail N.E. of Baroda; timber; tanneries. Pop. 27,000.

Göd'ing. See HODONIN.

Godmanchester (*god-man-chest'er* or *gum'sester*), munic. bor., Huntingdonshire, England, on R. Ouse; noted for cheese; flour mills. Pop. 2,000.

Gods'tone, par. and vil., Surrey, England, 4½ m. E. of Redhill; Roman remains. Pop. (par.) 2,950.

Godthaab (*got'hāb*), tn., W. Greenland; first Danish colony in Greenland, founded 1721; trading centre. Pop. *c.* 1,000.

God'win-Aus'ten, or DAPSANG (designated K² on Indian Survey Map), mt. peak, Mustagh Range, W. Himalayas, N. Kashmir, India; second highest peak in world (28,250 ft.).

Gog'ra, chief riv., United Provs., India; rises in Tibet; flows S.E.; joins Ganges at Chapra; navigable for 200 m.; length, 600 m.

Goil, LOCH, W. branch of Loch Long, Firth of Clyde, Scotland; length, 6 m.

Gol'borne, urb. dist., Lancs, England, 5 m. S. of Wigan; cotton manufacture and spinning; colliery. Pop. 7,300.

Golcar (*gō'kar*), urb. dist., W. Riding, Yorks, England, 3 m. S.W. of Huddersfield; woollen goods; mineral springs. Pop. 9,800.

Golcon'da, ruined city, Hyderabad, India, 7 m. W. of Hyderabad; centre of diamond cutting till 1687; now a small fortress serving as Nizam's treasury.

Gold Coast, Brit. crown colony and protectorate, including Ashanti and N. Territories, on Gulf of Guinea, W. Africa; surrounded by French terr., Ivory Coast on W., and Togoland on E. Climate hot and moist; surface rises to plateau; covered with forests; rivs. are Volta, Ankobra, and Prah; agriculture is staple occupation; chief export cocoa; other exports, gold, manganese, diamonds, kola nuts, mahogany, palm kernels; government botanical station at Aburi; chief railways from Takoradi and Accra to Kumasi; principal tns., Accra (cap.), Cape Coast, Sekondi; chief port, Takoradi; chief tn. in Ashanti, Kumasi. Area, *c.* 80,000 sq. m.; pop. *c.* 2,300,000 (Europeans, 2,500).

Golden Gate. See under SAN FRANCISCO.

Golden Horn. See under CONSTANTINOPLE.

Golds'boro, city and port, N. Carolina, U.S.A.; 50 m. S.E. of Raleigh; tobacco and cotton. Pop. 11,500.

Gol'spie, vil., Sutherland, Scotland, 17 m. S.W. of Helmsdale; fishing; Dunrobin Castle, seat of Duke of Sutherland, is in parish. Pop. 900.

Gomel', or HOMEL, tn., White Russia rep., U.S.S.R., 140 m. N. of Kiev; rly. jn.; agricultural machinery; sawmills. Pop. 86,500.

Gomera (*gō-mā'rā*), one of the Canary Is.; mountainous; cattle and dromedary rearing; chief port and tn., San Sebastian. Area, 144 sq. m.; pop. 23,000.

Gon'da. (1) Dist., United Provs., India; very fertile; rice, wheat, maize. Area, 2,875 sq. m.; pop. 1,500,000. (2) Chief tn. of above, 70 m. E.N.E. of Lucknow; important rly. jn.; trades in agricultural produce. Pop. 13,500.

Gondal'. (1) Indian state, Bombay, India, in Kathiawar peninsula; grain, cotton; silver and gold thread. Area, 1,024 sq. m.; pop. 167,000. (2) Cap. of above. Pop. 17,500.

Gon'dar, tn., Abyssinia, 20 m. N.E. of L. Tana; alt. 7,500 ft.; former cap.; cotton, gold, silver, and leather manufactures. Pop. 3,000.

Gondok'oro, trading post, s. Anglo-Egyptian Sudan, on R. Nile; unhealthy town.

Goodwick. See FISHGUARD.

Good'win Sands, dangerous shoals, off E. Kent, England; separated from mainland by the Downs; shifting sands, partly dry at low water; dangers now much reduced by lighting and buoying.

Good'wood, seat of Duke of Richmond, S. Downs, Sussex, England; famous racecourse 5 m. N. of Chichester.

Goole, mkt. tn. and port, W. Riding, Yorks, England, at confluence of R. Don with Ouse; extensive docks; iron foundries; shipbuilding, engineering, flour mills, chemical works. Pop. 20,200.

Göp'pingen, tn. and wat.-pl., Württemberg, Germany, 22 m. E.S.E. of Stuttgart; textiles, leather, machinery. Pop. 22,000.

Gorakhpur'. (1) Dist. and div., United Provinces, India; dist. flat, abounds in lakes and marshes; dense forests; chief rivs., Rapti, Gogra, Gandak; products, timber and rice. Area, 4,535 sq. m.; pop. 3,267,000. (2) Chief tn. of above, on Rapti, 100 m. N. of Benares; large riv. trade in timber and grain. Pop. 50,500.

Gori (*gō-rē'*), tn., Georgia, U.S.S.R., on R. Kura, 50 m. N.W. of Tiflis; timber, corn. Pop. 10,000.

Gorinchem (*gō'rink-em*), or GORKUM, fortified tn., S. Holland, on R. Merwede, 22 m. S.E. of Rotterdam; salmon fisheries; trade in grain, hemp, cattle. Pop. 14,000.

Gorizia (*go-rits'ē-a*), (German *Görz*), tn., N. Italy, on R. Isonzo, 12 m. N. of Gulf of Trieste; winter resort; silk mills. Scene of severe fighting during Great War. Pop. 26,500.

Gorleston-on-Sea (*gorls'ton*), wat.-pl., Suffolk (par. partly in Norfolk), England, 2 m. S. of Great Yarmouth. Pop. 20,400.

Gör'litz, tn., Silesia, Prussia, on R. Neisse, 90 m. W. of Breslau; textiles, machinery, glass. Pop. 86,000.

Gor'ton, tn., Lancs, England; E. suburb of Manchester; ironworks, cotton mills. Pop. 48,500.

Görz. See GORIZIA.

Gos'forth, urb. dist., Northumberland, England, 2 m. N. of Newcastle; annual race meeting in Gosforth Park. Pop. 18,000.

Gos'lar, tn., Hanover, Germany, 25 m. S. of Brunswick; silver, copper, lead, sulphur mines. Pop. 21,000.

Gos'port, port, Hants, England, opposite Portsmouth, with which it is connected by floating bridge; naval depot. Pop. 37,900.

Gosselies (*gos-lē'*), tn., Belgium, 5 m. N. of Charleroi; ironworks, coal mines. Pop. 10,000.

Gö'ta (*yu'ta*), riv., Sweden; drains L. Vener to Kattegat; length, 68 m.; navigable throughout. Göta Canal connects Baltic and Kattegat by way of Lakes Vener and Vetter.

Göteborg (*yu'te-bor*), port, Sweden, on Göta riv.; large commercial and industrial centre; traversed by numerous canals; fine harbour; electric railway to Stockholm; shipbuilding, machinery, textiles, wood pulp, sugar refining, brewing. Pop. 233,500.

Gotha (*gō'tä*), tn., W. Thuringia, Germany; manufactures sausages, toys, shoes, sugar. Pop. 46,000.

Goth'enburg. See GÖTEBORG.

Gotthard, ST. See ST. GOTTHARD PASS.

Göt'tingen, tn., Hanover, Germany, 60 m. S. of Hanover; book trade; univ.; manufactures scientific instruments, textiles, chemicals, sugar. Pop. 41,500.

Gott'land, isl., Baltic Sea; belongs to Sweden; coast is steep; interior mostly level, with large extent of forest; agriculture, sheep and cattle raising, fishing, cement making, and lime burning. Chief tn., Visby. Area, 1,150 sq. m.; pop. 35,000.

Gou'da, or TER GOUWE, tn., S. Holland, on R. Ysel; noted for cheese. Pop. 28,000.

Goulburn (*gōl'burn*). (1) Tn., New South Wales, Australia, 100 m. S.W. of Sydney; tanneries. Pop. 12,500.

(2) Riv., Victoria, Australia; trib. of R. Murray; irrigation works.

Gourock (*goo'rok*), tn., wat.-pl., Renfrewshire, Scotland, on Firth of Clyde; yachting centre; large steamer traffic. Pop. 8,800.

Govan (*guv'an*), par., Glasgow, Scotland, on Clyde; shipbuilding yards; engineering works; locomotive manufactures; incorporated with Glasgow (1912). Pop. 372,000.

Gow'er, or GWYR, peninsula, Glamorganshire, Wales; projects into Bristol Channel; chief tn., Swansea.

Gow'rie, CARSE OF, fertile alluvial belt, on N. side of Firth of Tay, Scotland; fruit; length, 15 m.

Go'ya, tn., Corrientes, Argentina, S. America, on Paraná; pastoral dist.; commercial centre. Pop. 16,000.

Goyan'a, or GOYANNA, tn., Brazil, S. America, on Goyana R., 40 m. N.N.W. of Recife; sugar, coffee, rum, tobacco, cotton, hides. Pop. 54,000.

Goyaz'. (1) State, Brazil, S. America, between Minas Geraes and Matto Grosso; mountainous; large tracts unexplored; forests; stock raising on campos; tobacco cultivated and gold mined; diamonds. Area, 254,834 sq. m.; pop. 640,500. (2) Cap. of above, 600 m. N.W. of Rio de Janeiro; trades in cattle, wine, cotton, coffee. Pop. 21,500.

Gozo (*gōts'ō*), isl., Mediterranean Sea, 4 m. N.W. of Malta, belongs to Britain; wheat, cotton, fruit, lace. Area, 26 sq. m.; pop. 23,000.

Graaff-Reinet (*grăf-rī'net*), tn., Cape of Good Hope prov., S. Africa, 140 m. N.N.W. of Port Elizabeth; alt., 2,463 ft.; vineyards and orchards; wool and mohair. Pop. 9,500, of whom half are whites.

Gräfrath (*gref'răt*), tn., Rhineland, Prussia, 12 m. E. of Düsseldorf; steel and iron works; silk and cotton manufactures. Pop. 11,000.

Graf'ton. (1) City, N.E. New South Wales, Australia, on Clarence R.; agricultural dist.; sugar mills. Pop. 6,500. (2) Tn., Massachusetts, U.S.A.; boots and shoes; residential suburb of Worcester. Pop. 7,000. (3) City, W. Virginia, U.S.A., 80 m. S. of Pittsburgh; coalfield; machinery shops, iron foundries, and flour mills. Pop. 9,000.

Gragnano (*grăn-yă'nō*), tn., Italy, 20 m. S.E. of Naples; trade in wine; manufactures macaroni. Pop. 15,500.

Graham Land, part of Antarctica; due S. of Cape Horn; mountainous and icebound; now believed to be a chain of islands.

Grahamstown, city, Cape Prov., S. Africa, 75 m. N.E. of Port Elizabeth; agricultural and pastoral dist.; ostrich farming; wool industry; is a health resort. Pop. 15,500 (7,650 whites).

Graian Alps (*gră'an*), portion of main Alpine chain, French-Italian frontier, between Savoy and Piedmont; peaks over 12,000 ft.

Grammichele (*gră-mē-kă'lă*), tn., Sicily, Italy, 33 m. S.W. of Catania; marble. Pop. 23,500.

Gram'pians, THE, mountains of the Central Highlands, Scotland; extends N.E. to S.W. from cos. of Banff and Aberdeen to Argyll and Dumbarton; highest summits, Ben Nevis (4,406 ft.), Ben Macdhui, Cairntoul, Braeriach, and Cairngorm.

Gran. See ESZTERGOM.

Granad'a. (1) Prov., S. Spain; traversed by Sierra Nevada; fertile plains and valleys; wheat, barley, wine, sugar, fruit; textile factories, ironworks, tanneries. Area, 4,928 sq. m.; pop. 602,000. (2) Cap. of above; has the Moorish palace of the Alhambra on fortified eminence; liqueurs, textiles, paper, soap, gloves, beet sugar, olives, and cereals are produced. Pop. 108,500. (3) City, Nicaragua, Central America, on L. Nicaragua; exp. indigo, hides, cocoa, coffee. Pop. 15,000.

Gran'by, tn., Quebec, Canada, 40 m. E. by S. of Montreal; saw and grist mills; paper, wooden goods, leather, tobacco. Pop. 7,000.

Gran Cha'co, EL ('the great hunting-ground'); extensive region, central S. America; comprising parts of Bolivia, Paraguay, Argentina; traversed by Pilcomayo, Bermejo, and other tribs. of Paraguay; surface mostly flat, with large tracts of forest, pastureland and swamp; exp. quebracho bark and extract; thinly populated by nomadic Indian tribes. Area, *c.* 300,000 sq. m.

Grand Bank, submarine plateau (500,000 sq. m.) extending S.E. from Newfoundland; most important cod-fishing ground in world—employs 100,000 fishermen; depth, 15 to 160 fathoms.

Grand Canal, China; extending from Hangchow to Tientsin; length, 850 m.; when constructed, Grand Canal was greatest engineering work of kind in world; fel. into disuse when steam traffic was introduced.

Grand Canary, one of the Canary Islands; belongs to Spain; volcanic origin; climate healthy; chief peak, Pico del Pozos (6,400 ft.); fertile valleys; fruit and early vegetables; mineral springs. Cap. Las Palmas. Area, 550 sq. m.; pop. 130,000.

Grand Cañon, gorge in plateau region, Arizona, U.S.A.; cut out by Colorado R.; extends W. *c.* 220 m. from confluence of Little Colorado R.; 4½ to 12 m. wide, and in some parts 6,000 ft. deep; walls descend in series of shelves with detached pillars and masses of rock; magnificent rock-colouring and countless side gorges.

Grand Falls, garden city, Newfoundland, on Exploits R.; founded in 1905 as centre for pulp and paper industry. Pop. 4,000.

Grand Forks. (1) Tn., S.E. Brit. Columbia, Canada, near U.S.A. boundary; gold and copper smelting works; saw and flour mills. Pop. 1,500. (2) City, N. Dakota, U.S.A., on Red R.; in wheat dist.; sugar beet; flour mills. Pop. 15,500.

Grand Island, city, Nebraska, U.S.A., 85 m. W. of Lincoln; railway works; beet-sugar factories. Pop. 14,000.

Grand Rapids. (1) City, Michigan, U.S.A., 30 m. E. of L. Michigan; furniture manufactures; flour and grist milling; foundry products; fruit growing. Pop. 169,000. (2) See WISCONSIN RAPIDS.

Grange′mouth, port, Stirlingshire, Scotland, on Firth of Forth; E. terminus of Forth and Clyde Canal; shipbuilding yards, sawmills; imports timber, pig-iron, iron ore; coal mined in vicinity; oil-pipe line from Dalmuir, on Clyde. Pop. 11,800.

Grange-over-Sands, holiday resort in Grange urb. dist., Lancs, England, on Morecambe Bay, 9 m. N.W. of Carnforth. Pop. 2,600.

Gran′ite City, city, Illinois, U.S.A., 6 m. N. of St. Louis; steel foundries; motor-cars. Pop. 25,000.

Granth′am, mkt. tn., S.W. Lincolnshire, England; rly. jn.; engines, electric plant, and agricultural machinery are manufactured; malting. Pop. 19,700.

Gran′ton, port, Edinburgh, Scotland; trawling centre; sawmills; ferry to Burntisland. Pop. 2,500.

Gran′town-on-Spey, burgh and mkt. tn., Moray, Scotland, 20 m. S. of Forres; health resort. Pop. 1,600.

Granville (1) (*gron-vēl′*). Fortified port, seaside resort, Manche, France, on Gulf of St. Malo; fisheries; shipbuilding; manufacture of chemicals. Pop. 10,000. (2) (*gran′vil*), Tn., New South Wales, Australia, 12 m. W. of Sydney; rly. jn.; ironworks, flour mills, and tanneries. Pop. 18,000.

Gras′litz. See KRASLICE.

Gras′mere, vil. and small picturesque lake, Westmorland, England, in Lake District; tourist centre. Pop. 1,000.

Grasse (*gräs*), tn., Alpes-Maritimes, France, 12 m. N.N.W. of Cannes; manufactures essences and perfumes; winter resort. Pop. 12,000.

Graudenz. See GRUDZIADZ.

Gravelines (*gräv-lēn′*), fortified port, Nord, France, 15 m. S.W. of Dunkirk; fisheries, shipbuilding, flax and hemp spinning, sugar refining. Pop. 2,000.

Graves′end, port, mkt. tn., munic. bor., Kent, England; part of Port of London; important shipping centre; boat building; paper making. Pop. 35,500.

Grays Thur′rock, urb. dist., Essex,

England, 3 m. N.W. of Tilbury Fort; lime, cement, bricks. Pop. 18,200.

Graz (*gräts*), tn., cap. Styria, S.E. Austria, on R. Mur; manufactures machinery, steel and iron ware, chemicals, soap; large rly. works. Pop. 153,000.

Greas'ley, par. and vil., Notts, England, 7 m. N.W. of Nottingham. Pop. (par.) 6,500.

Great Bar'rier Reef, coral reefs off E. coast, Queensland, Australia; length, 1,000 m.; distance from coast, 15 to 100 m.; built on former Australian coast-line; broken opposite riv. mouths by navigable channels.

Great Basin, THE, area of internal drainage, W. United States, between Wasatch Mts. and Sierra Nevada; contains Great Salt L. and Death Valley; much desert; sparse pop. Area, *c.* 200,000 sq. m.

Great Bear Lake, lake, Mackenzie, Canada; discharges through Great Bear R. into Mackenzie R. Area, *c.* 11,000 sq. m.

Great Brit'ain, large isl. off W. coast of Europe, consisting of England, Scotland, and Wales; extreme length, *c.* 605 m.; breadth, *c.* 320 m.; most northerly point is Dunnet Head, in Caithness; most easterly, Lowestoft Ness, Suffolk; most southerly, Lizard Point, Cornwall; most westerly, Ardnamurchan Point, Argyll; total area (including I. of Man and Channel Islands), 89,041 sq. m.; total pop. 43,000,000. See BRITISH ISLES.

Great Crosby. See CROSBY.

Great Falls, city, Montana, U.S.A., on Missouri R.; rich mining region; gold, copper, and silver smelting works; great wool trade. Pop. 29,000.

Great Fish River. (1) Riv., Cape Prov., S. Africa; has tortuous course; enters Indian Ocean; mouth closed by bar; length, 230 m. (2) Or BACK'S RIVER, riv., N.W. Terr., Canada; rises on N.E. of Great Slave Lake; flows N.E. to Arctic Ocean; relics of Franklin's expedition discovered in estuary (1859); length, 440 m.

Great Grimsby. See GRIMSBY.

Great Harwood, urb. dist., Lancs, England, 4½ m. N.E. of Blackburn; cotton mills; collieries. Pop. 12,800.

Great Lakes, THE, collective name for five fresh-water lakes—Superior, Michigan, Huron, Erie, and Ontario—situated between Canada and U.S.A.; form upper waters of St. Lawrence R. Superior, largest lake, is connected with Huron by St. Mary R.; Michigan (wholly in U.S.A.) joins Huron at Straits of Mackinac; Huron empties itself into Erie by St. Clair R. and Lake, and Detroit R.; between Erie and Ontario are Niagara R. and Falls. Lakes opened up to navigation, and differences of levels overcome by canals with numerous locks; lakes frozen for four or five months in winter; some of largest and most important tns. in N. America situated on shores; Chicago, on Michigan, and Buffalo, on Erie, share greater part of lake traffic; extensive coalfields, iron mines, fruit and grain-growing regions, especially on S. Area, 96,000 sq. m.

Great Orme's Head, headland, Carnarvonshire, Wales; lighthouse.

Great St. Ber'nard Pass, easiest pass over Pennine Alps (8,111 ft.); leads from Martigny in Switzerland to Italian valley of Aosta; since 12th cent. hospice has extended hospitality to travellers; St. Bernard dogs famous; carriage road across the pass.

Great Salt Lake, Utah, U.S.A., principal drainage centre of Great Basin; 4,218 ft. above sea-level; six times as salt as ocean; salt manufactured by evaporation of water; lake has no outlet; fed by Bear, Jordan, and Weber rivs.; contains several islands. Area, 1,500 sq. m., but subject to large fluctuations.

Great Slave Lake, N.W. Territories, Canada; irregular shores; numerous bays; drained by Mackenzie R.; frozen for six months annually. Length, *c.* 300 m.; breadth, 15 to 60 m.; area, *c.* 10,000 sq. m.

Greece, rep., S.E. Europe; consists of S. part of Balkan Peninsula and numerous islands—Eubœa, N. Sporades, Cyclades, etc., on E., Crete, Cerigo, etc., on S. Ionian Islands, on W.; bounded by Albania, Yugoslavia, and Bulgaria on N., and Turkey. Most S. part, the Morea, or Peloponnesus, is joined to mainland by narrow isthmus of Corinth. Coasts are high, rocky, and much indented. N. part consists of Macedonia and Thrace; farther S. is Thessaly; country is traversed on W. by Pindus Mts.; along E. coast a ridge runs through Olympus, Pelion, and Eubœa, enclosing plain of Thessaly; lower courses of Rs. Struma and Vardar in N. are in Greek terr. Climate is Mediterranean; snow lies above 4,000 ft.; rainfall heaviest on W.; marshlands are malarial. Below 1,500 ft. the cypress, myrtle, olive, and other evergreens prevail; vine, fig, orange, tobacco, cotton, and date flourish; above 1,500 ft. are oak and chestnut, beech and pine forests. Agriculture, which is backward, is predominant occupation; chief products are grapes for currants, olives, tobacco, figs; cereals are wheat, barley, rye, and maize; minerals are iron, lead, zinc, emery, magnesium, salt, and marble. Chief industries are smelting, and manufacture of textiles, olive oil, soap, leather. Exp. include currants, figs, olive oil, wines, tobacco, hides, ores, marble, and sponges. Athens is cap.; chief ports, Piræus, Salonika, Volo, Dede-Agatch. Area, 49,912 sq. m.; pop. 6,205,000.

Gree'ley, city, N. Colorado, U.S.A., on S. Platte riv.; coal mines; flour, sugar beet, and lumber mills. Pop. 11,000.

Green Bay, city, Wisconsin, U.S.A., on L. Michigan; coal trade; paper mills. Pop. 37,000.

Green'land, large isl., only colonial possession of Denmark; between Baffin Bay and Atlantic Ocean, N.E. of America; larger part within Arctic circle; extreme length, *c.* 1,650 m.; greatest breadth, *c.* 800 m.; interior completely buried under ice of great thickness; surface generally mountainous; highest peak, Petermann Spitze (*c.* 11,000 ft.), near Franz Josef Fjord; coast-line broken by numerous bays and fjords of great depth; Disko, on W. coast, is largest of many islands; drainage mainly by enormous glaciers, and small streams of melted snow and ice; part of N.E. and N.W. coasts still unexplored. Fauna includes lemming, musk-ox, white wolf, polar bear, reindeer, fox, and hare; numerous birds; whales, seals; copse-woods on coast, where some vegetables thrive; climate colder on E. coast owing to N. polar current; W. coast washed by Atlantic water. Principal settlements on the W. are Julianehaab (most S. station), Godthaab, Godhavn, and Upernivik; on the E. Angmagsalik, Scoresby. Principal exp.: whale and seal oil, eiderdown, fox and seal skins; cryolite; cod and haddock fisheries on W. coast; trade a monopoly of Danish government. Area, *c.* 825,000 sq. m., of which ice-free portion is *c.* 50,000 sq. m.; pop. 14,500 (Eskimos and *c.* 300 Danes).

Green'land Sea, part of Arctic Ocean, between Spitsbergen, Norway, Jan Mayen, Iceland, and Greenland; midway between Greenland and Spitsbergen it is 2,500 fathoms deep; much fog and ice in W. portion.

Green'law, vil., Berwickshire, Scotland, on R. Blackadder; co. tn. till 1882. Pop. 600.

Green Mountains. See APPALACHIANS.

Green'ock, port and manufacturing tn., Renfrewshire, Scotland, on Clyde estuary; sugar refining; shipbuilding, iron working; engineering works; woollen factories; rope works, tanneries; large foreign trade. Pop. 78,900.

Greenore', port and wat.-pl., Louth, I.F.S.; passenger steamer service with Holyhead, 80 m. S.E. Pop. 300.

Greens'boro, city, N. Carolina, U.S.A., 70 m. N.W. of Raleigh; iron and copper mines; cotton mills, blast furnaces, tobacco and furniture factories. Pop. 53,000.

Greens'burg, city, Pennsylvania, U.S.A., 30 m. S.E. of Pittsburgh; gas and bituminous coal and coke; steel manufactures. Pop. 15,000.

Green'ville, city, S. Carolina, U.S.A., 100 m. N.W. of Columbia; cotton market; textile factories. Pop. 29,000.

Greenwich (*grin'ij*), metropolitan and parl. bor., London, England; first meridian passes through Royal Astronomical Observatory, from which Greenwich time is reckoned; Royal Naval Coll. Pop. 100,900. (2) Tn., Connecticut, U.S.A.; summer resort and residential suburb of New York. Pop. 25,000.

Greetland, urb. dist., W. Riding, Yorks, England, 3 m. S.W. of Halifax; woollen manufacture. Pop. 4,300.

Greifswald (*grīfs'vält*), tn., Pomerania, Prussia, 20 m. S.E. of Stralsund; agricultural machines; surgical instruments; fish curing. Pop. 26,500.

Greiz (*grīts*), tn., Thuringia, Germany, 50 m. S. of Leipzig; dress fabrics; dyeing and tanning. Pop. 37,000.

Grenä'da, one of Brit. W. India Islands; most southerly of Windward group; volcanic origin; crater lakes; very fertile, good climate; chief products, cocoa, fruit, spices, cotton. Cap. St. George's. Area, 133 sq. m.; pop. 66,500.

Grenadines (*gren-a-dēnz'*), chain of small islands, Windward group, Brit. W. Indies; extend for 60 m. between St. Vincent and Grenada; exp. cotton. Pop. 7,500, mostly on Carriacou, the chief island.

Gren'chen, tn., Solothurn, Switzerland, 16 m. N. of Berne; watchmaking. Pop. 10,500.

Greno'ble, tn., cap. Isère, France, on R. Isère; fortress; tourist centre for French Alps; manufactures kid gloves, liqueurs, cement, straw hats, silk, and linen. Pop. 78,000.

Grenzmark (*grents'-*), prov., Prussia, on Polish frontier, lying between Pomerania and Silesia and divided into two portions by Brandenburg; consists of the remnants of the prewar provs. of W. Prussia and Poland; numerous small lakes; cattle; rye, potatoes. Cap. Schneidemühl. Area, 2,971 sq. m.; pop. 332,500.

Gret'na, township and par., Dumfriesshire, Scotland, on Solway Firth, and 9½ m. N.W. of Carlisle; includes Gretna Green, notorious for its runaway marriages. Pop. (par.) 3,000.

Grey'mouth, port, South Island, New Zealand, on W. coast; coal and gold. Pop. 6,000.

Grey'town. (1) Tn., Natal, S. Africa, 65 m. N. of Pietermaritzburg; mixed farming and wattle growing. Pop. 3,500. (2) Or SAN JUAN DEL NORTE, port, Nicaragua, Central America, on Caribbean Sea; exp. hides, rubber, mahogany, bananas; harbour protected by breakwater, partially silted up. Pop. *c.* 600.

Grims'by, or GREAT GRIMSBY, port, Lincolnshire, England, on R. Humber; great fishing port; many docks; exports coal; industries include shipbuilding, brewing, tanning. Pop. 92,500.

Grim'sel Pass, pass, Bernese Alps, Switzerland, between Rs. Aar and Rhone; alt. 7,100 ft.; traversed by carriage road; hospice at N. end (6,155 ft.), now submerged by the impounding of L. Grimsel for great hydro-electric scheme.

Grindelwald (*grēn'del-vält*), vil. and mountain valley, Bernese Oberland, Switzerland; tourist resort; winter sports.

Grin'stead, EAST, urb. dist., mkt. tn., Sussex, England, 17 m. S. of Croydon; brewing; bricks and tiles. Pop. 7,500.

Griqualand East and **Griqualand West** (*grēk'waw-land*), divs. of Cape Prov., Union of S. Africa. *Griqualand East,* part of Transkeian terrs., bounded by Natal, Basutoland, and Pondoland; fine pastures; exp. wool. Chief tn., Kokstad. Area, 6,602 sq. m.; pop. 265,000. *Griqualand West,* bounded by Bechuanaland, Transvaal and Orange Free State; pastoral plateau; diamond mines. Chief tn., Kimberley. Area, 15,197 sq. m.

Grisons (*grē-sōn'*), most easterly canton, Switzerland; largest, but most thinly populated; surface mountainous, with narrow valleys and forests; contains three sources of Rhine, and Engadine or upper course of Inn; cattle breeding; maize and chestnuts; wine; mineral springs; climate severe; tourist centres, esp. at Davos, Arosa, St. Moritz, and Engadine. Chief tn., Chur. Area, 2,746 sq. m.; pop. 123,000.

Grod'no, or GARDINAS. (1) Prov., claimed by Lithuania; partly occupied by Poland; surface flat, with pine forests and swamps; chief riv., Niemen; woollen industry. Area *c.* 14,900 sq. m.; pop. *c.* 2,000,000. (2) Fortified tn., Poland, on Niemen, in terr. claimed by Lithuania; important rly. jn.; manufactures tobacco; timber trade. Pop. 62,000.

Gron'ingen. (1) Prov., N.E. Holland; flat, with rich pastures; climate damp; agriculture, dairy farming, and grazing; some fishing and boat building. Area, 883 sq. m.; pop. 391,000. (2) Cap. of above; connected by canals with Dollart and Zuider Zee; chief tn. of N. Holland and great trading centre; manufactures woollen goods; boat building, rope making, sugar refining, tobacco, furniture, pianos. Pop. 101,500.

Grosseto (*grōs'sā-to*). (1) Prov., Tuscany, Italy; quicksilver, timber. Area, 1,735 sq. m.; pop. 165,000. (2) Cap. of above, 90 m. N.W. of Rome; mineral springs. Pop. 22,000.

Groz'nyi, tn., N. Caucasian Area, Russia, on S. trib. of R. Terek; naphtha wells and refineries. Pop. 97,000

Grudziadz (*gruj'yōnts*) (Ger., *Graudenz*), tn., Poland, on R. Vistula; machinery, tapestry, cigars, flour. Pop. 35,000.

Grün'berg, tn., N. Silesia, Prussia; textiles, machinery, paper; vineyards. Pop. 25,000.

Gruyère (*grü-yār'*), tn., Switzerland, 16 m. S. of Fribourg; dist. gives its name to Gruyère cheese. Pop. 2,000.

Guadalajara (*gwä-thä-lä-chä'rä*). (1) Prov., Spain, on Meseta; S. fertile; traversed by R. Tagus; produce chiefly agricultural; silver and salt deposits. Area, 4,676 sq. m.; pop. 208,000. (2) Cap. of above; woollens, leather. Pop. 14,000. (3) Tn., Jalisco, Mexico, 300 m. W.N.W. of Mexico; textiles, Indian pottery, leather. Pop. 143,500.

Guadalquivir (*gwä-thäl-kē-vēr'*), riv., S. Spain; rises in Sierra de Cazorla; flows S.W. for 360 m. into Atlantic; is navigable to Seville.

Guadeloupe (*gä-dē-loop'*), two islands separated by narrow channel, Leeward Islands, W. Indies, form French colony with five isl. dependencies; climate hot but healthy; soil fertile and well cultivated; exp. sugar, coffee, cocoa, rum, bananas, vanilla. Cap. Basse-Terre. Area, 688 sq. m.; pop. 243,500.

Guadiana (*gwä-thē-ä'nä*), riv., Spain and Portugal, rises in Meseta, flows into Atlantic; length, 500 m.; navigable 40 m.

Guadix (*gwä-thēch*), tn., Granada, Spain, 30 m. E.N.E. of Granada; trades in wool. Pop. 16,500.

Guaira, La. See LA GUAIRA.

Gualeguaychú (*gwä-lä-gwī-choo'*), riv. port, Entre Rios, Argentina, S. America, 100 m. N. of Buenos Aires; meat products, hides. Pop. 23,000.

Guam (*gwäm*), most southerly and largest of Marianas Archipelago, Pacific Ocean; belongs to U.S.A.; mountainous; well-watered, fertile; chief products, rice, maize, sugar, copra, timber. Cap. Agaña. Area, 210 sq. m.; pop. 18,000.

Guanajuato (*gwä-nä-chu-ä'tō*). (1) Inland state, Mexico; mountainous in N., fertile plain in S.; rich in minerals (gold, silver, lead, tin, iron); some cattle reared; tanneries. Area, 10,950 sq. m.; pop. 860,500. (2) SANTA FÉ DE GUANAJUATO, cap. of above; centre of mining dist.; manufactures cotton, pottery. Pop. 19,500.

Guantánamo (*gwän-tä'nä-mō*), city, S.E. Cuba, W. Indies; rich agricultural region; trade in sugar and bananas; American naval station. Pop. 20,000.

Guardafui (*gwär-dä-fwē'*), CAPE, N.E. extremity of the 'eastern horn of Africa,' at S. of entrance to Gulf of Aden.

Guardbridge', vil., Fife, Scotland, at

mouth of R. Eden, 4 m. N.W. of St. Andrews; paper mill. Pop. 770.

Guárico (*gwā-rē'kō*), inland state, Venezuela, S. America; cattle, cheese. Cap. Calabozo. Area, 25,000 sq. m.; pop. 125,500.

Guatemala (*gwā-tē-mä'lä*). (1) Rep., Central America; bounded by Mexico, Brit. Honduras, Gulf and Rep. of Honduras, Salvador, and Pacific Ocean. Surface consists of low-lying marshy plains along Pacific coast rising to Sierra Madre; many volcanoes, including Tajamulco (13,500 ft.); copious rainfall on Atlantic slope; vast forest lands; most important crop is coffee; sugar, rice, maize, and bananas also produced; gold, silver, lead, and copper mines; timber and chicle gum exported. Majority of the inhabitants are Indians; many half-castes, few Europeans. Cap. Guatemala. Area, 42,353 sq. m.; pop. 2,000,000. (2) Or GUATEMALA LA NUEVA (New Guatemala), cap. of above, on plain *c.* 5,000 ft. above sea-level, and 70 m. from its Pacific port, San José; centre of coffee trade. Pop. 116,000.

Guayaquil (*gwī-a-kēl'*), chief port, Ecuador, S. America; exp. cocoa, coffee, rubber, ivory nuts, Panama hats; shipyards; various manufactures; climate hot and unhealthy. Pop. 100,000.

Guayas (*gwī'äs*), coastal prov., Ecuador, S. America; most important (industrially and commercially) of the rep.; climate hot, humid, unhealthy; soil fertile; cocoa, coffee, tobacco, cane sugar, and rice. Cap. Guayaquil. Area, 8,331 sq. m.; pop. 150,000.

Gubbio (*goo'bē-ō*), city, Umbria, Italy, 20 m. N.N.E. of Perugia; at foot of Monte Calvo; majolica ware. Pop. (comm.) 30,500.

Guben (*goo'ben*), tn., Brandenburg, Prussia, 30 m. S. of Frankfurt-on-Oder; woollen cloth and yarn, pottery, paper. Pop. 41,000.

Guebwiller (*geb-vē'yā*), (German *Gebweiler*), tn., Haut Rhin (Alsace), France; textiles, machinery; wines. Pop. 11,500.

Guelderland. See GELDERLAND.

Guelph (*gwelf*), tn., Ontario, Canada, 40 m. W. of Toronto; market for agricultural and stock-raising dist.; flour and woollen mills; Ontario Agricultural Coll. Pop. 18,500.

Guéret (*gā-rā'*), chief tn., Creuse, central France, 48 m. by rail N.E. of Limoges; leather, hosiery. Pop. 6,000.

Guernsey (*gern'zē*), second largest of the Channel Islands; climate mild; health resort; large quantities of fruit, flowers, and vegetables (esp. tomatoes and grapes); famous breed of cattle; granite quarries; fishing. Cap. St. Peter Port. Area, 25 sq. m.; pop. 40,000.

Guerrero (*ger-rā'rō*), Pacific State, Mexico; mountainous; rich in minerals, but little worked; fertile; produces coffee, cereals, tobacco, cotton. Cap. Chilpancingo; chief port, Acapulco. Area, 25,279 sq. m.; pop. 567,000.

Guiana (*gē-ä'nä*), that part of S. America between Orinoco and Amazon rivs., but esp. Brit., Dutch, and French Guianas; flat, swampy tracts, with rich, fertile soil along coast; beyond this, land rises to undulating savannas, behind which are mts. covered with almost impenetrable forest; contains innumerable rivers, which form chief means of communication; larger streams are navigable up to rapids and falls; vegetation remarkably rich and luxuriant; sugar, coffee, rice, cocoa, fruits cultivated; forests yield fine timbers, balata, rubber, oil, balsams, gums, nuts; birds, particularly brilliant in plumage, include humming-birds and parrots; jaguars, tapirs, alligators, and great variety of insects; gold and diamonds are produced; inhabitants chiefly Indians, Negroes, and Europeans; climate not unhealthy though tropical.

BRITISH GUIANA, largest of the three colonies, is bounded on W. by Venezuela, S. by Brazil, and E. by Dutch Guiana; in W. are Pacaraima Mts., culminating in Mt. Roraima, on Venezuelan boundary; principal rivs.,

Essequibo, Courantine, Berbice, Demerara; rlys. connect Georgetown with New Amsterdam, and Demerara R. with Essequibo R., and line from Demerara a few miles along w. coast; principal exports, sugar, rum, rice, molasses, coffee, timber, balata, bauxite, diamonds, and gold. Chief tns., Georgetown (cap.) and New Amsterdam. Area, 89,480 sq. m.; pop. 308,000.

DUTCH GUIANA, or SURINAM, bounded on w. by Brit. Guiana, s. by Brazil, and E. by Fr. Guiana; great extent of dense forest and unexplored country; exports sugar, rum, coffee, cocoa. Cap. Paramaribo. Area, 54,291 sq. m.; pop. 150,000.

FRENCH GUIANA, or CAYENNE, bounded on w. by Dutch Guiana, s. and E. by Brazil; little agricultural industry; gold mining principal occupation; Fr. penal settlement. Cap. Cayenne. Area, 34,740 sq. m.; pop. 47,500.

Guienne (*gē-en'*), anc. prov., s.w. France; now divided into deps. of Gironde, Dordogne, Lot, Aveyron, Lot-et-Garonne, and Tarn-et-Garonne.

Guild'ford, mkt. tn., Surrey, England, on Wey; remains of Norman keep; important rly. jn.; grain and live-stock markets. Pop. 30,800.

Guin'ea, dist., w. Africa; along shores of Gulf of Guinea; originally included the coast lands from R. Gambia to Angola (C. Negro).

Guipuzcoa (*gē-pooth'kō-a*), maritime prov., N. Spain; surface mountainous; climate mild, healthy; fruit, maize, timber, cattle; rich in minerals (iron, zinc, lignite, copper); flourishing industries; fisheries; mineral springs. Cap. San Sebastian. Area, 728 sq. m.; pop. 291,000.

Guisborough (*giz'bur-o*), tn., N. Riding, Yorks, England, near Middlesbrough; iron, steel, alum; ruined priory. Pop. 6,300.

Guiseley (*giz'lē*), urb. dist., W. Riding, Yorks, England, 8 m. N.W. of Leeds; woollen goods. Pop. 5,600.

Gujarat (*gooj-rät'*), region, Bombay; comprising peninsulas of Kathiawar and Cutch, and a strip of mainland; produces cotton, millet, pulses, winter wheat. Area, 13,579 sq. m.; pop. 3,718,000.

Gujranwal'a. (1) Dist., Lahore, Punjab, India; chief river, Chenab; irrigation dist.; exp. cotton and grain. Area, 2,309 sq. m.; pop. 624,000. (2) Cap. of above, 40 m. N. of Lahore. Pop. 38,000.

Gujrat (*gooj-rät'*), tn., Punjab, India, on R. Chenab; makes cotton goods, brass-ware, and inlaid gold and silver articles. Pop. 22,000.

Gulbar'ga, tn., Hyderabad, India, 100 m. w. of Hyderabad; cotton industries. Pop. 36,000.

Gul'lane, vil., E. Lothian, Scotland, 15 m. N.E. of Edinburgh, on Firth of Forth; seaside and golfing resort. Pop. 1,500.

Gumti (*goom'tē*), riv., India; joins Ganges, 17 m. N.E. of Benares, after a general S.E. course of 500 m.

Guntur', tn. and dist., Madras, India; bounded on N. and E. by R. Kistna; cotton trade; ginning factories. Pop. (tn.) 48,000.

Güstrow (*goos'tro*), tn., Mecklenburg-Schwerin, N. Germany; ironworks; sugar, beer. Pop. 20,000.

Guth'rie, city, Oklahoma, U.S.A., 30 m. N. of Oklahoma city; fruit; dairying. Pop. 15,000.

Gwal'ior. (1) Largest Indian state in Central India; in basins of Rs. Chambal and Narbada; surface level in N., rising to Vindhya Mts. in s.; produces grain, oil-seeds, cane sugar, cotton; cotton ginning; muslins and carpets made; inhabitants mainly Hindus. Area, 26,357 sq. m.; pop. 3,186,000. (2) Ancient cap. of above, 60 m. s. of Agra; huge fortress on rock with sculptured caves. Consists of an old tn., and a new tn. known as Lashkar. Contains Maharajah's palace. Pop. 80,500.

Gwe'lo, mining centre, S. Rhodesia, S. Africa, 100 m. N.E. of Bulawayo; alt. 4,650 ft.; gold and diamonds. Pop. 1,230 whites.

Gwersylt (*goo-er'silt*), vil. and par., Denbighshire, Wales, 3 m. N.W. of

Wrexham; coal mines in neighbourhood. Pop. (par.) 6,000.

Gyangtse (*gē-äng'tse*), tn., Tibet, 10m. s.w. of Lhassa; on important trade route from India through Sikkim; caravan centre; market for woollens.

Gympie (*gim'pi*), tn., Queensland, Australia, 90 m. N. of Brisbane; gold mining. Pop. 9,000.

Gyöngyös (*dyon-dyosh'*), tn., Hungary, 40 m. N.E. of Budapest; wine, textiles. Pop. 20,000.

Györ' (*dyor*), or RAAB, tn., Hungary, 70 m. S.E. of Vienna; horse fairs; textiles; agricultural machinery. Pop. 50,000.

Gyula. See under BÉKÉS.

Gyula-Fehérvár. See ALBA-IULIA.

H

Haar'lem, tn., cap. of N. Holland, has collections in art and science, and an academy of science; textiles, printing, brewing; large trade in flower bulbs. Pop. 113,300.

Habana. See HAVANA.

Hack'ensack, tn., New Jersey, U.S.A., N.W. suburb of New York; iron foundries, silk factories; paper, jewellery. Pop. 26,000.

Hack'ney, metropolitan and parl. bor. of London, England, 3 m. N.E. of St. Paul's; formerly fashionable residential suburb. Pop. 215,400.

Had'dington, co. tn., E. Lothian, Scotland, on R. Tyne; 15th cent. church ('Lamp of Lothian'), and Knox Memorial Institute; grain mkt.; corn mills. Pop. 4,400.

Haddingtonshire. See EAST LOTHIAN.

Ha'derslev, tn., E. Schleswig, Denmark, on Haderslev Fjord; rly. jn.; tobacco, gloves; iron foundries, tanneries. Pop. 14,000.

Had'field, vil., Derbyshire, England, 1½ m. N.W. of Glossop; calico and print works. Pop. 6,000.

Hadhramaut (*hä-drä-mowt'*), prov. of S. Arabia; arid coast extends from Oman on E. to Yemen on W.; interior has fertile valleys; tobacco, frankincense, aloes, carpets, shawls. Cap. and chief port, Makalla. Pop. of prov. *c.* 150,000.

Had'leigh, mkt. tn., Suffolk, England, 70 m. N.E. of London; corn mills, malt houses. Pop. 3,000.

Had'ley, par. and vil., Shropshire, England, 10 m. W. of Ipswich; coal and iron mines. Pop. 3,200.

Hagen (*hä'gen*), tn., Westphalia, Prussia, 33 m. E. by N. of Düsseldorf; iron and steel works; textile industries; tanning, brewing, distilling. Pop. 100,000.

Hagenau. See HAGUENAU.

Ha'gerstown, city, Maryland, U.S.A., 72 m. N.W. of Baltimore; has machine shops, flour mills; furniture, chemicals. Pop. 31,000.

Hagonoy', tn., Luzon, Philippines, on Manila Bay; dist. produces rice and sugar; woven fabrics, hats; fishing. Pop. 22,000.

Hague (*hāg*), THE (Dutch, *'s Gravenhage*), cap. of Holland, 2 m. from North Sea; traversed by numerous canals; royal palace, castle of Counts of Holland (Dutch Parliament House), famous picture gallery, museums; Palace of Peace. Chief industries, copper and lead smelting, iron foundries, printing works; carriages, furniture; distilling. Pop. 425,000.

Haguenau (*hä'gen-ow*), tn., Bas Rhin (Alsace), France, on R. Moder; textiles, porcelain, soap, beer. Pop. 14,000.

Haidarabad. See HYDERABAD.

Haifa (*hī'fa*), port, Palestine, on Bay of Acre, at foot of Mt. Carmel; manufactures cement and soap; exports wheat. Pop. 25,000.

Hails'ham, mkt. tn., Sussex, England, 7 m. N. of Eastbourne; bricks, pottery; trade in agricultural produce. Pop. 4,900.

Hainan (*hī-nan'*), isl. in prov. of Kwang-tung, extreme s. of China, between China Sea and Gulf of Tongking; extending *c.* 150 by *c.* 100 m. Centre and s. are mountainous, densely wooded, yielding camphor, mahogany, rosewood; agriculture in coastal valleys, rice being main crop; stock raising; earthquakes and typhoons occur. Cap. Kiung-chow (with port Hoi-how). Area, *c.* 1,300 sq. m.; pop. *c.* 2,000,000.

Hainaut (*ā-nō'*), prov., Belgium; surface generally level, broken by spurs of Ardennes; traversed by Rs. Sambre, Schelde, Dender, and Haine; rich coalfields and iron mines; fertile soil. Cap. Mons. Area, 1,437 sq. m.; pop. 1,263,000.

Haiphong (*hī-fong'*), chief port, Tongking, Fr. Indo-China, on branch of Red R. delta; cotton thread, soap, oil. Pop. 20,000.

Haiti (*hă'ti*) or HAYTI. (1) Second largest isl. in W. Indies, separated from Cuba by Windward Passage, and from Porto Rico by Mona Passage. Surface is mountainous, highest peak Loma Tina (10,300 ft.). Mts. are covered with pine, oak, and other forests—much valuable timber being produced. Rivers are not navigable; many large lakes. Earthquakes frequent and hurricanes common; climate hot in low-lying parts, healthful elsewhere. Cotton, cocoa, tobacco, sugar, coffee are cultivated. Minerals as yet undeveloped. Isl. is divided into two republics—Haiti in w., and Santo Domingo in E. Area of isl., 29,536 sq. m.; pop. 3,197,600. (2) REPUBLIC, w. third of above isl.; formerly French colony, became rep. in 1804; under U.S.A. supervision since 1916. Chief products, coffee, cotton, sugar, cocoa, tobacco. Cap. and chief port, Port au Prince. Area, 10,204 sq. m.; pop. 2,300,000.

Hakodate (*ha-ko-dă'tā*), port, Hokkaido, Japan, on bay of Hakodate; splendid harbour; great fishing centre; exports sulphur, dried fish, beans, peas, timber, furs. Pop. 164,000.

Hal, tn., Brabant, Belgium, on R. Senne; sugar, paper, porcelain. Pop. 16,000.

Hal'berstadt, tn., Saxony, Germany, 29 m. s.w. of Magdeburg; sugar, cigars, machinery, paper, leather goods. Pop. 48,000.

Hal'den, formerly FREDRIKSHALD, tn., s. Norway, near Swedish boundary; wood pulp and paper mills, boots, shoes. Exp. granite. Pop. 11,000.

Hale, urb. dist., N. Cheshire, England, adjoining Altrincham. Pop. 10,700.

Haleb. See ALEPPO.

Halesowen (*hālz-ō'en*), urb. dist., Worcestershire, England, 7 m. s.w. of Birmingham; agricultural implements; iron and steel works; rails, chains. Pop. 31,100.

Halesworth, urb. dist., Suffolk, England, 9 m. s.w. of Beccles; mkt. tn. Pop. 2,000.

Halfa. See WADI HALFA.

Hal'ifax. (1) Co. bor., W. Riding, Yorks, England, on R. Calder; woollens and worsteds, also carpets, cotton, iron, and steel. Pop. 98,100. (2) Cap., Nova Scotia, Canada; E. terminus of Canadian National Rlys.; fine harbour, open all the year round; iron foundries, machinery, furniture, boots and shoes; large sea trade, especially in fish, apples, lumber, and agricultural produce. Seat of Dalhousie Univ. Pop. 58,000.

Halle (*hă'le*), tn., Saxony, Prussia, on R. Saale, 20 m. N.E. of Leipzig; flourishing Hanse town in Middle Ages; famous univ.; oldest industry is salt production; paraffin and sugar refining, engineering; printing and publishing. Pop. 195,000.

Halmahe'ra ('great land'), or GILOLO, isl., Dutch E. Indies, E. of Celebes; consists of four peninsulas, each traversed by well-forested mountain chain 3,000 to 4,000 ft. high; several active volcanoes; sago, spices, coconuts; trepang and pearl shells. Area, 6,500 sq. m.; pop. 103,000.

Halm'stad, port, Sweden, on Kattegat, 76 m. S.S.E. of Göteborg; breweries, cloth manufactures, sawmills; salmon fishing; exports granite, wood pulp, timber. Pop. 23,000.

Hal'stead, mkt. tn., Essex, England, on R. Colne; silk and crape mill. Pop. 5,900.

Haltwhistle, mkt. tn., Northumberland, England, 13 m. w. of Hexham; collieries. Pop. 3,900.

Ham, East. See East Ham.

Ham, West. See West Ham.

Hamadan', tn., Persia, 185 m. s.w. of Tehran; important entrepôt of trade; extensive manufactures of leather, rugs, shellac. Pop. 30,000.

Ham'burg, free city and state, Germany, on N. branch of R. Elbe; second city of Germany; greatest port and commercial town on Continent. Old town intersected by canals, and surrounded by fine promenades. Docks cover huge area; part of harbour is a free port. Trades chiefly with Britain and America; chief exports: iron and steel, machinery, chemical manures, china and glassware, sugar, paper; chief manufactures are foodstuffs, beer, tobacco; shipbuilding, machinery, motor-cars, chemicals, furniture, musical and scientific instruments. Important schools of navigation and commerce. Hamburg state (area, 158 sq. m.) includes Bergedorf and Cuxhaven. Land produces cereals, vegetables, fruit, potatoes. University founded (1919). Pop. (city) 1,079,000; (state) 1,134,000.

Ham'eln, tn., Hanover, Prussia, at junction of Rs. Hamel and Weser; famous for mediæval buildings and legend of Pied Piper; sugar, distilling, papermaking. Pop. 26,000.

Hami (*hä'mē*), tn., Sinkiang, China, just w. of Gobi Desert; important trading centre. Pop. *c.* 6,000

Ham'ilton. (1) Munic. bur., Lanarkshire, Scotland, 10 m. S.E. of Glasgow; centre of rich iron and coal field; iron and brass foundries; cotton mills. Pop. 37,900. (2) City, Ohio, U.S.A., 20 m. N. of Cincinnati, on Great Miami R.; tobacco, hay, grain, vegetables; paper, safes, locks, steam pumps. Pop. 52,000. (3) City, Ontario, Canada, at w. end of Lake Ontario, 40 m. s.w. of Toronto; in 'garden of Ontario'; fruit-raising dist.; great transport facilities; varied metal manufactures, especially agricultural implements. Pop. 127,000. (4) Tn., Victoria, Australia, on R. Wannon, 198 m. w. of Melbourne; agricultural centre, butter factory and meat-preserving works. Pop. 5,200.

Hamm, tn., Westphalia, Prussia, on R. Lippe, 18 m. N.E. of Dortmund; iron foundries, wireworks; brushes, baskets, oil, varnish; thermal baths. Pop. 50,000.

Ham'merfest, port, Norway, on island of Kvalö; the most northerly town in Europe; exports fish, fish oil, hides, and down. Pop. 3,500.

Ham'mersmith, metropolitan bor., on N. side of R. Thames; part of w. London; iron, motor, and dye works; lead and oil mills. Pop. 135,500.

Ham'mond, city, Indiana, U.S.A., on R. Calumet, 18 m. S.E. of Chicago; iron and railway industries; bookbinding. Pop. 65,000.

Hamp'shire, Southamptonshire, or Hants, mar. co., s. England, bounded N. by Berks, w. by Wilts and Dorset, s. by Eng. Channel, E. by Sussex and Surrey. Isle of Wight is included in county, but is distinct from it for administrative purposes. On coast are Portsmouth Harbour and Southampton Water; inland are fertile valleys, hills, and woods; crossed by North Downs, in N.W. and W.; w. of Southampton Water is New Forest. Principal rivs., Lymington, Test, and Itchen, famous trout streams. Agriculture, sheep, cattle, and horse rearing, fishing, shipbuilding, brewing, tanning are carried on. Chief tns., Southampton (co. tn.), Portsmouth, and Winchester; many seaside resorts; Aldershot, military training centre. Area, 1,645 sq. m.; pop. (including Isle of Wight) 1,102,500.

Hamp'stead, N.W. residential suburb of London; *Hampstead Heath* is a popular pleasure ground. Pop. 88,900.

Hamp'ton, urb. dist., Middlesex,

England; part of Greater London, on R. Thames. *Hampton Court*, a former royal residence; fine gallery of paintings. Pop. 13,100.

Hanau (*hä'now*), tn., Hesse-Nassau, Prussia, on R. Main; gold and silver work; diamond cutting; brewing; chemicals, hats, gloves. Pop. 38,500.

Hands'worth. (1) N.W. suburb of Birmingham, Warwickshire, England. Pop. 75,000. (2) Urb. dist., Yorks, England, 4 m. S.E. of Sheffield; collieries and quarries. Pop. 16,000.

Hangchow, port, Chekiang, China, on Tsien-Tang R.; centre of silk manufacture; rice mills; trading centre; univ. Pop. 427,000.

Han'ko, port, Finland, 50 m. S.W. of Helsinki; exports butter, wood, paper; seaside resort. Pop. 7,000.

Hankow', riv. port, Hupeh, China, on R. Han, at junction with Yangtze Kiang; accessible to ocean steamers; large transit trade; centre of commerce and finance; iron and steel works; textiles; rice, oil, and flour mills. Pop. *c.* 1,500,000.

Han'ley, tn., Staffordshire, England, part of Stoke-upon-Trent; extensive potteries; coal and iron mines. Pop. 78,000.

Han'nibal, city, Missouri, U.S.A., on Mississippi R.; exports lumber, agricultural produce; flour mills, tobacco factories. Pop. 20,000.

Hanoi', cap. of Tongking and of French Indo-China, on Songkoi or Red R.; silks, cottons, furniture, matches, tobacco, pottery. Pop. 103,000.

Han'over. (1) Maritime prov., N.W. Prussia, traversed by Harz Mountains in S.E.; remainder forms part of great N. German plain, with immense stretches of heath; chief rivs., Elbe, Weser, Ems; numerous canals; well-cultivated in more fertile areas; rye, flax, potatoes, hops, tobacco, beet; minerals include coal, salt, silver, copper, iron ore, lead, asphalt; sheep, cattle, and horses reared; famous poultry rearing (esp. geese); principal tns., Hanover (cap.), Hildesheim, Osnabrück, Göttingen. Area, 14,898 sq. m.; pop. 3,191,000. (2) Cap. of above, on R. Leine; fine parks and suburbs, picture galleries, museums, libraries; hardware, chemicals, machinery, pianos, tobacco, rubber. Pop. 423,000.

Han'thawaddy, dist., Lower Burma, India; great plain in which rice is largely grown. Chief tn., Rangoon. Area, 1,866 sq. m.; pop. 492,000.

Han'well, urb. dist., part of Greater London, 10 m. W. of St. Paul's; electric material and furniture; mental hospital. Pop. 21,000.

Han-yang, city, Hupeh, China, at junction of R. Han with Yangtze Kiang; ironworks. Pop. 450,000.

Har'ar, prov. and tn., Abyssinia, 230 m. E. of Addis Ababa; prov. is fertile and produces much coffee; tn. trades in durra, skins, hides, ivory, cattle, and mules. Pop. (tn.) 40,000.

Har'bin, tn., central Manchuria, China, on R. Sungari; important rly. jn.; flour mills, soya bean works, distilleries, tanneries. Pop. *c.* 200,000.

Harbour Grace, tn., Newfoundland, 24 m. W. by S. of St. John's; has large but exposed harbour; trades in furs, fish, cod-liver oil. Pop. 3,800.

Har'burg, port, Hanover, Prussia, on R. Elbe; manufactures palm oil, rubber goods, chemicals; brewing and shipbuilding. Pop. 73,000.

Har'danger Fjord, inlet on W. coast, Norway, S. of Bergen; magnificent scenery; tourist resort.

Hardoi'. (1) Dist., United Provinces, India; much of it jungle. Area, 2,331 sq. m.; pop. 1,092,800. (2) Cap. of above, 60 m. N.W. of Lucknow; saltpetre works, wood carving; exp. grain. Pop. 14,000.

Hardwar', tn., United Provinces, India, on R. Ganges, 110 m. N.N.E. of Delhi; place of pilgrimage; every twelfth year a sacred festival is held. Pop. 30,000.

Harefield, vil., Middlesex, England, 4 m. N. of Uxbridge; asbestos works. Pop. 3,000.

Harfleur (*ar-floor*), port, Seine-Inférieure, France, 5 m. E. of Havre; potteries, distilleries, chemical works. Pop. 3,300.

Hari-Rud (*rood*), riv., Asia, rises on w. slope of Hindu Kush; flows w. through Afghanistan, turns N., finally losing itself in Tejend sands, w. of Merv. Length, *c.* 650 m.

Har'lech, tn., Merionethshire, N. Wales, on Irish Sea; tourist centre. Pop. 1,100.

Har'lingen, port, Friesland, Holland, on Zuider Zee; exp. dairy and farm produce; flax, fish. Pop. 10,000.

Harlow, anc. mkt. tn., Essex, England, on R. Stort, 5 m. N. of Epping; annual fair. Pop. 3,000.

Har'penden, urb. dist., Herts, England, 5½ m. s. of Luton; agriculture; hats. Pop. 8,300.

Harrington, urb. dist., Cumberland, England, 2 m. s. of Workington; coal mined and exported. Pop. 4,100.

Harris. See LEWIS-WITH-HARRIS.

Har'risburg, city, Pennsylvania, U.S.A., on Susquehanna R.; beautiful scenery; handsome capitol; manufactures machinery and other steel and iron goods; flour, shoes, cigarettes, and cotton goods. Pop. 80,000.

Har'rismith, tn., Orange Free State, S. Africa, 54 m. N.W. of Ladysmith; wool and hides; woollen factory; health resort. Pop. 2,500 whites.

Har'rison, tn., New Jersey, U.S.A., on Passaic R., opposite Newark; iron, steel, and brass manufactures. Pop. 17,000.

Har'rogate, tn., W. Riding, Yorks, England, 15 m. N. of Leeds; health resort, noted for saline, chalybeate, and sulphur springs. Pop. 39,800.

Har'row-on-the-Hill, tn., Middlesex, England; a N.W. part of Greater London; famous public school founded by John Lyon (1571); printing works. Pop. 26,400.

Hart'ford, cap. of Connecticut, U.S.A., at head of navigation of Connecticut R. Buildings include state capitol, Trinity Coll. on outskirts; manufactures small arms, machines, hardware, typewriters, electric appliances, aeroplanes, silver plate; tobacco. Pop. 164,000.

Har'tlepool, port, co. Durham, England, including munic. bor. of Hartlepool and co. bor. of W. Hartlepool. Large trade; engineering works, shipbuilding, iron and brass foundries, flour and paper mills, soap works. Pop. 88,700 (including W. Hartlepool, 68,100).

Harwich (*har'ich*), port and wat.-pl., Essex, England; packet station for Holland; fine docks; large export and import trade; manufactures of cement and fertilizers. Pop. 12,700.

Harzburg (*harts'boorg*), tn., Brunswick, Germany, on N. side of Harz Mts., 26 m. s. of Brunswick; health resort with mineral springs; manufactures jewellery. Pop. 6,200.

Harz Mountains (*harts*), mt. range, Germany, extending through part of Prussia, Brunswick, and Anhalt; s. slopes well forested; highest peak, Brocken (3,745 ft.), ascended by railway; rich in iron, copper, lead, silver, sulphur; numerous mineral springs. Length, 57 m.; breadth, 20 m.; area, 784 sq. m.

Hasa, AL, E. coast dist., Nejd, Arabia, on Persian Gulf; dates, pearls; white donkeys. Area, *c.* 30,000 sq. m.; pop. *c.* 150,000.

Haskovo. See KHASKOVO.

Has'land, par. and vil., Derbyshire, England, 2 m. S.E. of Chesterfield; coal and ironstone. Pop. 3,000.

Haslemere (*hā'zel-mēr*), tn., Surrey, England, 12 m. S.W. of Guildford; residential centre. Pop. 4,300.

Has'lingden, tn., Lancs, England, 8 m. N. by W. of Bury; cotton goods; coal mines, ironworks. Pop. 16,600.

Haspe (*has'pe*), tn., Westphalia, Prussia, 10 m. N.E. of Barmen; iron, steel, and hardware. Pop. 26,000.

Has'san, dist., Mysore, India; prod. coffee, cereals. Chief tn., Hassan, 60 m. N.W. of Mysore. Area, 2,665 sq. m.; pop. 584,000.

Has'selt, tn., Limbourg, Belgium; distilleries and breweries. Pop. 21,200.

Hastings (*hāst'ings*). (1) Co. bor., Sussex, England; fashionable wat.-pl. and one of Cinque Ports; anc. castle and churches; joined to St.

Leonards, now incorporated with Hastings. Small shipbuilding and fishing industry. Pop. 65,200. (2) Tn., North Island, New Zealand, 12 m. s.s.w. of Napier; gelatine and refrigerating works. Severe earthquake, 1931. Pop. 15,500.

Hatch End, hamlet, Middlesex, England, 2 m. N.W. of Harrow; part of Greater London; coal wharf. Pop. 3,000.

Hat'field, or BISHOP'S HATFIELD, mkt. tn., Herts, England, on R. Lea, 17½ m. by rail N. of London; rly. centre; Queen Elizabeth was a prisoner in the old palace before her accession to the throne. Hatfield House, the seat of the Earl of Salisbury, contains many historical documents. Pop. 5,800.

Hath'ersage, par. and vil., Derbyshire, England, on R. Derwent, 10 m. N. of Bakewell; gritstone quarries; pins and steel wire; pre-Roman remains in vicinity. Pop. 2,000.

Hath'ras, tn., United Provs., India, 21 m. S. of Aligarh; exports sugar, grain, cotton, oil-seeds, and ghee; noted for carved work. Pop. 39,000.

Hat'teras, CAPE, low promontory, N. Carolina, U.S.A.; on sandbank; violent storms make navigation difficult.

Hat'tiesburg, tn., Mississippi, U.S.A., 105 m. N.E. of New Orleans; hardware; turpentine, resin. Pop. 13,000.

Hat'tingen, tn., Westphalia, Prussia, on R. Ruhr; iron and steel manufactures; tobacco. Pop. 14,000.

Haugesund (*how'ge-zoond*), port, Norway, 35 m. N. of Stavanger; fishing centre for herring, lobsters, and mackerel; woollen goods and margarine. Pop. 17,000.

Haute-Garonne (*ōt-ga-ron'*), dep., s.w. France, crossed by R. Garonne; produces timber, cereals, wine, and fruit; dairy farming; white marble quarries; mineral springs. Chief tn., Toulouse. Area, 2,457 sq. m.; pop. 425,000.

Haute-Loire (*ōt-lwär*), dep., S.E. France; surface mountainous; crossed by R. Loire; coal, timber, cereals, lace, silk, paper. Chief tn., Le Puy. Area, 1,930 sq. m.; pop. 269,000.

Haute-Marne (*ōt-marn'*), dep., N.E. France; surface slopes upwards from N. to plateau of Langres in S.; crossed by R. Marne; one-fourth covered by forests; cereals, vegetables, wine, and iron. Chief tn., Chaumont. Area, 2,420 sq. m.; pop. 199,000.

Hautes-Alpes (*ōtz-alp'*), dep., S.E. France; mountainous in E.; lower valleys have Mediterranean type of vegetation; drained by R. Durance; sheep and cattle are raised. Chief tn., Gap. Area, 2,178 sq. m.; pop. 89,300.

Haute-Saône (*ōt-sōn'*), dep., E. France; crossed by R. Saône; nearly half surface under cultivation; cereals, cherries, apples, plums, tobacco; iron, steel, and copper works, cotton manufacture; coal mined at Ronchamp. Chief tn., Vesoul. Area, 2,074 sq. m.; pop. 228,300.

Haute-Savoie (*ōt-sa-vwä'*), dep., E. France; mountainous; beautiful scenery; white wine; little agriculture; cattle, poultry; cheese. Chief tn., Annecy. Area, 1,774 sq. m.; pop. 236,000.

Hautes-Pyrénées (*ōt-pē-rā-nā'*), dep. s.w. France; southern part includes central group of Pyrenees; principal rivs., Gave de Pau, Adour, and Neste; mineral springs abound; lead, zinc, marble worked; cattle, sheep, horses; fruit growing and wine. Chief tns., Tarbes, Lourdes. Area, 1,750 sq. m.; pop. 186,000.

Haute-Vienne (*ōt-vē-en'*), dep., central France, crossed by Rs. Vienne, Isle; produces fruits, cereals, porcelain; chestnuts largely grown; cattle and sheep reared. Chief tn., Limoges. Area, 2,119 sq. m.; pop. 350,200.

Hautmont (*ō-mon'*), tn., Nord, France, 18 m. S.E. of Valenciennes; sugar, glass, pottery. Pop. 15,000.

Haut-Rhin. See ALSACE-LORRAINE.

Havä'na, or HABANA, cap. and port of Cuba, on N. coast; chief commercial city of W. Indies. Consists of old or inner town and well-laid-out new part. State univ.; splendid harbour with strong fortifications; chief industries: Havana cigars, sugar, chocolate, coffee, rum, molasses, woollen fabrics, and straw hats. Pop. 581,100.

Hav'ant, mkt. tn., Hants, England, 6 m. N.E. of Portsmouth; brewing, tanning; small trade in timber and coal. Pop. 4,300.

Hä'vel, riv., Prussia; rises in Mecklenburg; joined by R. Spree at Spandau; unites with R. Elbe above Wittenberge. Length, 220 m. Partly canalized.

Hav'erfordwest (or *här'ford-west*), port and mkt. tn., Pembroke, S. Wales; picturesque town built round castle; agricultural produce. Pop. 6,100.

Haverhill. (1) (*hāv'ril*) City, Massachusetts, U.S.A., 33 m. N. of Boston; boots and shoes; woollens; bricks. Pop. 49,000. (2) (*hā'ver-il*) Mkt. tn., Suffolk, England, on S.W. border; textiles, horse-hair cloth. Pop. 3,800.

Havre (*ä'vr*), or LE HAVRE DE GRACE, second port of France, on estuary of R. Seine; large shipbuilding yards; ropes, wire, machinery, oils, chemicals, cotton goods; petroleum pipe line to Paris. Pop. 158,000.

Hawaiian Islands (*ha-wī'ē-an*), called SANDWICH ISLANDS by Captain Cook, in midst of N. Pacific Ocean, form a terr. of U.S.A. There are twelve islands (eight inhabited), stretching 300 m. E.S.E. to W.N.W. The inhabited islands are: Hawaii (4,015 sq. m.), Maui, Oahu, Kauai, Molokai, Lanai, Niihau, Kahulaui. Hawaii has Mauna Loa ('Great Mt.'), the largest volcano in the world, still active, and extending about 75 by 50 m., and over 13,600 ft. in height; also Mauna Kea ('White Mt.'), 13,825 ft. About 16 m. S.E. lies hill called Kilauea, with crater over 8 m. in circumference. Maui (728 sq. m.) has two large mts., one of which, Mauna Haleakala (*c.* 10,030 ft.) has largest pit-crater in world (*c.* 19 sq. m. in area). Molokai, a small mountainous island, has a leper settlement. Climate is cool and healthy. There are large quantities of pumice, sandstone, sulphur; considerable forests, and soil is highly fertile. Irrigation is extensively used. Sugar and pineapples are most important products; coffee, honey, hides, fruit, rice, bananas, tobacco, cotton also exported. Stock ranching and dairy farming. Honololu, cap. of the group, lies on S. coast of Oahu. Total area, 6,449 sq. m.; pop. 256,000.

Hawarden (*här'den*), mkt. tn., Flint, N. Wales, 6 m. W. by S. of Chester; coal mines, clay fields; iron, and chemical works. Pop. 8,000.

Haw'ick, burgh, Roxburghshire, Scotland, on R. Teviot; hosiery, tweeds, blankets; dyeworks, tanneries; large live-stock sales. Pop. 17,100.

Hawk'hurst, tn., Kent, England, 12 m. S.E. of Tunbridge Wells; hop growing. Pop. 3,100.

Hä'worth, urb. dist. and tn., W. Riding, Yorks, England, 4 m. S.S.W. of Keighley; worsted, alpaca, and mohair factories. Residence of Brontë family. Pop. 5,900.

Hay'dock, tn., Lancs, England, 3 m. N.E. of St. Helens; iron working and coal mining. Pop. 10,400.

Hayes and Harlington, urb. dist., W. Middlesex, England; part of Greater London. Pop. 23,600.

Hayle (*hāl*), or HEYL, urb. dist. and port, Cornwall, England, 4 m. S.E. of St. Ives; engineering, shipbuilding; roperies; coal, iron, timber, and grain imported. Pop. 900.

Hayl'ing Island, isl., Hants, England, in S.E. of co.; seaside resort with fine sands; rly. bridge to mainland. Length, 4 m.; breadth, 1½ m.

Hay'ward's Heath, urb. dist., Sussex, England, 13 m. N. of Brighton; large cattle sale. Pop. 5,400.

Hazára, dist., N.W. Frontier Prov., India; lies between mountain ranges; bounded on W. by R. Indus; sheep and cattle raised; important forests. Area, 3,391 sq. m.; pop. 560,000.

Hazaribagh (*ha-za-rē-bag'*), dist., Bihar and Orissa, India; important coal and mica-producing area. Cap.

Hazaribagh, 210 m. N.W. of Calcutta. Area, 7,020 sq. m.; pop. 1,277,000.

Hazebrouck (*az-brook'*), tn., Nord, France, 25 m. S. of Dunkirk; rly. jn.; textiles; trade in grain and live-stock. Pop. 12,000.

Ha'zel Grove and Bramhall, urb. dist., N.E. Cheshire, England, 2¼ m. S.E. of Stockport; famous manor-house. Pop. 13,300.

Ha'zleton, tn., Pennsylvania, U.S.A., 34 m. S.S.W. of Scranton; centre of rich coal dist.; textiles, iron, sheet steel. Pop. 39,000.

Head'ington, par. and vil., Oxfordshire, England, 2½ m. E. of Oxford; building-stone quarries; favourite walk for Oxford students; hunting lodge of Saxon kings. Pop. (par.) 7,000.

Hean'or (or *hā'nor*), mkt. tn. and urb. dist., Derbyshire, England, 10 m. N.W. of Nottingham; coal, iron, and hosiery. Pop. 22,400.

Heart's Content, port, Avalon Peninsula, Newfoundland, 40 m. N.W. of St. John's; terminus of three Atlantic cables; excellent harbour; shipbuilding, fishing. Pop. 1,100.

Heath'field, par. and vil., Sussex, England, 8 m. N. of Hailsham; chicken rearing for London market. Pop. (par.) 6,000.

Heaton Norris, tn., Lancs, England; suburb of Stockport; iron, cotton, thread; bleaching. Pop. 11,000.

Heb'burn, tn., Durham, England, on R. Tyne, 4 m. N.E. of Gateshead; shipbuilding, engineering, cement, chemicals, ropes and sails. Pop. 24,100.

Heb'den Bridge, tn., W. Riding, Yorks, England, 9 m. N.W. of Halifax; textiles, dyeworks, foundries. Pop. 6,300.

Hebrides (*heb're-dēz*), or WESTERN ISLES, large group of islands extending over 200 m. along W. coast of Scotland; divided by Little Minch into *Outer Hebrides* (Lewis and Harris, N. Uist, Benbecula, S. Uist, and Barra) and *Inner Hebrides* (Skye, Rum, Eigg, Coll, Tyree, Mull, Staffa, Iona, Colonsay, Jura, and Islay). Scenery is wild and picturesque; climate mild and moist; industries: sheep rearing, fishing, home-spun tweeds, distilling. Large deer forests. Area, 2,812 sq. m.; pop. 70,500.

Hebrides, NEW. See NEW HEBRIDES.

He'bron, tn., Palestine, 20 m. S.S.W. of Jerusalem; contains traditional tomb of Abraham and other patriarchs. Modern city is called El Khalil, and manufactures glass and leather water-skins. Pop. 16,600.

Heck'mondwike, tn., W. Riding, Yorks, England, 10 m. S.W. of Leeds; blankets, woollens, carpets, rugs. Pop. 9,000.

Hed'on, bor., E. Riding, Yorks, England, 5 m. E. of Hull; formerly important seapt., now inland; famous church. Pop. 1,500.

Heerlen (*hār'len*), tn., Limburg, Holland, 9 m. N.N.W. of Aachen; in centre of new coalfield. Pop. 42,000.

Heidelberg (*hī'del-berg*). (1) City, Baden, Germany; beautifully situated on R. Neckar, surrounded by hills covered with forests and vineyards; anc. castle, with great vat capable of holding 50,000 gallons of wine; celebrated univ. (1385); beer, wine, and book industry; scientific instruments. Pop. 73,000. (2) Tn., Transvaal, S. Africa, 30 m. S.E. of Johannesburg; sanatorium. Pop. 3,500.

Heidenheim (*hī'den-hīm*), tn., Württemberg, Germany, 20 m. N.N.E. of Ulm; textiles, brewing, tobacco, dyeworks. Pop. 19,000.

Heilbron (*hīl'bron*), div. and tn., Orange Free State, S. Africa, 75 m. S. of Johannesburg; coal mines; livestock and maize. Pop. (tn.) 2,000.

Heilbronn', tn., Württemberg, Germany, on R. Neckar; gold, silver, and iron articles, machinery, motor-cars, beer, tobacco, chemicals. Pop. 46,000.

Hejaz (*hezh'az*), former kingdom, Arabia, on shores of Red Sea, now incorporated with Nejd. Almost all stony desert; in S. some cultivation, dates, wheat, and barley being chief products. Contains sacred cities of Mecca and Medina; chief seaports, Jidda and Yambu. Area, *c.* 150,000 sq. m.; pop. 800,000.

Hek'la ('mantle' or 'cap'), active volcano, Iceland, near S.W. coast, 5,108 ft. high.

Hel'der, fort. port, N. Holland, at W. entrance to Zuider Zee; protected against sea by embankments of enormous strength; prov. can be flooded from here. Pop. 30,000.

Hel'ena. (1) Cap. of Montana, U.S.A., centre of dist. rich in gold, silver, and iron, and in agricultural produce; smelting, quartz-mills. Pop. 14,000. (2) City, Arkansas, U.S.A., on R. Mississippi; head of ocean-going navigation; exports cotton and lumber. Pop. 9,000.

Hel'ensburgh, tn. and wat.-pl., Dumbartonshire, Scotland, on Firth of Clyde; mainly residential; close by is Craigendoran pier for Clyde steamer traffic. Pop. 8,900.

Hel'icon, mountain range, Bœotia, Greece; traditional home of Muses.

Hel'igoland, or HELGOLAND, isl., North Sea, 28 m. from mouth of R. Elbe; contains land-locked harbour capable of sheltering large ships; seaside resort. Ceded by Britain to Germany (1890); powerfully fortified by Germany. During Great War formed forward base for German fleet; by Treaty of Versailles the fortifications, harbours, and military establishments were destroyed, and defences prohibited for the future. Area, ¾ sq. m.; pop. 2,600.

Hellin (*āl-yēn'*), tn., S.E. Spain, 46 m. N.W. of Murcia; makes leather, pottery, cloth. Pop. 11,000.

Hel'mand, river, Afghanistan, rises in W. Hindu Kush, and flows for about 600 m. S.W., W., and N. to Lake Hamun.

Helmond (*hel'mont*), tn., N. Brabant, Holland, on R. Aa, 26 m. S.S.W. of Nijmegen; textile industries; margarine, soap, tobacco. Pop. 25,000.

Helms'dale, fishing port, Sutherlandshire, Scotland, 29 m. N.E. of Dornoch. Pop. 1,500

Helm'stedt, tn., Brunswick, Germany, 20 m. S.E. of Brunswick; furniture, soap, tobacco, earthenware. Pop. 17,000.

Hels'by, vil., Cheshire, England, 8 m. N.E. of Chester; rubber and cable manufactures. Pop. 2,000.

Hel'singborg, port, Sweden, on the Sound; exports dairy produce, timber, paper, and iron; manufactures pottery, and has copper works, india-rubber works, breweries, and sugar refineries. Pop. 53,000.

Helsingör', formerly ELSINORE, port, Denmark, on Zealand I.; sawmills, shipbuilding; exports agricultural produce. Pop. 15,000.

Helsink'i, formerly HELSINGFORS, cap. and port of Finland, on Gulf of Finland; splendid harbour, guarded by fortress of Sveaborg; exports timber, corn, and butter; manufactures sugar, beer, spirits, carpets; univ.; cathedral. Pop. 216,000.

Hel'ston, market tn., Cornwall, England, on R. Cober, 11 m. S.W. of Falmouth; dairy farming centre; summer resort. Pop. 2,500.

Helvel'lyn, mountain in Lake Dist., England, between Thirlmere and Ullswater. Height, 3,118 ft.

Hem'el Hemp'stead, mkt. tn., Herts, England, 5 m. W. of St. Albans; paper making, iron founding; corn and cattle trade. Pop. 15,100.

Hems'worth, urb. dist., W. Riding, Yorks, England, 8 m. S.E. of Wakefield; coal mining and bricks. Pop. 13,000.

Hen'derson, city, W. Kentucky, U.S.A., on R. Ohio; cotton, tobacco; coal mining. Pop. 12,200.

Hen'don, tn., Middlesex, England, on R. Brent; part of Greater London; important aviation centre; aeroplane factories and flying schools. Pop. 115,700.

Hengelo (*hen-he-lō'*), tn., Overyssel, Holland; cotton factories, dyeworks, breweries. Pop. 33,000.

Hénin-Liétard (*ā-nan-le-ā-tar'*), tn., Pas-de-Calais, France, 12 m. N.E. of Arras; coal mines, sugar refineries, and tanneries. Pop. 17,800.

Hen'ley-on-Thames, mkt. tn., Oxfordshire, England, on R. Thames; favourite summer resort, noted for its beautiful surroundings; famous annual regatta. Market gardening. Pop. 6,600.

Hennebont (*hen-bon'*), tn., Morbihan, N.W. France, 6 m. N.E. of Lorient; agricultural produce; tin-plating. Pop. 6,200.

Henzad'a. (1) Dist., Irrawaddy, Lower Burma; rice and tobacco. Area, 2,872 sq. m.; pop. 551,000. (2) Chief tn. of above, 75 m. N.N.W. of Rangoon; rice mills and sawmills. Pop. 24,000.

Herat', city, W. Afghanistan, situated on Hari Rud, 2,500 ft. above sea-level; once a large city with magnificent buildings, now a mass of ruins. Surrounding country fertile and well irrigated. Pop. *c.* 10,000.

Hérault (*ā-rō*), maritime dep., S. France; surface rises to Cévennes in N.W.; drained by Rs. Hérault, Orb; salt, wine, fruits, olives, chestnuts; sheep reared, and Roquefort cheese made from their milk. Chief tn., Montpellier. Area, 2,402 sq. m.; pop. 488,200.

Her'berton, tn., Queensland, Australia, 70 m. N.N.W. of Rockingham; tin, copper, bismuth. Pop. 2,800.

Hercegovina. See BOSNIA AND HERCEGOVINA.

Hercula'neum, anc. city, Italy, at E. base of Mt. Vesuvius. In A.D. 79 it was overwhelmed by an eruption. Since early 18th cent., excavations have been going on. The discoveries render possible the reconstruction of the domestic life of the ancients, and many beautiful wall-paintings and statues have been brought to light, as well as philosophical MSS., coins, mosaics. It was an important town at time of its destruction.

Her'cules, PILLARS OF, two rocks which stand on either side of Strait of Gibraltar, that on European side being Rock of Gibraltar, formerly called Calpe; and on African side Ceuta, formerly Abyla.

Her'eford ('ford of the army'), co. tn., Herefordshire, England, on R. Wye; beautiful cathedral with library of chained books; agricultural produce; cider. Pop. 24,200.

Her'efordshire, inland co., England, on Welsh border, bounded N. by Shropshire, E. by Worcestershire, S. by Gloucestershire and Monmouth, W. by Brecon and Radnor; rich, fertile county, well watered by R. Wye and its tribs.; in E. are Malvern Hills and in S.W. Black Mts. Wheat, barley, and hops; apple and pear orchards; celebrated cattle, sheep, and horses; cider-making main industry; salmon and trout fishing; limestone quarries at Ledbury; some iron foundries. Chief tns., Hereford (cap.), Leominster, Ross, and Ledbury. Area, 842 sq. m.; pop. 111,800.

Her'ford, tn., N.E. Westphalia, Prussia, 8 m. N.E. of Bielefeld; cotton and flax manufactures, carpets, furniture, cigars. Pop. 36,000.

Herisau (*hār'is-ow*), tn., N.E. Switzerland, 7 m. N.W. of Appenzell; muslin, embroidery; bleach and dye works. Pop. 15,000.

Hermannstadt. See SIBIU.

Her'mon (modern JEBEL ESH-SHEIKH), triple snow-clad peak, S. Syria, the highest mountain (9,200 ft.) of Anti-Lebanon range; is encircled with ruins of anc. temples dedicated to Baal.

Hermosillo (*her-mo-sēl'yo*), city, cap. of Sonora, Mexico, 80 m. N. of Guaymas; mint, distilleries, and flour mills; sugar, silver. Pop. *c.* 18,000.

Hermoupolis. See SYROS.

Her'ne, tn., Westphalia, Prussia, 12 m. W. of Dortmund; coal and coke; boiler and ammonia works. Pop. 68,000.

Herne Bay, wat.-pl., N. coast of Kent, England. Pop. 11,200.

Herne Hill, residential suburb of London, Surrey, England, 4 m. S. of St. Paul's.

Hernösand (*her'noo-sant*), tn. and port, Sweden, on Gulf of Bothnia; timber products are exported; engine factories and sawmills. Pop. 12,000.

Her'stal, tn., Belgium, 2 m. N. of

Liége; manufactures iron and steel goods. Pop. 23,000.

Hertford (*här'ford*), co. tn., Herts, England, 24 m. N. of London; 2 m. S. is Haileybury Coll.; brewing, malting; brushes, gloves. Pop. 11,400.

Hert'fordshire, or HERTS, inland co., England, bounded N. by Cambridge, E. by Essex, S. by Middlesex, S.W. by Buckingham, N.W. by Bedford. Beautiful undulating county of hills, valleys, parks, and woods; in N. is branch of Chiltern Hills. Principal rivs. are Lea, Stort, Colne, and artificial New River. Wheat is principal grain grown; water-cress, fruits, and roses cultivated; cattle raised; manufacturing industries small; brewing at Watford; straw hats, paper making, tanning, and brick making. Chief tns., Hertford (cap.), St. Albans, Hemel Hempstead, Watford, Hitchin, and Letchworth. Area, 632 sq. m.; pop. 401,200.

Hertogenbosch. See 'S HERTOGENBOSCH.

Herzegovina. See BOSNIA AND HERCEGOVINA.

Hes'se, republic of Germany, comprising the provinces Oberhessen, Starkenburg Rheinhessen, and eleven small enclaves; watered by Rs. Rhine, Lahn, Main, Fulda; cereals, root crops, fruit, tobacco, and vines; famous mineral springs; iron, salt, manganese ore; industries: leather goods, chemicals, furniture, hardware and machinery, tobacco, wine. Chief tns., Darmstadt (cap.), Mainz, Worms, Offenbach. Area, 2,970 sq. m.; pop. 1,347,000.

Hesse-Nassau (*hes'e-nas'ow*), prov., Prussia, Germany; surface mostly hilly; magnificent forests; wine, fruits; iron, coal, copper, manganese are mined; mineral springs; much manufacturing. Chief tns., Cassel (cap.) and Frankfurt on Main. Area, 6,063 sq. m.; pop. 2,397,000.

Hessle (*hes'el*), urb. dist., E. Riding, Yorks, England, W. suburb of Hull. Pop. 6,400.

Hes'ton and Isleworth (*i'zel-worth*), urb. dist. and outlying suburb of London, Middlesex, England, 12 m. W. by S. of St. Paul's; residential quarter; market gardening. Pop. 75,400.

Hes'wall, par. and vil., Cheshire, England, on estuary of R. Dee, 3½ m. N.W. of Neston; fisheries. Pop. (par.) 5,000.

Het'ton-le-Hole, par. and mkt. tn., Durham, England, 5 m. N.E. of Durham; coal mines. Pop. 17,700.

Hex'ham, tn., Northumberland, England, on R. Tyne, 20 m. W. of Newcastle; leather gloves; market gardening centre. Pop. 8,900.

Hey'sham, port and wat.-pl., Lancs, England, on Morecambe Bay; part of Morecambe; L.M.S. Rly. packet station for Ireland and Isle of Man. Pop. 5,000.

Heyst (*hīst*), or HEYST-SUR-MER, wat.-pl., W. Flanders, Belgium, 8 m. N. of Bruges; favourite seaside resort.

Hey'wood, munic. bor. and par., Lancs, England, 8 m. N.N.E. of Manchester; coal mining, cotton and chemical manufacture, boiler works, railway wagons. Pop. 26,000.

Hidalgo (*ē-dal'go*), state, Mexico; hilly in N. and E.; S. and W., undulating plain; stock raising, mining, and agriculture; produces silver, gold, copper, mercury; also cereals, coffee, beans, sugar, tobacco. Cap. Pachuca, 55 m. N.N.E. of Mexico city. Area, 8,637 sq. m.; pop. 622,000.

Hierro. See FERRO.

High'am Fer'rers, munic. bor., Northants, England, 5 m. E. of Wellingborough; boots and shoes. Pop. 2,900.

High'bridge, urb. dist., Somerset, England, on R. Brue, 6¼ m. by rail N. of Bridgwater; port; rly. jn.; makes bricks, roofing tiles, and drain pipes. Pop. 2,600.

Highgate, residential suburb of London, England, 4 m. N.W. of St. Paul's.

Highland Park, city, Michigan, U.S.A., near Detroit; motor-car factories; partly residential. Pop. 53,000.

High Point, city, N. Carolina, U.S.A., 80 m. W. of Raleigh; textiles, furniture, and wooden articles. Pop. 37,000.

High'worth, tn., Wilts, England, 6 m. N.E. of Swindon; formerly a mkt. tn. Pop. 2,150.

High Wycombe. See WYCOMBE.

Hi'iumaa, formerly DAGÖ, isl., Baltic Sea, belonging to Estonia; N. of Saare Maa; cattle rearing, fishing. Area, 367 sq. m. Pop. 15,000.

Hil'den, tn., Rhineland, Prussia, 8 m. S.E. of Düsseldorf; silk, cotton, printing; tanneries, brickworks. Pop. 20,000.

Hil'denborough, par. and vil., Kent, England, 2 m. N.W. of Tonbridge; makes cricket bats and balls. Pop. (par.) 1,750.

Hildesheim (*hil'des-hīm*), tn., Hanover, Prussia, at base of Harz Mts., with fine cathedral; chief industries: machinery, vehicles, agricultural implements, church bells, bricks, sugar refining, cigars, brewing, and tanning. Pop. 59,000.

Hil'la, tn., vilayet of Baghdad, Iraq, on R. Euphrates; trade in rice, barley, and wheat. Pop. *c.* 30,000.

Hill Tippera. See TRIPURA.

Hil'versum, tn., Holland, 16 m. S.E. of Amsterdam; floorcloth, carpets; summer resort. Pop. 52,000.

Himalayas (*him-äl'yas* or *him-a-lā'yas*), highest system of mountains in world, stretching, in irregular curve, almost 1,600 m. along N. boundary of India, with average breadth of 200 m.; they lie mainly between Rs. Indus and Brahmaputra. Rising steeply from Ganges plain is a range (some 4,000 to 5,000 ft.) between which and the higher ranges lie the fertile valleys of Nepal and Bhutan. The greater system, starting from the Pamir Plateau in extreme N.W., is divided into two main parallel chains, one lying N. of the other. The N. chain, forming a watershed between India and Tibet, has been little explored; its only part under 16,000 ft. is Dras Pass (*c.* 11,300 ft.), which leads to Kashmir; the Niti Pass (*c.* 16,700 ft.) connects India with Sinkiang. The S. chain, consisting of lofty snowclad peaks, includes the highest mountains in the world—many over 20,000 ft.; the highest is Mt. Everest (29,140 ft.); other peaks are K^2 or Mt. Godwin-Austen (*c.* 28,260 ft.); Kanchenjunga (*c.* 28,150 ft.). From this chain flow the Ganges, Indus, Brahmaputra, and many of their tribs.; on its slopes stand many hill-stations, including Simla, Darjeeling, Murree, Almora. There are numerous glaciers, and the snow-line is higher on the Indian side than on the Tibetan; metal ores exist and gold is worked in Tibet.

Hinck'ley, tn., Leicestershire, England, 13 m. S.W. of Leicester; hosiery, boots, pottery. Pop. 16,000.

Hindenburg (*hin'den-boorg*), formerly ZABRZE, tn., S.E. Silesia, Prussia, 7 m. S.W. of Beuthen; manufactures chemicals, beer, glass, wire; coal mining. Pop. 73,000.

Hind'erwell, urb. dist., N. Riding, Yorks, England, on coast N. of Whitby; iron mines and fisheries. Pop. 2,100.

Hindley (*hĭnd'ley*), urb. dist., Lancs, England, 2 m. S.E. of Wigan; cannel coal, cotton mills, iron works. Pop. 21,600.

Hindu Kush (*hin'doo koosh'*), range of mts. in Central Asia, stretching S.W. from Pamirs to N. of Kabul, over 350 m. long, with breadth of 200 m.; divides Kabul and Oxus basins. Contains sources of many important rivers; crossed by many passes. Tirach Mir (25,400 ft.), on frontier of Chitral, is highest peak.

Hinojosa del Duque (*ē-no-ho'sa-del-doo'kā*), tn., Cordoba, Spain, 48 m. N.N.W. of Cordoba; copper mining; linen and woollens. Pop. 11,000.

Hip'perholme (*-hōm*), urb. dist., W. Riding, Yorks, England, 2 m. N.E. of Halifax; tanning and stone quarrying. Pop. 5,400.

Hirosaki (*hē-ro-sä'ke*), tn., N. Honshu, Japan; green lacquer ware. Pop. 37,500.

Hiroshima (*hē-ro-she'ma*), tn., S.W. Honshu, Japan; lacquer and bronze manufactures; opposite tn. is sacred 'Island of Light,' with celebrated

Shinto temple, one of three wonders of Japan. Pop. 196,000.

Hirschberg (*hĕrsh'berg*), tn., Silesia, Prussia, 26 m. s.w. of Liegnitz; laces, linens, cotton, paper, porcelain, wine, and cider. Pop. 29,000.

Hirson (*ēr-son*), tn., Aisne, France, on R. Oise; has foundries, nail and glass works. Pop. 11,000.

Hissar'. (1) Dist., Brit. India, one of administrative divs. of Punjab; borders on Rajputana desert; inadequately watered and is subject to famines; produces in E. cattle, rice, barley, wheat, and sesame; saltpetre. Area, 5,217 sq. m.; pop. 817,000. (2) Cap. of above, 100 m. N.W. of Delhi; large cattle fairs. Pop. 22,000. (3) Mountainous prov., Tadzhik, U.S.S.R.; traversed by tribs. of Oxus; fertile valleys produce cereals, cotton, flax; alluvial gold. Cap. Hissar, 80 m. S.S.W. of Samarqand, famous for damascened swords. Pop. 10,000.

Hitch'in, urb. dist. and mkt. tn., N.W. Herts, England; lavender and peppermint; chalk working. Pop. 14,400.

Hjörring (*hyoor'ing*), tn., Denmark, 30 m. s.w. of the Skaw; textiles, engineering, bricks, tobacco. Pop. 11,000.

Hoang-ho. See HWANG-HO.

Ho'bart, cap. of Tasmania, on estuary of R. Derwent; centre of large fruit-growing dist.; excellent harbour; has Parliament House, Government House, and univ.; exports are fruit, hops, grain, timber, wool, and minerals; breweries, jam factories, flour and sawmills, potteries, iron foundries, and tanneries. Pop. (with suburbs) 59,000.

Ho'boken. (1) Tn., New Jersey, U.S.A., on R. Hudson; exp. coal; iron foundries; silk and lead pencil manufactures. Pop. 57,000. (2) Tn., Belgium, on R. Schelde; suburb of Antwerp; shipbuilding yards. Pop. 32,000.

Höchst (*hoochst*), tn., Hesse-Nassau, Prussia, on R. Main, 6 m. w. of Frankfurt; machinery, dyes, chemicals; tanning and brewing. Pop. 31,000.

Hoddesdon (*hodz'don*), tn., Herts, England, 4 m. S.E. of Hertford; an angling resort; brewing. Pop. 6,800.

Hodeida (*ho-dā'da*), fort. tn. and port, Yemen, Arabia, on Red Sea; exports coffee, grain, dates, cotton. Pop. 35,000.

Hod-Mezö-Vasarhely (*hōd-meyoo-vä'-shar-hā-ly*), tn., Hungary, 16 m. N.E. of Szeged; dist. very fertile; wheat, grapes, melons, tobacco; cattle, horses, pigs, and sheep are reared. Pop. 62,000.

Hodonin (*ho'don-yĕn*), formerly GÖDING, tn., Moravia, Czechoslovakia, 45 m. N. of Bratislava; manufactures tobacco, sugar, and glass; lignite mines. Pop. 12,000.

Hof (*hōf*), tn., N.E. Bavaria, Germany, on R. Saale, on N.E. slopes of Fichtelgebirge; manufactures textiles, sugar, dyes, chemicals, beer, machinery, hardware. Pop. 41,000.

Hohenlimburg (*ho'en-lim'boorg*), tn., Westphalia, Prussia, 12 m. S.S.E. of Dortmund; iron and steel goods, dyes, textiles. Pop. 16,000.

Hohensalza. See INOWROCLAW.

Hohenstein - Ernstthal (*ho'en-stīn-erns'täl*), tn., Saxony, Germany, 10 m. w. by s. of Chemnitz; textiles, machinery, needles; arsenic mines in vicinity. Pop. 17,000.

Hohenzollern Canal (*ho'en-tsol'ern*), runs 60 m. due N. from Berlin to R. Oder at Stettin; affords access for large vessels from the Baltic.

Hokitika (*hō-ke-tē'ka*), tn., w. coast, South Island, New Zealand; brewing, tanning; sawmills; great gold rush in 1865. Pop. 2,500.

Hokkai'do ('North Sea road'), N. part of Japanese Empire, including Hokkaido or Yezo I., the Kuriles, and adjacent islets; interior forested; timber cutting, fishing, paper making. Area, 34,084 sq. m.; pop. *c.* 2,000,000.

Hol'beach, mkt. tn., Lincs, England, formerly on Wash, now 6 m. inland; agricultural industries; brewing; mustard growing. Pop. 6,100.

Holborn (*hō'born*), central metropolitan bor., London, England; contains City Temple, Lincoln's Inn,

Gray's Inn, Brit. Museum, and many other public buildings. Pop. 38,800.

Hol'derness, flat and fertile peninsula, Yorks, England; a div. of the E. Riding. Pop. 56,000.

Hol'land, (1) or THE NETHERLANDS, mar. kingdom, N.W. Europe, consisting mainly of deltaic deposits of Rs. Rhine, Maas, and Schelde; much of surface below sea-level, and protected by embankments and sand dunes; highest point 655 ft. Bounded by Germany on E., Belgium on S., and elsewhere by North Sea. Within historic times sea invaded land, transforming Flevo lake into the Zuider Zee (South Sea); anc. continental coast-line lay along Frisian Islands, now separated by the Wadden (Shallows) from the mainland. Since 16th cent. over a million acres have been reclaimed from sea, lake, and river; work of reclaiming Zuider Zee was begun in 1924. Four separate areas to be drained cover total area of 523,000 acres, with fresh-water lake in centre. Estuary of Rs. Maas and Schelde contains many islands—*e.g.* N. and S. Beveland, Walcheren. Canals and waterways (2,000 m.) much more important than railways (2,300 m.) and metalled roads. Climate resembles that of England, but is more variable. Principal occupations are grazing and agriculture. Cattle of superior breeds give rise to trade in butter and cheese prepared in factories (esp. at Gouda and Edam); chief crops are rye, oats, potatoes, and sugar beets; horticulture, especially production of bulbs, flowers, and fruit, has been carried on for centuries; fisheries of some importance; chief industries are brewing, distilling, manufacture of tobacco, sugar, vinegar, bricks, and stoneware, margarine, machinery, cocoa, salt, diamond cutting, shipbuilding; coal mining in Limburg prov. is increasing; exports are food products and commodities mentioned above. Official cap., The Hague; Amsterdam is commercial cap., and Rotterdam and Flushing are chief ports. Area, 12,603 sq. m.; pop. 7,731,000. *Colonial Possessions*: Dutch East Indies. Area, 733,715 sq. m.; pop. 52,825,000. Dutch W. Indies comprise Dutch Guiana and Curaçao. (2) City, Michigan, U.S.A.; furnaces, furniture, pianos, shoes, drugs. Pop. 12,000. (3) NORTH and SOUTH. See NORTH HOLLAND and SOUTH HOLLAND. (4) PARTS OF. See LINCOLNSHIRE.

Hollingworth, urb. dist., N.E. Cheshire, England, 3 m. S.E. of Stalybridge; cotton manufacture. Pop. 2,300.

Hollywood. See LOS ANGELES.

Holme Cultram, urb. dist., Cumberland, England; contains wat.-pl. of Silloth, 18 m. W. of Carlisle. Pop. 4,700.

Holm'firth, tn., W. Riding, Yorks, England, 6 m. S. of Huddersfield; woollen mills. Pop. 10,400.

Holo', formerly SULU, archipelago, extending from N.E. Borneo to S. Philippines; larger islands volcanic, others of coral formation; teak, rice, coffee, cotton, saffron, sesame, indigo are grown, and pearl shell exported; group belongs to U.S.A. Cap. Holo, on Holo I. Area, *c.* 1,000 sq. m.; pop. *c.* 100,000.

Holstein. See SCHLESWIG-HOLSTEIN.

Holt, par. and mkt. tn., Norfolk, England, 10 m. W. by S. of Cromer. Pop. (par.) 2,250.

Holyhead, port, Holy Isle, Anglesey, N. Wales; chief mail-packet station for Ireland. Pop. 10,700.

Holy Island, or LINDISFARNE, isl. off Northumberland, England; connected with mainland at low tide by sandy tract; has ruined Benedictine monastery and a castle; small fishing village and summer resort in S.W. Area, 1,338 ac.; pop. 600.

Holy Land. See PALESTINE.

Holyoke (*hōl'yōk*), tn., Massachusetts, U.S.A., on Connecticut R., dammed here to supply water power; paper industry, textiles, machinery. Pop. 57,000.

Holytown, tn., Lanarkshire, Scotland, 11 m. E.S.E. of Glasgow; coal mines, steel works. Pop. 12,500.

Holywell, mkt. tn., Flint, Wales; zinc mines, cement works, hardware. Pop. 3,400.

Holywood, port, co. Down, N. Ireland, on Belfast Lough; bathing resort; residential area of Belfast. Pop. 4,000.

Holzminden (*holts'min-den*), tn., Brunswick, Germany, on R. Weser; ironworks, sawmills, chemicals, and manures. Pop. 12,000.

Homburg, or HOMBURG-VOR-DER-HÖHE (*hom'boorg-fŏr-dăr-hō'ā*), tn. and wat.-pl., Hesse-Nassau, Prussia, 10 m. N.W. of Frankfurt; saline and chalybeate springs; machinery, dye, and leather works, hats. Pop. 14,300.

Homel. See GOMEL.

Home'stead, tn., Pennsylvania, U.S.A., 6 m. S.E. of Pittsburgh; iron and steel works, engines, machinery, aeroplane propellers. Pop. 20,000.

Homs, tn., Syria, near R. Orontes; important point on trade route; manufactures silk, textiles, gold and silver thread. Pop. 53,000.

Honan', prov., Central China; greater part level; drained by Hwang-Ho; wheat, maize, beans, hemp, cotton; coal is worked. Chief tns., Kaifeng (cap.) and Honan. Area, 69,830 sq. m.; pop. *c.* 30,000,000.

Hondu'ras ('wave-like'). (1) Rep., Central America, bounded N. and E. by Caribbean Sea; S., Nicaragua, Pacific and Salvador; and W., Guatemala; coast-line *c.* 400 m. Surface, excepting narrow strip of swamp-land on the coast, is mountainous, traversed by Nicaraguan Cordillera, and forming elevated tableland with fertile plains and valleys, and rising in mountain ridges—highest point being Montaña de Salaque (*c.* 10,120 ft.); many streams, including Segovia (*c.* 350 m.) and Ulua. Climate is healthy in highlands, but oppressive in lowlands. Bananas are the most important product; coconuts, coffee, tobacco, and sugar are also produced; country rich in minerals: gold, copper, antimony, silver, iron; industries are cattle breeding and straw plaiting for hats. Cap. Tegucigalpa; tns. include La Esperanza, Santa Rosa, Amapala, and Tela (banana port). Area, 44,275 sq. m.; pop. 761,000. (2) BRITISH, crown colony, Central America; W. side of Gulf of Honduras, bounded N. by Yucatan, W. by Guatemala. Coast swampy, succeeded by rich plain and hills and mountains. Climate moist and hot. It produces cedar, mahogany, rosewood, logwood, chicle sugar, coffee, sarsaparilla, fruits, tortoiseshell, most of which are exported; imports cotton, yarn, cloth, hardware, general goods. Cap. Belize. Area, 8,598 sq. m.; pop. 45,300.

Honfleur (*on-fler'*), port and wat.-pl., Calvados, France, on estuary of R. Seine; shipbuilding, fishing, chemical manures. Pop. 8,200.

Hong Kong', island belonging to Britain, lying off S.E. coast of China at estuary of Canton R., along with small portion of mainland on peninsula of Kowloon, constitutes crown colony of Hong Kong; extreme length of isl. *c.* 11 m., and breadth 2 to 5 m.; separated from mainland by strait, which makes an excellent harbour. Interior barren and rocky. Chief exports, rice, sugar, tea, silk, and tin; univ. opened, 1912. Cap. Victoria. Area, 32 sq. m.; pop. 1,076,000.

Hon'iton, tn., Devon, England, on R. Otter, 16 m. E.N.E. of Exeter; noted for lace; brewing; sawmilling; butter. Pop. 3,000.

Hon'ley, urb. dist., W. Riding, Yorks, England, 3½ m. S. of Huddersfield; woollen mills. Pop. 4,600.

Honolu'lu, cap. and principal port of Hawaiian Islands, on S. coast of Oahu; pleasant, well-planned, and highly civilized town; pineapple canning; exp. coffee, sugar, and wool; coaling station. Pop. 116,000.

Honshu. See JAPAN.

Hooghly (*hoog'li*). (1) Most westerly mouth of R. Ganges, entering Indian Ocean. Trade to Calcutta passes up this branch. Has rapid tidal bore; navigation difficult. (2) Tn., Bengal, India, in dist. and on riv. of same name; has fine mosque. Pop. 30,000.

Dist. produces rice and jute. Area, 1,188 sq. m.; pop. 1,080,000.

Hoorn (*hōrn*), port, Holland, on Zuider Zee; famous cheese and cattle markets; boat building, sawmills; quaint old buildings. Pop. 12,000.

Hopeh, most N. province, China; divided in two by Great Wall; N. mountainous; has great extremes of climate; S. low, fertile, well-watered; produces wheat and millet; coal is found. Chief towns, Peking and Tientsin. Area, 115,830 sq. m.; pop. *c.* 32,000,000.

Hopkinsville, tn., W. Kentucky, U.S.A., 80 m. S. of Evansville, Indiana; great tobacco and live-stock markets; manufactures cigar boxes and furniture. Pop. 14,000.

Hoquiam (*hō'kwe-am*), tn., Washington, U.S.A., at mouth of R. Hoquiam, on Gray's Harbor; great sawmills and wood-working factories; canneries for fruit and salmon. Pop. 11,000.

Hor'bury, tn., W. Riding, Yorks, England, 3 m. S.W. of Wakefield; woollen goods, railway wagons. Pop. 7,800.

Hör'de, tn., Westphalia, Germany, 3 m. S.E. of Dortmund; iron and steel works, coal and iron mines. Pop. 35,000.

Hormuz', small isl., Strait of Hormuz, Persia, 11 m. S.E. of Bandar Abbas; chief products, red ochre and rock salt; great trading centre 14th to 16th cent.; trade transferred to Bandar Abbas.

Horn, CAPE, most S. point of S. America, on isl. of Tierra del Fuego; prevalent W. winds make navigation very difficult. Alt. 1,390 ft.

Horn'castle, mkt. tn., Lincolnshire, England, 18 m. E. by S. of Lincoln; great horse fair, and trade in agricultural produce. Pop. 3,500.

Hornchurch, urb. dist., Essex, England, 2 m. S.E. of Romford; manufactures bricks, tiles, etc. Pop. 28,400.

Hor'nell, city, New York, U.S.A., on Canisteo R., 70 m. S.E. of Buffalo; railway stock, furniture, silks, and electrical goods. Pop. 16,000.

Horn'sea, urb. dist., E. Riding, Yorks, England, on North Sea, 15½ m. by rail N.E. of Hull; wat.-pl.; fishing; Anglo-Saxon antiquities. Hornsea Mere (327.5 acres) is largest lake in co. Pop. 4,500.

Horn'sey, munic. bor., part of Greater London, 5 m. N. of St. Paul's; mainly working-class dist. Pop. 95,500.

Hor'sens, port, Jutland, Denmark, 22 m. S.W. of Aarhus; weaving, tobacco, soap, electrical goods, condensed milk, organs; dairy products exported. Pop. 28,000.

Horsforth, urb. dist., W. Riding, Yorks, England, 5 m. N.W. of Leeds; woollen manufacture. Pop. 11,800.

Hors'ham, mkt. tn., N. Sussex, England; iron and brass founding; bricks, pottery; brewing. Christ's Hospital (the Bluecoat School) housed near by. Pop. 13,600.

Hor'ten, port, Norway, on Oslo Fjord; shipbuilding; wat.-pl. Pop. 10,000.

Horwich (*hor'ich*), urb. dist., Lancs, England, 18 m. N.W. of Manchester; locomotive works, bleaching, cotton spinning, dyeing, calico printing; stone quarries, brick and tile works. Pop. 15,700.

Hoshangabad'. (1) Dist., Central Provinces, India, between R. Narbada and Satpura Mts.; wheat, linseed, cotton. Area, 3,681 sq. m.; pop. 445,000. (2) Chief tn. of above, on R. Narbada; brass-working, cotton industries. Pop. 12,000.

Hoshiarpur (*hōsh-yar-poor'*). (1) Dist., Punjab, India; rice, cotton, tobacco. Area, 2,247 sq. m.; pop. 927,000. (2) Cap. of above, 60 m. E. of Amritsar; lacquer, cottons, and ivory-inlaid articles. Pop. 21,000.

Hotin, tn., N. Romania, on R. Dniester; manufactures leather, candles, beer, bricks. Pop. 19,000.

Hot Springs, health resort, Arkansas, U.S.A., 55 m. S.W. of Little Rock; thermal mineral springs. Pop. 20,000.

Houghton-le-Spring (*hō'ton*), tn., co. Durham, England, 6 m. N.E. of Durham; collieries and limestone quarries. Pop. 10,500.

Houns'low, tn., Middlesex, England, 10 m. W.S.W. of London; part of Greater London; powder mills; Kneller Hall is headquarters of Royal Military School of Music. Hounslow Heath was a highwayman's haunt. Pop. 23,000.

Houston (*hoos'ton*), tn., Texas, U.S.A.; railway centre and port, connected by canal with Galveston Bay; large exp. of cotton; great oil refineries; rice mills; machinery; railway carriages. Pop. 290,000.

Hove, tn. Sussex, England; continuous with Brighton; popular resort. Pop. 55,000.

How'rah, tn., Bengal, India, opposite Calcutta; jute, cotton, shipbuilding. Pop. 195,000.

Howth (*hōth*), tn., co. Dublin, I.F.S., on Dublin Bay; summer resort; fishing. Pop. 3,100.

Hoy, mountainous isl., Orkney, Scotland; cliffs 1,140 ft. high; the 'Old Man of Hoy,' an isolated rock, rises to 450 ft. Has celebrated 'Dwarfie Stone,' in which are excavated rooms. Area, 53 sq. m.; pop. 1,000.

Hoy'lake, tn., Cheshire, England, 6 m. W. of Birkenhead; famous golf links; fishing. Pop. (with W. Kirby) 16,600.

Hoy'land, NETHER, tn., W. Riding, Yorks, England, 3 m. S.S.E. of Barnsley; coal mines, ironworks, brickworks. Pop. 15,200.

Hradec Králové (*hrad'ets krā'lo-vē*), formerly KÖNIGGRÄTZ, tn., Bohemia, Czechoslovakia, on R. Elbe; engineering, tanning, soap, candles, pianos. Scene of decisive victory of Prussia over Austria (1866), known as battle of Sadowa or Königgrätz. Pop. 13,000.

Hsi-an. See SIAN.

Huancavelica (*wan-ka-vā-lē'ka*), dep. central Peru; mountainous; silver, copper, lead, tungsten, mercury not developed owing to lack of communications; wheat, potatoes; alpacas reared. Cap. Huancavelica, 150 m. E.S.E. of Lima. Area, 8,297 sq. m.; pop. 230,000.

Huanuco (*wan-oo'ko*), dep., central Peru; mountainous; cotton, sugar-cane, coffee, grown in valleys; much mineral wealth unworked. Cap. Huanuco, 150 m. N.N.E. of Lima. Area, 15,425 sq. m.; pop. 200,000.

Huaraz (*wä-räth*), tn., cap. of Ancachs, Peru, 180 m. N.N.W. of Lima; mineral springs; silver, copper, and lead mines in vicinity. Pop. 20,000.

Hubli (*hoo'ble*), tn., s. Bombay, India, 15 m. S.E. of Dharwar; cotton and copper manufactures. Pop. 69,000.

Huchow', tn., Chekiang, China, 80 m. S.W. of Shanghai; silk centre. Pop. 100,000.

Huck'nall, urb. dist., Notts, England, 8 m. N.W. of Nottingham; hosiery; coal mines. Pop. 17,300.

Hud'dersfield, co. bor., W. Riding, Yorks, England, on R. Colne, in extensive coalfield; centre of 'fancy' woollen industry; silk and cotton goods; iron goods, machinery, locomotives. Pop. 113,500.

Hud'son, tn., New York, U.S.A., on Hudson R.; Portland cement, hosiery, and knitted goods. Pop. 11,400.

Hud'son Bay, great inland sea, N. of N. America; receives drainage of great part of Canada by Churchill, Nelson, Albany, and other rivers. Connected with Atlantic by Hudson Strait. Well stocked with salmon and cod. Hudson Strait is open to navigation for two or three months in each year. Area, 400,000 sq. m.

Hud'son River, riv., New York state, U.S.A.; rises in Adirondack Mts.; falls into Atlantic at New York; total length, *c.* 315 m. Principal trib. is R. Mohawk. The Hudson-Mohawk route across Appalachian Mts. with barge canal and rly. to L. Erie affords important means of communication between New York and Great Lakes.

Hué (*whā*), fort. tn., Fr. Indo-China, on Hué R., 9 m. from sea; cap. of Annam; produces glass and ivory goods. Pop. 41,000.

Huelva (*wel'va*). (1) Frontier prov., S.W. Spain; valuable copper mines; wine, fruit, esparto. Area, 3,913 sq. m.; pop. 379,000. (2) Cap. of above,

55 m. w. by s. of Seville; fishing; exp. copper and manganese. Pop. 44,000.

Huercal Overa (*wer-kal' o-vā'ra*), tn., S.E. Spain, 40 m. N.E. of Almeria; silver, copper, and lead mines. Pop. 16,000.

Huesca (*wes'ka*). (1) Prov., Spain; watered by Aragon and other affluents of R. Ebro; N. occupied by Pyrenees; mts. well forested; produces wine, grain, fruit. Area, 5,848 sq. m.; pop. 253,000. (2) Cap. of above; cathedral; leather, pottery; trade in wine, fruit, cereals. Pop. 14,000.

Hull. (1) Properly KINGSTON-ON-HULL, riv. port and co. bor., E. Riding, Yorks, England, at confluence of R. Hull with Humber; extensive docks; shipbuilding, machinery, chains, ropes, canvas, chemicals, vegetable oil, tanning, sugar refining, brewing; extensive trade with Continent; deep-sea fishing. Univ. college. Pop. 313,400. (2) Town, Quebec, Canada, opposite Ottawa; lumber, pulp, and paper mills; matches. Pop. 27,000.

Hum'ber, estuary of Rs. Trent and Yorkshire Ouse, E. coast of England, between Yorkshire and Lincolnshire.

Hunan' ('south of the lake'), prov., central China, in Yangtze Kiang basin; surface hilly; coal, zinc, antimony; tea, rice, wheat. Cap. Chang-sha. Area, 83,380 sq. m.; pop. 28,000,000.

Hun'gary, inland kingdom, central Europe, bounded N. by Czechoslovakia, E. by Romania, S. by Yugoslavia, W. by Austria. Surface is mainly plains of middle Danube and its trib. the Tisa (Theiss); the smaller plain, the 'Little Hungarian Alföld' (area *c.* 6,000 sq. m.), and the Great Hungarian Alföld, the largest plain in Europe (*c.* 37,000 sq. m.), are separated by the Bakony Wald, which lies between the R. Danube and Lake Balaton. The Danube enters Hungary below Bratislava, turns S., and flows through Hungary into Yugoslavia; is navigable for vessels drawing 6 ft.; R. Tisa rises in Carpathians, flows through Hungary, and crosses S. border below Szeged; navigable for steamers to Tokay; country subject to river floods; many marshes. Largest lake is Balaton (265 sq. m.). Climate is continental; rainfall of early summer is followed by remarkably dry period. Greater part of the Alföld consists of wide, open, treeless steppes called pusztas, with herds of horses, cattle, buffaloes, sheep, and swine; soil excellently adapted for the growing of wheat. Agriculture is chief occupation, and wheat, rye, barley, oats, maize, and potatoes of excellent quality are grown; tobacco, sugar beet, apples, apricots, grapes, peaches, pears, plums, and hops are largely produced; land is divided among peasant proprietors, who engage largely in bee-keeping and silk culture; forests yield oak, beech, and pine; chief minerals are coal, lignite, bauxite; salt is a state monopoly. Industries include brewing and distilling, wine making, sugar and flour milling, and tobacco. Agricultural implements, machinery, pig-iron, and steel are manufactured. Univs. at Budapest (cap.), Szeged, Pécs, and Debrecen. Area, 35,875 sq. m.; pop. 7,980,000.

Hungerford, tn., Berks and Wilts, England, 24 m. W. by S. of Reading; trout fishing, hunting. Pop. 2,800.

Hunstan'ton (or *hun'ston*), or NEW HUNSTANTON, urb. dist., Norfolk, England, on the Wash, 14 m. N. by E. of King's Lynn; seaside resort. Pop. 3,100.

Hunt'ingdon. (1) Co. tn., Hunts, England, on R. Ouse; has 13th-cent. grammar school; birthplace of Oliver Cromwell. Pop. 4,100. (2) Tn., Pennsylvania, U.S.A., 150 m. E. of Pittsburgh; flour, leather; coal, iron, and limestone. Pop. 7,000.

Hunt'ingdonshire (HUNTS), midland co., England, bounded N. and W. by Northants, S.W. by Beds, E. by Cambridge. Surface mostly level, with slight risings in S.E. In N.E. is fen district called Bedford Level. Principal rivs. are Nene and Ouse. Chiefly agricultural county; much pasture-land; wheat chief grain grown; market gardening and fruit growing, brewing, tanning, ironfounding, and manufactures of paper and parchment. Chief tns., Huntingdon (cap.), St. Ives, and Godmanchester. Area, 366 sq. m.; pop. 56,200.

Hunt'ington. (1) Tn., Indiana, U.S.A., 25 m. S.W. of Fort Wayne; shoes, gloves, and pianos; lime burning. Pop. 14,000. (2) Tn., Long Island, New York, U.S.A.; shipbuilding; market gardening; oyster fishing. Pop. 21,000. (3) Tn., W. Virginia, U.S.A., on R. Ohio; manufactures machinery; furniture, lumber. Pop. 76,000.

Hunt'ly, tn., Aberdeenshire, Scotland, 40 m. N.W. of Aberdeen; agriculture and woollens. Pop. 3,800.

Hupeh (*hoo-pā*), ('north of the lake'), prov., central China; a plain, watered by Yangtze and Han rivs.; tea, cotton, rice, wheat; coal mines. Cap. Wuchang. Area, 71,410 sq. m.; pop. 27,167,000.

Huron (*hū'ron*). (1) One of Great Lakes, N. America, connected with Lakes Superior, Michigan, and Erie by St. Mary R., Mackinac Strait, and St. Clair R. respectively. Area, 23,010 sq. m. (2) Tn., S. Dakota, on James or Dakota R., 105 m. E. of Pierre; meat products, dairy produce. Pop. 10,000.

Hurstmonceux (*hurst-mon-soo'*), vil., Sussex, England, 7 m. N.E. of Eastbourne; ruined castle; willow baskets made. Pop. 1,500.

Hurst'pierpoint, mkt. tn., Sussex, England, 8 m. N. of Brighton; anc. Brit. camp and remains of Roman villa. Pop. 3,100.

Husi (*hoo'shi*), tn., Moldavia, Romania, near R. Prut; wine, tobacco, and live-stock. Pop. 17,000.

Husum (*hoo'zoom*), tn., Schleswig-Holstein, Germany, 100 m. N.W. of Hamburg; cattle markets; oyster fisheries. Pop. 10,000.

Hutch'inson, city, Kansas, U.S.A., on Arkansas R.; salt-works; creameries and flour mills. Pop. 27,000.

Huy (*oo'ē*), tn., Liége, Belgium, on R. Meuse; distilleries; paper mills. Pop. 14,500.

Hwang-Hai. See YELLOW SEA.

Hwang-Ho ('yellow river'), one of the chief rivers of China; rises near sources of Yangtze Kiang in Tibet, and flowing N.E., traverses N.W. China and part of Mongolia; re-enters China, flowing S., E., and N.E.; enters Gulf of Pohai or Pe-chih-li; drains basin of 600,000 sq. m., and is *c.* 2,500 m. long. Liable to destructive floods, hence known as 'China's Sorrow.'

Hyde (*hīd*), munic. bor., Cheshire, England, 7 m. E. of Manchester; cotton spinning and weaving; engineering; margarine. Pop. 32,100.

Hyderabad'. (1) Principal Indian state in India, lying in Deccan between provs. of Madras and Bombay. Country fertile, but poorly cultivated. Chief rivs., Godavari and Kistna. Rice, wheat, maize, cotton are grown. Considerable undeveloped mineral wealth. Area, 82,698 sq. m.; pop. 12,472,000. (2) Cap. of above, on R. Musi; surrounded by walls; important commercial centre; fourth largest town in India. Pop. 404,000. (3) City, cap. of dist. of same name, Sind, Bombay, Brit. India; near E. bk. of R. Indus; arsenal; manufactures silks, gold and silver work, pottery. Pop. 82,000.

Hyères (*ē-ār*), winter health resort, Var, France, on Riviera, 11 m. E. of Toulon and 3 m. from sea; climate mild and dry; picturesque old town; vineyards, palms, orange groves, and rose and flower cultivation; saltpans in dist.; market gardening, early fruit and vegetables. Pop. (including suburb of Costebelle), 21,300.

Hyogo. See under KOBE.

Hythe (*hīth*), wat.-pl., Kent, England, one of the Cinque Ports; fine beach and golf course. Pop. 8,400.

I

Ibadan′, tn., Yoruba, s. Nigeria, 124 m. by rail N.N.E. of Lagos; has Brit. resident and is station for Hausa troops; market for cotton; silk made and tobacco grown. Pop. *c.* 175,000.

Ibagué (*ē-bä′gā*), or SAN BONIFACIO DE IBAGUÉ, tn., Colombia, S. America, 100 m. w. of Bogota; cocoa, tobacco, and sugar-cane. Pop. 30,000.

Ibarra (*ē-bar′a*), tn., Ecuador, S. America, at foot of volcano of Imbabura, 50 m. N.N.E. of Quito; cotton and woollen industries. Pop. *c.* 10,000.

Ibe′rian Peninsula, name applied to Spain and Portugal taken together; derived from the Iberian people who lived along the river Ebro (Latin *Iberus*); separated from rest of Europe by the Pyrenees; flora and fauna resemble those of N. Africa, hence it is frequently stated that 'Africa begins at the Pyrenees.' Area, 229,054 sq. m.; pop. 28,635,000. See SPAIN; PORTUGAL.

Ib′stock, par. and vil., Leicestershire, England, 5 m. N. of Market Bosworth; coal mines, brick and tile works. Pop. (par.) 5,200.

Ice′land, isl. in North Sea, *c.* 500 m. N.W. of Shetland Islands and 250 m. S.E. of Greenland; N., E., and W. shores much indented by fiords; surface consists of ice-covered plateaus 1,500 to 2,000 ft., and mts. culminating in Oräfa Jökull (6,425 ft.), near S.E. coast; numerous small lakes, many being crater basins or moraine lakes. Glacier fields cover 5,000 sq. m.; in interior are large areas covered by recent lavas. Over twenty of the many volcanoes have been active in modern times; the best known are Hecla (5,108 ft.), Katla, and Askja; hot springs and geysers are common. Chief industry is breeding of cattle and sheep; principal exports: salt fish (esp. cod), butter, oil, mutton, and wool. Only *c.* 7,000 sq. m. of area are habitable; there are no railways. Iceland is independent state, governed by King of Denmark. Cap. Reykjavik. Area, 39,709 sq. m.; pop. 95,000.

Ichang′, treaty port, Hupeh, China, on Yangtze Kiang, 10 m. below Ichang gorges; opened in 1877; tranships cargo to and from Szechwan; trades in cotton, cotton goods, rice, and oil. Pop. 110,000.

Iconium (*ī-kō′ni-um*) (modern *Konia*), anc. city, Asia Minor. Cap. of Lycaonia under Romans; three times visited by Paul and Barnabas. See KONIA.

Ida (*ī′da*). (1) Mt. range, Mysia, N.W. Asia Minor, at foot of which lay anc. plain of Troy. Granicus, Simois, Scamander, and other streams of classic story rise in it; now known as Kaz Dagh (highest point, 5,750 ft.). (2) Mt., centre of Crete, alt. 8,050 ft.; Zeus said to have been born in one of its caves; modern name Psiloriti.

Idaho (*ī′da-hō*), W. State, U.S.A., bounded N. by British Columbia, Montana, E. by Montana and Wyoming, S. by Utah and Nevada, W. by Oregon and Washington. Surface mainly rugged and mountainous; S.E. region lies in Great Basin of U.S.A., while the rest, some 70,000 sq. m., lies in drainage basin of Columbia R.; in N. and E. is part of Rocky Mt. system, the Salmon R. range, separating Idaho from Montana; other ranges are the Saw Tooth and Baisé; the Snake R. Plains are large stretches covered with drifting sand. Abundant vegetation in N. and centre. Climate is healthy. Mineral deposits include gold, copper, lead, silver, zinc, and coal, while in the S.E. soda, gypsum, and sulphur are found; there are many state forests; grain farming is mostly confined to river valleys, but extensive irrigation works have been carried out; most important crop is wheat; other crops are oats, barley, potatoes, hay; principal industries are lumber and timber working, flour and grist milling; stock raising is carried on. Cap. Boise. Area, 83,888 sq. m.; pop. 432,000.

Idle, par. in co. bor. of Bradford, W. Riding, Yorkshire, England; woollen trade; stone quarrying and brickmaking. Pop. 7,900.

Iglau. See JIHLAVA.

Iglesias (*ē-glä'sē-äs*), tn., Sardinia, Italy, 34 m. W. by N. of Cagliari; lead and zinc mines worked since Roman times; cathedral (1285); old walls and towers; castle (1325). Pop. 20,000.

Igualada (*ēg-wa-lä'da*), city, prov. Barcelona, Spain, 32 m. N.W. of Barcelona; leather and textiles; centre of rich agricultural and wine-producing dist. Pop. 12,000.

Ilagan (*ē-la-gän'*), cap. Isabela prov., Luzon, Philippines, 175 m. N.N.E. of Manila; centre of tobacco industry. Pop. 23,000.

Il'chester, tn., Somerset, England, 5 m. N.W. of Yeovil; anc. Roman station; important town in Saxon times; Roger Bacon born in or near town. Pop. 500.

Ile-de-France, anc. prov., France, bounded by rivers Seine, Oise, Thève, Beuvronne, and Marne.

Ile du Diable (*ēl doo dē-abl'*), one of the group of Iles du Salut, off coast of Fr. Guiana, 50 m. N.W. of Cayenne; convict settlement.

Iles du Salut. See SALUT, ILES DU.

Iletsk (*ē-letsk'*), tn., Orenburg, Russia, on riv. Ilek, trib. of Ural R., 40 m. S. of Orenburg; important salt mines; salt and brine baths. Pop. 11,000.

Ilford, or GREAT ILFORD, urban dist. and tn., Essex, England, part of Greater London; residential suburb; paper mills and photographic works. Pop. 131,000.

Ilfracombe (*il'fra-coom*), urban dist., mkt. tn., and seaside resort, Devon, England, on Bristol Channel; fishing and small coasting trade. Pop. 9,200.

Ilhavo (*ēl-yä'vō*), seaport, Beira, Portugal, 37 m. S. of Oporto, on lagoon; exports salt; fisheries; factory of Vista-Alegre famous for glass and porcelain. Pop. 13,000.

Ili, riv., central Asia, rises in Tien Shan Mts.; flows N.W. and falls by several mouths into Lake Balkhash. Length, *c.* 900 m.; navigable between Balkhash and Iliisk.

Ilkeston (*ilks'ton*), munic. bor., Derbyshire, England, 9 m. E.N.E. of Derby; hosiery, lace; earthenware, bricks; ironworks, ironstone mines, and collieries. Pop. 32,800.

Ilkley (*ilk'lā*), urb. dist., W. Riding, Yorkshire, England, on R. Wharfe; famous mineral springs; Roman and Saxon remains; Bolton Abbey within 5 m. Pop. 9,700.

Illawarra (*il-la-wär'ra*), dist., New South Wales, Australia, forming belt of land between the S. tableland and the coast; very fertile; rich coal seams; dairy farming; coal, iron ore, fireclay, and freestone are mined. Lake Illawarra, salt lagoon, 9 m. by 3 m., frequented for scenery and fishing. Chief towns, Wollongong, Bulli, Kiama, and Geringong.

Ille-et-Vilaine (*ēl-ā-vē-lān'*), mar. dep., N.W. France, part of anc. Brittany; watered by rivs. Ille and Vilaine; temperate, humid climate; not naturally fertile, but greatly improved by careful tillage; chief crops, wheat, buckwheat, oats, and barley; market gardening; potatoes, early vegetables, flax, and hemp are largely grown, as well as apples and pears, cider being made; large numbers of horses and cattle reared; manufactures unimportant; iron, lead, zinc, slate, granite obtained; fishing on coast. Chief tns., Rennes (cap.), St. Malo, Dinard. Area, 2,697 sq. m.; pop. 562,000.

Illinois (*il-i-noi'* or *il-i-noiz'*), N. Central State of U.S.A., bounded N. by Wisconsin, E. by Lake Michigan and Indiana, S.E. and S. by Ohio R., S.W. and W. by Mississippi R. Situated in prairie-plain region, touching Great Lake dist. in N.E.; average height above sea-level 600 ft. Watered by rivs. Mississippi, Ohio, and tribs.;

most important river is Illinois, at times broadening into vast lakes—notably Peoria Lake. Climate extreme. Illinois is richest agricultural state of U.S.A., chief cereal crops being maize, wheat, oats, and hay; active live-stock industry carried on. Minerals are important, chief mineral product being coal, of which Illinois is third largest producer in U.S.A.; many petroleum wells; zinc is worked, also lead, limestone, salt, and fluorspar. Chief industries are slaughtering and meat packing, iron and steel foundries. Cap. Springfield. Chicago, the largest city, is second largest in America; other cities, Peoria, East St. Louis, Quincy, Rockford, Joliet, and Decatur. Area, 56,665 sq. m.; pop. 6,500,000.

Illogan (*il-ug'an*), par. and vil., Cornwall, England, 2 m. N.W. of Redruth; tin and copper mines. Pop. (par.) 8,300.

Illyr'ia, name applied to coastal region along Adriatic Sea from Fiume in N. to Albania in S., and stretching inland as far as rivs. Danube and Morava. Mainly part of Yugoslavia.

Il'men, large fresh-water lake, N.W. Russia, immediately S. of city of Novgorod. Area, 360 sq. m.; 93 ft. above Baltic level; flat, marshy shores; discharges into Lake Ladoga by R. Volkhov; productive fisheries.

Ilmenau (*ēl'me-nou*), tn., summer resort, Thuringia, Germany, at N. base of Thüringer Wald, 20 m. S.S.E. of Gotha; porcelain, toys, glass, papier-maché, and steel goods. Pop. 14,000.

Il'minster, urb. district, Somerset, England, 10 m. S.E. of Taunton; manufactures lace, shirts, and collars; agricultural centre. Pop. 2,200.

Iloilo (*ē-lō-ē'lo*), town, cap. prov. Iloilo, Panay I., Philippines; one of chief ports of archipelago; exports sugar, tobacco, rice. Pop. 49,000.

Ilorin (*il-aw'rin*), chief tn., native amirate, N. Nigeria, 170 m. N.N.E. of Lagos; connected by rail with coast (248 m.); 30 m. E., at Aguji, is government experimental and forestry station; agricultural centre; extensive caravan trade. Pop. 73,000.

Ils'ley, EAST, mkt. tn., Berkshire, England, 11 m. S. of Abingdon; sheep markets and fairs; race-horses trained. Pop. 400. West Ilsley is 2 m. to the N.W.

Imatra Falls. See FINLAND.

Im'bros, Turkish isl., N.E. Ægean Sea, 14 m. W. of entrance to Dardanelles; of volcanic origin; cereals, fruit, and olives grown. Kastron (N. coast), chief tn. Area, 100 sq. m.; pop. *c.* 9,000.

Im'mingham, port, Lincolnshire, England, 4 m. from Grimsby; largest dock on E. coast. Pop. 2,200.

Imola (*ē'mō-la*), tn., Italy, 21 m. by rail S.E. of Bologna; manufactures glass and pottery; 12th cent. cathedral. Pop. 37,000.

Imphal. See MANIPUR (2).

Ince - in - Makerfield, urban dist., Lancashire, England, 1 m. S.E. of Wigan; collieries, ironworks, railway workshops, and cotton mills. Pop. 21,800.

Inchcape. See BELL ROCK.

Inchcolm (*insh-kōm'*), ('island of Columba'), small isl. in Firth of Forth, Scotland, now national property; ruins of monastery founded by Alexander I. (1123).

Inchgar'vie, rocky islet, Firth of Forth, Scotland, between N. and S. Queensferry; forms central support of the two great spans of Forth Bridge.

Inchkeith', isl., Firth of Forth, 2¾ m. S. of Kinghorn, Fife, Scotland; lighthouse on the highest point; can be seen 21 m.; strongly fortified; now government property.

Independence, city, Missouri, U.S.A., 10 m. E. of Kansas City; iron foundries, flour mills; agricultural produce. Pop. 12,000.

In'dia, the central peninsula of S. Asia, includes terr. over which Brit. king as Emperor of India exercises dominion or suzerainty. Four distinct regions are recognized: (1) the mountainous north, (2) the Indo-Gangetic valley, (3) the Deccan, (4) Burma.

(1) The Himalayas protect India on

N.W. frontier, and act as barrier between Assam and Burma. On N.W frontier the mountains are pierced by passes, most important of which are that through which Kabul R. passes, Khyber pass, and Bolan pass. See HIMALAYAS.

(2) Alluvial plains, richest and most densely populated part of India, stretching from Arabian Sea to Bay of Bengal, owe their fertility to Rs. Indus, Jumna, Ganges, and Brahmaputra.

(3) The Deccan plateau (average height 1,500–2,000 ft.) enclosed on E. and W. by E. and W. Ghats respectively. Drainage of this area is mainly to E., chief rivs. being Mahanadi, Godavari, Kistna, and Cauvery. N. of Surat, Rs. Narbada and Tapti drain to W. from slopes of Vindhya hills, which form roughly-defined N. boundary of the tableland.

(4) Burma, N. part of Indo-Chinese peninsula. See BURMA.

Climate, which is typically monsoon, varies from cold of Himalayas to intense, moist heat of plains and dry heat of Deccan. The S.W. (summer) and N.E. (winter) monsoons are much modified by local configuration. The three seasons are: hot (March to May), wet (June to Oct., later in S. Madras), and cool. Rainfall varies from 8 in. in Sind and Cutch to over 500 in. at Cherrapunji in Assam. Any failure of the regular rains is disastrous and leads to serious famine. Agriculture is chief industry, nearly three-fourths of total pop. being engaged in it. Much use is made of irrigation, and large tracts of land have been made productive by this means. The government irrigation works water *c.* 28,000,000 acres. Most important crops are rice, pulses, wheat, millet, and other grains; cotton, jute, oil-seeds; tea and sugar. Special attention is paid to afforestation by the state; most important timber is teak, found at its best in Burma. Mining is important: coal, petroleum (chiefly in Burma and Assam), manganese, gold, lead, silver, iron, copper; salt and saltpetre are mined. Cotton is manufactured in Bombay; jute in Bengal; iron in Bihar and Orissa; woollen and silk goods, paper, and timber.

The sea-borne trade of India is second only to that of U.K. in Brit. Empire. Chief exports: jute, raw and manufactured; cotton, raw and manufactured; grain, pulses, and flour; tea; oil-seeds and oils; leather, hides, and skins. Trade is mainly with U.K., Japan, and U.S.A. There is a land trade with Nepal and the Shan States. Most of the railways are state owned. Good roads run in all directions. The largest ports are Calcutta, Bombay, Karachi, Rangoon, and Madras.

British India is divided into 15 provinces; Ajmer-Merwara, Andaman and Nicobar Islands, Assam, Baluchistan, Bengal, Bihar and Orissa, Bombay, Burma, Central Provinces and Berar, Coorg, Delhi, Madras, North-West Frontier Province, Punjab, United Provinces. There are also many Indian states, the largest being Rajputana, Kashmir, Hyderabad. France and Portugal have also small possessions in India. Tns. with over 200,000 inhabitants are the former cap., Calcutta (1,132,000, with suburbs), Bombay, Madras, Hyderabad, Rangoon, Lucknow, Delhi (cap. since 1911), Lahore, Ahmedabad, Bangalore, Karachi, Cawnpore, Poona. Area of all India, 1,805,332 sq. m.; pop. 318,942,500.

India, FRENCH. See FRENCH INDIA.

India, PORTUGUESE. Port. possessions in India comprise Diu, Daman, and Goa. Area, 1,638 sq. m.; pop. 550,000.

India'na, N. Central State of U.S.A., lying between L. Michigan and Ohio R.; bounded N. by lake and state of Michigan, E. by Ohio, S. by Kentucky, W. by Illinois. Surface mostly undulating prairie, having range of sand-hills in N.; S. of this country is flat and marshy with shallow lakes; along Ohio R. a chain of hills ('Knobs') rises steeply. Most important rivers are the Ohio and its trib. the Wabash. Climate equable, soil, excepting sandy region s. of Lake Michigan, exceedingly fertile, especially Wabash valley. Land is largely agricultural; chief crops, maize, wheat, oats, hay, and potatoes; also tobacco and fruits and vegetables of all varieties. Minerals include coal, limestone, and clay. Manufactures and industries are important, and include iron and steel foundries, slaughtering and meat packing, as well as woollen works and manufacturing of agricultural implements. Natural facilities for transport are provided by the Ohio and Wabash rivers and Lake Michigan. Cap. Indianapolis; other tns., Fort Wayne, Evansville, South Bend. Area, 36,354 sq. m.; pop. 2,930,400.

Indianap'olis, cap. of Indiana, U.S.A., on White R., 100 m. N.W. of Cincinnati. Public buildings include federal building, state capitol, court house, and city hall. Important railway centre; large trade in agricultural produce; large slaughtering and meat-packing establishments, foundries, and machine shops. Pop. 364,000.

Indian Ocean, bounded W. by Africa, N. by Asia, E. by Malay Archipelago and Australia, divided in N. by India into Bay of Bengal (E.) and Arabian Sea (W.); mean depth, *c.* 2,300 fathoms; area, 29,340,000 sq. m. N. of the equator, direction of currents varies with monsoons; receives many important rivers from Asia; chief islands are Madagascar, Mauritius, Réunion, and Ceylon.

Indo-China, FRENCH. See FRENCH INDO-CHINA.

Indore. (1) Indian state in S.W. Central India; in N. is watered by R. Chambal and its tribs., and in S. by R. Narbada; traversed from E. to W. by Vindhya range. Principal products, poppy, raw cotton, wheat, tobacco, and valuable timber; chief manufactures, cotton and opium. Area, 9,519 sq. m.; pop. 1,151,600. (2) Cap. of above; cotton manufacture; residence of Agent-General of Central India. Pop. 93,000.

Indre (*an'dr*). (1) Riv., France, trib. of Loire, in departments of Indre and Indre-et-Loire, rises on borders of dep. Creuse; length, 150 m. (2) Dep., central France; watered by Cher, Indre, and Creuse. Produces cereals, vines, sugar-beet; sheep are reared, iron ore is worked, and dep. furnishes best lithographic stones in France. Chief tn., Châteauroux. Area, 2,664 sq. m.; pop. 255,000.

Indre-et-Loire (*an-dr-ā-lwär*), dep., central France; drained by R. Loire and tribs. Grain, vines, beetroot, and hemp cultivated; wine, silk, pottery, and bar iron manufactured. Chief tn., Tours. Area, 2,377 sq. m.; pop. 334,000.

In'dus, riv., N. India, rises in Tibet, N. of Himalayas, near sources of Brahmaputra and Sutlej; flows N.W. through Tibet and Kashmir and enters Punjab; receives the waters of Rs. Jhelum, Chenab, Ravi, Beas, and Sutlej, and flowing S.W., enters Arabian Sea by delta. Length, *c.* 1,500 m.; drainage area, 372,000 sq. m. Is outlet for productions of N.W. India; one of best bridged rivers in India; subject to great floods; navigable to Attock in N.W. Frontier Prov.

Ing'ersoll, tn., Ontario, Canada, 19 m. E.N.E. of Hamilton; rly. jn. Pop. 5,000.

Ing'leborough, hill, W. Yorkshire, England, in Pennine Chain; rises from limestone plateau in which are numerous pot-holes, extensive caverns, and underground watercourses; alt. 2,373 ft.

Ing'leton, par. and vil., W. Yorkshire, England, 10 m. N.W. of Settle; centre for geologists and tourists. Pop. (par.) 2,400.

In'golstadt, tn., Bavaria, Germany, on R. Danube; univ., founded 1472; ironfounding; locomotives and machinery. Pop. 27,000.

Inhambane (*ēn-yam-bä'nä*). (1) Dist., Portuguese E. Africa; coconuts, sugar-cane, rubber, and coffee. Area, 33,000 sq. m.; pop. *c.* 1,000,000. (2) Seapt. in above; exp. mafurra, oilseeds, copra, and sugar. Pop. 20,000.

Inishmore′, largest of Aran Isles, Galway, I.F.S., 30 m. S.W. of Galway; fishing. Pop. 1,800.

Ink′erman, vil., Crimea, Russia, near E. extremity of Sevastopol harbour; here Anglo-French troops defeated Russian army (1854).

Inland Sea, Japan, narrow, island-studded sea separating Kyushu and Shikoku from Honshu; the three straits—Shimonoseki, Bungo, and Kii—are narrow and dangerous but strongly fortified, and sea is thus a safe and sheltered highway for Japan's commerce. Chief ports, Hiroshima, Okayama, Kobe. Length, *c.* 250 m.; width, 10 to 40 m.

Inn, Alpine trib. of R. Danube; rises in Grisons canton, Switzerland, flows N.E. through Engadine, Austrian Tirol, and S.E. Bavaria to enter Danube at Passau. Length, 315 m.

Innerleith′en, tn., Peeblesshire, Scotland, 5 m. S.E. of Peebles; woollen manufactures; saline springs, said to be the St. Ronan's Well of Scott's novel of that name. Pop. 2,400.

Innerle′ven. See BUCKHAVEN.

Innsbrück (*ēns′brook*), tn., Austria, cap. of Tirol, beautifully situated on R. Inn at head of Brenner Pass; tourist centre; univ. (founded 1677). Franciscan church (with monument to Maximilian I.), imperial castle, and Ferdinandeum museum; textile, glass-painting, and mosaic industries. Pop. 56,000.

Inowroclaw (*in-ov-rots′waf*), formerly HOHENSALZA, tn., Poland, 60 m. N.E. of Poznan; salt works; iron-founding and manufacture of machinery and chemicals. Pop. 24,000.

Insterburg (*ēn′ster-boorg*), tn., E. Prussia, Germany, on R. Pregel, 35 m. E. of Königsberg; linen, machinery, leather, and beer. Pop. 39,000.

Interlaken (*ēn-ter-lä′ken*), tn., Berne, Switzerland, between Ls. Thun and Brienz; tourist resort. Pop. 3,000.

Invera′ray, co. tn., Argyllshire, Scotland; on Loch Fyne; castle (rebuilt 1880) is seat of dukes of Argyll; fishing. Pop. 500.

Inverbervie. See BERVIE.

Invercar′gill, tn., New Zealand, in extreme S. of S. Island; sawmills, foundries, meat-freezing works. Pop. 23,000.

Inverell′, tn., N. New South Wales, Australia, 280 m. N. of Sydney; centre of wheat and maize dist.; wine; silver, tin, and diamond deposits in vicinity. Pop. 5,000.

Inveresk′, par. and vil., Midlothian, Scotland, near Musselburgh; paper mills. Pop. of par. 21,200.

Invergor′don, seapt., Ross and Cromarty, Scotland, 13 m. N.E. of Dingwall; naval base during Great War. Pop. 1,400.

Inverkeithing, royal burgh, Fife, Scotland, on Firth of Forth; shipbuilding, paper works. Pop. 3,200.

Inverkip′, par. and vil., Renfrewshire, Scotland, 6 m. S.W. of Greenock; par. contains Gourock; wat.-pl. Pop. (par.) 13,000; (vil.) 600.

Inverness′, royal burgh, seapt., and co. tn., Inverness-shire, Scotland, on R. Ness; 'cap. of the Highlands;' at end of Caledonian Canal; has coasting trade, woollen industries, engineering works, distilleries; rly. centre; important wool fair. Anc. Pictish cap. Pop. 22,600.

Inverness′-shire, Highland co., Scotland, extending from Moray Firth on N.E. to Atlantic and Outer Hebrides on W. Surface is mostly wooded country, rough hill-grazing, heath, peat, and stony waste little cultivated; deer forests and grouse moors; excellent fishing; many wild glens. It is largest and most mountainous co. in Scotland; flat strip near Inverness gradually rises into mountain-land, culminating in Ben Nevis (4,406 ft.) in S.W. There are many rivers, the largest being Spey, Findhorn, Ness, Beauly, and Lochy. Among the numerous lochs are Ness, Morar (deepest in Brit. Isles), Shiel, Arkaig, Lochy, Ericht, and Laggan. Water-power used in great hydro-electric schemes. Caledonian Canal traverses the county, through Glenmore, along line of geological 'fault.' Co. tn., Inverness. Area, 4,211 sq. m.; pop. 82,100.

Inverurie (*in-ver-oor'i*), royal burgh, Aberdeenshire, Scotland, at confluence of Don and Ury; cattle trade; manufactures paper, mineral waters; rly. workshops. Pop. 4,500.

Iona, or Icolmkill (*ī-ō'na* or *ī-kŏm-kil'*), isl. at s.w. corner of Mull, Scotland, about 3½ m. long and 1½ m. wide; coast rocky and surface mostly rough. Associated with St. Columba and introduction of Christianity into Scotland; great centre of learning and religion from 6th cent. onwards; restored ruins of cathedral; chapel of St. Oran; Columba's tomb; numerous crosses and carved stones. Area, *c.* 2,000 ac.; pop. 200.

Ionian Islands (*ī-ō'ni-an*), group of islands on w. coast of Greece, consisting of seven islands, Corfu, Cephalonia, Paxos, Santa Maura (Leukas), Ithaca, Cerigo (Cythera), Zante (Zakynthos); surface mountainous; highest peak, Monte Nero, 5,310 ft., in Cephalonia; subject to frequent earthquakes; rich in marble, sulphur, salt, coal, wine, olives, currants, fruit. Area, *c.* 1,100 sq. m.; pop. *c.* 265,000.

Iowa (*ī'ō-wa*), N. Central State, U.S.A.; bounded N. by Minnesota; E. by Mississippi R., which separates it from Wisconsin and Illinois; s. by Missouri; w. by Rs. Missouri and Big Sioux (separating it from Nebraska and S. Dakota). Surface mostly prairie (average elevation 1,000 ft.). Iowa is divided into two drainage systems; the larger, on E., drained by tribs. of R. Mississippi; and that on w. by tribs. of R. Missouri. Climate is one of great extremes of heat and cold, but is healthy. Chief industry agriculture; maize, wheat, barley, oats, rye, potatoes, hay; live-stock; meat packing; dairy farming and poultry keeping. Valuable deposits of coal; other important minerals, gypsum, limestone, and clay. Chief tns., Des Moines (cap.), Dubuque, Sioux, Davenport, Council Bluffs, and Cedar Rapids. Area, 56,147 sq. m.; pop. 2,420,000.

I'owa City, city, Iowa, U.S.A., 120 m. E. of Des Moines; seat of Iowa State Univ.; centre of rich farming and stock-breeding district. Pop. 15,000.

Ipek. See Pec.

Ipoh (*ē'pō*), tn., Perak, Malay Peninsula, *c.* 125 m. by rail N.W. of Kuala Lumpur; centre of tin mining. Pop. 38,000.

Ipswich (*ips'wich*). (1) Co. bor. and seapt., Suffolk, England, near head of Orwell estuary; several fine churches, including St. Mary-at-the-Tower; principal industries, manufacture of agricultural implements and chemical manures, engineering, brewing, and tanning. Pop. 87,600. (2) Tn., Queensland, Australia, 23 m. w. of Brisbane; originally known as Limestone; is the centre of agricultural and coal-mining dist. Pop. 20,500.

Iquique (*ē-kē'kā*), seapt., Chile; exports large quantities of nitrate of soda. Has been frequently devastated by earthquakes. Pop. 37,000.

Iquitos (*ē-kē'tos*), tn. and riv. port, Peru, on Upper Amazon R.; has shipyard and floating dock; exports include rubber, tobacco, cotton, and soap. Pop. *c.* 10,000.

Irapuato (*ē-rap-wat'ō*), tn., Guanajuato, central Mexico, 170 m. N.W. of Mexico City; anc. churches and convents; in mining and agricultural dist.; rly. jn. Pop. 21,000.

Iraq (*ē-räk'*), official name for Mesopotamia, kingdom lying mainly between rivers Euphrates and Tigris, but with important desert region stretching westward to Trans Jordan. Surface consists of low-lying plain. Climate hot and dry in summer, cold in winter; rainfall, mainly in winter, very scanty. Cultivation is possible chiefly under irrigation. Schemes to restore anc. canals and to develop new areas will vastly increase productive area. Communications are being rapidly extended. Chief railway is that between Basra and Baghdad. Chief products are dates, rice, wheat, barley, fruits, live-stock, and cotton. Important oil-fields. Chief town is Baghdad, and chief port, Basra. Area, 143,250 sq. m.; pop. 2,849,000.

Irbit (*ĕr-bēt'*), town, Ural Area, Russia, E. of Ural Mts., 100 m. N.E. of Sverdlovsk; great fair (instituted 1643), second only to that of Nijni Novgorod. Pop. 12,000.

Ire'land, one of Brit. Isles, W. of Great Britain, bounded N., W., and S. by Atlantic Ocean, N.E. by North Channel, E. by Irish Sea and St. George's Channel. Coast-line about 2,200 m., no place more than 50 m. from sea. Island has basin-shaped central plain, 250 to 300 ft. in height, nearly surrounded by mountainous coasts; this configuration results in large area of bogland. Rivers are (N.) Foyle, Bann; (E.) Laggan, Boyne, Liffey; (S.) Barrow, Suir, Blackwater, Lee; (centre and W.) Erne, Moy, Galway, and Shannon. Chief lakes (loughs): Neagh, Erne, Allen, Ree, Derg, Conn, Mask, Corrib, Killarney. Climate is generally moist and warm, with more rainfall and warmth on W. than on E. About 3,000,000 ac. are mountain-land, peat bog, or marsh; greater part of remainder permanent grassland; breeding and rearing of live-stock of great importance; pig-breeding gives rise to valuable trade in bacon, ham, and pork. Trade in dairy produce is increasing. Chief crops, oats, potatoes, turnips, and flax. On E. coast there are valuable fisheries (mackerel, cod, ling, and herring); salmon fisheries on coasts and rivers. Minerals include coal, slate, marble, iron, bauxite, and silver, but these are not worked to any great extent. The lack of coal has been a great handicap to Irish industry, but a considerable linen industry has developed round Belfast and in Londonderry. Dublin manufactures poplin. Domestic and convent industries in hand-made lace and embroidery; spinning of wool and hand-loom weaving of woollens, carpets, rugs, are noted. Brewing of porter and ale and distilling are also important. Belfast and Londonderry have shipbuilding.

There are 3,750 m. of rly. operated by six companies. The largest is the Great Southern Railways Co., which controls all the lines entirely within the I.F.S.; next in importance is the Great Northern Railway Co., which has lines running from Belfast to Dublin and Londonderry and to the S. part of N. Ireland. The N. cos. of N. Ireland are served by the London, Midland, and Scottish Rly. Co. under the control of the Northern Counties Committee. The other groups are the Donegal Rly. Co., Londonderry and Lough Swilly Rly. Co., and the Belfast and Co. Down Rly. Co. There is an excellent canal system 848 m. in length. Two canals (Royal, *c.* 100 m.; and Grand, 208 m. including branches) connect Dublin with the Shannon, which is itself navigable, with the aid of a canal near Limerick, from Lough Allen to the sea. Atlantic liners by the N. passage call at Moville, those by the S. at Cobh (Queenstown).

Ireland is divided politically into Northern Ireland (consisting of the counties of Antrim, Armagh, Down, Fermanagh, Londonderry, and Tyrone), and the Irish Free State (counties Cavan, Donegal, Monaghan, Carlow, Dublin, Kildare, Kilkenny, Offaly, Longford, Louth, Meath, Leix, Westmeath, Wexford, Wicklow, Clare, Cork, Kerry, Limerick, Tipperary, Waterford, Galway, Leitrim, Mayo, Roscommon, and Sligo). N. Ireland has a parliament of its own and also sends representatives to Westminster. The I.F.S. has the status of a Brit. Dominion. The area of Northern Ireland is 5,236 sq. m.; pop. (1926) 1,256,000; Belfast (cap.), 415,000. Area of Irish Free State, 26,600 sq. m.; pop. (1926) 2,971,000; Dublin (cap.) 419,000.

Irish Free State. See IRELAND.

Irish Sea, sea between Great Britain and Ireland, connected with Atlantic Ocean by St. George's Channel on S. and by North (or St. Patrick's) Channel on N. Length, 110 m.; breadth, 150 m.; maximum depth, 850 ft.

Irkutsk (*ĕr-kootsk'*), tn., Siberian Area, U.S.S.R., on R. Angara, on Trans-Siberian railway; chief trade centre of E. Siberia, with important traffic in tea and furs. Chief industries are brewing, timber cutting, flour milling, and manufacture of leather goods. Pop. 99,000.

Ir'lam, urb. dist., Lancs, England, 8 m. S.W. of Manchester; candles, glycerine, and soap. Pop. 12,900.

Ironbridge, tn., Salop, England, 13¾ m. by rail S.E. of Shrewsbury; forms part of tn. of Madeley; named from bridge over R. Severn, the first iron bridge ever built; collieries and ironworks in vicinity. Pop. 2,900.

I'ronton, city, Ohio, U.S.A., 100 m. S.E. of Columbus; iron, coal, and fireclay; foundries, manufacture of machinery. Pop. 14,000.

I'ronwood, city, Michigan, U.S.A., 7 m. S.W. of Bessemer; iron mining and lumbering. Pop. 16,000.

Irrawaddy, great river, Burma, formed by junction of two streams which rise in N. of province; general course from N. to S.; discharges into Bay of Bengal between Gulf of Martaban and Cape Negrais through extensive delta. Main tributary, Chindwin. Riv. is main highway of commerce, being navigable from its mouth as far as Bhamo (*c.* 900 m.) for large steamers, and of enormous potential value for irrigation. Tns. on its banks, Rangoon, Bassein, Mandalay, Bhamo. Length, *c.* 1,300 m.

Irth'lingborough, urb. dist., Northamptonshire, England, 4 m. N.E. of Wellingborough; boots and shoes; ironstone quarries. Pop. 4,700.

Ir'tish, trib. of R. Ob; rising in Altai Mts., flows N.W. through Lake Zaisan, joins Ob after course of *c.* 2,600 m., of which 2,000 m. are navigable for about two-thirds of the year; passes many important towns, including Omsk, where it is crossed by Trans-Siberian railway.

Irun (*ē-roon'*), frontier tn., Spain, 8 m. E. of San Sebastian; important custom-house; hot mineral springs; ironworks, potteries, and paper mills. Pop. 14,000.

Ir'vine. (1) Royal bur. and seapt., Ayrshire, Scotland; shipbuilding, engineering, foundries, and chemical works. Pop. 12,000. (2) Riv., Ayrshire, Scotland; rises near Drumclog, and flows W. to Firth of Clyde; length, 30 m.; Kilmarnock, Galston, and Irvine on its banks.

Ir'vington, tn., New Jersey, U.S.A.; residential suburb of Newark; smelting; lumber mills. Pop. 57,000.

Isabela (*iz-a-bā'la*), province, Luzon, Philippines; mountainous and forest-clad; rice, maize, sugar, coffee, tobacco. Cap. Ilagan. Area, *c.* 4,000 sq. m.; pop. 113,000.

Isbarta (*ēs-bar'ta*), (anc. BARIS), tn., Konia, Asia Minor, 64 m. N. of Adalia; vines and poppies cultivated; carpet weaving. Pop. 45,000.

Ischia (*is'ki-a*), volcanic isl. at N. entrance of Bay of Naples, Italy; produces fruit and corn; wine and oil; straw plaiting and fishing are chief industries; subject to earthquakes. Area, 26 sq. m.; pop. 28,000. Chief tn., Ischia. Pop. 8,000.

Ischl (*ish'l*), or BAD-ISCHL, wat.-pl., Upper Austria, 30 m. S.E. of Salzburg; saline baths; salt produced from brine; villa of the former imperial family. Pop. 10,000.

Iseghem (*ē'se-gem*), tn., W. Flanders, Belgium, *c.* 10 m. N. by W. of Courtrai; manufactures textiles. Pop. *c.* 14,000.

Isère (*ē-zār'*). (1) Riv., France, trib. of Rhone; flows through Savoie, Isère, and Drôme; length, 180 m. (2) Dep., S.E. France; mountainous, especially towards S.; produces cereals, wine, fruit, hemp, butter, and cheese; rich in minerals, having mines of iron, coal, lead, silver, and copper; principal industry, glove-making, is centred in Grenoble; other industries: metal working, paper making, silk weaving, cement works. Cap. Grenoble. Area, 3,178 sq. m.; pop. 558,000.

Iserlohn (*ē-zer-lōn'*), tn., Westphalia, Prussia, 14 m. S.E. of Dortmund; iron, steel, and metal works; needles, chemicals, and furniture. Pop. 30,000.

Isfahan (*ēs-fa-hän'*), tn., Persia, on Zaindeh R., 210 m. S. of Tehran; former cap. of Persia; surrounded by gardens and orchards; manufactures include woven fabrics, gold, silver, and leather ware. Pop. *c.* 100,000.

Ishpeming (*ish'pem-ing*), city, Michigan, U.S.A., 15 m. w.s.w. of Marquette, its port on Lake Superior; iron-mining centre, gold, silver, and marble; manufactures machinery, lumber, etc. Pop. 11,000.

Iskanderun. See ALEXANDRETTA.

Iskelib (*is'kel-ib*), tn., Angora, Asia Minor, 100 m. N.E. of Angora; salt springs. Pop. 54,000.

Islay (*ī'lā*), isl., Argyllshire, Scotland; one of Inner Hebrides; dairy farming, stock raising, whisky distilling; slate and marble; popular summer resort. Chief tn., Bowmore. Area, 235 sq. m.; pop. 6,500.

Isle of Dogs, peninsula on l. bk. of Thames, London, England, included in bor. of Poplar; here are W. India and Millwall docks and large shipbuilding yards.

Isle of Man. See MAN, ISLE OF.

Isle of Wight. See WIGHT, ISLE OF.

Isleworth (*īz'ĕl-wŭrth*), par. and vil., Middlesex, England, 10 m. s.w. of St. Paul's; part of Greater London; centre of great fruit and flower growing dist.; soap works. Pop. (par.) 30,000.

Islington (*iz'ling-ton*), metropolitan bor. and par., London, England, 2 m. N. of St. Paul's. Annual horse and cattle shows; metropolitan cattle market; London Fever Hospital, and Holloway and Pentonville prisons. Pop. 321,700.

Islip (*iz'lip*), tn., Long I., New York, U.S.A.; summer resort. Pop. 21,000.

Ismail or **Izmail,** tn., Bessarabia, Romania, on an arm of R. Danube, 40 m. from Black Sea; cereals, wool, tallow, and hides; flour milling. Pop. 37,000.

Ismailia (*is-ma-ē'li-a*), tn., Lower Egypt, on N. shore of Lake Timsah and w. bank of Suez Canal; is seat of administration of Suez Canal. Pop. *c.* 10,000.

Isonzo, riv. of Illyria, Italy; enters Gulf of Trieste by two mouths; length, 81 m. Very important during Great War.

Issiq Köl (*is'ik kool*), lake, Khirgiz, U.S.S.R., lies between spurs of the Tien Shan mountains, 250 m. s. of Balkash; length, 115 m.; breadth, 38 m.

Issoudun (*ēs-oo-dun'*), tn., Indre, France, 22 m. w.s.w. of Bourges; manufactures leather, parchment, woollens, linen, and agricultural implements. Pop. 10,000.

Issy (*ē-sē'*), tn., Seine, France, 3 m. s.w. of Paris; distilleries, brass and chemical works; silk and oil cloths. Pop. 23,000.

Istambul. See CONSTANTINOPLE.

Is'tria, peninsula in N.E. Adriatic, formerly a margravate of Austria now part of Italian province of Pola; rocky coasts; country generally mountainous; olive oil, wine, fruits; mining, cattle raising, fishing. Area, 1,549 sq. m.; pop. 299,000.

Italy, kingdom in s. Europe; peninsula *c.* 700 m. long, and from 100 to 150 m. broad. It is bounded on N. by the long chain of the Alps. The islands of Sicily, Sardinia, Elba, and *c.* seventy small ones belong to Italy. The N. (Lombardy) is largely the basin of the Po. Just N. of the mouth of the Po is that of the Adige. The long chain of the Apennines, a continuation of the Alps, runs through the peninsula. The Apennines spread out into a number of ranges in Central Italy, and have thus broken up the country and delayed political union. The two rivers of Central Italy are the Arno and the Tiber. The Po is the only Italian river that surpasses the Arno in size. S. of Rome is the Campagna, an open plain. S. Italy is mostly mountainous, particularly Calabria. The only important lakes are Ls. Garda, Maggiore, and Como in the N.

Climate varies greatly. The N. in summer is as hot as the S., but in winter it is as cold as N. Europe. Oranges and lemons grow on the coast of Calabria, but a few miles inland the climate resembles that of England.

The great scourge of the s. is malaria, which is, however, being fought and reduced. Earthquakes at intervals convulse the s. (especially Calabria and Sicily); Vesuvius and Etna are active volcanoes.

Agriculture is the principal industry; chief crops are maize and rice (in N.). wheat, vines, olives, oranges, lemons, chestnuts, almonds; flax and hemp are grown, and tobacco under state control. Manufactures are silk, cotton, and motor-cars, woollens, furniture, glass (at Venice), porcelain, beet sugar, olive oil, paper. Coral- and tunny-fishing employ over 26,000 fishermen. Minerals are plentiful, the most important being sulphur ore, lead, and zinc. Carrara and Massa produce marble. Exports: silk and artificial silk, cotton, vegetables and fruit, wool, milk and cheese products, vehicles, hemp, hides, sulphur, flour, wheat pulp. Cap. Rome. Area, 119,710 sq. m.; pop. 41,168,000.

Italy has several overseas possessions, which include Eritrea, part of Somaliland, and Italian Libya, in Africa.

Itasca Lake. See MISSISSIPPI.

Ithaca (*ith'a-ka*). (1) Now THIAKI, one of Ionian islands, Greece; currants and oil; supposed to have been home of Odysseus. Area, 44 sq. m. (2) City, New York, U.S.A., 45 m. S.S.W. of Syracuse; seat of Cornell Univ.; manufactures include guns, typewriters, and clocks. Pop. 19,000.

Itzehoe (*it'zā-hō*), tn., Schleswig-Holstein, Prussia, 32 m. N.W. of Hamburg; oldest town in Holstein (founded 809); 12th cent. church; metal-founding and shipbuilding; sugar, chicory, tobacco. Pop. 20,000.

Ivanovo-Voznesensk (*ē-van-ōv'ō vos-nes'ensk*). (1) Prov., central Russia; drained by R. Volga; much of it forested; in S.W. rye, oats, wheat, and barley are grown. (2) Chief tn. in above, 150 m. N.E. of Moscow; consists of Ivanov on r. bk. of Uvod, and Voznesensk on l. bk.; cotton trade; woollen, iron, and chemical works. Pop. 111,000.

Iveston (*īvs'ton*), par. and vil., Durham, England, 9 m. N.W. of Durham; coal mines and iron foundries. Pop. (par.) 5,100.

Iviza (*ē-vē'tha* or *ē-vē'sa*). (1) One of Balearic Islands, Mediterranean Sea; hilly and well-wooded; salt (produced by evaporation), cereals, fruit. Area, 230 sq. m.; pop. 24,000. (2) Cap. of above; has cathedral and a fortress built by Philip V. Pop. 7,000.

Ivory Coast, or CÔTE D'IVOIRE, Fr. colony, N. coast of Gulf of Guinea, between Liberia and Gold Coast, part of Fr. West Africa. Surface rises from the low coastal region to mountainous Kong terr. in N.E.; much of interior densely forested. Maize, fruit, gold, coffee, cocoa, rubber, mahogany are among products. Among largest tns. are Grand Bassam, Bingerville (cap.), Abidjan, Assinie. Area, *c.* 122,000 sq. m.; pop. 1,725,000.

Ivrea (*ē-vrā'a*), tn., Piedmont, Italy, 28 m. N.N.E. of Turin; 10th cent. cathedral; silk and cotton manufactures; large markets. Pop. 12,000.

Ivry-sur-Seine (*ē-vrē'soor-sān*), tn., Seine, France, 3 m. S.E. of Paris; organs, rubber, chemicals; iron and steel works. Pop. 41,000.

I'vybridge, urb. dist., Devon, England, 10 m. E. of Plymouth; paper mills. Pop. 1,600.

Ixmiquilpan (*ēs-mē-kēl-pän'*), town, Mexico, 80 m. N. of Mexico City; silver mines. Pop. *c.* 13,000.

Izhevsk', tn., Votiak Terr., Russia, 150 m. S.W. of Perm; iron foundries. Pop. 63,000.

Iz'mid, tn., Asia Minor, near head of Gulf of Izmid, Sea of Marmara; cereals, silk, and tobacco; on Anatolian railway. Pop. 56,000.

Izmir. See SMYRNA.

J

Jabalpur. See JUBBULPORE.

Jablonec (nad Nisou) (*yäb'lon-ets näd nyē'sō*) (German *Gablonz*), tn., N. Bohemia, Czechoslovakia, 7 m. S.E. of Liberec; glass industries; textiles; Gablonz ware. Pop. 27,000.

Jack'son. (1) City, Michigan, U.S.A., 63 m. W. of Detroit; manufactures locomotives, automobiles, machinery. Pop. 55,000. (2) City, Tennessee, U.S.A., 86 m. N.E. of Memphis; large cotton trade; manufactures engines, cotton-seed oil, sewing machines. Pop. 19,000. (3) City, cap. of Mississippi, U.S.A.; centre of rich cotton-growing region, and manufactures cotton-seed products and agricultural implements. Pop. 48,000.

Jack'sonville. (1) City, N. Florida, U.S.A., on St. John's R.; commercial centre of state; exports lumber, naval stores, kaolin, phosphates, fish, fruit. Pop. 130,000. (2) City, Illinois, U.S.A., 35 m. W. of Springfield; rly. shops, woollen mills. Pop. 15,500.

Jacobabad', frontier tn., N. Sind, Bombay, India; hottest place in India; caravan trade. Pop. 11,000.

Jade (*yä'dä*), or JAHDE, bay, N.W. Oldenburg, Germany, a few miles W. of Weser estuary; on W. is Wilhelmshaven; area of bay, 75 sq. m.

Jaen (*hä-en'*). (1) Prov., S. Spain, on S. slopes of Sierra Morena; watered by Guadalquivir, Segura, etc.; one of most fertile dists. of Spain, producing oil, wine, and almonds; has lead, silver, and iron mines. Area, 5,203 sq. m.; pop. 637,500. (2) Cap. of above; Moorish ruins; leather, soap, weaving, and milling; exp. wine, fruit, and vegetables. Pop. 36,000.

Jaf'fa, or JOPPA, port, Palestine; rly. to Jerusalem; exp. fruit (esp. oranges), olive oil, barley, sesame, and wine; occupied by Allenby's forces on march to Jerusalem, 1917. Pop. 48,000.

Jaff'na, tn. and port on isl. of same name, N. Ceylon; tobacco, curry stuffs, mangoes. Pop. 42,500.

Jägerndorf. See KRNOV.

Jagersfontein (*yä-gers-fon-tīn'*), tn., Orange Free State, S. Africa, 60 m. S.W. of Bloemfontein; in neighbourhood are Klipfontein diamond mines. Pop. 4,000.

Jah'rum, tn., Fars, Persia, 100 m. S.E. of Shiraz; dates and tobacco. Pop. 15,000.

Jaipur (*jī-poor'*). (1) Indian state, Rajputana, India; greater part is vast sandy plain; rich in mineral deposits; copper, marble, iron, cobalt, and salt; one of wealthiest and best administered of Indian states. Area, 15,579 sq. m.; pop. 2,340,000. (2) Cap. of above, 150 m. S.W. of Delhi; the 'rose-red city'; manufactures gold enamelled work, Oriental metal work, carpets, and muslin; much visited by tourists. Pop. 120,500.

Jalalabad', or JELLALABAD, tn., Afghanistan, near Khyber Pass, between Kabul and Peshawar; trades in fruit and timber. Pop. *c.* 6,000.

Jalapa (*hä-läp'ä*), tn., Mexico, 50 m. N.W. of Vera Cruz; pottery, leather; medicinal plant from which jalap is prepared grows wild in dist. Pop. 28,000.

Jalisco (*hä-lis'ko*), Pacific state, Mexico; chief riv. Lerma (Santiago); partly volcanic; unhealthy coast lands; mining, stock raising, cereals. Cap. Guadalajara. Area, 33,492 sq. m.; pop. 1,200,000.

Jal'na, tn., N.W. Hyderabad, India, 38 m. E. of Aurangabad; famous fruit gardens. Pop. 17,000.

Jalpaiguri (*jul-pī'goor-i*). (1) Dist., Bengal, India, adjoining Bhutan; fertile; tea, rice, jute, timber. Area, 2,962 sq. m.; pop. 936,500. (2) Tn., cap. of above; trading centre. Pop. 15,000.

Jamai'ca, largest and most important of Brit. W. Indies; surface mountainous, being crossed from E. to W. by Blue Mts., rising to 7,423 ft.; climate pleasant and healthy; produces fruits (especially bananas), sugar, coconuts, coffee, ginger, pimento, cocoa, rum, and timber; cattle and horses raised; inhabitants include whites, Negroes, Indians, Chinese, half-breeds; rly. mileage is 210. Cap. Kingston. Area, 4,450 sq. m.; pop. 858,000.

James'town. (1) City, New York, U.S.A., 60 m. S.W. of Buffalo; furniture, woollen goods; summer resort. Pop. 45,000. (2) Tn., cap. of isl. of St. Helena; coaling station. Pop. 2,500.

Jamkhandi (*jum-kăn'dē*), Indian state, Bombay, India; cereals produced and cotton manufactured. Cap. Jamkhandi, 110 m. N.E. of Goa. Pop. of tn., 13,000; of state, 101,500.

Jamrud', fort and cantonment, N.W. Frontier Prov., India, at mouth of Khyber Pass. Pop. 6,500.

Jamshedpur', tn., Bihar and Orissa, India, 150 m. W. of Calcutta; has Tata iron and steel works. Pop. 57,000.

Janes'ville, city, S. Wisconsin, U.S.A.; machinery, textiles, shoes. Pop. 18,500.

Janina. See YANNINA.

Janiuay (*hä-nē-wī'*), tn., Panay I., Philippines, 19 m. N.W. of Iloilo; silk and cotton; sugar mills. Pop. 25,000.

Janjira', Indian maritime state, Bombay, India; rice, coconuts; fishing. Chief tn., Janjira, 40 m. S. of Bombay. Area, 324 sq. m.; pop. 88,000.

Jan Mayen (*yăn mī'en*), isl. between Iceland and Spitsbergen; annexed by Norway, 1929; volcanic origin (Beerenberg, 8,000 ft., is extinct volcano); glaciers; seal and whale fisheries. Length, 35 m.

Ja'ora. (1) Indian state, Central India; millet, cotton, maize. Area, 600 sq. m.; pop. 86,000. (2) Cap. of above, 75 m. N.W. of Indore. Pop. 17,500.

Japan' (Jap. *Nippon*, 'eastern land'), empire, E. Asia; consists of Japan Proper, a chain of islands including Kuriles (Jap. *Chishima*), Hokkaido, Honshu, Shikoku, Kyushu, and Ryukyu group, also S. Sakhalin (Jap. *Karafuto*), Formosa (Jap. *Taiwan*), Pescadores (Jap. *Bokoto*), Korea (Jap. *Chosen*) on mainland, Caroline, Marshall, and Ladrone groups in N. Pacific Ocean. To these may be added Kwantung, S. Liaotung pen. (including Port Arthur and Dairen), leased from China.

Surface generally mountainous, with many active and dormant volcanoes, and country is subject to frequent earthquake shocks, that of Sept. 1923 being especially destructive; among highest peaks is beautifully shaped cone of Fuji-san (12,400 ft.); hot mineral springs abound. The outline of all the islands is much broken; rivs. short and rapid, and in summer torrential, from the heavy rains and melting of snow; useful for irrigation, but not for navigation. Climate varies greatly with the latitude; in main islands, temp. ranges from *c.* 5° F. to 80° in N., and from 42° to 98° in S.; rainfall increases from 40 in. in N. to over 80 in S., and in some places rises to 150; N. Pacific current, known as the Kuro Siwo ('black tide'), passing N. along whole S.E. coast, makes this much warmer than N.W.; typhoons are most destructive in autumn; snowfall very heavy in N.W.

Trees include oak, beech, pine, elm, cedar, wax tree, chestnut, maple, sago-palm, and bamboo; cherry tree largely cultivated, and paper-mulberry and lacquer tree are characteristic and of great economic value; fruits include oranges, grapes, persimmons, and peaches. Principal industries are agriculture, silk production, forestry, and fisheries; agriculture employs *c.* 60 per cent. of inhabitants; cultivation greatly hampered by difficulties of communication. Of cultivated area (exclusive of Formosa) *c.* 60 per cent. is under rice; two or three crops raised on same field every year;

cattle, horses, pigs, and goats are reared, but few sheep. Minerals are important; coal production is increasing, and silver, copper, antimony, gold, sulphur, iron, graphite, and china-clay are worked, as well as petroleum; manufactures include cotton, silk, lacquer-ware, bronzes, mats, carpets and rugs, porcelain, pottery, bamboo and cane work, matches, glass; shipbuilding; iron and steel.

Japan is one of great naval powers of the world; has large mercantile marine; chief exports: silk and silk goods, cotton goods, and pottery; principal exports to United Kingdom are silk, fish, tinned peas, soya bean oil; principal imports from U.K. are textiles, iron and steel, chemicals and dyes, machinery.

The Japanese are of Mongoloid stock, and a striking difference exists between the upper and lower classes; former are white or light yellow in colour, with oval face, obliquely set eyes and small mouth; the latter are darker in complexion and stronger in build, and have coarser features and straight eyes.

The largest tns. are Osaka, Tokyo (cap.), Nagoya, Kyoto, Kobé, Yokohama; most important ports, Yokohama, Kobé, Osaka, Moji, and Nagasaki. Area of Japan Proper, 152,357 sq. m.; pop. 59,700,000. Total area of empire, 265,129 sq. m.; total pop. *c.* 83,500,000.

Jaroslav. See YAROSLAVL.

Jaroslaw (*yä-rō'swaf*), tn., Galicia, Poland, on R. San, 60 m. W.N.W. of Lwow; pottery, cloth, brandy, confectionery. Pop. 20,500.

Jar'row, tn. and riv. port, Durham, England, on r. bk. of R. Tyne; shipbuilding, foundries, paper, and chemical works. Pop. 32,000.

Jashpur'. (1) Indian state, Central Provs., India; ebony and other timber. Area, 1,963 sq. m.; pop. 154,500. (2) Cap. of above, 85 m. N. by E. of Sambalpur. Pop. 1,700.

Jassy (*yäsh'ē*), cap., dep. of same name, Romania, on R. Prut; trade in cereals, petroleum, salt, metals, fruits, wine, cattle. Pop. 185,000.

Játiva (*hä'tē-va*), city, E. Spain, 35 m. S.S.W. of Valencia; fruit culture; oil, wine. Pop. 14,500.

Jauer (*you'er*), tn., Silesia, Prussia, 38 m. W. of Breslau; leather, carpets, machinery. Pop. 12,500.

Jaunpur'. (1) Dist., United Provs., India; traversed by R. Gumti; highly cultivated; rice, sugar-cane, tobacco. Area, 1,551 sq. m.; pop. 1,155,000. (2) Tn., cap. of above, on R. Gumti, 35 m. N.W. of Benares; perfumes, papier-mâché. Pop. 33,000.

Ja'va, isl., Dutch E. Indies; volcanic mts. run from end to end of isl.; many active volcanoes, some peaks reaching 12,000 ft.; in N. are fertile alluvial plains; rivs. short and commercially unimportant; climate unhealthy in low-lying dists., hot and damp, but heat tempered by regular sea breezes; average temp. in lower parts is 78° F.; rainfall about 75 in. Mts. covered with trees to 10,000 ft.; forests produce teak, coconuts, palms, bamboos, spice trees; cultivated products include rice, maize, cassava, sugar, coffee, tea, tobacco, rubber; minerals include petroleum, coal, salt, sulphur; exports, chiefly to Holland, include sugar, rubber, coffee, tea, tobacco, cinchona, tin; trade mainly carried on by Arabs and Chinese, the native inhabitants being engaged chiefly in agriculture; manufacture of coarse cloth, mats, and soap. Cap. Batavia. Area, 50,811 sq. m.; pop. 37,434,000.

Jaworów (*yä-vor'ov*), tn., Galicia, Poland, 30 m. W.N.W. of Lwow; brewing, pottery. Pop. 9,000.

Jaworzno (*yä-vozh'no*), tn., Poland, 30 m. N.W. of Cracow; coal mines, petroleum wells; zinc-smelting works. Pop. 13,000.

Jaxartes. See SIR DARYA.

Jazira, AL (*jäz-ē'rä*), country between rivs. Tigris and Euphrates, N.W. of Baghdad.

Jed'burgh, royal burgh, Roxburghshire, Scotland; ruins of beautiful abbey, founded 1118; tweeds and other woollens; tanning. Pop. 3,100.

Jedda. See JIDDA.

Jef'ferson City, cap. of Missouri, U.S.A.; agricultural implements, shoes, clothing, tiles; rly. workshops. Pop. 14,500.

Jef'fersonville, city, s. Indiana, U.S.A.; rly. engineering works. Pop. 11,000.

Jelgava (*yel'ga-va*), formerly MITAU, tn., Latvia, 30 m. s.w. of Riga; linen factories; soap works. Pop. 28,500.

Jellalabad. See JALALABAD.

Jemappes (*zhĕ-măp'*), tn., Belgium, 3 m. w. of Mons; coal and iron mining. Famous for victory of French over Austrians (1792). Pop. 15,000.

Jena (*yā'nä*), tn., Thuringia, Germany, on R. Saale; univ. founded in 1558; trade in books, pianos, and optical instruments. Scene of defeat of Prussians by Napoleon (1806). Pop. 54,000.

Jer'ablus (anc. *Carchemish*), tn., N. Syria, Asia, on R. Euphrates, 65 m. N.E. of Aleppo; Baghdad rly. crosses river here.

Jer'ba, isl., Gulf of Qabes, off Tunisian coast, Africa; 'isl. of lotus-eaters'; sponges, dates, olives, silk-and-wool material. Area, 425 sq. m.; pop. *c.* 90,000.

Jerez, or JEREZ DE LA FRONTERA (*hā-reth' dā la fron-tā'ra*), formerly XERES, tn., Cadiz, Spain; famous for *sherry* (name derived from *Jerez*); relics of Moorish occupation. Pop. 65,000.

Jer'icho, vil., Palestine, 5 m. N. of Dead Sea; taken by Israelites under Joshua; later destroyed by Romans; rebuilt by Hadrian; ruined during Crusades; captured by Brit. forces in Great War (Feb. 21, 1918). Pop. 1,000.

Jer'sey, largest of Channel Islands; surface undulating, mostly cultivated; potatoes, tomatoes; good fishing; famous cattle; dairy produce; holiday resort. Chief tn., St. Helier. Area, 45 sq. m.; pop. 50,000.

Jer'sey City, tn., New Jersey, U.S.A., on R. Hudson, practically a suburb of New York; important rly. terminus; excellent harbour; meat packing; iron, steel, machinery, chemicals, tobacco, pottery. Pop. 16,000.

Jeru'salem, cap., Palestine; stands on hills of Zion, Acra, Moriah, and Bezetha, and thus a natural fortress almost impregnable in ancient times; sacred city of Jews and Christians; in Great War Jerusalem was surrendered by Turks to Allenby (Dec. 9, 1917); many improvements carried out in and around the city; univ. (on Mt. Scopus) opened in 1925 for Jewish and Oriental studies. Pop. 63,000.

Jervis Bay, detached portion of Federal Terr., on coast of New South Wales, Australia; naval college; future port of Canberra, 123 m. distant by rail. Area, *c.* 4,000 ac.

Jes'selton, port, Brit. N. Borneo, on S. China Sea; rly. to interior.

Jhang. (1) Dist., Punjab, India; drained by Rs. Chenab, Jhelum, and Ravi; grain, cotton, oil-seeds. Area, 3,452 sq. m.; pop. 571,000. (2) Tn., cap. of above; leather, soap, brass work. Pop. 30,500.

Jhansi (*jăn'sē*). (1) Dist., United Provs., India, between E. and W. section of Central India; produces cereals and cotton; frequently suffers from famine. Area, 3,634 sq. m.; pop. 606,500. (2) Cap. of above, 110 m. s.w. of Cawnpore; rly. jn.; has fort. Pop. 66,500.

Jhelum (*jā'lum*), or JEHLAM. (1) Riv., India; unites with Chenab; one of the 'five rivers' of Punjab; irrigates large areas. (2) Dist., Punjab, India, crossed by Salt Range and Jhelum R.; cereals, oil-seeds. Area, 2,773 sq. m.; pop. 477,000. (3) Tn., cap. of above, on R. Jhelum, 100 m. N. of Lahore; trades with Kashmir. Pop. 18,500.

Jibuti (*zhē-boo'tē*), cap., Fr. Somaliland, Africa, on Gulf of Aden; fine harbour; exports coffee, rubber, ivory, live-stock; rly. to Abyssinia. Pop. 8,500.

Jichin (*yēch'ēn*), tn., Bohemia, Czechoslovakia, 60 m. N.E. of Prague; agricultural machinery, leather. Pop. 10,500.

Jid'da, port, Hejaz, Arabia, on Red Sea, 50 m. W. by N. of Mecca; pilgrims for Mecca land here; extensive harbour; exports mother-of-pearl, coffee, carpets, balsams. Pop. 25,000.

Jihlava (*yē'lävä*), formerly IGLAU, tn., Moravia, Czechoslovakia, 50 m. W. of Brno; trades in timber and grain; textiles, leather, glass. Pop. 28,500.

Jind (*jēnd*), Indian state, Punjab, India; chief products, grain and cotton; principal manufactures, gold and silver jewellery, cloth, leather. Cap. Sangrur (pop. 12,000); former cap. Jind, 75 m. N. of Delhi (pop. 11,000). Area, 1,259 sq. m.; pop. 308,500.

Jitomir (*zhē-tō-mēr'*), tn., Ukraine, U.S.S.R., 70 m. W. of Kiev; iron smelting. Pop. 77,000.

Joachimsthal (*yō'ä-chims-täl*), tn., Bohemia, Czechoslovakia, on S. slopes of Erzgebirge, 10 m. N. of Carlsbad; mines yield silver, nickel, bismuth, uranium; first German silver dollars ('thalers') coined here. Pop. 8,000.

Jodhpur (*jod-poor'*), or MARWAR. (1) Indian state, Rajputana, India; largely desolate, sandy country, watered by Luni and its affluents; produces salt (from Sambhar and other salt lakes), tin, iron, marble, cereals. Area, 34,963 sq. m.; pop. 1,842,000. (2) Cap. of above; walled town; has a fortress. Pop. 73,500.

Johan'nesburg, tn., Transvaal, S. Africa; largest city in S. Africa; commercial and gold-mining centre; in Witwatersrand goldfield; alt. 5,740 ft.; founded in 1886 on discovery of gold; rly. centre; other industries: printing, milling, brewing, and iron and brass founding. Pop. 302,000 (171,000 whites).

Johannisberg (*yō-han'-*), vil. and castle, Hesse-Nassau, Prussia, 12 m. W. of Mainz; vineyards (52 ac.) produce the famous Johannisberger wine.

John o' Groats, or **John o' Groat's House**, 2 m. W. of Duncansby Head, Caithness, Scotland; used to denote most N. part of Great Britain; named from former octagonal house of John Groat, who received royal grant of the lands and ferry of Duncansby, *c.* 1600.

John'son City, city, E. Tennessee, U.S.A., 90 m. E. of Knoxville; tourist centre; foundries; produces leather and furniture. Pop. 25,000.

Johns'tone, tn., Renfrew, Scotland, 3 m. W. by S. of Paisley; cotton, flax, iron, machinery, shoe laces; collieries in vicinity. Pop. 12,800.

Johns'town. (1) Tn., Pennsylvania, U.S.A., 55 m. E. of Pittsburgh; iron and steel manufactures. Pop. 67,000. (2) Tn., New York, U.S.A., 40 m. N.W. of Albany; manufactures gloves, clothing. Pop. 11,000.

Johore (*jō-hōr'*), or JOHOR, independent sultanate (under Brit. protection), S. extremity of Malay Pen., Asia; surface low-lying; forested; produces rubber, timber, coffee, sago, pepper; rly. (120 m.). Cap. Johore. Area, 7,678 sq. m.; pop. 330,500.

Jokjakar'ta, or JOKYAKARTA, residency, Java, Dutch E. Indies; sugar, tobacco. Cap. Jokjakarta (110,000), 260 m. E.S.E. of Batavia; large citadel. Pop. 1,400,000.

Jo'liet, city, Illinois, U.S.A., 30 m. S.W. of Chicago; iron and steel manufactures. Pop. 42,000.

Joliette, city, Quebec, Canada, 43 m. N. of Montreal; woollen, paper, and tobacco manufactures. Pop. 11,000.

Jönköping (*yon-cho'ping*), tn., Sweden, on S. end of L. Vetter; manufactures matches, carpets, paper, arms. Pop. 30,000.

Jop'lin, tn., Missouri, U.S.A., 140 m. S. of Kansas City; zinc and lead; smelting works. Pop. 33,000.

Joppa. See JAFFA.

Jor'dan, riv., Palestine, rises on slopes of Mt. Hermon; flows through Sea of Galilee and rift valley into Dead Sea.

Juan de Fuca. See FUCA.

Juan Fernandez Islands (*hwän fernän'däth*), volcanic group (belonging to Chile), S. Pacific Ocean; largest is Mas-a-Tierra, where Alexander Selkirk, prototype of Robinson Crusoe, lived (1704–9); wireless station; *c.* 300 inhabitants.

Juba (*joo'ba* or *yoo'ba*), or JUB, riv., E. Africa, rising in the highlands of Abyssinia, Africa; traverses Galla country and Italian Somaliland, reaching Indian Ocean near Kismayu; in lower reaches fringed by a narrow fertile belt. Length, *c.* 1,000 m.

Jubbulpore', or JABALPUR. (1) Most northerly div., Central Provs., India; generally hilly. Area, 18,950 sq. m.; pop. *c.* 2,000,000. (2) Dist. in above, largely in rich plain of Narbada riv.; wheat, millet, oil-seeds. Area, 3,912 sq. m.; pop. 746,000. (3) Cap. of div.; cottons, carpets, pottery; oil and flour mills; military station; important rly. jn. Pop. 108,000.

Judæ'a, term applied to S. Palestine in time of Christ.

Ju'dah, dist. of ancient Palestine, between Philistia and Dead Sea.

Jug'gernaut. See PURI.

Jugo-Slavia. See YUGOSLAVIA.

Jujuy (*hoo-hwē'*), prov., N. Argentina, S. America; mountainous in E., with fertile valleys; dry plateau in W.; sugar-cane, cereals, fruit. Cap. Jujuy (8,000). Area, 14,802 sq. m.; pop. 90,000.

Jullundur', or JALANDHAR, tn., Punjab, India, 50 m. S.E. of Amritsar; flour mills, cotton and silk factories. Pop. 71,000.

Jumilla (*hoo-mē'lyă*), tn., E. Spain, 40 m. N. by W. of Murcia; coarse cloth and esparto fabrics. Pop. 20,500.

Jum'na, riv., N. India; rises in Himalayas; forms boundary between Punjab and United Provs.; crosses United Provs., and unites with Ganges below Allahabad. Chief cities on banks: Delhi, Agra, Muttra, Allahabad. Length, 860 m.

Junagarh (*joo-nă-gur'*), or JUNAGAD, tn., Kathiawar Peninsula, Bombay, India; ancient citadel. Pop. 33,500.

Juneau (*joo-nō'*), cap., Alaska, *c.* 320 m. N.W. of Prince Rupert; gold-mining and fishing centre; lumber products. Pop. 3,500.

Jung-Bunzlau. See MLADA BOLESLAV.

Jungfrau (*yoong-frou'*), mt., Bernese Oberland, Switzerland; alt. 13,669 ft.; name means the 'maiden'; first ascended in 1811; electric railway up to 11,340 ft.

Junin (*hoo-nēn'*), central dep., Peru, S. America; copper, silver, lead. Cap. Cerro de Pasco. Area, 22,814 sq. m.; pop. 450,000.

Ju'ra. (1) Mountainous isl., Inner Hebrides, Scotland; nearly bisected by Loch Tarbert; highest point, Paps of Jura, 2,571 ft.; sheep farming and agriculture; fishing; quarrying. Area, 143 sq. m.; pop. 500. (2) Mt. range, along borders of France and Switzerland; length over 150 m., breadth *c.* 40 m.; chiefly limestone; forms a high plateau rising in several parallel chains. (3) Dep., E. France; mainly mountainous; drained by R. Doubs; large forests; vines, cereals, cheese; rock salt and iron mines; clocks, watches, toys. Cap. Lons-le-Saunier. Area, 1,951 sq. m.; pop. 231,000.

Jutigalpa (*hoo-tē-găl'pa*), or JUTICALPA, tn., Honduras, Central America; centre of rich mining and agricultural district. Pop. 10,000.

Jut'land, pen., forming continental part of Denmark. See DENMARK.

K

K². See GODWIN-AUSTEN.

Kabar'din-Bal'kar, area between North Caucasian Area and Georgia, U.S.S.R.; Kabardin is plain and hilly; Balkar is mountainous, including loftiest part of Caucasus Mts. (Mt. Elbruz, 18,465 ft.); numerous streams; main occupations are herding cattle and sheep, and agriculture (maize, sunflowers, potatoes, and vegetables). Chief tn., Nalchik. Area, *c.* 3,600 sq. m.; pop. 204,000.

Kab'ba, prov., N. Nigeria, W. Africa; valleys fertile and stretches of dense forest; watered by Rs. Niger and Benue; cereals, rubber, tobacco, indigo, and cotton. Chief tns., Zungeru (cap.) and Lokoja. Area, 10,382 sq. m.; pop. 411,000.

Kabin'da. (1) Part of Belgian Congo, w. Africa, N. of mouth of R. Congo; very fertile; has flourishing plantations and orange groves. Area, *c.* 3,000 sq. m. (2) Cap. of above, on the coast; formerly a famous slave mart. Pop. *c.* 10,000.

Kabul (*kä'bool*). (1) Riv., Afghanistan; source in Hindu Kush; joins Indus; length, 300 m. (2) Cap., Afghanistan, on Kabul R.; 6,900 ft. above sea-level; an anc. town commanding passes N. and W.; on trade route between Central Asia and Punjab; large transit trade in carpets, shawls, soap, silk, and cotton. Pop. *c.* 100,000.

Kach'hi, level dist., Baluchistan, between Brit. Baluchistan and native state; fertile where irrigated; leather and pottery. Area, 5,300 sq. m.; pop. 75,000.

Kachin' Hills, hill region, N. Burma; crossed by several mountain chains; watered by Irrawaddy; inhabited by lawless native tribes. Area, *c.* 19,180 sq. m.; pop. 64,000.

Kadur', dist., Mysore, India; mostly hilly; well forested; rice and coffee. Chief tn., Chikmagalur, 80 m. N.W. of Mysore. Area, 2,788 sq. m.; pop. 334,000.

Kaf'fa, dist. in S.W. of Abyssinia, Africa; mountainous and thickly wooded; coffee grown on mt. slopes. Area, *c.* 5,000 sq. m.

Kaffra'ria ('land of the Kaffirs'), former name for Transkeian Territories, S. Africa; name sometimes restricted to dist. between Great Fish and Great Kei Rs.; annexed to Cape Colony in 1865 as Brit. Kaffraria.

Kafiristan', dist., N.E. Afghanistan, on S. slope of Hindu Kush; mountainous; watered by tribs. of Rs. Indus and Kabul; many great forests. The inhabitants, pastoral tribes, are backward in civilization. The country commands the passes of the Hindu Kush. Area, *c.* 5,000 sq. m.; pop. *c.* 175,000.

Kagē'ra, riv., E. Africa, headwater of Nile; enters Lake Victoria; lower reaches navigable for shallow draught steamers; length, about 430 m.

Kagoshima (*kä-go-shē'ma*), tn., S. Kyushu, Japan, on Kagoshima Gulf; arms, cotton, pottery, glass, cigarettes. Pop. 125,000.

Kaietur Fall (*kī'ē-toor*), waterfall, Potaro riv., Brit. Guiana, S. America; alt. of great fall, 741 ft.; of small falls, 81 ft.

Kai-feng (*kī-feng*), walled tn., cap. of Honan, China, near Hwang-Ho R., from floods of which it has often suffered; centre of important agricultural area; cotton factories. Pop. 200,000.

Kaira (*kī'ra*), dist., Bombay, India, N. of Gulf of Cambay; largely plain; chief crops, cotton, millet, rice, pulse; bauxite mined; exports ghee (clarified butter). Chief tn., Kaira. Area, 1,608 sq. m.; pop. 711,000.

Kairwan. See QAIRWAN.

Kaiseng (*kī'seng*), or SONG-DO, tn., Korea, 35 m. N.W. of Seoul; was cap. from 910 to 1232; ginseng and oiled paper. Pop. 60,000.

Kaiserslautern (*kī'zers-lou'tern*), tn., Bavaria, Germany, on R. Waldauter, 42 m. W. of Mannheim; manufactures iron goods, cotton, woollens, beer, tobacco, sugar. Pop. 59,000.

Kaiser Wilhelm's Land. See NEW GUINEA.

Kaithal (*kī-tul'*), tn., Punjab, India, 50 m. S.W. by S. of Ambala; saltpetre, lac ornaments, toys. Pop. 16,000.

Kalahar'i Desert, vast steppe region in Bechuanaland and S.W. Africa; elevation of 3,000 to 4,000 ft.; almost waterless; inhabited by agricultural race and by nomadic Bushmen or hunters; many parts covered with vegetation; cattle raised in E. portion and crops grown; big game abundant. Area, 120,000 sq. m.; pop. *c.* 50,000.

Kalamat'a, seapt., S. Greece; important fig centre; exports silk, olive oil, currants, and fruit. Pop. 29,000.

Kalamazoo′, tn., s. Michigan, U.S.A.; railway centre; machinery, paper; much celery and fruit (esp. grapes). Pop. 54,000.

Kalat′. (1) State, Baluchistan; mountainous, with fertile valleys; salt. Area, 73,278 sq. m.; pop. 328,000. (2) Cap. of above; khan's palace. Pop. 15,000.

Kal′be, tn., Saxony, Prussia, on R. Saale, 17 m. s. of Magdeburg; rly. jn.; manufactures textiles, paper, and sugar. Pop. 11,000.

Kalgan′, fort, tn., Hopeh, China, 100 m. N.W. of Peking; extensive transit trade; centre for wool, furs, skins, and tea. Pop. 76,500.

Kalgoor′lie, tn., W. Australia, 340 m. E.N.E. of Perth; goldfields; water supply pumped from Perth; now linked by rly. with Port Augusta, S. Australia. Pop. 5,300.

Kalimpong, tn., Bengal, India, in Darjeeling dist.; health station (alt. 3,933 ft.) with Church of Scotland Homes for poor European and Eurasian children (1900); mkt. tn. for Tibetan wool and mules; agricultural fairs.

Kalisz (*kä′lish*). (1) Prov., Poland; flat and sandy; many lakes and marshes; cereals, cattle raising. Area, 4,377 sq. m.; pop. 1,342,400. (2) Cap. of above, 50 m. w. of Lodz; brewing and tanning; ribbons, sugar. Pop. 45,000.

Kal′mar, port and cathedral tn., Sweden, opposite Öland I.; shipbuilding and timber products. Pop. 19,000.

Kal′muck, Autonomous Area, Russia, N.W. of Caspian Sea and s. of R. Volga; a plain, most of which is below sea-level; not well watered; stock raising; inhabited by Mongols. Chief tn., Astrakhan. Area, 27,850 sq. m.; pop. 153,000.

Kalocsa (*kol′och-ä*), tn., Hungary, near l. bk. of R. Danube; fine cathedral, archbishop's palace, and observatory; wine, fruit, flax, cereals. Pop. 12,000.

Kaluga (*kä-loo′gä*). (1) Prov., central Russia, bounded by Moscow on N. Iron and coal mined; rye, oats, potatoes, flax, cucumbers, and vegetables are cultivated. Area, 10,282 sq. m.; pop. 1,152,000. (2) Cap. of above, on R. Oka; leather goods, beer, bricks, and sausages. Pop. 52,000.

Kamchat′ka, peninsula, E. Siberia, E. of Sea of Okhotsk; traversed by mountain range with volcanic peaks; drained by Kamchatka and other streams; severe climate; thermal springs; valuable furs; minerals in mountains; abundant fish; salmon canneries; reindeer bred. Area, *c.* 104,280 sq. m.; pop. *c.* 20,000.

Kam′enets Podolskiy′, or PODOLIAN KAMENETS, tn., Ukraine, U.S.S.R., 250 m. N.W. of Odessa; tobacco and brewing. Pop. 30,000.

Kamenz (*kä′ments*), tn., Saxony, Germany, on R. Schwarz Elster, 21 m. N.E. of Dresden; leather, glass, stoneware. Pop. 11,000.

Kamerun. See CAMEROONS.

Kam′et, MOUNT, Himalayan peak, United Provs., India, 210 m. N.E. of Delhi; first climbed by Brit. party under Frank Smythe, June 21, 1931; highest summit yet attained by man. Alt. 25,447 ft.

Kam′loops, tn., British Columbia, Canada, on Thompson R., 150 m. N.E. of Vancouver; brewing and fruit preserving; cigars, bricks. Pop. 4,500.

Kam′pen, tn., Overyssel, Holland, near mouth of R. Ijssel; cigars; trade in hay and dairy produce. Pop. 20,000.

Kampot, tn., s.w. Cambodia, Asia, on Gulf of Siam; principal seaport. Pop. 3,000.

Kamp′ti, tn., Central Provs., India, 9 m. N.E. of Nagpur; cotton. Pop. 50,000.

Kamrup′, dist., Assam, India, on both sides of R. Brahmaputra; rice is the chief crop. Chief tn., Gauhati. Area, 3,863 sq. m.; pop. 762,000.

Kamyshin′, tn., Saratov, Russia, on R. Volga; exports cereals and salt; timber and flour mills. Pop. 18,000.

Kan'ara. (1) NORTH, strip of country between W. Ghats and Arabian Sea, Bombay, India; hills well wooded; rice, coconuts, cardamoms, pepper, teak. Area, 3,946 sq. m.; pop. 402,000. (2) SOUTH, terr., Madras, s. of above; rice, coconuts, coffee, areca nuts, spices; manufactures tiles. Area, 4,021 sq. m.; pop. 1,247,000.

Kanazawa (*kă-nă-ză'wă*), tn., Honshu, Japan, on W. coast, 125 m. N.E. of Kyoto; porcelain, silks, inlaid bronzes. Pop. 147,500.

Kanchenjung'a, highest peak in Nepal Himalayas, N. India; over 28,000 ft.

Kandahar', tn., Afghanistan, commanding entrance of Bolan Pass. On main route between India and Persia, trades largely with Herat, Samarqand, Bukhara, and Bombay; silks and felts produced; exports wool, fruit, vegetables, provisions; encircled by walls; on high rock to N. is strong fortress. Pop. 60,000.

Kan'dy, old cap., Ceylon, near centre of isl.; picturesque; native temples (one containing Buddha's tooth); tea, cocoa, pepper. Pop. 33,000.

Kan'gra. (1) Dist., Punjab, India; tea, rice, honey, spices. Chief tn., Dharmsala, 100 m. N.E. of Amritsar. Area, 9,978 sq. m.; pop. 766,000. (2) Tn. in above, former cap.; destroyed by earthquake (1905). Pop. 5,000.

Kankakee', tn., Illinois, U.S.A., on Kankakee R., 56 m. s. of Chicago; agricultural implements, furniture, machinery, incubators. Pop. 17,000.

Kannstatt', tn., Württemberg, Germany, on R. Neckar, 2½ m. from Stuttgart; mineral springs; chemicals, motor-cars, and machinery. Pop. 21,000.

Kano (*kă'no*). (1) Prov., N. Nigeria, Africa; mainly well-cultivated plain. Area, *c.* 20,000 sq. m.; pop. 2,300,000. (2) Cap. of above; walled; great trading centre; manufactures cotton, Hausa gowns, embroidered goods, and leather articles. Pop. 50,000.

Kan'sas, a central state of U.S.A.; bounded N. by Nebraska, E. by Missouri, S. by Oklahoma, W. by Colorado. Surface generally consists of undulating prairie, rising from 800 ft. in S.E. to 4,000 ft. in N.W.; drained by Rs. Kansas and Arkansas and their tribs. Climate is healthy, although subject to occasional extremes of both heat and cold. Kansas is pre-eminently agricultural (irrigation required in W.), and produces large crops of maize, wheat, oats, alfalfa, potatoes, barley, flax. Live-stock is largely raised; dairy farming flourishes in W. Minerals include vast quantities of coal; oil, petroleum, natural gas, zinc, limestone, lead, salt, gypsum also found. Industries include meat packing, flour milling, dairying. Chief tns., Kansas City, Topeka (cap.), and Wichita. Area, 82,158 sq. m.; pop. 1,852,000.

Kan'sas City. (1) Tn., Missouri, U.S.A., on r. bk. of Missouri R., adjoining Kansas City, Kansas; important railway and trading centre; has grain elevators, stockyards, meat-packing houses; butter substitutes, butter, eggs, lumber, grain; important annual live-stock show. Pop. 399,000. (2) Tn., Kansas, U.S.A., on R. Missouri; practically part of above; meat-packing and live-stock trade; flour milling; locomotives; soap. Pop. 122,000.

Kansk, tn., Siberian Area, U.S.S.R., on Trans-Siberian Rly., 130 m. E. of Krasnoyarsk; near iron, gold, and coal fields; leather working and distilling. Pop. 19,000.

Kansu', prov., China, drained by Hwang-Ho; mountainous parts well timbered; in E., loess regions produce poppy; cereals, fruits; gold, mercury, petroleum, and coal are found. Cap. Lanchow. Area, 125,450 sq. m.; pop. 5,928,000.

Kantara, now QANTARA. See SUEZ CANAL.

Kapur'thala, Indian state, Punjab, India, 35 m. S.E. of Amritsar; cotton, sugar, wheat, tobacco. Area, 630 sq. m.; pop. 284,000.

Kara, dist., Far E. Area, U.S.S.R., 300 m. E. of Chita; gold mines.

Karachi (*karä'chi*), port, Sind, India, N.W. of Indus delta; outlet for N.W. India; rly. terminus; excellent harbour; nearest Indian port to Europe; air port; exports wheat, hides, tallow, wool. Pop. 217,000.

Kara-Hissar' Sharki, or SHABIN KARA-HISSAR, tn., Asia Minor, 85 m. S.W. of Trebizond; alum mines. Pop. 18,000.

Kara-Kalpak', an area, part of Kazak Rep., U.S.S.R., lying S.E. of Sea of Aral along N. bk. of R. Oxus; largely desert; fertile soils along Oxus; producing figs, melons, fruits, and some wheat, maize, cotton. Area, 45,200 sq. m.; pop. 303,000.

Karako'ram Mts., or MUSTAGH RANGE, range of mts. 450 m. long, in Central Asia, N. of Kashmir, between Hindu Kush and Kunlun mts.; great glaciers; highest peak, Mt. Godwin-Austen.

Kara-kul', GREAT, salt lake, Ferghana, Central Asia, on Pamir plateau; *c.* 13,000 ft. above sea-level; 12 m. by 10 m.; no outlet, and was formerly much larger.

Kara-kum'. See QARA QUM.

Kara Sea (*kä'ra*), branch of Arctic Ocean; 170 m. by 300 m.; between Novaya Zemlya and N.W. Siberia; navigation open from July to Sept.

Karasu-Bazar (*ka-rä'soo-ba-zär'*), tn., Crimea, Russia; manufactures morocco leather goods, embroidery; exports fruit. Pop. 13,000.

Karateghin (*kä-rä-tä-gēn'*), former khanate of Bukhara, now included in Tajik Rep., U.S.S.R.; good pasture. Area, 8,000 sq. m. Pop. *c.* 300,000.

Karauli (*kä-rou'li*), Indian state, Rajputana, India; hilly, richly timbered; agriculture, cattle raising; iron ore. Chief tn., Karauli, 70 m. S.E. of Jaipur. Area, 1,242 sq. m.; pop. 134,000.

Karbala (*kar-bä'la*), tn., Iraq, 60 m. S.S.W. of Baghdad; a holy city and a centre of pilgrimage; exports cereals, dates, and hides. Pop. 55,000.

Kare'lia, rep., Russia, between Finland and White Sea; contains Lake Onega and many other lakes and marshes; stretches of forest; little agriculture; timber industries. Chief tn., Petrozavodsk, on W. shore of L. Onega. Area, 53,890 sq. m.; pop. 267,000.

Karen'ni, region between Siam and Lower Burma; drained by Salween R.; consisting of number of small native states under Brit. control; inhabited by Red Karens and other tribes; produces teak, rice, lac, hides, areca nuts. Area, 4,280 sq. m.; pop. 63,000.

Karikal'. (1) Fr. possession, Coromandel coast, India; very fertile; irrigated by branches of Cauvery R. Area, 53 sq. m.; pop. 58,000. (2) Cap. of above; exports rice, pottery, and ground-nuts. Pop. 17,000.

Karlovac (*kar'lo-vats*), tn., Croatia-Slavonia, Yugoslavia, 30 m. S.W. of Zagreb; chemicals, woollens, leather. Pop. 17,000.

Karlovci Sremski (*kar'lov-tsi*), formerly KARLOWITZ, tn. and archiepisc. see, Croatia-Slavonia, Yugoslavia, N.W. of Belgrade, near R. Danube; wine and plum brandy. Pop. 5,700.

Karlsbad. See CARLSBAD.

Karlsburg. See ALBA-IULIA.

Karlskro'na, or CARLSCRONA, port, S. Sweden; headquarters of Swedish fleet; felt hats, leather, canvas; exports timber, fish, dairy produce. Pop. 27,000.

Karlsruhe (*karls-roo'e*), cap. of Baden, Germany, 30 m. S. of Heidelberg; palace, picture gallery, and academy of art; railway stock, machinery, hardware, surgical instruments, chemicals, carpets, beer, perfumes, tobacco. Pop. 146,000.

Karl'stad, tn., Sweden, on isl. N. end of L. Vener; timber trade; matches, machinery, tobacco; agreement dissolving union of Norway and Sweden signed here (1905). Pop. 20,000.

Karnak', vil., Egypt, on R. Nile, where anc. Thebes stood; site of great temple and other ruins.

Kar'nal. (1) Dist., Punjab, India,

N. of Delhi; alluvial plain producing cotton, sugar, cereals. Area, 3,125 sq. m.; pop. 829,000. (2) Cap. of above; manufactures cotton, blankets, boots. Pop. 23,000.

Karroo. See under CAPE OF GOOD HOPE.

Kars. (1) Vilayet, Turkey-in-Asia, in extreme N.E.; elevated plateau crossed by mts.; thickly wooded; extreme climate; agriculture and cattle rearing; extensive deposits of salt. Area, 7,238 sq. m.; pop. 205,000. (2) Fortress and cathedral tn., cap. of above, 110 m. S.E. of Batum; coarse woollens, carpets, felt. Pop. 24,000.

Karun (*kä-roon'*), river, Persia, rises in Bakhtiari Mts., flows W. and S., and joins the Shatt-al-Arab below Basra. Length, *c.* 470 m.

Kasai', riv., Africa; source in Portuguese W. Africa, which it separates from Belgian Congo; then flowing N.W. unites with Kwango and joins Congo near Ngato. Length, *c.* 900 m.

Kashan', tn., Persia, 95 m. N. of Isfahan; manufactures silk, copper vessels; rose-water exported. Pop. over 15,000.

Kashgar', tn., W. Sinkiang, China, on trade route between India, China, and Russia; manufactures leather goods, pottery, felt, textiles; oil refining. Pop. (est.) 80,000.

Kashmir, Indian state, N.W. India. Surface consists of mountains and rich valleys, the latter 5,000 ft. above sea-level; includes basin of Upper Indus, and is crossed by R. Jhelum (which widens into several lakes) and its tribs. Agricultural and pastoral; extensive forests; woollen cloth, shawls, silver work, and wood carving. Fine climate; health resort. Cap. Srinagar. Area, 84,258 sq. m.; pop. 3,331,000.

Kasi. See BENARES.

Kasimov (*ka-sē'mov*), tn., central Russia, on R. Oka; leather goods, ropes, linen; annual fair. Pop. 13,000.

Kassa. See KOSICE.

Kassal'a, fort. tn., Anglo-Egyptian Sudan, E. of Khartum; trading centre for ivory, gold dust, hides. Pop. 20,000.

Kassel. See CASSEL.

Kastamu'ni, or KASTAMO'NU. (1) Vilayet, N. Asia Minor; cereals, fruits, cotton, mohair, and tobacco; much mineral wealth and timber. Area, 19,570 sq. m.; pop. 336,000. (2) Cap. of above; manufactures copper ware. Pop. 63,000.

Kasto'ria, tn., Greece, N.W. Macedonia; trade in grain; remains of Byzantine walls. Pop. 10,000.

Kasur', tn., Punjab, India, 34 m. S.E. of Lahore; grain, cotton, leather. Pop. 31,000.

Katan'ga, prov., Belgian Congo, N. of Rhodesia; rich in copper and radium; other minerals are coal, tin, iron, diamonds, gold; cattle raising; connected by rail with Cape Town and Lobito Bay on W. coast, and Beira on E. coast. Area, 180,000 sq. m.; pop. *c.* 1,000,000.

Katha', region, Upper Burma, drained by R. Irrawaddy; hilly; forested; rubies and other gems; rice, tea, cotton. Chief tn., Katha. Area, 8,917 sq. m.; pop. 254,000.

Kathiawar', peninsula, W. coast, India, between Gulf of Cambay and Gulf of Cutch; produces cotton. Area, 20,882 sq. m.; pop. 2,542,000.

Katmandu', cap. of Nepal, India, on Baghmati R.; numerous temples. Pop. 90,000.

Katowice (*kä-to-vit'se*), tn., Poland, 45 m. W.N.W. of Cracow; ironworks, machinery; zinc and coal in vicinity. Pop. 105,000.

Katrine (*kat'rin*), LOCH, Stirlingshire and Perthshire, Scotland; 8 m. long; scene of Scott's *Lady of the Lake*; supplies Glasgow with water.

Kat'tegat, sound between Sweden and Denmark. Length, 150 m.; breadth, from 40 to 70 m.

Kattowitz. See KATOWICE.

Kauai. See HAWAIIAN ISLANDS.

Kaunas (*kou'nas*), formerly KOVNO, present cap. of Lithuania, on R. Niemen; bone meal, metal goods, soap, and candles. Pop. 96,000.

Kaval'la, port, Greece, on Kavalla Bay, Macedonia; exports tobacco. Pop. 50,000.

Kaveri. See CAUVERY.

Kawardha', Indian state, Central Provinces, India; chiefly well-forested hills with fertile areas producing wheat, rice, cotton. Cap. Kawardha, 110 m. S.E. of Jubbulpore. Area, 798 sq. m.; pop. 62,000.

Kayes (*kās*), tn., French Sudan, Africa, at head of navigation of R. Senegal; fortified; on rly. and air route from Dakar. Pop. 11,500.

Kazak', rep., R.S.F.S.R., bordered by Ural Area, Siberian Area, China, Turkmen Rep., Caspian Sea, and European Russia. Most of it is 'steppe' country, with numbers of salt lakes. Live-stock rearing and agriculture are chief occupations. Area, 1,169,975 sq. m. Pop. 6,531,000. Chief tns., Kzyl-orda (cap.), Semipalatinsk, Alma-Ata, Petropavlovsk, and Uralsk.

Kazan', cap. of Tatar Republic, Russia, near R. Volga, *c.* 200 m. E. of Nijni-Novgorod; has fortress containing governor's castle, arsenal, monastery, cathedral; univ.; soap, candles, felt boots, morocco leather, tobacco, textiles; brewing. Pop. 180,000.

Kazerun', tn., Persia, 50 m. W. of Shiraz; has famous garden with orange groves. Dist. produces rice, cotton, opium. Pop. *c.* 7,000.

Kazvin (*kaz-vēn'*), tn., Persia, 90 m. N.W. of Tehran; produces grain, silks, fruit; important transit trade. Pop. 50,000.

Kearny (*kär'ne*), tn., New Jersey, U.S.A., opposite Newark; thread, linoleum, celluloid, photographic material; railway shops and slaughter houses. Pop. 41,000.

Kears'ley, urb. dist., Lancs, England, 4 m. S.E. of Bolton; coal, cotton; bleaching and dyeing. Pop. 9,700.

Kecskemet (*kech'kem-āt*), tn., Hungary, 65 m. S.E. of Budapest; fruit preserving; flour milling; tanning; wine, apples, apricots, and tobacco. Pop. 79,000.

Kedah', state, W. coast of Malay Peninsula, under Brit. protection; drained by R. Kedah; rice, rubber, tapioca, coconuts. Cap. Alor Star. Area, 3,648 sq. m.; pop. 339,000.

Kediri (*kā-dē'rē*), residency, E. Java, Dutch E. Indies; much of it mountainous; rice, cassava, sugar, tapioca, teak. Area, 2,847 sq. m.; pop. 2,154,000.

Kedu', residency, central Java, Dutch E. Indies; mountainous, with fertile valley of R. Praga; rice, sugar-cane, tobacco, coconuts, groundnuts; rubber, timber. Area, 2,197 sq. m.; pop. 2,448,000.

Keeling Islands. See COCOS ISLANDS.

Keene, tn., New Hampshire, U.S.A., 40 m. S.W. of Concord; manufactures furniture, boots; large trade in lumber and maple sugar; winter sports resort. Pop. 11,000.

Keewat'in, provisional dist., N.W. Terr., Canada, between Hudson Bay and 102° W.; in 'Barren Land' region; abounds in game. Area, 228,000 sq. m.

Keg'worth, tn., Leicestershire, England, 5½ m. N.W. of Loughborough; hosiery and embroidery. Pop. 2,100.

Keighley (*kēth'lē*), tn., W. Riding, Yorks, England, 9 m. N.W. of Bradford; manufactures woollen stuffs, machinery, and tools; ironfounding. Pop. 40,400.

Kei Islands (*kā'ē*), group in Molucca Islands, Dutch E. Indies; all thickly wooded; maize, yams, rice, plantains cultivated; fishing. Area, 572 sq. m.; pop. 36,000.

Keith, tn., Banffshire, Scotland, on R. Isla; distilleries, flour mills, blankets, and agricultural implements; horse and cattle fairs. Pop. 4,400.

Kelan'tan, state, E. coast of Malay Peninsula, under Brit. protection; drained by R. Kelantan; rice, coconuts, rubber, live-stock. Cap. Kota Bharu. Area, 5,713 sq. m.; pop. 309,000.

Kells, mkt. tn., co. Meath, I.F.S., 38 m. N.W. of Dublin; illuminated

Book of Kells was prepared here in 10th cent. Pop. 2,200.

Kel'so, mkt. tn., Roxburghshire, Scotland, on R. Tweed; ruins of abbey; coach building; manufactures agricultural machinery and fishing tackle. Pop. 3,900.

Kempston, urb. dist., Beds, England, adjoining Bedford. Pop. 5,400.

Kemp'ten, tn., s.w. Bavaria, Germany, on R. Iller; textiles, paper, matches, machinery; cement; brewing. Pop. 22,000.

Ken'dal, tn., Westmorland, England, on R. Kent; woollens, hosiery, boots and shoes, gunpowder. Pop. 15,600.

Keneh, or KENA. See QENA.

Keng-tung. See TUNG KENG.

Ken'ilworth, mkt. tn., Warwickshire, England, 4 m. N. of Warwick; famous ruined castle; tanning. Pop. 7,600.

Ken'more, par. and vil., Perthshire, Scotland, on L. Tay; popular tourist resort. Pop. (par.) 1,000.

Ken'nington, suburb of London, Surrey, England, 2 m. S.S.W. of St. Paul's. Kennington Oval, S. of Vauxhall Bridge, is ground of Surrey Cricket Club. Pop. 72,700.

Keno'ra, tn., Ontario, Canada, on L. of the Woods; lumbering, flour milling, fishing; gold mining in vicinity. Pop. 6,000.

Keno'sha, tn., Wisconsin, U.S.A., on Lake Michigan; good harbour; motor-cars, hosiery, bedsteads. Pop. 50,000.

Ken'sington, bor. of London, contains Kensington Gardens and Palace, Natural History and South Kensington Museums, and Brompton Oratory. Pop. 180,700.

Kent, co. in S.E. extremity of England, between Thames estuary and Eng. Channel; surface undulating in interior, rising in the Downs to over 800 ft.; drained by Rs. Thames, Medway, Stour, Darent; in S.E. is marshy district, and in S. is region known as the Weald; N.W. corner is practically a suburb of London, with Woolwich Arsenal and government dockyards of Sheerness and Chatham. Kent is called the 'garden of England'; large tracts of woodland, with oaks and other valuable trees. Agriculture is chief industry; cereals, hops, fruits, vegetables; sheep and cattle; dairying and market gardening; coal mined. At Whitstable and Faversham are oyster beds. Manufactures include gunpowder, bricks, cement, paper, shipbuilding; fishing round coasts. Most important tns. are Gillingham, Chatham, Maidstone (co. tn.), Tunbridge Wells, Folkestone, Dover, Margate, Ramsgate, Canterbury. Area, 1,525 sq. m.; pop. 1,218,600.

Kentuck'y, S. Central State, U.S.A., bounded N. by Illinois, Indiana, and Ohio; E. by W. Virginia and Virginia; S. by Tennessee; W. by Missouri. Surface undulating, rising to about 3,000 ft. in Alleghany plateau. In S.W. are great cypress swamps. Principal rivs. are Ohio, which forms N. boundary, and its tribs.; R. Mississippi forms part of W. boundary. There are some remarkable caves. Climate is temperate. Kentucky is largely agricultural, esp. Blue Grass country; produces more tobacco and hemp than any other dist. of U.S.A.; also maize, wheat, and fruit. Especially famous for horses; mules, cattle, sheep, pigs also raised. There are large forests containing valuable timber. Extensive coalfields in both E. and W., also iron, lead, salt, fluorspar, sandstone, natural gas, petroleum. Among principal industries are lumbering, flour milling, tanning, manufacture of cotton-seed oil, hardware, clothing, cigars. Chief tns. are Frankfort (cap.), Louisville, Covington, Lexington, Newport. Area, 40,598 sq. m.; pop. 2,553,000.

Ke'nya, MT., volcanic peak, Kenya Colony, Africa; was first climbed by H. J. Mackinder (1899); lower slopes are forested. Height, 17,040 ft.

Ke'nya Colony and Protectorate, formerly BRITISH EAST AFRICA, country in E. Africa, bounded by Abyssinia (N.), Uganda Protectorate (W.), Tanganyika Terr. (S.), Indian

Ocean and Italian Somaliland (E.); seaboard *c.* 400 m. Protectorate consists of coastal strip rented from Sultan of Zanzibar. Coast regions are flat and unhealthy; high parts of interior fit for white occupation; traversed by volcanic mt. ranges; highest peak, Mt. Kenya; chief rivs., Tana and Sabaki; part of L. Rudolf in N.W. and of L. Victoria in W. In interior are valuable forests and fine pasture lands; S. and N.E. dists. are fertile. Chief products of highlands are coffee, maize, wheat, sisal; of wet lowlands, rice, coconuts, cotton, cassava, sugar, ground-nuts; dairying and wool industries in highlands. Mineral resources are not yet exploited. Rly. from Mombasa to L. Victoria and through Uganda to R. Nile. Cap. Nairobi; chief port, Mombasa. Area, 224,960 sq. m.; pop. 2,892,000 (including 12,500 Europeans).

Ke'okuk, city, S.E. Iowa, U.S.A., on Mississippi R., receiving water-power from Des Moines rapids; centre of rich agricultural area; butter; manufacture of starch, glucose, and patent medicines. Pop. 14,000.

Kerbela. See KARBALA.

Kerch, port, Crimea, Russia; is situated on Strait of Kerch, connecting Black Sea and Sea of Azov, and is strongly fortified; wheat, linseed, wool, hides, and caviare; sturgeon fishing. Pop. 34,000.

Kerguelen Land (*ker'ge-len*), or DESOLATION ISLAND, a mountainous uninhabited isl. in extreme S. of Indian Ocean. The Kerguelen cabbage is much valued by sailors as a preventive of scurvy. Annexed by France (1893). Area, *c.* 1,400 sq. m.

Kerkrade (*kerk'rā-dā*), tn., Limburg, Holland, on German frontier; coal-mining centre. Pop. 35,000.

Kerkuk. See KIRKUK.

Kermadec' Islands, volcanic group, Pacific Ocean, 600 m. N.E. of Auckland, New Zealand; luxuriant vegetation; attempts at settlement have failed; group annexed to New Zealand (1887). Area, 8,208 ac.

Kerman'. (1) Prov., S. Persia, with Baluchistan on E. and Gulf of Oman on S. Country mostly desert, with fertile uplands and valleys; cotton, gums, dates, wools, carpets, and shawls. Area, *c.* 60,000 sq. m.; pop. *c.* 700,000. (2) Tn., cap. of above; carpets and felts; brass work. Pop. 40,000.

Kermanshah', cap. of prov. of same name, Persia, on route between Tehran and Baghdad; considerable trade in silk yarns, opium, gum, raw hides, carpets. Prov. produces wheat, maize, rice, fruits. Pop. (prov.) *c.* 400,000; (tn.) 40,000.

Ker'ry, W. mar. co., Munster, I.F.S., bounded N. by R. Shannon, E. by Limerick and Cork, S. by Cork, W. by Atlantic; coast deeply indented; surface, generally mountainous, is crossed by Macgillicuddy's Reeks, rising to 3,414 ft. in Carrantuohill, highest peak in Ireland. Rivs. are unimportant. Kerry contains the celebrated Lakes of Killarney. Mineral springs occur in various parts. Potatoes, oats, slate; well-known strain of cattle; dairy farming and coast fishing. Co. tn., Tralee. Area, 1,815 sq. m.; pop. 149,200.

Kes'singland, par. and vil., Suffolk, England, 4½ m. S. of Lowestoft; wat.-pl.; fishing. Pop. (par.) 2,500.

Keste'ven, PARTS OF. See LINCOLNSHIRE.

Keswick (*kez'ik*), mkt. tn., Cumberland, England, near L. Derwentwater; tourist centre; lead pencils. Pop. 4,600.

Ketch'ikan, tn., S.W. Alaska, N. America; important halibut and salmon fisheries; timber; fox farming. Pop. 2,500.

Ket'ley, vil., Salop, England, 13 m. E. of Shrewsbury; coal mines; ironworks. Pop. 2,200.

Ket'tering, mkt. tn., Northants, England; boots, shoes, brushes; leather dressing and ironfounding. Pop. 31,200.

Kew (*kū*), suburban dist. of London, included in Richmond bor., Surrey, England; famous for the Royal Botanic Garden. Pop. 4,400.

Kewanee (*ke-wä'nē*), tn., Illinois, U.S.A., 130 m. w.s.w. of Chicago; agricultural implements; coal mining in vicinity. Pop. 16,000.

Keynsham (*kān'shăm*), mkt. tn., Somerset, England, on R. Avon, 5 m. S.E. of Bristol; remains of abbey founded 1172. Pop. 3,850.

Key West ('bone reef'), city and port, Florida, U.S.A.; situated on Florida Keys; important U.S. naval station; connected with mainland by rly.; popular winter and health resort; exports cigars, sponges, turtles, fruit, and salt. Pop. 13,700.

Khabarovsk', tn., Far Eastern Area, U.S.S.R., on R. Amur; chief centre of sable trade; tanning, fur dressing, brewing, distilling. Pop. 44,000.

Khaibar Pass. See KHYBER PASS.

Khairagarh (*kīr-a-gur'*), Indian state, Central Provinces, India; soil extremely fertile; wheat and rice grown; large forest area with teak and bamboo. Chief tn., Khairagarh, 125 m. N.E. of Nagpur. Area, 930 sq. m.; pop. 124,000.

Khairpur (*kīr-poor'*). (1) State, Sind, Bombay, India; rich, fertile plain round Indus, otherwise sterile sandhill ridges; wheat, pulses, and cotton are grown. Area, 6,050 sq. m.; pop. 193,000. (2) Cap. of above, 150 m. N. of Hyderabad; weaving and dyeing; firearms, swords, and carpets. Pop. 16,000.

Khamga'on, tn., Berar, India, 25 m. W. of Akola; cotton factories and cotton market. Pop. 20,000.

Khandesh', dist., Bombay, India; surface generally flat; rugged and thickly wooded in N.W.; drained by R. Tapti; cotton extensively grown; oil-seeds and indigo exported. Area, 10,952 sq. m.; pop. 1,718,000.

Khand'wa, tn., Central Provinces, India, 70 m. S.E. of Johore; exports raw cotton; oil-pressing. Pop. 27,000.

Khania. See CANEA.

Khar'ga, great oasis, Libyan Desert, Egypt; palm groves; cereals and lucerne; mat and basket making. Area, *c.* 1,800 sq. m.; pop. *c.* 10,000.

Kharkov'. (1) Dist., Ukraine, U.S.S.R.; low tableland; drained by Rs. Dnieper, Don, Donetz; in 'black earth' zone; agriculture is principal occupation; beetroot, tobacco, flax, hemp, silk; chief minerals are iron, coal, salt, chalk. Area, 21,040 sq. m.; pop. 3,452,000. (2) Cap. of above; important railway centre; four annual fairs; woollens, sugar, iron goods, agricultural implements; chemicals. Pop. 417,000.

Kharput', tn., Turkey, Asia, on R. E. Euphrates; contains American Protestant college; Jacobite convent with a collection of rare manuscripts. Pop. 81,000.

Khartoum (*kar-toom'*), cap., Anglo-Egyptian Sudan, Africa; near jn. of Blue and White Niles; connected by rail with Upper Egypt and Port Suakin on Red Sea. For nearly a century emporium for ivory and gum of Sudan and great slave market; Gordon besieged and killed here (1885); retaken by Kitchener (1898); contains Gordon Memorial Coll. Pop. (including suburbs) 45,000.

Khasi and Jaintia Hills, dist., Assam, India; elevated plateau 4,000 to 6,000 ft. high; well timbered; oranges, betel nuts, pineapples, potatoes. Area, 6,022 sq. m.; pop. 243,000.

Khasko'vo, or HASKOVO (Turkish *Khaskoi*), tn., S. Bulgaria; carpets, woollen goods, silk, and tobacco. Pop. 26,000.

Kheri (*ke-rē'*). (1) Dist., United Provinces, India; sugar-cane, wheat, rice; important cattle-breeding centre. Area, 2,976 sq. m.; pop. 913,000. (2) Tn. in above, 75 m. N. of Lucknow.

Kherson'. (1) Dist., Ukraine, U.S.S.R.; surface flat; drained by Rs. Dnieper, Dniester, Bug; agriculture and cattle raising. Area, 27,337 sq. m.; pop. 3,807,000. (2) Port, cap. of above, on R. Dnieper; flour, beer, machinery; trade in timber, wool, cereals, hides. Pop. 59,000.

Khingan' Mountains, two ranges in E. Asia. (1) GREAT KHINGAN; important orographical, climatic, and economic boundary; separates Mongolian plateau from Manchuria; rises to 8,000 ft. (2) LITTLE KHINGAN, E. of above; crossed by Amur R.

Khiva (*kē'va*), cap. of former state of Khiva, now absorbed in Uzbek Rep., U.S.S.R., Asia, 25 m. w. of R. Oxus; has lost much of its former importance; silks, cottons, and carpets. Pop. 20,000.

Khoi (*koy*), tn., N.W. Persia; transit trade in wheat, barley, cotton, fruit. Pop. *c*. 30,000.

Khōjend', tn., Uzbek Rep., U.S.S.R., Asia, on R. Sir Darya; silk, cotton, textiles, coarse porcelain; fruit, vines. Pop. 37,000.

Kho'qand, town, Uzbek Rep., U.S.S.R., Asia, near R. Sir Darya, 120 m. S.E. of Tashkent; important trade centre; cotton factories and flour mills; exports silk. Pop. 68,000.

Khorasan. See KHURASAN.

Khotan', tn. and oasis, Sinkiang, China, in basin of R. Tarim; cereals, cotton, fruits; carpets, silk, metal work, and jade. Pop. *c*. 5,000. Dist. has area of 400 sq. m.; pop. *c*. 200,000.

Khul'na. (1) Dist., Bengal, India, largely deltaic; rice, jute; manufactures sugar and molasses from date-palm juice. Area, 2,011 sq. m.; pop. 1,453,000. (2) Chief tn. of above, 75 m. N.E. of Calcutta; trades in salt, rice, and sugar. Pop. 16,000.

Khunsar', tn., Persia, 100 m. N.W. of Isfahan; fine orchards; trades in dried fruits. Pop. *c*. 10,000.

Khurasan', formerly KHORASAN, prov., N.E. Persia; surface generally mountainous in N. and E., remainder of country mainly salt, marshy desert; here and there are fertile valleys; produces best wool in Persia; valleys yield rice, wheat, cotton, tobacco, opium, and fruits; turquoise mines at Maadan. Cap. Meshed. Area, *c*. 150,000 sq. m.; pop. *c*. 1,000,000.

Khurja (*koor'jä*), tn., United Provinces, India, 50 m. S.E. of Delhi; important commercial centre; cotton ginning and pottery. Pop. 26,000.

Khuzistan (*kooz-i-stän'*), formerly ARABISTAN, prov., S.W. Persia; mostly mountainous in N., but soil in valleys very fertile; S. part largely plains and marshes; rice, maize, barley, cotton, wool, are produced. Extensive petroleum fields. Area, 25,700 sq. m.; pop. *c*. 350,000. Cap. Shustar; pop. 10,000.

Khyber Pass (*kī'ber*), or KHAIBAR, great pass from India to Afghanistan, through Safed Koh and Sulaiman mts.; 33 m. long, 40 to 450 ft. wide, with rocky precipices rising on each side to heights of from 1,400 to over 3,300 ft. Summit of pass is at Landi Kotal. Now traversed by railway from Peshawar.

Kiakhta. See TROITSOKOSAVSK.

Kiangsi', prov., Central China, Asia; consists mainly of mountain ridges with intervening valleys; rice, wheat, silk, cotton, tea, tobacco; much valuable timber. Cap. Nanchang. Area, 69,480 sq. m.; pop. 24,467,000.

Kiangsu', mar. prov., China; numerous large lakes; intersected by canals; S. portion is 'garden of China'; alluvial soil produces rice, wheat, melons; cotton and silk are grown. Cap. Chinkiang. Area, 38,600 sq. m.; pop. 33,800,000.

Kiaochou Bay (*kē-ou-chou'*), bay and terr., Shantung, China; leased by China to Germany (1898), captured by Japanese (1914), returned to China (1922); railway from chief port Tsingtao to Tsinan. Area of concession, *c*. 200 sq. m.

Kid'derminster, mkt. tn., Worcestershire, England, on R. Stour; carpet manufacture is the staple industry; worsted spinning and dyeing; iron and tinplate. Pop. 28,900.

Kids'grove, urb. dist., Staffs, England, in the Potteries; has coal mines and ironworks. Pop. 9,900.

Kid'welly, port, mkt. tn., Carmarthenshire, Wales, near Carmarthen Bay; coal mines and brick works. Pop. 3,200.

Kiel (*kēl*), port, Schleswig-Holstein, Prussia, on inlet of Baltic Sea; at entrance to Kiel Canal; Ger. naval station; fine harbour; univ.; observatory; shipbuilding, foundries, breweries, oil and chemical works. Pop. 214,000.

Kiel Canal extends through Schleswig-Holstein from Brunsbüttel on Elbe to Kiel Bay, thus uniting North Sea with Baltic. Breadth at bottom, 72 ft.; at surface, 213 ft.; depth, 36 ft. Harbourage of Ger. High Seas Fleet during most of the Great War; now open to vessels of all nations at peace with Germany.

Kielce (*kyel'tsa*). (1) County, Poland; mostly plateau, rising to 1,350 ft.; iron, coal, zinc, lead, and cereals. Area, 9,937 sq. m.; pop. 2,536,000. (2) Cap. of above, 100 m. S. of Warsaw; ropes, dyes, cottons, cement. Pop. 41,000.

Kiev (*kē'yev*), tn., Ukraine, U.S.S.R., on R. Dnieper; once cap. of Muscovite empire; cathedral of St. Sophia is oldest in Russia; commercial centre for S.W. Russia; machinery, hydraulic presses, grain elevators; tobacco, flour; sugar industry. Pop. 514,000.

Kikinda, VELIKA (*kik'in-dä vel'ik-a*), formerly NAGY KIKINDA, tn., Yugoslavia, 70 m. N. of Belgrade; agricultural and stock-raising centre; flour. Pop. 25,000.

Kikuyu (*ki-koo'yoo*), prov., Kenya Colony, bordering Uganda on the W. It includes Mt. Kenya; elevation between 4,500 and 18,600 ft.; climate temperate. Cap. Nyeri. Pop. (est.) 323,000.

Kilauea (*kē-lou-ā'a*), largest active volcano in world, S.E. Hawaii, E. slope of Mauna Loa; elevation, 4,400 ft.; circumference, 8 m.

Kilbarchan (*kil-bar'kan*), par., tn., Renfrewshire, Scotland, 5 m. W. of Paisley; linen factory; silk and cotton fabrics, Paisley shawls. Pop. (par.) 7,500.

Kilbir'nie, tn. and par., N. Ayrshire, Scotland, on R. Garnock, 17 m. S.W. of Glasgow; flax spinning, linen thread, weaving of fishing nets. Pop. (par.) 8,000.

Kildare'. (1) Co., Leinster, I.F.S.; most of surface flat, with bogs in N.; watered by Rs. Liffey, Boyne, Barrow, and crossed by two canals; plain of Curragh is in centre; chief industry agriculture; potatoes, oats, barley; live-stock. Brewing and distilling. Area, 654 sq. m.; pop. 58,000. (2) Mkt. tn., cap. of above; cathedral; remains of castle and Carmelite friary. Pop. 2,100.

Kilimanjar'o, extinct volcanic mountain to E. of Lake Victoria, Tanganyika Terr., E. Africa; highest point is volcanic cone of Kibo (19,324 ft.); large glaciers.

Kilindini'. See MOMBASA.

Kilkee', tn., co. Clare, I.F.S., 8 m. W.N.W. of Kilrush; popular seaside resort; fishing. Pop. 1,700.

Kilkenny. (1) Co., Leinster, I.F.S.; undulating, rising in N.E. to over 1,000 ft.; drained by Rs. Barrow, Nore, Suir. Produces black marble, anthracite coal; manufactures beer, whisky, flour, leather; much arable and grazing land. Area, 796 sq. m.; pop. 71,000. (2) Chief tn. of above, on R. Nore; has R.C. cathedral; marble works and tanneries; brewing, bacon curing. Pop. 10,000.

Killaloe (*kil-la-loo'*), tn., co. Clare, I.F.S., on R. Shannon; important salmon fishing. Pop. 900.

Killar'ney ('church of sloes'), mkt. tn., co. Kerry, I.F.S.; R.C. cathedral; bog-oak souvenirs. In vicinity are Lakes of Killarney, famous for beautiful scenery. Pop. 5,300.

Killiecrank'ie, PASS OF, Perthshire, Scotland, through which R. Garry flows; 3 m. S.E. of Blair Atholl. In battle of Killiecrankie Claverhouse defeated Mackay, but was himself slain (1689).

Killin', par. and vil., Perthshire, Scotland, near head of Loch Tay; tourist centre; woollens. Pop. (par.) 1,500.

Killis', tn., Aleppo, Syria, 35 m. N. of Aleppo; olives cultivated. Pop. 20,000.

Killyleagh', port and par., co. Down, N. Ireland, on Strangford Lough; linen manufactured; exports agricultural produce. Pop. (par.) 4,300.

Kilmar'nock, munic. burgh and tn., Ayrshire, Scotland, on Kilmarnock

Water; in one of richest mineral fields of Scotland; iron is staple trade; manufactures carpets, textiles, boots and shoes, porcelain and fireclay goods, railway stock, and machinery. Pop. 38,100.

Kilmaurs', tn. and par., Ayrshire, Scotland, on R. Carmel, 2 m. N.W. of Kilmarnock; hosiery and shoes; coal mining. Pop. (par.) 4,600.

Kilpat'rick. (1) NEW, or EAST, par., Dumbartonshire, Scotland; contains Bearsden, residential suburb of Glasgow. Pop. 13,900. (2) OLD, par., Dumbartonshire, Scotland, contains Clydebank. Pop. 56,000.

Kilren'ny and An'struther, royal burgh, Fife, Scotland, on Firth of Forth; fisheries. Pop. 3,300.

Kilrush', port, co. Clare, I.F.S., on R. Shannon; slate quarries; fisheries. Pop. 3,300.

Kilsyth (*kil'sīth'*), tn., Stirlingshire, Scotland, 10 m. W. of Falkirk; limestone and sandstone quarries, coal and iron mines in vicinity; cotton factory. Pop. 7,600.

Kilwin'ning, tn., Ayrshire, Scotland, on R. Garnock, 4 m. E. of Ardrossan; engineering, iron smelting and founding, coal mining, and woollen manufactures. Traditional home of Freemasonry in Scotland. Pop. 5,300.

Kim'berley. (1) Chief tn., Griqualand West, Cape Prov., S. Africa; chief diamond-mining centre of the world. Pop. 40,000 (17,000 Europeans). (2) Tn., Notts, England, 5 m. N.W. of Nottingham; coal mines; brewing and knitting industries. Pop. 5,500.

Kincar'dine O'Neil, par. and vil., Aberdeenshire, Scotland, on R. Dee, 26 m. W. of Aberdeen; holiday resort; annual fairs. Pop. (par.) 2,040.

Kincar'dineshire, or THE MEARNS, mar. co., E. Scotland; rises from coast to Grampian Mts.; deer forests, grouse moors; watered by Rs. North Esk, Bervie, Dee, and other streams; produces oats, barley, wheat; cattle and sheep raised; fishing important. Chief tns., Stonehaven (cap.), Laurencekirk, Bervie, Banchory. Area, 382 sq. m.; pop. 39,900.

Kinchinjun'ga. See KANCHENJUNGA.

Kin'der Scout, highest summit, Peak dist., N.W. Derbyshire, England; alt. 2,088 ft.; often called The Peak.

King'horn, royal burgh and seaside resort, Fife, Scotland, 3 m. S.W. of Kirkcaldy. Golf clubs made. Alexander III. of Scotland fell over cliffs and was killed (1286). Pop. 2,000.

Kings'bridge, port, S. Devon, England, on R. Salcombe; fishing; coasting trade; mild climate. Pop. 3,000.

Kings'clere, mkt. tn., N. Hants, England; malting, brewing, rope making; large training stables for racehorses. Pop. 2,200.

King's County. See OFFALY.

King's Lang'ley, par. and vil., Herts, England, 21 m. N.W. of London; site of anc. palace; remains of Dominican friary; paper mills. Pop. 2,000.

King's Lynn, port, Norfolk, England, on R. Great Ouse; has several buildings of antiquarian interest; fisheries; corn and cake mills; motor carriage and coach works; agricultural implements; shipbuilding. Pop. 20,600.

King's Norton, par. and tn., Worcestershire, England; suburb of Birmingham; paper, metal, and screw nails; par. contains model vil. of Bournville, with Cadbury's cocoa and chocolate works. Pop. (par.) 7,500.

King'ston. (1) Tn., New York, U.S.A., on Hudson R.; railway and canal terminus; railway repairing shops; manufactures shirts, cigars, and bricks. Pop. 28,000. (2) Tn., N.E. Pennsylvania, U.S.A., on R. Susquehanna, opposite Wilkes-Barre; anthracite coal mining; machinery; hosiery. Pop. 9,000. (3) Tn., Ontario, Canada, on Lake Ontario; shipyards and engine works; univ. Pop. 22,000. (4) Cap. and port, Jamaica, W. Indies; greatly damaged by earthquake (1907). Pop. 63,000.

Kingston-upon-Hull. See HULL.

Kings'ton-upon-Thames, munic. bor. and mkt. tn., Surrey, England, part of

Greater London; riverside resort; market gardening; paper, machinery. Pop. 39,100.

Kings'town. (1) DUN LAOGHAIRE (*lē'ri*), tn. and mail-packet station, co. Dublin, I.F.S.; has spacious harbour; steamer service with Holyhead; sea-fishing centre; yachting rendezvous and favourite winter resort. Pop. 19,000. (2) Cap. and port, s.w. coast of St. Vincent, W. Indies; cotton, arrowroot, sugar, coconuts. Pop. 3,800.

Kings'winford, par. and vil., Staffs, England, 3½ m. w. of Dudley; coal and iron mining; brick, tiles, iron goods, and glass. Pop. (par.) 22,000.

Kings'wood, urb. dist., Glos, England, 3½ m. N.E. of Bristol; boots and shoes; market gardening. Pop. 13,300.

King-te-Chen', tn., N.E. Kiangsi, China, 85 m. N.E. of Nang-chang; famous since 11th cent. for porcelain ware; rice bowls. Pop. *c.* 300,000.

Kingussie (*king-ū'si*), burgh, Inverness-shire, Scotland, on R. Spey; favourite summer resort; annual fairs. Pop. 1,100.

King William's Town, tn., Cape Prov., S. Africa, on Buffalo R., 30 m. w. by N. of East London. Important commercial centre, with large trade in wool, hides, grain; jam, confectionery, soap, candles, and leather. Pop. 6,500 (Europeans).

Kinross', cap., Kinross-shire, Scotland, on Loch Leven; woollens; famous trout-fishing centre. Pop. 2,500.

Kinross'-shire, inland co., Scotland; surface consists of hills encircling central plain in which is Loch Leven; higher ground is adapted for sheep and cattle grazing. County produces grain, turnips, potatoes; coal, fireclay, and limestone. Co. tn., Kinross. Area, 82 sq. m.; pop. 7,500.

Kinsale', port, co. Cork, I.F.S., on Kinsale Harbour; popular health resort; headquarters of S. of Ireland Fishing Co. Pop. 2,700.

Kintyre (*kin-tīr'*), or CANTIRE, peninsular dist., Argyllshire, Scotland; about 42 m. long and 4 to 11 m. broad, and terminates at s. in bold promontory called Mull of Kintyre, only 13 m. from Ireland. Chief industries: distilling, dairy-farming, and stone quarrying. Chief tn., Campbeltown. Pop. 6,700.

Kioto. See KYOTO.

Kirchheim-unter-Teck (*kērch'hīm*), tn., Württemberg, Germany, 15 m. S.E. of Stuttgart; hosiery, chemicals, soap, cement, machinery. Pop. 5,000.

Kirghiz Republic (*kir-gēz'*), rep., U.S.S.R., central Asia, lying S.E. of Kazak and w. of China. Mountainous with a number of glaciers; extensive grazing ground for fat-tailed sheep, cattle, and goats; some agriculture and silkworm rearing. Cap. Frunze. Area, 98,400 sq. m.; pop. 990,000.

Kirin'. (1) Prov., Manchuria, China; well watered and fertile; tobacco, pulse, millet, maize, wheat, barley, potatoes, the poppy. Area, 105,000 sq. m.; pop. 7,500,000. (2) Cap. of above; river port on Sungari R., with important dockyards. Pop. *c.* 100,000.

Kirkbur'ton, urb. dist., W. Riding, Yorks, England, 5 m. S.E. of Huddersfield; woollen and fancy goods; coal and iron mines. Pop. 3,200.

Kirk'by-in-Ash'field, urb. dist., Notts, England, 12 m. N.W. of Nottingham; coal mines. Pop. 17,800.

Kirkby Lons'dale (*kir'bi*), urb. dist. and mkt. tn., Westmorland, England, on R. Lune; grammar school; flagstones. Pop. 1,400.

Kirkby Moor'side (*kir'bi*), par. and mkt. tn., N. Riding, Yorks, England, 18 m. s.w. of Whitby; agricultural implements, bricks, and tiles. Pop. (par.) 1,700.

Kirkby Ste'phen (*kir'bi*), par. and mkt. tn., Westmorland, England, on R. Eden; slate quarries in neighbourhood. Pop. (par.) 1,500.

Kirkcaldy (*kir-kaw'de*), port, royal burgh, Fife, Scotland, on Firth of Forth; called the 'lang toon' from its great length; linoleum and floorcloth, linen manufacture, bleaching, ironfounding, oilcake making; potteries, breweries, and engineering works. Pop. 43,900.

Kirkcudbright (*kir-koo'brā*), co. tn. and royal burgh, Kirkcudbrightshire, Scotland, on R. Dee, 6 m. from Solway Firth; agricultural produce. Pop. 2,300.

Kirkcudbrightshire, mar. co., S.W. Scotland; rocky coast with numerous caves; surface hilly, rising in N.W. to over 2,760 ft. in Mt. Merrick; drained by Rs. Dee, Fleet, Ken, Urr; great part of surface is under grass; cattle, sheep, and horses raised; dairy farming carried on; large quantities of granite quarried. Chief tns., Kirkcudbright (co. tn.), Maxwelltown, Dalbeattie, Castle-Douglas. Area, 900 sq. m.; pop. 30,300.

Kirkheaton, urb. dist., W. Riding, Yorks, England, 2 m. E. of Huddersfield; woollen manufactures. Pop. 2,600.

Kirkintil'loch, burgh, Dumbartonshire, Scotland, on Luggie Water, 6 m. N.E. of Glasgow; chemical works and iron foundries. Pop. 11,800.

Kirk-Kilis'se, tn., European Turkey, 50 m. E. of Adrianople; chief trading station between Constantinople and Balkans; butter, cheese, wine, tobacco, and cereals. Bulgarians defeated Turks here (1912). Pop. 16,000.

Kirk'land Lake, tn., Ontario, Canada, 60 m. N. of Cobalt; rich gold mines. Pop. 4,000.

Kirk'ley, coast par., Suffolk, England; included in munic. bor. of Lowestoft; fishing. Pop. 10,000.

Kirklis'ton, par. and vil., W. Lothian and Midlothian, Scotland, on R. Almond; distilling, malt extract. Pop. (par.) 5,400.

Kirkmai'den, par. in Rhinns of Galloway, Wigtownshire, forming peninsular southern extremity of Scotland, terminating in Mull of Galloway; dairy farming. Pop. 1,800.

Kirkos'wald, par. and vil., Ayrshire, Scotland, 4 m. S.W. of Maybole; famous as residence of originals of Robert Burns's 'Tam o' Shanter' and 'Souter Johnny.' Pop. (par.) 2,200.

Kirk'stall, par., W. Riding, Yorks, England; part of Leeds; ironworks, brewing, and tanning. Pop. 5,500.

Kirkuk (*kir-kook'*), or KERKUK, tn., Iraq, 150 m. N. of Baghdad; great market centre trading in hides, salt, silks, cottons, fruit; petroleum wells. Pop. over 20,000.

Kirk'wall, city and royal burgh, port, and chief tn. of Orkney, Scotland; cathedral of St. Magnus, 12th cent.; market tn.; distilling. Pop. 3,500.

Kirriemuir', mkt. tn., Angus, Scotland, 5 m. N.W. of Forfar; birthplace of Sir J. M. Barrie, who has made it world-famous as 'Thrums'; linen. Pop. 3,300.

Kirsanov (*kēr-sä'nov*), tn., Russia, 300 m. S.E. of Moscow; iron smelting and flour milling. Pop. 25,000.

Kir Sheher (*kēr shār'*), tn., Asiatic Turkey, 85 m. S.E. of Angora; fine mosque; carpets. Pop. 68,000.

Kirt'on-in-Lind'sey, mkt. tn. and par., Lincolnshire, England, 9 m. N.E. of Gainsborough; cattle markets and large fairs; corn mills. Pop. (par.) 1,600.

Kish. See QAIS.

Kishangarh (*kish-un-gur'*). (1) Indian state, Rajputana, India; produces millet, barley, maize, cotton; garnets and marble. Area, 858 sq. m.; pop. 78,000. (2) Cap. of above, 18 m. N.E. of Ajmer; weaving, dyeing, cutting of precious stones. Pop. 9,500.

Kishinev'. See CHISINAU.

Kishm. See QISHM.

Kish'on, riv. of central Palestine which drains Plain of Esdraelon and flows into Bay of Acre.

Kiskunfelegyhaza. See FÉLEGYHÁZA.

Kislovodsk (*kēs-lo-vodsk'*), tn., N. Caucasian Area, Russia, U.S.S.R., 80 m. S.E. of Stavropol; mineral wells. Pop. 31,000.

Kis'singen, tn., Bavaria, Germany, 62 m. E. of Frankfurt-on-Main; mineral springs. Pop. 6,600.

Kistna. (1) Riv. of S. India, rises in W. Ghats, and flows E. to Bay of Bengal; not navigable, but of great use for irrigation. Length, 800 m.

(2) Dist., Madras Presidency, India; drained by R. Kistna; rich agriculturally, producing cereals, cotton, tobacco, salt along coast. Cap. Masulipatam. Area, 5,907 sq. m.; pop. 2,133,000.

Kisu'mu, formerly PORT FLORENCE, port, L. Victoria, Kenya Colony, Africa; former terminus of Uganda Rly., with steamer service to Uganda ports; new line from Uganda Rly. into Uganda will lessen importance of tn. Pop. includes 150 whites and 1,200 Asiatics.

Kit'chener, formerly BERLIN, city and port, Ontario, Canada, 60 m. W. of Toronto; manufactures furniture, boots and shoes, iron goods, motor-cars; sugar refining. Utilizes Niagara water-power. Pop. 22,000.

Kit'zingen, tn., Bavaria, Germany, on R. Main, 10 m. S.E. of Wurzburg; brewing, coopering, horse-hair spinning; cement; river trade. Pop. 10,000.

Kiukiang, port, Kiangsi, China, on Yangtze Kiang; exports green tea, porcelain, beans, grasscloth, cotton, camphor. Pop. 71,000.

Kiushiu. See KYUSHU.

Kivu (*kē'voo*), lake, Belgian Congo, Central Africa, discharging into Lake Tanganyika by R. Russisi; contains numerous islands. Alt. 5,000 ft.; area, 1,100 sq. m.

Kiz'il Irmak' ('red river'), largest riv. of Asia Minor; rises in the Kizil Dagh, and flows into Black Sea. Length, *c.* 600 m.

Kiz'il-Kum. See QIZIL QUM.

Kizlyar', tn., Daghestan, U.S.S.R., on delta of R. Terek, near Caspian Sea; famous wine. Pop. 9,600.

Klad'no, tn., Bohemia, Czechoslovakia, 16 m. W.N.W. of Prague; coal and iron mines; iron, steel, and bridge-building works. Pop. 19,000.

Klag'enfurt, cap. of Carinthia, Austria, on R. Glan; iron foundries; machinery; white lead. Pop. 27,000.

Klaipe'da, formerly MEMEL, port, Lithuania, on Kurisches Haff; centre of Baltic timber trade; shipbuilding, ironfounding, brewing; chemicals, soap; herring fisheries. Pop. 37,000.

Klausenburg. See CLUJ.

Klausthal (*klous'täl*), tn., Hanover, Prussia, in Harz Mts., 30 m. S.E. of Hildesheim; silver and lead mining. Pop. 12,000.

Klerks'dorp, tn., Transvaal, S. Africa, on trib. of R. Vaal, 100 m. S.W. of Johannesburg; important cattle centre; gold. Pop. 5,700.

Kleve. See CLEVE.

Klon'dike, small riv., Yukon Terr., Canada, which joins Yukon R. at Dawson City; gives its name to gold-bearing dist., which in 1896 drew diggers from all parts of the world; output of gold greatly decreased.

Klosterneuburg (*klos-ter-noi'boorg*), tn., Austria, on R. Danube, near Vienna; wines and cement. Pop. 14,000.

Knares'borough, mkt. tn., W. Riding, Yorks, England, on R. Nidd, 3 m. N.E. of Harrogate; agricultural produce, linen, and leather. Famous petrifying dropping well. Pop. 5,900.

Knin, tn. and fortress, Dalmatia, Yugoslavia; on rly., 36 m. N. of Split; centre of agricultural dist. Pop. 23,000.

Knocke-sur-Mer, wat.-pl., W. Flanders, Belgium, 11 m. N.E. of Bruges; favourite holiday resort.

Knot'tingley, urb. dist., W. Riding, Yorks, England, on R. Aire, 14 m. S.E. of Leeds; breweries, potteries, roperies, and bottle works; limestone. Pop. 6,800.

Knox'ville, city, Tennessee, U.S.A., on Tennessee R.; has marble quarrying, and coal, iron, zinc, and copper mines; textiles, furniture; iron foundries and rolling mills. Pop. 106,000.

Knuts'ford, urb. dist. and mkt. tn., Cheshire, England, 10 m. S.W. of Manchester; favourite residence of Manchester merchants; leather, cotton, worsted. Pop. 5,900.

Kob'do, tn., N.W. Mongolia, Asia; important cattle market; trade in wool, skins, and sheep. Pop. 6,000.

Ko'be, tn., Honshu, Japan, on

Osaka Bay; now includes Hiogo; fine harbour, important seaport; shipbuilding. Pop. 644,000.

Koblenz. See COBLENZ.

Ko′chi, tn., Shikoku, Japan; noted for coral, and long-tailed fowls; paper making. Pop. 66,000.

Kodok, formerly FASHODA, tn., Anglo-Egyptian Sudan, on White Nile; dist. produces cotton under irrigation.

Koffyfon′tein, tn., Orange Free State, S. Africa, 45 m. S.S.E. of Kimberley; diamond mine of same name in vicinity. Pop. 3,300.

Kofu (*ko′foo*), tn., Honshu, Japan, 80 m. W. of Tokyo; silk and sweetmeats. Pop. 68,000.

Kohat′. (1) Dist., N.W. Frontier Province, India; mountainous with many rivers; salt mines, petroleum, and sulphur. Area, 2,694 sq. m.; pop. 220,000. (2) Cap. of above, 37 m. S. of Peshawar; commands Kurran Pass from Afghanistan. Pop. 28,000.

Kohistan′ ('country of the hills'), geographical name applied to several mountainous districts of Asia. (1) Mountain mass in central Persia, surrounded by deserts. (2) High valleys to N. and E. of Kabul, Afghanistan, whose inhabitants, the Kohistani, stubbornly resisted Brit. occupation of Kabul. (3) Mountainous dist. which separates Afghanistan from upper valley of Indus on Peshawar border. (4) Tract of barren and sparsely populated country, extending from W. of Sind into Baluchistan.

Kokand. See KHOQAND.

Ko′komo, city, Indiana, U.S.A., 50 m. N. of Indianapolis; glass, lumber products, rubber goods, steel wire. Pop. 33,000.

Koko-Nor, lake, N.E. Tibet, central Asia; alt. 9,950 ft.; length, 60 m.; breadth, 40 m.

Kok′stad, tn., Griqualand East, N.E. Cape Prov., S. Africa; health resort; centre of good grazing country; cheese making. Pop. 3,300.

Ko′la, peninsula, N. Russia, between Barents Sea and White Sea; mainly plateau (*c.* 700 ft.); numerous lakes, rivers, and marshes; unproductive soil; cattle and pigs in some of the valleys; reindeer raised; herring and salmon. Chief tn., Murmansk. Area, 50,000 sq. m.; pop. 23,000.

Kolaba′, dist., Bombay Presidency, India, lying between W. Ghats and sea; hilly; coast fringe produces coconuts and betel nuts; rice further inland; salt manufacture. Cap. Alibagh, 20 m. S. of Bombay. Area, 2,169 sq. m.; pop. 563,000.

Kolar′. (1) Dist., Mysore, India; most important gold-producing dist. in India; sugar, molasses, silk, cotton. Area, 3,149 sq. m.; pop. 705,000. (2) Cap. of above, 40 m. N.E. of Bangalore; manufactures coarse blankets. Pop. 13,000.

Kol′berg, tn., Pomerania, Prussia, on Baltic Sea; foundries and machine-works, distilleries; salmon and lamprey fishing. Pop. 30,000.

Kol′ding, mkt. tn., E. coast of Jutland, Denmark; woollen cloth; exports cattle. Pop. 17,000.

Kolhapur′. (1) Indian state, S. Bombay, India; hilly in W., plateau in E.; rice, millet, sugar, tobacco, and cotton. Area, 3,217 sq. m.; pop. 834,000. (2) Cap. of above, 80 m. N.E. of Goa; manufactures cotton, lace, paper, and pottery. Pop. 56,000.

Kolin (*kō-lēn′*), tn., Bohemia, Czechoslovakia, on R. Elbe, 38 m. E. of Prague; sugar, flour, chemicals, beer, starch. Pop. 16,000.

Kolmar. See COLMAR.

Köln. See COLOGNE.

Kolomea. See KOLOMYJA.

Kolom′na, tn., Moscow, Russia, on R. Moskva, 60 m. S.E. of Moscow; agricultural products; locomotives and railway wagons. Pop. 18,000.

Kolomyja (*kō-lo-mē′a*), formerly KOLOMEA, tn., Poland, on R. Prut, 100 m. S.E. of Lwow; agricultural products, pottery, candles; great rly. centre. Pop. 32,000.

Kolozsvar. See CLUJ.

Komarom′, tn., Czechoslovakia, on R. Danube; cereals, tobacco, timber, and cattle; good harbour, and river craft built. Pop. 18,000.

Komati (*kō-mä'tē*), riv., S.E. Africa; rises in Transvaal and enters Indian Ocean at Delagoa Bay. Length, *c.* 500 m.

Komatsu', tn., W. coast of Honshu, Japan; silk and gauze; supplies most of the clay for Terai and Kanazawa potteries. Pop. 12,000.

Komi, or ZIRIAN, dist., N. Russia, lying W. of Ural Mts.; half of it N. of Arctic Circle. In N. is tundra, where large herds of reindeer are bred; farther S. is taiga forest, mostly pine; tar, pitch, timber products; hunting fur-bearing animals. Area, 171,399 sq. m.; pop. 207,000.

Komotau. See CHOMUTOV.

Konakri (*kon-ä-krē'*), port and cap. of French Guinea, W. Africa; rubber, coffee, ground-nuts, and gum; terminus of French Guinea Rly. Pop. 9,000.

Kong, inland tn., French Ivory Coast, W. Africa; indigo, kola nuts, cloth, and salt. Pop. 15,000.

Kongs'berg, tn., Norway, on R. Laagen, 60 m. W.S.W. of Oslo; silver mines, smelting, and royal mint. Pop. 7,500.

Kō'nia, or KONYA. (1) Vilayet, Asia Minor, with Taurus Mts. in S.; opium, gold, chrome ore, and mercury. Area, 39,410 sq. m.; pop. 504,000. (2) Cap. of above, on rly. to Baghdad, anc. ICONIUM; plum and apricot orchards; carpets and silks. Pop. 47,000.

Königgrätz. See HRADEC KRÁLOVÉ.

Königsberg (*ke'nigz-berg*), cap. of E. Prussia, on R. Pregel; commercial and industrial centre of E. Germany; great tea centre of Europe; univ.; 14th cent. cathedral; shipbuilding. Machinery, wood pulp, chemicals, sugar, tobacco, beer, amber articles manufactured. Exports cereals, timber, flax, hemp, flour. Pop. 280,000.

Königshütte. See KROLEWSKA HUTA.

Königssee (*ke'nigz-zā*), lake, Bavaria, Germany, 15 m. S. of Salzburg; elevation, 1,850 ft.; almost enclosed by precipitous limestone mts.; well stocked with salmon and Alpine trout.

Konitz. See CHOJNICE.

Konstanz (*kon-stants'*), formerly CONSTANCE, tn., Baden, Germany, at exit of R. Rhine from L. Constance; 11th cent. cathedral; textiles, machinery, chemicals. Pop. 31,000.

Koorin'ga, tn., S. Australia, 85 m. N. of Adelaide; centre of wheat dist.; famous Burra-Burra copper mine, now closed, is near the town. Pop. 2,600.

Koot'enay. (1) Riv., Brit. Columbia, Canada; rises in Rocky Mts., loops into Montana and Idaho (U.S.A.), flows through Kootenay Lake, and joins Columbia R. Length, 400 m. (2) Lake, Brit. Columbia; 60 m. long, 1 to 4 m. wide. (3) Dist., Brit. Columbia, drained by Kootenay R.; mountainous, diversified by valleys and lakes; famous fruit-farming area; great mineral wealth; coal, iron, gold. Chief tn., Nelson. Area, 26,346 sq. m.

Kö'penick, tn., Brandenburg, Prussia, on isl. in R. Spree; suburb of Berlin; cotton, carpets; chemicals, sealing wax, glass. Pop. 31,000.

Köprülü. See VELES.

Kordofan', prov., Anglo-Egyptian Sudan, W. of White Nile; rolling plains, with peaks rising to 2,600 ft.; no rivers except in S.E.; millet, gums; cattle and camels reared; exports gum, hides, ivory, ostrich feathers. Cap. El Obeid. Area, 130,000 sq. m.; pop. (est.) 671,000.

Kore'a (Jap. *Chosen*), peninsular country with many islands, E. coast of Asia; lies between Yellow Sea and Sea of Japan. Annexed by Japan in 1910. Surface is mountainous, drained by Rs. Han, Tai-dong, Yalu, Tumen, and other streams. Principal industry is agriculture, but methods are extremely primitive. Rice, barley, wheat, and other grains, tobacco, cotton, cattle are produced. There is some whale-fishing, and many small fishing colonies are round shores. Minerals include gold, which is extensively worked, coal, copper, iron, graphite, mica. Cap. Seoul. Rly. mileage, *c.* 2,000. Area, 84,949 sq. m.; pop. 19,200,000.

Koritsa (*kor'che*), tn., S.E. Albania; flour, and tobacco factories; woollens and carpets. Pop. 26,000.

Kos. See Cos.

Kosciusko (*kos-ē-us'ko*), mt. peak, Australian Alps, New South Wales; highest peak in Australia (7,336 ft.); has meteorological station; home of Australian Alpine sports.

Kosice (*ko'shit-se*), formerly KASSA, tn., E. Slovakia, Czechoslovakia, on R. Hernad; woollen goods; distilling, brewing, sawmilling. Pop. 53,000.

Kös'lin, tn., Pomerania, Prussia; brewing, textiles, soap, tobacco. Pop. 29,000.

Kostroma'. (1) Prov., central Russia; surface is undulating plateau; winter severe; dairying and agriculture; timber; cotton and linen manufactures. Area, 13,340 sq. m.; pop. 810,000. (2) Cap. of above, on R. Volga; linen, tobacco, wooden articles; univ. Pop. 68,000.

Ko'tah. (1) Indian state, Rajputana, India; cereals, tobacco. Area, 5,684 sq. m.; pop. 630,000. (2) Cap. of above, 120 m. S. of Jaipur; muslins. Pop. 32,000.

Köthen. See CÖTHEN.

Kot'ka, port, Finland, on Gulf of Finland; exports wood pulp and timber. Pop. 16,000.

Ko'tor, formerly CATTARO, tn., port, Montenegro, Yugoslavia, on Adriatic; fine natural harbour; lace making; trade in cheese. Pop. 2,800.

Kottbus (*kot'boos*), tn., Prussia, on R. Spree, 70 m. S.E. of Berlin; cloth making; tobacco, brandy, machinery. Pop. 50,000.

Kovno. See KAUNAS.

Kovrov', tn., Vladimir, Russia, 95 m. W. of Nijni-Novgorod; textiles, railway stock; timber mills, copper, and iron foundries. Pop. 26,000.

Koweit. See KUWAIT.

Kow'loon, peninsula, China, opposite Hong Kong, and now part of it politically; ceded to Gt. Britain in 1860. Area, 376 sq. m.; pop. 264,000.

Kozlov', tn., central Russia, 150 m. S.E. of Tula; important rly. jn.; railway workshops and flour mills; sausages; large trade in eggs, cattle, meat, hides. Pop. 54,000.

Kragujevac (*krä'goo-yā-vats*), tn., Serbia, Yugoslavia, 60 m. S.S.E. of Belgrade; government arsenal; textiles; flour mills. Pop. 16,000.

Krajova. See CRAIOVA.

Krakata'o, volcanic isl., Strait of Sunda, between Sumatra and Java, where one of most terrible volcanic eruptions occurred in 1883, when greater part of isl. was blown up; followed by enormous ocean waves which destroyed several hundred villages and caused great loss of life. The ascending dust gave rise to a succession of widely distributed brilliant sunsets in the following winter and spring.

Kraslice (*kras'lit-se*), formerly GRASLITZ, tn., Bohemia, Czechoslovakia, in Erzgebirge; musical instruments, lace, buttons, clocks. Pop. 10,000.

Krasnodar', formerly EKATERINODAR, tn., N. Caucasian Area, U.S.S.R., on R. Kuban; glass, chemicals, tobacco; naphtha. Pop. 163,000.

Krasnovodsk', tn., Turkmen Rep., U.S.S.R., on E. shore of Caspian Sea, opposite Baku; terminus of Trans-Caspian Rly.; 69 ft. below sea-level; exports cotton and dried fruits. Pop. 10,000.

Krasnoyarsk', tn., Siberian Area, U.S.S.R., on Trans-Siberian Railway and R. Yenisei; gold refining; leather, porcelain, machinery. Pop. 72,000.

Krä'wang, residency, W. Java, Dutch E. Indies. Mainly flat, but hilly in S.E. Rice, coconuts, rubber, tea, cinchona; extensive forests. Area, 19,872 sq. m.; pop. 800,000.

Krefeld. See CREFELD.

Kremenchug', tn., Ukraine, U.S.S.R.; important river port on R. Dnieper; centre for grain and timber; flour, tobacco, and agricultural machinery. Pop. 58,000.

Krems, tn., Austria, on R. Danube; white lead, mustard, vinegar. Pop. 18,000.

Kremsier. See KROMERIZ.

Kreuzburg (*kroits'boorg*), tn., Prussian Silesia, 59 m. E. of Breslau; sugar, machinery, flour. Pop. 12,000.

Kreuznach (*kroits'nach*), tn., Rhineland, Germany, 28 m. S.W. of Mainz; mineral springs; tobacco, chemicals, leather. Pop. 25,000.

Krimmitschau. See CRIMMITSCHAU.

Krishnag'ar, tn., Bengal, India, 55 m. N. of Calcutta; artistic clay figures. Pop. 25,000.

Kristiansand. See CHRISTIANSAND.

Kris'tianstad, port, S. Sweden; engineering, distilling; sugar factories. Pop. 13,000.

Krivoi' Rog, tn., Ukraine, U.S.S.R., 100 m. N.E. of Kherson; centre of dist. rich in iron, copper, coal, slate, lithographic stone; chemicals. Pop. 31,000.

Krk (*kerk*) (Italian *Veglia*), island, Adriatic; belongs to Yugoslavia; red wine. Area, 156 sq. m.; pop. 29,000.

Krnov (*kur'nof*), formerly JAGERNDORF, tn., Silesia, Czechoslovakia, on R. Opava; woollens and machinery. Pop. 21,000.

Krolewska Huta (*kru-lef'ska*), formerly KÖNIGSHÜTTE, tn., Poland, adjoining Prussian Silesia; centre of Upper Silesian coal and iron dist.; foundries, rolling mills; bricks and glass. Pop. 73,000.

Kromeriz (*krōm'yer-zhēzh*), tn., Moravia, Czechoslovakia, on R. Morava; fruit, cereal, and cattle market; agricultural machinery, flour, beer. Pop. 57,000.

Kro'nenberg, tn., Rhineland, Prussia, 7 m. S.S.W. of Elberfeld; foundries, steel works. Pop. 14,000.

Kron'stadt. (1) Port, fortress, and great naval arsenal, Russia, on isl. at head of Gulf of Finland; ice-bound from December till end of May. Pop. 62,000. (2) See BRASOV.

Krotoszyn (*krō-to-shēn'*), tn., Poland, 55 m. S.E. of Poznan; sawmills, breweries; trade in grain, wool, cloth, furs. Pop. 13,000.

Kru'gersdorp, tn., Transvaal, S. Africa, 20 m. W. of Johannesburg; gold-mining centre. Pop. 14,500 whites.

Krusevac (*kru'she-vats*), tn., Serbia, Yugoslavia, 35 m. N.W. of Nish; cap. of Serbia till 1389; explosives, railway trucks. Pop. 6,500.

Kual'a Lum'pur, cap. of Selangor, Malay States; centre of tin mining; rubber, rice, pepper, tapioca. Pop. *c.* 80,000.

Kuban'. (1) Riv., S. Russia, 450 m. long; rises on Mt. Elbruz; enters Black Sea S. of Taman peninsula, and sends a branch N. to Sea of Azov. (2) Prov., N. Caucasian Area, U.S.S.R.; includes valley of R. Kuban and N. slope of Caucasus range with coast of Sea of Azov; agriculture; horses and cattle; petroleum, coal, salt. Area, 36,645 sq. m.; pop. 2,626,000.

Kuch Behar. See COOCH BEHAR.

Kuen-lun. See KUNLUN.

Kuka (*koo'kä*), tn., Bornu, Nigeria, on W. shore of Lake Chad; formerly great slave-trading centre; caravan trade. Pop. (est.) 60,000.

Kuldja (*kool'yä*), prov. of Sinkiang, China; plateau crossed by mountains; drained by R. Ili; grains, fruits, vines, cotton; stock rearing. Cap. Kuldja. Pop. 10,000.

Kulm. See CHELMNO.

Kulmbach (*koolm'bach*), tn., Bavaria, Germany, 11 m. N.W. of Bayreuth; textiles; chemicals; black beer. Pop. 12,000.

Kum. See QUM.

Kumamo'to, city, Kyushu, Japan, 50 m. N.E. of Nagasaki; ruined 16th cent. castle; much-frequented Buddhist temple outside town. Pop. 147,500.

Kumasi (*koo-mä'sē*), cap., Ashanti, Gold Coast, W. Africa; on rocky eminence; trading centre. Pop. *c.* 25,000.

Kumaun (*koo-mä'oon*), div., United Provinces, India; greater part occupied by southern Himalayas; important forested areas; fruit, rice, wheat in valleys. Chief tn., Naini Tal. Area, 13,725 sq. m.; pop. *c.* 1,300,000.

Kumbako'nam, sacred city, S.E. Madras, India, 25 m. N.E. of Tanjore;

metal-ware, silk and cotton fabrics, sugar, pottery. Pop. 61,000.

Kune'ne, riv., Angola, W. Africa; rises in Benguella plateau (5,800 ft.); enters Atlantic Ocean; for 200 m. from mouth forms boundary between Angola and S.W. Africa; sandbanks at mouth; length, 720 m.

Kungur (*koong-goor'*), tn., Ural Area, Russia, 58 m. S.S.E. of Perm; tanneries, soap and shoe factories; important fair; alabaster quarries. Pop. 20,000.

Kunlun Mountains (*koon-loon'*), mt. system, forming one of loftiest ranges in Asia, and constituting N. wall of Tibetan plateau; general direction W. to E.; length, *c.* 2,300 m.; main chain divides into parallel chains: (1) Western, from Pamir to Tashdavan pass in Altyn-Tagh section of range, where trade route from Tarim valley to Lhasa crosses mts. (2) Central, from Lhasa-Tarim route to S. of Lan-chow. (3) Eastern, lying wholly in China from S. of Lan-chow to a little E. of Ho-nan city. System continued by mts. of N. China (Ku-liang, Ala-shan, and In-shan), to join highlands of N.E. Asia in the Greater Khingan range.

Kuopio (*koo-o'pe-o*). (1) Dept., central Finland; dairy farming and cattle rearing; iron obtained. Area, 13,984 sq. m., excluding water; pop. 377,000. (2) Cap. of above, on Lake Kallavesi; important trading centre. Pop. 24,000.

Kurdistan', extensive mountainous region of W. Asia, extending southwards from the riv. Aras to the plains of Iraq, and from the Euphrates E. to Urmia in Persia. Much of it is grass-covered tableland where sheep are raised in large numbers. Watered by tribs. of Rs. Euphrates and Tigris. Inhabitants are the turbulent Kurds. Persia, Iraq, and Turkey claim portions of the territory. Area, *c.* 52,000 sq. m.; pop. *c.* 1,500,000.

Kurgan', tn., Ural Area, R.S.F.S.R., on R. Tobol; on Trans-Siberian Rly.; agricultural machinery, leather, flour; exports butter; annual fairs. Pop. 28,000.

Kuria-Muria (*koo're-a-moo're-a*), group of rocky islands off S.E. coast of Arabia; attached to Aden; guano.

Kuril Islands (*koo'rēl*), series of thirty-two small volcanic islands between Kamchatka and Japan; ceded to Japan by Russia (1875); largest are Kunashiri and Etorop; generally fog-bound; numerous hot springs; seal hunting and salmon fishing. Area, 6,169 sq. m.; pop. *c.* 4,500.

Kur'isches Haff, shallow lagoon on S. coast of Baltic Sea, partly in E. Prussia and partly in Lithuania; about 60 m. long; almost separated by line of sand dunes from sea. Area, 680 sq. m.

Kurnool'. (1) Dist., Madras, India; watered by Kistna and other rivs.; immense forests; iron ore, steatite, lead, not much worked; millet, cotton, oil-seeds; subject to drought. Area, 7,580 sq. m.; pop. 915,000. (2) Cap. of above, 105 m. S. of Hyderabad; carpets and coarse cotton cloth. Pop. 28,000.

Kursk (*koorsk*). (1) Prov., Russia, N. of Ukraine; rich soil, drained by numerous streams; rye, oats, potatoes, hemp, wheat, millet, beetroot; beautiful orchards; flour milling, sugar refining, distilling. Area, 17,266 sq. m.; pop. 2,904,000. (2) Cap. of above, 330 m. S. by W. of Moscow; confectionery, soap, tobacco; distilleries, iron foundries, flour mills; annual fair. Pop. 99,000.

Kurume (*koo-roo-mā'*), tn., Kyushu, Japan, 55 m. N.N.E. of Nagasaki; extensive manufacture of blue cotton fabric. Pop. 72,000.

Kushiro', open port, S.E. Hokkaido, Japan; large timber export; important fisheries. Pop. 16,000.

Kustanaisk (*koos-ta-nīsk'*), tn., Kazak Rep., U.S.S.R., on R. Tobol, 250 m. S.W. of Petropavlovsk; tanneries, flour mills, and tallow manufacture; important centre of trade in fertile steppe. Pop. 25,000.

Küstrin (*koos-trēn'*), tn., Prussia, Germany, at confluence of rivs. Warthe and Oder, 52 m. by rail E. of Berlin; rly. jn.; formerly forti-

fied; machinery, hardware. Pop. 18,000.

Kutaiah (*koo-tī'yă*), tn., Asia Minor, 75 m. S.E. of Brusa; manufactures carpets and earthenware. Pop. 70,000.

Kutais (*koo-tīs'*). (1) Government of Georgia, U.S.S.R.; valuable timber, chiefly walnut; wheat, maize, tobacco; eucalyptus and camellia; gold, silver, copper, lead, and manganese ores, also naphtha wells. Chief port, Batum. Area, 8,145 sq. m.; pop. 1,070,300. (2) Cap. of above; silks; trade in fruit. Pop. 46,000.

Kut-al-Imara (*koot-el-i-mă'ră*), small tn., Iraq, almost surrounded by R. Tigris. During Great War captured by Brit. from Turks; recaptured (1916) by Turks after long siege; finally captured by Brit. (1917). Carpets. Pop. *c.* 6,000.

Kut'na Hor'a, formerly KUTTENBERG, tn., Bohemia, Czechoslovakia, 45 m. E. by S. of Prague; tobacco, sugar. Pop. 14,000.

Kutno (*koot'no*), tn., Warsaw govt., Poland, 69 m. W. of Warsaw; breweries and distilleries. Pop. 11,000.

Kuttenberg. See KUTNA HORA.

Kuwait', AL, formerly KOWEIT, port, Arabia, head of Persian Gulf; fine natural harbour; exports horses, sheep, wool. Pop. 50,000.

Kuznetsk', tn., Saratov prov., Russia, 160 m. S.W. of Samara; agricultural implements, leather, ropes, bricks. Pop. 30,000.

Kwanchengtze. See CHANG-CHUN.

Kwangchow-wan, bay and terr., S.E. China; free port; exports pigs, cattle, straw, ground-nuts, sugar; leased to France (1898) for 99 years, and under govt. of French Indo-China. Cap. Fort Bayard. Area, 190 sq. m.; pop. 250,000.

Kwangsi', prov., S. China, consisting of upper part of basin of Si-kiang; produces cassia, sugar, tobacco, rice, hemp, indigo, and silk; cinnamon, and camphor trees. Cap. Kweilin. Area, 77,200 sq. m.; pop. 12,260,000.

Kwangtung'. (1) Mar. prov. of S. China; crossed by mt. ranges except in lower basin of Si-kiang; produces rice, tea, sugar, sub-tropical fruits, mulberry, salt and fresh water fish. Cap. Canton. Area, 99,970 sq. m.; pop. 37,000,000. (2) S. portion of Liaotung Peninsula, S. Manchuria, China; leased to Japan by China; produces maize, millet, beans, wheat, tobacco, hemp, vegetables; important fisheries. Area, 1,438 sq. m.; pop. 1,147,000.

Kwan'za, river, Angola, W. Africa; rises in Bihé plateau and enters Atlantic. Course broken by rapids and falls. Length, 700 m.

Kweichow', inland prov. of S.W. China; mainly hilly; well watered; gold, silver, and quicksilver; cereals, goatskins, wild silk, and timber. Cap. Kweiyang. Area, 67,160 sq. m.; pop. 11,115,000.

Kweilin', cap. of Kwangsi prov., China, on R. Kwei; trade in silks and skins. Pop. 100,000.

Kweiyang, cap. of Kweichow prov., China; trade centre. Pop. *c.* 100,000.

Kyauksē'. (1) Dist., Burma, irrigated by nine canals; chief crop, rice. Area, 1,282 sq. m.; pop. 143,000. (2) Cap. of above, 30 m. S. of Mandalay. Pop. 6,000.

Kyles of Bute, narrow, winding arm of Firth of Clyde, between Bute I. and Argyllshire, Scotland; favourite steamer route in summer; picturesque scenery.

Kyneton, tn., Victoria, Australia, 50 m. N.W. of Melbourne; school of mines; agricultural implements. Pop. 3,400.

Kyoto (*kē-ŏ'tō*), city, S. Honshu, Japan; former cap.; beautiful temples and shrines; univ.; pottery, porcelain, bronzes, silks, fans, embroidery, enamel ware. Pop. 680,000.

Kyushu (*kyoo'shyoo*), formerly KIUSHIU, most southerly of the four large islands of Japan; mountainous and volcanic; hot springs and solfataras; rice, tea, tobacco; coal; famous pottery; chief port, Nagasaki; rly. tunnel being constructed to connect isl. with Honshu. Area, 16,201 sq. m.; pop. 7,750,000.

Kyustendil′, tn., Bulgaria, 43 m. s.w. of Sofia; hot mineral springs; vicinity raises fruit, vines, tobacco. Pop. 15,000.

Kzyl-Orda (*ki-zēl′*), cap., Kazak Rep., U.S.S.R., on R. Sir Darya, and Central Asian Rly.; 310 m. N.W. of Tashkent. Pop. 8,500.